The Criminological Foundations
of Penal Policy

CLARENDON STUDIES IN CRIMINOLOGY
Published under the auspices of the Institute of Criminology,
University of Cambridge, the Mannheim Centre, London School of
Economics, and the Centre for Criminological Research,
University of Oxford.

GENERAL EDITOR: PER-OLOF WIKSTRÖM (*University of Cambridge*)

EDITORS: ALISON LIEBLING AND MANUEL EISNER
(*University of Cambridge*)

DAVID DOWNES, PAUL ROCK, AND JILL PEAY
(*London School of Economics*)

ROGER HOOD, LUCIA ZEDNER, AND RICHARD YOUNG
(*University of Oxford*)

Professor Roger Hood CBE, QC (Hon), PhD, DCL, FBA
Director, University of Oxford Centre for Criminological Research
and Fellow of All Souls College

The Criminological Foundations of Penal Policy

Essays in Honour of Roger Hood

Edited by

Lucia Zedner

and

Andrew Ashworth

OXFORD

UNIVERSITY PRESS

OXFORD

UNIVERSITY PRESS

Great Clarendon Street, Oxford OX2 6DP

Oxford University Press is a department of the University of Oxford.
It furthers the University's objective of excellence in research, scholarship,
and education by publishing worldwide in

Oxford New York

Auckland Bangkok Buenos Aires Cape Town Chennai
Dar es Salaam Delhi Hong Kong Istanbul Karachi Kolkata
Kuala Lumpur Madrid Melbourne Mexico City Mumbai Nairobi
São Paulo Shanghai Taipei Tokyo Toronto

Oxford is a registered trade mark of Oxford University Press
in the UK and in certain other countries

Published in the United States
by Oxford University Press Inc., New York

© The various contributors 2003

The moral rights of the authors have been asserted
Database right Oxford University Press (maker)

First published 2003

British Library Cataloguing in Publication Data
Data available

Library of Congress Cataloging in Publication Data
Data available

ISBN 0-19-926509-7

1 3 5 7 9 10 8 6 4 2

Typeset by Kolam Information Services Pvt. Ltd. Pondicherry, India
Printed in Great Britain on acid-free paper by
Biddles Ltd, Guildford and King's Lynn

General Editor's Introduction

The *Clarendon Studies in Criminology* was inaugurated in 1994 under the auspices of the centres of criminology at the Universities of Cambridge and Oxford and the London School of Economics. It is the successor to the *Cambridge Studies in Criminology*, founded by Sir Leon Radzinowicz and J.W.C. Turner almost sixty years ago.

To celebrate Roger Hood's distinguished and ongoing contribution to British Criminology, the *Clarendon Studies in Criminology* is proud to add to the series *The Criminological Foundations of Penal Policy*, edited by Zedner and Ashworth. It is particularly appropriate that this collection be included in the *Clarendon Studies in Criminology* as Roger Hood was the first general editor of the series. He has also worked at all three of the institutes (Cambridge, Oxford, and LSE) involved with the series.

This book is not only a Festschrift in honour of Roger Hood, but also in its own right an important contribution to the discussion about the criminological foundations of penal policy. Zedner and Ashworth have succeeded in assembling an impressive selection of contributions on this topic by colleagues, students, and friends of Roger Hood.

On behalf of the *Clarendon Studies in Criminology*, and its editorial board, we welcome this latest addition to the series as a fitting tribute to the work of our eminent colleague.

Per-Olof H Wikström
University of Cambridge

Contents

Notes on Contributors

ANDREW ASHWORTH is Vinerian Professor of English Law, University of Oxford.

Sir ANTHONY E. BOTTOMS is Wolfson Professor of Criminology, University of Cambridge and Professorial Fellow in Criminology, University of Sheffield.

RICHARD V. ERICSON is Principal of Green College, and Professor of Law and Sociology, University of British Columbia.

DAVID A. GREEN is a Ph.D. candidate in the Institute of Criminology, University of Cambridge.

RICHARD HARDING is Inspector of Custodial Services for the State of Western Australia and Emeritus Professor at the University of Western Australia.

HEIKE JUNG is Professor of Criminal Law, University of the Saarland, Saarbrücken.

NICOLA LACEY is Professor of Criminal Law, London School of Economics, and Adjunct Professor, Social and Political Theory Program, Research School of Social Sciences, Australian National University.

SEÁN MCCONVILLE is Professor of Criminal Justice, Queen Mary, University of London.

ANDREW SANDERS is Professor of Criminal Law and Criminology, University of Manchester.

STEPHEN SHUTE is Professor of Criminal Law and Criminal Justice, University of Birmingham.

MICHAEL TONRY is Director of the Institute of Criminology and Professor of Law and Public Policy, University of Cambridge, and Sonosky Professor of Law and Public Policy, University of Minnesota.

LORD WINDLESHAM was formerly Principal of Brasenose College, Oxford, 1989–2002.

RICHARD YOUNG is Reader in Criminal Justice and Assistant Director, Centre for Criminological Research, University of Oxford.

LUCIA ZEDNER is Reader in Criminal Justice, University of Oxford.

Editors' Introduction

Lucia Zedner and Andrew Ashworth

This volume brings together an international group of criminologists to celebrate Roger Hood's immense contribution to the development of criminology. When plans for the volume were taking shape, we discussed them with Sir Leon Radzinowicz—the founding father of British criminology—who was first Roger Hood's mentor and then a collaborator in various joint projects. Sir Leon was enthusiastic about the plan, and was keen to write an appreciation of Roger Hood which would open the volume. When it became apparent that his advancing illness would not permit him to accomplish this, he expressed great regret that he would be unable to do what Roger Hood had done for him, and write a fitting tribute to open this *Festschrift*. However, he reminded us of the high regard in which he held Roger Hood's scholarship, of his early and public recognition of the exceptional nature of his talent for criminology.[1] In the preface to his *Adventures in Criminology*,[2] Sir Leon wrote of their great friendship, paid tribute to Roger Hood's 'exceptional' work in curbing his self-confessed tendency towards over-writing, and added that 'the fact that he [Roger Hood] knows the dark corners of our discipline so well made his task so much less strenuous'.

In this introduction we begin by describing the range of Roger Hood's writings on criminology; we then focus particularly on his writings on the relationship between criminological research and the development of policy, which is the theme of the volume; and we conclude with a discussion of the twelve essays in the volume.

---

[1] See Sir Leon's preface to Roger Hood, *Borstal Re-Assessed* (London: Heinemann, 1965).

[2] L. Radzinowicz, *Adventures in Criminology* (London: Routledge, 1999) p. xiv.

Roger Hood's Contributions to Criminological Literature

The purpose of this first section is not to discuss every one of Roger Hood's writings, but rather to identify some seven major areas of criminology—in addition to that which forms the theme of this volume—where his contributions have already been telling. When dealing with someone who has been director of a major criminological research centre for thirty years and who has already been honoured widely for his work by his peers (for example, the Presidency of the British Society of Criminology from 1987 to 1989, and the Sellin-Glueck Award for Distinguished International Contributions to Criminology, from the American Society of Criminology in 1986), we have to be selective.[3] But, even at that, the breadth and depth of Roger Hood's research and writings are awesome. Here are some prominent examples from the fields of sentencing, parole, race, penal effectiveness, custody, penal history, and the death penalty.

Sentencing

Roger Hood's first book was *Sentencing in Magistrates' Courts*,[4] in which he described and interpreted the data from empirical research into sentencing patterns of twelve magistrates' courts. The study was characterized by a sophisticated analysis of the meaning and existence of sentencing disparity, and concluded with challenging suggestions about the causes of the different approaches he found—that they appeared to stem from different bench traditions and, possibly, from the differing social characteristics of localities. The Magistrates' Association subsequently encouraged Roger Hood to investigate these issues further, in the specific context of motoring offences. In *Sentencing the Motoring Offender*[5] he demonstrated not only that these local variations persisted when magistrates completed questionnaires and sentencing exercises on their own, away from their colleagues, but also that variations were greater as the features of the case became more unusual. The sophisticated framework for this study, only briefly mentioned here,[6] is reflected in, or is a reflection

---

[3] There has also been significant public recognition, in the award of the C.B.E. for services to criminology.

[4] (London: Tavistock, 1962).

[5] (London: Heinemann, 1972).

[6] It is discussed further in Chapter 7 below.

of, the fine fifth chapter of that world-renowned book of 1970 with Richard F. Sparks, *Key Issues in Criminology*.[7] This chapter not only assessed the state of research into decision-making in sentencing, but also developed a number of important new themes. The normative dimension of Roger Hood's interest in sentencing was pursued in rousing style in his influential lecture on 'Tolerance and the Tariff',[8] where he began by challenging the role of parole authorities in effectively fixing the time to be spent in custody, and then argued in favour of returning the key decisions to the judges whilst urging them to be much more explicit about the normative evaluations underlying their sentencing practices.

In collaboration with Sir Leon Radzinowicz, Roger Hood continued his criticism of a group of proposed sentencing reforms for their neglect of central issues of evaluation. The recommendations of the Advisory Council on the Penal System for reform of the English 'approach' to maximum prison sentences were castigated for failing to tackle the essential question of the relative seriousness of offences, and for attempting to develop a sentencing structure without this foundation.[9] Both the Advisory Council's proposals and those of the Floud Committee on sentences for 'dangerous' offenders were attacked strenuously for their nebulous and expansive definitions of 'danger' and for their proposals to introduce new measures in respect of this elusive category rather than refining the criteria and safeguards in existing procedures.[10] The two co-authors further elaborated these themes in their masterly appraisal of the early sentencing guidelines movement in the United States,[11] pointing to the perils of closely constraining judicial sentencing and of the intrusion of bureaucratic commissions into key decisions about the imposition of the state's coercive powers. Subsequently Roger Hood

---

[7] In the World University Library series (London: Weidenfeld and Nicolson, 1970).

[8] 'Tolerance and the Tariff: Some Reflections on Fixing the Time Prisoners Spend in Custody', NACRO Reprint No. 11 (London: NACRO, 1974), abstracted in J. Baldwin and A.K. Bottomley (eds.), *Criminal Justice: Selected Readings* (Oxford: Martin Robertson, 1978).

[9] L. Radzinowicz and R. Hood, 'A Dangerous Direction for Sentencing Reform' [1978] *Crim.L.R.* 713.

[10] Ibid.; and also L. Radzinowicz and R. Hood, 'Dangerousness and Criminal Justice: A Few Reflections' [1981] *Crim.L.R.* 756.

[11] In their essay on 'The American Volte-face in Sentencing Thought and Practice' in C. Tapper (ed.), *Crime, Proof and Punishment: Essays in Memory of Rupert Cross* (London: Butterworths, 1981).

himself returned to empirical sentencing research with his large-scale study on *Race and Sentencing*, discussed under 'Race' below, and then participated in the vigorous debate that surrounded the proposal of the then government to introduce mandatory sentences in the 1990s. He and his co-researcher, Stephen Shute, brought some of the evidence from their empirical research on parole and early release to bear on the government's claims about the protective effect of the proposed automatic sentence of life imprisonment and other proposals.[12] In their article they gave a cool and devastating demonstration of the fallacies underlying the government's claims, and argued against the simplistic nature of the government's package of proposed reforms. Sadly, their efforts proved to be yet another illustration of the widening gulf between criminological research findings and criminal justice policy during that decade, as legislation on the automatic life sentence was enacted without significant alteration.

Parole and Release from Custody

It is evident that a number of Roger Hood's writings on sentencing are closely, and rightly, tied into discussions of the criteria on which release from custodial sentences ought to be determined. In three overlapping but differently directed essays in the early 1970s,[13] he argued powerfully against the tendency for parole decisions to represent a form of re-sentencing in secret, against proposals to allow even greater executive discretion over release from custody, and in favour of the reinstatement of judicial determination of the time to be served in custody. He was then invited to engage in public service which could be expected to influence policies on release from custody, and he accepted appointment to the Carlisle Committee in the late 1980s. In its report,[14] the committee proposed the removal of discretionary release from sentences less than four years long, and a much more structured system for the release of those serving sen-

[12] R. Hood and S. Shute, 'Protecting the Public: Automatic Life Sentences, Parole and High Risk Offenders' [1996] *Crim.L.R.* 788.

[13] In his 'Tolerance and the Tariff' (n. 8 above); in 'Some Fundamental Dilemmas of the English Parole System and a Suggestion for an Alternative Structure' in D.A. Thomas (ed.), *Parole: Its Implications for the Penal and Criminal Justice Systems* (Cambridge: Institute of Criminology, 1974); and in one of three commentaries on the report of the Younger Committee on Young Adult Offenders, 'Young Adults Offenders: I, The Custodial Sector' (1974) 14 *British Journal of Criminology* 388.

[14] Report of the Review Committee, *The Parole System in England and Wales*, Cm. 532 (London: HMSO, 1988).

tences of four years and over. The committee also—and one detects Roger Hood's hand here—made a strong plea for the reconsideration of sentencing practices if its proposals on early release were to be implemented, and also emphasized the need for restraint in the use of imprisonment. These cautionary notes seem not to have made a great impression on the politicians, but most of the committee's recommendations on early release were enacted by the Criminal Justice Act 1991. Roger Hood then had the opportunity to study the implementation of the new system. In an important series of publications based on their thorough empirical study,[15] he and his co-researcher, Stephen Shute, demonstrated how the post-1991 system of early release had the effect of lengthening the proportion of sentence spent inside by prisoners, and thus of increasing the prison population (as the Carlisle Committee had predicted would happen if sentence lengths were not reduced). They also demonstrated, among other things, how the greater emphasis on risk as the primary criterion appears to have led the Parole Board to take a more cautious approach, well beyond the actuarial predictions of risk. More about this research and its policy context can be found in Chapter 9 below.

Race

In the late 1980s Roger Hood had conversations with Navnit (now Lord) Dholakia in which he indicated his interest in carrying out empirical research into the way in which ethnic minorities were dealt with in the courts. The Commission for Racial Equality agreed to fund the research, and the Lord Chancellor's Department granted access to Crown Court records in the West Midlands, where the research was carried out. The study involved over 3,000 cases at five Crown Court centres, the largest sentencing study carried out in this country. Research on this subject was always likely to prove

---

[15] R. Hood and S. Shute, *Parole in Transition: Evaluating the Impact and Effects of Changes in the Parole System. Phase One: Establishing the Base-Line* (Oxford: Centre for Criminological Research Occasional Paper No. 13, 1994); R. Hood and S. Shute, *Parole in Transition: Evaluating the Impact and Effects of Changes in the Parole System. Phase Two: Paroling with new Criteria* (Oxford: Centre for Criminological Research Occasional Paper No. 16, 1995); R. Hood and S. Shute, 'Parole Criteria, Parole Decisions and the Prison Population: Evaluating the Impact of the Criminal Justice Act 1991' [1996] *Crim.L.R.* 77; and R. Hood and S. Shute, *The Parole System at Work: A Study of Risk-based Decision-making*, Home Office Research Study 202 (London: Home Office, 2000).

sensitive, and when the results began to come out in late 1992, followed by the publication of *Race and Sentencing*,[16] there was considerable public furore. Inevitably the carefully circumscribed findings were misinterpreted or taken out of context by some. Aggregate differences in the use of imprisonment for black offenders were found, but Hood attributed these largely to the larger number of black offenders convicted of serious offences, and to the tendency to plead not guilty and thus (if convicted) to forfeit the discount for pleading guilty. Only some 7 per cent of the difference was unaccounted for—a possible 'race effect'—and the difference was much more in evidence in one court than in the others. The Commission for Racial Equality publicized the findings widely, and they became a central topic of public discussion. Roger Hood spoke to a wide range of different audiences to explain his findings. On the one hand some sections of the media had rushed to accuse the judiciary of racism (whereas Hood was careful to state his findings more circumspectly), while on the other hand some judges undoubtedly indulged in a whispering campaign against the findings. Some of the judicial misgivings emerged in a more sophisticated form in a short article by a Cambridge research student published in 1995, to which Roger Hood was able to write a strong, clear, and compelling response.[17] *Race and Sentencing* remains the leading piece of research on racial issues, and it has recently been complemented by Roger Hood's research (with Stephen Shute) on ethnic minorities' perceptions of the fairness of criminal courts.[17a]

Effectiveness of Penal Measures

At an early stage in his career Roger Hood took part in a criminological colloquium organized by the Council of Europe on the effectiveness of penal measures. The paper he produced on that

---

[16] R. Hood in collaboration with G. Cordovil, *Race and Sentencing* (Oxford: Oxford University Press, 1992); the C.R.E. also produced a short summary of the research, as *A Question of Judgement: Race and Sentencing* (London: Commission for Racial Equality, 1992).

[17] T. Halevy, 'Racial Discrimination in Sentencing? A Study with Dubious Conclusions' [1995] *Crim.L.R.* 267, and R. Hood, 'Race and Sentencing: A Reply' [1995] *Crim.L.R.* 272.

[17a] R. Hood, S. Shute, and F. Seemungal, *Ethnic Minorities in the Criminal Courts: Perceptions of Fairness and Equality of Treatment* (London: Lord Chancellor's Department, Research Series No. 2/03, 2003).

occasion,[18] an astute and judicious assessment of the research and some of its pitfalls, stood for many years as a most penetrating analysis of effectiveness studies. It was the foundation for many of the points developed in Chapters 6 and 7 of *Key Issues in Criminology*.[19] Interestingly, Hood took the opportunity to return to the subject a quarter of a century later, again under the auspices of the Council of Europe, when he accepted appointment as general *rapporteur* for a project on *Psychosocial Interventions in the Criminal Justice System*.[20] This enabled him to reflect on the deep changes in policy, principle, and even criminological fashion that had taken place in the intervening years. He noted how, after the decline of rehabilitation and the rise of neo-classical rationales in the 1970s, the early 1990s were witnessing a revival of emphasis on the management of dangerous offenders and of enthusiasm for the effectiveness of treatment. From the very beginning, he pointed out the 'dangers that such claims will be influential, the lessons of the past ignored, and some of the benefits which have flowed from the adoption of just deserts reversed'.[21] His measured assessment identifies both the advantages to be gained and the pitfalls to be avoided in what has become known as the 'What Works' movement.

Custody

Roger Hood's second book, based on his doctoral thesis, was *Borstal Re-Assessed*.[22] This traced the various stages in the development of the borstal system from the early years of the century, and assembled evidence about its effectiveness. The book appraises the borstal system through the lenses of early criminological theory and then contemporary penal policy, and demonstrates how the later development of borstals and of other measures for young offenders was constrained by sensitivity to public opinion and by some judicial

---

[18] R. Hood, 'Research on the Effectiveness of Punishments and Treatments' in Council of Europe, *Collected Studies in Criminological Research* (Strasbourg: Council of Europe, 1967) i, 73.

[19] N. 7 above.

[20] Council of Europe, *Psychosocial Interventions in the Criminal Justice System*, Collected Studies in Criminological Research, xxxi (Strasbourg: Council of Europe, 1996); Hood's written contributions are to be found in his Introduction and his Conclusions.

[21] Ibid., 13.

[22] R. Hood, *Borstal Re-Assessed* (Cambridge Studies in Criminology, London: Heinemann, 1965).

conservatism. This research also gave rise to the short book on *Homeless Borstal Boys*,[23] which involved a follow-up of borstal boys and an examination of factors relevant to their reconviction. Hood's sophisticated understanding of the processes at work during custodial sentences was also evident from the final chapter of *Key Issues in Criminology*,[24] with its searching assessment of the then current state of research on the effects of custody on the individuals subjected to it.

History of Criminal Justice

Research and writing on penal history provided the focus of Roger Hood's work for several years in the late 1970s and early 1980s. This was not the first time he had engaged in serious historical work: for example, the whole thrust of his *Borstal Re-Assessed* involved tracing the history of borstals through original sources such as reports of the Prison Commissioners, in order to identify the official objectives of the institutions before assessing the extent to which those objectives were achieved. However, his collaboration with Sir Leon Radzinowicz in the monumental task of writing the fifth volume of *A History of English Criminal Law and its Administration from 1750* took him deep into the details and the interpretation of nineteenth-century penal history. A team of researchers trawled the primary sources, and Radzinowicz and Hood then set about the task of collating, interpreting, writing, and revising. Along the way they published major journal articles arising from the research, dealing with the approach to political prisoners,[25] with the various initiatives towards the structuring of sentencing,[26] and with the various attempts to deal with habitual criminals.[27] Volume 5 of 'the History' was published in 1986,[28] to considerable

---

[23] R. Hood, *Homeless Borstal Boys* (London: G. Bell & Sons, 1966).

[24] See n. 7 above.

[25] L. Radzinowicz and R. Hood, 'The Status of Political Prisoners in England: the Struggle for Recognition' (1979) 65 *Virginia Law Review* 1421.

[26] L. Radzinowicz and R. Hood, 'Judicial Discretion and Sentencing Standards: Victorian Attempts to Solve a Perennial Problem' (1979) 127 *University of Pennsylvania Law Review* 1288.

[27] L. Radzinowicz and R. Hood, 'Incapacitating the Habitual Criminal: The English Experience' (1980) 78 *Michigan Law Review* 1305.

[28] L. Radzinowicz and R. Hood, *A History of English Criminal Law: volume V, The Emergence of Penal Policy in Victorian and Edwardian England* (London: Stevens, 1986); the volume was reprinted in paperback, without the extensive bibliography, by Oxford University Press in 1990.

acclaim.[29] From the outset there was no doubt that it would stand the test of time to become the standard work, such is its degree of detail and the sureness of its interpretations. It ranges over theories of criminality, the problems of measuring crime, early efforts to deal specially with young offenders, the abiding problem of recidivists, the history of transportation and the evolution of the prison system, the range of punishments from death, through flogging to noncustodial alternatives, and the attempts to rationalize sentencing. It is an immense achievement, not least because the elegance and clarity of the writing make it a pleasure to read. A decade later Roger Hood was drawn back into the study of penal history when he obtained a research grant to carry out oral historical research into the experience of crime and social change of three generations of people in the East End of London. The report of this research demonstrates how offending and victimization were parts of everyday life in all three generations, but that various forms of social restraints were loosened and individual expectations tended to heighten as the last century wore on.[30]

The Death Penalty

One particular sphere of criminal policy in which Roger Hood's international reputation came to him relatively late in his career is his expertise in matters of capital punishment. Although he took an interest in it in earlier years, particularly during the period when he spent a month or so each year as Visiting Distinguished Professor of Law at the University of Virginia, it was not until the late 1980s that he was commissioned by the United Nations to prepare a report on the extent to which capital punishment was still used in member states. That report was presented to the tenth session of the United Nations Committee on Crime Prevention and Control in 1988, and it formed the basis of his monograph on the death penalty, now in its third edition.[31] The book is a comprehensive criminological study, examining such matters as the progress of the abolitionist movement, the observance of safeguards, the problems of a restricted

---

[29] Excerpts from reviews may be found on the back cover of the paperback edition of 1990.

[30] The most accessible publication from this research is R. Hood and K. Joyce, 'Three Generations: Oral Histories on Crime and Social Change in London's East End' (1999) 39 *British Journal of Criminology* 136.

[31] R. Hood, *The Death Penalty: A World-Wide Perspective* (3rd edn., Oxford: Oxford University Press, 2002).

use of capital punishment, and issues relating to public opinion. Probably its most potent arguments are to be found in its analysis of the evidence on the deterrent effect of capital punishment. The book pays particular attention to certain details of the policies in the United States, where the death penalty has come to be used more frequently in recent years. However, one of the abiding difficulties is to obtain accurate information about the numbers of executions in various countries across the world: even the United Nations often cannot succeed in getting replies to its questions, and so it has taken all Roger Hood's powers to ensure that what he writes is as accurate as can be. The great success of his work on capital punishment leads him frequently on to the international stage, with visits to various countries, often at the request of the British Foreign Office, to argue the case for abolition in accordance with United Nations policy.

* * *

From this selective and relatively brief survey of Roger Hood's work, the sheer breadth of his contributions to criminology comes clear. His research is at the forefront of criminological knowledge on several fronts, and it has had a distinct influence on policy in many fields—notably sentencing, parole, race, and capital punishment. And yet the degree of influence has not always been commensurate with the quality of the research and the robustness of its findings, and this has led Roger Hood to reflect on the relationship between criminology and penal policy. It is this theme, which draws from all the fields of his criminological research, that forms the focal point of this volume in his honour.

Roger Hood on Criminology and Penal Policy

The relationship between criminological research and penal policy is a subject that has long been a matter of concern to Roger Hood. He has written about this relationship on at least four separate occasions spanning twenty-eight years.[32] These four articles provide a fascinating insight into his own attitudes to the role of criminological

---

[32] R. Hood, 'Criminology and Penal Change: A Case Study of the Nature and Impact of Some Recent Advice to Governments' in R. Hood (ed.), *Crime, Criminology and Public Policy: Essays in Honour of Sir Leon Radzinowicz* (London: Heinemann, 1974) 375; R. Hood, 'Some Reflections on the Role of Criminology in Public Policy'

research, its import for penal policy, and changes in the nature of the relationship itself.

Writing in 1974,[33] Roger Hood applauded the fundamental premise of the 1959 White Paper, *Penal Practice in a Changing Society*,[34] that penal policy should be based on criminological research into the nature of offending, the efficacy of existing penal measures, and a review of penal philosophy.[35] The White Paper did not envisage a quick technological fix and regarded the funding of long-term research as essential.[36] It is important to remember that criminology was still in its infancy in Britain well into the 1950s. One academic who began teaching the subject in 1955 is reported to have been surprised to find himself inhabiting 'an empty discipline'.[37] The role of the Home Office in breathing life into the discipline—both in the setting up of its own Research Unit and in the funding of the Institute of Criminology in Cambridge—was pivotal. The fine words and financial muscle of the Home Office could not, however, ensure that subsequent penal policy-makers took note or made use of the very criminological output it had sought to encourage. Roger Hood lamented the repeated failure of post-war penal policy to base itself on the findings of criminological research. In the introduction of the suspended sentence,[38] for example, he regretted that 'the part played by criminological analysis, theory and research was minimal'.[39] And similarly, in respect of the introduction of community service, he criticized the unfounded assumption that working alongside volunteers could readily influence offenders.

[1987] *Crim.L.R.* 527; R. Hood, 'Penal Policy and Criminological Challenges in the New Millennium' (2001) 34 *The Australian and New Zealand Journal of Criminology* 1; R. Hood, 'Criminology and Penal Policy: The Vital Role of Empirical Research' in A. Bottoms and M. Tonry (eds.), *Ideology, Crime and Criminal Justice: A symposium in honour of Sir Leon Radzinowicz* (Cullompton: Willan Publishing, 2002) 153.

[33] In the *Festschrift* edited by him in honour of Sir Leon Radzinowicz, n. 32 above.

[34] Home Office, *Penal Practice in a Changing Society*, Cmd. 645 (London: HMSO, 1959) 7.

[35] Hood, 'Criminology and Penal Change', n. 32 above, 384.

[36] '[R]apid progress cannot be expected. Research Projects in this field are inevitably complex and take time to complete': Home Office, n. 34 above, 8–9.

[37] Quoted in P. Rock, 'The Social Organization of British Criminology' in M. Maguire *et al.* (eds.), *The Oxford Handbook of Criminology* (Oxford: Oxford University Press, 1994) 131.

[38] First introduced in the Criminal Justice Act 1967 and subsequently re-enacted in the Powers of the Criminal Courts Act 1973.

[39] Hood, 'Criminology and Penal Change', n. 32 above, 380.

'Where', he asked, 'was the consideration of the problem in the light of criminological ideas and knowledge?'[40] His argument was not that community service was necessarily wrong-headed, but rather that there had been no recourse to criminological research in order to assess how it might be expected to work, for what types of offender it might be suitable, and so on.

This failure to base policy development upon criminological research appeared to Roger Hood to be an abandonment of the fundamental principles of the 1959 White Paper. Instead, government committees[41] repeatedly eschewed consideration of research in favour of policy developments based largely on political expediency and mere opinion. In so far as criminological research had a place at all it was in the evaluation of penal measures already introduced. Roger Hood was by no means hostile to 'careful evaluation of new penal measures—if possible through controlled experimental conditions'. He insisted, however, that experimental innovation would be likely to result in 'a series of ineffectual remedies' if not based upon a reasoned consideration of why each '*might* be a useful and just addition to the penal measures already available'[42]—the word 'addition' sounding an early warning against the unco-ordinated burgeoning of different forms of non-custodial penalty. The absence of 'coherent and convincing criminological argument' was, he concluded, in part the structural failing of government advisory bodies called upon to operate without facilities for research or academic enquiry.[43] In the absence of research facilities, the recommendations made were no more than 'a potpourri of intelligent suggestions' whose acceptance was dependent more on their political appeal than their likely efficacy in providing a viable alternative to imprisonment. His conclusion was gloomy, even fatalistic: 'the belief that expert advice based on criminological and penological research is the foundation for penal change, is only a screen behind which ideological and political factors, perhaps inevitably, shape those attitudes which imbue legislation'.[44] This seminal quotation is used in several of the contributions to this volume: its characterization of criminological research as no more than 'a screen' for ideo-

[40]   Hood, 'Criminology and Penal Change', n. 32 above, 411.
[41]   And particularly the Wootton Committee.
[42]   Hood, 'Criminology and Penal Change', n. 32 above, 390.
[43]   Ibid., 417.
[44]   Ibid.

logically and politically driven penal policies suggests a most super-ficial presentational role. But it would be wrong to conclude that Hood sees no greater role for criminology, as his later publications attest.

He returned to the question of the role of criminology in a plenary address to the American Society of Criminology in 1986.[45] Here again he was concerned with the interplay between research and policy and, in particular, with the problematic nature of this rela-tionship. But he seemed to have overcome some of his earlier pes-simism to argue strongly that criminology did have a role to play in the formulation of policy. He declared 'startling' Stanley Cohen's view that 'it is simply not our professional job to advise, consult, recommend, or make decisions'.[46] And he rejected as false Cohen's analogy with the sociologist of religion acting as priest. A better analogy, he suggested, was between economics and fiscal policy. His point was that criminology should not be seen as synonymous with a particular approach but, at its best, as a means of challenging ortho-doxies, exposing myths, destroying stereotypes, and exposing injust-ices. In this critical role, it would be much harder to characterize criminologists as the handmaidens of government or as apologists for state repression.

More importantly still, Roger Hood insisted 'that, by its very nature, crime cannot be logically separated from the study of crim-inal policy... criminal behaviour as a social entity does not exist independently of the policy and legal and administrative apparatus which defines it, classifies it, labels and interacts with it'.[47] He thus framed policy formulation both as a legitimate outcome and as a necessary subject of criminological enquiry. In doing so he was extremely wary of the dangers that policy would drive (and con-strain) research, and he deplored the criminological peddling of simplified solutions to fundamental social problems. In particular, he regretted the increasing sway that governments held over aca-demic research. The distinction between internal Home Office re-search and that conducted 'outside' by academics was being eroded by changes in patterns of funding, the rise of the 'customer-

---

[45] Hood (1987), n. 32 above.
[46] S. Cohen, *Visions of Social Control* (Cambridge: Polity Press, 1985) 238.
[47] Hood (1987), n. 32 above, at 530.

contractor' principle in the commission of research, and the direct political control of the research agenda by ministers. He identified the dangers arising from a criminological agenda controlled by policy interests as the promotion of 'narrow, often excessively narrow, technical evaluation of administrative procedures or decisions'; concentration on 'short to mid-term problems'; the pressure to find solutions; and 'research programmes truncated to meet administrative schedules for the receipt of "answers" '.[48] This, he concluded, 'surely cannot be good for the intellectual development of any discipline'. No doubt he was reflecting, with all too painful self-awareness, on the dilemmas he daily faced as the Director of the Oxford Centre for Criminological Research, as he went on to observe that 'for the community of researchers, their product, and their future hopes of contracts, run the risk of being assessed by the criterion of how useful—and perhaps how palatable—their findings and recommendations are to the authorities'.[49] The most important source of resistance to these pressures lay, he argued, in greater financial independence from government funding which might enable academics to pursue research free from the pressures of policy relevance.

In this address, Roger Hood appeared torn. He saw criminology's role in informing policy as central to its task, and went so far as to concur 'wholeheartedly' with Sir Leon Radzinowicz's argument that 'to rob criminology of this practical function is to render it sterile'.[50] This is a strong statement and it envisages a particular brand of criminology that cannot but have in mind the practical ramifications of its knowledge. But Hood was equally impressed by the costs of policy relevance. He saw the pressures of policy-driven research as inimical to intellectual integrity and the present organization of government funding as hostile to criminology's critical role. His support for the 'practical function' of criminology would ensure that he did not call for the complete severing of connections between university research and government agendas. The problem was, and is, one of ensuring a relationship that acknowledges, and goes some way towards satisfying, the legitimate interests of both.

It is striking that writing at the beginning of the new century, Roger Hood depicted an even more hostile climate for crimino-

---

[48] Hood (1987), n. 32 above, 536–7.   [49] Ibid., 537.
[50] L. Radzinowicz, *In Search of Criminology* (London: Heinemann, 1961) 168.

logical research than that which had prevailed at the time of his previous articles. In his keynote address to the Australian and New Zealand Society of Criminology in 1999, he wrote of a 'crisis' in the relationship between academic criminology and penal policy-making, arising from the ascendancy of ideological and political considerations over the findings of research.[51] Reflecting on this historic shift he argued, '[t]here can be no doubt that the gulf between criminological research and penal policy has now become yet more acute'.[52] He had identified this gulf in his 1974 essay. He attributed its widening to the disproportionate prominence given to popular opinion in the formation of penal policy (a prominence all the more curious when compared, by him, to the reliance of health policy on medical science, not public opinion). The impact of 'populist punitiveness' (to borrow from Bottoms[53]) had downgraded the influence of criminological knowledge, and Hood found himself in good criminological company in bemoaning the widening gap between criminology and penal policy.

Reflecting historically, Roger Hood saw the period of his own criminological education as one in which 'the view that criminology was a social scientific discipline that would provide the evidence for "rational improvement" was unquestioned'.[54] Accepting that this assumption was politically naïve, he was nevertheless disinclined to accept that it was wrongheaded. What, then, had happened to bring about the abandonment of this basic assumption? Looking back, he discerned three key factors: growing public intolerance of high crime rates; loss of confidence in the ability of the state to deal with crime through progressive or welfare measures; and the distancing of the liberal, humanitarian aspirations of most criminologists from the hard-headed realism of politicians anxious for public support.

These political shifts are well beyond the scope of the academy to control, but Roger Hood also wondered 'whether criminologists themselves have not had some part to play in the growing disillusionment with criminological knowledge'.[55] In particular he drew attention to the fundamental ambivalence of criminologists about their

---

[51] Hood (2001), n. 32 above.

[52] Ibid., 2.

[53] A. Bottoms, 'The Philosophy and Politics of Punishment' in C. Clarkson and R. Morgan (eds.), *The Politics of Sentencing Reform* (Oxford: Clarendon Press, 1995).

[54] Hood (2001), n. 32 above, 6.   [55] Ibid., 7.

involvement in the penal system. First, criminologists tended to distinguish between the role of criminological knowledge in informing penal policy and the quite separate task of deciding that policy. Indeed, as Hood and Sparks themselves argued as early as 1970, there are severe limits to what criminology can properly claim to do—'[w]hat it cannot do is to decide what the *aims* of penal policy should be'.[56] This self-limiting ordinance constituted a powerful constraint on the impact criminology might properly seek to make. Secondly, the widespread rejection of 'correctionalism' by criminologists created a critical climate in which any exercise of state power was viewed with suspicion. In this climate, criminology was readily characterized as 'useful knowledge' destined 'to legitimise and extend modern penal power'.[57] Hood saw this as distorting what criminology stood for, and as effectively depriving criminologists of any critical role—a painful irony, given that many became criminologists precisely in the 'belief that they wanted improve the criminal justice system'. Thirdly, while he accepted Nils Christie's characterization of criminology's role as 'problem raising' as much as 'problem solving', he regretted that the 'nothing works' school had had a 'depressing effect on both criminologists and policy makers'.[58] Fourthly, he cited the common distaste amongst criminologists for empirical study of difficult subjects linked to punitive policies, for example, deterrence, risk assessment, and privatization. Fifthly, he criticized the trend for dominating fashions in methodology rather than the acceptance of different, competing approaches as appropriate for different purposes. This last trend manifested itself chiefly as a rejection of 'number-crunching' and of positivism (a term, he suggested, 'often used for its damning effect, rather than denoting a wholesale rejection of scientific method') in favour of qualitative work. Finally, he regretted the withdrawal of many criminologists from empirical research generally: 'without empirical enquiry, the ability of criminology to influence penal policies and practices will be greatly reduced'.[59]

---

[56] R. Hood and R. Sparks, *Key Issues in Criminology* (London: Weidenfeld and Nicolson, 1970) 8–9.

[57] D. Garland, 'Criminological Knowledge and its Relation to Power' (1992) 36 *British Journal of Criminology* 403.

[58] Hood (2001), n. 32 above, 9.   [59] Ibid., 12.

Similarly, in his contribution to a volume of essays in honour of his friend and mentor Sir Leon Radzinowicz,[60] Roger Hood took issue with the distinction drawn by David Garland and Richard Sparks between criminologists operating 'as a kind of specialist underlabourer' and those who engage in 'more lofty and wide ranging debates'.[61] He insisted that 'criminologists will be heard only if they can speak in their "wider ranging role" from a firm base of empirical research, and research that can make claims to be scientifically rigorous, in the sense that it is repeatable, reliable and valid. This is what distinguishes criminology from other types of discourse about crime. Unless legitimacy can be claimed for this view, the "criminologist" will be treated as just another person with an "opinion" on the subject'.[62] In so arguing, Roger Hood did not seek to separate the empirical and the discursive; indeed, he insisted that 'one cannot be done convincingly without the other'.[63] But he was equally clear that criminology will gain acceptance in the public sphere only if the scientific legitimacy of its findings is beyond question. Where criminologists fail to defend the prestige of their discipline, or where they cave in to the pressure to 'bring in research funds', and conduct research which they know to be methodologically flawed, or accept contracts for research which is 'quick and dirty',[64] they undermine the professional integrity of their work. In so arguing, he came again to the same conclusion as in his Australian address, namely that 'some of the problems that confront us as criminologists are due to our own failings'.[65]

Although Roger Hood regards the development of theory as a legitimate criminological enterprise, he has tended to emphasize the importance of empirical contributions in order to counteract what he sees as inadequately grounded theorizing or policy prescriptions. As his earlier writings confirm, his view is that criminal justice policy should be based 'on criminological research into the nature of offending, the efficacy of existing penal measures, and a review of penal philosophy'.[66] It is noticeable that this assumes a notion of the criminological enterprise that goes much wider than the empirical. The same assumption shines through his criticism of the way in

---

[60] Hood, 'Criminology and Penal Policy: The Vital Role of Empirical Research', n. 32 above.

[61] Quoted in ibid., 158.   [62] Ibid., 159.   [63] Ibid.   [64] Ibid., 168.

[65] Ibid., 161.   [66] See n. 4 above.

which the suspended sentence was introduced: in commenting that 'the part played by criminological analysis, theory and research was minimal',[67] he clearly included two aspects of the criminological enterprise apart from empirical research. Both of these deserve further discussion.

The first is 'theory', itself a wide-ranging notion which, in this context, is used to refer to both the matters of 'penal philosophy' indicated earlier and social interpretations of trends and tendencies. It is true that some of the debates about penal philosophies have an inevitable empirical dimension: it is important to examine the extent to which, and the conditions under which, individual or general deterrence may be expected to work; it is necessary to put to an empirical test the claims of those who promote incapacitation as a goal; empirical findings on rehabilitative measures have long been the subject of evaluation and re-evaluation by criminologists; and the same should happen in relation to restorative justice. But the empirical dimension is only part of the debate. There are also the questions of principle raised by the various rationales for punishment, and the issues of social meaning and social effects. There were criminologists at the forefront of the rehabilitative movement in the 1960s, and there are still many who find this approach persuasive in principle. There were also, for example, criminologists who argued for or who supported the intended shift towards 'just deserts' in the 1980s and early 1990s. These instances can be advanced in support of the importance of work in penal philosophy and of its relevance to policy. Moreover, such work does not need to be done at the level of 'macro-theory': as Roger Hood advocated in his powerful essay on 'Tolerance and the Tariff',[68] it is also necessary to scrutinize the arguments for regarding certain offences as more serious than others. This should fall with the scope of the normative dimension of criminology.

'Theory' also has another dimension, which looks not so much to the justifications for taking coercive measures against those convicted of offending as to interpretations of trends and tendencies in penal policy. In recent years there has been considerable preoccupation with this kind of approach in criminological writings. Although

---

[67] See n. 8 above.

[68] R. Hood, 'Tolerance and the Tariff: Some Reflections on Fixing the Time Prisoners Serve in Custody' (London: NACRO, 1974).

Roger Hood condemned 'broad overviews and predictions' whose captivating prophecies of 'net-widening' and 'dispersal of discipline' were, in his view, 'better examples of penal rhetoric than descriptions of penal practice',[69] it is doubtful whether he would reject this whole *genre* of theorizing. Its gist is to identify and to characterize drifts or trends of policy, often (though not always) as a prelude to a critical argument. That critical argument may have specific empirical components (is there evidence of significant net-widening as a result of certain policy initiatives?), but it is more likely to be a question of the 'general fit' of the characterization—to what extent do we live in a 'risk society'? Is the actuarial approach a prominent aspect of penal policy? Has there been a movement from the corporal to the carceral? Is 'responsibilization' a major or a minor aspect of current penal policy? In raising questions of this kind, criminologists are trying to make sense of social developments. Imaginative theorizing that is grounded in sound empirical understanding is to be valued highly. The value of this kind of theorizing surely transcends the empirically verifiable: it is more a question of making sense of what is going on, about which lively debate is always possible. The premises of those who develop such theories must be subjected to rigorous scrutiny, of course, but there is also a place for imaginative theorizing in criminology.

   The other aspect of the criminological enterprise identified by Roger Hood in his earlier writings was 'criminological analysis', which might suggest the use of a body of criminological 'knowledge' to scrutinize the foundations of any penal policy proposal. The obvious question, then, is what counts as criminological 'knowledge'. The findings of quantitative empirical research clearly fall into this category, even if we must recall that such findings often incorporate elements of judgement, classification, and other normative aspects. There must also be a central place for the findings of qualitative empirical research, although Roger Hood has been implicitly critical of those who favour the 'qualitative' appreciation of sentiments, actions, and 'meaning' over quantitative work.[70] It is true this kind of work does not produce ' "hard", verifiable and repeatable observations'. It is, however, arguable that more radical changes in penal policy will be brought about not by demonstrating the superior efficacy of one sanction over another, but by understanding

[69] Hood, n. 51 above, 11.   [70] Ibid., 10.

and thereby changing social perceptions of crime. We would at least conclude that the findings of both quantitative and qualitative research should be regarded as forming part of criminological 'knowledge', subject to the usual scrutiny of their integrity and of the inferences to be drawn from them.

How should this 'criminological analysis, theory and research' be deployed? It should be brought to bear on policy debates not only through the writings of criminologists but also, Roger Hood has argued, through their engagement in advisory and policy-making groups. He acknowledges the legitimacy of criminological involvement in government committees, commissions, and the boards of state and voluntary organizations, to say nothing of 'lobbying by criminologists in favour of reducing the prison population'.[71] He would also go further: his point is not merely that engagement with penal policy is a legitimate and (probably) laudable role for the criminologist, but also that this kind of engagement is part of the criminologist's duty to her or his profession. However, Roger Hood has not sought to lay blame for the breakdown of the relationship between criminology and penal policy solely at the door of academic criminologists. He has also been severely critical of changes in the promotion, commissioning, and funding of research whether within the Home Office, the Research Councils, or other Foundations. He commented critically that '[t]hose who fund research have gathered to themselves greater and greater power to set the agenda, to control access to information, to specify the scope of the work through tender documents and to approve the reports before final payment'.[72] He condemned also the increasingly narrow conception of 'policy relevance' being promoted by managerialist pressures; the inadequacy of resources; and shortness of time-scales truncated to meet administrative schedules. And he deplored the inevitable negative impact both on the quality of research produced and on those attracted into the discipline. His principal solution lay in structural change: the creation of a Criminological Research Council to ensure independence of funding and to protect criminology from the manacles of government.

Roger Hood's conception of criminology is expansive, catholic (in the sense of admitting many brands of the faith), and yet personally, decidedly pragmatic. As he has argued elsewhere '*talking* about

---

[71] R. Hood, 'Tolerance and the Tariff: Some Reflections on Fixing the Time Prisoners Serve in Custody' (London: NACRO, 1974) 9.   [72] Ibid., 12.

criminology is not the same thing as *doing* criminology. Both are necessary and both should support each other'.[73] His pragmatism derives from a strong sense of conscience and the obligation owed by academics to achieving 'a more just, equitable, non-discriminatory and effective penal response to crime'.[74] It manifests itself also in the belief that seeking larger social and economic change is but an ambition. Since 'crime and criminals will be with us', 'we are duty bound to contribute our knowledge to achieve, as best we can, a just and effective penal policy for the many who will continue to fall within the grasp of the criminal justice system'. For Roger Hood that duty is best discharged by seeking to attain the highest standards of scientific legitimacy and by securing sufficient independence within the academy for criminologists to pursue their research unfettered by the narrow demands of policy relevance.

The Essays

The contributions to this volume reflect upon the relationship between criminological research and the development of policy. In their different ways the essays draw upon Roger Hood's own reflections upon this relationship and reflect upon the contribution of his research to policy formation during his long career as a criminologist. The twelve essays are grouped into four sections, which examine in turn the theoretical relationships between criminological research and policy; the historical development of these relationships; case studies of policy change; and finally, perspectives on international comparisons.

The first, theory section opens with an analysis by Richard Ericson of the culture and power of criminological knowledge. Contrary to prevailing perceptions, Ericson argues that criminologists have a powerful influence on policy, both by providing the rhetoric in which policy is enunciated and by furnishing the applied knowledge and the technologies through which policing systems are constructed. His central premise is that criminology is simultaneously a policy field, a legal field, and part of a system of academic disciplines. The import of these categories is that criminologists can escape neither policy nor law: the one forms both the subject and the very *raison d'être* of criminology, the other the frame within which

---

[73] Hood (2002), n. 32 above, 156.   [74] Hood, n. 51 above, 6.

criminology exists. As an academic discipline, criminology inevitably competes for the primacy of its jurisdiction over the problems of crime and its control. It is this competition that generates the sense of powerlessness so bemoaned by criminologists.

In the second essay, Nicola Lacey addresses the absence of a principled framework for criminal justice reform and the inhibition on principled policy-making imposed by the increasing politicization of criminal justice. Lacey explains the growing political salience of crime by reference to larger changes in the political, cultural, and economic structure of late modern societies. In the political struggles brought about by these changes, governments identify crime control as a useful tool to maintain their legitimacy. The effects of politicization are for Lacey worrying, not least in the misplaced emphasis consequently given to punishment as a means of controlling crime. She concludes by considering how normative penal philosophies may be adapted to establish the principles that should underlie penal institutions and practice, and how these might relate to larger questions of social justice.

In the third essay, Anthony Bottoms offers theoretical reflections on the interaction between policy and research in the evolution of the 'Incentives and Earned Privileges' (IEP) policy introduced into English prisons and young offender institutions in 1995. He begins by explaining the avowed purposes of IEP—in short to improve prisoners' behaviour—and the procedures by which it was introduced. The central core of the chapter reports the findings of the Cambridge research (in which Bottoms had special responsibility for theoretical issues) in five very different penal institutions during the first year in which IEP was implemented, drawing on compliance theory in order to interpret the results. Although the implementation of IEP differed significantly from institution to institution, in general the research found little evidence of success in improving prisoners' behaviour. Bottoms concludes by examining the reception of these research findings by policy-makers and by reflecting upon on the possibilities and limits of penal policies, such as this, that are based upon rational choice theory.

The essays in the second section examine the historical relationship between criminological research and policy formation from three quite different perspectives. In the opening essay Lucia Zedner examines the history of British criminology in the post-war period. She argues that the prevailing sense that criminology has failed to influence policy formation is exacerbated by disagreement over the discipline's role and purpose. Zedner contends that this fractured intellectual history owes much to its institutional origins; that intellectual and institutional rivalry has obscured the value of *rapprochement*; and that the schism is itself based on a shared delusion that only policy-oriented research is capable of influencing policy. Finally, she rejects the presumption that criminology has failed by arguing that its larger influence lies in providing the language, the key concepts, and the theoretical and normative frameworks in which policy is developed.

Seán McConville's essay takes its theme from Roger Hood's major historical contribution with Sir Leon Radzinowicz in *A History of English Criminal Law and its Administration*.[75] It examines the effects on penal policy of the activities of political prisoners in the years around the First World War. The position of political prisoners, contends McConville, rendered them peculiarly well placed to write powerful accounts of their experiences of prison life, to mobilize supporters, to attract publicity, and to lobby parliament. Some even went on to attain personal positions of political influence or power. Given the unusually rich source of data about prison life they provided and the strength of their political power, one might have expected political prisoners to have exerted considerable influence on subsequent penal policy. That so little change eventuated is a puzzle that McConville explains partly by reference to the fact that there was little by way of criminological enterprise in Britain in the 1920s able to harness this rich resource effectively.

In the final essay in this section, Lord Windlesham transports us to the end of the twentieth century to examine the influences on penal policy formation in the years 1997–2001. The essay analyses how the objectives of New Labour were translated into criminal justice policy and practice in the party's first term of office. The Labour government was particularly anxious to make political capital of research evidence from the British Crime Survey which partially confirmed the downward trend in recorded crime. Windlesham analyses the political and institutional influences behind the major reform programme pushed through by the Labour administration. He pays particular attention to the two far-reaching reviews it

[75] *Volume V. The Emergence of Penal Policy in Victorian and Edwardian England* (London: Stevens, 1986).

commissioned: one dealing with the relationships between the courts and the wider criminal justice system carried out by Court of Appeal judge Sir Robin Auld, and one dealing with the sentencing framework conducted by senior civil servant John Halliday. He observes that the emphasis on the expertise of the reviewer in each case, together with the tight timetable imposed, meant that there was less reliance upon criminological research than, for example, in previous Royal Commissions. He concludes that political imperatives rather than criminological research drove legislative change in this period.

The essays in the third section address three case studies that highlight particular aspects of the research–policy relationship. The first, by Andrew Ashworth, explores the impact of criminological research upon English sentencing policy. Opening with the crisis in judicial legitimacy as a major theme in late twentieth-century criminal justice history, Ashworth suggests that this crisis is better understood as a deficit in public confidence. Ashworth goes on to explore the effect of research findings on the innovations in sentencing policy and on the rise or fall of particular rationales for sentencing, and also the effect of research findings on sentencing practice in the magistrates' courts and the Crown Court. He observes that criminological research evidence has had minimal influence on the introduction of new forms of sentence. By contrast the growth of academic interest in penal philosophy has spawned vigorous debates around rehabilitation, proportionality, incapacitation, and restorative justice which have, in turn, influenced the rise and fall of these various rationales for punishment. From analysis of policy formation, Ashworth moves to examine the impact of research on sentencing practice, observing, in particular, the differing receptiveness of the magistracy and the judiciary to empirical research. Whereas the former has shown itself open to research and interested in its findings, there remains a serious reluctance among the judiciary to allow empirical research into their working practices, thereby closing off a major sphere of public administration from understanding and from independent scrutiny.

The second essay, by Andrew Sanders and Richard Young, takes the case of police research, policy, and practice as its subject. Examining the impact on policy and practice of three empirical studies of policing in which the authors were themselves involved, they explore how far their varying influence was due to the different origins, style, results, or publication of the research. Their contention is not that one research style or another is to be preferred, but rather that different styles are complementary and that the persuasiveness of criminological research is bolstered by a synthesis of approaches. Advocating oscillation between different levels of theory, research styles, and publication fora, Sanders and Young conclude that critical/theoretical research and policy-led evaluation are in reality complementary rather than antithetical.

In the final essay in this section, Stephen Shute examines the role of research in the development of parole. He charts the origins, the rise, and the subsequent reforms of the parole system, and demonstrates the various respects in which criminological research contributed. He identifies the considerable influence of empirical research at the early stages, on such matters as the composition and dynamics of Local Review Committees and the incongruity between risk of reconviction and LRC recommendations. He draws attention to the many ways in which scholarly writings on parole policy in the 1970s—Roger Hood's prominent among them—presaged reforms of the early release system that were introduced sooner or later. The essay lays bare the penal ambiguity of parole, and shows how a system with no clearly accepted rationale has been blown one way or another by winds from different directions—the need to control the prison population, the use of information about risk of re-offending, and caution about the consequences of mistaken releases. Although he establishes that criminological research has influenced parole policy in various ways, Shute concludes that the future shape of the early release system remains profoundly uncertain.

The final section offers three sets of international observations on the research/policy relationship. The first essay, by Heike Jung, reconstructs the campaign in Germany to promote the place of the victim in criminal justice policy. Recognizing that the German victims' movement has been embedded in and influenced by international developments, Jung nonetheless argues that the particular orientation of the debate has been structured by German legal and philosophical traditions and existing laws. Jung suggests that the palpable influence of victimologists in promoting victims' policies appears to run counter to Hood's diagnosis of a 'widening gulf' in the relationship between criminology and penal policy. But Jung is equally quick to point out both that criminologists had influence because their demands happened fortuitously to coincide with popular sentiment and that the results of that influence were not always those they had intended or desired.

The second essay in the section, by Richard Harding, explores the successes and failures of criminological research in Australia. Some successes were immediate, some delayed, some were direct, others indirect and diffuse. The essay examines what factors determined whether research findings were taken up or ignored, and the relationship between take-up of research findings and proximity to the policy-makers. Although he observes a broad correlation between the proximity of the researchers to the official agencies and the take-up of that research, it is by no means uniform. Other important factors in determining the efficacy of research in the Australian case are the socio-political context in which research is carried out and the timeliness of its proposals. In short where the socio-political environment is conducive, the research impact tends to be greatest. Harding also observes other means by which criminological influence can be effectual, not least in the criminologist's various roles as activist, teacher, author, consultant, and bureaucrat: of these some have parallels in Britain, others take distinct and more influential forms in Australia. Not surprisingly, he too concludes that criminologists tend to underestimate the influence they have.

The final essay, by Michael Tonry and David Green, examines the ways in which systematic criminological knowledge (as opposed to researcher preference) has influenced policy in the USA and UK. Tonry and Green observe that knowledge is filtered through existing paradigms, prevailing ideology, short-term political considerations, and bureaucratic inertia. This is not to say that research does not have influence, but that its influence is often indirect and partial. Whilst criminological knowledge is institutionally supported, funded, sought, and valued, politicians and citizens nonetheless tend to think that crime policy is a matter of common sense not reliant on specialist knowledge or expertise. Moreover the 'two communities' occupied by researchers and policy-makers have divergent cultures that often impede effective communication. Tonry and Green conclude that 'research findings are influential in relation to policy-making on most subjects at least some of the time, and on many subjects most of the time'. They argue that, while the case for an independent national research institute is strong, there are ample opportunities within the present funding structure for academic researchers to exert an influence if they use robust research designs and publish their findings in a style accessible to policy-makers.

The essays in this volume were inspired by Roger Hood's writings on the relationship between criminology and public policy. Collectively they in turn raise a number of questions about this relationship and its implications for future criminological scholarship. What do we mean when we talk of criminological research? What is the relationship between empirical research and critical, theoretical, and normative enquiry? Can and should criminologists claim a special scientific expertise and thereby authority? What is and what ought to be the relationship between criminological research and the development of penal policy? What power and what scope does criminology have to influence policy? What are the other competitors for influence, and can that competition be overcome? It will come as no surprise to discover that the authors differ widely in the answers they give to these and other questions. That their essays reveal such diversity of opinion, of inclination, and of expertise is testimony to the rich, if conflicted, nature of contemporary criminology.

Upon one issue alone does there appear to be common accord: namely that there is an indivisible relationship between criminology and penal policy. To the extent that criminologists think that influencing policy is a valid or even a primary role, the question inevitably arises how best the impact of their work can be maximized. Several themes emerge, notably: the timeliness of research; its relevance to current policy concerns; its accessibility to those who might use it; the mode of its distribution; and the importance of pursuing several different paths of influence simultaneously to maximize impact. In all these regards Roger Hood must be regarded as a master of the art. His sensitivity to the political moment, the clarity of his writing, the persuasiveness of his argument, and his rigorous defence of even the most unpalatable truths have ensured that the message of his various important research studies cannot easily be ignored.

We dedicate this collection of essays to Roger Hood as an expression of our admiration for his outstanding scholarship and promotion of criminology. The contributors all responded with great enthusiasm to our invitation and the quality of their essays testifies to the importance they attached to honouring its subject. Together we offer this book as a tribute to the past, present, and future scholarship of our friend Professor Roger Hood CBE, QC (hon), PhD, DCL, FBA, AcSS.

Part 1

The Theoretical Relationships between Research and Policy

1

The Culture and Power of Criminological Research

Richard V. Ericson

Introduction

This chapter explores the research culture and influence of criminology. It makes three claims about criminology. First, regardless of its manifestations across academic disciplines, criminology is a policy field. Its primary research focus is principled courses of action that are or should be taken regarding conduct that is or could be criminalized. Secondly, criminology is a legal field. Its primary question is whether conduct that can be criminalized is best dealt with through the criminal justice system compared to other institutions, for example medicine, business, education, family, insurance, or welfare. Thirdly, criminology is a system of academic disciplines, each with its professional constituency and institutional base in society. These disciplines, professions, and institutions offer competing policy rhetorics and policing alternatives in efforts to gain jurisdiction over problems of crime and security.

Criminologists are in perpetual motion among empirical research, policy rhetorics, and policing initiatives. In moving from research to policy criminologists engage in a process of translation that has three dimensions. First, they shift from the authority of complexity in their research culture to the authority of simplicity in public culture. The messiness of empirical research and theoretical abstractions must be tidied up in order to be pointed at policy. Secondly, they experience chaos. A given criminological inquiry escapes its author as it enters into new professional and institutional contexts where there are competing discourses articulating different interests. Thirdly, simplification and chaos entail loss of autonomy.

The criminologist has his or her research taken by others to use in their own practical contexts for addressing crime and security problems.

The experience of loss of autonomy leads criminologists to complain that their research has little influence on policy. Indeed this perception of lack of influence pervades the culture of criminological research. An opposing viewpoint is advanced in this chapter. Criminologists have powerful influence at the level of both policy rhetorics and policing initiatives. However, because they must compete in the system of criminology, they often find that their own policy preferences are not as hegemonic as those of other criminologists representing different disciplines, professions, and institutions. For example, complaints of lack of influence are pervasive among criminologists whose careers began during the era of the strong welfare state. These criminologists now find their research questions and policy preferences diminished in competition with those who favour rational choice and situational opportunity models of crime reduction and security provision. These models oppose welfarism, and promote self-governance of crime risks by organizations, communities, and individuals beyond the state.

The power of criminological rhetoric is analysed. Criminologists are like legal practitioners in deploying figurative language to urge principled courses of action. Through vivid tropes of crime as blight, illness, opportunism, risk, and so on, criminologists express their preferred cause of crime as it relates to the practical solution that they envisage. Crime is also used as a powerful trope for addressing intractable problems of institutional failure. For example, youth crime is used as a metaphor for failure of the family as the responsible locus for human welfare and the improvement of populations.

The figures of quantitative data also provide figurative language for policy directions. Criminologists help to 'make crime count' by networking with government statistical agents, criminal justice system officials, and journalists to advance particular interests. Data pointing to causal responsibility for crime and security problems are mobilized to influence the response ability of political and legal systems. Moral determinations are made in the selection and interpretation of facts, and data are dramatized to make policy preferences seem urgent.

The power of criminological policing is also analysed. The influence of criminology is found not only at the level of abstract policy rhetoric, but also in how it constitutes policing systems. Indeed the word policy is rooted in policing: the routine practices of surveillance, classification, and regulation used to govern conduct.

Criminology is increasingly a field of applied knowledge and social necessity directed at specific risk-management problems on behalf of particular clients. New criminologies of everyday life draw upon rational choice and routine activity models of criminal offending to invent technologies of situational crime prevention. This technocratic criminology is driven by the policing needs of its professional and institutional constituents, especially those in private business enterprise. Whatever expertise criminologists offer is rapidly de-skilled into the surveillance systems and pragmatic routines of security operatives.

While the primary thrust of criminological policing is preventive security, there are applications throughout the process of criminalization. Powerful new technologies for the policing of risk have been invented and applied by criminologists to determine gradations of restriction on offenders and to justify extra punishment of those de-selected as dangerous. With the aid of these criminological technologies, probation has shifted from welfare to surveillance, imprisonment from rehabilitation to incapacitation, and parole from reintegration to risk minimization.

Criminological policing of risk is also turned onto criminal justice agents themselves. Criminologists invent surveillance, audit, and performance-indicator technologies to monitor the procedural propriety and efficiency of criminal justice operations. In this policing capacity they use their research culture and power to influence the culture and power of the criminal justice system itself.

Criminology as a Policy Field

Criminology is an academic field devoted to the study of policy. Policy is a principled course of action. Criminology both researches and recommends principled courses of action taken by various units of society: institutions, organizations, communities, and individuals. With a focus on how action is principled, criminology is obviously normative. In particular, action is assessed with regard to its pragmatic, sagacious, and prudent qualities. A principled course of action is one which uses practical wisdom to produce desired consequences.

Policy operates at the level of rhetoric. It involves persuasive discourses about preferred courses of action that are intended to move people to act in accordance with the expressed preferences. As such policy is itself a form of action. It is formulated with the intention of being accepted as reality and becoming embedded in routines.

Principles of action are perpetually contested among the myriad institutions, organizations, communities, and individuals that constitute society. Criminologists are part of this contestation for two reasons. First, as analysts of principled courses of action they cannot escape making choices among preferred principles. They make such choices in the topics they choose to research, the classifications they construct, the analyses they undertake, and the techniques through which they structure their research communications. Secondly, their choices are structured by the system of criminology, the academic disciplines, professions, and institutions that constitute the field. For example, there is quite different policy as rhetoric emanating from a criminology that is based in medicine, with its figurative language of disease and resultant model of delinquency and treatment; a criminology based in social science, with its figurative language of community and resultant model of integration and restorative justice; and a criminology based in business enterprise, with its figurative language of risk management and resultant model of loss reduction and loss acceptance.

No criminologist stands outside policy as rhetoric. The criminologist who claims to be doing so through 'pure' quantitative analyses loses sight of the fact that such analyses are based on probability statistics aimed at delineating the normal. What is constituted as the standard or norm through probability statistics bears both factual and moral imprints. 'The norm may be what is usual or typical, yet our most powerful ethical constraints are also called norms'.[1] Probability statistics 'make up people'[2] in the sense of telling them both where they fit within a 'normal' population and what their normative obligations are as a result. That is, people experience the facts of probability statistics as normative obligations

---

[1] I. Hacking, *The Taming of Chance* (Cambridge: Cambridge University Press, 1990), 104.

[2] I. Hacking, 'Making up People' in T. Heller *et al.* (eds.), *Reconstructing Individualism* (Stanford, Cal.: Stanford University Press, 1986).

and therefore as scripts for principled action. They entail 'a power as old as Aristotle to bridge the fact/value distinction, whispering in your ear that what is normal is also all right'.[3]

The criminologist who claims to be standing outside policy as rhetoric through 'pure' theory loses sight of the fact that all theory as abstraction has rhetorical force. This point is not only acknowledged by leading social theorists who have had the greatest influence on criminology, but is also exemplified in their writing. For example, as Garland[4] observes, 'Foucault's inquiries always carried with them a critical, normative dimension, urging us to identify the dangers and harms implicit in the contemporary scheme of things, and to indicate how our present social arrangements might have been—and might still be—differently arranged'. As a leading synthesizer of social theory into criminology, Garland himself readily accepts the normative force of his writing as policy rhetoric.[5]

Criminology is characterized by moral rhetorics of justice. In this respect it is consistent with other social sciences. Abbott[6] reminds us 'that it is of the nature of our perception of moral and political affairs to see—in any social system whatever—a dialogue of good and bad, or inclusion or exclusion, or whatever. Our very mode of judgment dooms us to perpetual dissatisfaction . . . there is no good society, but rather a universal straining after justice in any situation'. Abbott contends that more explicit moral discourse has increased in the social sciences. '[A]n empirical analysis of current sociological writing and teaching would find a level of explicitly moral statements—on any reasonable coding of moral versus nonmoral statements—much higher than in the scholarships of the 1950s'.[7]

Policy also operates at the level of policing. The policing dimension of policy addresses the actual courses of action taken to achieve desirable outcomes. Indeed policing is an action verb, connoting attempts to govern courses of action in preferred directions. The

[3] Hacking, n. 1 above, 170.

[4] D. Garland, *The Culture of Control: Crime and Social Order in Contemporary Society* (Oxford: Oxford University Press, 2001), 3.

[5] Ibid., and D. Garland, 'Of Crimes and Criminals: The Development of Criminology in Britain' in M. Maguire *et al.* (eds.), *The Oxford Handbook of Criminology* (Oxford: Oxford University Press, 1997), 11.

[6] A. Abbott, *Chaos of Disciplines* (Chicago, Ill.: University of Chicago Press, 2001), 218, 229.

[7] Ibid., 204.

policing action may involve coercion or manipulation, and thus be based on a negative logic. But it can also be grounded in the promotion of health, well-being, and social improvement, and thus based on a positive logic.

The early modern conception of policy was coincident with policing. Policing referred to a body of principled courses of action for all aspects of government regarding security, health, education, and material prosperity.[8] It was underpinned by 'police science', a branch of political economy practised by Beccaria, Bentham, Colquhoun, and Adam Smith, among many others. Known also as the 'science of government' and the 'science of happiness', police science aimed to address 'everything . . . unregulated, everything that can be said . . . to lack order or form'.[9] For example, among seventeenth- and eighteenth-century German works on police science was Frank's six-volume *System for a Complete Medical Policing*, which included detailed regulations designed to 'prevent evils through wise ordinances', and covered every then imaginable aspect of health care.[10] Von Justi, in his 1768 treatise entitled *Eléments généreaux de police*, said that 'the science of policing consists . . . in regulating everything that relates to the present condition of society, in strengthening and improving it, in seeing that all things . . . contributed to the welfare of members that compose it'. Karl Marx, writing in 1843, restated the eighteenth-century view that '[s]ecurity is the supreme social concept of civil society, the concept of police, the concept that the whole society exists only to guarantee to each of its members the preservation of his person, his rights, and his property'.[11]

[8] L. Radzinowicz, *The History of the English Criminal Law and its Administration* (London: Stevens, 1956), iii, 417–38; C. Oestreich, *Neostoicism and the Early Modern State* (London: Hutchinson, 1982); D. Andrew, *Philanthropy and Police: London Charity in the Eighteenth Century* (Princeton, NJ: Princeton University Press, 1989); M. Foucault, 'Governmentality' in G. Burchell *et al.* (eds.), *The Foucault Effect: Studies in Governmentality* (Chicago, Ill.: University of Chicago Press, 1991), 87; P. Pasquino, 'Theatricum Politicum: The Genealogy of Capital—Police and the State of Prosperity' in G. Gordon *et al.* (eds.), *The Foucault Effect: Studies in Governmentality* (Chicago, Ill.: University of Chicago Press, 1991), 105; R. Ericson and K. Haggerty, *Policing the Risk Society* (Oxford: Clarendon, 1997), 46–8.

[9] Pasquino, n. 8 above, III.

[10] S. Bok, *Lying: Moral Choice in Public and Private Life* (New York: Vintage, 1979), 215–16.

[11] K. Marx, *Writings of the Young Marx on Philosophy and Society*, ed. L. Easton and K. Guddat (New York: Anchor, 1967), 236.

This conception of policing has endured. It is central to contemporary criminology, which is careful not to limit research on policing to the activities of the public police or coercive social control.[12] Policing is conceived as courses of action that govern conduct in the name of security. Criminologists are among those who take such courses of action, and therefore they are part of the policing system. Their research is motivated by a desire to create novel analytical frameworks, classifications, risk-assessment tools, and the like that govern how people think and act in principled ways. The *raison d'être* of criminology and other human sciences is their contributions to the policing of organized life, to surveillance defined simply as the production of knowledge useful in the administration and well-being of populations.[13]

Policy as rhetoric and policy as policing are entwined. They are mutually constitutive as discourse and practice, thought and action. The influence of criminology is found not only at the level of rhetorics or ways of thinking, but also in how it constitutes regulatory practices which in turn have their own rhetorical force. As Giddens[14] remarks, 'the practical impact of social science and sociological theories is enormous, and sociological concepts and findings are constitutively involved in what modernity is'. While criminologists as academics are more thinkers than doers, 'research works within morally freighted categories, and implicitly or explicitly urges certain kinds of action. Having decided on careers as thinkers, modern social scientists fill their scholarship with explicit attempts to act—to right wrongs by identifying and then labelling them as such'.[15]

---

[12] C. Shearing, 'The Relation between Public and Private Policing' in M. Tonry and N. Morris (eds.), *Modern Policing* (Chicago, Ill.: University of Chicago Press, 1992); Ericson and Haggerty, n. 12 above; I. Loader, 'Consumer Culture and the Commodification of Policing and Security' (1999) 33 *Sociology* 373; I. Loader and N. Walker, 'Policing as a Public Good: Reconstituting the Connections between Policing and the State' (2001) 5 *Theoretical Criminology* 9.

[13] C. Dandeker, *Surveillance, Power and Modernity: Bureaucracy and Discipline from 1700 to the Present Day* (New York: St Martin's Press, 1990); M. Poster, *The Mode of Information: Poststructuralism and Social Context* (Cambridge: Polity Press, 1990).

[14] A. Giddens, *The Consequences of Modernity* (Cambridge: Polity, 1990), 16.

[15] Abbott, n. 6 above, 203.

Criminology as a Legal Field

Criminology is also a legal field. This is obviously the case because criminology addresses behaviours that are, or could be, treated as violations of criminal law and procedure. When criminologists are called upon to offer a pithy definition of the field, they typically refer first and foremost to the sagacious role of criminology as part of the criminal justice system. For example, in her 1990 presidential address to the American Society of Criminology (ASC), Petersilia[16] states that the formation of criminology as a field and the foundation of the Society itself were 'strongly grounded in the practical concerns of the criminal justice system . . . [criminology] is defined by a major social phenomenon—crime—and the system and agencies established to address that phenomenon'. In his 1992 presidential address, Blumstein[17] declares that 'an important mission of the ASC and its members involves the generation of knowledge that is useful in dealing with crime and the operation of the criminal justice system . . . and then helping public officials to use that knowledge intelligently and effectively'.

Criminology is a legal field for more profound reasons. Any field concerned with principled courses of action must consider the role of law. Criminologists are perpetually figuring out the shifting place of criminal law and procedure compared to other branches of law, and to other principled bases of action for dealing with undesirable conduct. In this respect they conduct what Lowi[18] refers to as 'real policy evaluation', in contrast to narrow risk management and cost-benefit analyses. Real policy evaluation is 'understood as the study of the legally definable possibilities, institutional limits and unanticipated consequences'.[19] What can criminal law and procedure do and not do in governing conduct? What are the capacities of other branches of law in governing conduct? What are the capacities for governing conduct beyond the law, for example through health, education, business, family, and welfare institutions? What are the unanticipated consequences of pursuing principled courses of action, whether legal or extra-legal?

[16] J. Petersilia, 'Policy Relevance and the Future of Criminology—The American Society of Criminology 1990 Presidential Address' (1991) 31 *Criminology* 1.

[17] A. Blumstein, 'Making Rationality Relevant—The American Society of Criminology 1992 Presidential Address' (1993) 33 *Criminology* 1.

[18] T. Lowi, 'Risks and Rights in the History of American Governments' (1990) 119 *Daedalus* 17, 38–9.

[19] Ibid.

Legally principled action is never autonomous, but rather operates through inter-institutional networks. As Foucault observed, 'law operates more and more as a norm, and the juridical institution is increasingly incorporated into a continuum of apparatuses (medical, administrative and so on) whose functions are for the most part regulatory'. In referring to law as a 'norm', Foucault emphasizes that law functions not only as a policing mechanism—prescribing through imposed rules of conduct—but also as policy rhetoric. Through the articulation of policing prescriptions that have symbolic and legitimation value as well as regulatory force, law instructs not only on what to do but also on who to be. Law as policy prescription is especially evident in declaratory legislation such as the Canadian Charter of Rights and Freedoms.[20]

Perhaps as good a definition of a criminologist as any is someone who uses abstractions of crime and security to establish disciplinary, professional, and institutional jurisdiction over the governance of human conduct.[21] Through such efforts, criminologists participate directly in how the criminal law institution does or does not relate to other institutions in the fundamental public policy tasks of allocating resources (for example, guaranteeing and protecting relationships; intervening to enforce policies and programmes), resolving conflicts (for example, by providing principles and mechanisms for doing so), and keeping the peace (for example, establishing rules of behaviour and enforcing violations with sanctions).

Criminologists study how the mechanisms of criminal law co-ordinate social institutions and help to constitute society's authority system. While criminal law is an interpretive practice that is obviously central to the legitimation of the state's penal apparatus,[22] it also helps legitimate other social institutions. Criminologists are part of the interpretive practice, bringing the legitimacy of scientific inquiry and university-based research to the enterprise.[23]

---

[20] J. Bakan, *Just Words* (Toronto: University of Toronto Press, 1997).

[21] R. Ericson and K. Carriere, 'The Fragmentation of Criminology' in D. Nelken (ed.), *The Futures of Criminology* (London: Sage, 1994), 89; R. Ericson, 'Making Criminology' (1996) 8 *Current Issues in Criminal Justice* 14.

[22] N. Lacey, 'Criminology, Criminal Law, and Criminalisation' in M. Maguire *et al.* (eds.), *The Oxford Handbook of Criminology* (Oxford: Oxford University Press, 1997), 437 at 445.

[23] Garland, n. 5 above, 46–7.

Contemporary institutions are possessed by bureaucracies and therefore obsessed with procedure.[24] There is reciprocal influence between criminal procedure and the procedures used in other forms of law, social institutions, organizations, and groups. Procedures combine with moral considerations to provide a discourse of procedural propriety—principled course of action—that sustains the legitimacy of institutions. Criminology addresses the extent to which the procedural conceptions of criminal law permeate other institutions and thereby affect their autonomy, result in a merging of practices, and influence the interchangeability of both their professional staffs and their clienteles.[25] There is also concern with how the conceptions of procedure fostered by criminal law relate to accountability and legitimacy in various institutions, and thus to the constitution of institutional roles and authority.[26]

Criminological research that examines wrongdoing and its regulation in other institutions uses criminal law as a template: Should the activity be criminalized? Could it be criminalized? What are the implications of criminalizing it? This research effort helps to define the institutional and professional boundaries of criminal law and its place in the division of expert knowledge and labour of crime management and security provision. As Lacey emphasizes:

'Criminalization' constitutes an appropriate conceptual framework within which to gather together the constellation of social practices which form the subject matter of criminology, criminal law, and criminal justice studies ... the ideal of criminalization captures the dynamic nature of the field as a set of interlocking practices in which the moments of 'defining' and 'responding to' crime can rarely be completely distinguished. It accommodates the full range of relevant institutions within which those practices take shape and the disciplines which might be brought to bear upon their analysis.... Within the framework of criminalization, we may therefore accommodate the relevant practices of a variety of social actors and institutions: citizens, the media, the police, prosecution agencies, courts, judges and lawyers, social workers, probation officers and those working in the

[24] J. Habermas, *Legitimation Crisis* (Boston, Mass.: Beacon, 1975); Dandeker, n. 13 above.

[25] D. Garland, *Punishment and Welfare: A History of Penal Strategies* (Aldershot: Gower, 1985); J. Lowman, R. Menzies, and T. Palys (eds.), *Transcarceration: Essays in the Sociology of Social Control* (Aldershot: Gower, 1987); D. Chunn, *From Punishment to Doing Good* (Toronto: University of Toronto Press, 1992).

[26] P. Stenning (ed.), *Accountability for Criminal Justice* (Toronto: University of Toronto Press, 1995).

penal and mental health systems, legislators, and key members of the executive. We are also able to acknowledge the relevance of a wide variety of disciplines to the analysis of these institutions: sociology, psychology, political science, economics, legal studies, moral and political philosophy, and anthropology, to name only the most obvious.[27]

Criminologists have documented that criminalization is minimal compared to other options for regulating conduct that could be criminalized. Ironically, criminologists have de-centred criminal law and the criminal justice system. They have shown that most conduct which could be criminalized is unknown to the police, although it is known and dealt with by people in other institutions such as family, education, business enterprise and healthcare. Even when crime is known to the police, it is most often dealt with by simply distributing the knowledge of it to other institutions where the problem is addressed more directly. On the rare occasions when culprits are known to police, most are diverted to other institutions.[28]

Business enterprise is illustrative. In this sphere the emphasis is usually on keeping crime out of criminal law jurisdiction. The preference is for private security mechanisms that minimize property loss. There is also some acceptance of property loss so as not to disrupt the smooth flow of commercial relationships. When enforcement does seem necessary, the preference is for compliance mechanisms. While a few criminologists struggle to extend the jurisdiction of criminal law in the private corporate sphere,[29] most underpin the significance of alternatives using compliance law enforcement

---

[27] Lacey, n. 22 above, 448–9; see also N. Lacey, 'Contingency and Criminalisation' in I. Loveland (ed.), *Frontiers of Criminality* (London: Sweet & Maxwell, 1995), 1.

[28] A. Ashworth, 'The Decline of English Sentencing and Other Stories' in M. Tonry and R. Frase (eds), *Sentencing and Sanctions in Western Countries* (New York: Oxford University Press, 2001), 62; Ericson and Haggerty, n. 8 above; R. Ericson and K. Haggerty, 'The Policing of Risk' in T. Baker and J. Simon (eds.), *Embracing Risk: The Changing Culture of Insurance and Responsibility* (Chicago, Ill.: University of Chicago Press, 2002).

[29] F. Pearce and S. Toombs, 'Ideology, Hegemony and Empiricism: Compliance Theories of Regulation' (1990) 30 *British Journal of Criminology* 423; F. Pearce and S. Toombs, 'Policing Corporate "Skid Rows": A Reply to Keith Hawkins' (1991) 31 *British Journal of Criminology* 415; F. Pearce and L. Snider, *Corporate Crime: Contemporary Debates* (Toronto: University of Toronto Press, 1995).

models[30] or mechanisms internal to the specific business enterprise concerned.[31]

To the extent that it does focus on criminal law and criminal justice administration for controlling wrongful conduct, criminology is a 'governmental project'.[32] It is 'an academic project closely aligned with government institutions and the production of applied knowledge for state policy and practice... Criminology's ongoing struggles for a discipline or academic specialization has required practical expressions for government-centred initiatives'.[33] As such criminology is administrative, a branch of management science concerned with the regulation of populations through efficient, just and humane practices. It is entwined with public administration and 'heavily influenced by immediate policy needs'.[34] It deploys traditional policy analysis which assumes the state's legally authorized officials are the principal actors.

In contrast, recognizing the limits of criminalization and the fact that the regulation of wrongful conduct is mainly embedded in other social institutions, some criminologists advance the governance project.[35] The governance project studies the deployment of administrative and regulatory systems that foster self-governance in institutions, organizations, communities, and individuals beyond the state legal apparatus. Some criminologists suggest that analysis of such systems belongs to other disciplines. For example

[30] K. Hawkins, *Environment and Enforcement: Regulation and the Social Definition of Pollution* (Oxford: Oxford University Press, 1984); K. Hawkins, 'Compliance Strategy, Prosecution, Policy, and Aunt Sally: A Comment on Pearce and Toombs' (1990) 30 *British Journal of Criminology* 444; K. Hawkins, 'Enforcing Regulation: More of the Same From Pearce and Toombs' (1991) 31 *British Journal of Criminology* 427; M. Tonry and A. Reiss (eds.), *Beyond the Law: Crime in Complex Organizations* (Chicago, Ill.: University of Chicago Press, 1993).

[31] In the case of insurance fraud see R. Ericson, D. Barry, and A. Doyle, 'The Moral Hazards of Neo-Liberalism: Lessons From the Private Insurance Industry' (2000) 29 *Economy and Society* 532; R. Ericson, A. Doyle, and D. Barry, *Insurance as Governance* (Toronto: University of Toronto Press, 2003).

[32] Garland, n. 5 above.

[33] R. Walters, 'Social Defence and International Reconstruction: Illustrating the Governance of Post-War Criminological Discourse' (2001) 5 *Theoretical Criminology* 203 at 206.

[34] Garland, n. 5 above, 47.

[35] N. Rose, *Powers of Freedom: Reframing Political Thought* (Cambridge: Cambridge University Press, 1999); N. Rose and M. Valverde, 'Governed by Law?' (1998) 7 *Social and Legal Studies* 541.

Garland[36] asserts that criminology's 'claim to be an empirically grounded, scientific understanding sets it apart from moral and legal discourses, while its focus upon crime differentiates it from other social scientific genres, such as the sociology of deviance and control, whose objects of study are broader and not defined by criminal law'. Garland's demarcation is too sharp. Governance beyond the state and its criminal law apparatus is not a separate sphere requiring a separate discipline. Rather, it is entwined with the policies of government, including those of the criminal justice system itself. Moreover, criminologists routinely blend scientific, moral, and legal discourses in their research and policy work. The governmental project and the governance project intersect. This intersection can be illuminated further if we analyse criminology as a system of disciplines, professions, and institutions.

Criminology as a System

Criminology is part of a system which includes other academic disciplines, professions associated with each discipline, and institutions associated with each profession. These disciplines, professions, and institutions compete for jurisdiction in dealing with wrongful conduct that has the potential to be criminalized. The criminologist is best conceived as someone who uses abstractions of crime and security to establish disciplinary, professional, and institutional jurisdiction. Crime thrives as a metaphor for social ills of all types, and security thrives as a metaphor for control problems of all types. Crime and security are therefore the loci for policy rhetorics and policing actions from myriad disciplinary, professional, and institutional standpoints.

The most obvious sign that criminology is a multi-disciplinary, multi-professional, multi-institutional field is the fact that it is organized in so many different ways in the institution of higher education itself. In each local university context, the organization of criminology depends on the particular people involved and how they make their subject fit within prevailing organizational structures. For example, criminology has been organized in separate university departments (Keele, Montreal), as part of law faculties (Oxford, Cambridge), within socio-legal studies programmes (Berkeley), in business schools (Pennsylvania), in interdisciplinary

[36] Garland, n. 5 above, 11.

graduate programmes (LSE, Toronto), and in sociology departments (many North American universities), to name only some manifestations. Attendance at major conferences, such as those of the British Society of Criminology or the American Society of Criminology, makes evident the disciplinary array. Professors of sociology, political science, economics, anthropology, psychology, medicine, philosophy, law, business, history, education, communications, and so on join those who are actually identified with criminology and criminal justice studies departments. Even more disciplines are likely to be added in the future because the new 'what works' questions regarding crime and security are increasingly technical, focusing for example on the surveillance capacities of information technology, the certainty of DNA testing, and the docility capacity of pharmaceutical products for those suffering from clinically-defined behavioural disorders. Indeed if the technocratic turn persists, physical, biological, and applied sciences may increasingly sideline social sciences in the interdisciplinary struggle over crime and security jurisdiction.[37]

Garland[38] observes that '[m]odern criminology is a composite, eclectic, multidisciplinary enterprise . . . [O]ne of the major dynamics of modern criminology is the incessant raiding of other disciplines or ideologies for new ideas with which to pursue (and renew) the criminological project . . . [M]odern criminology is highly differentiated in its theoretical, methodological and empirical concerns'. This 'raiding' and differentiation are not only motivated by a search for ideas, academic status, and defensible space in disciplinary turf wars. They are also part of the ongoing struggles over policy jurisdiction in the division of expert knowledge and labour among disciplines, professions, and institutions.[39] Criminological jurisdiction rises and falls according to how it is located in university organization (e.g. prestigious faculties); paradigms (e.g. the success of abstractions of crime and security in taking jurisdiction from others and creating new jurisdiction); research funding (e.g. access to and influence over major foundations and other funding agencies); publication (e.g. prestigious publishers and a hierarchy of professional

[37] K. Haggerty, 'Displaced Expertise: Three Limitations on the Policy Relevance of Criminological Thought' (unpublished paper, Department of Sociology, University of Alberta, 2001).

[38] Garland, n. 5 above, 19.

[39] A. Abbott, *The System of Professions: An Essay on the Division of Expert Labor* (Chicago, Ill.: University of Chicago Press, 1988); Abbott, n. 6 above.

journals); and professional associations (e.g. associations with professional power, such as law and medicine). Academics from different disciplines fiercely compete for financial capital (research
grants), for symbolic capital (the authority to define), and social
capital (networks of influence)[40] that will enhance their professional
powers in policy rhetoric and policing.

Criminology does not stand apart from the professional and institutional worlds of crime and regulation it analyses, but participates
in and helps to form those worlds. Each discipline related to the field
of criminology makes its professional and institutional choices, and
then helps its preferred choices to draw the necessary boundary to
get the policy job done. It is this boundary that defines the profession
and institution as much as the specialized disciplinary knowledge
that it encloses. At the same time the specialized disciplinary knowledge is bolstered by the firmly drawn and well-guarded boundaries
among professions and institutions. This boundary patrol work is
one of the major cultural functions of disciplines, helping to structure professions and institutions and to give them power to act.

[A] cultural function of disciplines is that of preventing knowledge from
becoming too abstract or overwhelming. Disciplines legitimate our necessarily partial knowledge. They define what is permissible not to
know. . . . They provide a specific tradition and lineage. They provide
common sets of research practices that unify groups with diverse substantive interests. Often . . . these various limits are quite arbitrary.[41]

Abbott[42] proceeds to observe that disciplines, especially those
associated with the social sciences, are not very differentiated with
respect to the subject matters they address. While variation occurs in
how each discipline analyses a given subject matter, there is extensive
overlap in the substantive topics studied. One result is relatively little
*inter*disciplinarity, as different disciplines work on the same topic
with an 'amazing lack of reciprocal knowledge'[43] across disciplines.
Another result is that different disciplines compete for the authority
to define the significance of the substantive topic and to influence
policy regarding it. 'Bodies of academic work are perpetually being

---

[40] P. Bourdieu, *Homo Academicus* (Cambridge: Polity Press, 1988), 78–9; P.
Bourdieu and L. Wacquant, *An Invitation to Reflexive Sociology* (Cambridge: Polity
Press, 1992), 76; J. Chan, 'Globalisation, Reflexivity and the Practice of Criminology'
(2000) 33 *The Australian and New Zealand Journal of Criminology* 118, at 119.
[41] Abbott, n. 6 above, 130.   [42] Ibid., 142.   [43] Ibid.

redefined, reshaped, and recast by the activities of disciplines trying to take work from one another or to dominate one another.'[44] There is variation in this regard, depending on how contested a substantive topic itself may be in political culture. For example, the study of money flows is relatively uncontested and therefore a stable topic, the almost exclusive jurisdiction of economics. On the other hand, fields such as ethnic studies and criminology are highly contested and unstable, and therefore open to a broad range of competing disciplines.[45]

Abbott also makes the point that problem-oriented fields, which largely consist of empirical studies and produce local knowledge, do not create enduring academic fields 'except in areas with stable and strong institutionalized external clienteles like criminology. Even there, the status differences seem to keep the disciplines in superior power. Criminology departments hire from sociology departments, but seldom vice versa'.[46] 'Problem-portable knowledge' of basic disciplines is more competitive than 'problem-based knowledge' because it has the power of abstraction to address a range of problems and is more efficient.[47] Thus fields such as criminology 'are ultimately dependent on specialized disciplines to generate their theories and methods. Interdisciplinarity presupposes disciplines'.[48]

It is criminology's clienteles in different professions and institutions that sustain its disciplinary force as a policy field. A necessarily brief and partial overview of some of these clienteles illustrates how criminology participates in the division of expert knowledge and labour in the system of professions and institutions.

As stated previously, there are many institutions that respond to conduct that has the potential for criminalization. Criminology has origins in a series of claims by health professionals as to why they should have jurisdiction over criminality.[49] Inspired by the European Social Defence movement,[50] the model was not of crime–responsibility–punishment, but rather symptom–malaise–treatment.

---

[44] Abbott, n. 6 above, 137.   [45] Ibid., 138.   [46] Ibid., 134.

[47] Ibid., 135.   [48] Ibid.

[49] D. Garland, 'British Criminology Before 1935' in P. Rock (ed.), *A History of British Criminology* (Oxford: Oxford University Press, 1988),1; Garland, n. 5 above; T. Morris, 'British Criminology: 1935–1948' in P. Rock (ed.), *A History of British Criminology* (Oxford: Oxford University Press, 1988), 20.

[50] B. Wooton, *Social Science and Social Pathology* (London: Allen and Unwin, 1959); Walters, n. 33 above.

The influence of this model was profound. For example, juvenile delinquency legislation constituted young offenders in a 'condition of delinquency' that required treatment, rather than as persons who should be criminally prosecuted for a crime. 'Dangerous offenders' were designated as having diminished or no responsibility, and therefore to be medicalized as well as criminalized. More recently other areas, such as domestic violence, have been medicalized,[51] and the influence of the medical institution over criminological jurisdiction remains strong.

When social welfare was more at the forefront of state initiatives, criminologists played a significant role in conceptualizing and rationalizing the effort, and in implementing the associated programmes. Following the Second World War, criminologists underpinned the

colonization of a formerly legal terrain by 'social' authorities and professional groups. . . . 'Progress in penal reform,' whatever else it involved, was a matter of increasing the numbers and the jurisdictions of social experts on delinquency. This grant of discretionary power to unaccountable professionals, whose decisions were typically issued without explanation and without being subject to judicial review, is an indication of the degree of trust that these professional groups then commanded, and also of the way in which their powers were perceived.[52]

For example, sociological theories of strain and opportunity helped generate various 'war on poverty' and 'opportunities for youth' initiatives.[53] Labelling theorists explicitly sided with the underdog, including the criminalized, in a policy positioning aimed at greater social welfare and justice as well as shifting of dominant paradigms in the discipline.[54] With the more recent shift toward neo-liberal governance and downsizing of the welfare state,

[51] I. Hacking, *Rewriting the Soul: Multiple Personality and the Sciences of Memory* (Princeton, NJ: Princeton University Press, 1995).

[52] Garland, n. 4 above, 36.

[53] R. Merton, *Social Theory and Social Structure* (New York: The Free Press, 1968); R. Cloward and L. Ohlin, *Delinquency and Opportunity* (New York: The Free Press, 1960); A. Cohen, *Delinquent Boys: The Culture of the Gang* (New York: The Free Press, 1955); D. Downes, *The Delinquent Solution: A Study in Subcultural Theory* (London: Routledge and Kegan Paul, 1966).

[54] E. Schur, *Labeling Deviant Behavior: Its Sociological Implications* (New York: Harper and Row, 1971); R. Ericson, *Criminal Reactions: The Labelling Perspective* (Farnborough: Saxon House, 1975); Abbott, n. 6 above, 68 ff.

criminologists have, with some exceptions,[55] duly abandoned the welfare arena, or concentrated their efforts on research that aids the process of welfare programme de-selection and regulation. Age-old questions resurface of who are the deserving poor, and of the extent to which the criminalization of welfare fraud and of other economic survival tactics should be used to uphold the integrity of what is left of welfare systems.

The movement away from welfarism and toward neo-liberalism has led a number of criminologists to examine the private insurance industry as an important institution in the prevention and regulation of crime.[56] The institution of insurance has become increasingly pervasive as contemporary society assumes insurance risk logics in a wide range of institutional contexts. The insurance industry governs efforts at loss prevention and harm minimization in all spheres of social life. The extremely low clearance-by-arrest rate for property crime means that the police primarily serve as information brokers to the insurance industry's own systems of loss prevention and indemnification. Moreover, the operative law is more the law of the insurance contract rather than criminal law, as it uses differential contract conditions and premium rates to create incentives to policyholders to be their own policing agents. The insurance industry has substantial and sophisticated private policing operations to address the extensive fraud and other criminal activity generated by its own commercial relations. This is managed almost exclusively through the insurance industry's own private justice system beyond the law.

The mass media have a pervasive influence in shaping crime, law, and justice, and criminologists are giving renewed attention to their

---

[55]   e.g. P. Carlen, *Jigsaw—A Political Criminology of Youth Homelessness* (Buckingham: Open University Press, 1996).

[56]   N. Reichman, 'Managing Crime Risks: Towards an Insurance Based Model of Social Control' in S. Spitzer and A. Scull (eds.), *Research in Law, Deviance and Social Control* (Greenwich, Conn.: JAI Press, 1986); J. Simon, 'The Emergence of Risk Society: Insurance, Law and the State' (1987) 95 *Socialist Review* 61; J. Simon, 'The Ideological Effects of Actuarial Practice' (1988) 22 *Law and Society Review* 772; P. O'Malley, 'Legal Networks and Domestic Security' (1991) 21 *Studies in Law, Politics and Society* 252; M. Clarke, 'The Control of Insurance Fraud: A Comparative View' (1990) 30 *British Journal of Criminology* 1; M. Clarke, *Citizens' Financial Futures: The Regulation of Retail Financial Services in Britain* (Aldershot: Gower, 1999); Ericson and Haggerty, n. 8 above; Ericson and Haggerty, n. 28 above; Ericson, Barry, and Doyle, n. 31 above; Ericson, Doyle, and Barry, n. 31 above.

effects.[57] They seek an understanding of how the mass media frame particular events and issues as criminal or not; who influences that framing; and, the consequences of that framing. They examine ways in which the mass media use crime and security to produce morality plays about political culture.[58] Such analyses of mass media are designed to contest media framing of crime and security. Criminologists also see the mass media as direct participants in processes of enforcement.[59] Of course criminologists themselves are also direct players in the mass media and its constructions of crime and regulation.[60] They serve regularly as expert authorized knowers in the news. Indeed, research on the role of criminologists as news sources would be revealing of their place in the division of expert knowledge and labour regarding crime and security. It would indicate how their frameworks of understanding fare in comparison to those of others (for example, police, politicians, reform advocacy groups, doctors, and journalists themselves), their place in the knowledge hierarchies involved in shaping crime and security policies.

An understanding of how crime and security are mediated by other institutions does not push the policy rhetoric and policing capacities of criminal law to the sidelines. Rather, criminal law is

[57] e.g. R. Ericson, 'Mass Media, Crime, Law and Justice: An Institutional Approach' (1991) 30 *British Journal of Criminology* 219; R. Ericson (ed.), *Crime and the Media* (Aldershot: Dartmouth, 1995); R. Ericson, P. Baranek, and J. Chan, *Visualizing Deviance: A Study of News Organization* (Toronto: University of Toronto Press, 1987); R. Ericson, P. Baranek, and J. Chan, *Negotiating Control: A Study of News Sources* (Toronto: University of Toronto Press, 1989); R. Ericson, P. Baranek, and J. Chan, *Representing Order: Crime, Law and Justice in the News Media* (Toronto: University of Toronto Press, 1991); R. Sparks, *Television and the Drama of Crime: Moral Tales and the Place of Crime in Public Life* (Milton Keynes: Open University Press, 1992); P. Schlesinger and H. Tumber, *Reporting Crime: The Media Politics of Criminal Justice* (Oxford: Clarendon, 1994).

[58] R. Wagner-Pacifici, *The Moro Morality Play: Terrorism as Social Drama* (Chicago, Ill.: University of Chicago Press, 1986); J. Katz, 'What Makes Crime News?' (1987) 9 *Media, Culture and Society* 47; Sparks, n. 57 above.

[59] Ericson, Baranek, and Chan, *Negotiating Control*, n. 57 above; Schlesinger and Tumber, n. 57 above; A. Doyle, *Arresting Images. Crime and Policing in Front of the Television Camera* (Toronto: University of Toronto Press, 2003).

[60] K. Daly, 'Celebrated Crime Cases and the Public's Imagination: From Bad Press to Bad Policy' (1995) *The Australian and New Zealand Journal of Criminology*, Special Supplementary Issue, 6; J. Chan, 'Systematically Distorted Communication? Criminological Knowledge, Media Representation and Public Policy' [1995] *The Australian and New Zealand Journal of Criminology*, Special Supplementary Issue, 23.

one player in the field of institutional players. Moreover, it can be highly influential, gaining the upper hand in inter-institutional processes of criminalisation.

The study of criminal law reform has been especially fruitful in illustrating that crime is defined politically, and therefore connects to political concerns and interests well beyond the regulation of undesirable conduct.[61] Perhaps the best illustration of this point is research on victims' movements.[62] Political and professional groups use criminalisation debates as a vehicle for creating their role on the political stage, a role that in turn allows them some purchase on how crime and other aspects of social life are morally understood and governed.

Another fruitful line of criminological research concerns the mechanisms through which the criminal law institution regulates knowledge possession and use, resulting in the accretion of power/ knowledge advantages to some over others. For example, criminal law patrols its own institutional boundaries with respect to the types of expertise it allows as evidence in dispute settlement.[63] Some institutions and their discourses are given more licence than others. For example, medical discourse tends to be mitigating, while sociological discourse is often aggravating in the criminal courts. At the same time, even with respect to more permissible discourses, rules of evidence, judgments and discretion are used to protect the authority of legal reasoning and discourse over the claims of other professional experts and their peculiar reasoning and discourse. The institutional hegemony of law is managed by protecting its ways of producing meaning, its own knowledge systems in the wider environment of other professional and institutional discourses with claims to

[61] J. Gusfield, *The Culture of Public Problems: Drinking, Driving and the Symbolic Order* (Chicago, Ill.: University of Chicago Press, 1981); J. Simon, 'Governing through Crime' in G. Fisher and L. Friedman (eds.), *The Crime Conundrum: Essays on Criminal Justice* (Boulder, Colo.: Westview, 1997).

[62] P. Rock, *A View From the Shadows* (Oxford: Oxford University Press, 1986); P. Rock, *Helping Victims of Crime: The Home Office and the Rise of Victim Support in England and Wales* (Oxford: Oxford University Press, 1990); L. Zedner, 'Victims' in M. Maguire *et al.* (eds.), *The Oxford Handbook of Criminology* (Oxford: Oxford University Press, 1997).

[63] E. Freidson, *Professional Powers: A Study of the Institutionalization of Formal Knowledge* (Chicago, Ill.: University of Chicago Press, 1986); D. Nelken, 'The Truth about Law's Truth', EUI Working Paper (Florence: European University Institute, 1990).

authority.[64] The more general question here is again the division of expert knowledge and labour among institutions and associated professions, as this relates to criminal law jurisdiction. As the courts recognize in granting professional privilege and standing to expert witnesses, it is not professional formal education, credentials, and institutionalization that are most important, but rather abstract knowledge combined with skill and practical experience.[65] Lacey makes the point well in observing that

evidence in criminal trials—sociological or psychological knowledges, for example, are subtly invalidated or else modified in the course of 'translation' into the terms of legal discourse. A good example here is the slow and partial legal recognition of evidence about the effects of long-term violence in 'domestic' homicide cases. Whilst recent cases have begun to accept such evidence as relevant, its force is inevitably limited by the need to shape it to fit the conceptual straightjackets of legal defences such as provocation, self-defence, and diminished responsibility. For instance, there is a legal requirement that, to qualify as provocation or self-defence, a violent response must follow immediately upon provocative or threatening conduct. This has posed difficulties in several cases in which defendants (most of them women) who have been subject to 'domestic' violence kill their abusers, yet in which there is no immediate relation between the ultimate killing and the particular attack. The result is that defence lawyers have been forced to reconstruct the relevant evidence in psychiatric terms which accord with a diminished responsibility defence which misrepresents the defendant's position. Such transformations of non-legal knowledges in the legal process have generally been invisible to conventional legal analysis and have received only partial recognition and understanding in socio-legal scholarship.[66]

Professionals in the institutions mentioned to this point—health, welfare, insurance, mass media, politics, and criminal law—pressure criminology to stay grounded, providing local knowledge of practical significance. In consequence criminology's 'epistemological threshold is a low one, making it susceptible to pressures and interests generated elsewhere'.[67] Criminology faces the additional

[64] R. Ericson and P. Baranek, *The Ordering of Justice: A Study of Accused Persons as Dependants in the Criminal Process* (Toronto: University of Toronto Press, 1982).

[65] Freidson, n. 63 above; R. Smith and B. Wynne (eds.), *Expert Evidence: Interpreting Science in Law* (London: Routledge, 1989); D. Mayo and R. Hollander (eds.), *Acceptable Evidence: Science and Values in Risk Management* (New York: Oxford University Press, 1991).

[66] Lacey, n. 22 above, 446.   [67] Garland, n. 5 above, 24.

pressure that everyone has a strong personal interest in, and significant knowledge about, its subject matter. This personal interest and knowledge are based in both popular culture and everyday experiences of crime victimization and (in)security.[68] Experiential, common-sense knowledge is entwined with criminological knowledge, and criminological categories and analyses readily slip into practical wisdom and common sense.

While such slippage is a feature of social scientific knowledge in general,[69] it is accentuated in the case of criminology and the popular engagement with its subject matter. As Garland records,[70] this slippage has been evident since the founding of criminology. For example, Lombroso's ideas permeated journalistic articles and popular fiction because they resonated with the political culture of an urban middle class that increasingly feared criminal classes in its midst. With the more recent proliferation of public media and the obsession with crime and security, the influences of popular and political cultures on criminology are accentuated. Indeed many of the explanatory structures used by criminologists are very similar to the narrative structures of everyday discourse about crime, criminality, and security.[71]

As a policy field feeding upon and into so many professions and institutions, criminology must produce knowledge that is 'socially robust'.[72] Social robustness is judged by myriad 'sprawling socio-scientific constituencies with open frontiers'.[73] The specific judgement of robustness is based on policy relevance in each context of application. It is never predetermined, but rather the outcome of 'intensive (and continuous) interaction between results and their

---

[68] Zedner, n. 62 above; L. Zedner, 'The Pursuit of Security' in T. Hope and R. Sparks (eds.), *Crime, Risk and Insecurity: Law and Order in Everyday Life and Political Discourse* (London: Routledge, 2000).

[69] N. Stehr and A. Simmons, 'The Diversity of Discourse' (1979) 16 *Society* 45; N. Stehr and R. Ericson (eds.), *The Culture and Power of Knowledge: Inquiries into Contemporary Societies* (Berlin and New York: de Gruyter, 1992); N. Stehr, *Practical Knowledge: Applying the Social Sciences* (London: Sage, 1992); N. Stehr, *Knowledge Societies* (London: Sage, 1994).

[70] Garland, n. 5 above, 31–4.

[71] D. Matza, *Delinquency and Drift* (Englewood Cliffs, NJ: Prentice Hall, 1964); D. Matza, *Becoming Deviant* (Englewood Cliffs, NJ: Prentice Hall, 1969).

[72] H. Nowotny, P. Scott, and M. Gibbons, *Re-Thinking Science: Knowledge and the Public in an Age of Uncertainty* (Cambridge: Polity Press, 2001), 258–9.

[73] Ibid.

interpretation, people and environments, applications and implications'.[74]

The need for social validation of knowledge in various professions and institutions means that criminology has an interstitial quality. It fills gaps left by its professional and institutional constituencies in their efforts to address problems of crime and security. It rushes into new fields of inquiry and research topics because its primary orientation is problem solving, and because it does not have intellectually rigorous ways of denying demands for its services. Its fluidity is also related to the ways in which abstractions of crime and security can be used to address a very broad range of questions regarding human behaviour and organization.

The fluidity of criminology makes it messy. Its messiness is compounded by the fact that it is based on empirical inquiries and policy relevance, both of which throw up perpetual knowledge conundrums. Messy and not pure, it is at the margins of the basic disciplines that it draws upon and flows into for academic sustenance. As Abbott remarks about the division of expert knowledge more generally:

Specialists in knowledge tend to withdraw into pure work because the complexity of the thing known eventually tends to get in the way of the knowledge system itself. So the object of knowledge is gradually disregarded. This process is familiar throughout the professions, where applied work ranks below academic work because the complexities of professional practice make practical knowledge messy and 'unprofessional.' But we see the process in academia itself; much of the very-high status discipline of economics is quite unconcerned with empirical reality. Similarly, it was the gradual withdrawal of sociology and anthropology into inward, professional concerns that left the terrain of social commentary open to humanists, who have invaded it with vigor and insight, if not always accuracy and intelligibility.[75]

From Criminology to Policy

The system of criminology requires criminologists to serve as translators. They are in perpetual motion from empirical research to policy rhetorics and policing initiatives, and back again. Translation has three dimensions. First, there is a process of *simplification* to

---

[74] Ibid., 258.   [75] Abbott, n. 6 above, 22.

meet the requirements of professional and institutional constituencies. The messiness of empirical research and theoretical abstractions must be tidied up in order to be pointed at policy. Secondly, translation is *chaotic*. A given criminological inquiry escapes its author as it enters into new professional and institutional contexts where there are competing interests, and competing discourses articulating those interests. Thirdly, simplification and chaos yield *loss of autonomy*. The criminological researcher has his or her knowledge taken over by others to use in their own practical contexts of moving people to action through policy rhetoric and policing.

In order to have their research judged socially robust by their professional and institutional constituencies, criminologists must translate it into simplified frameworks and concepts. They must shift from 'the authority of complexity'[76] in the world of academic scholarship to the practical knowledge needed to shape the worlds beyond. '[T]he practical value of social scientific knowledge is not dependent on a faithful, in the sense of complete, representation of social reality. Instead, social science knowledge that wants to optimize its practicality has to attend and attach itself to elements of social situations that can be altered or are actionable.'[77]

In spite of academic claims about complexity, social scientists often provide very simple accounts, even reducing their analysis to a single dimension to explain something forcefully: for example, rational choice, economic needs, relations of production, social division of labour, psychological drives, and so on. They also communicate through simple binary oppositions—for example, autonomy/constraint, security/insecurity, order/chaos, authority/power, equality/inequality—in a manner akin to journalists.[78]

As Stehr and Grundmann illustrate,[79] Keynes was a successful economist because he combined a highly polemical style with a simple idea that investment decisions are an important basis of employment levels in a national economy. Keynes' policy rhetoric based on a simple idea fostered policing of the 'institutional conditions which lead to lower interest rates and contribute to expect-

---

[76] N. Stehr and R. Grundmann, 'The Authority of Complexity' (2001) 52 *British Journal of Sociology* 313.

[77] Ibid., 313.

[78] Ibid.; R. Ericson, 'How Journalists Visualize Fact' (1998) 560 *Annals of the American Academy of Political and Social Sciences* 83; Abbott, n. 6 above.

[79] Stehr and Grundmann, n. 76 above, 322 ff.; see also Stehr, n. 69 above.

ations about economic growth which in turn stimulate investments',[80] and of public expenditure as a way of supporting demand.
Keynes' simple policy rhetoric and policing initiatives were highly
successful for over two decades following the Second World War, in
the context of strong economic sovereignty within states. They lost
force only with the expansion of economic globalization.

Stehr and Grundmann[81] note that 'for Keynes economics is ultimately a moral and not a natural science. Keynes[82] therefore does
not hesitate to recommend his theory and its implied economic
policies as measures which serve multiple political and moral aims
in a harmonious manner'. In a letter to George Bernard Shaw in
1935, Keynes stated, ' "when my new theory has been duly assimilated and mixed with politics and feeling and passions, I can't predict
what the final upshot will be in its effects on action and affairs. But
there will be a great change" '.[83] The Keynesian theory of economic
action also ramified into other fields, including the social reconstruction criminology that developed after the Second World War.[84]

While criminologists also effectively simplify their research into
policy, they are prone to be simplistic. They are drawn into oversim-
plification because their research is expected to resonate with the
common sense of popular culture and with governance issues in
political culture. Even some scholars with prominent positions in
the most prestigious universities use their institutional positions to
fuel the popular sense rather than to treat it as problematic or a
subject for research inquiry in its own right. Thus Garland[85] quotes
Harvard professor James Q. Wilson who asserts ' "Wicked people
exist. Nothing avails except to set them apart from innocent
people"—a claim that simultaneously reasserts the most simplistic
common sense, gives up on social and rehabilitative programmes,
and dismisses the whole project of a social scientific criminology'.
Indeed criminologists sometimes join the 'common sense revolution'
of neo-liberal regimes and invoke the rhetoric of common sense itself
as a justification for their policy pronouncements.

[80] Stehr and Grundmann, n. 76 above, 322.
[81] Ibid., 325.
[82] J. Keynes, *The General Theory of Employment, Interest and Money* (London:
Macmillan, 1936), 381.
[83] Quoted by Stehr and Grundmann, n. 76 above, 325.
[84] Garland, n. 5 above, 48.
[85] Garland, n. 4 above, 131.

Criminologists frequently complain that their research has not had any direct impact on the policy field it was aimed at. In this refrain they sound much like the news source who complains that her thoughtful analysis of a newsworthy event has been turned into a sound bite, taken out of context, or even used against her position.[86] They also sound much like police officers who complain that police work is supposed to be concerned with criminal law enforcement but rarely is, and that the police therefore do not have much impact on crime control.[87]

Observable direct impact of criminological research is rare. Like the news source, the criminologist's research report escapes her authorship as it enters into new contexts of interpretation and use. As elaborated in the next section, the criminological contribution is often only at the level of rhetoric, providing tropes and marshalling data for persuasive purposes in a culture of public argument. Moreover, criminological rhetoric is contested vehemently because there are so many competing disciplines, professions, and institutions involved in addressing problems of crime and security. Indeed there are quite contradictory positions taken by the state and other policy seekers, because crime and security problems are increasingly pervasive and have not abated through the growth of expert knowledge and range of institutions that have addressed them.

Criminologists fail to perceive the direct impact of their research because a lot of their work is technocratic and invisibly absorbed into routine administrative systems and practices. The criminologist's case study report escapes her authorship as it moves through the administrative system. While technocratic studies may lead to new rules, classifications, and protocols in policing systems, it is usually not possible to observe directly what impact these new procedures have on the behaviour of those who are supposed to be responding to them.[88] Again the research effort dissipates, this time into the chaos of policing systems regarding crime and security.

Criminologists fret a great deal about the chaos and their perceived lack of influence on policy as rhetoric and policing. They see their field as fragmented and even fractured by the pull in so many directions by different professions and institutions. They often fail to

[86] Ericson, Baranek, and Chan, *Negotiating Control*, n. 57 above.
[87] Ericson and Haggerty, n. 8 above.
[88] C. Shearing and R. Ericson, 'Culture as Figurative Action' (1991) 42 *British Journal of Sociology* 481.

appreciate the inevitability of such chaos, its positive dimensions, and their real influence on policy. The best feature of criminology is its multidisciplinary ability to slip and slide among various institutional and professional discourses and practices. The cacophony of competing policies in the division of expert knowledge about crime and security is what makes criminology vital. As Alan Hunt observes,[89] 'It is a field of academic study sufficient unto itself, ignoring and contemptuous of cognate disciplines, that is in terminal crisis. The fact that criminology is unsure of its precise location and its relation to the wider project of social science is what keeps it relevant and engaged.'

Because they must simplify their research, experience chaos in the culture of argument about crime and security, and feel that they have no direct influence on policy, criminologists inevitably complain about loss of autonomy. This complaint is accompanied by rhetoric in favour of more autonomy, including autonomy from policy concerns. This response is ironic because criminology exists only as a policy field.

Some criminologists claim autonomy by arguing for a policy-free zone that is purely academic. They contend that true social scientists do not have to be normative about their subject matter, let alone advocates or participants. For example, Hagan argues against criminology as a separate discipline precisely because it is a policy field. Pure criminology is simply a branch of sociology, above policy concerns.

The structural approach outlined in this volume is inherently opposed to the separation of criminology from sociology, arguing instead that the structural foundations of sociology make its explanatory role necessary for an understanding of crime and delinquency. The policy analysis of crime leaves off where the sociological study of crime and delinquency began. Sociologists, it seems, may still be uniquely suited to pursue the causes of these behaviors regarded by others as disreputable.[90]

Criminologists themselves have often asserted the need to be distant from the fray of policy rhetoric. Nigel Walker[91] positions

[89] A. Hunt, 'Criminology: What's in a Name? A Response to Clifford Shearing' (1990) 32 *Canadian Journal of Criminology* 657.

[90] J. Hagan, *Structural Criminology* (Cambridge: Polity Press, 1989), 257–8.

[91] N. Walker, *Crime and Punishment in Britain* (Edinburgh: Edinburgh University Press, 1965), pp. i–ii.

the criminologist by saying 'it is no more his function to attack or defend the death penalty than it is the function of the political scientist to take part in an election campaign'. Surely criminologists who study the death penalty intend to influence the debates and bring about change,[92] just as political scientists who study elections regularly serve as pollsters and media commentators during election campaigns and thereby influence the election process.

A second claim to autonomy is the special place of the university as a context for independent inquiry. For example, in the early days of criminological research in Britain, both the Home Office and university-based scholars emphasized the importance of the detached, scientific inquiry that a university infrastructure offers.[93] In spite of its inevitable entanglements with myriad institutions and professions, criminology in the academy still has a special place and relative autonomy. Criminologists usually have considerable time to develop their ideas and research, compared to the immediacy experienced by practical actors in criminal justice agencies and other contexts of criminalization. Their requirements of closure, authoritative certainty, and practical action are also different. Practical actors in criminal justice must work efficiently toward finality and clear-cut solutions, accompanied by expressions of authoritative certainty. Therefore they act on partial or weak accounts and eschew more abstract explanations. In contrast, academic criminologists can cultivate deliberate ambiguity and play with abstractions. They have the freedom to do so because of their *relative* autonomy from other institutional contexts of practical action and their ability to act at a distance. They also have different audiences to persuade compared to practical actors directly involved in regulating crime. In turn they have a different role in institutional and professional legitimation processes.

A third claim to autonomy is research resources that are independent of sponsorship by those seeking specific policy outcomes.[94] The strong influence of external sponsors with a specific policy

---

[92] e.g. R. Hood, *The Death Penalty: A World-Wide Perspective* (Oxford: Oxford University Press, 1996).

[93] L. Radzinowicz, *The Cambridge Institute: Its Background and Scope* (London: HMSO, 1988); L. Radzinowicz, *Adventures in Criminology* (London: Routledge, 1999).

[94] R. Hood, 'Penal Policy and Criminological Challenges in the New Millennium' (2001) 34 *The Australian and New Zealand Journal of Criminology* 1.

agenda has always been a significant issue for independent criminological inquiry.[95] Independence of university-based researchers has been compromised in recent years because universities have shrinking resources; social science research councils have increasingly earmarked their funds for policy-relevant research, often in direct partnership with the agencies concerned about specific policies; and most funding resides with government foundations interested in specific policy questions and immediate needs. Furthermore, research grants are increasingly subject to audit, with new definitions of principled courses of action for researchers. Janet Chan observes that:

academic criminologists are 'propelled' by resource-starved universities to seek consultancies and research grants to satisfy external demands for relevance, value for money and contractual accountability. The same logic of performance and contractualism has led to a new emphasis on evaluation of criminal justice programs and policies as part of the policy process (O'Malley 1996: 35; see also Hogg and Brown 1998: 193; Israel 2000: 10–11). The distinction between 'academic' and 'administrative' criminologies, once sharply demarcated, is becoming much less clear-cut (O'Malley 1996). These new technologies of governance—marketisation, consumerism, managerialism and accountability—also raise serious questions in relation to intellectual property, political independence, and the future direction of criminological research (Israel 2000).[96]

Criminologists lament this state of affairs, and even assert that 'scientific research should not be part of the governmental apparatus'[97]—and indeed in most fields it is not'.[98] Of course scientific research in all fields is controlled by external sponsors, in industry as well as government, a matter of great consternation to scientists in many disciplines.[99] Scientific research is entwined with the governmental apparatus, especially in the Foucauldian sense as described above by Chan. It is peculiar to argue that criminology should be more policy relevant—governmental—but at the same time claim that the way to achieve this is an autonomously funded science that somehow exists outside governmental processes.

[95] Garland, n. 5 above.   [96] Chan, n. 40 above, 130.
[97] See G. Geis, '"This Sort of Thing Isn't Helpful": The Dilemma of the Australian Institute of Criminology' (1994) 27 *The Australian and New Zealand Journal of Criminology* 282.
[98] Hood, n. 94 above, 14.
[99] J. Pelikan, *The Idea of the University: A Reexamination* (New Haven, Conn.: Yale University Press, 1992).

A fourth claim to autonomy is the superiority of expert knowledge over lay knowledge. There is a blurring of expert and lay knowledge regarding crime and security because policy as rhetoric is increasingly driven by popular and political cultures.[100] Criminologists frequently complain that the scientific rationality of criminological research is distorted or simply ignored in favour of political solutions embedded in the common sense of public culture. For example, Garland protests[101] that the war on drugs in the United States disregards criminological expertise. This expertise shows a decline in illegal drug use, the fact that criminalization does not alter drug use, and the fact that criminalization fosters other problems such as violence, disrespect for authorities, and discrimination against minorities. More generally, Garland complains vehemently that:

The policy-making process has become profoundly *politicized* and *populist*. Policy measures are constituted in ways that appear to value political advantage and public opinion over the views of experts and the evidence of research. The professional groups who once dominated the policy-making process are increasingly disenfranchised as policy comes to be formulated by political action committees and political advisors.... Crime control strategies and criminological ideas are not adopted because they are known to solve problems. The evidence runs out well before their effects can be known with any certainty. They are adapted and they succeed because they characterize problems and identify solutions in ways that fit with dominant culture and the power structure upon which it rests.[102]

Chan[103] makes the important point that consumers of expert knowledge are often co-producers of that knowledge. Moreover, they can readily discredit unwelcome results through the mobilization of other experts who can usually find methodological flaws because of the limits of science itself. 'Not only are practitioners and politicians able to choose between expert groups, but those groups can also be *played off against each other* within and between disciplines, and in this way the autonomy of customers is increased.'[104]

In spite of its perpetual and necessary positioning for more autonomy, criminology cannot get away with representing itself as a distanced form of independent scientific inquiry. It loses credibility if it tries to do so because it is the non-scientific policy constituencies

[100] U. Beck, *Risk Society: Toward a New Modernity* (London: Sage, 1992), 154.
[101] D. Garland, n. 4 above, 132.   [102] Garland, n. 4 above, 13, 26.
[103] Chan, n. 40 above, 128.   [104] Ibid.

served by the criminologist that give her the credibility to claim a privileged standpoint. At the same time criminologists generally avoid making open declarations of what I am indicating here: that the field is highly relative and biased toward the institutional interests of its policy constituencies. Such a declaration might undermine the persuasive force of 'academic' and 'scientific' accounts when they come in handy to those constituencies. Institutions restrict individual authorship. They tend to do our thinking for us.[105] The success of any move within an institutional discourse and practice depends on criteria internal to the institution: good moves are defined internally in the course of producing the discourse and practice.[106]

Of course criminology is also part of the institution of higher education, and in this domain it does retain some distinctive features of its own discourse and practice. One dominant feature is a negative logic. Criminologists focus on the pathologies of aberrant people and on crime risks as threats to security. They also focus on the failure of institutions to provide security and justice, even to the extreme of declaring that 'nothing works'. Criminologists turn this negative logic on their own enterprise. The failure of criminology to influence policy, let alone create a better world, is now a recurrent theme.[107]

---

[105] M. Douglas, *How Institutions Think* (Syracuse, NY: Syracuse University Press, 1986).

[106] D. Nelken, 'Reflexive Criminology?' in D. Nelken (ed.), *The Futures of Criminology* (London: Sage, 1994), 24, referring to the ideas of Stanley Fish.

[107] R. Hood, 'Criminology and Penal Change: A Case Study of the Nature and Impact of Some Recent Advice to Governments' in R. Hood (ed.), *Crime, Criminology and Public Policy: Essays in Honor of Sir Leon Radzinowicz* (London: Heinemann, 1974); R. Hood, 'Some Reflections on the Role of Criminology in Public Policy' [1987] *Crim.L.R.* 527; Hood, n. 94 above; S. Cohen, *Visions of Social Control* (Cambridge: Polity Press, 1985); S. Cohen, *Against Criminology* (New Brunswick, NJ: Transaction Books, 1988); S. Cohen, 'If Nothing Works, What is our Work?' (1994) 27 *The Australian and New Zealand Journal of Criminology* 104; J. Braithwaite, 'The State of Criminology: Theoretical Decay or Renaissance?' (1989) 22 *The Australian and New Zealand Journal of Criminology* 129; Nelken, n. 106 above; A. Bottoms, 'The Philosophy and Politics of Punishment' in C. Clarkson and R. Morgan (eds.), *The Politics of Sentencing Reform* (Oxford: Clarendon, 1995); A. Blumstein, 'Probing the Connection between Crime and Punishment in the United States' (1995) 5 *Criminal Behavior and Mental Health* 67; D. Dixon, 'Crime, Criminology and Public Policy' (1995) 28 *The Australian and New Zealand Journal of Criminology* 1; F. Zimring, 'Populism, Democratic Government, and the Decline of Expert Authority: Some Reflections on "Three Strikes" in California' (1996) 28 *Pacific Law Journal* 243; Chan, n. 40 above; Garland, n. 4 above.

This long list of scholars who have turned the negative logic of criminology onto the criminological enterprise itself entered the field in the heyday of welfarism. They have experienced the ascendancy of politicized and populist influences on policy, and an accompanying decline of their conception of policy as resulting from a rational process aided by detached scientific inquiry. They have also witnessed the failure of their own welfarist policy preferences. Worse still, they have seen the growing hegemony of anti-welfarist criminologies based on models of rational choice and individual responsibility, rhetorics of zero tolerance, and reconceptualization of the least fortunate members of society as an undeserving underclass. They have also experienced the diminishment of their role as a buffer between troubled people and the punitive urges of the populace, in keeping with the declining role of criminal justice practitioners themselves in this regard.

Perhaps most troubling of all, this generation of criminologists ironically contributed to some aspects of their own diminishment. Committed to the scientific ethos, they exposed the limits of social science in explaining human behaviour, assessing the effectiveness of criminal justice programmes and advancing policies. They documented the many ways in which the criminal justice system is neither effective nor humane, for example through empirical investigations of the backstage realities of discount justice, discrimination, and administrative convenience that compromise and even scandalize lofty principles of justice and welfare. They devised technologies of risk management and auditing that cramped the innovative capacities of the criminal justice system. They documented that in any case the criminal justice system is only a minor player in crime control and security provision, that most crime is dealt with through the private 'justice' systems of other institutions, and that even when it does come to police and prosecutorial attention crime is most often funnelled back through these other institutions.

In this depressed state, some criminologists have tried to seal the hermeneutic circle of their academic institution and eschew explicit policy concerns. They 'have comprised boutique knowledges within a corpus of criminological work focused on the production of solutions to specific crime problems'.[108] In the American context, recent studies of the journal *Social Problems*, which is a leading outlet for

---

[108] Walters, n. 33 above, 216.

research on crime and deviance,[109] reveal that there has been a substantial decline over twenty years in the number of articles that make explicit policy recommendations.[110] Moving away from its original welfarist policy orientation on behalf of the less fortunate,[111] *Social Problems* has more recently focused on studies of the construction of social problems, and of subject positions or identities in relation to processes of construction.[112]

Of course those who emphasize social constructionism and identity politics are themselves committed to taking apart the organizations they study in order to advance alternative policies. They themselves are constructionists, deploying their own rhetoric and policing preferences to advance different frameworks for positive action. Their realization of success comes when they have unseated the undesirable policy framework they deconstruct. However, at this point the new policy reality they represent becomes orthodoxy and is itself open to constructionist analysis by competitors. 'Constructionism as an argument is attractive for its cleansing, destructive powers until a particular end, for a particular group of people, is established. Then constructionism becomes intellectual embarrassment to those very people.'[113]

Efforts to circle the wagons of the academy from policy constituencies are not successful. The academic institution is not merely porous but fluid, with outside institutions charged with getting the world's work done, including the very difficult work of dealing with crime and security. Any academic discourse of crime and security necessarily feeds into the activities of people and the institutions they populate by virtue of the fact that they are audiences for that discourse at all. While some criminology has a very restricted audience—largely limited to a few fellow specialists in the academy—it is never hermetic.

It seems peculiar to take the view that the enormous apparatus of criminology—its academic departments, journals, expert services,

---

[109] M. Karides, J. Misra, I. Kennelly, and S. Moller, 'Representing the Discipline: *Social Problems* Compared to *ASR* and *AJS*' (2001) 48 *Social Problems* 111.

[110] W. Brekus, K. Brekus, and J. Galliher, 'Social Problems in *Social Problems*: The Theory and Method of Justice' (2001) 48 *Social Problems* 137.

[111] Abbott, n. 6 above, 68 ff.

[112] Brekus, Brekus, and Galliher, n. 110 above.

[113] Abbott, n. 4 above, 87–8. See generally I. Hacking, *The Social Construction of What?* (Cambridge, Mass.: Harvard University Press, 1999).

and conferences with casts of thousands—is supported primarily as a grand scheme of self-referentiality among academics. It is preferable to understand how it is supported because it does make real contributions to policy as rhetoric and policing.

Criminological Rhetoric

The research communications of criminologists are highly rhetorical. They are intended to move their audiences to more principled courses of action in dealing with crime and security. While criminological publications appear in the scholarly formats of academic journals and books, they are often tract-like and infused with discourses of moral reform. Even academics who otherwise claim a detached analytical stance wish their analyses to have rhetorical force on the world. Consider the following statement by John Beattie, an historian of crime and criminal justice in seventeenth- and eighteenth-century England,[114] who expresses the desire that his work, and that of other time-and-place historians, will influence present-day policies regarding crime and security.

As crime, especially violent crime, has appeared to increase sharply in Western Europe and North America over the last 30 years or so, the history of crime and of policing and punishment has taken on a particular urgency. This wider public concern surely helps to explain why historians have become interested in studying crime and past societies' responses to it, and why there has been a recent explosion in writing on the criminal law and the administration of justice.[115]

The empirical research and expositions of revisionist historians in the 1970s had enormous influence and continue to do so.[116] These

[114] J. Beattie, *Crime and the Courts in England, 1660–1800* (Princeton, NJ: Princeton University Press, 1986).

[115] J. Beattie, 'Crime, Policing and Punishment in England 1550–1850' in J. Gladstone, R. Ericson, and C. Shearing (eds.), *Criminology: A Reader's Guide* (Toronto: Centre of Criminology, University of Toronto, 1991).

[116] e.g. E. Thompson, *Whigs and Hunters: The Origin of the Black Act* (London: Allen Lone, 1975); D. Hay, P. Linebaugh, and E. Thompson (eds.), *Albion's Fatal Tree: Crime and Society in Eighteenth-Century England* (New York: Pantheon, 1975); M. Foucault, *Discipline and Punish: The Birth of the Prison* (New York: Pantheon Books, 1977); M. Ignatieff, *A Just Measure of Pain: The Penitentiary in the Industrial Revolution, 1750–1850* (New York: Pantheon, 1978); D. Rothman, *Conscience and Convenience: The Asylum and its Alternatives in Progressive America* (Boston, Mass.: Little, Brown, 1980).

historians for the present devised rhetorical structures and strategies for understanding penal crises so that their research could feed into contemporary penal reform movements. For example, Foucault was a penal reform advocate. His advocacy shaped *Discipline and Punish*, which in turn was used by him as a history for the present to force people radically to rethink the fundamental question, 'Why prisons?' Foucault was widely criticized for his lack of attention to historical specificity and empirical detail, yet his rhetorical strategy has profoundly influenced how the penal apparatus is now understood and used.

In their desire rhetorically to force more principled courses of action, criminologists are consistent with legal practitioners. Law is itself a culture of argument, full of literary devices and figurative language aimed at effecting authoritative certainty and closure over decisions, and at moving people to act under its descriptions.[117] Criminal legal cases are 'texts whose rhetorical structure is at least as important as their superficial legal content.... [This rhetorical structure reveals] the significant symbolic aspect of the power of criminal law, along with the implicit yet powerful images of wrong-doing and rightful conduct, normal and abnormal subjects, guilt and innocence which legal discourse draws upon and produces'.[118]

Criminologists deploy figurative language in their rhetorical invocations.[119] They champion tropes that lead their audiences to see crime problems and security solutions in one way as opposed to others, and to act accordingly. As such they produce ideology as a procedure not to know.[120] Consider how medicine has used its disease metaphor to colonize the definition and treatment of

---

[117] L. Fuller, *Legal Fictions* (Stanford, Cal.: Stanford University Press, 1967); J. White, *When Words Lose their Meaning: Constitutions and Reconstitutions of Language, Character and Community* (Chicago, Ill.: University of Chicago Press, 1984); P. Goodrich, *Reading the Law* (Oxford: Blackwell, 1986); R. Posner, *Law and Literature: A Misunderstood Relation* (Cambridge, Mass.: Harvard University Press, 1988); K. Scheppele, *Legal Secrets: Equality and Efficiency in Common Law* (Chicago, Ill.: University of Chicago Press, 1988); A. Norrie, *Crime, Reason and History* (London: Butterworths, 1993); R. Ericson, 'Why Law is Like News' in D. Nelken (ed.), *Law as Communication* (Aldershot: Dartmouth, 1996).

[118] See Lacey, n. 22 above. See also N. Lacey, 'A Clear Concept of Intention: Elusive or Illusory?' (1993) 56 *Modern Law Review* 621.

[119] A. Ortony (ed.), *Metaphor and Thought* (Cambridge: Cambridge University Press, 1979).

[120] D. Smith, 'The Ideological Practice of Sociology' (1974) 8 *Catalyst* 39.

delinquency, child abuse, dangerousness, and so on.[121] Consider how urban planners have used metaphors of crime as blight,[122] and the association of 'broken windows' with fear of crime,[123] to bulldoze communities and remake them. Consider how sociologists have used tropes of 'blocked opportunities' for youth as a means of enhancing educational and occupational access.[124] Consider how economists have used the metaphor of 'bowling alone' to depict the decline of civic engagement and the need to enhance social capital as a means of reducing crime and other social ills.[125]

These examples suggest how the rhetorical force of criminological discourse typically reaches beyond the control of crime *per se*. Crime itself is a trope for addressing intractable problems of human behaviour, well-being, and security. For example crime, and in particular youth crime, is used to address failures in the institution of the family as the responsible locus for human welfare and the improvement of populations.[126] Governments as well as institutions in civil society seek to 'govern through crime'[127] by using criminological rhetorics of crime to influence more principled courses of action regarding human security and welfare.

Successful tropes are those that become embedded in practices, which in turn reinforce the tropes and the principled courses of action they urge.[128] For example, criminological sponsorship of the 'broken windows' trope is intended to foster better-kept communities, while each act of repair 'proves' the discourse of orderliness. This discourse also feeds into broader 'community' initiatives for self-policing, for example in the form of electronic security technologies and private policing agents. When present, these technologies

[121] Abbott, n. 39 above; Hacking, n. 51 above.

[122] D. Schön, 'Generative Metaphor: A Perspective on Problem-Setting in Social Policy' in A. Ortony (ed.), *Metaphor and Thought* (Cambridge: Cambridge University Press, 1979).

[123] J. Wilson and G. Kelling, 'Broken Windows: The Police and Neighborhood Safety' [1982] *Atlantic Monthly*, March, 29; G. Kelling and C. Coles, *Fixing Broken Windows* (New York: Free Press, 1996).

[124] Cloward and Ohlin, n. 53 above.

[125] R. Putnam, *Bowling Alone* (New York: Touchstone, 2000).

[126] J. Donzelot, *The Policing of Families* (New York: Pantheon, 1979); Garland, n. 4 above, 84.

[127] Simon, n. 56 above.

[128] M. Valverde, *The Age of Light, Soap and Water: Moral Reform in English Canada* (Toronto: McClelland and Stewart, 1991).

and agents are a perpetual reminder of the (in)security that prompted them into existence and seems to make them necessary. They become part of the rhetoric. Fear proves itself.[129]

Criminologists also use quantitative data in the service of policy rhetoric. As Porter[130] remarks regarding the social sciences in general and psychology in particular, the softer the science, the harder the data. Thus in criminology we find 'the enduring popularity of the politically disinterested, methodologically rigorous model of criminological research, usually based on "hard" quantitative data'.[131] The rhetorical strategy is to infuse trust in numbers to legitimate research analyses and the policy directions they urge. Furthermore, the analytical models derive from the natural sciences which also provide legitimation and underpin the power of criminological rhetoric.[132]

Statistics are open to a great deal of rhetorical manipulation at all stages of the research process, from initial criteria of relevance used to create categories and classify, through analytical techniques and interpretations.[133] Haggerty[134] demonstrates how criminologists join with government statistical agents, criminal justice system operatives, and mass media journalists in 'making crime count' for particular institutional interests. Crime statistics are a practical accomplishment in the context of institutional regimes and processes, influenced by extra-scientific factors, networks of interest, and the desire to persuade. In particular, figures are used as figurative language to dramatize crime problems and create a sense of urgency for law enforcement resolutions.[135]

[129] Zedner, n. 68 above; Ericson and Haggerty, n. 28 above.

[130] T. Porter, *Trust in Numbers: The Pursuit of Objectivity in Science and Public Life* (Princeton, NJ: Princeton University Press, 1995).

[131] Chan, n. 40 above, 120.

[132] M. Foucault, *The Order of Things: An Archaeology of the Human Sciences* (New York: Random House, 1972); P. Bourdieu, 'The Specificity of Scientific Field and the Social Conditions of the Progress of Reason' (1975) 14(6) *Social Science Information* 19.

[133] D. Dorling and S. Simpson (eds.), *Statistics and Society: The Arithmetic of Politics* (London: Arnold, 1999); J. Best, *Damned Lies and Statistics: Untangling Numbers from the Media, Politicians and Activists* (Berkeley, Cal.: University of California Press, 2001).

[134] K. Haggerty, *Making Crime Count* (Toronto: University of Toronto Press, 2001).

[135] J. Orcutt and J. Turner, 'Shocking Numbers and Graphic Accounts: Quantified Images of Drug Problems in the Print Media' (1993) 40 *Social Problems* 190.

Statistical research on human populations and their problems inevitably has a moral character that urges particular courses of action. Moral assessments guide the selection of risks to focus on and how to mitigate them.[136] Moral judgements are built into statistical norms that establish what is normal about a population, and what is not.[137] Moreover, in having to move from factual construction to authoritative certainty regarding the locus of a problem and its resolution, researchers must pinpoint *a* cause and urge *a* policy solution in relation to that cause. This point is made brilliantly by Gusfield[138] through his analysis of how impaired driving is singled out as a central cause of road accidents. 'The rapidity with which alcohol is perceived as villain exemplifies the moral character of factual construction. Without the moral direction the transformation of data into policy directives is difficult.'[139] The criminologist must mobilize data of causal responsibility in order to shape response ability within the political and legal systems. This process inevitably entails moral determinations of how rhetorically to mould and interpret the facts.

As we know from actor network analysis in the social study of science,[140] the success of policy rhetoric depends on how the scientist is connected to powerful social networks in other institutions, in particular the political and business constituencies interested in the research, and sometimes the news media. Criminologists are no exception in having to rely on powerful social networks to advance their research. They join their policy constituencies and the news media in mobilizing consent to their way of seeing a crime problem and a response that hopefully will yield more justice and security.

A well analysed example of criminological research in this regard is the work of Sherman and Berk[141] on law enforcement responses to

[136] M. Douglas, 'Risk as a Forensic Resource' (1990) 119(4) *Daedalus* 1; M. Douglas, *Risk and Blame* (London: Routledge, 1992).

[137] Hacking, n. 1 above.

[138] Gusfield, n. 61 above.

[139] Ibid., 74.

[140] e.g. A. Cambrosio, C. Limoges, and E. Hoffman, 'Expertise as a Network: A Case Study of the Controversies over the Environmental Release of Genetically Engineered Organisms' in N. Stehr and R. Ericson (eds.), *The Culture and Power of Knowledge: Inquiries into Contemporary Societies* (Berlin and New York: de Gruyter, 1992); Beck, n. 100 above, 168–9.

[141] L. Sherman and R. Berk, 'The Specific Deterrent Effects of Arrest for Domestic Assault' (1984) 49 *American Sociological Review* 261; L. Sherman and R. Berk, 'The

domestic violence. As Binder and Meeker[142] and Binder and Binder[143] show, Sherman and Berk used their experimental field research on police responses to domestic violence to advocate a strict policy of criminalization in this area. This advocacy helped shape a policy of criminalization in many American jurisdictions, in spite of the very limited and methodologically flawed research on which it was based. The rhetorical success of Berk and Sherman was partly attributable to the way in which their policy preference resonated with politically correct approaches to domestic violence in public culture. But it also related to their efforts to communicate their criminological research and policy rhetoric through other networks and media. For example, they wrote a tract for the Police Foundation[144] which favoured criminalization of domestic violence. Binder and Binder[145] refer to this tract as a 'high-pressure sales' tool that was distributed to police departments throughout the United States. 'That was followed by a press release and many other efforts at influencing media coverage.' In the words of Sherman and another colleague[146] the research was 'actively promoted' and there was an attempt to 'orchestrate the release of experimental results for maximum press coverage'.[147]

Criminologists come to believe their own rhetoric, leading to a narrowness of focus and sometimes a misdirected influence on policy. This process occurred through the infamous rhetoric of

Minneapolis Domestic Violence Experiment', *Police Foundation Reports* No. 1 (Washington, DC: Police Foundation, 1984).

[142] A. Binder and J. Meeker, 'Experiments as Reforms' (1988) 16 *Journal of Criminal Justice* 347; A. Binder and J. Meeker, 'Arrest as a Method to Control Spousal Abuse' in E. Buzawa and C. Buzawa (eds.), *Domestic Violence: The Changing Criminal Justice Response* (Westport, Conn.: Arburn House, 1992); A. Binder and J. Meeker, 'On the Policy Implications of the Domestic Violence Experiment Replications' (1993) 58 *American Sociological Review* 886.

[143] A. Binder and V. Binder, 'The Relationship between Research Results and Public Policy' in H. Pontell and D. Shuchor (eds.), *Contemporary Issues in Crime and Criminal Justice: Essays in Honor of Gilbert Geis* (Upper Saddle River, NJ: Prentice Hall, 2001).

[144] Sherman and Berk, n. 141 above.

[145] Binder and Binder, n. 143 above, 42.

[146] L. Sherman and E. Cohn, *Police Policy on Domestic Violence, 1985: A National Survey*, Crime Control Reports No. 1 (Washington, DC: Crime Control Institute, 1989).

[147] Ibid., 120; Binder and Binder, n. 143 above, 42.

'nothing works', first advanced by Martinson[148] and then taken up in the extreme negative logic of many researchers examining the effectiveness of the correctional system (myself included).[149] Martinson[150] himself later cautioned about the limitations of his original analysis, and complained about the ways in which his text had escaped him as it became misused by various criminologists who supported anti-correctionalist reformers. 'Nothing works' was a rhetorical force that fed on a wider political culture that was eroding the very capacity of the state to provide security against crime and distribute welfare.

This aggressively disappointed reaction, with its emphatic overstatement of negative data and its suppression of all contrary evidence, was less an informed view of the system than a cathartic reaction to the problems and conflicts the system entailed. That such an emotive overreaction could so quickly become conventional wisdom suggests there were other interests and emotions involved in shaping this response—forces that had little time for criminological details or the careful interpretation of empirical research.[151]

In retrospect we can witness the unintended consequences of some criminological rhetoric. Criminologists can be swept up in reform movements that are not of their own making, but nevertheless lead them to make inferential leaps from their data and use figurative language that is unwarranted. Thus, contrary to the view of many who say their research has little influence on policy, other criminologists warn that there is sometimes too much influence, and that researchers should therefore be circumspect with their figurative language, whether it involves words or numbers as symbolic power. In his presidential address to the American Society of Criminology, Charles Wellford stated:

---

[148]   R. Martinson, 'What Works?—Questions and Answers about Prison Reform' (1974) 35 *The Public Interest* 22.

[149]   See J. Chan and R. Ericson, *Decarceration and the Economy of Penal Reform* (Toronto: Centre of Criminology, University of Toronto, 1981); and the critique by M. McMahon, 'Net-Widening: Vagaries in the Use of a Concept' (1990) 30 *British Journal of Criminology* 121; M. McMahon, *The Persistent Prison?: Rethinking Decarceration and Penal Reform* (Toronto: University of Toronto Press, 1992).

[150]   R. Martinson, 'New Findings, New Views: A Note of Caution Regarding Sentencing Reform' (1979) 7 *Hofstra Law Review* 242.

[151]   Garland, n. 4 above, 69.

We should be concerned about the fact that we have far more impact on public policy than we deserve. Someone produces a modestly adequate piece of research demonstrating that some type of program has some kind of positive effect on some kind of crime in some place for limited time, and suddenly the program is adapted as a national model.... Later on...we conduct some evaluation research and demonstrate that the program has very modest, if any, consequences and yet the program continues to be used.[152]

Abbott[153] expresses the view that 'Social Scientists remain completely in control of policy advice to governments on matters of American social life'. While this itself is an exaggeration—especially if we examine criminological research and American policy on crime and security[154]—it nevertheless indicates why a huge social science apparatus continues to be supported in the United States. Research rhetoric does help form new realities, especially at the level of policy as policing.

Criminological Policing

Criminologists tend to regard policy as some grander scheme of government or fundamental principles or laws. In this regard they are close to one definition of policy in the *Oxford English Dictionary* as 'a fundamental truth or law as the basis of reasoning or action'. But policy is also rooted in its original meaning of 'policing', involving the everyday practices of classification, surveillance, and regulation used to govern conduct. As Giddens has stressed,[155] the influence of social science is found not only at the level of abstract policies or frameworks for thinking, but also in how it constitutes institutional classification schemes, regulations, and routine practices of bureaucratic surveillance.[156] Criminological research also contributes to policy as policing in these ways. In doing so it obtains its official warrant from various crime control authorities and their bases of institutional power. In their policing capacity, criminological 'categories actually constitute their criminal objects in the very act of comprehending them. They are ... truth-producing categories that provide the discursive conditions for real social

---

[152] C. Wellford, 'Controlling Crime and Achieving Justice—The American Society of Criminology 1996 Presidential Address' (1997) 35 *Criminology* 1, 3.

[153] Abbott, n. 6 above, 146.   [154] Garland, n. 4 above.

[155] Giddens, n. 14 above, 14, 16.   [156] See also Poster, n. 13 above.

practices. These categories are themselves a product (and a functioning aspect) of the same cultures and social structures that produce the criminal behaviours and individuals to which they refer'.[157]

In this view criminological research is part of the governmental apparatus in the Foucauldian sense.[158] That is, it participates in 'calculated means of the direction of how we behave and act ... [carried out] by various authorities and agencies, involving particular forms of truth, and using definite resources, means and techniques'.[159] As such governmental work is not restricted to the state, but also involves governance throughout civil society and private sector institutions. Thus it includes what may be termed private policy (and private policing) as well as public policy (and public policing). It also entails governing governments—that is, policing the activities of government itself—as a core element of its practices. Governing government is central to liberalism,[160] and is valued and actively sponsored by government itself, for example through research grants to scholars or funding to non-governmental organizations committed to social change.

Criminological policing as part of the governmental apparatus has intensified in the past two decades. Criminology is increasingly a field of applied knowledge and social necessity directed at very local and specific risk-management problems on behalf of particular institutions. This trend is underpinned by theoretical developments in criminology and the social sciences more generally. Theoretical work, embracing postmodern social science in one form or another, supports institutional fragmentation and ideologies of self-governance. Postmodern theories reject grand totalizing and meta-theory as pragmatic guides to action. In doing so they undermine theoretical warrants for broader policy projects and social intervention such as welfarism—some grander scheme of government or fundamental principles or laws—and instead privilege local and institution-specific discourses of risk. These local, institution-specific discourses create a utilitarian, single problem, single cause, single solution frame of risk expertise that ignores systemic aspects and their consequences.

---

[157] Garland, n. 4 above, 25.   [158] Foucault, n. 8 above.
[159] M. Dean, *Governmentality: Power and Rule in Modern Society* (London: Sage, 1999), 2, 3.
[160] Rose, n. 35 above.

This theoretical shift and the risk-management practices it underwrites articulate broader social changes toward governance beyond the state and its basis in local knowledge of risk. Included in this shift is a repositioning of the criminal justice system in regulatory space, a space that is now being constructed through concerns of vulnerability, risk, efficiency, and accountability. Discourses and technologies of risk penetrate a range of institutions and have a bearing upon how the criminal justice system and its operatives think and act.[161] Criminologists have inevitably become part of this risk enterprise and its mechanisms of policing.

This new theoretical infrastructure of criminological policing is augmented on the methodological side by a resurgence of quantitative research. Anchored in 'actuarial justice',[162] criminological policing relies in particular on probability statistics as a powerful technology of standardization and a means of ordering populations. As Hacking[163] documents so brilliantly, probability statistics produce laws of their own that force people to act under their descriptions of risk.

We obtain data about a governed class whose deportment is offensive, and then attempt to alter what we guess are relevant conditions of that class in order to change the laws of statistics that the class obeys. This is the essence of the style of government that in the United States is called 'liberal.' As in the nineteenth century, the intentions of such legislation are benevolent. The *we* who know best change the statistical laws that affect *them*.[164]

In the very process of legislating the lives of their subjects, probability statistics also bring order to criminology. In a field otherwise highly fractured among disciplines, professions, and institutions, probability statistics offer precise classifications, reduced ambiguity, direct links to policy constituencies, and real effects.

Quantification is a powerful agency of standardization because it imposes order on hazy thinking, but this depends on the license it provides to ignore or reconfigure much of what is difficult or obscure. Whenever a reasoning process can be made computable, we can be confident that we are dealing

---

[161] M. Feeley and J. Simon, 'Actuarial Justice: The Emerging New Criminal Law' in D. Nelken (ed.), *The Futures Criminology* (London: Sage, 1994); Ericson and Haggerty, n. 8 above; P. O'Malley (ed.), *Crime and the Risk Society* (Aldershot: Dartmouth, 1998).

[162] Feeley and Simon, n. 161 above.   [163] Hacking, n. 1 above.

[164] Ibid., 119.

with something that has been universalised, with knowledge effectively detailed from the individuality of its makers. As nineteenth century statisticians like to boast, their science averaged away everything contingent, accidental, inexplicable, or personal, and left only large-scale regularities. It is important to add that quantification has the virtues of its vices. The remarkable ability of numbers and calculations to defy disciplinary and even rational boundaries and link academic to political discourse owes much to this ability to bypass deep issues. In intellectual exchange, as in property economic transactions, numbers are the medium through which dissimilar desires, needs, and expectations are somehow made commensurable.[165]

Criminological policing of risk is focused on crime prevention in particular. The new criminologies of everyday life draw upon rational choice and routine activity models of criminal offending to invent technologies of situational crime prevention. They accept the findings of police researchers that the public police and criminal justice system have very limited capacity to know about or effectively deal with crime, and that most governance of crime occurs through the institutions of civil society beyond the state.[166] They take the view that much crime, especially property crime, is part of normal social and economic routines, and as such must be managed so as not to disrupt those routines. This management includes acceptance of the view that some crime is caused by the way social and economic routines are structured by the institution concerned, and therefore must be tolerated as an inevitable aspect of those routines. The policing of insurance fraud is a classic case in point.[167] As Garland shows,[168] the criminology of everyday life 'has become a major resource for policy makers in the last two decades. . . . Crime avoidance remains a prominent organising principle of everyday life. . . . Crime has come to be regarded as an everyday risk that must be routinely assessed and managed in much the same way that we come to deal with road traffic'.

This emphasis on the policing of crime risks in everyday life has fostered a substantial sub-field of criminology devoted to police studies. This sub-field now has its own specialized journals, university departments, and degree programmes. Research is not limited to

---

[165] Porter, n. 130 above, 85.
[166] Ericson and Haggerty, n. 8 above; Ericson and Haggerty, n. 28 above.
[167] Ericson, Doyle, and Barry, n. 31 above.
[168] Garland, n. 4 above, 16, 106.

the public police, but rather addresses policing in the broad sense of sustaining social and economic routines through the governance of populations in a variety of institutions. Private policing is seen as especially salient because it is strategically placed to deal with the minutiae of situational crime prevention in private spaces that the public police cannot routinely access. The public police are reconfigured as information brokers and advisors to private policing operatives, and as aggressive eradicators of minor offending in public spaces when required by business enterprise.[169]

As Garland observes,[170] much of the inventiveness of situational crime prevention and private policing drives from the security operatives themselves. Criminologists such as Clarke,[171] Wilson,[172] Kelling and Coles,[173] and Felson[174] provide abstractions, systematization, and rhetoric to justify the practices and smooth the way for their proliferation.

In what is a very Foucauldian story, this dispersed, disorganised, field of recipes and crime control techniques—composed of a multitude of small-scale inventions, some of them ingenious, most of them quite mundane, all of them growing out of situated problem-solving activities rather than abstract analyses—come to be taken up and developed by criminological experts. Criminologists rationalized and systematized these ideas and techniques, creating new criminological theories, and persuading public agencies (the Home Office, the National Institute of Justice, the police) to adapt these ways of thinking. These theories are then fed back through preventative partnerships and crime prevention advice—into practical locales, where they help lay practitioners to systematize their practice, to become self-conscious about what they do, and to learn from accumulated data and proven best practice.[175]

[169] L. Huey, K. Haggerty, and R. Ericson, *Policing Fantasy City* (unpublished research report to the Law Commission of Canada, 2001).

[170] Garland, n. 4 above, 160–1.

[171] R. Clarke, 'Situational Crime Prevention: Its Theoretical Basis and Practical Scope' in M. Tonry and N. Morris (eds.), *Crime and Justice: An Annual Review of Research* (Chicago, Ill.: University of Chicago Press, 1983).

[172] J. Wilson, 'Crime and Public Policy' in J. Wilson and J. Petersilia (eds.), *Crime* (San Francisco, Cal.: Institute for Contemporary Studies, 1995).

[173] Kelling and Coles, n. 123 above.

[174] M. Felson, *Crime and Everyday Life* (2nd edn., Thousand Oaks, Cal.: Pine Forge Press, 1998).

[175] Garland, n. 4 above, 161.

Brodeur[176] protests this state of affairs, observing that 'technical expertise applied on a routine basis by low-ranking professionals is playing an increasing role in criminal justice, at the expense of scientific and research expertise'. The new criminologies of everyday life are indeed subservient to the technicians of security. Whatever expertise they offer is rapidly de-skilled into the pragmatic routines of security operatives. Moreover, expertise is emerging outside the social sciences entirely, as applied scientists and engineers continue to invent security technologies that go in search of uses.

Victimology has arisen as another sub-field that specializes in preventive security.[177] For victimologists, criminology is victim consumerism. That is, victimization and fear of crime surveys are used to constitute community interests and to argue how the criminal justice system compared to other institutions can meet these interests better. These surveys and other forms of risk analysis are also used to augment the self-policing capacities of everyone as potential victims. For example, potential victims are made more aware of the routine crime risks in their environment and what preventive security arrangements they can put in place to minimize them.

While the primary thrust of criminological policing is preventive security, there are applications throughout the criminalization process. Powerful new technologies for the policing of risk have been invented by criminologists to determine gradations of restriction on offenders, and justify extra punishment to those de-selected as 'dangerous'. For example, there is 'the well-documented movement to transform the probation service from an individualised welfare-oriented service towards a more systematised, centralised organisation whose task is to provide surveillance and control of offenders in the community.... More striking still is the development of electronic technologies for monitoring offenders' movements, and the possibilities of such means being available to track and control their behaviour'.[178] Criminologists have also been highly successful at having penal authorities adopt their dangerousness assessment

---

[176] J. P. Brodeur, 'Expertise Not Wanted: The Case of the Criminal Law' (unpublished paper to the Schloessman Seminar on the Expert in Modern Societies: Historical and Contemporary Perspectives (Berlin: Max Planck Institute, 1998), 30.

[177] Zedner, n. 62 above; Zedner, n. 68 above.

[178] Hood, n. 94 above, 4.

tools.[179] Indeed the entire system of penal operatives now thinks and acts only in the language of policing risk. Parole boards have been 'recast, in effect, as risk assessment tribunals'.[180]

Criminological policing of risk has also turned onto criminal justice system operatives themselves. Criminal justice system operatives such as the police are subject to a panoply of surveillance and auditing technologies.[181] The concern is not only the traditional one of monitoring due process, but also bureaucratic efficiency regarding risk communication.[182] That is, criminal justice system operatives are themselves policed with regard to their own practices of preventive security, including how they communicate risks promptly and in proper form.[183]

Conclusions

This chapter makes a number of claims about criminology and policy that are intended to influence the culture of criminological research. Hopefully these claims will lead criminologists to reflect upon and debate their research enterprise and its relation to policy.

Criminologists must accept that there is no escape from policy. Criminology is inevitably a policy field because the research focus is invariably on principled courses of action that are or should be taken regarding conduct that is or could be criminalized. Criminologists must also accept that they cannot escape the law. Even when they are researching the alternative policing mechanisms of other institutions, the template is always the criminal law and whether criminalization may be an option for governance of the conduct in question.

Criminologists need to appreciate their role in the system of criminology. They are part of a system of academic disciplines, professions, and institutions in which they compete for jurisdiction

---

[179] R. Hare, *Manual for the Hare Psychopathy Checklist—Revised* (Toronto: Multi-Health Systems, 1991); C. Webster, G. Harris, M. Rice, C. Cormier, and V. Quinsey, *The Violence Prediction Scheme* (Toronto: Centre of Criminology, University of Toronto, 1994).

[180] Hood, n. 94 above, 3. See also R. Hood and S. Shute, *The Parole System at Work: A Study of Risk Based Decision-Making* (London: Home Office, 2000).

[181] Ericson and Haggerty, n. 8 above, part v.

[182] Ibid.

[183] R. Ericson, 'The Royal Commission on Criminal Justice System Surveillance' in M. McConville and L. Bridges (eds.), *Criminal Justice in Crisis* (Aldershot: Edward Elgar, 1994).

over problems of crime and security. The competitive process is hegemonic, requiring criminologists to pit their authority against that of other disciplines, professions, and institutions whose frameworks of understanding and values they fundamentally disagree with or even deplore. The competitive process also requires criminologists to translate their research results into the criteria of relevance of their policy constituencies. Translation results in simplification of research results; chaos in facing the cacophony of voices from other disciplines, professions, and institutions with divergent views on problems of crime and security; and loss of autonomy of one's own voice in policy processes. While criminologists will complain vehemently about their loss of autonomy, they should appreciate that it is an inevitable component of their competitive participation in the system of criminology.

Ironically, in the very process of complaining that they lack power in policy processes, criminologists may be giving testimony to the fact that their research can be influential. Relative lack of power simply reflects that a criminologist's preferred disciplinary, professional, and institutional affiliation has been less successful in hegemonic processes of advancing policy rhetorics and policing initiatives. The only principled course of action for the criminologist is to devise better policy rhetorics and policing initiatives that will more clearly demonstrate their value. This entails development of better research, using figurative language that is more carefully chosen, for example with regard to words and numbers that have greater symbolic power. It also entails development of better communication networks among professional and institutional constituencies who will traffic in the research results as a means of advancing their policy preferences. It is only through such research efforts and communication networks that the criminologist can hope that his or her own principled courses of action will take effect in processes of criminalization. Indeed it is only through such research efforts and communication networks that criminology has any reason to exist at all.

2

Principles, Politics, and Criminal Justice

Nicola Lacey

This chapter addresses three issues concerning the relationship between criminological scholarship (broadly conceived) and criminal
justice policy. It examines the lack of any clear, agreed framework of
principle for the conduct or reform of criminal justice practices; it
considers the increasing politicization of criminal justice within
national politics; and it analyses the impact of this politicization on
the project—widely endorsed by criminal justice scholars but rarely
realized in policy development—of moving towards a more principled, transparent, and legitimate criminal justice practice.[1] I shall
begin by reviewing some of the evidence of, and explanations for, the
politicization of crime and criminal justice in the UK, and by considering some of the implications of this politicization for the development of theoretically informed criminal justice policy. Moving on
to a more general analysis of the relationship between criminal
justice philosophy and criminal justice policy, I shall suggest that
the structure of normative criminal justice theories might be adapted

[1] The recent Halliday Report on sentencing reform (*Making Punishments Work:
Report of a Review of the Sentencing Framework for England and Wales* (London:
Home Office Communication Directorate, 2001) available online at www.homeof-
fice.gov.uk/cpg/halliday/htm) provides a good example of these implications: as Neil
Hutton has observed, while the Report correctly identifies confusion in the organizing
principles of sentencing and provides 'a more systematic set of principles', it nonetheless 'create[s] a different blend of obfuscation as to the purpose of punishment . . . and
will leave the lay reader with no clearer idea of what the system is trying to achieve. In
the politically sensitive field of sentencing and punishment', Hutton concluded, 'this is
probably a strength rather than a weakness': 'Making Punishments Work?' (2001) 34
Socio-Legal Newsletter (July), 1 at 2.

so as to foster a more productive relationship with policy debate. I shall then move on to analyse the conditions—social, cultural, and institutional—under which a dialogue between criminal justice theory and criminal justice policy might most fruitfully take place. I shall conclude with some reflections on an apparent paradox: that a certain degree of politicization seems necessary in order to motivate public debate and institutional reform; yet that politicization is potentially inimical to the rational development and consistent implementation of policy. In developing this argument, I hope to develop our understanding of the conditions under which criminological knowledge may inform criminal justice policy; a project to which Roger Hood's work has made such an important contribution, across a wide range of fields, over the last forty years.[2]

Crime and Politics in the UK

The proposition that crime and criminal justice policy have become increasingly politicized issues in the UK over the last twenty years will be accepted not only by criminal justice scholars and practitioners but also by any reasonably reflective observer of the national political scene. On her election in 1979, Conservative Prime Minister Margaret Thatcher made 'law and order' one of her central political platforms, exploiting a perceived vulnerability in the Labour Party's tendency to locate the causes of crime in broad socio-economic conditions rather than individual responsible action. The fact that—as the 'Left Realist' movement in criminology was soon also to identify[3]—the impact of crime was almost as unequally socially distributed as the incidence of crime itself entailed that the Labour stance was potentially unpopular even among its natural constituencies. Thatcher's astute identification of tough criminal justice policy as a vote-winner undoubtedly ushered in a new era of what we might call populist-led policy development in

---

[2] See in particular on this topic 'Some Reflections on the Role of Criminology in Public Policy' [1987] *Crim.L.R.* 527. Hood's recent 'Capital Punishment: A Global Perspective' (2001) 3 *Punishment and Society* 331 sets out, in relation to capital punishment, several of the comparative questions which I raise in this chapter in relation to criminal justice policy more generally.

[3] J. Lea and J. Young, *What is to be Done about Law and Order?* (Harmondsworth: Penguin, 1984); R. Kinsey, J. Lea, and J. Young, *Losing the Fight against Crime* (Oxford: Blackwell, 1986).

the criminal justice field.[4] Spurred on by the perceived need to respond vigorously to the (albeit localized) public disorder occasioned by the miners' strike of the early 1980s, the next decade saw a massive programme of legislative reform and policy development in fields such as public order law, police powers, prosecution structure, and penal arrangements. All were designed, in one way or another, to make the criminal justice system more efficient and more effective in the 'fight against crime'.

This drive for effectiveness was underpinned at every turn not merely by a principled concern about the various costs, human and economic, of relatively high levels of crime, but also by politicians' perception of the strategy's popularity with voters.[5] A key index of this political orientation was the remarkable about-turn of the Labour Party on the topic following the appointment of Tony Blair as Shadow Home Secretary. Recognizing the Party's perceived 'softness' on crime as a political 'Achilles' Heel', Blair swiftly began framing a new stance in terms of being '[t]ough on crime, tough on the causes of crime'. It was, of course, a framework which cleverly combined the Party's traditional concern with the social roots of crime with a more contemporary recognition of the popular demand for decisive and punitive state action in response to offending. At the level of rhetoric, this framework has been sustained seamlessly by the Party since its election to Government in 1997 under the stewardship of first Jack Straw and then David Blunkett in the Home Office. At the level of policy, however, it is the 'tough on crime' half of the equation which has been increasingly to the fore.

Although my focus in this chapter will be the position in Britain, it is important to my argument to note that this accentuated political salience has also occurred in some other countries. For example,

---

[4] See D. Downes and R. Morgan, 'Dumping the "Hostages to Fortune"? The Politics of Law and Order in Post-War Britain' in M. Maguire, R. Morgan, and R. Reiner (eds.), *The Oxford Handbook of Criminology* (3rd edn., Oxford: Oxford University Press, 2002), 286.

[5] One exception to policy pragmatism was the Criminal Justice Act 1991, discussed below. The unhappy fate of key aspects of the legislation at the hands of judges, magistrates, and the popular press provides however an instructive example of the limits of principled reform even under strong leadership at the Home Office: see N. Lacey, 'Government as Manager, Citizen as Consumer' (1994) 57 *Modern Law Review* 534.

David Garland's recent *The Culture of Control*[6] documents the rise and rise of 'the new politics of law and order' in the United States as well as in Britain. Garland draws on a range of indices—levels of punishment and policing, to name but two—to diagnose a fundamental shift in the nature of criminal justice's salience in 'late modernity'.[7] In broad terms, Garland's argument is that in the context of late modern social and economic conditions—conditions such as relatively high levels of crime, geographical mobility, short-term relations, and insecurity in the economy—crime and responses to crime come to have a special salience in the production of images of social order. In an argument which is more than reminiscent of Durkheim's, but which is closely focussed on specific social developments, Garland charts the development of a criminal justice policy which veers between 'adaptation, denial and acting out': a blend of managerialism and rationalization mixes with a return to the expressive, symbolic dimension of criminal justice policy, producing a distinctive 'culture of control'. While from the perspective of criminal justice theory the resulting mix of institutional responses may look incoherent and chaotic, there may well—as Garland shows—be a deeper logic which pins apparently disparate policies together and enables them to fulfil certain instrumental and symbolic functions.

It would be wrong, however, to exaggerate the seamlessness of either the pre-existing 'penal-welfarist' consensus or of the tough 'law and order' approach in British policy of the last two decades. For example, in the area of youth justice, initiatives have continued to balance older penal-welfarist with retributive concerns and, most recently, have begun to blend these with tentative moves towards elements of restorative justice. Moreover, notwithstanding the formal reconstruction of probation as a form of punishment, and attempts to reorient the professional ideology of the probation ser-

---

[6] (Oxford: Oxford University Press, 2001).

[7] As I argue below, while the framework of 'late modernity' is suggestive, Garland's approach over-generalizes, extrapolating from conditions which are likely to be specific to his two case studies, Britain and the USA. Notwithstanding his reference to differences between the USA and Europe, much the same is true of Jock Young's deployment of the same framework: while US/European differences in the exclusionary dynamics of later modernity are emphasized in the first chapter of *The Exclusive Society* (London: Sage, 1999), especially 22–3, 27, the analysis of the rest of the book is firmly centred on UK and US examples, with occasional continental European reference points serving to bolster the 'late modern' typology (see e.g. 65).

vice, it seems likely that, at the level of daily practice, the work of probation officers and others involved in the execution of community sentences, even including the new intensive supervision orders, remains substantially welfare-oriented. Similarly, at the same time as politicians have been endorsing—and stoking—the popular demand that prisons should be 'no holiday camps', there has been no discernible reduction in the emphasis—at the level of policy aspiration if not of practice—on training and, particularly in the area of drug abuse, accredited rehabilitative programmes in prisons. Moreover, the trenchant reports of David Ramsbotham during his tenure as Chief Inspector of Prisons reflected a continuing commitment in public (if not official) discourse to the ideas underlying the penal welfarism which Garland takes decisively to have been overthrown. At various points over the last twenty years diversionary practices such as cautioning have been systematically adapted to filter less serious cases out of the criminal justice system altogether. Current pilot schemes expanding restorative justice initiatives suggest the political possibility of yet more radical moves in a diversionary direction. And we should add into the picture the empirically dominant phenomenon of relatively non-moralized 'regulatory' crime, with distinctive and far less politicized and punitive enforcement regimes, which fit uneasily with Garland's tripartite framework, and which always floated outside what he characterizes as the penal welfarist consensus. At the level of criminal justice practice, in short, reports of the demise of penal welfarism have almost certainly been exaggerated.

Also significant for any attempt to explain the political salience of criminal justice policy, it must be remembered that the intensity of the 'acting out' aspects of the 'culture of control' have varied markedly over the last twenty years. For example, there was a marked toning down of the rhetorical and indeed material ferocity of the political 'fight against crime' in the late 1980s. During Douglas Hurd's period as Home Secretary, the thrust of policy—perhaps most vividly exemplified by, but not confined to, the Criminal Justice Act 1991—was towards a moderation of penal and legislative severity, the goal being to rationalize criminal justice power within a consistent framework based on the principle of proportionality in punishment. This doubtless had not a little to do with Hurd's temperate, 'one-nation' style of conservatism. But it also had to do with a recognition in Government of the difficulties of meeting the extraordinary expectations about effectiveness in general and crime reduction in particular which had been created by the political promises made during the early part of the decade. The moderation of the Hurd era was, admittedly, short-lived: his successors in the Home Office, notably David Waddington and Michael Howard, swiftly returned to an axiomatic 'tougher punishment means more effective criminal justice policy' stance, perhaps most vividly exemplified in Howard's oft-repeated assertion that 'prison works'. From a scholarly perspective, it is tempting to describe the assertion as wilfully ignorant in the face of overwhelming contrary evidence. This would, to a significant degree, be a mistake. For there is a sense in which Howard's claim might be thought true: at the level of popular satisfaction, if not of crime-reduction. Prison works, in other words, *politically*.

Notwithstanding the New Labour Government's greater commitment to 'evidence-led' policy development, the difficulty of identifying a politically viable alternative to inexorable expansion of the prison system continues to haunt the Home Office. The supposed political inevitability of such an expansion is much in evidence, albeit particularly in relation to repeat and serious offenders, in the Halliday Report.[8] In this as in other respects, the change in government since 1997 has made relatively little difference to the levels of politicians' anxiety about reducing severity and punitiveness in the handling of crime. Perhaps the most poignant recent example of confidence not only in the popularity but also in the effectiveness of increased criminalization and punitiveness was David Blunkett's decision, less than a year after the implementation of what can only be described as an extremely modest human rights framework in domestic law, that some of its provisions would have to be suspended in response to the threat of international terrorism.[9] While, particularly in relation to Britain, Garland's diagnosis of a radical shift in penal ideology is somewhat overdrawn, there is therefore reason to think that we have witnessed a set of changes in the conditions of criminal justice policy-making which are of sufficient quantitative and qualitative importance to call for the kind of macro-sociological explanation which Garland attempts.

Like Garland, I would therefore suggest that certain developments in the political, cultural, and economic structure of late

---

[8]   *Making Punishments Work*, n. 1 above.
[9]   One should add the fact that political opposition to this move has been relatively restricted.

modern societies such as Britain and the United States are currently having a distinctive impact on the role which criminal justice policy plays in politics. I would, however, give a slightly different analysis, along with a great deal more attention to the specificities of different late modern societies. Let me therefore sketch my own, very general account. I want to suggest, first, that the state's criminal justice power may be becoming (relatively) more important in establishing governments' legitimacy and credibility, and to offer some speculative reasons why that might be the case. Secondly, I shall examine the difficulties posed for governments by high levels of popular concern about crime and by governments' commitment to responding to such popular demands.

The Political Salience of Criminal Justice: Penal Populism and Political Economy

There are many reasons to think that criminal justice policy and the institutions through which that policy is realized have a particular importance in establishing the legitimacy and credibility of governments. For a start, leaving aside the example of war, the power to convict and punish represents the most vivid exercise of state force in relation to individual citizens. Furthermore, and partly because of this, the nature of criminal justice power may be seen as a telling index of how humane and civilized a society really is. This is why evidence about matters such as the racial inequalities which mark the enforcement of criminal law—evidence which is depressingly plentiful in this country[10]—cause such widespread concern. Neither of these features is, however, new: these would have been reasons to think of criminal justice as posing especially salient legitimation questions, at least since the inception of liberal ideals of the proper limits of state power and of the importance of respect for human rights. The fact that such legitimation questions appear to have been managed rather easily by most national governments, and that criminal justice policy remained until recently relatively insulated from the pressures of party politics, is perhaps testimony to the strength of the penal welfarist consensus identified by Garland.[11]

---

[10] See R. Hood, *Race and Sentencing* (Oxford: Clarendon Press, 1992).
[11] Garland, n. 6 above, Chapter 2.

In this context, I would argue that globalization, in the specific sense of the increasing interdependence of national economies, provides a clue to the particular salience which criminal justice policy now enjoys—or perhaps suffers from—in countries such as Britain and the USA. As governments struggle to establish their legitimacy in a world in which a range of policy questions are no longer within their exclusive power, decisive criminal justice policies become a useful tool in establishing the credibility and identity of an administration—whether at national or state level. Particularly when a relatively weak government, operating in the context of relatively weak institutions of civil society, is confronted with relatively high levels of popular concern about crime,[12] there is a strong temptation to respond directly in terms of legislative initiatives expanding the reach of criminal law, or policy initiatives designed to make the processes of prosecution and punishment more effective in terms of, for example, crime reduction. Other factors canvassed in the literature on this topic include the increasing focus on risk-management, often fostered by technology, as a governmental strategy, and the weakening of traditional party affiliations, along with a consequent increase in the proportion of 'floating voters' whom political parties must try to attract with a variety of, often highly emotive, policy responses.[13]

It is crucial to recognize, however, that the salience and politicization of criminal justice vary from country to country, with countries such as the USA at one end of the spectrum and those such as the Netherlands at the other.[14] At an anecdotal level, this was brought home to me when, six years ago, Lucia Zedner and I employed a German research assistant to work on a project on community-based crime prevention. One of his tasks was to track and compare newspaper crime reporting in Britain and Germany. A week into this task he was in a state of shock. In Germany, he had not encountered

---

[12] On the different conditions pertaining in Germany in relation to this variable see L. Zedner, 'Dangers of Dystopias in Penal Theory' [2002] *Oxford Journal of Legal Studies* 341.

[13] See P. O'Malley, 'Risk, Power and Crime Prevention' [1992] *Economy and Society* 252; R. Hogg and D. Brown, *Rethinking Law and Order* (London: Pluto Press, 1998), 116–120.

[14] See F. Adler, *Nations Not Obsessed by Crime* (Littleton, Colo.: F.B. Rothman, 1983); see also Hogg and Brown, n. 13 above, 135–7; D. Downes, *Contrasts in Tolerance* (Oxford: Oxford University Press, 1988).

the sensational crime reporting which now pervades even the 'quality' press in Britain. As Michael Tonry has argued, the state of criminological knowledge of the explanations for these persisting national differences is, to put it mildly, incomplete.[15] Research on these differences announces, however, one common, intriguing, fact: that the more successfully socially integrated a society is, the less obsessed it tends to be with law and order.[16] Furthermore, even where the social equilibrium is unsettled by major structural change—as in the case of German unification in 1989—the existence of institutions which guarantee high levels of social solidarity and employment security for a critical mass of the population appears to enable a country to avoid extreme politicization of criminal justice, along with all its attendant difficulties.

The Elusive Promise of Crime Reduction through Criminalization

In Britain in recent years the popular law and order dynamic has spawned a range of developments, both expanding the terrain of criminalization and increasing the severity of punishment. These pragmatic responses range from legislation specifically geared to controlling dangerous dogs and 'raves' through to mandatory sentencing for offenders who have repeated certain serious offences.[17] While not all of these developments are necessarily oriented to delivering greater severity—a recent example being measures designed to expand the range of sentences available for young offenders, with a view to keeping them out of custody where possible[18]—the overall tendency is both to expand the terrain of criminal regulation and to increase the severity of the range of punishments available to the courts. The articulated justification

[15] M. Tonry, 'Symbol, Substance and Severity in Western Penal Policies' (2001) 3 *Punishment and Society* 517.

[16] For a thoughtful comparative case study analysing the relationship between crime rates, responses to crime, and social structure see J. Braithwaite, 'Crime in a Convict Republic' (2001) 54 *Modern Law Review* 11; see also D. Melossi, 'Translating Social Control' and W. de Haan, 'Explaining the Absence of Violence: A Comparative Approach' in S. Karstedt and K.-D. Bussmann, *Social Dynamics of Crime and Control* (Oxford: Hart Publishing, 2000) at 143 and 189 respectively.

[17] Criminal Justice and Public Order Act 1994; Crime (Sentences) Act 1997.

[18] Crime and Disorder Act 1998 ss. 67–68.

for these developments towards greater penal severity is the promise of crime reduction through incapacitation or deterrence and the satisfaction of crime victims' grievances by meting out punishments which are seen as deserved. But can these promises be delivered, and, if so, can they be delivered consistently with a civilized and rights-respecting criminal justice policy?

It is not only inevitable but, of course, perfectly appropriate that democratic governments should seek to respond to the concerns of their electorates. However, it must equally be recognized that government-generated information and publicity is one of the most potent influences on popular perception of crime problems. Moreover, where governments manage information so as to stoke rather than soothe popular concern about crime, and respond to the resultant popular demands by promising things which cannot be delivered through criminal justice policy, they create long-term problems for themselves and for their citizens. In Britain, an intriguing example was provided by the plight, already adverted to above, of the successive conservative administrations from 1979 to 1997.[19] In its early years, the Thatcher government attempted to pursue the vigorous 'law and order' policy which had undoubtedly helped to elect it. As the 1980s passed, it began to realize that it was confronting a double bind presented by the high expectations which that policy stance had created. Notwithstanding significantly increased spending on criminal justice and in particular an expansion in police numbers and the prison system, crime rates were rising sharply. None of this came as any surprise to criminal justice scholars and practitioners. Even leaving aside relevant factors such as levels of unemployment and poverty, headlines such as 'Crime rates rise despite increased spending on police' reveal some very basic misunderstandings—notably a failure to grasp the fact that the immediate effect of putting more resources into policing and prosecution will be likely to be some such rise in recorded crime, as citizens are encouraged to report crime and a better resourced enforcement system becomes better equipped to record and pursue it.

But such headlines—which are still common in this country—reveal something very important about the nature of our public

---

[19] For further discussion of these developments see N. Lacey, 'Government as Manager, Citizen as Consumer: The Case of the Criminal Justice Act 1991', n. 5 above.

debate about crime. This is that it is extremely unsophisticated. For it is premised on the idea that the majority of crime is processed by the criminal justice system, and hence that governments can achieve decisive changes in the extent and severity of crime *by modifying the criminal law, the criminal process, and the penal system*. This premise, as any first-year criminology student knows, is a false one: a vast proportion of offending behaviour never comes to the notice of the formal authorities, and a large proportion of that which does is either not proceeded against at all or is dealt with by informal or managerial strategies.[20] The inevitable conclusion is that social policy and social institutions beyond the criminal process are the context in which the vast majority of crime problems are managed.

As we have seen, the New Labour administration has tried to refine its approach to criminal justice policy by teaming the principle of being 'tough on crime' with that of being 'tough on the causes of crime'. Nonetheless, when the Home Secretary comments upon or responds to the latest figures of recorded crime or the results of the annual British Crime Survey (which is based on self-report and victimization studies), his approach is invariably to proffer policy initiatives within the criminal process.[21] The causes of crime—social disintegration, poor housing and education, social exclusion—are, inevitably, complex political issues which lend themselves to the media sound bite far less readily than does the promise of being tough on crime. Policies to tackle the sorts of social problems— structural social exclusion, the effects of long-term discrimination, drug abuse, poor education, and housing—which we know to be implicated in crime levels are costly, and their effects are both hard to measure and medium or long term in their impact. For these reasons, governments are constantly tempted to confine their responses to

[20] On the attrition process see M. Maguire, 'Crime Statistics and A. Sanders and R. Young, 'From Suspect to Trial' in Maguire *et al.* (eds.), n. 4 above, at 322 and 1034 respectively; see generally N. Lacey and C. Wells, *Reconstructing Criminal Law* (2nd edn., London: Butterworths, 1998) Chapter I.III.b.

[21] See, most recently, *Criminal Justice: The Way Ahead* (Cm 5074, London: HMSO, 2001). A central feature of this document, which is effectively the Government's election manifesto in the criminal justice field, is an ambitious target for crime reduction. Other notable features include the pervasiveness of the managerial language of efficiency, performance indicators, and targets; and the fact that the document was published in advance of three significant public reports on aspects of criminal justice (Lord Justice Auld's review of criminal courts; the Law Commission's report on double jeopardy and the Halliday report on sentencing, n. 1 above).

crime to the toughening or modification of the criminal justice system, asserting that criminal justice policies themselves can deliver deterrence, reform, and incapacitation. This is not to say that there are no other social policies which have an impact on crime: for example, the history of community crime prevention in this country illustrates the blurred boundaries between criminal justice and broader social policies concerning, for example, housing.[22] However, the Government's framing of the issues increasingly focuses on discrete criminal justice policies as the answer to 'the crime problem'.

The social conditions which foster this difficulty include the discipline of electoral politics and the social fragmentation which attenuates the capacity of institutions in civil society to contribute to social ordering in such a way as to make reliance on the hard end of the state criminal justice process less necessary, and hence less politically compelling. Significantly, these are undoubtedly less characteristic of some countries than of others. Even taking Garland's two principal examples, Britain and the USA, we can perceive significant variations in the political salience and tractability of criminal justice: one obvious index would be capital punishment which, while still attracting a majority of popular support in Britain, is something which politicians are able to keep away from their reform agenda without any undue sacrifice of popularity.

Let us take, however, two further examples: Australia and Germany—one an Anglo-Saxon-style political economy, the other a corporatist-style economy, but each with markedly lower policitization of criminal justice than Britain or the USA. In Australia, levels of social integration, as measured by a variety of social and economic indices, are higher than they are in Britain or the USA.[23] This undoubtedly gives Australia a greater capacity to pursue the socially less disintegrative routes available in the development of criminal justice policy and institutions. This is not to say, however, that there are not some worrying signs of a law and order politics comparable to that in Britain emerging. The obvious example is in the area of drug-related crime, where the long-standing 'harm-minimization' policy appears to be being eroded by a 'tough on drugs', zero-

[22] See K. Pease, 'Crime Prevention' in Maguire *et al.* (eds.), n. 4 above, 947.

[23] See F. Gruen, 'The Quality of Life and Economic Performance' in P. Sheehan, B. Grewal, and M. Kumnick (eds.), *Dialogues on Australia's Future* (Melbourne: Centre for Strategic Economic Studies, 1996); see Hogg and Brown, n. 13 above, 161–5.

tolerance approach.[24] The new measures announced in 2001 in New South Wales, in which a swingeing set of new police powers, penalties, and offences designed to tackle a social problem in Cabramatta will be applied across the state, as well as the emphasis on tough minimum prison sentences for a range of offences in the recent Labour Party election campaign in New South Wales provide instructive examples of the dangers of pragmatic, populist policy-making.[25] Though one should not be too quick to take drug policy as the archetype for criminal justice policy as a whole, the fact that it is one of the few federally directed areas of Australian criminal policy gives it a special significance in both practical and symbolic terms.

Germany provides a more decisive counter-example to the late modern condition diagnosed by Garland and, with a slightly different inflection, by Young.[26] Notwithstanding a heightened level of popular concern about crime consequent on social and economic changes following unification in 1989, German criminal justice and penal policy remains, by British or US standards, temperate in both tone and substance.[27] It can hardly be doubted that broader features relating to social structure—the predominance of long-term relations in the labour market, higher levels of social solidarity, and a muscular constitutional framework governing the development even of more detailed matters such as prison policy—have been important factors in inhibiting the politicization of crime and punishment in post-war Germany.[28]

In short, while a broad, socio-theoretic explanation such as Garland's is surely necessary to our analysis of the contemporary politicization of criminal justice and, by implication, to our assessment of the scope for modifying it, a successful analysis would have to be yet more ambitious in at least one respect: it would have to be informed

[24] See S. Bronitt and B. McSherry, *Principles of Criminal Law* (Sydney: Law Book Company, 2001) 821–833.

[25] *Sydney Morning Herald*, 28 Mar. 2001, 1.

[26] N. 7 above.

[27] See Zedner, n. 12 above; L. Lazarus, *Contrasting Prisoners' Rights* (forthcoming, Oxford University Press); see generally Michael Tonry and R.S. Frase (eds.), *Sentencing and Sanctions in Western Countries* (Oxford: Oxford University Press, 2001).

[28] See N. Lacey and L. Zedner, 'Discourses of Community in Criminal Justice' [1995] *Journal of Law and Society* 93, 'Community in German Criminal Justice: A Significant Absence?' [1998] *Social and Legal Studies* 7; and '"Community" and Governance: A Cultural Comparison' in Karstedt and Bussman (eds.), n. 16 above.

by, and tested out in the light of, some comparative models and data. In this respect, the model recently developed by Hall, Soskice, and others may be of potential relevance to comparative research in criminal justice. Their 'varieties of capitalism' approach develops a typology distinguishing liberal from co-ordinated market economies.[29] Liberal market economies include Britain, the USA and, broadly, Australia, while Sweden, Japan and Germany would be key examples of co-ordinated market economies. Significant differences in these two basic types of capitalism concern both the capacity for consensual policy-making and implementation and a wide range of economic, political, and social institutions which have provided distinctive paths through the economic restructuring necessitated by changes in world markets and by technological developments over the last thirty years. These include institutions as diverse as education and training systems, labour market regulation, and financial systems. Crucially for criminal justice, the varieties of capitalism analysis suggest that a combination of interlocking factors in the liberal market economies has significantly accelerated disparities of wealth and social and spatial disintegration, while co-ordinated market economies have been more successful in maintaining relatively high levels of social integration and relatively low levels of inequality. This seems a particularly promising framework for pushing through at an analytic level the broad diagnosis offered by Young's vision of 'the exclusive society'.[30] While this would clearly need to be tested empirically across a range of variables, the nature of these systematic differences between liberal and co-ordinated market economies seem *a priori* to be highly likely to correlate both to levels of crime and to the strength and distribution of demands for punishment.

Criminal Justice Principles

Principles and Contemporary Penal Policy

I now want to step aside from this social analysis to consider the principles which might usefully govern the development of criminal justice policy in particular in late modern, social democratic soci-

---

[29] See e.g. Peter A. Hall and David Soskice (eds.), *Varieties of Capitalism* (Oxford: Oxford University Press, 2001).

[30] See n. 7 above.

eties, and to consider why it is that the burgeoning literature on normative principles of criminal justice has had so relatively little impact on public debate about crime and punishment. This is, at first sight, surprising for a number of reasons. In a broadly liberal order, punishment is, after all, a practice which poses a considerable burden of justification for the state. Even leaving aside the obvious disparity of power between state institutions and individual offenders, criminalization is, on the face of it, a social evil: a practice which is costly in both human and financial terms, and one whose practical and moral advantages are often uncertain. One of the most important preconditions for any reasoned public debate about criminal justice policy is the recognition that a society has difficult choices to make about forms and levels of criminalization. These choices include decisions about how many of our limited public resources should be devoted to the costly practice of criminalization as opposed to other social policies such as education, employment, health, and housing—each of which may have important practical implications for crime. The controversies about proper forms and levels of state punishment which surface regularly in political debate cannot themselves be analysed except in terms of some broader view of the rationale for the criminal justice system. For example, the argument for a reduction in the use of imprisonment, or for the introduction of a new penalty such as electronic curfew or reparation orders, takes place against the backcloth of more general views about the functions of criminal justice, and about the proper limits of state power. Yet, as compared with debates about other important social institutions—the taxation system and the health system, to name just two—the debate about the justice of criminal justice power in this country today seems curiously arid. This aridity is fostered by the fact that the normative literature continues to focus on punishment as a discrete issue rather than on criminalization as an integrated set of social practices.[31]

In the British context, I would argue that the poor quality of public debate engendered by both political context and the lack of proper interaction between theory and policy design has given rise to three specific myths structuring criminal justice policy development.

---

[31] On the need to integrate questions of punishment with broader questions of normative political theory and social justice see N. Lacey, *State Punishment* (London: Routledge, 1998); J. Braithwaite and P. Pettit, *Not Just Deserts* (Oxford: Clarendon Press, 1990).

These in turn have fostered the unfortunate tendency for governments to respond to what they perceive as popular concern about crime[32] by making commitments to crime reduction based on empirically dubious claims about the criminal justice system.

First, in the context of rising crime, an almost irresistible fantasy for government is the idea that crime reduction can be improved by the identification and selective incapacitation of a small group of especially 'dangerous' or simply persistent offenders who are responsible for a disproportionate amount of crime. This myth has become particularly powerful in relation to drug-related crime. Over the years, its central claim has been investigated in a number of empirical studies, none of which has been able to produce criteria of identification which provide anything like the kind of accuracy which could make such a selective policy acceptable from the human rights perspective which the government claims to espouse.[33] In the absence of such evidence, the claim amounts to an attribution of a global disposition of 'dangerousness' rather than a rigorous assessment of the likelihood of serious reoffending. This has not, unfortunately, prevented governments in a number of countries from introducing selective incapacitation policies through the back door via mandatory sentencing systems.

A second myth has to do with the capacity for increased deterrence to be gained by increasing levels of sentence. A careful study of the facts about offending puts in doubt the argument that there is untapped potential for deterrence through increased severity.[34] In this context, too, the introduction of forms of mandatory sentencing in the USA, in Britain, and in parts of Australia—policies which had been marketed in terms of deterrence as much as incapacitation—

[32] The decisive role of the media in shaping these concerns should not be overlooked: see e.g. R. Sparks, *Television and the Drama of Crime* (Milton Keynes: Open University Press, 1992); S. Cohen and J. Young (eds.), *The Manufacture of News* (London: Constable, 1973); R. Ericson (ed.), *Crime and the Media* (Aldershot: Dartmouth, 1995); R. Reiner, 'Media Made Criminality' in Maguire *et al.* (eds.), n. 4 above, 376.

[33] R. Tarling, *Analysing Offending: Data, Models and Interpretation* (London: HMSO, 1993); J.E. Floud and W. Young, *Dangerousness and Criminal Justice* (London: Heinemann, 1981); A. von Hirsch, *Past or Future Crimes* (Manchester: Manchester University Press, 1985).

[34] For a review of the literature on deterrence see A. von Hirsch, A. Bottoms, E. Burney, and P.-O. Wikström, *Criminal Deterrence and Sentencing Severity: An Analysis of Recent Research* (Oxford: Hart Publishing, 1999).

represent one of the most retrogressive policy developments in contemporary criminal justice.

A final myth has to do with the reductive potential of incapacitative punishments over the long term.[35] Since the vast majority of the prison population is released into the community within a relatively short space of time, the disruptive effects of imprisonment in terms of personal and employment relationships, housing, and so on suggest that the long-term effects of imprisonment are counter to the interests of public protection. It is important not to lose sight of the fact that the social costs of penal severity reach well beyond the pecuniary costs of prison sentences; those sentenced to custody return to the community, and incapacitative effects are therefore smaller than political rhetoric implies. It is apposite to note that there is strong reason to think that the indirect costs of imprisonment are especially high for women.[36] This is so not least because social structures which still accord women primary responsibility for domestic labour and child-rearing, along with the growing number of female-headed households, mean that the practical and emotional implications of a woman's imprisonment for her family is often utterly devastating. The effect on the intergenerational transmission of social exclusion is of particular concern.[37]

Leaving aside for a moment the inhospitable political context for a reasoned debate about crime and punishment, I would like to suggest three specific reasons for the aridity of the political debate in Britain today. First, criminologists—and particularly those working in policy-relevant institutions such as the Home Office—have shown relatively little interest in penal principles, and have concentrated on empirical research focussed on particular practices.[38] Secondly, both the normative and the practical/empirical work in the field have tended to be marked by an unfortunately narrow orientation: an orientation to crime and punishment as

[35] For a general discussion of incapacitation see Tarling, n. 33 above.

[36] T. Wolfe, *Counting the Cost: The Social and Financial Consequences of Women's Imprisonment* (London: Prison Reform Trust, 1999: a summary appears as Appendix D of *Justice for Women: The Case for Reform* (London: Prison Reform Trust, 2000).

[37] See J. Hobcraft, *Intergenerational and Life Course Transmission of Social Exclusion*, LSE Centre for the Analysis of Social Exclusion Working Paper 15 (London: LSE, 1998).

[38] On the history of, and explanations for, this set of attitudes see L. Zedner (this volume).

discrete issues rather than as instances of more general questions of social justice and social design.[39] As I shall try to show, this is particularly unfortunate—and particularly puzzling—in the light of the current Government's broad commitment to tacking social exclusion. For the implication of the development of penal policy in isolation from broader questions—normative questions about social justice, empirical questions about institutional and social structure—is likely to be a blunting of our appreciation of the contribution of criminal justice as currently configured to social exclusion,[40] and hence a failure to develop and exploit what is likely to be one of the most effective political arguments for penal moderation. Finally, much of the normative literature about punishment operates at a level of philosophical abstraction which makes its implications for actual practices opaque. With honourable exceptions,[41] philosophers of criminal justice have exhibited little interest in the design of criminal justice institutions, let alone in their political, cultural, and economic conditions of possibility.

This difficulty about what we might call the institutional deficit of penal philosophy can best be illustrated by means of a brief review of the main arguments in the field. The first set of arguments may be described as *backward-looking* or *retributive*: they advance the idea that punishment should be proportional to the offender's deserts, and that proportional punishments are required by justice. Retributive arguments have moved on from the ancient *lex talionis* which spoke in terms of 'an eye for an eye'—and today argue—consistently with modern notions of human responsibility—that the measure of punishment should reflect not only the gravity of the harm or wrong done by an offender but also the degree of her culpability in doing it.[42] Nonetheless, the modern theory of just deserts shares one key feature with the ancient approach to retribution: in looking exclu-

---

[39] For an honourable exception see B.A. Hudson, *Penal Policy and Social Justice* (Basingstoke: Macmillan, 1993).

[40] See Young, n. 7 above.

[41] See R.A. Duff, *Punishment, Communication and Community* (Oxford: Oxford University Press, 2001).

[42] For a modern statement of desert theory see A. von Hirsch, *Doing Justice: The Choice of Punishments* (New York: Hill and Wang, 1976); for von Hirsch's revised statement of desert theory, which accommodates forward-looking elements and hence amounts to a mixed theory, see his *Censure and Sanctions* (Oxford: Clarendon Press, 1993).

sively backwards to the offence, each implies that there is some intrinsic moral worth to the practice of punishment which cancels out its *prima facie* wrongfulness, *irrespective of its having any further beneficial social consequences.*

By contrast, *forward-looking or goal-oriented* approaches start out from the idea that punishment is evil and must be justified by compensating good effects.[43] Such effects come in narrower and broader, more or less crime-oriented forms. Specific goals include the deterrence of actual offenders through the experience of punishment or the general deterrence of potential offenders through fear of punishment; the incapacitation of offenders in the name of public protection; and the use of punishment as an occasion for reform or rehabilitation. Broader ambitions are espoused by approaches which see punishment as a potentially socializing institution whose educative effects go beyond mere deterrence or coercion and reach the inculcation of values enshrined in criminal law.[44]

Unfortunately, these general principles of punishment are notorious for saying little about what form punishment should take. Views differ as to what desert requires: the calculation of actual or probable consequences of punishment is difficult to assess. This poses some limits to the help which we can get from the two 'pure' retributive and utilitarian approaches to punishment in shaping principles governing the use of, for example, imprisonment. Certainly, a focus on a concrete question such as imprisonment suggests that the forward-looking approach has some discrete advantages over its retributive rival. Clearly, either principle has to take into account the uniquely intrusive, stigmatizing, psychologically painful, and expensive nature of prison as a penalty. Yet while on the forward-looking approach, the deterrent, rehabilitative, incapacitative, and other effects of imprisonment can in principle be assessed, the relation between a certain prison term and a certain level of culpability or desert is subject to no objective metric. It is therefore vulnerable to swings in popular or political reaction to crime. Conversely, the forward-looking approach also suffers from its own peculiar

---

[43] The classic statement of this approach is to be found in Jeremy Bentham's utilitarian philosophy: see *An Introduction to the Principles of Morals and Legislation* (ed. J.H. Burns and H.L.A. Hart, London: Methuen, 1983; first published 1789).

[44] See J. Braithwaite, *Crime, Shame and Reintegration* (Cambridge: Cambridge University Press, 1989); R.A. Duff, 'Punishment as Communication' (1999) 1 *Punishment and Society* 27.

weakness in the context of contemporary law and order politics: especially when the utilitarian argument is applied narrowly to criminal justice issues, it invariably suggests, at a rhetorical level, that punishment has potential instrumental effectiveness. Though in principle measurable, these instrumental effects are in practice of course very difficult to assess. The inevitable result is that deterrent or incapacitative effectiveness tends to become a rhetorical axiom rather than a scientific question.[45]

In view of the remarkable revival of retributive thinking in criminal justice policy over the last twenty years, it is perhaps worth reflecting in a little more detail on the capacity of the idea of desert both to provide a plausible rationale for punishment and to temper some of the potential excesses of the incapacitative and deterrent goals which have also persisted in penal policy discourse. It might be thought that the move in many countries towards a more desert-based approach to punishment would have provided an effective limit on the pursuit of incapacitative and deterrent policies. Indeed, the move towards sentencing guidelines was shaped in part precisely by scepticism about the reductive effect of sentencing, and by an awareness of the civil libertarian implications of an unlimited pursuit of reductive goals—whether by rehabilitation, deterrence, or incapacitation—at the level of individual sentencing.

There are unfortunately, however, several reasons why desert-based interpretation of penal policy cannot deliver these necessary limits. First, the desert criterion is relatively indeterminate: it fails to establish any very constraining guidelines as to the proper measure of punishment. It gives no reason for sentences of imprisonment as opposed, say, to corporal punishments such as those prescribed in the Islamic tradition. Secondly, and following from this, in the context of insistent popular anxiety about crime, the desert criterion offers no firm basis for a principled resistance to increased, ineffective severity in punishment. Indeed it sits happily with a political rhetoric which celebrates rather than tempers the retributive emotions and the demand for vengeance. In this context, arguments about the incommensurability of current levels of punishment become a matter not of reasoned judgement but of convention and

---

[45]   See Roger Hood's recent contribution to this question: 'Penal Policy and Criminological Challenges in the New Millennium' (2001) 34 *The Australian and New Zealand Journal of Criminology* 1.

intuitive appeal. While almost all academic defenders of desert theory also espouse a principle of parsimony,[46] when unleashed in political rhetoric in the context of high anxiety about crime, the relationship between desert and parsimony becomes impossible to sustain. Thirdly, this upward drift in levels of punishment—and notably in the use of imprisonment—is susceptible of no evaluation or assessment: it is simply presented as justified irrespective of its social costs or consequences. Hence, finally, the desert framework tends to become diluted by the judicial and legislative introduction of a number of goal-oriented considerations—principles whose pragmatic and piecemeal adoption results in a fragmented and ultimately incoherent penal policy. While this failure is not a necessary theoretical implication of the desert model, in the specific political context in which it has been operating in Britain and the USA over the last fifteen years, it is near to a political inevitability.

The strengths and weaknesses of each of these approaches mirror, therefore, those of the other. While desert-based approaches appear to offer certain prescriptions about the proper scale of punishment, and fit with certain pervasive moral intuitions, the suspicion remains that the imposition of punishment irrespective of beneficial social consequences equates either to a form of vengeance or—perhaps more charitably—to the proposition that two wrongs make a right. Conversely, the goal-oriented approach to punishment, while its cost-benefit principle appears to have transparency and efficiency on its side, has difficulty in generating persuasive principles for the distribution or quantum of punishment. Why not punish an innocent person if the deterrent consequences would outweigh her suffering? Why not merely pretend to punish if this would achieve deterrence without incurring cost? Why not threaten draconian penalties for trivial offences if this would effectively prevent them? These complementary strengths and weaknesses mean that penal policy in real social orders rarely reflects a purely desert-based or consequence-oriented approach. Yet ideas about rationales of punishment incontrovertibly inform government policy and penal practice.

Finally, and most importantly from my point of view, in their most common forms, each of the pure theories tends to ignore the interaction between criminal justice and broad questions of social

---

[46] See e.g. von Hirsch, *Censure and Sanctions*, n. 42 above.

policy: how far is an offender's just desert for crime affected by broader social injustice? May the short-term and direct pursuit of policies of crime reduction through increased punishment turn out to be counter-productive in the longer term and in the light of broader policy objectives?

Revising our Normative Thinking about Criminal Justice

In thinking normatively about punishment in the broader context of criminal justice and other social institutions, I argue that it is necessary to move beyond a debate structured in terms of the opposition between, or some combination of, these two basic theories. As a starting point, it is appropriate to make three very broad assumptions. First, and ideally, the principles governing criminal justice would appeal to values widely shared across the political community. In the real world of diverse societies, such consensus is rarely attainable. However, it is relatively uncontroversial that criminal justice practices should be designed so as to recognize and respect the rights and responsibilities of all members of the community to the greatest degree which is compatible with a similar respect for others. In short, criminal justice must be compatible with the basic ideals of civic reciprocity in a liberal and democratic society.[47]

Secondly, the goals and values informing criminal justice practice should be consistent with those informing other important areas of social policy. Thus although the specific context of criminal justice poses its own distinctive political and moral demands, a criminal justice practice which flew in the face of other valued social principles—the minimization of social exclusion, for example—would be vulnerable to objection. Many crime problems simply cannot be resolved exclusively in terms of criminal justice policy. Without the substantial benefits of civic co-existence—employment, decent housing, good education—many offenders have an insufficient stake in society to give them adequate incentives to avoid future offending. In this context, penalties such as imprisonment have little effect, and such effect as they have consists in short-term incapacitation combined with longer-term stigmatization, which is liable to

---

[47] See S. Benhabib, *Situating the Self* (Oxford: Polity Press, 1992), Chapter 5; I. M. Young, *Intersecting Voices* (Princeton, NJ: Princeton University Press, 1997), Chapters 2 and 3.

destroy any chance of reintegration.[48] Yet, in the context of wide-spread social exclusion, even restorative, deliberately reintegrative penalties have little hope of making a serious impact on rates of reoffending. The scope for genuine reintegration purely through criminal justice is severely circumscribed: the best that can be done is to design penalties so as to limit their disintegrative effects and to provide opportunities, where possible, for social reintegration. This is precisely why criminal justice policy must be integrated with other goals of social policy—with good education, adequate housing, decent welfare safety nets, and high levels of employment. Hence government initiatives in fields such as housing and education, to name but two of the most obvious, should be seen as integral to criminal justice policy.

Thirdly, principles of criminal justice and practices of punishment should be such as to be capable of being applied in an equitable and non-discriminatory way to members of different social groups. I assume, in particular, that the same general principles of punishment should be applied to different groups of citizens—to men and women, to members of different ethnic groups, to young and adult offenders. However, the equitable treatment of different groups does not in itself imply equal treatment in a literal sense.[49] Rather, equity is to be understood in terms of treatment *as an equal*—an idea which implies a respect for social difference. Hence facts about social context of offending among certain groups and about specificities in patterns and forms of offending are of direct relevance to proper penal policy for those groups. To take the example of gender, to the extent that women offenders present lower levels of social danger—both qualitatively, in the sense of the seriousness of the crimes they commit, and quantitatively, in terms of their levels of offending and likelihood of reoffending—this implies substantially different treatment for women in the criminal justice system.[50]

---

[48] The most influential statement of a reintegrative approach to punishment is to be found in the work of John Braithwaite: see his *Crime, Shame and Reintegration*, n. 44 above; John Braithwaite, *Restorative Justice and Responsive Regulation* (Oxford: Oxford University Press, 2002); Braithwaite and Pettit, n. 31 above; J. Braithwaite and K. Daly, 'Masculinities and Communitarian Control' in T. Newburn and E. Stanko (eds.), *Just Boys Doing Business?* (London: Routledge, 1994): see also Duff, *Trials and Punishments* (Cambridge: Cambridge University Press, 1986).

[49] P. Carlen, *Sledgehammer* (London: MacMillan, 1998).

[50] See *Justice for Women* (London: Prison Reform Trust, 2000), Chapters 1, 4, and 5.

Perhaps more controversially, the idea that criminal justice should cohere with other social values suggests that on occasion facts about the social context of offending may affect the legitimacy or at least the proper extent of state punishment. If a large proportion of certain groups of offenders are people whose basic citizenship rights—such as the right to physical or sexual integrity—have been violated by abuses from which the state has failed to protect them, this must be a relevant factor in determining the nature, if not the fact, of their punishment.[51] For example, the fact that a very high proportion of women in prison have suffered serious abuse as children would, on this view, raise distinctive questions about the legitimacy of their punishment. Similarly, at a yet more basic level, where an offender has received less than his fair share of public resources such as education, this should affect the state's investment in the educational or other relevant aspects of his sentence. Though criminal justice creates its own moral imperatives, these can never be entirely insulated from broader questions of social justice. As I shall try to demonstrate below, this argument of principle, if realized in practice, would promise substantial social benefits, not least in alerting us to what it is realistic to expect of penal practices. Our criminal justice theorizing should therefore, I would argue, proceed on the basis of the three assumptions of reciprocity, policy integration, and non-discrimination; should be grounded in a proper social-scientific understanding of the conditions of existence of particular sets of institutions; and should attend far more closely than has traditionally been the case to questions of institutional design and of interaction effects between criminal justice and other social institutions.

From Principles to Practices: Social Resources for an Integrated Criminal Justice Policy

Let me now move back to the political issues canvassed in the first part of this chapter. The normative assumptions of reciprocity, policy integration, and non-discrimination which I have described are grounded in intuitions, commitments, and values which are widely shared in contemporary Britain. Yet their application in the

---

[51] See B.A. Hudson, 'Mitigation for Socially Deprived Offenders' in A. von Hirsch and A. Ashworth (eds.), *Principled Sentencing* (Oxford: Hart Publishing, 1998), 205.

field of criminal justice is vulnerable to increases in the popular demand for expanded criminalization and greater severity in punishment. This demand is itself fostered by governments whose policies assert, in recognition of the misery caused by crime, the validity of the retributive emotions, and—crucially—go on to make extravagant promises about their own capacity to reduce crime through criminal justice policy as traditionally—i.e. narrowly—conceived.

In modern electoral democracies, perhaps the most important barrier to parsimonious and enlightened penal policy lies in the quality of public debate about crime. A responsible government is one which makes available the facts on the basis of which that electorate can make informed decisions; filtering and interpretation by the media are, however, inevitable. In a culture such as Britain's, in which police practices geared to enhancing clear-up rates and crime reduction through selective recording of reported offences come as a shock to the public, there is clearly a problem about the quality of information on the basis of which perceptions of the crime problem—and hence demands for punishment—are being formed. There is a need for honesty and realism on the part of both government and media: honesty about the proportion of crime processed by the official system, and realism about the impossibility of 'perfect enforcement'; honesty about the consequences of punishment, and realism about its potential to reduce crime.

If governments effectively both construct and promise to satisfy the retributive demands of an anxious populace, irrespective of the social consequences of doing so, it appears as if we have, as a society, no choices in this area. We simply have to expand the criminal law and punish to the extent of (what is at the particular moment regarded as) desert, and the necessary prison places must be provided. In this context, the prison budget becomes effectively ring-fenced—a situation which is exacerbated in countries such as Britain and the USA by the possibility of privatization, which distances the immediate fiscal implications of prison expansion.

The development of a criminal justice policy which is genuinely integrated with broader social policies presents, however, a complex challenge to any government whose electorate not only cares deeply about crime but has been encouraged to think that it can be solved by punishment. Let me turn, finally, then, to the resources available in different late modern societies for the pursuit of criminal justice policy and the shaping of criminal justice institutions.

In this context, I argue that countries like Germany have a number of decisive advantages over Britain. First, it may be an advantage of Germany's particular federal systems that criminal justice policy rests primarily at the state level, where a variety of interest groups and views can more easily find a voice in the policy-making process. It is not clear, of course—as the US example shows—that this is sufficient to prevent crime from becoming a political football in the pursuit of electoral goal-scoring, and it must be admitted that the federal system, conversely, presents obstacles to the development of an integrated nation-wide criminal justice policy. One would like to think, however, that the federal-state relationship in criminal justice policy might develop, particularly in the context of increasing international influence on and co-operation in criminal justice strategy, towards a realignment in which the advantages of localism are combined with a more coherent approach at the federal level. Secondly, Germany's dense institutions of civil society, relative to Britain's, and their traditions of local initiative and independence, may have the capacity to foster the involvement of a wide variety of social institutions in the fields such as crime prevention and—notably in the restorative justice movement—the management of social disputes more generally. These underlying social conditions might be expected to facilitate precisely the kind of reintegrative criminal justice policy for which I have been arguing, along with the integration of criminal justice with broader social institutions, at least at the local level.

Though the British experience provides instructive examples of possible pitfalls, we must therefore always be wary of taking histories from one country as unambiguous lessons for another. But I would like to conclude with a very broad question of social policy and social theory. It is worth asking how far it is possible for British practice to move in a reintegrative direction; and whether it is a serious danger that countries like Germany will be drawn further along the politicized, disintegrative route diagnosed by Garland which characterizes current British policy. To the extent that the integrative route depends on the existence of a rich set of institutions in civil society, it is hard to see how effective practices of restorative justice and other 'community-based' initiatives can be implemented successfully in Britain. There is a painful irony, it seems to me, in the resurgence of an appeal to 'community' in the construction of British and American social policy at just the time when government policies and economic forces had effected a decisive decline in the vitality of the local, intermediate institutions which might have formed the infrastructure for the realization of such policies.[52]

Conversely, it is depressingly easy to see how current trends in the development of the economy in countries like Germany—trends which are already bringing with them an increase in unemployment and in casual and insecure part-time labour, and a widening of wage differentials and hence of the gap between rich and poor—might over time disrupt the levels of social integration which foster a relatively liberal criminal policy.[53] We can also imagine how a fragmentation of civil society might damage the infrastructure which fosters a criminal justice policy relatively integrated with social policy and social institutions. In this respect, at the level of practice, support for institutions intermediate between individuals and state, and a recognition of their relevance to the long-term management of crime problems, appears one of the most important questions in criminal justice policy throughout the world. At the level of research, only by means of rigorous comparative study will it be possible to improve our grasp of the potential in different systems for countering the increasingly politicized, exclusionary, and repressive dynamics of criminal justice which David Garland and Jock Young have generalized as the features of 'late modern' penality.

[52] See N. Lacey and L. Zedner, 'Discourses of Community in Criminal Justice' [1995] *Journal of Law and Society* 301.

[53] See Hogg and Brown, n. 13 above, 142–60.

3

Theoretical Reflections on the Evaluation of a Penal Policy Initiative

Anthony E. Bottoms

In the mid-nineteenth century, it was necessary for macro-political reasons for the English penal system to replace transportation to the colonies by what was called penal servitude in penitentiaries at home. The original blueprint for the new system was created by Lieutenant-Colonel Joshua Jebb, and it is described in the following way by Leon Radzinowicz and Roger Hood in their magisterial *Emergence of Penal Policy in Victorian and Edwardian England*:[1]

The regime would be grounded on a progressive stage system, through which prisoners would advance according to the marks they earned for industry and good conduct. This would provide [according to Jebb] 'the best record of the prisoners' actual position with reference to character'. As a 'stimulus to industry, good conduct and moral improvement', they would be rewarded by an extra allowance varying from 3d to 9d per week to spend on [various] luxuries.

Jebb's 'progressive stage system' had both antecedents and rivals in Victorian penality, and these are particularly associated with the names of (respectively) Alexander Maconochie in Norfolk Island, Australia,[2] and Walter Crofton in

---

[1] L. Radzinowicz and R. Hood, *The Emergence of Penal Policy in Victorian and Edwardian England* (Oxford: Clarendon Press, paperback edn., 1990) 493. Quotations within this passage are from a report by Jebb in 1846.

[2] On Maconochie see J.V. Barry, *Alexander Maconochie of Norfolk Island* (Oxford: Oxford University Press, 1958); also Norval Morris's recent 'fictionalized history': N. Morris, *Maconochie's Gentlemen: The Story of Norfolk Island and the*

Ireland.[3] In due course, Victorian penality evolved into the Edwardian penal system, one of the major achievements of which was
the creation of the English borstal system.[4] As Radzinowicz
and Hood describe, there was real continuity between the regime
principles of the borstal system and some of the earlier developments:[5]

The [borstal] regime was constructed around the classic reformatory principles of Maconochie and Crofton, classification and progressive stages.
The boy would begin in the ordinary grade. He could be demoted for bad
conduct to a penal grade, where he would lose all privileges of diet and
correspondence and be put to work stone-breaking. . . . But he was continu-
ously encouraged to earn marks for industry and good conduct by the
prospect of being promoted . . . to 'special grade', where he would wear a
different uniform and receive various privileges, including association
during meal times and in the evening three times a week, a better diet
and a larger gratuity. In this grade an appeal was made 'to higher and better
instincts', as he was put upon his trust. . . . However, to get there was a 'very
severe ordeal', taking at least nine months.

As these brief introductory remarks amply illustrate, the English
penal system has, in the last 150 years, not infrequently had recourse
to various policies in which it was hoped that the provision of
incentives (and disincentives) would spur prisoners on to improve
their behaviour, make progress in their prison sentences, and/or
accelerate their release with a view to improved chances of eventual
rehabilitation.[6] Roger Hood, in his long and distinguished research
career, has frequently touched on such issues, not only in his

Roots of Modern Prison Reform (Oxford: Oxford University Press, 2002). On the
relationship of Maconochie's 'marks system' to Jebb's 'system of marks' see Radzinowicz and Hood, n. 1 above, 493 n. 11.

[3] On the conflict between Jebb's English system and Crofton's Irish system see
Radzinowicz and Hood, n. 1 above, 515–21.

[4] Named after the village of Borstal, near Rochester, where the first borstal institution was located.

[5] Radzinowicz and Hood, n. 1 above, 392–3. Quotations within this passage are
from a 1909 official report.

[6] On the incentive of release as a spur to reform see the argument in the White Paper
which first proposed the modern English parole system: 'a prisoner's date of release
should be largely dependent on his response to training and his likely behaviour on
release . . . these arrangements would afford the strongest incentive to reform': *The
Adult Offender* (Cmnd. 2852, London: HMSO, 1965).

historiographical collaboration with Sir Leon Radzinowicz (see above), but also in his classic early work on the history of the borstal system,[7] and more recently in his many involvements with research and policy-making relating to the parole system.[8]

The most recent English penal policy initiative to make explicit use of the language of incentives has been the so-called 'Incentives and Earned Privileges' (IEP) policy, introduced into English prisons and young offender institutions in 1995. The implementation of that policy was, in its first full year of operation, carefully researched by a team from the Cambridge Institute of Criminology. I was a member of this research team (which was very ably led by my colleague Dr Alison Liebling[9]), and in the years since the research was completed[10] I have fairly frequently utilized the results of the IEP evaluation as an example when lecturing and writing on the topic of compliance with the law, a subject that increasingly preoccupies me.[11] In the light of this background, coupled with Roger Hood's

[7] R. Hood, *Borstal Re-Assessed* (London: Heinemann, 1965).

[8] Professor Hood was a member of the Parole Review Committee, chaired by Lord Carlisle, which reported in 1988 (*The Parole System in England and Wales: Report of the Review Committee*, Cm. 532 (London: HMSO, 1988). Subsequent research work includes R. Hood and S. Shute, *Parole in Transition* (Oxford: Oxford Centre for Criminological Research, 1994); R. Hood and S. Shute, *Evaluating the Impact and Effects of Changes in the Parole System* (Oxford: Oxford Centre for Criminological Research, 1995); R. Hood and S. Shute, *The Parole System at Work: A Study of Risk Based Decision-Making*, Home Office Research Study 202 (London: Home Office, 2002).

[9] The academic research team, in full, consisted of: Alison Liebling (project director), who led the team in all four principal phases of the research (research design, fieldwork, analysis, and writing up); Grant Muir (research assistant and principal fieldworker); Gerry Rose (methodology adviser and research statistician); and myself (senior adviser to the research at all stages, with no participation in the fieldwork but a special responsibility for theoretical issues). We were very fully supported on policy and practical issues and interpretation by Andy Barclay, a former governor of HM Prison, Whitemoor, who was at the time on partial secondment to the Cambridge Institute of Criminology.

[10] The Final Report of the research (A. Liebling, G. Muir, G. Rose, and A.E. Bottoms,'An Evaluation of Incentives and Earned Privileges: Final Report to the Prison Service') was submitted to the research sponsors in July 1997. A copy of the report is now lodged in the Radzinowicz Library of Criminology at the Institute of Criminology, University of Cambridge.

[11] See e.g. A.E. Bottoms, 'Compliance and Community Penalties' in A.E. Bottoms, L.R. Gelsthorpe, and S. Rex (eds.), *Community Penalties: Change and Challenges* (Cullompton: Willan Publishing, 2001) at 113–14.

several research explorations into incentives-related themes, it seemed particularly appropriate—given the very welcome opportunity to contribute to this volume—that I should focus in this chapter on the theoretical lessons to be learned from the results of the IEP evaluation.

That task is, however, made more complex by the fact that the full research results of the IEP evaluation have not been formally published.[12] I am therefore particularly grateful to Alison Liebling for allowing me, in the middle part of this chapter, to summarize these results.[13] Before that, I shall describe the IEP policy, and then in the final part of the chapter I shall offer some theoretical reflections that arise from the research results.

It is my hope that the chapter makes a contribution to the overall theme of this volume (as described by the editors in their introduction) in two ways: first, by considering the interaction between policy and research in the creation and evolution of the IEP policy; and secondly, through a theoretical discussion of the possibilities and the limits of penal policies based (as the IEP policy was and is) on rational choice theory. These various reflections are offered in warm tribute to the enormous contribution that Roger Hood has made to the development of criminology and penal policy in Britain in the last forty years.

The IEP Policy: Background and Context

In 1990, a major disturbance took place at Manchester Prison, followed by a series of incidents elsewhere. This led to a

[12] Only a short summary of the research findings has been published: see A. Liebling, G. Muir, G. Rose, and A.E. Bottoms, 'Incentives and Earned Privileges for Prisoners: An Evaluation', *Home Office Research Findings No. 87* (London: Home Office, 1999). The unpublished Final Report (n. 10 above) has however been available to interested enquirers since 1999. Two published papers by Alison Liebling also draw selectively on the IEP research findings: see A. Liebling, 'Prison Officers and the Use of Discretion' (2000) 4 *Theoretical Criminology* 333; A. Liebling, 'A "Liberal Regime within a Secure Perimeter?": Dispersal Prisons and Penal Practice in the Late Twentieth Century' in A.E. Bottoms and M. Tonry (eds.), *Ideology, Crime and Criminal Justice: A Symposium in Honour of Sir Leon Radzinowicz* (Cullompton: Willan Publishing, 2002).

[13] I also wish to express my indebtedness to Alison Liebling for her detailed and constructive comments on earlier drafts of this chapter.

judicial inquiry (the Woolf Inquiry)[14] and a subsequent White Paper,[15] together widely perceived as steering prisons policy towards a more justice-oriented, constructive, and perhaps liberal set of targets.[16] It was in this post-Woolf Inquiry period that the English Prison Service began once again to examine particularly carefully the concept of incentives.[17] By 1994, the Service's three-year forward planning document (the *Corporate Plan 1994–97*) included the following statement:[18]

One of the most important aspects of this [Corporate Plan]...will be to develop a system of properly structured incentives and sanctions based on prisoners' behaviour and willingness to co-operate. Facilities and privileges over and above the minimum should be earned by responsible behaviour and hard work. Governors will be encouraged and enabled to operate differential regimes which reflect these principles.

There were three main themes incorporated within this approach, all of which can be discerned in the above quotation. First, the Plan, building on the earlier White Paper, accepted in principle the Woolf Report's emphasis on a 'Code of Standards', 'intended to provide a clear benchmark as to the level of [minimum] standards which ought to be achieved and a means of encouraging the Prison Service to

[14] Rt. Hon. Lord Justice Woolf and His Honour Judge Stephen Tumim, *Prison Disturbances April 1990: Report of an Inquiry*, Cm. 1456 (London: HMSO, 1991).

[15] Home Office, *Custody, Care and Justice*, Cm. 1647 (London: HMSO, 1991).

[16] See E. Player and M. Jenkins (eds.), *Prisons After Woolf: Reform Through Riot* (London: Routledge, 1994).

[17] During what David Garland has termed the era of 'penal welfarism', which flourished especially in the mid-twentieth century, there was often less emphasis on an incentives-based approach: see D. Garland, *The Culture of Control* (Oxford: Oxford University Press, 2001). A good indication of the reasoning behind penal welfarism's approach to incentives and privileges was given by Sir Lionel Fox, then the Chairman of the Prison Commissioners, in 1952: '[in] so far as the "privileges" had a value as elements of training, the sooner a prisoner was able to profit by them the better; and in so far as they were useful as aids to discipline, a prisoner might be more affected by the loss of something that he was actually enjoying than by deferment of the hope of enjoying it. Accordingly it was decided that since good reading, the stimulation of industry by earning, and the maintenance of family relations by letters and visits were all valuable for training, they should be divorced from the stage system and made available to all prisoners from the beginning of their sentences': L.W. Fox, *The English Prison and Borstal Systems* (London: Routledge and Kegan Paul, 1952) 149–50.

[18] *HM Prison Service Corporate Plan 1994–97* (London: HMSO, 1994), Preface. The White Paper is at n. 15 above.

achieve them'.[19] Secondly, and congruently with the Woolf Report's espousal of 'contracts' or 'compacts',[20] the Corporate Plan took the view that facilities and privileges above this minimum level should be earned by 'responsible behaviour and hard work'. In consequence, as the Plan itself put the matter, the Prison Service needed to become more active in 'developing and extending prisoner compacts which set out the facilities and opportunities available to prisoners and the obligations and responsibilities which they must discharge in return'.[21] Thirdly, the Corporate Plan envisaged the development of a system of 'differential regimes' in prisons, with movement within or between establishments (or clusters of establishments) based on a structured system of incentives, thus hopefully 'linking prisoners' progress through the prison system more closely with their behaviour and performance'.[22]

As will be apparent from the language and tone of the preceding paragraph, the purpose of these developments was not seen as primarily restrictive or coercive. Instead, it was intended to support the development of constructive and positive regime provision, and to encourage prisoners to engage more fully with regime opportunities and challenges. In considering the Prison Service's policy approach at this time, one must also remember two other related facts. First, concurrently with the publication of the Woolf Report but

[19] Woolf and Tumim, n. 14 above, para. 12.117. The *Corporate Plan 1994–97* (n. 18 above), 16 spoke of 'Operating Standards' and emphasized that 'prisoners will be treated with fairness, justice and respect as individuals', concepts that were said to be 'particularly relevant to the physical environment in which prisoners are held and the way their needs are met'.

[20] Ibid., paras. 12.120–12.129. The Woolf Report recommended that prisoners should, on an individual basis, be offered the opportunity of entering into a 'contract' or 'compact' with the institution in which they were housed. It was anticipated that prisoners might receive progressively more under these compacts as they moved through the system, although these advantages could be lost if there were subsequent bad behaviour. Compacts would 'therefore be a way of introducing greater incentives into the system' (para. 12.122), and they would be subject to regular review. Prisoners would not be obliged to enter into compacts, but the Report considered that it would be in their interests to do so as certain opportunities might be open only to those on compacts. The Report concluded that a 'compact' of this kind 'would underline both the prisoner's and the establishment's responsibilities in relation to the way an inmate serves his sentence'. It could also 'substantially improve the position of the inmate since it would make clear what were his legitimate expectations', and it would 'assist in providing a structure to an inmate's imprisonment' (para. 12.129).

[21] *Corporate Plan 1994–97*, n. 18 above, 19.   [22] Ibid.

unconnected with it, Parliament had made provision for the management of prisons (and of prisoner escorts) by private-sector companies,[23] which in turn had had the effect of stimulating competition, innovation, and market-testing in the public-sector prisons.[24] Secondly, the Woolf Report had arisen out of a major prison disturbance (in which staff had lost control of the prison for an extended period of time), yet the proposals of the report were—for reasons of justice[25]—frequently seeking to extend the rights of and the facilities available to prisoners.[26] In order, in the future, to maintain control while moving towards more generous rights and facilities, the Prison Service—like the Woolf Report itself[27]—saw merit in the development of a properly structured system of incentives.

To summarize, therefore, in the post-Woolf era the main aims of an incentives-based approach, seen in the context of other then-recent developments, could reasonably be described as follows: 'improved regime and prisoner "performance"; the development of more constructive regimes; and the achievement of better control'.[28]

---

[23] Criminal Justice Act 1991, Part IV. See also Lord Windlesham, *Responses to Crime, Volume 2: Penal Policy in the Making* (Oxford: Clarendon Press, 1993) 271–307 and 420–7.

[24] For an evaluation of the early stages of prison privatization in England see A.K. Bottomley, A. James, E. Clare, and A. Liebling, *Monitoring and Evaluation of Wolds Remand Prison and Comparisons with Public Sector Prisons, in particular HMP Woodhill* (London: Home Office, 1997).

[25] At the end of Section 14 of the Woolf Report (entitled 'Prisoners', and including sections on education, physical education, work, food, family ties, visits, telephones, disciplinary procedures, etc.), it is indicated that the suggestions in the Section 'are directed to one of the themes which has run through this report, the theme of justice in prisons secured through the exercise of responsibility and respect. The achievement of justice will itself enhance security and control. These themes must come together in the programmes provided for prisoners and in the way they are treated in prison': Woolf and Tumim, n. 14 above, para. 14.437. This approach was built on the earlier finding of the Woolf Inquiry that '[a] recurring theme in the evidence from prisoners who may have instigated, and who were involved in, the riots was that their actions were a response to the manner in which they were treated by the prison system. Although they did not always use these terms, they felt a lack of justice': ibid., para. 9.24.

[26] See in particular the recommendations in Section 14 of the Woolf Report, which are summarized in Woolf and Tumim, n. 14 above, paras. 15.67–15.85.

[27] See Woolf and Tumim, n. 14 above, 374–8, discussed more fully later in this chapter.

[28] M. Bosworth and A. Liebling, *Incentives in Prison Regimes: A Review of the Literature* (Cambridge: Cambridge Institute of Criminology, 1995) 11.

In the summer of 1994, the Prison Service commissioned the Cambridge Institute of Criminology to conduct a very rapid (two-month) review of the available research literature on incentives-based regimes. The review was completed by Alison Liebling and a research assistant (Mary Bosworth), and was subsequently published by the Institute in March 1995.[29] In their conclusions, the authors of this report drew attention to the many historical antecedents of incentives-based prison regimes, and argued that 'on the whole, they have failed', partly because they had sometimes been 'over-simplistic', and partly because their aims had often been unclear. Developing the point about 'over-simplistic' approaches, it was stated that 'research shows that prisoners may react in ways more complex and less predictable than [those] assumed by rational choice perspectives of human behaviour'.[30] In support of this statement, Bosworth and Liebling had earlier presented two 'models' of incentives in prison regimes, reproduced here (in a slightly edited form) as Figure 3:1. The first part of this Figure shows what Bosworth and Liebling called the 'simple model' of incentives, that is the idea that, given the rational choice theory foundations of an incentives-based approach, incentives will normally have straightforwardly beneficial effects on prisoners' behaviour. The second part of the Figure presents the authors' 'complex model', which takes greater account of the many interconnecting features of prison life.[31] In their supporting text, Bosworth and Liebling argued that the complex model gives a more realistic account of 'the real prison world', and 'shows how incentives can only work if they are seen as part of the whole regime'. Hence, in their view, 'an incentives-based approach should build upon and will be dependent upon other important features of prison life'.[32]

[29] Bosworth and Liebling, n. 28 above.

[30] Ibid., 138.

[31] The 'complex model' shown in Figure 3:1 is reproduced here as originally presented by Bosworth and Liebling, and therefore as part of the historical record of the relationship between research and policy in the development of the IEP policy. The model should not be treated as a final statement of all the relevant factors that need to be considered in introducing incentives into prison regimes. For later accounts of the complexities of social order in prisons see e.g. A.E. Bottoms, 'Interpersonal Violence and Social Order in Prisons' (1999) 23 *Crime and Justice: A Review of Research* 205; Liebling (2000) and (2002), n. 12 above. A fuller account by Alison Liebling is in preparation, in a volume provisionally entitled *Prisons and their Moral Performance*.

[32] Bosworth and Liebling, n. 28 above, 137.

(a)   <u>The simple model</u>

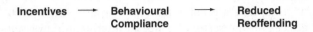

(b)   <u>The complex model</u>

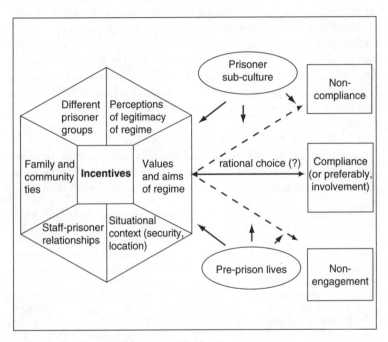

Source: Bosworth and Liebling, see n.28, 136–7.

FIGURE 3:1. Bosworth and Liebling's Two Models of Incentives in Prison Regimes (1995)

Soon after these words were written, however, the penal policy climate in England began to change radically, in a way that was to affect significantly the final character of the IEP policy. A new Home Secretary (Michael Howard, appointed in the summer of 1993) had already begun to make it clear that his approach to prison regimes diverged significantly from that of Lord Woolf.[33] Then, in the autumn and winter of 1994–5, there occurred within the space of four months two major (and very embarrassing) escapes of groups of prisoners from separate maximum security prisons, in each case linked directly or indirectly to a liberal interpretation of standing instructions on prisoners' possession and privilege entitlements. These events placed the Prison Service severely on the defensive, and prison policy shifted rapidly towards a strong new emphasis on security and control.[34] Among the raft of new policies introduced at this time, the most important were: (i) increased physical security and increased searching of prisoners' cells, property, etc.; (ii) mandatory drug testing;[35] (iii) restrictions on prisoners' possessions through a policy of 'volumetric control';[36] (iv) the ending of handing in of property by prisoners' visitors; and (v) restrictions (entailing significant reductions) in the availability of temporary release and home leave.

The IEP policy was formally introduced in 1995, concurrently with most of these other policies. However, although the foundations of the IEP policy had been laid at an earlier time (see above), in the political climate of 1995 it inevitably acquired some dimensions

[33] In a speech to the Conservative Party Annual Conference in October 1993, Michael Howard expressed the opinion that prison regimes should be 'decent but austere'. Later, in August 1994, he was reported as holding the view that 'prisoners enjoy a standard of comfort that taxpayers would find hard to understand' (*Observer*, 22 Aug. 1994). Elements of Michael Howard's views, including the phrase 'decent but austere', can already be found in the *Corporate Plan 1994–97*, n. 18 above, 5 (cf. the phrase 'decent but not lavish conditions' in the 1991 White Paper, n. 15 above, 59: the White Paper however also emphasized that prison conditions had 'for many years failed to achieve' such standards). See generally R. Sparks, A.E. Bottoms, and W. Hay, *Prisons and the Problem of Order* (Oxford: Clarendon Press, 1996) Chapter 1.

[34] See Sir John Woodcock, *Report of the Enquiry into the Escape of Six Prisoners from the Special Security Unit at Whitemoor Prison, Cambridgeshire, on Friday 9th September 1994*, Cm. 2741 (London: HMSO, 1994); and General Sir John Learmont, *Review of Prison Service Security in England and Wales and the Escape from Parkhurst Prison on Tuesday 3rd January 1995*, Cm. 3020 (London: HMSO, 1995).

[35] The introduction of mandatory drug testing was evaluated by researchers from the Oxford University Centre of Criminological Research: see K. Edgar and I. O'Donnell, *Mandatory Drug Testing in Prisons: The Relationship Between MDT and the Level and Nature of Drug Misuse*, Home Office Research Study No. 189 (London: Home Office, 1998).

[36] The policy of 'volumetric control' involved a restriction of prisoners' possessions (apart from one large item) to what would fit within the volume of a standard-sized box.

more in keeping with the new philosophy. This different emphasis was made very clear in a speech by Michael Howard to the Prison Service Conference early in 1997; while the first few sentences of the following quotation set out the basic features of any prison incentives scheme, the second paragraph unambiguously sets the IEP policy in the context of the other changes of the mid-1990s:

Privileges should be earned, not enjoyed as of right. Prisoners who behave well should benefit and those who behave badly should face sanction. And once earned, privileges should not necessarily be permanent. They will be lost if a prisoner's behaviour deteriorates. The new system is transparently fair.

This means real progress towards meeting public expectations about what kind of place prison should be. The general public could never comprehend—let alone condone—what they used to hear about prisoners living with luxuries and free from control. Nor could I. I am pleased that we are making such stories a thing of the past.[37]

Three things followed from this change in political direction. First, many of the factors that had underpinned the concept of an incentives policy in the post-Woolf period (such as guaranteed minimum standards, and 'compacts') were, by 1995, of considerably reduced significance; and this meant, among other things, that the threshold of prisoners' basic entitlements was reduced below the level that the Woolf Report had had in mind in speaking of a 'Code of Standards'. Secondly, and linked to the first point, the character of the IEP policy changed somewhat in emphasis, away from what Bosworth and Liebling (see Figure 3:1) had termed the 'complex model', and to a greater extent (though not completely) towards the 'simple model'. And thirdly, those required to research the effectiveness of the IEP policy inevitably had to take account of this new context of prisons policy.

The IEP Policy: Purposes, Frameworks, and Procedures

It is now time to discuss the 1995 IEP policy initiative in detail. I shall first consider the formal purposes of the policy, its basic frameworks, and the procedures that were intended to support it. Then, in the next sections, I shall go on to describe the Cambridge research and its results.

[37] Quoted in Prison Reform Trust, *Prison Incentives Schemes: Briefing Paper* (London: Prison Reform Trust, 1999), 7.

Purposes

The IEP policy was formally set out in a Prison Service Instruction to Governors (IG), issued in June 1995.[38] This document stated that IEP 'seeks to ensure that prisoners earn privileges by responsible behaviour and participation in hard work and other constructive activity'. Within this overall purpose, five specific aims were identified:

  (i)   to provide that privileges generally are earned by prisoners through good behaviour and performance and are removable if prisoners fail to maintain acceptable standards;

  (ii) to encourage responsible behaviour by prisoners;

  (iii) to encourage hard work and other constructive activity by prisoners;

  (iv) to encourage sentenced prisoners' progress through the prison system; and

  (v)   to create a more disciplined, better controlled, and safer environment for prisoners and staff.

From these formal aims, three principal goals of the IEP policy can be usefully distilled. The first was to *improve individual prisoners' behaviour* through an incentives-based system. It was intended that by making privileges dependent on good behaviour, because prisoners would value and seek to achieve the privileges on offer, their rational response would be to improve their behaviour and work harder. Secondly, IEP was intended to *create more orderly prisons* ('a more disciplined, better controlled and safer environment'). This would occur partly because of the hoped-for aggregate effects of individuals changing their behaviour in response to incentives (see above); and partly because, in the particular context in which it was eventually introduced, IEP was seen as complementing, and usefully interacting with, other policies such as mandatory drug testing[39] and enhanced security[40]—the new policies taken together

---

[38] HM Prison Service, *Incentives and Earned Privileges for Prisoners: National Framework* (IG 74/1995).

[39] e.g., as part of the new drugs strategy in prisons (of which mandatory drug testing was a part), some prisons were encouraged to develop 'drug-free wings' for prisoners who volunteered to be 'drug-free' throughout their sentence. It was anticipated that allocation to such wings could be linked to the IEP system.

[40] e.g., as will be seen in more detail later, at one of the research prisons ('CatC'), a new system of controlled movements (to enhance security and order) was introduced

would therefore, it was hoped, enhance the orderliness of prisons.[41] Thirdly, and as indicated in the fourth of the formal aims set out in the 1995 IG (see above), IEP was intended *to encourage sentenced prisoners' progress through the system.* This third aim, of course, had originally been formulated at an earlier stage of policy development (see the discussion of the *1994–97 Corporate Plan,* above), but it was repeated in the 1995 Instruction to Governors despite now having a decreased prominence in policy thinking. Within its new context, however, this third objective raised some important issues which must be explored briefly.

In introducing the 1995 version of the IEP policy, the Prison Service was keen to emphasize that a given prisoner should not be denied access to certain constructive activities (which were intended to be rehabilitative) just because he/she was on a low privilege level. As the Instruction to Governors put it:

Sentence planning should take place irrespective of the level of privileges or regime in which a prisoner is placed: education, training, employment and offending behaviour programmes set to meet sentence planning objectives are not privileges.[42]

This explicit conceptual separation between sentence planning and privilege level was very different from the policy emphasis in the post-Woolf Report context, in which an incentives policy had originally been formulated. The conceptual separation creates a

at the same time as IEP, and the two policies were seen by managers in that prison as very usefully complementing each other. Comparing the old system with the new, one governor-grade at CatC commented: 'inmates could go where they liked and do what they wanted, so to change the entire ethos from that to incentives-driven regime and controlled movements was quite a big undertaking. It has changed the whole ethos of the place.'

[41] There was also a more system-wide dimension to this strand of policy: the creation of a *national framework* for privileges, in conjunction with the other new initiatives, was seen from Prison Service Headquarters as helping to 'address a perceived and uneven drift in many establishments towards a liberal interpretation of policy on privilege entitlement', and also as contributing towards 'a "reform-as-control" context, in which policy changes and new management systems were being introduced in order to change the way prisons were organized, and to improve "performance" and compliance with instructions at all levels': *Final Report to the Prison Service,* n. 10 above, p. xi.

[42] N. 38 above, 2. Note the clear echoes in this quotation of Fox's penal-welfarism (n. 17 above), but here existing *alongside* a formal system of incentives, in what is in effect a dual-track approach.

distinction between *constructive activities* and *material privileges* (access to private cash, wearing of own clothes, etc.), the latter seen as making life in prison more comfortable, but not necessarily more constructive. The separation is, clearly, based upon a wish not to hinder 'constructive activities' at any time in a prisoner's sentence. However, the relationship between the fourth formal aim of the IEP scheme ('to encourage sentenced prisoners' progress through the prison system') and the constructive activities/material privileges distinction set out later in the IG, is obviously not at all straightforward. In practice, also, the Cambridge research showed that most prisons found it very difficult to draw hard and fast lines between 'material privileges' and 'constructive activities'.

Frameworks

Having decided on the IEP policy, the Government wanted it to be implemented quickly. As indicated above, the Prison Service Instruction to Governors (IG) on IEP was issued in June 1995 (although, given the earlier statements in the *1994–97 Corporate Plan*, an incentives scheme of some kind had been anticipated for some time before that by most people in the Prison Service). The IG required immediate implementation of the new policy in thirty-two 'first phase establishments', and subsequent implementation in all other establishments by December 1995, only seven months later. Thus, the implementation timescale was extremely short.

The IG set out a policy framework that was to be followed nationally, but significant scope was left to local discretion in developing the details of the scheme.

There was to be a nationally uniform framework of three privilege levels, to be termed (in ascending order) the *basic*, *standard*, and *enhanced* levels. The IG also specified six 'key earnable privileges' which prison establishments might include within the ambit of their local IEP scheme: these key earnables were extra and improved visits; access to private cash; eligibility to participate in enhanced earning schemes; wearing own clothes; extra time out of cell; and earned community visits (that is, visits outside the prison, though these were to be subject to standard sentence-eligibility criteria and to appropriate risk assessments). However, it was recognized by Prison Service Headquarters that not all of these 'key earnables' would be relevant in all prisons (for example, all women prisoners already wore their own clothes, and there were no plans to change this; long-term prisoners in conditions of maximum security could not expect community visits). Hence, only two of the six 'key earnable privileges' were required to be included in the schemes of all establishments—these were extra/improved visits and access to private cash. Establishments could also, if they wished, include other appropriate earnable privileges (outside the national list of six 'key earnables') within their local IEP scheme.

No instructions were given from Headquarters about the proportion of prisoners (in any given category of prison) who should be classified as 'basic', 'standard', or 'enhanced'; this was left to local discretion, although the IG did comment generally that 'a standard level of privileges assumes a reasonable level of behaviour, and should normally apply to the majority of prisoners in a particular establishment'.[43] Also left to local discretion were two other matters which proved to be very important in practice. The first of these was the *entry level*: individual establishments were allowed by the IG to choose whether convicted receptions to their prison should begin at basic level or at standard level.[44] Secondly, the IG explicitly allowed individual establishments to decide whether, and if so to what extent, their scheme was to be '*location based*'; that is, grouping together prisoners on a particular level in a specific location such as an 'enhanced wing'.[45]

Procedures

The 1995 IG advised prison governors that 'effective implementation...depends critically on agreement by staff, at all levels and from all disciplines within the establishment, that the scheme is consistent with the goals and values of the Service and has the potential to create positive improvement in their areas of work'. It also recommended wide consultation in the design of schemes, and 'clear communication of its aims and methods of operation' to ensure 'staff engagement in its successful development'.[46] It was not, however, made clear how these admirable suggestions could be

---

[43] Ibid., 13.

[44] Unconvicted prisoners were required to have an entry level of 'standard'.

[45] There was however an important proviso on this point in the IG, namely that governors retained a responsibility to ensure that the total accommodation in their establishments was fully and efficiently used. As we shall see later, in location-based schemes there was sometimes a tension between the IEP philosophy and the operational requirements of this proviso.

[46] N. 38 above, 2.

fully squared with the speed with which governors were required to implement IEP (see above).

The IG required governors to ensure that decisions relating to a move in level 'should be taken on general, objective and published grounds, and should be seen as following from a particular pattern of performance and behaviour'.[47] The instruction advised that local schemes should operate fairly and consistently, and establishments were told to publish details of the different privilege levels, the criteria for earning and retention, and the procedures under which decisions would be made. They were also instructed to provide review boards. Establishments could either include a separate local IEP appeals system in addition to the normal requests and complaints procedure, or they could handle appeals using their existing procedures.

The Research

In May 1995, the University of Cambridge Institute of Criminology was commissioned by the Home Office (on behalf of the Prison Service) to undertake a research evaluation of the IEP policy. The short time-scale of this commission was consistent with the general sense of urgency about the introduction of the IEP policy (see above).[48]

The research comprised both an *outcome* and a *process* dimension. The outcome dimension was focussed on the extent to which the IEP policy had, in its first full year of operation, achieved its objectives, especially those of improving prisoners' behaviour and creating more orderly prisons (see above). Two principal methods were used for the outcome study. The first and most important was a set of detailed structured interviews with random samples of prisoners (about 100 in each prison studied), using a thirty-page interview schedule. These interviews were carried out twice: a 'before' administration in May/June 1995 (Time 1), and an 'after' administration a

---

[47] N. 38 above, 12.

[48] The Institute had, of course, conducted a literature review in the preceding year (n. 28 above), and there had been some interim discussions about possible evaluation research. Nevertheless, the final commissioning of the research was both sudden and late, and a research team had to be put into the field to conduct the 'before' outcome interviews (using lengthy structured interview schedules that had to be designed very rapidly) within a month of the research being commissioned.

year later (Time 2), the aim being to capture significant changes in self-reported behaviour and attitudes during this period.[49] These self-report measures were supplemented by collecting data from the administrative records of each prison on matters such as numbers and types of disciplinary adjudications, assaults, use of formal restraints, prisoners' requests and complaints, and so on.

The outcome research therefore followed a broadly quasi-experimental before–after design, although without the benefit of any control sample, since the Home Secretary had decided it was essential to introduce IEP into all English prisons at the earliest opportunity, and no prison was therefore available to act as a control.[50] However, since before–after quasi-experimental research designs are well known to be open to the objection that they may insufficiently capture the complexity and lived reality of particular social contexts,[51] the quasi-experimental outcome research was deliberately supplemented by what we described as 'process research', which was carried out in each prison between the 'before' and the 'after' administrations of the structured research interviews for the outcome study. This process research was intended to provide a 'thick description' of the operation of IEP in each prison studied.[52]

[49] The 'after' interviews were conducted with a fresh random sample in each prison studied; there was therefore no 'panel' element to the sampling, this being impracticable in most of the prisons studied because of considerable population turnover. Response rates for the structured interviews were high at both Time 1 and Time 2. A structured interview was preferred to a self-completion questionnaire, despite the higher costs, for a number of reasons including: (i) anticipated higher response rates; (ii) ability to explain questions that were not immediately understood (there are relatively high levels of non-literacy among prisoners); (iii) better control over 'circulation' of the research questions between different respondents; and (iv) ensuring that virtually all questions were answered by each respondent.

[50] In one other important respect, the evaluation did not conform to a classical quasi-experimental research design. In such designs, the policy change being evaluated should ideally be the only significant alteration in the chosen social context, so reducing the 'threats to validity' in inferences drawn about the causes of any behavioural changes that are observed between Time 1 and Time 2. In the IEP research, this ideal requirement was simply not available, given the plethora of new prison policies introduced simultaneously with IEP. Appropriate care therefore has to be taken when interpreting the research results.

[51] See R. Pawson and N. Tilley, *Realistic Evaluation* (London: Sage, 1997), although I would not endorse many of the other criticisms of quasi-experimental methodology that are made by these authors.

[52] The methodology for the process study drew heavily on Alison Liebling's previous research on prison suicides and attempted suicides. See especially A. Liebling,

The process research used a mixture of participant observation (lasting several weeks) and process-oriented interviews in each prison. The participant observation involved attendance at management and operational meetings; plus careful and extensive observation of and participation in the life of selected wings or blocks in each prison (including many informal conversations, and weekend as well as weekday presence); plus perusal of available documents such as internal reports and correspondence. Special arrangements were also made to speak to persons less centrally involved in the day-to-day life of the prison, such as staff in specialist departments and Board of Visitors members. This thorough immersion in the life of each prison was supplemented by twenty lengthy interviews with prisoners, and twenty-five with staff, in each prison studied. These were semi-structured interviews, less formal and structured than the outcome study interviews, but deliberately long, detailed, and sensitive. Staff process interviews focussed on their experiences and attitudes concerning prisoners' behaviour and motivation, and the development and operation of incentives-based regimes.[53] Prisoner process interviews focussed on reactions to the use of the 'basic', 'standard', and 'enhanced' categories in that particular prison, and prisoners' views about how the incentives strategy might have altered their own and others' behaviour. Neither staff nor prisoner process interviews were (unlike the outcome study interviews) based on randomly chosen samples; rather, the method adopted for sample selection was more akin to quota sampling (for example, the researchers ensured that appropriate numbers of different categories of staff, and of prisoners on the three different IEP 'levels', were included in the process interview samples).

It should be noted at this stage that, in developing the structured interview schedule for the outcome interviews and the semi-structured interview guide for the process interviews, the Cambridge research team worked essentially within the conceptual framework of the 'complex model' that had been presented by Bosworth and

Suicides in Prison (London: Routledge, 1992) and A. Liebling and H. Krarup, *Suicide Attempts in Male Prisons* (London: Home Office, 1993).

[53] The research team also distributed an eight-page self-completion questionnaire to staff at all five establishments at both Time 1 and Time 2 (except CatC at Time 1, for operational reasons). Return rates varied, and the questionnaires were therefore treated mainly as a supplementary source of data for the process study—as, in effect, a 'volunteer sample' of staff opinions.

Liebling in their earlier literature review (see Figure 3:1). Thus, the questions in both interviews were deliberately wide-ranging, and this approach was approved by the Prison Service personnel who were liaising with the Cambridge research team. In particular, a number of questions on prisoners' perceptions of the fairness of different aspects of prison life were incorporated into both the outcome and process interviews with prisoners, congruently with the inclusion of 'legitimacy' in Figure 3:1, and deliberately drawing on previous Cambridge research which had strongly pointed to the importance of issues of legitimacy and fairness in the maintenance of order in prisons.[54]

The research was principally conducted in five Prison Service establishments of varying type,[55] namely:

- A 'dispersal' (maximum security) prison[56] [Full Sutton];
- A large local prison in London[57] [Wormwood Scrubs];
- A Category C training prison[58] [Highpoint];
- A young offenders' institution [Stoke Heath];
- An open prison for women [Drake Hall].

[54] Sparks, Bottoms, and Hay, n. 33 above; S. Ahmad, 'Fairness in Prison', unpublished PhD thesis, University of Cambridge, 1996.

[55] The research team also collected some much more limited information from seven other establishments (five prisons and two Young Offender Institutions (YOIs)), in order to help assess the degree to which the research results could be taken to reflect the more general picture of the implementation of IEP across the country. (For details, see the Final Report, n. 10 above, 32–42.) However, no rigorous evaluative research was conducted in these seven establishments, so they are not further discussed in this chapter.

[56] On the origins and more recent development of the so-called 'dispersal prisons' in England, see Liebling (2002), n. 12 above.

[57] 'Local prisons' in England fulfil certain distinctive functions within the overall prison system. Normally located within cities or towns, they house prisoners on remand, who are 'produced' from the local prison at courts in the area when required. Local prisons are also typically the first location for prisoners who have just been sentenced; and each local prison contains an Observation, Categorization, and Allocation (OCA) Unit which then allocates sentenced prisoners to other prisons on the basis of their security categorization and other factors (for a recent study of this activity see D. Price, 'Security Categorisation in the English Prison System', unpublished PhD thesis, University of Cambridge, 2000). In most local prisons, some short-sentence prisoners are retained in the prison after the allocation process, and may serve the whole of their sentences in that institution.

[58] Prisoners in England are classified into one of four security categories, from A (maximum security required) to D (considered suitable for allocation to an open prison). Category C prisons are more numerous than open (Category D) prisons or Category B prisons.

There were significant constraints in the choice of prisons for the research. All included prisons had to be among the thirty-two 'first phase' IEP establishments, which comprised only a quarter of the total prison estate; and, since there was also a wish by the Prison Service to include establishments of several types in the evaluation, on occasion the choice was heavily restricted.[59] Also, given the speed with which the research had to be set up, the researchers were in practice heavily dependent on Prison Service advice in the choice of research sites.

Section A of Table 3:1 presents some basic details of accommodation and population in the chosen prisons. Section E of the same table gives the research team's carefully considered view—using a five-point scale where '5' equals 'very full IEP implementation'—of the extent of implementation of the IEP policy in each prison, both at the beginning of the research fieldwork (May–June 1995, 'Time 1') and at its end (May–June 1996, 'Time 2'). Not surprisingly, in four of the establishments, little IEP implementation had taken place at Time 1, but at the young offenders' institution (YOI) a fully-fledged IEP scheme was already in operation when the research started.[60] The establishments then made varying progress during the first full year of the IEP policy, with one prison (the London local prison) advancing least towards IEP implementation. This variation in implementation proved to be important in interpreting the research findings, especially in the absence of a control prison; there were no formal controls, but we were able to compare various indicators of behaviour and attitudes at Time 1 and Time 2 for prisons which had manifestly reached very different points on the continuum of IEP implementation, both at the beginning and the end of the year. In particular, in what follows I shall on occasion use the following two comparisons:

(a)   'Good IEP implementation' versus 'less good IEP implementation' prisons. This comparison is based on the research team's overall assessment, using the ratings on the five-point scale (see above) at Time 2. 'Good IEP implementation' prisons are those which were, at Time 2,

---

[59] e.g., only one dispersal prison (see n. 56 above) was among the 32 'first phase' establishments, so that prison (Full Sutton) had to be included in the evaluation if the research team wished—as we did—to include a maximum security prison within the research.

[60] This is more fully explained later in the chapter.

TABLE 3:1   IEP in Five Prisons: Basic Data

	London Local	CatC	Women's Open	MaxSec	YOI
A. Prison Size and Population*					
CNA	702	679	268	603	372
Operational Capacity	805	679	268	583	360
Prisoner pop. Time 1	764	634	213	550	260
Prisoner pop. Time 2	842	647	205	546	307
B. Features of Local IEP scheme					
Entry Level	Standard	Basic	Basic	Standard	Basic
Locational/ Non-locational	Non-Loc	Loc	Non-Loc	Non-Loc	Partly Loc
C. Distribution of Prisoners by Level (%)[†]	(Main) (Lifer)				(YO) (Juv)
Basic	1 0	16	46	8	42 75
Standard	89 10	67	22	43	35 25
Enhanced	10 90	16	32	49	23 n/a
D. Criteria and Scoring Systems					
(a) Criteria	No formal criteria in most wings (see text)	No formal criteria except when already on Enhanced, then: 1 Works Staff assessment 2 Wing Staff assessment (on both cell inspection and 'attitude to staff and other prisoners')	[Basic to Standard] 1 Personal hygiene 2 Attitude to staff 3 Performance at work 4 General behaviour [Standard to Enhanced] The above, plus: 5 House behaviour 6 Addressing offending behaviour 7 Attendance at evening classes 8 Positive contribution	1 Conforming to regime 2 Behaviour 3 Attendance and performance at work 4 Attitude towards staff/ inmates 5 Complying with sentence plan 6 Complying with compact	1 Attitude to staff 2 Attitude to peers 3 Discipline record 4 Response to sentence plan 5 Attitude to employment 6 Hygiene
(b) Scoring	No formal system in most wings (see text)	For Enhanced prisoners only: Works Staff 30 pts Wing Staff 20 pts	Good Acceptable Poor (on each criterion)	High Good Poor (on each criterion)	Five-point numerical scale (on each criterion)
E. Researchers' Overall Rating of IEP Implementation (five point scale)	(Main) (Lifer)				
Time 1	n/a n/a	1	n/a	n/a	5
Time 2	1 2	3	4	4	5

Notes: *CNA ('Certified Normal Accommodation') is the number of bed-spaces available when there is full use of accommodation but no overcrowding in the prison. 'Operational capacity' may be below this figure (e.g. when some cells are temporarily out of commission) or above it (e.g. where the Prison Service will allow a degree of 'doubling up' in cells in that prison at times of population pressure). Prisoner population figures are the average daily population over the six months prior to the research fieldwork at Time 1 and Time 2.
[†]At the time of the 'process' fieldwork in each prison.

awarded a score of at least four on the scale of effective IEP implementation (see Table 3:1E). There were three 'good implementation' prisons: the YOI, MaxSec and Women's Open.[61]

(b) *'High IEP Change' versus 'Less High IEP Change' prisons.* This comparison, unlike the first, considers the change in the research team's assessment of IEP implementation from Time 1 to Time 2. Prisons which had 'less good IEP implementation' at Time 2 (London Local, CatC) are also classified as 'less high IEP change', because the implementation of IEP procedures had been only partial in these establishments, and thus there had been relatively little change from Time 1 to Time 2. But one 'good IEP implementation' prison—the YOI—was also a 'low change' establishment on this second criterion, precisely because its IEP implementation was so advanced at Time 1.[62] Hence, the two prisons which experienced the greatest IEP change from Time 1 to Time 2 were Women's Open and MaxSec.

Implementation in Five Prisons

It would be inappropriate, in a chapter of this character, to provide a great deal of detail about the implementation of the IEP policy in the research prisons. However, a certain amount of basic contextual information must be provided in order to make adequate sense of the research findings to be discussed later.[63]

[61] As will have been noticed, the research at no stage attempted to disguise the identities of the five research prisons, and in the Final Report (n. 10 above) they are referred to throughout by their real names. However, to assist readers who are less familiar with the English prison system, I have in this chapter chosen to refer to the five prisons principally by names which briefly encapsulate their function within the system. It should also be noted that, in all five prisons studied, significant changes have occurred since the research was carried out, so descriptions of regimes contained in this chapter should not be taken as representing current conditions in these prisons.

[62] Given that the research design focussed on change between Time 1 and Time 2, the inclusion of this particular YOI (where change in IEP implementation between Time 1 and Time 2 was limited because of advanced IEP implementation at Time 1) was not ideal in research terms. The institution was included because the Prison Service was very keen to include within the five research establishments one that they already saw as an 'IEP leader' at the commencement of the research.

[63] Readers seeking further information should consult the Final Report, n. 10 above.

Careful study of sections B, C, and D of Table 3:1 will immediately show that there were major differences in the way that IEP was implemented in the research prisons. Thus, for example, on the key issue of *entry level*, three prisons chose a 'basic' and two a 'standard' entry point. The scheme in one prison (CatC) was wholly *location-based*, and the YOI ran a partly location-based scheme, but in the other three prisons IEP was operated on a non-locational basis. The distribution of prisoners by level varied dramatically by prison, with Women's Open and the YOI having high proportions (over 40 per cent) on basic level, and MaxSec and the lifer wing of London Local having high proportions on enhanced.[64] In fact, ironically only the two 'less good IEP implementation' prisons (CatC and the main part of London Local) had followed the suggestion of the 1995 IG that 'a standard level of privileges... should normally apply to the majority of prisoners in a particular establishment' (see above).[65]

As section D of Table 3:1 shows, formal criteria and scoring systems existed in the three 'good IEP implementation' prisons, but not the other two. However, as will be noted from the table, the criteria differed in detail in different prisons. There were also other important differences between prisons (not shown in the table), such as the details of the privileges available on each level, the extent of mobility between levels, and the time taken for such moves to occur. The extent to which formal procedures (such as review boards and appeal procedures) were in place also varied by prison, although as a

[64] It is not accidental that the highest proportions of enhanced level prisoners were found in the two prisons housing primarily long-term inmates. Historically, high privilege levels have been granted to long-term prisoners to offset the deprivations of lengthy imprisonment; with the shift to an IEP policy, local managements in prisons for long-termers tended to want to maintain these traditional practices within the new IEP structure.

[65] Variations between prisons in the proportion of prisoners on different levels continued beyond the date of the research. See e.g. the data provided by the Home Office in response to a Parliamentary Question in 1998 (HC Deb. vol. 317, cols. 826–827(Written Answers), 31 July 1998), reproduced and commented on in the Prison Reform Trust's 1999 Briefing Paper, n. 37 above. These data included (as the Cambridge research data necessarily could not) examples of the same kinds of prisons (e.g. local prisons) with markedly different distributions of prisoners on different levels. The PRT Briefing Paper commented that it seemed 'such discrepancies are far more to do with variations in the way schemes are operated in individual prisons... than they are with the behaviour of prisoners themselves' (ibid., 13).

generalization it would be fair to say that such procedures were under-developed in most of the research establishments.

To supplement Table 3:1, a brief narrative portrait of the implementation of IEP in the five research prisons will now be given. For this purpose, the prisons are treated in the same order as in the columns of Table 3:1, which means that they are also treated in ascending order of the researchers' overall rating of IEP implementation at Time 2 (see the bottom row of the table).

London Local

London Local (Wormwood Scrubs) is a prison built in the Victorian era. Historically, it comprised four completely physically separate cellblocks, running parallel to one another, but more recently these cellblocks have been joined together by a linking 'spine' at one end of the original blocks (as in the vertical of a capital 'E'). At the time of the research, the four Victorian cellblocks were used for the traditional local prison functions of housing remand and shorter-sentence prisoners, while the linking spine (E wing) was a national 'main lifer centre' for life-sentence prisoners,[66] and as such fulfilled completely different functions from the rest of the prison.[67]

As with some other older local prisons, by tradition London Local had a strong staff culture and an active branch of the Prison Officers' Association. It was regarded by prisoners as basically 'run by staff', with little senior management presence. Given this background, key members of the senior management team were somewhat resistant to the introduction of IEP, because they were worried about staff abusing the scheme.[68]

There was also a tradition in the prison of the semi-independence of the four main wings. Thus, when the IEP scheme was introduced

[66] See n. 57 above. But Category A (maximum security) life sentence prisoners were not allocated to E Wing, because it did not have the necessary level of physical security.

[67] For this reason, the research team originally wished to exclude E Wing from the IEP research evaluation. This idea was not well received by local management, who regarded the lifer wing as the major 'flagship' of the prison; we changed our plans accordingly.

[68] A governor grade at London Local said to the research team: 'Management has no faith in the policy. It has no value; there is no necessity for it. We are seen as being difficult, but it has no value for management. Officers want it because it's punitive. Management don't want it because it's punitive, but we are having to hand it to staff'.

in these wings in January 1996,[69] each wing was allowed to devise its own scheme. Two began with numerical scoring systems, but these quickly fell into disuse.[70] One wing (A Wing) developed a carefully-monitored 'three strikes and you're out' policy for downgrading from standard to basic,[71] but otherwise there were few formal criteria or procedures for this kind of movement—an officer would simply have a word with a senior or principal officer, requesting that a 'problem prisoner' be put on basic, usually for a strictly limited period of a week or less.[72] Movement from standard to enhanced was, on all four wings, associated with certain prison jobs (wing cleaners, servery workers, and orderlies) and was decided by wing staff on a wholly discretionary basis, with no formal criteria.

Standard level was the 'entry level' at London Local (Table 3:1C). Since most movements to basic were temporary, and enhanced was associated with a limited number of prison jobs (see above), in practice there was very little movement between levels, with about 90 per cent of the prisoners in the main wings being on standard level.[73]

In the Lifer wing (E Wing), IEP was introduced earlier than in the main wings, in June 1995. It was decided that all prisoners already in the wing at the implementation date should be placed on enhanced level, with newcomers being placed on standard. However, a review

[69] This implementation date was well behind schedule for a 'first phase' establishment; the delay was created largely by the reluctance of senior management to sign up to the IEP scheme: n. 68 above.

[70] In one case because of a 'decanting' operation that required a relocation of prisoners during building works.

[71] That is, three adverse reports within a two-week period. This scheme was carefully monitored by the wing Senior Officers and the wing governor-grade.

[72] Because of these limited periods on basic, most prisoners on basic in London Local did not lose out on either visits or private cash. Many prisoners, while disliking basic, therefore considered that it was better than being placed on a formal disciplinary charge, which would involve having a blot on their records, going 'down the block' (segregation unit) for a few days, and possibly having some days added to their sentence length.

[73] In the Time 2 research interviews for the outcome study we included a question asking prisoners to what privilege level they were currently allocated. At London Local, no fewer than 46 % gave an answer other than 'basic', 'standard', or 'enhanced' (10 % said 'don't know', and 36 % gave other answers). In the remaining four prisons, the highest comparable figure was 7 %. The clear conclusion has to be that IEP had made relatively little impact on the prison at London Local, with a significant proportion of prisoners not even knowing what their official privilege level was.

procedure was established to consider a new prisoner's situation after three months. In practice, virtually all prisoners were upgraded to enhanced at this point, and there was almost no subsequent downgrading (either of existing or new prisoners). Hence, as with the main part of the prison, there was very little overall movement between levels, and 90 per cent of prisoners were on one level (though in E Wing this was enhanced rather than standard).

In summary, therefore, IEP was not a priority for senior management at London Local; there was a marked amount of discretion at wing level, and very few formal procedures; and in practice there was very little movement between levels, either in the main prison or the lifer wing. In short, it is easy to understand why London Local was classified by the research team as a 'less good IEP implementation' prison.[74]

CatC

The Category C prison included in the research (Highpoint Prison) was, at the time of the study, unusual in that it comprised two different geographical sites (North and South), separated by a main road.[75] It was also, traditionally, somewhat notorious as a prison with minimal supervision and a 'free flow' of prisoner movements; this had resulted in high levels of theft and bullying, and a colloquial name of 'Knifepoint'.

Senior management in the prison used the general national tightening up of security (see the earlier section) as a lever to abolish 'free flow' and to introduce more controlled movement. For

[74] Those familiar with the English prison system will know that local prisons (see n. 57 above) have, over the years, faced rather special problems. They are the prisons that are most likely to be overcrowded (i.e. with prisoner population above 'certified normal accommodation': see Table 3:1A, which shows that London Local was the only overcrowded prison in the Cambridge research sample). Successive reports of Chief Inspectors of Prisons have also frequently commented on insufficient work, lack of time out of cells, etc., in local prisons because of overcrowding and staffing difficulties. Given this background, it might be thought that any local prison, especially a large one like London Local, might find it difficult to implement IEP. In fact, however, the evidence suggests that some local prisons did implement IEP much more fully than did London Local. That was true of Hull (a smaller prison), which was the only local prison among the seven 'supplementary prisons' considered in the Cambridge research (n. 55 above). According to internal Prison Service evaluations, it was also true of Wandsworth Prison which, like Wormwood Scrubs ('London Local'), is a large local prison in the capital.

[75] It is now two separate prisons, one for men and one for women.

example, new fences were put up inside the grounds, there was increased staff supervision of prisoners' movements to and from work, and greater control at the serving of meals. IEP was welcomed by senior management as a complement to this process (see note 40 above), and it was introduced with only a few days' notice in July 1995.

Two key features of the CatC IEP scheme were, first, that the entry level was basic rather than standard; and, secondly, that the scheme was fully 'locational' (see Table 3:1B), that is, all housing units in the prison were specifically designated for prisoners of a particular privilege level. Of the four housing units on the South site, one was designated for basic level accommodation, one became an enhanced unit, and the other two were 'standard'. All accommodation on the (smaller) North site was designated 'standard-plus', in a local refinement of the national scheme. All new receptions began on basic, and were held in an induction unit for not more than two weeks; this was a deliberate policy based on a version of rational choice principles.[76] At the end of the induction period, a prisoner would be allocated either to one of the 'standard' wings in South, or to a 'standard-plus' unit in North. In theory, this allocation was made on the basis of behaviour while on induction (the better-behaved got standard-plus); but in practice the decision was often made on the basis of bed-space availability (an inevitable feature of location-based schemes: see further below), or sometimes because of a prisoner's expressed preference of work or education (opportunities varied on the two sites).

All prisoners on standard or standard-plus were eligible for consideration for promotion to the enhanced unit on the South site (hence, it was not necessary to go through standard-plus to achieve enhanced). In practice, however, most of those who were allocated to the North site (standard plus) had no wish to move to the enhanced unit. The formal incentives for such a move were extra visits and higher private cash; but in the particular context of CatC, these were regarded by North site prisoners as being outweighed by the less formal staff supervision and better staff–prisoner relations on

---

[76] A governor-grade explained: 'They can see what the bottom end of life offers, . . . and I would imagine that most of them think it's pretty poxy. They don't like it, and therefore that's also an encouragement. Let them get a quick sniff of the whole thing and then move them up, as it were.'

North,[77] plus a greater availability of work (because of budgetary cuts, there was during the period of the research a significant reduction of work opportunities on the South site[78]). All this is an excellent illustration of the point, regularly made in the deterrence literature, that incentive and disincentive schemes are dependent on the subjective assessments of those at whom they are aimed, and that sometimes the *subjective* assessments of such persons turn out to differ from those that had been anticipated by the people who devised the scheme.[79]

Another very important feature of the CatC IEP scheme was the existence of the 'BRU', or 'Basic Regime Unit', which comprised about one-third of the bed-spaces in the housing unit on the South site that was reserved for prisoners on basic level (most of the rest were on induction—see above). This unit had been operating for some time before CatC's general adoption of IEP in July 1995, but it was then fully assimilated within the IEP framework. In practice if not in theory, the BRU had largely replaced the prison's segregation unit,[80] and being moved to the BRU was widely regarded by prisoners as a punishment. Prisoners could be placed in the BRU, as a result of deterioration in behaviour, from anywhere else in the prison, but they had to be notified (in writing) by a governor-grade of the

[77] e.g., the North site had a good personal officer scheme, and, because of the design of the housing units, prisoners were allowed keys to their own 'rooms' and could come and go all night if they wished within the confines of their particular sub-unit.

[78] On the South site, budgetary cuts between Time 1 and Time 2 nearly halved the number of prisoners in full-time education (from 67 to 35), reduced numbers in formal work parties (from 143 to 110), and reduced the average number of working hours per week (from a target of 27 per week to a reduced target of 18 per week).

[79] On subjectivity in relation to deterrence see e.g. D. Beyleveld, 'Identifying, Explaining and Predicting Deterrence' (1979) 19 *British Journal of Criminology* 205; A. von Hirsch, A.E. Bottoms, E. Burney, and P.-O. Wikström, *Criminal Deterrence and Sentence Severity* (Oxford: Hart Publishing, 1999).

[80] The segregation unit remained in existence, but was not used except to house recaptured escapees before transferring them to a higher-security prison. Technically, there was a different unit for persons placed on formal administrative segregation ('Rule 43 Good Order and Discipline'), but this was located in the same housing unit as the BRU, and the regime for both was identical. Rule 43 prisoners were, however, more likely to be transferred to more secure prisons, and in principle this status was reserved for persons considered to have engaged in more serious 'subversive activities' than those in the BRU.

reasons for such a move.[81] The minimum period in the BRU was two weeks, after which a decision could be made to transfer a prisoner to a standard wing; but in practice it was not uncommon for prisoners to be in the BRU for substantially longer than two weeks (cf. London Local, where very temporary stays on basic were the norm). Indeed, a small number were retained in the BRU for several months, and there was a reluctance by staff to transfer such prisoners to another prison, that being perceived as a 'reward' for bad behaviour. There was often considerable disruption in the BRU, including a series of cell and sanitation destructions.[82]

Turning now to procedures, in CatC these were mostly purely informal and discretionary. The only exceptions were the BRU, and the enhanced wing on the South site. Procedures for entry into the BRU have been described above, and had at least an element of formality; however, exit from the BRU was conducted very informally, by the wing governor in consultation with BRU staff. Reviews of eligible BRU prisoners were held weekly, but not on any set day of the week, and prisoners were not asked to make representations to the review. Although the decisions in these reviews were formally those of the wing governor, in practice he relied heavily on staff opinions. The enhanced wing ran a more formal points system, described in Table 3:1D, but this operated only once a prisoner was on enhanced, not to get him there in the first place. Essentially, a prisoner had to score a certain minimum number of points to remain on enhanced; if he failed to do so for three weeks running, or had three adjudications in a three-month period, he would be downgraded to standard (not standard-plus).

In summary, therefore, at CatC senior management were enthusiastic about the IEP policy because they saw it as assisting the process, already under way, of helping to 'get the prison under control'. The IEP scheme adopted was location-based, which in itself largely determined the numbers on each level. However, prisoners' subjective perceptions did not match the official version of the locations. Additionally, procedures were mostly very informal, and fell well short of the procedural ideals outlined in the 1995 Prison Service

[81] The procedure was, however, significantly less formal than those involved in traditional disciplinary procedures or administrative segregation; it could amount to no more than a telephone call to a governor-grade and the subsequent issuing of a written notification.

[82] The reasons for behaviour of this kind are discussed in a later section.

Instruction to Governors. The BRU was a special (and contentious) feature of the scheme.

Women's Open

The implementation of IEP in Women's Open (Drake Hall) was complicated by the concurrent existence of a building programme in the prison, which in due course led to the replacement of most of the existing (1940s) housing units by single-storey 'cottages' with single rooms to which prisoners had their own keys. Because most of these cottages did not have staff offices in them, the building programme had the effect of making staff somewhat more distant from prisoners at Time 2 than Time 1; however, this was against a background where both Prison Service Headquarters and the Prison Inspectorate rated the prison as a 'best practice' establishment with an enthusiastic staff team and good sentence planning arrangements.

The implementation of IEP coincided with the new national policy on restrictions of home leave/temporary release (see above), which had a particular impact on open prisons. In other words, an incentive scheme was introduced in Women's Open just after the effective removal of the greatest potential incentive that was available. Despite this, Women's Open entered fully into the spirit of the IEP policy and introduced major changes.

The IEP scheme introduced was not location-based. Like CatC, Women's Open started most new arrivals (except lifers) on basic grade,[83] with a review after a set period. However, in Women's Open the initial period on basic was longer than in CatC (four to five weeks, rather than two). As the prison housed many short-term inmates who remained in the prison for only a limited period, this had the overall effect that the proportion of the total population who were on basic was much higher than at CatC (see Table 3:1C). Once on standard level, a prisoner had to remain on that level for two months before consideration for upgrading to enhanced; hence, the IEP policy in Women's Open was strongly 'time-based'. Enhanced-level privileges hinged very largely on visits and private cash, and visits in particular were highly prized in a women's prison where

---

[83] Lifers were automatically placed on enhanced level. Senior managers in the prison had a policy whereby incoming prisoners on standard or enhanced in their previous prison could continue on their previous privilege level, but in practice most such prisoners started on basic because their record did not state their previous level.

family ties (especially with children) were valued by prisoners even more than in most men's prisons.[84]

The prison had a formal system for IEP upgrading. A single review board met weekly and considered all prisoners who were time-eligible, against an official set of criteria which was formally rated by staff (see Table 3:1D). Prisoners were allowed to see the comments and ratings by staff prior to the review board meeting, and to make any representations that they wished in writing (but not to be present at the board). The review board's decision was also given in writing to the prisoner; and theoretically there was an opportunity for the prisoner to appeal this decision, but at the time of our fieldwork no one had done so.

Most time-eligible prisoners were raised from basic to standard, but the standard to enhanced movement involved a more elaborate set of criteria (see Table 3:1D) and was less automatic. Curiously, there were no regular reviews for considering whether a prisoner should remain on a higher level once she had achieved it, and in practice there were virtually no downward-level movements.[85] If a prisoner became a problem, she was more likely to be transferred back to a closed prison than downgraded to a lower IEP level.

There was a good deal of resentment among prisoners about the initial period on basic: most felt they had 'earned their way' from a closed prison to an open prison, and should not have to 'start earning again' once they arrived there. (Many described it as like 'starting your sentence again'.) This issue will be discussed further in a later section.

In summary, Women's Open had a relatively formal IEP system, though with very few downgradings. Its 'basic entry level' character was seen as unfair by most prisoners, especially in the context of an open prison. Prisoners also disliked the severe reductions in the major incentive of home leave/temporary release. Many staff agreed with prisoners on both these points.

---

[84] However, as is common in women's prisons because there are fewer of them, there were sometimes difficulties in arranging visits because some families had to travel very long distances to the prison.

[85] Prisoners were not usually downgraded even after a disciplinary offence or a positive test during mandatory drugs testing, though such events might well delay upgradings.

MaxSec

The maximum security (dispersal) prison included in the research (Full Sutton) had been operating as a prison for only eight years in 1995. It had had a turbulent early history (typical of new dispersal prisons), but had then become more stable and controlled. Like most dispersal prisons, it had a high level of activities and programmes, and it was the only establishment in the research sample not to suffer budgetary cuts during the research period. At Time 1, staff–prisoner relations seemed good, and there was an impressive senior management team in place.

Dispersal prisons in general have had a history of control problems, though these had diminished somewhat in the 1990s.[86] However, the two sets of high-profile escapes that threw the prison system into national prominence in the mid-1990s (see the earlier discussion) had both occurred in dispersal prisons, and there was a determination at the highest levels in government to bring dispersal prisons in particular under tighter control.[87] At the beginning of the research period, Max-Sec was therefore poised to introduce a dramatic collection of changes and restrictions, including IEP, which was seen as part of the overall 'package'. There was anxiety within the prison about the possible effects of this 'package', particularly among wing staff, who quite often during this period felt themselves to be sandwiched between angry prisoners and a determined senior management team. In the event, MaxSec did successfully implement its whole package of change, but with two significant temporary losses of order, in November 1995 (one wing)[88] and January 1997 (two wings). However, because of the restrictive character of most of the changes being introduced (volumetric control of property, tighter security, etc.), management took the precaution of carefully describing the privileges policy as an 'earned privileges' policy, deliberately dropping the term 'incentives'.[89]

---

[86] Home Office, *Managing the Long-Term Prison System: The Report of the Control Review Committee* (London: HMSO, 1984); A.E. Bottoms and R. Light (eds.), *Problems of Long-Term Imprisonment* (London: Gower, 1987); Liebling (2002), n. 12 above.

[87] See generally Liebling (2002), n. 12 above.

[88] Our research team was carrying out fieldwork in MaxSec at this time. For a vivid account of the problems of conducting research in such a context see A. Liebling, 'Doing Research in Prison: Breaking the Silence' (1999) 3 *Theoretical Criminology* 147.

[89] A particular reason for this was that private cash spending in most dispersal prisons (including MaxSec) had 'drifted' furthest from officially stipulated levels, and would therefore need to be reined in with the formal introduction of IEP.

At the time of the implementation of IEP in MaxSec, every prisoner was assessed by his personal officer and his workshop or education supervisor on six formal criteria, each scored 'poor', 'good', or 'high' (see Table 3:1D). These reports were then reviewed by the wing principal officer and a senior officer, and a grading decision made. Thereafter, privilege levels were deliberately tied to sentence planning (more so than in any other prison in our research sample), and were automatically reviewed at the prisoner's annual sentence plan review, or at six months if the prisoner or his personal officer chose to make a formal request at that time.[90] The annual Sentence Review Boards were very transparent, with the prisoner encouraged to attend, and able to hear and comment on all reports written about him.

MaxSec therefore had the most procedurally formal IEP scheme of our five establishments,[91] and also by far the highest level of prior planning and consultation with prisoners as the scheme was introduced. Much of this was associated with an anticipated negative reaction from prisoners (which duly materialized), and a determination by management to be able to defend the scheme as legitimate in the face of such reactions. It undoubtedly assisted the successful introduction of IEP at MaxSec that the entry level was 'standard', that very few prisoners were placed on basic level, and that half of the population was granted enhanced status (see Table 3:1, B and C). Nevertheless, some of the group discussions between staff and prisoners at the time of the introduction of IEP were very tense and emotive.[92]

It was also the case that the way the IEP scheme was introduced placed a heavy onus of assessment on senior wing staff (see above). There was clear evidence that this resulted initially in significant variations in assessments and detailed procedures between wings, a point that inevitably raised fairness objections (though these were being addressed at the end of the research period). There was also a tendency by staff to 'try out' some of the more unwelcome policies initially in MaxSec's Vulnerable Prisoner Unit

[90] There was also an appeal system in place, and during the initial assessments about 10–12 prisoners per wing appealed, but very few were successful.

[91] Despite the apparently very formal system, however, there was evidence of some prisoners receiving an upgrading outside the prescribed procedures, with the approval of the wing Principal Officer. This is a further example of the pervasiveness, in our research prisons, of discretionary decision-making relating to IEP.

[92] See further Liebling, n. 88 above.

(VPU),[93] where prisoners were seen as more compliant (so the policy would be tested first in a less hostile environment). This however led to some resentment among VPU prisoners, who felt that they were being treated as 'guinea pigs' in unwelcome experiments; this was seen as particularly unfair since, they argued, they did indeed generally behave better than those in the main prison, and therefore did not deserve to be the first to be subjected to increased restrictions.[94]

In summary, the introduction of the new privileges policy into MaxSec was more fraught than in any of the other prisons. The scheme introduced had a high element of formality, but there was still significant variation between wings (for example, in the extent of staff resort to the use of basic level), a point that led to accusations of unfairness.

YOI

Like MaxSec, the YOI (Young Offender Institution) in our research sample (Stoke Heath) had had a troubled history in the not-too-distant past, but had stabilized by the beginning of the research. It was regarded by both Prison Service Headquarters and the Prisons Inspectorate as a 'best practice' YOI, although (as with a number of YOIs) there remained some concern about bullying in the establishment. Our research fieldworkers were however less sure about whether the institution could reasonably be described as a 'best practice' establishment.[95]

The Governor had introduced a so-called 'compacts system' in 1994, based on incentives principles, and in line with the *Prison*

[93] Vulnerable Prisoner Units are for prisoners who are considered for some reason to be at risk of potential attacks from other inmates. Sex offenders constitute the largest single category of offenders in VPUs, but others (e.g. those with unpaid prison debts) are also to be found there. VPUs exist in dispersal prisons because quite a few Category A (maximum security) prisoners are sex offenders.

[94] For rather similar research evidence from another dispersal prison at an earlier date see Sparks, Bottoms, and Hay, n. 33 above, Chapter 6.

[95] Among the reasons for these doubts were: (i) an apparently over-enthusiastic security department, which placed about 5% of prisoners (in a YOI) on 'closed visits'; (ii) the low visibility of senior management in the institution (see n. 102 below); and (iii) a philosophy held by many staff, described by them as 'care with a firm hand'. Examples of this philosophy could readily be found in conversations with staff ('We treat them with contempt; we bully them, given them a bit of their own medicine'; 'We're not psychologists but we can tell when we've gone too far; then we stop'), though our fieldworkers considered that such 'macho' language was not always reflected in actual staff behaviour.

Service Corporate Plan 1994–97 (see the earlier section). By the beginning of the research period, this system was well established; it carried the overwhelming endorsement of staff, and was also generally accepted by the prisoners (although prisoners were mostly unenthusiastic about the attitudes that staff displayed in implementing the system).[96] Given this background, the formal arrival of the national IEP policy made very little difference to operational practice at YOI.

YOI included in its population both 'young offenders' (aged 18–21) and 'juveniles' (aged 15–18), and ran separate incentives systems for each, although along similar principles. For simplicity, I shall describe in detail only the system for young offenders, who constituted the majority of the population.[97] It is important to note, however, that the number of juvenile sentenced inmates rose significantly between Time 1 and Time 2,[98] with various side effects that were to prove of some importance in interpreting the Time 1/Time 2 research comparison.[99]

The IEP system for offenders over 18 was partly location-based, and the entry level was basic. All new arrivals were sent initially to an induction wing (basic level), from which progression could be made to the main wings, namely C wing (which had a mixed population of basic and standard levels) and D wing (mixed standard and

---

[96] e.g., '[i]f they say jump, you've got to jump'; '[t]hey love picking on certain people, like they've got people they don't like and they try to degrade them as much as possible'. Our research fieldworkers were also concerned about some of the language used by staff about prisoners ('horrible juvenile shit-bags', etc.).

[97] The juvenile system was based on similar principles, but with differences of detail. The most important of these were: *first*, during our fieldwork the juvenile part of the YOI operated with only two levels (basic and standard) instead of three (see Table 3:1B), though this was altered to three in the year after our Time 2 fieldwork; and, *secondly*, on the juvenile wing there were two separate points systems in operation—see n. 100 below.

[98] From 40 at Time 1 to 106 at Time 2. This change occurred because the YOI had a remand function at Time 1 but had lost this function by Time 2, with a consequential increase in sentenced juveniles.

[99] Principally (i) because at Time 2 there were in total more juvenile prisoners, various ways in which juveniles were disadvantaged (such as having only two privilege levels instead of three: see Table 3:1B) were felt more acutely; and (ii) because the establishment had a higher proportion of juveniles, staff shifted the 'tone' of the operation of IEP from a balanced combination of positive encouragement and negative deterrence towards a heavier emphasis on the latter. These issues are discussed more fully in a later section.

enhanced). Movement up or down levels was determined by an elaborate points score, calculated on a weekly basis (see Table 3:1D). For example, to be considered for upgrading from standard to enhanced, prisoners had to score eighteen points or more (out of thirty) for six consecutive weeks; and if they then scored fewer than twenty points for two consecutive weeks while on enhanced, they were downgraded. In addition to the points system, anyone suspected of bullying could be placed on administrative segregation ('good order and discipline': see note 80 above), and would subsequently revert to basic level. This combination of factors (that is, the basic entry level; upgrading requiring a certain number of consecutive weeks with particular scores; and the fact that upgrading was not permanent when achieved) meant that in practice YOI had nearly as high a proportion of its offenders aged 18+ on basic as did Women's Open (see Table 3:1C).[100]

One privilege of particular significance in the IEP scheme at YOI was footwear. Standard and enhanced level prisoners were allowed to wear their own trainers, but basic-level prisoners had to wear prison-issue shoes (referred to locally as 'baccy tins') which were deeply unpopular. Highly prized incentives on the enhanced level were the fact that prisoners were allowed pocket TVs, and they had the possibility of moving into six-bedded dormitories where they were allowed to watch TV after lights-out. Thus, incentives at YOI were genuinely meaningful to the prisoners.

The IEP review process was not conducted by a review board. Rather, the levels were intended to be determined entirely by the weekly scores. Since these scores were based principally on assessments by wing staff (see the criteria in Table 3:1D), this meant that in practice a large amount of discretion was delegated to wing staff,[101]

---

[100] For juveniles, in addition to the weekly points score, there was a completely separate daily points system. Each prisoner started each day with 15 points and, if he lost all these points during the day for minor misdemeanours (e.g. 'skylarking', 'improper use of cell bell') then that evening the prisoner remained in his cell instead of being allowed out for 'evening association'. This second system usually meant about 15–20 prisoners 'banged up' in the evening in the juvenile wing (which had a capacity of 120). Our research fieldworkers considered that staff sometimes used this points system to limit the number of prisoners on evening association in the juvenile wing (and thus make the wing easier to control).

[101] One of the six criteria ('attitude to employment') depended on assessments by works staff. Wing staff did not always approve of the marks awarded by works staff for this part of the weekly score.

although an appeal to a principal officer or a governor-grade was built into the system. This delegation to wing staff was deliberate policy, and in line with the more general policy approach of senior management at YOI, which was to empower basic-grade staff to the greatest extent possible, although within guidelines set by management.[102]

In summary, then, at YOI there was a 'compacts' scheme which predated the national IEP policy and which remained in place largely unchanged. The policy was enthusiastically supported by staff, and had become part of the institution's corporate identity. The details of the scheme were clear, elaborate, well-publicized, and well-known by prisoners; but prisoners were less accepting of staff attitudes in implementing the scheme. There was no review board, and much discretion was vested in wing staff, but the weekly wing decisions could be appealed to a higher-grade staff member.

Concluding Comment

From these brief pen-portraits of the implementation of IEP in the five research prisons, it will not be difficult for the reader to discern why the final Cambridge research report contains the comment: 'we were struck by the scale of the differences between our prisons'. The 1995 Prison Service Instruction to Governors (IG) had allowed a significant degree of local discretion in the development of the IEP policy. Inevitably, local managements often shaped the implementation of the policy to their own wider philosophies, and/or what they perceived to be the particular needs of their institution; and this resulted in considerable cross-establishment variations. Against this complex and varied background, we now need to consider the findings of the Cambridge research.

Research Results

I shall summarize the formal results of the research evaluation under three main headings—prisoners' perceptions of IEP, the process

---

[102] Senior management had derived this approach from management styles observed in private prisons. In favour of the approach there was undoubtedly a great deal of specialist knowledge available within the staff group at YOI, and training provision was also good, as the establishment incorporated a regional staff training centre. Our research fieldworkers, however, had doubts about the low visibility of senior management at YOI (n. 95 above), since they considered that this sometimes led to insufficient accountability of wing staff for their behaviour and decision-making.

study results, and the outcome study results. I shall then briefly consider the initial reception of the research results by the research sponsors.

Prisoners' Perceptions of IEP

In the outcome study, at both Time 1 and Time 2, the research team took the opportunity to ask a number of questions about prisoners' perceptions of IEP. Some of the results are shown in Tables 3:2 and 3:3.

The principal official message of the IEP policy (that to a greater extent than previously privileges had to be earned) was clearly received by prisoners. In four of the five prisons, there was a statistically significant increase, from Time 1 to Time 2, in prisoners'

TABLE 3:2   Prisoners' Perceptions of Aspects of IEP*

	London Local	CatC	Women's Open	MaxSec	YOI
(a) Do you agree with the policy that privileges should be earned?					
Time 1	18	6	7	7	91
Time 2	33	37	81	50	92
Movement	↑↑	↑↑	↑↑	↑↑	–
(b) Do you think the staff expect hard-working behaviour in this prison?					
Time 1	31	68	80	34	72
Time 2	53	49	78	44	82
Movement	↑↑	↓↓	–	(↑)	(↑)
(c) Clear info given about privileges and how they can be earned?					
Time 1	22	24	32	20	67
Time 2	20	39	20	38	70
Movement	–	↑	(↓)	↑↑	–
(d) Do privileges reflect how you behave?					
Time 1	19	24	23	15	67
Time 2	31	23	44	23	51
Movement	(↑)	–	↑↑	–	↓↓

*Data from Outcome Study at Time 1 and Time 2. Arrows on the 'movement' line represent the amount and direction of change between Time 1 and Time 2; for a full explanation, see the later discussion of Table 3:4.

acceptance of this key point (Table 3:2(a)), the exception being the YOI where awareness of the point was already extremely high at Time 1. Interestingly, the greatest increase between Time 1 and Time 2 came in the two 'high IEP change' prisons, Women's Open and MaxSec. However, in the two 'less good IEP implementation' prisons (London Local and CatC) only a minority of prisoners endorsed the 'privileges have to be earned' policy even at Time 2. There was a generally similar, but less clear-cut upward movement from Time 1 to Time 2 in perceptions that the staff expected hard-working behaviour from prisoners (Table 3:2(b)). The major exception in this regard was CatC, where the budgetary cuts that resulted in a significant diminution of work opportunities on the South site (see note 78 above) actually led to a significant *reduction*, at Time 2, in the proportion of respondents believing that the staff expected hardworking behaviour. This is a good illustration of the point, previously made by the Cambridge literature review,[103] that penal policies like IEP cannot be viewed in isolation, but must—at least to an extent—be understood and evaluated in the way that they are seen by prisoners, that is, as simply one element of a complex overall prison environment.

As previously indicated, the IEP policy was introduced into English prisons simultaneously with a range of other new initiatives, all of which were of a restrictive character. In the outcome study at Time 2, prisoners were asked to rate 'how fair it has been to introduce' each of five policies, including IEP (Table 3:3); thus, the question asked about the in-principle fairness of the new policy in question. Generally speaking, IEP fared well in this comparison. It was the only new policy to receive more 'fair' than 'unfair' responses in four of our prisons (the exception being MaxSec). In terms of comparative ratings within each prison (see the figures in parentheses in Table 3:3), IEP was well received, by comparison with other policies, in three prisons. It was however less well rated in MaxSec and Women's Open, the two prisons where its introduction had been—for different reasons—the most contentious (see the previous section).

So, the official message of the IEP policy came across in most prisons (Table 3:2, (a) and (b)), and the policy itself was generally perceived in principle as reasonably fair (Table 3:3). None of this means, however, that *in practice* and *as implemented* the IEP policy

---

[103] Bosworth and Liebling, n. 28 above.

TABLE 3:3   Prisoners' Fairness Ratings* for Five New Policies in Five Prisons

	London Local	CatC	Women's Open	MaxSec	YOI
IEP	+34(1)	+8(1)	+4(3)	−38(4)	+32(2)
Mandatory Drug Testing	+13(3)	−1(2)	+36(1=)	−11(1)	+26(3)
Increased Security	+28(2)	−14(3=)	+36(1=)	−35(2)	+39(1)
Volumetric Control	−7(4)	−14(3=)	−20(5)	−37(3)	−13(4)
Restrictions on Temp. Release/Home Leave	−51(5)	−71(5)	−8(4)	−71(5)	−59(5)

[Figures in brackets show the rank order of the fairness ratings in each prison]
*In the Outcome Study at Time 2 prisoners were asked to rate the overall fairness of each of five policies on a five-point scale from 'very fair' to 'very unfair'. This 'fairness rating' is derived from these data; it measures the difference between 'fair' and 'unfair' ratings for each policy for each prison, disregarding neutral answers. For example, in London Local 63 per cent of prisoners rated IEP as 'very fair' or 'fair', as against 29 per cent rating it 'not very fair' or 'very unfair'; this produces a 'fairness rating' of 63–29=+34.

achieved its objectives. The data in Table 3:2(c) and (d) begin to raise some worrying doubts in these respects. A rational-choice-based incentives policy requires, for maximum effectiveness, good communication to participants about how one can gain the rewards on offer. At Time 2, however, only in one prison (the YOI) did a majority of prisoners consider they had clear information about how to gain privileges (Table 3:2(c)). On the further question whether the privileges awarded actually reflected behaviour, again only in the YOI did a majority answer in the affirmative (though with a significant reduction in positive responses from Time 1 to Time 2), and only in Women's Open was there an unambiguously significant positive movement from Time 1 to Time 2 on this variable.[104]

[104] These data refer to prisoners' perceptions. The research team also constructed a measure of self-reported prisoner misbehaviour (see the later discussion), and it was found that in most prisons this measure was significantly correlated with privilege levels (basic-level prisoners reporting the highest levels of misbehaviour, and so on). The only exception to this pattern was at Women's Open, where there were no significant differences by privilege level on the misbehaviour score, probably because the entry level was basic, and few were subsequently downgraded (see earlier discussion). Ironically, however, in Table 3:2(d) Women's Open is the only prison to show a significant increase in prisoners' perceptions that privilege levels 'reflect how you behave'.

Process Study Results

The extent and depth of the process study generated much data and many insights. Within the framework of this chapter, I can offer only the barest headline results from this work, which I shall do in seven key points.[105]

First, the policy was officially described as an 'IEP' policy, but in truth there were not too many incentives available. Because of the general context in which IEP was introduced, some privileges (for example temporary release; freedom of movement within prisons) were in many prisons being withdrawn or restricted. MaxSec was therefore honest in describing its policy as an 'earned privileges' and not an 'IEP' policy (see above); and it was the 'privileges have to be earned' message that was most prominently received by prisoners (see also Table 3:2(a)). Linked to these points, our research fieldworkers noticed a frequent tendency, in the operation of the IEP policy in practice, for many staff to *respond to bad behaviour* in operating the policy, rather than specifically to *reward good behaviour*.

Secondly, staff in most prisons were very positive about the IEP policy. During the process interviews, in four prisons two-thirds or more of staff interviewed thought the policy as it was implemented was 'good' or 'OK',[106] a view that was markedly more favourable than that of the prisoners. A clear majority of staff at the YOI, CatC, and Women's Open thought that the policy had improved prisoners' behaviour, and that view was also held by a third of staff in the other two prisons. An important feature in these positive responses was the perception that IEP had contributed to overall improvements in control and orderliness in the prisons, and more specifically to the armouries of control of basic grade staff. A governor-grade in one prison put this last point well:

I think it's been a good thing because staff do feel they can quite easily... have some control over these inmates because the inmates know it's the staff at the bottom level who are making the decisions rather than like an adjudication when they go in to the Governor.[107] And it's important that

---

[105] Credit for the process research belongs to Alison Liebling and Grant Muir, with support from Andy Barclay: see n. 9 above.

[106] The exception was London Local, where 55% of staff thought that the current operation of the IEP policy was 'poor'.

[107] The reference is to formal proceedings for a prison disciplinary offence, which are heard by a governor-grade with staff as prosecution witness(es).

they behave on a day-to-day level with the staff that they work with because that's where the comments are coming from.

It follows from the above, of course, that the advent of IEP also increased the *discretionary power* of basic-grade staff. How that power was exercised therefore became a crucial issue in the implementation of the scheme, and I shall return to this point later.

Thirdly, in procedural terms there were a number of weaknesses, particularly in some prisons (see the previous section). The high aspirations of the IG in these respects were often not put into practice. The IG had recommended wide consultation with staff in the introduction of schemes, and clear communication with both prisoners and staff. In practice, however, schemes were mostly introduced hurriedly (except at MaxSec), with little consultation, and clear communication with prisoners did not always occur (see for example Table 3:2(c)). Similarly, while prisons were told in the IG to publish clear criteria for the earning and retention of privileges, only three of the research prisons did so (Table 3:1D), and even in those prisons the process research suggested that the criteria were by no means always applied consistently, for example in different wings. Again, the IG had required the introduction of review boards and appeal procedures in all prisons, but these were conspicuously absent in several of our prisons. The implications of all this for perceptions of fairness will be considered shortly.

Fourthly, a number of prisons had difficulty, in practice, in separating 'material privileges' and 'constructive activities', as recommended by the IG. Linked to this point, the most hotly contested single feature of the IEP policy, for prisoners in most prisons, was the inclusion of additional family visits (above the statutory minimum entitlement) as a key 'earned privilege', rather than as a legitimate expectation. Some argued that this approach was contrary to the Prison Service's commitment to the maintenance of the family ties of those imprisoned, as an aid to rehabilitation (a view which, of course, would tend towards the conclusion that family visits were 'constructive activities' rather than 'material privileges', in terms of the distinction between these concepts drawn by the IG[108]). More simply, many prisoners thought that this aspect of the IEP policy was

---

[108] It is worth noting that Sir Lionel Fox had taken this view about family visits in 1952 (n. 17 above): 'since the maintenance of family relations by letters and visits [was] valuable for training, [these] should be divorced from the stage system'.

straightforwardly unfair on them and their families, a view with which a number of staff expressed considerable sympathy.

Fifthly, many comments were made during the process research fieldwork on the variations among the prisons on *entry level* and on whether the scheme was or was not *location-based* (see Table 3:1B). Three of the research prisons had an entry level of 'basic', and there was a widespread perception among prisoners that insisting on such an entry level for transferees who had been 'standard' or 'enhanced' in their previous prison was very unfair. This feeling was especially strong at Women's Open, in view of the fact that most women felt they had 'progressed' by being transferred to an open prison, but then 'knocked back' by having to start again on basic. As for locational schemes, these operated at CatC and (in part) at the YOI. There are some theoretical advantages to location-based schemes: in particular (i) staffing levels can be varied to suit the population (fewer staff are needed on enhanced wings); (ii) physical comfort distinctions are easier to make if they are tied to distinct locations; and (iii) the prison could expect some trouble-free areas (as a governor-grade put it at CatC, the BRU 'is the price we have to pay for peace and quiet in the rest of the prison'). On the other hand, linking location to privilege level has an inbuilt tendency to produce a 'quota' system for a given privilege level, and at a time of population pressures this can produce distortions on the strict 'good behaviour = higher privilege level' approach, as the following quotations indicate:

Now this is where it falls down really because it's bums on beds.... So you can possibly get five inmates which are suitable for North [standard-plus] and possibly four which you'd really rather send to South 1 and 2 [standard] but we need to fill bed spaces so [they all go to North], and it falls down there (Officer at CatC).

At times you get bulges and some of them are not really worth level 2s but to maintain the full occupancy of the wing you've got to bend the figures and bend the points because we've got to maintain a wing of 60 (Officer at YOI).

Indeed, at CatC even the BRU was noted by our fieldwork team sometimes to 'tout for business' in order to fill spaces. Thus, population pressures in location-based IEP establishments could significantly distort some of the intended basic messages of the IEP scheme.

Sixthly, there was in several prisons a perception—contrary to the official message of the IEP policy—that basic level was essentially a punitive grade. It is not hard to see how such a view developed. If the 'standard' grade is indeed standard, and should (as the 1995 IG had suggested[109]) apply to the majority of prisoners in most prisons, then it seems to follow that basic level is—in reality, even if not according to the official rhetoric—a *sub-standard* level.[110] The most conspicuous example of this mind-set in the five research prisons was to be found in CatC, where the BRU had effectively replaced the segregation unit (see earlier discussion). But traces of a similar view could also be discerned in all the other prisons except Women's Open and the Lifer wing of London Local (neither of which used downgradings to basic at all). Indeed, it was because of its perceived punitive character that senior management at London Local were so reluctant to support the IEP policy.[111]

Issues of fairness and unfairness have been raised on a number of occasions in this subsection, and as a seventh and final point arising from the process research I shall address such issues more directly. Our research fieldworkers found that, while most prisoners were not hostile to an IEP policy in principle, and regarded it as basically fair (see Table 3:3), there were widespread feelings that various aspects of the IEP policy *as operationalized* were unfair. (This latter opinion was held by the majority of prisoners interviewed in the process research at all five prisons.) Even the minority of prisoners who felt that IEP was, in its operation, basically fair often added a qualification to the effect that some particular aspect of the scheme was unfair. Not surprisingly, perceptions of operational fairness were correlated with the prisoners' level (enhanced prisoners were more likely to rate the operation as IEP as fair), but even this was not universal:

[Q: Do you think the procedure is fair] No, it's obviously not, is it? Otherwise why am I sitting here as an enhanced inmate on enhanced privileges? It's very subjective, you know, I can name at least two other people on enhanced who have exactly the same attitude as me and state it

[109] N. 38 above, 13 (see text to n. 43 above).

[110] Indeed, in the early borstal system this was explicit (see the introduction to this chapter). As Radzinowicz and Hood (n. 1 above, 392) had put it: 'The boy would begin in the ordinary grade. He could be demoted for bad conduct *to a penal grade....*' (emphasis added).

[111] See n. 68 above.

as well, not prepared to get involved in the establishment's games as we see it (Prisoner at MaxSec).

So, what were the principal reasons for the widespread perception about unfairness in the operation of IEP schemes? They included the following:

- widely-held perceptions about the subjectivity, inconsistency, and unchecked character of decisions by staff about allocations to levels;[112]
- the use of basic level as a punitive device in some prisons, despite the rhetoric of IEP that the policy was not punitive;
- certain issues which were specific to particular establishments, especially the starting of new receptions on basic at Women's Open and the operation of the BRU at CatC;
- the inclusion of family visits among the key earnable privileges;
- the lack of an adequate 'reward' component in the scheme, leading to the perception that the scheme was basically unfair, and linked to a general 'deepening' of the experience of imprisonment through the concurrent increases in security.

This is an important and powerful list, which—as we shall see—has to be taken fully into account in interpreting the outcome effects of the new IEP policy.[113] Some of these points also raise serious doubts about the in-practice validity of the then Home Secretary's claim, in 1997, that 'the new system is transparently fair'.[114]

Summarizing the findings of the IEP process research study, we find a complex *mélange* of results including: the emphasis in practice on 'earned privileges' rather than 'incentives'; the greater empowerment of staff, leading also to greater discretion vested in them; a number of procedural weaknesses; some difficulties in distinguishing between 'constructive activities' and 'material privileges'; and specific issues relating to punitiveness, entry levels, and locational versus non-locational schemes. However, perhaps most importantly,

---

[112] As indicated earlier in this chapter, IG 74/1995, n. 38 above, had placed a greater emphasis on procedures and processes than actually materialized 'on the ground'. There was, for the most part, little understanding of this context at establishment level, and this undoubtedly contributed to the perceptions of prisoners as reported here.

[113] Note that the list includes items relating to both procedural and distributive justice: see later discussion.

[114] See text to n. 37 above.

there was a widespread (but not universal) consensus among prisoners on two propositions: that the basic concept of an IEP policy is in principle defensible and fair, but that IEP as it operated in practice had many features that were unfair.

Outcome Study Results

The outcome study was principally developed using a series of so-called 'composite variables' derived from questions in the formal outcome study interviews at Time 1 and Time 2. The use of composite variables is a standard research technique in analyses of this type; in essence, it consists of constructing a number of new variables, each of which is a composite of several different single items from the interview schedule or questionnaire utilized. Individual items contributing to composite variables are selected by researchers on the grounds that they are considered to reflect theoretically and empirically an aspect of the key outcome indicator being explored; in addition, however, individual items are included within a composite variable only if they can be shown, by rigorous statistical tests, to be reliable, and consistent with the other selected items in the composite variable in question.[115]

In the IEP research, the research team constructed ten composite variables,[116] of which nine are used in this chapter.[117] The individual items comprising these composite variables are not detailed here, but are fully set out in the Final Report of the research.[118] It should be noted also that the raw data for each composite variable were reprocessed in two respects. First, they were *standardized*, that is, related to a 'base', setting the mean value for the whole sample (all five prisons combined) at 10.0 at Time 1 for each composite variable. (Thus, by looking to see whether individual prisons had results above or below 10.0 at Time 1, one can observe cross-prison differ-

---

[115] For fuller details of these statistical procedures see Appendix C of the Final Report, n. 10 above.

[116] Although this work was fully discussed and agreed collectively within the research team, the principal technical credit for these analyses belongs to Gerry Rose, the team's statistician. As he would be the first to point out, however, statistical analyses of this sort depend heavily on the quality of the questionnaire being analysed, and all members of the research team had contributed to the design of the outcome study questionnaires at both Time 1 and Time 2.

[117] I have omitted a composite variable entitled 'Rating of Living Conditions', which is of limited relevance for the purposes of this chapter.

[118] Final Report, n. 10 above, 101.

ences; similarly, Time 1 – Time 2 differences can be noted bearing in mind that the mean value for all prisons combined at Time 1 is 10.0.) Secondly, for most analyses the composite variable data were also used in an *adjusted form*, to take account of changes in the composition of the research samples from Time 1 to Time 2.[119]

The principal results from the composite variables analysis are set out in Table 3:4. The columns of this table show not only the five prisons in the study, but also important within-prison differentiations, as discussed in an earlier section (for example the South and North sites at CatC; the main prison and the VPU at MaxSec; the young offender and juvenile sections of YOI). Results in Table 3:4 are shown in the form of arrows, indicating both the direction of Time 1/Time 2 change ($\uparrow$ = increase; $\downarrow$ = decrease) and the extent of change (two arrows = change of a greater magnitude). These arrows are a summary of much rigorous statistical testing, normally based on the use of several different statistical methods;[120] the arrows represent the best judgement of the research team's statistician concerning the overall interpretation of the data. This also explains the use of parentheses in the table; parentheses indicate a degree of uncertainty in the overall interpretation.

For presentational purposes, the composite variables can usefully be grouped into four clusters: attitude to IEP (one composite variable); behaviour and order (two variables); fairness and justice (four variables); and progress and participation (two variables).

'Attitudes to IEP' showed no overall change across the five prisons taken as a whole (the right-hand column of Table 3:4), and a mixed picture in individual establishments, though with MaxSec showing a significantly less positive attitude from Time 1 to Time 2 in both parts of the prison.

On the key variables relating to behaviour and order, there was also no overall change when the five prisons were taken together. There were however a number of important individual results which

---

[119] e.g., it was found that, overall, the Time 2 sample had higher levels of previous criminality than the Time 1 sample, and this difference was obviously of potential importance in relation to matters such as prison behaviour. For the adjusted version of the composite variables, corrections to the scores were made to take account of this change in the nature of the population from Time 1 to Time 2. In all, adjustments were made in respect of seven background factors of this kind, including previous criminality.

[120] Principally analysis of variance, t-tests, and chi-squared tests.

TABLE 3:4 Overview of Time 1/Time 2 Outcome Effects Based on Nine Composite Variables

	London Local		CatC			Women's Open	MaxSec		YOI		All prisons
	Convicted	Remand	Life	South	North		Dispersal	VPU	YO	Juv.	
A. ATTITUDE TO IEP											
1. Attitude to IEP	—	↑↑	—	↓↓	↑	—	↓	↓	↑	—	—
B. BEHAVIOUR AND ORDER											
2. Misbehaviour	↑↑	↑	—	↑	↓↓	—	—	↑	—	↑↑	—
3. Orderly Regime	—	—	—	↑↑	↑↑	↓	↑↑	—	—	—	—
C. FAIRNESS AND JUSTICE											
4. Staff Fairness	↓	↓	(—)	↓	(—)	↓	↓	↓(↓)	↓	↓(↓)	↓
5. Regime Fairness	↓	↓	↓	↓	↑↑	↓	↓	↓(↓)	↓	↓(↓)	↓
6. Justice Dimension	↓(↓)	—	—	↓	↑↑	↓(↓)	↓	↓↓	(—)	↓(↓)	↓
7. Relations with Staff	↓	↓	—	↓	↑↑	↓↓	↑	↓↓	↓	↓↓	↓
D. PROGRESS AND PARTICIPATION											
8. Making Progress	↓	↓	↓(↓)	↓(↓)	(↑)	↓	(—)	↓	↓(↓)	↓	↓
9. Participation	↓	↓	↓↓	↓↓	↑	—	—	—	↓↓	↓	↓

Key: (a) ↑/↓: Significant change (increase or decrease) between Time 1 and Time 2.
(b) ↑↑/↓↓: Significant but larger change (increase or decrease) between Time 1 and Time 2.
(c) Where arrows (or a blank) are enclosed in brackets, the results show the research team's best judgement, but there is some degree of uncertainty based on statistical tests.
(d) For this analysis, composite variables are both standardized and adjusted: see text for details.

merit more detailed attention, and I shall return to consider these below.

The fairness and justice composite variables presented a more consistent (if not very encouraging) picture. Taking the five prisons together, all four variables showed a significant reduction in levels from Time 1 to Time 2 (the right-hand column); and in general the individual prisons demonstrated a high degree of consistency with this overall picture. The most notable exception was the North site at CatC,[121] which showed a marked improvement from Time 1 to Time 2 in staff–prisoner relationships, and some uncertain but possible improvements on two other variables.[122]

Finally, there were the 'progress and participation' variables. Again, these showed mainly significant downward trends, with the exception of the North site at CatC, where there were improvements.

Let us now turn to a more detailed examination of the behaviour and order composite variables. Detailed scores relating to these variables are given in Table 3:5, distinguishing between the two 'high IEP change' prisons (MaxSec, Women's Open) and the other three establishments (see earlier discussion). Taking the misbehaviour variable and looking first at the 'high IEP change' prisons, there was an observable but not statistically significant reduction in misbehaviour at Women's Open, but on further examination this turned out to be fully accounted for by a reduction in staff reporting of misbehaviour,[123] almost certainly resulting from the change in the architecture of the house units from Time 1 to Time 2, and the consequently greater distance between prisoners and staff (see the

---

[121] Another (less strong) exception is that staff–prisoner relationships in the main part of MaxSec showed a small improvement.

[122] The strong improvements in staff–prisoner relations at CatC North further help to explain the reluctance of the 'standard-plus' prisoners on this site to move to the enhanced unit on the South site of CatC (see earlier section). Note also that results on the 'attitude to IEP' composite variable differed in the two parts of CatC: the South site showed a significant decrease from Time 1 to Time 2 in positive appraisals of IEP, while the North site showed an increase.

[123] The 'misbehaviour' composite variable consisted of some straightforward self-reports of prisoners' behaviour (e.g. hit/tried to hit another prisoner), and some variables based on staff reactions (e.g. warned by staff on behaviour). In further analyses, the research team was able to disaggregate these two dimensions of the misbehaviour score.

TABLE 3:5   Details of Time 1/Time 2 Outcome Effects for the Behaviour and Order Composite Variables, distinguishing between Higher and Lower 'IEP Change' Prisons*

A.   Self-Reported Misbehaviour
1.   *High 'IEP Change' Prisons*

			MaxSec	
	Women's Open	Dispersal	VPU	All
Time 1	9.87	10.07	9.83	9.98
Time 2	9.47	9.87	10.76	10.19
Movement	—	—	↑	—

2.   *Lower 'IEP Change' Prisons*

	London Local				CatC			YOI		
	Convicted	Remand	Life	All	South	North	All	YO	Juv	All
Time 1	9.79	10.00	9.24	9.71	10.49	9.64	10.14	10.57	9.68	10.37
Time 2	11.06	10.94	9.68	10.64	9.71	8.42	9.26	10.15	10.80	10.29
Movement	↑↑	↑	—	↑	↓	↓↓	↓	—	↑↑	—

B.   Orderly Regime
1.   *High 'IEP Change' Prisons*

			MaxSec	
	Women's Open	Dispersal	VPU	All
Time 1	10.77	9.33	9.94	9.55
Time 2	10.02	10.50	10.35	10.45
Movement	↓	↑	—	↑

2.   *Lower 'IEP Change' Prisons*

	London Local				CatC			YOI		
	Convicted	Remand	Life	All	South	North	All	YO	Juv	All
Time 1	9.79	9.76	10.69	10.04	8.60	10.00	9.17	10.59	10.22	10.51
Time 2	9.97	9.74	10.52	10.03	10.00	11.40	10.49	10.26	10.31	10.27
Movement	—	—	—	—	↑↑	↑↑	↑↑	—	—	—

*Using standardized and adjusted scores (see text for details).

earlier section). MaxSec main prison showed no change in self-reported misbehaviour, but there was an *increase* in such misbehaviour in the VPU (which experienced identical regime changes). Thus, there is no evidence from these results that the two prisons exhibiting the greatest amount of IEP change from Time 1 to Time 2 were benefiting from improved prisoner behaviour.

Turning to the lower IEP change prisons, we note immediately that both parts of CatC showed a significantly reduced level of self-reported misbehaviour from Time 1 to Time 2. Is it plausible that this can be causally attributed to the IEP policy? The answer is almost certainly in the negative. CatC was a 'less good IEP implementation' prison, with poorly developed IEP criteria and procedures, and some significant dysfunctions in its IEP policy (for example, most North site prisoners on standard-plus did not want to move to the enhanced wing; the locational character of the IEP policy meant that there was a significant degree of arbitrariness of the 'bums on beds' variety; and because of budgetary cuts prisoners' perception was that at Time 2 staff expected *less* hardworking behaviour than at Time 1 (see Table 3:2(b)). Moreover, the BRU was in place at Time 1 as well as Time 2 (see earlier section), so Time 1/Time 2 differences cannot be credibly attributed to any possible deterrent value of this unit. Given all this, it is therefore much more likely that the significant improvement in self-reported behaviour in both parts of CatC was attributable to the introduction of more controlled movements in the prison (for example greater control at mealtimes and less 'free flow' of prisoners in the grounds). In other words, the reduction in misbehaviour at CatC was probably the result of a prison-based version of 'situational crime prevention'[124] rather than the incentives-based approach of IEP, especially given the weak implementation of IEP at CatC.

What of self-reported misbehaviour in the other two 'lower IEP change' prisons (London Local and YOI)? Both showed some evidence of increased misbehaviour, but this probably had different causes in the two institutions. Given the very low IEP implementation level in the main wings of London Local, the worsening of behaviour there is almost certainly unconnected with the arrival of IEP. YOI, however, was a 'high IEP implementation' but 'low IEP change' prison, and it is therefore intriguing that self-reported misbehaviour significantly increased from Time 1 to Time 2 in the

---

[124] On 'situational crime prevention' see generally R.V.G. Clarke, 'Situational Crime Prevention' (1995) 19 *Crime and Justice: A Review of Research* 91. See also A.E. Bottoms, W. Hay, and R. Sparks, 'Situational and Social Approaches to the Prevention of Disorder in Long-Term Prisons' in T. Flanagan (ed.), *Long Term Imprisonment* (London: Sage, 1995).

juvenile wing, but not in the rest of the institution.[125] Possible reasons for this finding will be explored in a later subsection.

When we turn to the 'orderly regime' composite variable (Part B of Table 3:5), a not dissimilar overall picture emerges. Among the 'high IEP change' prisons, there was a perceived decrease in orderliness at Women's Open, offset by a perceived increase in MaxSec. There is no consistent pattern here, and the results are probably attributable to decreased and enhanced staff surveillance respectively. Among the lower IEP change prisons, there was a very marked increase in perceptions of orderliness on both sites at CatC, but no significant change anywhere else.

Overall, therefore, the composite variable analysis lends very little support to the hypothesis that the advent of IEP improved prisoners' behaviour. This is because there was no consistent overall change in self-reported misbehaviour or orderliness across the five prisons, and also no clear distinctions between the 'high IEP change' and 'lower IEP change' prisons. The principal improvement that was observed (at CatC) was almost certainly attributable principally to factors other than IEP.

Is this interpretation confirmed when one considers officially-collected institutional data, rather than the composite variables derived from interviews with prisoners? Table 3:6 provides information with which one can address this question; and to aid interpretation I have grouped the data for the two 'high IEP change' prisons on the right-hand side of the table.[126]

The results from Table 3:6 are broadly consistent with those of Table 3:5. In Women's Open, the main significant difference from Time 1 to Time 2 is a halving of the number of disciplinary adjudications, almost certainly as a result of the architectural changes and the lower staff surveillance. In MaxSec, on the other hand, staff surveillance increased, as evidenced by the massive increase in security information reports by staff (and, concomitantly, complaints by prisoners). There was also a reduction in assaults, whether measured by official assault data or by reference to hospital data on prisoners'

---

[125] It will be recalled that the numbers of prisoners in the juvenile wing increased sharply from Time 1 to Time 2 (n. 98 above), but the increase in misbehaviour shown in Tables 3:4 and 3:5 has controlled for this numerical difference.

[126] Within-prison regime differences are not shown in Table 3:6 (cf. Tables 3:4 and 3:5) because the relevant data were not consistently available to the researchers on a disaggregated basis.

TABLE 3:6   Details of Time 1/Time 2 Prisoners' Behaviour Data: Selected Institutional Data (adjusted to Annual Rates per 100 Prisoners)*

	London Local	CatC	YOI	Women's Open	Max Sec
1. Recorded assaults					
Time 1	9.03	7.4	24.6	0.5	13.3
Time 2	8.31	4.9	31.3	1.5	7.9
Movement	—	↓	↑	—	↓
2. Adjudications					
Time 1	117.0	321.8	283.1	181.2	201.5
Time 2	115.7	188.6	261.9	97.6	228.2
Movement	—	↓	—	↓	—
3. Head Injuries**					
Time 1	8.1	n/k	n/k	12.2	11.3
Time 2	13.1	4.3	n/k	11.7	5.9
Movement	↑	n/a	n/a	—	↓
4. Use of C & R (three-person teams)					
Time 1	5.5	8.5	10.0	10.9	0
Time 2	7.8	1.9	16.9	12.5	2.9
Movement	↑	↓	↑	—	—
5. Reportable Incidents					
Time 1	54.2	20.5	66.9	n/k	31.3
Time 2	38.7	14.2	40.4	195.1	32.6
Movement	↓	↓	↓	n/a	—
6. Security Information Reports					
Time 1	219.1	n/k	170.0	n/k	205.8
Time 2	223.3	n/k	162.9	172.7	489.4
Movement	—	n/a	—	n/a	↑
7. Requests & Complaints					
Time 1	52.9	213.2	15.4	109.9	105.5
Time 2	45.1	201.2	5.2	61.5	193.4
Movement	—	—	↓	↓	↑

Notes:
*   All data (except recorded assaults) are based on figures for the six months immediately before the Outcome Study fieldwork at Time 1 and Time 2 respectively, adjusted to annual rates per 100 prisoners. Recorded assault data are based on the KPI data for the year.
**Unlike all the other indicators in this table, head injuries data are not routinely collected in prisons. Data shown here were specially collected by the research team from prison hospital records; see n. 127 for a further comment.

head injuries.[127] This very encouraging result is consistent with the improved sense of orderliness discernible among prisoners in the main wings of MaxSec on the 'orderly regime' composite variable.

[127] The use of prison hospital records to throw light on the hidden world of prisoner–prisoner violence was pioneered in a study of Birmingham prisons in the

However, as with that variable, it seems more likely to have been the product of enhanced staff surveillance rather than IEP, though some supporting contribution from IEP cannot be ruled out. Among the 'less high IEP change' prisons, the most consistent results are again from CatC, which on all available indicators showed the largest improvements in prisoners' behaviour and orderliness from Time 1 to Time 2, though as we have seen it is very difficult to attribute these to IEP.

In summary, then, the outcome research analysis provided very little support for the view that the advent of IEP had consistently contributed to improvements in prisoners' behaviour in the five research prisons. The research did, however, show that the clutch of policies introduced concurrently with IEP (including IEP itself) resulted in improved orderliness in two prisons (CatC and the main wings in MaxSec). However, this group of policies also produced consistent reductions in fairness ratings from Time 1 to Time 2 in all prisons except CatC North; and from the process research (see earlier discussion), it is virtually certain that at least some of that perceived reduction in fairness was attributable to the operation (as opposed to the principle) of the IEP policy itself.

Initial Reception of the Research Results

The Final Report of the Cambridge University research into IEP was delivered to the research sponsors in July 1997. Although no technical criticisms of the research analyses were made, it cannot be said that the report was enthusiastically received.[128] The main reason for

early 1980s: W. Davies, 'Violence in Prisons' in M.P. Feldman (ed.), *Developments in the Study of Criminal Behaviour* (Chichester: John Wiley, 1982), ii. Sparks, Bottoms, and Hay, n. 33 above, 261–2 attempted to replicate this strategy in their study of two dispersal prisons, but reported that 'in view of the fragmentary nature of some of the hospital records we cannot be confident that the data we obtained are wholly reliable'. A similar *caveat* should be applied in respect of the head injury data shown in Table 3:6, perhaps not least in view of the high rate of reported injuries at Women's Open.

[128] Although the research analysis itself was not challenged, it was at one stage claimed that the research results could not be trusted because some 'most unrepresentative' prisons had been selected for the research. We were unimpressed by this comment, as (see earlier section) the research establishments had been chosen largely on Prison Service advice. This is not to deny that some other prisons might have implemented IEP in a way that did result in improvements in behaviour; this possibility is discussed in the conclusion to this chapter.

this initial lack of enthusiasm was the findings of the study on the behaviour and order variables: as one official put it to the present author in a subsequent discussion, these findings appeared 'counter-intuitive'. It was largely for these reasons that there was an eighteen-month delay before the findings of the research study were made public (in summary form) by the Home Office[129]—a delay that did not go unnoticed in some informed circles.[130] At this later date, however, some changes were made to the IEP policy in the light of the Cambridge research results; I shall discuss these changes more fully later.

In the final and theoretical part of this chapter, I shall argue that the official quoted above was wrong, and that the principal results of the study were not counterintuitive (or at least, they are readily explicable, and therefore should not have been regarded as counter-intuitive). To understand these points fully, however, it will be necessary to probe quite deeply into the reasons why human beings exhibit what the IEP policy called 'good behaviour'.

Theoretical Discussion: Preliminary Issues

The central purpose of the theoretical discussion that follows is to address, and seek to explain, the result that the Home Office official described as counterintuitive: that is, the apparent lack of effect of the IEP policy on prisoners' behaviour. However, before tackling that issue directly, I want to consider two preliminary matters that I believe will assist the later discussion; namely, the Woolf Report and subjectivity.

The Woolf Report

As previously indicated, in the aftermath of the Woolf Report, and before the security clampdown in English prisons in the mid-1990s, the issues of incentives and privileges were already being considered by the Prisons Board, and they featured prominently in their *Corporate Plan 1994–97*. It may therefore be instructive, in the wake of the 1995 IEP policy and the subsequent Cambridge research, to return at this stage to the *fons et origo* of the 1990s incentives developments, the Woolf Report itself.

[129] Liebling *et al.*, (1999) n. 12 above.
[130] See Prison Reform Trust, n. 37 above, 8.

The report devoted four pages to a section on 'incentives and disincentives'.[131] This began with the statement that '[i]t seems to us incontrovertible that prisoners are likely to behave more responsibly, and to make the best use of their time in prison, if they feel that their responsibility and effort will be in some way rewarded. Those who have a high investment in the system are not likely to seek to destroy it'.[132] Thus, the authors of the report were willing in principle to adopt an incentives-based approach. Shortly afterwards, however, two qualifications were made. First, it was suggested that there is some danger in the concept of 'privileges'. There are some things, the report stated, which should not be privileges, but 'the normal expectation of all prisoners ... who have not had such facilities withdrawn for clear and good reasons'.[133] Secondly, the report expressed distinct unease about the degree of discretion then available to prison governors with regard to privileges (including, at that date, personal possessions). The result of this wide discretion, it was suggested, 'has been the creation of a system which many prisoners see, *with justification*, as arbitrary... [and] this has led to a deep sense of injustice and grievance'.[134]

The report gave a specific example of this last point. In one prison, the Woolf Inquiry team had heard:[135]

a long and heartfelt explanation by one prisoner of a dispute with a prison officer over him having a box of tissues. The dispute eventually led that prisoner to spending time in the segregation unit. The problem, according to him, was that the prison from which he had come allowed him to have a box of tissues in his cell—and his present prison did not. He was not prepared easily to give up his tissues.... Such things may seem petty, but they are important. In this case, it led to a sense of grievance which was a factor in the disturbance which followed. Arbitrariness of this sort can lead prisoners to a feeling of unfairness and powerlessness which is unhealthy for the life and stability of the institution.

In other words, in the Woolf Report we have a suggestion that a system of privileges, if administered arbitrarily, could actually contribute to a major prison disorder (and thus could certainly lead to bad behaviour of a lesser kind).

[131] Woolf and Tumim, n. 14 above, 374–8.
[132] Ibid., para. 14.23.
[133] Ibid., para. 14.32.
[134] Ibid., para. 14.36 (emphasis added).
[135] Ibid., paras. 14.37–14.38.

These various lines of reasoning led the authors of the Woolf Report to develop some quite precise views on incentives and privileges. First, they said, many things should be entitlements, not privileges. Secondly, there were significant dangers in a system of 'personal and minor incentives', since this would be 'hard to administer fairly' and would 'put an additional burden on prison officers in trying to form nice judgements about who could have what privilege'. It would therefore 'risk itself becoming a disincentive rather than an incentive to good behaviour'.[136] Thirdly, however, incentives remained highly relevant to the major features of a prison sentence (as opposed to 'personal and minor incentives': see above), and the Woolf Report explicitly endorsed the view that 'incentives can be deliberately developed as a matter of policy in order to make progression through the [prison] system a consistent and psychologically credible process'.[137] This last point was elaborated as follows:[138]

It should be possible for each prisoner to have the incentive of knowing that he or she will build up a record of activity and behaviour during his time in prison which increasingly allows him greater freedom and greater opportunities until such time as he is discharged. Any regression during a prisoner's time in prison should be as a result of his own behaviour. Such a set-back should be temporary. In time, he should have the opportunity to get back on the ladder of progress.

It will be apparent that the Woolf Report's approach was very different, in some ways, from the subsequent IEP policy. Some of these differences are similar to the varying emphases of the *1994–97 Corporate Plan*, as contrasted with the 1995 IG (see the earlier section), and I shall not go over this ground again. But when we go right back to the Woolf Report, we find two other important differences that are worthy of special comment. First, the 1995 version of IEP actually *required* prison officers, in most prisons, to take on what the Woolf Report had called the 'burden' of 'trying to form nice judgements about who could have what privilege' with regard to incentives that were very often 'personal and minor'. (In practice, however, most officers actually welcomed this 'burden' because of

---

[136] Ibid., para. 14.42.
[137] Control Review Committee (n. 86 above); endorsed in the Woolf Report, n. 14 above, at para. 14.46.
[138] Ibid., para. 14.46.

the extra control leverage which it gave them: see the earlier discussion.) Secondly, the Woolf Report had explicitly raised the possibility that if a privileges system is seen as unjust and arbitrary, this can lead to a real sense of grievance, *and therefore can have counterproductive effects on behaviour.* This is an important suggestion that is given added point, in the present context, by the fact that the results of the Cambridge research showed increased perceptions of unfairness, from Time 1 to Time 2, in all the research prisons except CatC North (see Table 3:4). Yet it is also important to note that what we might describe as the potential 'unfairness counterproductivity' of incentives systems, so clearly raised in the Woolf Report, was virtually ignored in both the *1994–97 Corporate Plan* and the 1995 IG versions of IEP. It will be an important task, in the remainder of this chapter, to explicate in more detail the mechanisms of behaviour that might be involved in the 'unfairness counterproductivity' potential of incentives systems.

Subjectivity

In discussing IEP in operation at CatC, I described how most prisoners on the standard-plus wings on the North site had no wish to move to the enhanced wing on the South site; and I indicated that this was illustrative of the issue of subjectivity, regularly raised in the deterrence literature.

It is worth pursuing this point in a little more detail. Coleman and Fararo, in the introduction to their very useful edited collection on rational choice theory, note that this theoretical tradition contains one element 'that differentiates it from nearly all other theoretical approaches in sociology', namely *optimization*.[139] Elaborating the point, the authors comment:[140]

[Rational choice] theory specifies that in acting rationally, an actor is engaging in some kind of optimization. This is sometimes expressed as maximizing utility, sometimes as minimizing cost, sometimes in other ways. But however expressed, it is this that gives rational choice theory its power: It compares actions according to their expected outcomes for the actor and postulates that the actor will choose the action with the best outcome. At its most explicit, it requires that benefits and costs of all courses of action be specified, then postulating that the actor takes the

---

[139] J.S. Coleman and T.J. Fararo, 'Introduction' in J.S. Coleman and T.J. Fararo (eds.), *Rational Choice Theory: Advocacy and Critique* (London: Sage, 1992), p. xi.
[140] Ibid.

'optimal' action, the action that maximizes the differences between benefits and costs.

But what, for a given actor, is the 'best outcome'? This is where the element of subjectivity enters the picture. Those conducting a rational choice-based theoretical analysis of a given situation might *assume* that for actors A, B, C . . . Q, condition X is the best outcome; and national policy-makers or a local prison management team might make similar assumptions. But at the end of the day, what matters is not the assumptions of the theoreticians or policy-makers, it is what the 'best outcome' is adjudged to be by the particular people in the situation. Sometimes, policy-makers or managers wrongly second-guess what the real actors in the real situation will think; this is what happened in CatC, and more spectacularly on an earlier occasion in the famous English 'short sharp shock' detention centre experiment.[141] An analysis of subjective reactions is, therefore, essential in the full evaluation of schemes based on incentives or disincentives.

So far I have discussed the subjectivity of real-life actors only as rational calculators of optimum outcomes. They are indeed this, but they also have other characteristics; for example, they may have normative bonds to loved ones that might affect their choices, or, in a given situation, they might become very angry indeed because of perceived unfairness in the way that they have been treated by persons in power (see the 'box of tissues' case discussed above). Therefore, if we are interested in subjectivity—and in the context of incentives schemes *we have to be* so interested—then our analysis

---

[141] See D. Thornton, L. Curran, D. Grayson, and V. Holloway, *Tougher Regimes in Detention Centres* (London: Home Office, 1984). This volume reports research on experimental 'short sharp shock' detention centres in England in the early 1980s, intended to act as a deterrent to the young men who were sent there. However, against a control group of 'ordinary' detention centre trainees, no deterrent effect could be discerned in the evaluation. Announcing the scheme in 1979, the then Home Secretary said: 'Much greater emphasis will be put on hard and constructive activities, on discipline and tidiness, on . . . respect for those in authority. We will introduce on a regular basis drill, parades, and inspections. . . . [T]hese will be no holiday camps' (quoted in Thornton *et al.*, 1). The subjective reaction of the prisoners was, however, different. For example, in one detention centre it was reported by the researchers that 'the "new" activities (drill, extra physical education, etc.) reduced the amount of time spent on work. Work tended to be less popular than these new activities, hence the change [of regime] *involved the displacement of a relatively unpopular activity by a relatively popular one*' (ibid., 203, emphasis added).

of subjectivity needs to take account not only of subjective assessments of optimal outcomes, but also of other potentially important subjective motivations of human behaviour, such as normative attachments and/or resentment at perceived injustices. These wider issues—some of which, as previously explained, were included from the outset in the Cambridge research design—will be pursued more fully in what follows.

Theoretical Discussion: Rational Choice Theory

It is now time to confront the central explanatory issue: why, in the five research prisons, was the IEP policy less successful in reducing misbehaviour than the Prison Service had hoped? I shall begin this discussion within the parameters of rational choice theory, and subsequently move on to some wider issues of the kind raised in the Woolf Report.

Optimization

Remaining strictly within the 'optimization' framework of rational choice theory, there are a number of questions that can be raised concerning the incentives structures that were put in place in the research prisons, and whether in principle they were likely to produce a change in prisoners' behaviour. I shall consider these questions one by one.

First, *was there, in principle, sufficient change in the incentives/ disincentives structures to produce a change in behaviour?* In the two 'less good IEP implementation' prisons, there are serious grounds for doubts about this question. As we have seen, the IEP policy was particularly poorly implemented at London Local, to such an extent that in the main prison (non-lifer wings) at Time 2, a sizeable proportion of prisoners were unable to state what 'level' (basic, standard, or enhanced) they were currently on.[142] The weaknesses of IEP at CatC have also been commented on above, in explaining why it is unlikely that the Time 1/Time 2 reductions in misbehaviour (and increased orderliness) in that prison were attributable to IEP.

This first objection, however, cannot reasonably be raised concerning the two 'high IEP change' prisons, Women's Open and MaxSec. That is why, in discussing the outcome study results, care

---

[142] See n. 73 above.

was taken to differentiate the 'high IEP change' prisons from the others.

Secondly, *even where the incentives structure changed significantly, were the incentives on offer strong enough and meaningful enough to motivate prisoners?* The actual incentives on offer for the three 'levels' differed from prison to prison, and have not been discussed in detail in this chapter. This second question is, however, worth raising in broad terms, for a number of reasons. A famous phrase in one of the most important prison sociology books ever written referred to 'the pathetic collection of rewards and punishments to induce compliance' in that particular prison;[143] and the security context in which IEP was introduced meant that some previously-available real incentives (notably home leave) were now much less available than before. Against this, there are data from the research suggesting that most of the available 'key earnables' (extra visits, private cash, etc.) would not be regarded as meaningless (or 'pathetic') by most prisoners (see Table 3:7).[144] However, there were clearly exceptions, as the unwillingness of North site prisoners at CatC to move to the enhanced wing demonstrates. There is also other evidence from the research data that there were important Time 1/Time 2 differences between types of prisoners on attitudes to IEP as the policy became embedded—in particular, older prisoners and those with educational qualifications were less supportive of IEP at Time 2 than at Time 1, by comparison with younger and no-qualification prisoners respectively.[145] The full explanation of these results lies outside the scope of this chapter, but they clearly could reflect a growing feeling on the part of, for example, older prisoners that the IEP reward structure was simply part of the 'establishment's games', to use the words of a long-term prisoner quoted earlier, and thus not to be treated too seriously as an incentive.

[143] G. M. Sykes, *The Society of Captives* (Princeton, NJ: Princeton University Press, 1958), 61. Sykes's study was of Trenton Prison, NJ.

[144] On the importance to prisoners of what might seem to outside observers like small matters see T. Mathiesen, *The Defences of the Weak* (London: Tavistock, 1965). On the contrast between Sykes (n. 142 above) and Mathiesen on these issues see Sparks, Bottoms, and Hay, n. 33 above, 38–50.

[145] It is important to note that these are *time-based variables*. The research analysis showed that several individual-difference variables were significantly correlated with the mean scores for various of our 'composite variables': see n. 119 above. However, what is reported in the text is not this, but rather differential individual-difference effects on Time 1/Time 2 change.

TABLE 3:7   Prisoners' Perceptions of Meaningfulness of Various Incentives in Encouraging Good Behaviour (%) (Outcome Study, Time 2)

	London Local	CatC	Women's Open	MaxSec	YOI
(a) *Visits*					
Extra visits	55	63	81	69	78
Improved quality visits	76	68	77	86	70
Community visits	85	89	89	81	91
(b) *Prison-based privileges*					
Private cash	49	55	78	46	66
In-cell TV	87	80	72	78	95
Earnings schemes	77	74	78	55	73
Own clothes	54	45	75	51	82
Cooking facilities	62	63	74	65	58
Time out of cell	62	57	76	51	63

In summary, therefore, it is not possible to answer this second question definitively. There are good grounds for believing that most of the incentives on offer were meaningful for most prisoners (Table 3:7), but the evidence also suggests that there was a minority of prisoners who were less impressed, and that older and better-qualified prisoners were more likely to join this minority as time went on.

Thirdly, *was the information available on how to gain incentives sufficiently clear to prisoners?* As previously noted, the data available on this point are not encouraging (see Table 3:2(c)). Even at Time 2, only 37 per cent of all prisoners reported that they had clear information on how to gain privileges, and only in YOI did a clear majority of prisoners think this (the 'points system' in that institution had clearly made its mark). These are important data: in an incentives system that is based on the principle of subjects making rational choices, they need full and clear information on how to exercise those choices so as to 'make progress up the ladder'. In this instance, the majority of prisoners did not feel they had such information. This could have been *either* because the formal systems were deficient in providing information of this kind (as they clearly were at London Local and CatC: see Table 3:1D); *or* because, although there were formal systems, they were not adequately communicated to prisoners; *or* because, although there were formal systems, they were felt to be so subjective and/or arbitrary that in practice the prisoner had few clear guidelines.[146] Whichever of these possibilities

[146] e.g., in Women's Open the IEP criteria included the items 'attitude to staff' and 'personal hygiene' (Table 3:1D). It is obvious that different staff members might

was true, from a rational choice perspective the IEP policy was clearly not being optimally communicated in four of the five prisons.

Fourthly, *did rewards always follow from good behaviour, and downgrading from bad behaviour?* Whereas the third question focuses on information to prisoners (formal or informal), this final question focuses on the system in practice, as it seemed to prisoners. (Moreover, the subjective character of all incentives and deterrence-based schemes means that it is the perceptions of the subjects at whom the scheme is aimed that are crucial: see above.) Again as previously noted, Table 3:2(d) shows that only in the YOI did a majority of prisoners believe that the privileges awarded actually reflect behaviour at either Time 1 or Time 2,[147] and that at Time 2 this was believed by only a third of prisoners in all establishments combined. Clearly, this is disappointing from the point of view of the IEP policy. It suggests that there was a significant amount of cynicism in most of the prisons about the way that the IEP system was working in practice, and also a belief that there was a degree of arbitrariness about the system. These comments are, of course, also consistent with the previously-reported perceptions by prisoners about unfairness in the IEP policy, to which I shall return shortly; but at this stage, I am focusing only on the rational-choice (optimization) dimensions of IEP, and not on fairness. From a rational-choice perspective, if there is a perceived degree of arbitrariness about the system, so that privilege enhancement does not necessarily seem to follow from better behaviour (and vice versa), then clearly that will reduce the incentive to participants to engage in good behaviour, because the promised rewards might not follow.[148]

Having considered the four questions listed above, it is clear that from a rational-choice perspective the IEP policy was not optimally

interpret such criteria differentially, leading to possible perceptions of inconsistency and arbitrariness in the criteria.

[147] However, note also that in YOI there was a significant *reduction* from Time 1 to Time 2 in the proportion of prisoners holding this view. This was probably due to the different population mix (more juveniles) in YOI at Time 2, and some of the changes that this population shift seemed to cause: n. 99 above.

[148] One must also bear in mind that the risk of detection for some kinds of officially-defined 'bad behaviour' (e.g. bullying within the prisoner subculture) might well be low. This also would lead to a perception that downgrading might not result from bad behaviour.

implemented in our five prisons, and that this could easily have reduced (and probably did reduce) its hoped-for effectiveness in improving prisoners' behaviour. This, it seems, is therefore a necessary element of the answer to the major explanatory issue concerning IEP's relative ineffectiveness. I shall go on to argue, however, that it is probably not in itself a sufficient explanation.

Is Rational Choice Theory Sufficient?

It is at this point that we enter intellectually contentious terrain. Rational choice theory has been of growing importance in sociology in the last decade, to the point where some of its critics have published a book with the subtitle 'Resisting Colonization'.[149] For present purposes, the key question is: given that the central explanatory question can, to an extent, be answered in terms of rational choice, is anything to be gained by exploring other theoretical approaches?

Useful perspectives on this key question can be obtained by consulting the two concluding essays in the important Coleman/Fararo collection mentioned above.[150] Peter Abell, while well aware of the criticisms of 'rational action theory' (or RAT, as he calls it), nevertheless argues that this theory should provide a 'point of departure' for social scientific explanation, and be 'accorded pride of place in our thinking'—a kind of 'paradigmatic privilege'.[151] He continues:

It is barely necessary to mention [the] achievements [of RAT] in economics and now in political science. . . . Furthermore, there is little evidence of any serious competitor. If we were to restrict our interpretation of RAT to individual objective optimality with exogenous preferences, then this might not take us too far. But . . . we can add much fruitfully to this stark picture while staying within the spirit of the theory. RAT is indeed a rational choice of theory—it is at the moment our least worst choice of framework. It rests . . . upon four primary assumptions. . . . In the final analysis, though, it is the assumption of optimality—people, given their information (and so on) choose a best course of action—that has to be preserved if the framework is to keep its cutting edge. Putting it another way, if the predictions of our theory fail, then we should at least initially assume that

---

[149] M.S. Archer and J.Q. Tritter (eds.), *Rational Choice Theory: Resisting Colonization* (London: Routledge, 2000).

[150] Coleman and Fararo, n. 139 above.

[151] P. Abell, 'Is Rational Choice Theory a Rational Choice of Theory?' in Coleman and Fararo (eds.), n. 139 above, 203.

we have modelled the preferences incorrectly rather than assume a suboptimal choice. This in the final analysis is all that RAT requires of us.

There is significant merit in what Abell here argues. In particular, his final suggestion is important in reminding us that we can indeed take account of subjectivity while remaining within rational-choice theory—for example, in the present study, by remodelling prisoners' choices in a more sophisticated way to take account of the decisions that led most standard-plus prisoners at CatC not to want to transfer to the enhanced wing on the South site.[152] Nevertheless, even when all this has been taken into account, there may yet be more to say.

To see why, let us begin with the work of Jon Elster on social order. Elster believes that, in considering why individuals behave in ways that sustain social order (and we may note in passing that the enhancement of such behaviour is a central objective of the IEP policy), it is sensible to begin with the 'logically most simple type of motivation: rational, selfish, outcome-oriented behaviour'.[153] Yet, after a technically very impressive discussion, Elster concludes ('with some reluctance' because of the loss of parsimony in explanation) that the maintenance of social order cannot be adequately explained by using rational self-interest as a sole motivational assumption.[154] In particular, he convincingly develops the twin arguments, first that social norms of various kinds independently motivate individuals' order-related behaviour, and secondly that such norms are 'autonomous', in the sense that they cannot be regarded as merely rationalisations of self-interest.[155]

It is this kind of scholarship that underpins the chapter (by James Bohman) that is counterposed with that of Peter Abell at the conclusion of the Coleman/Fararo volume. Bohman highlights a number of limitations to rational-choice theory, including 'an important area of social behavior that has given the theory enormous difficulty: the problem of social norms and rules'.[156] His conclusion is not that rational-choice theory is false; rather, 'its explanations are

---

[152] This would, however, require considerable awareness and skill by senior prison managers if it were to be attempted in operational practice.

[153] J. Elster, *The Cement of Society: A Study of Social Order* (Cambridge: Cambridge University Press, 1989), 37.

[154] Ibid., 250.

[155] Ibid., Chapter 3.

[156] J. Bohman, 'The Limits of Rational Choice Explanation' in Coleman and Fararo (eds.), n. 139 above, 218.

adequate within its own domain'.[157] He further argues, however, that it would be a mistake to try to revise rational choice theory in order to make it more complete and comprehensive:[158]

> It is precisely because it makes such strong assumptions that the theory can explain phenomena in its domain. But its very strengths (and source of its quantitative structure) also set clear limits, and good rational choice explanations stay within them as narrowly as possible. Broadening the theory to include nonintentional maximization, future interests or stabilizing norms only leads to bad explanations.

Ultimately, Bohman concludes, while rational-choice theory has a great deal to offer to social science, 'the limits of its explanations show that it is an incomplete theory of social action and that it can remain vital only by incorporating other theories at different levels of explanation'.[159]

It is this approach that is adopted here, together with the view (following Elster) that social norms cannot be reduced to the framework of rational maximization.

Theoretical Discussion: Fairness, Resentment, and Legitimacy

In reporting the results of the Cambridge IEP evaluation, the language of 'fairness' and (especially) 'unfairness' was frequently used. In the composite variables analysis in the outcome study, in most prisons there was a significant deterioration from Time 1 to Time 2 in the 'fairness' results (Table 3:4). Given the general prison policy context in which IEP was introduced (with several fresh and non-trivial restrictions on prisoners, many of which were regarded by them as more unfair than IEP: see Table 3:3), some of this measured decline in perceived fairness was undoubtedly attributable to aspects of prison policy other than IEP. Nevertheless, the in-depth process study in the Cambridge evaluation also showed clearly that many aspects of the operation of IEP itself were widely regarded as unfair (even though most prisoners thought that the principle of the policy was fair). These perceptions deserve serious attention in the theoretical analysis of what I have called the central explanatory question arising from the IEP research, namely, why was the policy less

---

[157] J. Bohman, 'The Limits of Rational Choice Explanation' in Coleman and Fararo (eds.), n. 139 above, 224.   [158] Ibid.   [159] Ibid., 225.

successful in reducing misbehaviour than the Prison Service had hoped? To develop the analysis, I shall consider separately the three linked concepts of fairness, resentment and legitimacy.

Fairness and Unfairness

To describe something as unfair is to pass a normative judgement upon it, grounded in a conception of what is 'fair' or 'just'.[160] In beginning to speak of 'unfairness', therefore, we have moved away from rational-choice theory and into the realm of the normative. Hence, the key question for present purposes is whether in the implementation of the IEP policy in our five prisons judgements of the fairness or unfairness of IEP did in fact motivate prisoners' *behaviour* (as opposed to simply being an expressed attitude). If they did, given that judgements of unfairness outweighed those of fairness, they probably motivated behaviour in a negative direction. In that event, any benefit from increased good behaviour arising from the operation of rational-choice incentive-oriented behaviour might have been cancelled out by less good behaviour arising out of perceptions of unfairness. It will be recalled that this was, precisely, the danger that was raised in the Woolf Report's discussion of incentives schemes.

There is now a considerable literature in social psychology suggesting that subjects' behaviour in response to the requirements of persons in authority, and subjects' co-operative behaviour in groups, is in significant part influenced by non-instrumental considerations, and in particular by judgements of the extent to which the authorities in question deal with cases in a *procedurally fair* way.[161] This literature further suggests that perceived fairness of *outcomes* (or 'distributive justice') also affects subjects' co-operative and compliant behaviour, but usually not as much as does perceived procedural

---

[160] On justice as fairness see J. Rawls, 'Justice as Fairness' (1958) 67 *Philosophical Review* 169; J. Rawls, *A Theory of Justice* (Oxford: Oxford University Press, 1972). On legitimacy and fairness as contributors to normative legal compliance see A.E. Bottoms, 'Morality, Crime, Compliance and Public Policy' in A.E. Bottoms and M. Tonry (eds.), *Ideology, Crime and Criminal Justice: A Symposium in Honour of Sir Leon Radzinowicz* (Cullompton: Willan Publishing, 2002).
[161] T.R. Tyler, *Why People Obey the Law* (Princeton, NJ: Yale University Press, 1990); T.R. Tyler and S.L. Blader, *Co-operation in Groups: Procedural Justice, Social Identity and Behavioral Engagement* (Philadelphia, Penn.: Psychology Press, 2000); T.R. Tyler and Y.J. Huo, *Trust in the Law* (New York: Russell Sage, 2002).

justice.[162] Indeed, people are often able to accept an adverse outcome, while retaining intact their prior view of the legitimacy of authorities, provided that they feel that their case has been dealt with in a procedurally fair way, and that they have been accorded respect by the authorities in their dealings with them. It is clear that this body of literature is potentially highly relevant to our central explanatory question, notwithstanding that it was given little emphasis by those who formulated the 1995 IEP policy, and even less in the on-the-ground implementation of the policy above.[163]

What, then, in more detail, do most subjects in most research contexts regard as 'fair procedures'? Paternoster and his colleagues, in a much-cited article on procedural justice and spouse assault, list descriptively six major features of procedural justice.[164] Paraphrasing, they are:

(i) *Participation/representation* The opportunity adequately to put one's case to decision-maker(s) before a judgement is made by him/her/them.

(ii) *Dignity and respect* Being treated by the authorities as a human being, with rights, feelings, and status.

(iii) *Neutrality* The authority being willing and able to exercise an appropriate degree of neutrality and independence in handling the case.

(iv) *Competence* The authority appearing to be able to make high-quality decisions, and to explain them.

(v) *Consistency* The authority not acting arbitrarily, and, if different cases are judged differently, being able to explain why this is so.

(vi) *Correctability* The opportunity for initially unfair judgements to be corrected (for example, on appeal).

---

[162] See the references cited in n. 161, above.

[163] See n. 112 above. But see the literature review by Bosworth and Liebling, n. 28 above, which explicitly drew the attention of the Prison Service to this strand of literature.

[164] R. Paternoster, R. Brame, R. Bachman, and L.W. Sherman, 'Do Fair Procedures Matter? The Effect of Procedural Justice on Spouse Assault' (1997) 31 *Law and Society Review* 163.

Using similar ideas, but different language, Tyler and Blader have subsequently suggested that the key descriptive elements of procedural justice are *status recognition* (roughly equivalent to (i) and (ii) in the above list); *neutrality* (equivalent to (iii)); and the *trustworthiness of authorities* to make good judgements (equivalent to (iv)–(vi)).[165]

Most of these aspects of procedural justice are highly relevant to the IEP evaluation. In different prisons, the schemes could easily be accused of lack of consistency in decision-making (across prisons, across wings, and by different officers); lack of correctability; quite frequently (although not in MaxSec or Women's Open) lack of participation/representation; at times lack of neutrality (for example 'picking on certain people', note 96 above), or of competence by individual officers; and at times lack of dignity or respect afforded to prisoners by individual officers, perhaps particularly for juveniles in YOI.

There was, then, a good deal of perceived procedural unfairness in the operation of IEP, of a kind that can be explicitly related to other research literature on procedural justice. To this we must add that *distributive* (or outcome) justice was sometimes also seen as deficient in the operation of IEP, most notably in the automatic starting of prisoners on 'basic' in a new establishment (a particular problem at Women's Open), but also in feelings about the lack of an adequate 'reward' element in the schemes and the inappropriate use of basic level as a punishment.

Given the complexity of what was occurring in English prisons at the time of the IEP research, it is impossible to prove definitively that the widespread perception by prisoners of lack of fairness in the operation of IEP schemes was directly related to the absence of any measurable improvement in prisoners' behaviour in the Cambridge IEP research. However, one can certainly say that such a result would be fully consistent with the earlier research literature. It therefore seems entirely reasonable to assume such a result as a working hypothesis—in conjunction, of course, with the previously-stated conclusion that, from a rational choice perspective, the IEP policy was not optimally implemented in the research prisons, and that this probably reduced its hoped-for effectiveness

[165] Tyler and Blader, n. 161 above. In this text, Tyler and Blader also put forward a more analytic conceptualisation of procedural justice: ibid., 11–13.

in improving behaviour. In the light of this working hypothesis, I now want to explore two other concepts that are closely related to perceptions of fairness and unfairness, namely *resentment* and *legitimacy*.

Resentment

In speaking of resentment, the nature of the discourse changes again, for resentment is an *emotion*. Had a chapter of this kind been written twenty years ago, it is almost certain that it would have contained no subsection of this sort, because historically the disciplines of both criminology and sociology have institutionally suppressed emotions categories in their mainstream analyses.[166] In both disciplines, however, in recent years this situation has begun to show welcome signs of change.

'Resentment' is the emotion that has been highlighted for discussion here because it was the most prominent emotion noted by our fieldworkers in relation to the implementation of IEP. For those familiar with the literature on justice, such an observation immediately recalls the work of the Oxford philosopher J.R. Lucas.[167] For Lucas, there is an important difference between the concepts of justice and of injustice. Justice is a 'cold virtue, which can be manifested without feeling'.[168] But 'injustice is something we soon get steamed up about', that is we become emotional. Lucas continues:[169]

If I talk only about justice I am in danger if relapsing into platitudes; it is when I get hot under the collar about some specific piece of unfairness that my eloquence has an edge to it, and I really know what is getting my goat.

---

[166] The reasons for this are, however, different in the two disciplines. In the case of criminology, this feature developed originally because of the historical dominance of positivism. In the case of sociology, what Barbalet has called the 'expulsion of emotion from sociology' arose, in his analysis, from the fact that in conventional sociological accounts 'emotion is held to deform reason', and reason 'comes to be seen as an expanding web which is both produced by and supports social organization': J.M. Barbalet, *Emotion, Social Theory and Social Structure: A Macrosociological Approach* (Cambridge: Cambridge University Press, 1998) 13.

[167] J.R. Lucas, *On Justice* (Oxford: Clarendon Press, 1980).

[168] Ibid., 5. Indeed, those who dispense justice are frequently expected to suppress emotion, and to reach their decisions in what we significantly describe as a *dispassionate* manner, acting *without fear or favour*.

[169] Ibid. (emphasis added).

And . . . the contrast between the mild favour I feel towards fairness and the intense fury that unfairness arouses in my breast is symptomatic of a basic *asymmetry* between justice and injustice.

For Lucas, therefore, justice and injustice require separate analysis. Moreover, for social institutions to engage our allegiance, it is not enough that they should be fair and just (they must be other things too); yet if they display 'injustice or unfairness, [that] is a fundamental defect'. To cry 'unfair' is thus to make a fundamental protest, and we make such a protest when we consider that someone (ourselves or another) has been 'done down' (that is, someone, maybe myself, has been given less than his/her due by another person).[170] While Lucas has previously spoken of 'fury' in relation to injustice, he now refines the emotional analysis; for, as he points out, we can be angry when we are hurt, but '*indignation is the conceptually appropriate response to injustice*', to the process of having been unjustifiably 'done down'.[171] This is because 'injustice betokens an absence of respect . . . to understand it properly we have to construe it as an affront which belittles the worth of the [person] who suffers it'.[172]

These observations mesh well with an analysis of resentment in one of the most important recent sociological discussions of emotion, by Jack Barbalet.[173] Barbalet's book has two special features. First, it focuses on certain key macro-structural concepts in sociology (such as rationality, class structure, and social change), and considers how they are related to emotions categories. Thus, the author rightly refuses to confine the discussion of emotions to microsociology. Secondly, Barbalet's focus is not on emotions in social life in general, but on certain specific emotions, two of which are resentment and vindictiveness. As he points out, in unreflective discussions these two emotions are 'widely regarded as negative forces'. However, he shrewdly adds, 'it is pointless to describe an emotion as negative before knowing to what it is directed. To resent injustice is not negative'.[174]

---

[170] Ibid.

[171] Ibid., 7 (emphasis added). Note the conceptual similarity of 'indignation' and 'resentment', as shown in the following definitions from the *Longman Dictionary of the English Language* (Harlow: Longman, 1984): (i) 'Indignation' = 'anger aroused by something judged unjust, unworthy or mean'; (ii) 'Resentment' = 'a feeling of bitterness or persistent hurt and indignation at something regarded as insult, injury or injustice'. It is noteworthy also that injustice appears explicitly in both definitions.

[172] Lucas, n. 167 above, 7.   [173] Barbalet, n. 166 above.   [174] Ibid., 128.

Barbalet's discussion of resentment is linked to the macrosocio-logical concept of 'basic rights', but for present purposes it is not necessary to enter into the complexities of that topic. Rather, I shall focus on some 'basic propositions' with which Barbalet concludes his chapter on resentment and vindictiveness. The second and third of these propositions are both highly relevant to the present discussion:[175]

First, social action is best understood as an emotional process. Emotions are emergent in social relationships and constitute a source of change within them. Second, a basic human need is for social existence. The boundaries of individual social being are the extent of a social actor's propensities and capacities. For social being to be secure, the boundaries of and standing within collective and cooperative activity are experienced as inviolable.

These two propositions combine to produce a third, namely that violations of the conditions of social being generate emotional patterns which direct the action of the injured actor to restore their social standing.

I shall treat the first of these propositions as a given. Moving swiftly to the second, Barbalet is here emphasizing—as social anthro-pologists also frequently do—the fact that 'wherever we encounter them, . . . humans are invariably social, or better stated societal beings'.[176] In considering human needs it is therefore—according to Barbalet—a mistake to restrict ourselves to purely physical needs (food, water, etc.) and nurturing needs (the need for love and respect). There is, he argues, a third kind of need, 'the need for society, the need for collective and co-operative activity'.[177] Breaches of 'established practices or rules of social cooperation' therefore often provoke in individuals a real sense of violation,[178] since normally an adult human being 'occupies a status position through being located in

[175] Barbalet, n. 166 above, 148.

[176] M. Fortes, *Rules and the Emergence of Society* (London: Royal Anthropo-logical Institute, 1983), 1.

[177] Barbalet, n. 166 above, 141. The author adds that 'this category of need is often overlooked because of the unfounded but continuing separation', in much philosoph-ical and social scientific literature, of the concepts of 'nature' and 'society'.

[178] Barbalet illustrates this point through a discussion of Garfinkel's ethnometh-odological 'breaching experiments', rarely discussed with full attention to their emo-tional significance. See Barbalet, n. 166 above, 142–3; H. Garfinkel, *Studies in Ethnomethodology* (Englewood Cliffs, NJ: Prentice-Hall, 1967).

various socially cooperative activities . . . that are basic to . . . social existence'.[179] And naturally enough, when status is seen as violated by breaches of 'established practices or rules of social cooperation', this can lead to emotional reactions, especially of resentment or vengefulness. The difference between these two emotions, in Barbalet's analysis, is itself instructive for present purposes.[180] Vengefulness seeks to *avenge* an injury suffered by the subject; it is driven by self-regard, and is an emotion rooted in power relations, aiming to redress in a punitive manner the subject's perceived dispossession. Resentment, by contrast, 'is driven by regard for an externally accepted set of standards, values or norms', and is 'an emotional apprehension of departure from acceptable, desirable, proper and rightful *outcomes and procedures*'[181] (that is, it may be triggered by both procedural and distributive deviations from what are perceived as acceptable norms). So stated, the congruence between Barbalet's analysis, the social psychological literature on (especially) procedural justice, and Lucas's philosophical analysis (neither of which is discussed by Barbalet) is truly striking. The social psychological literature emphasizes the real sense of unfairness, and the sense of diminution of oneself as a human (social) being, when *procedurally* (and regardless of the outcome) one is not treated with respect by authorities, when one is brushed aside and not given an opportunity to put one's case, or when the authority seems to act arbitrarily or with partiality (in other words, what Tyler and Blader call status recognition, the trustworthiness of authorities, and their neutrality[182]). For Lucas, an injustice 'betokens an absence of respect' and a feeling of being 'done down'. All of these things, one can see more clearly in the light of Barbalet's analysis, are seen by subjects as breaches of the basic ground rules of social existence. They are *perceived normative breaches*, and they lead quite naturally to

---

[179] Barbalet, n. 166 above, 142. The concept 'status', as used here, is not confined to stratificatory status: ibid., 143–4.

[180] Ibid., 136–8.

[181] Ibid., 138, emphasis added. Note however that initial resentment may lead subsequently to vengefulness. It should be observed that Barbalet's conceptual discussion of resentment seems deficient in apparently limiting 'the interactional basis of resentment' to a third party's gain in status which a social actor evaluates as undeserved (ibid., 137). As the IEP research showed, resentment can be felt where there is 'an emotional apprehension of departure from acceptable, desirable, proper and rightful outcomes and procedures' even where no third party gains in status.

[182] Tyler and Blader, n. 161 above.

resentment. Moreover, resentment, as previously indicated, can lead to less compliant behaviour.

Two particular features of the IEP research results are worth returning to in the light of this theoretical analysis of resentment; each will help to develop the analysis further, at any rate on a suggestive basis.

The first concerns the within-prison differentiation of results on the misbehaviour composite variable at two of the prisons, YOI and MaxSec. In each case, the results for the main part of the institution (the 'dispersal' wings at MaxSec, the 18+ wings at YOI) showed no significant difference from Time 1 to Time 2; but self-reported misbehaviour worsened significantly in the minority section of both institutions (the VPU at MaxSec, the juvenile wing at YOI: see Table 3:5). These results seem likely to be explicable by reference to specific resentments about unfair treatment in the respective minority sections of the two prisons. Statistically, the strongest result was at YOI, where the juvenile wing showed a very significant rise in self-reported misbehaviour. Relevant to the explanation of this finding seemed to be factors such as:

- a growing resentment among the juvenile population (who were much more numerous at Time 2 than at Time 1) about their relative disadvantages by comparison with young offenders over 18;[183]
- the existence of the daily points system in the juvenile wing, but not in the wings for older offenders, coupled with evidence that this system was sometimes used arbitrarily and as a control device by wing staff (see note 100 above);
- because the establishment had a higher proportion of juveniles at Time 2, staff seemed to shift the 'tone' of the operation of IEP from a balanced combination of positive encouragement

---

[183] See n. 98 above. In particular (i) juveniles were not allowed to smoke, and (ii) juveniles had, at the time of the research, only two levels, not three (n. 99 and Table 3:1B above), so were denied access to 'enhanced' privileges (such as pocket TVs) available to those aged 18+ on the enhanced level. The institution's justification for this latter policy was that juveniles usually served shorter sentences; they were unlikely to have access to the higher levels of private cash allowed to those aged 18+ on the enhanced level; and there was only a small number of juveniles in the YOI, so there would by definition be very few who would reach the enhanced level. However, after the end of our research fieldwork, the case for change was conceded and a third level was introduced for juveniles: n. 97 above.

and negative deterrence towards a heavier emphasis on the latter, particularly in the juvenile wing.[184]

Consistently with the above interpretation, examination of the results for the two parts of YOI on the four 'fairness and justice' composite variables showed that in each case the juvenile wing showed the greater deterioration in fairness perceptions from Time 1 to Time 2 (Table 3:4).

A very similar pattern of results was also evident with regard to the VPU and the main dispersal wings at MaxSec (see again Table 3:4). As noted in an earlier section, because in MaxSec IEP and other newly-introduced restrictive policies were often 'piloted' in the VPU, prisoners in that Unit had a sense that they were being treated as 'guinea pigs' in unwelcome experiments, despite their historically more compliant behaviour. Additionally, Table 3:4 shows that the greatest Time 1/Time 2 contrast between the two parts of MaxSec came in the 'relations with staff' composite variable (which showed an improvement in such relations on the main wings, but a sharp deterioration in the VPU). This finding is difficult to interpret confidently on the data available to the research team,[185] but speculatively one can hypothesize that the much heavier staff policing of the prison at Time 2 (see earlier section) was the subject of significantly greater resentment in the VPU. This could have been particularly the case since VPUs have almost never, within the dispersal system, been the sites of major security or control problems, yet at the time of the research VPU prisoners were—in the wake of two major escapes from dispersal prisons—as much subject to the new restrictive policies as those in the rest of the prison.[186]

'Resentment', in dictionary definition, is a feeling of 'bitterness or persistent hurt and indignation at something regarded as insult, injury, or injustice'.[187] I have suggested earlier[188] that it can be felt

---

[184] See, in this regard, the staff's 'care with a firm hand' philosophy: n. 95 above. It is possible that this became accentuated with the arrival of more juveniles, given the greater power differential between staff and juvenile offenders as opposed to offenders aged 18+.

[185] Because the process research at MaxSec was conducted relatively early, and well before the Time 2 outcome interviews.

[186] On the troubled history of the dispersal system, in terms of both escapes and control disturbances, see the references cited at n. 86 above.

[187] See n. 170 above.   [188] See n. 181 above.

even where no third party is involved. But it is perhaps worth recalling Lucas's comment that 'it is when I get hot under the collar about some specific piece of unfairness that . . . I really know what is getting my goat'.[189] Maybe there is nothing more specific, in this sense, than a feeling that one is being treated very unfairly *by comparison with a third party*, and perhaps this is what is particularly suggested by the data on internal differentiation at MaxSec and (especially) YOI.[190]

The second element of the IEP research results worth returning to at this stage concerns the BRU at CatC. What was in evidence in the functioning of this unit was a clash of two incompatible philosophies. Management and staff were determined to maintain the BRU within what they understood to be the logic of incentives and rational choice. Hence, if a prisoner did not improve his behaviour while in the BRU, he stayed there; and, as previously noted, there was a reluctance by staff to transfer such prisoners to another prison, even one of a higher security category, that being perceived as a 'reward' for bad behaviour. BRU prisoners often saw matters completely differently. A few refused to play the game at all, and regarded the BRU as grossly unjust. In their pride, they remained there for several months, with cell and sanitation destructions being not uncommon, in a pattern with which all prison governors will be familiar. Here we see resentment at perceived injustice being transmuted into open *defiance*. Since defiance has been the subject of important theoretical analyses elsewhere by distinguished criminologists,[191] I shall say very little specifically about it here. It would, however, I believe be universally acknowledged that our empirically-validated knowledge of the conditions under which defiance arises remains meagre.[192] The main point of introducing the matter at this stage of my argument is to emphasize—as few have previously

---

[189] Lucas, n. 167 above, 5.

[190] For the avoidance of doubt, my argument is that a third party's gain in status is not a necessary interactional component of resentment (cf. n. 181 above), but that the existence of such a third-party comparison may sharpen and exacerbate feelings of resentment.

[191] L.W. Sherman, 'Defiance, Deterrence and Irrelevance: A Theory of the Criminal Sanction' (1993) 30 *Journal of Research in Crime and Delinquency* 445; J. Braithwaite, *Restorative Justice and Responsive Regulation* (Oxford: Oxford University Press, 2002), 81ff.

[192] Sherman's interesting 'falsifiable hypothesis' about defiance is as follows: 'sanctions provoke *defiance* of the law (persistence, more frequent or more serious

done—that resentment is a different (and obviously less extreme) reaction from defiance; that we know little about the conditions which make it likely that resentment will turn into defiance; yet that resentment itself, without turning into defiance, may still lead to a withdrawal of co-operative behaviour by the prisoner, in a way that could itself defeat the intentions of schemes such as IEP. In addition, however, it is worth noting that when a pattern of defiant behaviour sets in, in a segregation unit or a BRU, it will never be solved by remaining strictly within the logics of incentives and disincentives. Experienced prison governors know that the most promising way to break the cycle of such behaviour is to try to re-engage with the recalcitrant prisoner on a *normative* basis, to bring him back in to some kind of (at least minimal) normative consensus from which constructive dialogue about the future can begin.[193] Thus the BRU (like segregation units, 'close supervision units' and the like in prison systems across the world) is ultimately testimony to the fact that a wise approach to prison control uses incentives as a part, but not the whole, of its armoury of control.[194] I shall develop this point shortly, in a discussion of the multifaceted and inter-actional character of compliant behaviour.

violations) to the extent that offenders experience sanctioning conduct as illegitimate, that offenders have weak bonds to the sanctioning agent and community, and that offenders deny their shame and become proud of their isolation from the sanctioning community': Sherman, n. 191 above, 448.

[193] Of course, some prisoners of this kind have the characteristics described by Toch and Adams as those of the 'disturbed-disruptive inmates' (DDI). That does not, however, preclude strategies of the kind described. Indeed, in their concluding chapter Toch and Adams comment that: '[b]ehavior control may, of course, in some instances constructively affect conduct. But we have recorded many instances in which this strategy has not worked, or has proved counterproductive. In such instances it would not be unreasonable to attempt a different strategy, which combines self-examination with the rehearsal of more effective approaches to life situations, including those one can test in the prison. We assume the prisoner can become a participant in this self-reform strategy': H. Toch and K. Adams, *Coping: Maladaptation in Prisons* (New Brunswick, NJ: Transaction Publishers, 1989), 267–8.

[194] See the conclusion by Wright that in prisons 'more structured, more authoritarian settings may engender more disruptive behavior': K.N. Wright, 'A Study of Individual, Environmental and Interactive Effects in Explaining Adjustment to Prison' (1991) 8 *Justice Quarterly* 217 at 235; see also Bottoms (1999), n. 31 above, 261–3. For research into close supervision units in England see E. Clare and K. Bottomley, *Evaluation of Close Supervision Centres*, Home Office Research Study 219 (London: Home Office, 2001).

Legitimacy

With colleagues, I have elsewhere argued for the view that questions of *legitimate authority* are central to the maintenance of order in prisons.[195] I shall not repeat those arguments here, but it is appropriate to note that in developing this approach we relied centrally on David Beetham's conceptual reconsideration of legitimacy;[196] and I want now to argue that Beetham's work is highly relevant to the present discussion.

For Beetham, the content of legitimacy beliefs and principles is extremely historically and culturally variable, but he argues that we can nevertheless identify a common underlying structure that is very general. That underlying structure has three dimensions or criteria, in terms of which the legitimacy of any actually existing distribution of power and resources can be expressed and evaluated. These criteria of legitimacy are, in any given specific social context, almost never perfectly fulfilled; hence, each dimension of legitimacy also has a corresponding form of non-legitimate power. Beetham's diagrammatic representation of this scheme is reproduced in Figure 3:2.

The three dimensions shown in Figure 3:2 roughly correspond to the traditional preoccupations of three different academic specialisms which have considered issues of legitimacy: first, lawyers (has power been legally acquired, and is it being exercised within the law?); next, political philosophers (are the power relations at issue morally justifiable?); and finally, social scientists (what are the actual beliefs of subjects about issues of legitimacy in that particular society?).[197] However, a central plank of Beetham's argument is that social scientists have been wrong to follow Max Weber[198] in defining legitimacy as simply belief in legitimacy on the part of the relevant social agents.[199] To adopt this view, Beetham argues, is to leave social science with no adequate means of explaining why subjects may acknowledge the legitimacy of the powerful in one social context, but not in another. Beetham accordingly suggests

---

[195] R. Sparks and A.E. Bottoms, 'Legitimacy and Order in Prisons' (1995) 46 *British Journal of Sociology* 45; Sparks, Bottoms, and Hay, n. 33 above, especially chapters 2 and 9.

[196] D. Beetham, *The Legitimation of Power* (London: Macmillan, 1991).

[197] Ibid., 4 ff.

[198] M. Weber, *Economy and Society* (Berkeley, Cal.: University of California Press, 1968).

[199] Beetham, n. 196 above, 6.

Criteria of legitimacy	Corresponding form of non-legitimate power
1. Conformity to rules (legal validity)	Illegitimacy (breach of rules)
2. Justifiability of rules in terms of shared beliefs	Legitimacy deficit (discrepancy between rules and supporting shared beliefs, absence of shared beliefs)
3. Legitimation through expressed consent	Delegitimation (withdrawal of consent)

Source: Beetham, n. 196 above, 20.

FIGURE 3:2. Beetham's Dimensions of Legitimacy

an alternative formulation of the social-scientific view of legitimacy—'a given power relationship is not legitimate because people believe in its legitimacy, but because it can be justified in terms of their beliefs'.[200] This may seem to introduce a rather fine distinction, but the alternative formulation is seen by Beetham as fundamental because it injects a crucial element of moral judgement into the definition.[201]

What is crucial about this reformulation is its emphasis upon the moral assessment by citizens of the rules and acts of persons in authority in the light of the *justifiability of those acts and rules in terms of the beliefs of citizens; and since those are normative beliefs, they are also normally based on shared beliefs in that society* (see the language of Beetham's second criterion of legitimacy: Figure 3:2). Shared normative beliefs do indeed vary widely across societies, both historically and at any given time (compare, for example,

[200] Ibid., 11.
[201] Additionally, Beetham suggests that the simple 'belief in legitimacy' view takes no account of those aspects of legitimacy that have little to do with beliefs at all, such as the authorities' conformity to pre-existing legal rules: ibid., 12.

contemporary Britain with contemporary Saudi Arabia). But in any given society, what is particularly damaging to the legitimacy of an authority is when it acts in ways contrary to the shared moral beliefs of that particular community.

This conceptual reformulation is crucial as the theoretical analysis of this section moves on from the first two concepts considered (fairness/unfairness; resentment) to the third (legitimacy). In this connection, it is also important to realize that what was occurring at the time of the initial implementation of IEP was extremely complex. The national government was not only introducing an incentives scheme, it was trying to rein in previous levels of privileges, and it believed it was politically and morally justified in promoting this change (see the speech by Michael Howard quoted earlier in this chapter). There were, therefore, two kinds of legitimacy at issue in this situation: the *internal* legitimacy of the new prison policies (including IEP) *vis-à-vis* the subject group (the prisoners), and the *external* legitimacy of altered prison policies *vis-à-vis* the wider audience of citizens at large. There was, also, a deliberate attempt by the national government to promote a policy change based on a *fresh set of normative perspectives*, that is to change (in certain respects) what Beetham calls the 'shared beliefs' of the society.

As we have seen, perceptions of unfairness, and emotions of resentment, tend to arise when a *perceived normative breach* has taken place; and these normative breaches can (among other possibilities) be based on breaches of the understood ground-rules of social existence in that particular social context. In the light of this background, it is instructive to consider carefully what happened at MaxSec, the prison in our sample where the advent of IEP was the most hotly contested. In this prison, the reining in of previous levels of privilege entitlement was widely regarded by prisoners as unfair, for it was indeed a departure from the ground-rules of their previous social life in the prison. But this departure was justified by governor-grades in the prison as constituting a set of new ground-rules introduced by a democratically elected government, which believed (almost certainly rightly) that they could carry public opinion with them on this particular issue. Overall, therefore, what was apparent in this prison was a temporary legitimacy deficit for management *vis-à-vis* the prisoners, trumped eventually by an appeal to a wider political legitimacy, which prisoners were in the end forced to accept.[202] The temporary legitimacy deficit could still have led for a time to worse behaviour by the prisoners, based on their feelings of injustice and resentment.[203] But these initial perceptions of unfairness could be successfully 'faced down' by the authorities in the light of their appeals to a wider political audience.

There were, however, many other claims of injustice by prisoners at the time of the implementation of IEP, and the eventual resolution of some of these claims was interestingly different from that described above. The key event in this respect was the publication on 28 January 2000 of a fresh national framework for incentives and earned privileges, superseding and replacing the original 1995 IG, and making a number of important modifications to the original scheme.[204] A few months prior to the official publication of these new guidelines, Alison Liebling had received a formal letter from Prison Service Headquarters, alerting her to the proposed changes in the scheme. These changes, it was stated, had been agreed 'in the light of [the Cambridge] research and other feedback . . .[205] since your study concluded'.[206] In particular, the letter continued, the modifications aimed to:

- standardize entries to prisons at the 'Standard' level (reducing unfairness to prisoners who may currently find themselves on basic through no fault of their own);
- ensure that the IEP schemes are fully differentiated from the formal disciplinary system and are not used as a pseudo punishment;

---

[202] Indeed, it is quite interesting that in the main wings at MaxSec staff–prisoner relations actually showed a significant improvement from Time 1 to Time 2, despite the traumas at the time of the introduction of IEP. It is possible, though this interpretation is somewhat speculative, that prisoners accepted the staff had been obliged to introduce the unwelcome changes to the regime, and were considered to have done so as reasonably as possible in the circumstances.

[203] An implication of this line of thought would, of course, be that worsened behaviour could have been temporary, and that a later measurement could have shown an improvement.

[204] *Incentives and Earned Privileges; Earned Community Visits and Compacts* (Prison Service Order 4000, 2000).

[205] The specific reference in the letter is to feedback from HM Inspectorate of Prisons and from local Boards of Visitors. See also Prison Reform Trust, n. 37 above.

[206] 'Incentives and Earned Privileges', letter from Linda Robinson to Alison Liebling, 7 June 1999.

- ensure that basic regimes are not equivalent to 'segregation/punish-ment' conditions but provide all statutory facilities to at least the minimum level specified;
- ensure that IEP schemes are more fully woven into the fabric of prison life and integrated with other initiatives such as sentence planning, anti-bullying, drugs free wings, etc.;
- ensure that evaluation processes are fair and just (that is, removing opportunities for undue and unfair influence by individual officers, ensuring adequate management oversight etc.).

What is striking about this list is that four of the five specified points (i.e. all except the fourth) amount to an admission that in certain respects the 1995 version of IEP had been operating unfairly in many prisons.[207] The prison authorities felt that they could no longer defend these practices, and were taking steps to improve them significantly. In Beetham's language, they had acknowledged a 'legitimacy deficit' in the operation of IEP, which they were seeking to correct. In so doing, they were of course also acknowledging the validity of one of the central findings of the Cambridge research.

So, what differentiated these claims of injustice (which were conceded) from the claims of injustice based on the reining in of privilege levels at MaxSec (which were faced down)? The answer seems straightforward in the light of Beetham's analysis. The claims that were conceded were based on principles of distribu-tive or procedural justice that were widely shared in society at large (prisoners arriving at a new prison and being put on basic 'through no fault of their own'; basic being used as a 'pseudo-punishment'; inconsistent and arbitrary decision-making by staff). These were *genuine legitimacy deficits*, which the prison authorities felt they had to correct; they could not adequately defend them in the court of public opinion. The reining in of privilege levels at MaxSec could, however, be faced down by appealing to a wider political constituency which did not regard this change as unfair.[208]

---

[207] The fourth point, although not directly about fairness, is also a concession that the 1995 IEP policy took insufficient account of Bosworth and Liebling's 1994 literature review (n. 28 above), and the 'complex model' to which it had drawn attention (see Figure 3:1).

[208] On similar issues see also Sparks, Bottoms, and Hay, n. 33 above, 329–36.

Conclusions I: The Interactional Character of Legal Compliance

In the introduction to this chapter, I indicated that I have sometimes used the results of the IEP research as an example when lecturing and writing about legal compliance. In drawing the chapter to a close, it is appropriate to return to that broad theme.

Figure 3:3 reproduces my provisional conclusions concerning the principal basic mechanisms underpinning legal compliance. The argument is that there are four such principal mechanisms, namely instrumental-prudential compliance; constraint-based compliance; normative compliance; and compliance based on habit or routine.[209] The IEP research excellently illustrates each of these mechanisms in operation. The incentives policy itself appeals to instrumental-prudential mechanisms. The legitimacy deficits in the way that IEP was implemented discouraged normative compliance, legitimacy being now well-established in the research literature as encouraging compliant behaviour on normative grounds.[210] The improvements to behaviour and order at CatC between Time 1 and Time 2 were largely attributable to a prison-based version of situational crime prevention, which is a type of constraint-based compliance.[211] And finally—although I have said very little about these results in this chapter[212]—there were important findings in the study about individual differences between prisoners, and their effects on behaviour and misbehaviour; these results relate to individual propensities, that is compliance or non-compliance based on habitual and routine patterns of behaviour.

What is crucial in understanding legally compliant behaviour, however, is not merely to formulate a reasonably precise taxonomy of the principal mechanisms of compliance, but also to specify how these mechanisms might interact with one another.[213] For example, successful situational crime prevention of the 'target hardening' variety has its immediate impact by (perforce) strengthening constraint-based compliance; but, as news of the strengthened defence

---

[209] Bottoms (2002), n. 160 above.

[210] See the references at n. 161 above.

[211] On situational crime prevention see Clarke, n. 124 above.

[212] But see nn. 119 and 145 above.

[213] On the importance of interactive effects in studying legal compliance see Bottoms (2002), n. 160 above, 31–3.

A. Instrumental/Prudential Compliance

    1. Incentives
    2. Disincentives

B. Constraint-Based Compliance

    1. Physical Constraints
       (a) Physical restrictions on individuals leading to compliance
       (b) Physical restrictions on accessibility of target
    2. Social-Structural Constraints

C. Normative Compliance

    1. Acceptance of or belief in social norm
    2. Attachment leading to compliance
    3. Legitimacy

D. Compliance Based on Habit or Routine

Source: Bottoms (2002), n. 160 above, 30.

FIGURE 3:3   An Outline of the Principal Mechanisms Underpinning Legally Compliant Behaviour

of the relevant target spreads among potential offenders, there may well also be a deterrent (instrumental) effect.

The principal contribution of the IEP research, in this context, is to illustrate a particular kind of interaction between instrumental and normative mechanisms. One example of instrumental-normative interaction is well known to those versed in the literature on deterrence: in summary, it is that *deterrence works best among these with strong normative bonds to law-abiding members of the community* (sometimes expressed as 'stakes in conformity').[214] The present study differs from that example in two ways: first, as regards instrumental mechanisms, it focuses on incentives rather than disincentives; and secondly, as regards normative mechanisms, it focuses on legitimacy rather than attachment.[215] We can formulate the interaction effect that is illustrated by the IEP research in something like the following language: *incentive-based policies may be partially or wholly undermined in their intended effects if they are administered in what the subjects of the policy regard as an unfair*

[214] Von Hirsch *et al.*, n. 79 above, sections 7 and 8.
[215] On legitimacy as a sub-type of normative compliance see Bottoms (2002), n. 160 above.

way, and especially if these perceptions can be shown to be justified in terms of widely-shared moral beliefs in the society in question.

When, on a previous occasion, I presented an earlier version of these arguments, I was asked by a senior colleague (paraphrasing) 'do you believe that a criminal policy cannot/ought never to be founded purely on rational choice theory, since perceptions of fairness and legitimacy will always have a significant effect in practice?' I was glad to be asked the question, and to have the opportunity to answer in the negative. My approach is, rather, akin to that of James Bohman, namely that rational choice theory can indeed 'explain phenomena in its own domain', but it is an 'incomplete theory of social action and . . . can remain vital only by incorporating other theories at different levels of explanation'.[216] Thus, *incentives policies in criminal justice can be successful*, but those who formulate them must always remember that legal compliance is multifaceted, and that an incentives policy, as operationalized, may well have interactive links with other potential mechanisms of compliance or non-compliance, notably those of fairness and legitimacy (see Figure 3:3). If unfairness in operation (for example arbitrary and inconsistent decision-making) can be avoided, then there is no reason to suppose that an incentives policy will fail. It is therefore certainly possible, in principle, that IEP itself, in its original 1995 implementation (that is, before the 2000 reformulation) could have been more successful in some prisons than it was in the five that were studied by the Cambridge research team.[217]

In relation to IEP in the five research prisons, we should note one final point. I have argued, I believe correctly, that instrumental mechanisms of compliance are in principle separable from normative mechanisms. But in the earlier section of this chapter on rational-choice theory, I asked questions such as 'was the information available on how to gain incentives sufficiently clear to prisoners?', and 'did rewards always follow from good behaviour, and downgrading from bad behaviour?'. The answers to these questions were not straightforwardly positive, and part of the reason for this was a

[216] Bohman n. 156 above, 225.

[217] Hence, there is no reason *in principle* to cast doubt on evaluations of IEP that have reported more positive results than those in the Cambridge research (such as that in Garth Prison: see G. Beck, 'Some Issues and Results from an Ongoing Evaluation of an Incentives and Earned Privileges System in a High Security Long Term Prison' (1997) 3 *Prison Research and Development Bulletin* 3).

degree of arbitrariness and inconsistency in the systems in practice, which sent out unclear messages to prisoners. From a strictly rational-choice perspective arbitrariness and inconsistency constitute inefficiency; but to those who are subjected to them, they are also often seen as unfair. Thus, certain kinds of *inefficiencies in a rational choice approach can themselves generate normative disengagement*, and perhaps even help to trigger a wider delegitimation of the authority.

Conclusions II: Research and Policy

I turn, finally, to the lessons that may be derived from the IEP research with regard to one of the central themes of this volume, that is, the relationship between research and criminal justice policy.

Roger Hood's stimulating contribution to the Radzinowicz Memorial Symposium in 2001 was entitled 'Criminology and Penal Policy: The Vital Role of Empirical Research'.[218] In an important passage in this paper, he articulated two key propositions. First, criminologists, 'in pursuing empirical research, especially when it is related to the evaluation of criminal justice systems and policies', should not work simply as 'technicians', but rather adopt a wider role, placing their evaluations within a broader theoretical, social, and political context.[219] But secondly:[220]

the voices of criminologists will be heard only if they can speak in their 'wider-ranging role' from a firm base of empirical research, and research that can make claims to be scientifically rigorous, in the sense that it is repeatable, reliable, and valid. This is what distinguishes criminology from other types of discourse about crime. Unless legitimacy can be claimed for this view, the 'criminologist' will be treated as just another person with an 'opinion' on the subject.

---

[218] R. Hood, 'Criminology and Penal Policy: The Vital Role of Empirical Research' in A.E. Bottoms and M. Tonry (eds.), *Ideology, Crime and Criminal Justice: A Symposium in Honour of Sir Leon Radzinowicz* (Cullompton: Willan Publishing, 2002).

[219] Ibid., 158. On the relationship between theory and empirical research in criminology see also A.E. Bottoms, 'The Relationship between Theory and Research in Criminology' in R.D. King and E. Wincup (eds.), *Doing Research in Crime and Justice* (Oxford: Oxford University Press, 2000).

[220] Hood, n. 218 above, 159.

As this chapter has illustrated, there is on occasion a far from straightforward relationship between researchers, on the one hand, and policy-makers and criminal justice managers, on the other hand. This is so even when—as in this instance—personal relationships among those involved remain throughout very cordial. Roger Hood's prescriptions on how criminologists should conduct themselves in these contexts are, in my judgement, absolutely correct. In the case of the IEP research, there were in retrospect two key moments in the research–policy interface. In the first (the research design stage), the research team declined to operate simply as 'technicians' (that is, to the narrow agenda of IEG 74/1995) but decided—with the at least tacit support of our Prison Service liaison personnel—to set the research within the broader theoretical understandings of prison life that had developed during a series of Cambridge research projects on the internal life of prisons.[221] This decision was, I believe, wholly justified by subsequent events; had we not taken this wider view, the 'fairness' agenda, so vital in the eventual research results, could not have been developed empirically in the way that it was.

The second key moment in the research–policy interface came in the year after our report was presented. As indicated earlier in this chapter, some of the principal empirical results were greeted with dismay by the research sponsors. It was a difficult time for the research team, but we held our ground, saying in effect: 'yes, the result is disappointing, but you paid us to carry out an independent empirical examination, and this is what we have found'. In such stand-offs, in the end the empirical research—unless it can be discredited on technical grounds—speaks for itself. And the research did eventually influence policy in the specific field of incentives and earned privileges, that is in its influence on the new Prison Service Order in 2000.[222]

At the end of the day, however, research results are more important if they can be legitimately generalized beyond their immediate context. My reason for writing about the IEP research in this volume is, therefore, only in part because of a continuing interest in prisons-based incentives policies. More generally, I would wish to claim that

---

[221] Sparks, Bottoms, and Hay, n. 33 above; Liebling (1992), n. 52 above; Liebling and Krarup, n. 52 above; Bosworth and Liebling, n. 28 above; Ahmad, n. 54 above.

[222] See n. 204 above.

the IEP research contributes significantly to continuing and important debates about the possibilities and the limits of rational-choice-
based criminal justice policies, and the ways in which they may
interact with issues of fairness and legitimacy. Whether or not I
have made out such a claim is, of course, for others to judge.

Part 2

The Historical Development of Criminology as a Basis for Criminal Justice Policy

4

Useful Knowledge? Debating the Role of Criminology in Post-war Britain

Lucia Zedner

The Discontents of Contemporary Criminology

Contemporary British criminology suffers from two salient sources of discontent. Both derive directly from the relationship between the discipline and the world of policy formation. First, it is divided between two irreconcilable conceptions of itself, roughly: criminology as an empirical, pragmatic, and purposive science versus criminology as a branch of critical social theory. Secondly, in the face of the ever-growing prominence given to crime and crime control, criminology appears impotent to have influence beyond the walls of the academy. Arguably, the conflicted nature of the discipline arises directly out of ambivalence about its relationship to the 'outside' world of policy. Perhaps criminology overstates its discontents. It certainly suffers from a peculiar preoccupation with its own ailments—to which, of course, this contribution also falls prey. More than one criminologist has commented on the 'sad evidence of chronic academic navel-watching'[1] amongst criminologists. And, if anything, this has grown worse.[2] Whatever the causes of its disgruntlement, there can be few disciplines whose leading

[1] A.E. Bottoms, 'Comment' on D. Downes, 'Promise and Performance in British Criminology' (1978) 29 *British Journal of Sociology* 503.

[2] Perhaps the most depressingly meaningless manifestation of this introspection is E. Cohen and D. Farrington, 'Who are the Most Influential Criminologists in the English-speaking World?' (1994) 34 *British Journal of Criminology* 204.

protagonists are so ready to denounce their common project as a failure.[3]

Those who call themselves criminologists have failed to agree about what criminology is, still less what it is for. And whilst diversity of thought, approach, and purpose are signs of a discipline's vitality, there exists a level of disagreement beyond which its practitioners can no longer happily co-exist. Whether this intellectual rift is as deep or as impassable as criminologists have led themselves to believe, and whether criminology is as lacking in influence as is commonly supposed, will be the subjects of this chapter. If these discontents are not soundly based, why have they arisen and from whence? My contention is that the causes are historical in origin, and it is to the history of criminology in post-war Britain that we must look to understand the sources of its present fractures and perceived failure. Before turning to this history, I will sketch briefly the nature of its present discontents.

Rival Conceptions of Criminology

Even to talk of criminology presumes a disciplinary coherence that its multiple historical manifestations seem to belie. These include classical and positivist criminology, penology, and penal theory, the various sociologies of deviance, criminologies of the state (Marxist, radical, and critical), left and right realism, feminist criminology, victimology, studies in criminal justice, and, more recently, in risk, trust, and security. Nor has it had the benefit of an enduring institutional context.[4] It has been practised and taught in departments (and their respective degree programmes) of medicine, psychology, sociology, social administration, urban planning, law, and, only recently, in dedicated departments of criminology and criminal justice. Lacking coherence of founding assumptions, approach, methodology, or institutional setting, it is questionable whether the term discipline properly applies to criminology. Though its practitioners share a substantive interest in crime and

[3] J. Young 'The Failure of Criminology' in R. Matthews and J. Young (eds.), *Confronting Crime* (London: Sage, 1986); S. Cohen, *Against Criminology* (New Brunswick, NJ: Transaction Books, 1988); C. Sumner, *The Sociology of Deviance: An Obituary* (Buckingham: Open University Press, 1994) 300.

[4] Of the sort that Abbott argues is essential to the flourishing of disciplines: A. Abbott, *Chaos of Disciplines* (Chicago, Ill.: University of Chicago Press, 2001) 122–31.

its control,[5] this alone is not sufficient to distinguish it from other disciplines. As Ericson has argued (this volume at 57), '[p]ure criminology is simply a branch of sociology, above policy concerns'. In this observation lies the clue to its distinctive character. What distinguishes criminology from sociology proper is its historical engagement with policy. Ericson goes so far as to define criminology as 'an academic field devoted to the study of policy' (this volume at 6). Accepting this definition, I would argue nonetheless that the appropriate manner of this devotion has been one of the most contested issues in the discipline's development.

The perceived polarity between 'useful' empirical, pragmatic, policy-orientated, or evaluative criminological research and abstract, theoretical, radical, critical, and from the policy point of view therefore 'useless', criminological knowledge has been a defining characteristic of debate within criminology in the post-war period.[6] It mirrors a gulf in criminologists' self-conception of their individual role—roughly between those who see their purpose as being to inform policy and those who see their primary function as interpreting and explaining changes in the governance of crime (rather than informing or promoting those changes).[7] Crudely put, policy-orientated researchers tend to define their work as pragmatic, feet on the ground, and purposive.[8] They seek knowledge not just for its own sake but to the extent that it has practical application. Equally crudely, more theoretically minded researchers regard criminological knowledge as something to be obtained for its own sake, and see their endeavours as analytical and interpretative rather than functional. Although their focus is no less on policy development, the worth of their labours is validated above all by acknowledgement within the academy, rather than by its take-up in the policy arena. These multi-layered divisions have riven colleagues one from

[5] S. Walklate, *Understanding Criminology* (Buckingham: Open University Press, 1998) 13.

[6] How one describes this polarity depends, of course, on where one's allegiances lie. It has been variously described as lying between administrative and radical criminology, subsidized and unfunded research, and official and academic research.

[7] Or as Pawson and Tilley observe, criminological labour is segregated: 'theorists theorize, ethnographers empathize, statisticians soothsay, and so on': R. Pawson and N. Tilley, 'What Works in Evaluation Research?' (1994) 34 *British Journal of Criminology* 291.

[8] R.V.G. Clarke and D.B. Cornish, *Crime Control in Britain: A Review of Policy Research* (Albany, NY: State University of New York Press, 1983).

another, created intellectual rivalry, and even hostility. If 'British criminologists are no longer incessantly at one another's throats',[9] the sense of schism persists none the less.

Whereas many criminologists uncritically accept this division of labour and define their endeavours accordingly, Roger Hood has consistently sought to challenge the empirical/pragmatic versus theoretical/critical distinction. He takes issue with the line drawn by Garland and Sparks between the criminologist as 'a kind of specialist underlabourer, a technical specialist' and their 'more critical, ... more public, more wide-ranging role'.[10] He argues that the very claim of the criminologist to an authority greater than that of another person with an opinion on the subject lies precisely in the firm base of his opinion in empirical, 'scientifically rigorous' research.[11] And he insists that 'the "two possibilities", the empirical and the discursive must not ... be regarded as a division of labour: for one cannot be done convincingly without the other'.[12] Roger Hood is particularly critical of criminologists who assert the truth of a particular position, yet who are unwilling (principally for ideological reasons) to undertake the research necessary to substantiate or disprove that position.[13] For example, criminologists have, historically, tended to be sceptical about deterrence. They are quick to dismiss it as an ideological cover for punitivism, and reluctant to undertake the detailed statistical enquiry necessary to establish

[9] P. Rock, 'The Social Organization of British Criminology' in M. Maguire *et al.* (eds.), *Oxford Handbook of Criminology* (Oxford: Oxford University Press, 1994) 142.

[10] R. Hood, 'Criminology and Penal Policy: The Vital Role of Empirical Research' in A.E. Bottoms and M. Tonry (eds.), *Ideology, Crime and Criminal Justice* (Cullompton: Willan, 2002) 158. Hood is here quoting D. Garland and R. Sparks, 'Criminology, Social Theory and the Challenge of Our Times' in D. Garland and R. Sparks (eds.), *Criminology and Social Theory* (Oxford: Oxford University Press, 2000) 18.

[11] Hood, n. 10 above, 159.

[12] Ibid. Hood's thinking suggests a less dogmatic conception of the discipline than that of his mentor Sir Leon Radzinowicz, who insisted: 'we should not allow ourselves to be intimidated by those who contrast, with a supercilious air, so-called basic or pure research with applied research ... on closer examination attempts to distinguish between "criminology proper" and "administrative criminology" fail to reveal any difference in substance. Rather they convey an unattractive air of condescension': L. Radzinowicz, *Adventures in Criminology* (London: Routledge, 1999) 457–8. Radzinowicz himself tended to look down on the 'vague pretensions' of his more theoretically minded colleagues: at 223.

[13] Hood, n. 10 above, 161.

whether different penalties deter, under what conditions, and in respect of which categories of offenders.[14]

The corollary of Hood's insistence that theory be tested through research is, of course, that research itself is dependent on theory. As Pawson and Tilley conclude: 'research can be no more sophisticated than the theory which underlies it. The same, come to think of it, goes for policy making.'[15] Far from being dichotomously arrayed, policy research and theoretical enquiry are at best heavily interdependent. Only bad research and poor theory can claim independence of each other. None the less, there can be little doubt that, historically, this self-inflicted schism has served as an inhibition against exactly the marriage between research and theory that Roger Hood, for one, would like to see occur.

The Impotence of Criminology

Since its founding, criminology has taken its power to influence as a key, and at certain times and in certain places *the* key, evidence of its flourishing.[16] Paradoxically, perhaps, this preoccupation with criminology's wider influence is not confined to those who define themselves as policy-researchers.[17] Despite their rejection of instrumental conceptions of their discipline, theoretically minded criminologists are also quick to castigate themselves and their colleagues for their collective failure to inform penal change. The pressures to policy relevance appear to be both external and self-imposed. Even those most resolutely committed to theoretical approaches are swayed by 'the lure of relevance',[18] not merely under externally driven pressures to obtain funding. And yet, it is not self-evident why any discipline should judge its worth according to its

[14] On the poverty of deterrence research see A. von Hirsch, A.E. Bottoms, E. Burney, and P.-O. Wikström, *Crime Deterrence and Sentencing Severity: An Analysis of Recent Research* (Oxford: Hart Publishing, 1999).

[15] Pawson and Tilley, n. 7 above, 306.

[16] There are of course exceptions: see e.g. R. Hogg: 'the effects of criminology need not be measured only using a barometer of progress towards a crime-free society'. Hogg advocates a healthy ambivalence toward 'such confident enlightenment projects': R. Hogg, 'Crime, Criminology and Government' in P. Walton and J. Young (eds.), *The New Criminology Revisited* (Basingstoke: Palgrave, 1998) 158.

[17] See I. Loader, 'Criminology and the Public Sphere: Arguments for Utopian Realism', in ibid.

[18] K. Laster, 'The Lure of Relevance' (1994) 27 *The Australian and New Zealand Journal of Criminology* 3–4.

influence on policies developed in respect of the phenomenon studied. There is no absolute reason why the ability of criminology to inform or influence policy-making should be taken as a measure of success; any more than one would judge Durkheim by his influence on suicide levels.

Given the extraordinary expansion of the discipline over recent decades, it is difficult to concur with the conclusion that criminology has failed. Yet the sense of failure persists. And Roger Hood has not been immune from it: 'most developments in penal policy over the last decade have emerged not through the influence of criminological ideas or from the application of findings from research ... but from ideological and political considerations fuelled by populist concerns and impulses.'[19] The sense of failure is, if anything, exacerbated by the parallel vigour with which the criminological enterprise within the academy has grown.[20] Take one recent analysis of the discipline's health: 'the bullishness and even boastfulness that accompanies the apparent vitality of criminology as an academic discipline ... is at odds with criminology's more limited success in shaping the public discussion of "its" issues and its faltering influence on public policy and decision making.'[21]

That, as criminology flourishes within universities, its influence outside appears to decline is not so paradoxical as may first appear. As Petersilia has argued, '[t]he potential for policy "irrelevance" is inherent in the scientific advancement of which we are justly proud. It is also inherent in how we are trained, how we do our research, how we communicate our results, and how we are rewarded.'[22] Junior academics seeking tenure, and more established scholars seeking the recognition of their peers, are not rewarded for the impact their work has on policy, and certainly not for publication in policy papers.[23] Indeed to publish in practitioner journals, to engage in action research, or the training of criminal justice officials

[19] R. Hood, 'Penal Policy and Criminological Challenges in the New Millennium' (2001) 34 *The Australian and New Zealand Journal of Criminology* 1. In this article he returns to what has clearly been a matter of longstanding concern. See R. Hood, 'Some Reflections on the Role of Criminology in Public Policy' [1987] *Crim. L.R.* 527.

[20] T. Jefferson and J. Shapland, 'Criminal Justice and the Production of Order and Control' (1994) 34 *British Journal of Criminology* 265 at 283–4.

[21] Garland and Sparks, n. 10 above, 3.

[22] J. Petersilia, 'Policy Relevance and the Future of Criminology' (1991) 29 *Criminology* 8.

[23] On this point see Young and Sanders (this volume).

is to call into question the scholarly status of one's work. In short, the desire of criminologists to secure the respect of their peers according to academic criteria of pursuing basic research appears, on the face of it, irreconcilable with their simultaneous desire to influence policy formation.

Understood this way, the growing irrelevance of criminology (if indeed it is such) arises partly because, not in spite, of its flourishing within the academy. As opportunities for academic promotion and fora for intellectual engagement proliferate, the criteria of academic excellence hold increasing sway. The growth of academic criminology distances it from its policy-led roots; strengthens its scientific status as a 'pure' discipline (as opposed to a body of applied knowledge); and isolates it increasingly from the need to seek validation through intercourse with or influence upon practitioners. As Roger Hood has pointed out, it is easy to overstate the standing that criminology now has within universities.[24] And to the extent that it is still seeking to attain academic credibility, it simply cannot risk the appellation of hired hand to the policy analyst.[25]

Before we can begin to diagnose the sources of criminology's supposed impotence, we need some measure by which to estimate its influence. As one former Home Office researcher has observed: 'one problem in specifying the relationship of research to policy is that yesterday's research becomes today's accepted wisdom'.[26] Tracing the historic sources of that wisdom is not only difficult, it may not even be in the policy-makers' interests. Another problem is the assumption of a simple, unilinear causal relationship between the criminological enterprise and the formation of policy. In practice, even the most rarefied of academic criminology is influenced by the political and policy environment in which it is conducted. In short, it is informed by, quite as much as it informs, policy developments. Given the two-way traffic between the academy and the realm of policy, it is often difficult to ascertain whence ideas sprang or from what materials the building blocks of policy development were hewn.

[24] Hood, n. 19 above, 161.

[25] On similar dilemmas faced by criminological colleagues in Australia see G. Geiss, 'This Sort of Thing Isn't Helpful: The Dilemmas of the Australian Institute of Criminology' (1994) 27 *The Australian and New Zealand Journal of Criminology* 295.

[26] R. Tarling, 'Research, Politics and Criminal Justice' (1986) 25 *The Howard Journal of Criminal Justice* 113.

Criminologists are never happier than when identifying problems and crises. Arguably it is a psychological interest in the darker side of human nature and society that draws them to the discipline. No wonder then that they see ideological crisis in the legitimacy of the criminal process, material crisis in the conditions of the penal estate, and moral crisis in the reactions of the public.[27] They are prone also to seeing their discipline as being in crisis.[28] In what follows I will reject the suggestion that criminology is in crisis. By analysing debates about the role of criminology in post-war Britain, I will argue that our present discontents arise principally from a failure of historical understanding.

A Short History of Present Discontents

All disciplines are shaped by their history. For more established disciplines, that history is so long and so complex it is scarcely possible to excavate the key turns, institutional developments, and decisive individual contributions that shape their evolution. But criminology is a young discipline and its brief life makes it possible to examine how history has influenced its present configuration. Several versions of the intellectual history of criminology can be told. One is as a series of paradigm shifts from positivism through the sociology of deviance to the new criminologies and, later, studies in criminal justice to 'cultural studies' of crime control.[29] Another is as a succession of political allegiances. Roughly speaking, conservatism dominated the immediate post-war period of reconstruction and the emerging 'affluent society'; liberalism the progressive revolution of the 1960s; radicalism the 1970s; and, depending on one's view, some combination of neo-liberalism and conservatism the Thatcher/Reagan era of the 1980s and beyond.[30] Debates about paradigm shifts and periodization dominate the intellectual history

[27] e.g., M. Cavadino and J. Dignan, *The Penal System* (London: Sage, 2002), chap. 1.

[28] Roger Hood included: 'the relationship between criminology as an academic discipline and penal policy makers is also facing a crisis': Hood, n. 19 above. See also Jock Young's lament that 'it would be difficult to exaggerate the crisis of criminology at this time': Young, n. 3 above, 5.

[29] D. Downes, 'Promise and Performance in British Criminology' (1978) 29 *British Journal of Sociology* 483.

[30] R.R. Sullivan, 'The Schizophrenic Self: Neo-liberal Criminal Justice' in K. Stenson and R.R. Sullivan (eds.), *Crime, Risk and Justice; The Politics of Crime Control in Liberal Democracies* (Cullompton: Willan Publishing, 2001) 29.

of the discipline.[31] Fascinating as they are, my historical interest here is more constrained. I want to ask two historical questions. First, from when and for what reasons did the dichotomous arrangement of the discipline between 'underlabourers' and 'theorists' emerge? And secondly, why, how, and in what measure has the power of criminology to inform policy development come to define the discipline's role?[32] The two questions are not entirely separable. The dichotomy that is the subject of the first question arises directly from differing conceptions of what the discipline is for and what its relationship to the world of policy should be; whilst different conceptions of criminology's purpose inform arguments about how best it is to be achieved.

In attempting to answer these questions, I shall confine myself to the analysis of developments in post-war Britain. Obviously, criminology has a much longer and larger history,[33] but it is possible to argue that British criminology consolidated itself only in the middle years of the last century. Focusing on this period, it is possible to reconnect accounts of dominant paradigms and political allegiances to underlying structural changes in the way the subject was conceived, supported, and sustained. Such an account acknowledges the importance of individual contributions, particular events, and institutional developments,[34] but suggests that their import can be understood only by excavating the deeper structures that constrained the discipline's intellectual development. Recognizing the limits of the structuralist account, I will also attempt to identify those points of rupture or discontinuity that ushered in radical

---

[31] L. Radzinowicz, *In Search of Criminology* (London: Heinemann, 1961); D. Garland, 'The Criminal and his Science' (1985) 25 *British Journal of Criminology* 109; P. Rock (ed.), *A History of British Criminology* (Oxford: Oxford University Press, 1988); D. Garland, 'Of Crimes and Criminals: The Development of Criminology in Britain' in Maguire *et al.* (eds.), n. 9 above, 11.

[32] In a way that was not true of the sociology of deviance.

[33] Comparative analysis of the parallel development of the discipline in different countries would be fascinating but is beyond the scope of this chapter.

[34] e.g., the establishment of research institutes, changes in patterns of funding, the growth of the research community in and, later, outside government. As Garland has argued, '[i]ntellectual history can never be detached from the social and cultural settings in which ideas and sentences occur, and this is particularly true in respect of criminology which is so deeply marked by its institutional location': D. Garland, 'Criminological Knowledge and Its Relation to Power: Foucault's Genealogy and Criminology Today' (1992) 32 *British Journal of Criminology* 414.

changes in the way criminology was perceived and performed. My hope is that this historical analysis will reveal the origins of criminology's present discontents and also make manifest the constraints operating upon contemporary conceptions of criminology.

Founding the British Criminological Establishment

The (always hypothetical) standard account rightly recognizes Sir Leon Radzinowicz at Cambridge, Hermann Mannheim at the LSE, and Max Grünhut at Oxford as the founders of modern British criminology. And much effort has gone into identifying the extent and nature of their contribution to its development.[35] More interesting for our purposes is the underlying intellectual framework or, as some would have it, 'discursive formations' that shaped their world view. Although they could hardly be described as engaged upon a close or collaborative venture, they shared a common vision of the discipline as scientific, practical, empirical, and purposive. Its purpose was, above all, to secure by scientific investigation a body of knowledge about crime and criminals that would provide the foundations of informed policy development. Their legacy was a curious marriage of Continental positivism and English empiricism that was mutually reinforcing in its faith in 'science'.

Of the vital importance of pursuing criminological knowledge as a basis for policy formation, Radzinowicz was, to the end of his life, convinced.[36] In part, then, the conception of the discipline as useful knowledge was self-imposed by its founders. But environmental, institutional, and political factors were also important in promoting this utilitarian conception. The entrenchment of criminology as an academic discipline in post-war Britain is inseparable from its relation to the founding of the welfare state. Criminology, as Garland and Sparks have observed, 'developed as part of a governmental response to a specific problem of order... a small part of the social solution to the problems of industrial society'.[37]

Institutionally, criminology owes its birth to the commitment made in the Government White Paper, *Penal Practices in a Changing*

---

[35] Not least, reflexively, by Radzinowicz himself: Radzinowicz, n. 12 above. See also contributions by L. Radzinowicz, J.P. Martin, and D. Downes in Rock (ed.), n. 31 above, 35–44.

[36] Radzinowicz, n. 12 above, Chapter 18.

[37] Garland and Sparks, n. 10 above, 12.

Society,[38] to fund both an internal research programme within the Home Office and independent academic research as an essential part of criminal justice policy. The vital role of the then Home Secretary, R.A. Butler, in promoting research as a basis for informed policy development has been vigorously attested to by Radzinowicz.[39] But his success is attributable also to cross-party political support for the funding of criminological research. This broad political commitment was underpinned by a generalized faith in scientific discovery as the solution to modern ills. Drawing direct, and revealing, parallels with the importance of research in the fields of science and technology, the White Paper called not merely for expanded funding but for the creation of structures that would provide a permanent institutional basis for research. Offering no prospect of funding for theoretical work, its purpose in promoting criminological research was transparently instrumental. It was thought that 'the expense incurred would be easily recoverable through the considerable reduction of crime that would be achieved through the application of the findings of such research'.[40] Radzinowicz's own view was that the search for the causes of crime was a 'sterile' and fiscally driven endeavour.[41] None the less, the belief that criminology could solve the crime problem was essential in securing political, and therefore financial, support. As the Home Secretary, Lord Butler, observed, the case for funding research relied directly upon the promise of reducing the vast social costs of crime and law enforcement: 'the money spent on research...could be expected to earn "enormous dividends", not least by reducing crime'.[42] This faith in the ameliorative potential of research appeared to presume that it was possible to discover both the causes of crime and the means of its treatment. And yet, perhaps paradoxically, Butler identified as one of the strengths of the early research 'that from the start it has recognised the elusiveness of finding the causes of crime or effective measures to

---

[38] Home Office, *Penal Practices in a Changing Society*, Cmnd 645 (London: HMSO, 1959).

[39] 'I firmly believe that it would have been impossible to seek out another prominent political figure of the ruling party who at that time would have evinced the desire and the courage to be the captain of such a hazardous enterprise': Radzinowicz, n. 12 above, 169.

[40] Ibid., 445.

[41] Ibid., 441.

[42] R.A. Butler, 'The Foundation of the Institute of Criminology in Cambridge' in R. Hood (ed.), *Crime, Criminology and Public Policy* (London: Heinemann, 1974) 2.

combat it'.[43] Curiously, criminology was first promoted to achieve goals that, in all probability, neither its promoters nor its practitioners believed possible.

Given that both Grünhut and Mannheim were approaching retirement, leaving Radzinowicz and a handful of other researchers, the importance of Butler's decision, to fund research both within the Home Office and more importantly outside, should not be underestimated. Without this commitment, the continued development of academic criminology within the universities appeared at the time to be under threat. That the nature of the commitment being made, and the conception of criminological research it espoused, was narrowly instrumental was clear. And that the first head of the Home Office Research Unit, T.S. Lodge, was neither a criminologist nor a sociologist but an actuarial statistician confirms this instrumentalism, not least, as a response to bureaucratic concern about the inadequacies of existing criminal statistics. Lodge's appointment[44] also played a major part in the Unit's future orientation toward the collation of 'authoritative' quantitative data. A later comment by Lodge, on the sharp line drawn between data and its interpretation, illustrates the prevailing mentality: 'the only restriction placed on Research Unit staff . . . has been that they were not usually allowed to add to research reports expositions of their personal views, as distinct from conclusions derived from the research being reported combined with earlier authentic research. It may well be claimed that this has positive advantages, for it is not always easy, in reading academic publications to which this restriction does not apply, to see precisely where reasonable deductions from the data stop and the personal views of the author begin.'[45]

Understanding this mentality is crucial to understanding the intellectual environment in which academic criminology was founded. Lodge's comments are founded on assumptions about the hardness of hard data; the force of deductive reasoning; and the partiality of 'academic' interpretation that underpinned the aspiration to scien-

---

[43] R.A. Butler, 'The Foundation of the Institute of Criminology in Cambridge' in R. Hood (ed.), *Crime, Criminology and Public Policy* (London: Heinemann, 1974) 9.

[44] Together with that of the brilliant statistician Leslie Wilkins as Deputy Statistical Advisor to the Home Office. See the account in J.P. Martin, 'The Development of Criminology in Britain 1948–60' in Rock (ed.), n. 31 above, 40–1.

[45] T.S. Lodge, 'The Founding of the Home Office Research Unit' in R. Hood (ed.), *Crime, Criminology and Public Policy* (London: Heinemann, 1974) 11–24 at 22.

tific detachment of Home Office research at the time. In part it reflected bureaucratic doubts about the detachment and rigour of academic research. In part it created a pragmatic division of labour. Lodge recognized an obligation on the Home Office Research Unit to undertake 'dry and tedious research that universities would not always be willing to carry out'.[46] Ironically, however, in thus institutionalizing this division of labour, the Home Office fostered a breach that was to continue to divide criminology up to the present.

The breach was further entrenched by the expectations placed upon the Home Office Research Unit. It was to undertake *ad hoc* research on demand; to provide data needed to answer parliamentary questions; to provide facts as required by civil servants in the development of policy; to respond to requests for information by Royal Commissions, departmental committees, and other bodies of enquiry. All these demands took priority over its own internal research programme and limited its ability to develop an independent research agenda.[47] As enduring structural constraints, they were pivotal in framing what has come to be labelled, often somewhat derisively, 'administrative criminology'.[48]

Despite official reservations about the 'amateurism' and lack of 'objectivity' of academic research, the White Paper's promise to promote external (i.e. university-based) research was quickly fulfilled. In 1959 the first university-based Institute of Criminology in Britain was established at the University of Cambridge.[49] Under the powerful direction of Sir Leon Radzinowicz it set about a determinedly scientific programme of research—'[o]ur duty was to examine the many aspects of the subject-matter in a manner as dispassionate and objective as possible'.[50] Political allegiances were not merely suppressed but their very expression outlawed. And yet, despite these strictures and its avowed apoliticism, it is clear that the Institute's research programme took its very *raison*

---

[46] Ibid., 22.

[47] In the longer term, the Unit fought to overcome these strictures and has been remarkably proactive in determining its own research agenda.

[48] A term applied both to Home Office research and to research undertaken by academic criminologists funded by government and working under similar constraints: see Walklate, n. 5 above, 42–4.

[49] One of its very first Ph.D students was a young sociology graduate from the London School of Economics, Roger Hood.

[50] Radzinowicz, n. 12 above, 199.

d'être from the political framework of post-war social democratic welfarism. It was ideologically configured also by the accompanying belief that social problems were best solved by centralized bureaucratic endeavour to secure rational solutions informed by expert knowledge. Although situated within the University of Cambridge, the Institute appears to have lacked many of the ordinary features of academic life. Only one of its founding staff had had an academic background, few staff seminars were held, and 'general discussion was in short supply'.[51] It is hardly surprising, therefore, that one of the three Assistant Directors of Research, J.P. Martin, recalled 'the Institute in its early days was a centre of criminological research but not of criminological thought'.[52]

The Cambridge Institute's early years coincided with the heyday of the post-war welfare state: the highpoint of modernism and its confidence in the capacity of the state for social engineering.[53] Faith in the power of scientific knowledge as the lynchpin of this grand project was shared and promoted by the scientists themselves. This faith was rewarded by historically low levels of crime, an achievement that was readily credited to the research informed policies of the welfare state.[54] But in the 1960s, as crime rates began, seemingly inexorably, to rise, many of the presumptions of the criminological project were thrown into doubt. As Jock Young has observed: 'all of the factors which should have led to a drop in delinquency, if mainstream criminology were even half-correct, were being ameliorated and yet precisely the opposite effect was occurring'.[55] It is not clear how far this 'aetiological crisis', as Young tags it,[56] threatened the sense of purpose prevailing in Cambridge and within the Home Office Research Unit.[57] What is clear is that it was a major factor

[51] Martin, n. 44 above, 43.   [52] Ibid., 43.

[53] D. Garland, *The Culture of Control: Crime and Social Order in Contemporary Society* (Oxford: Oxford University Press, 2001).

[54] Ibid., 33.

[55] Young, n. 3 above, 5–6.

[56] J. Young, 'Radical Criminology in Britain' in Rock (ed.), n. 31 above, 167.

[57] Stanley Cohen, for one, certainly doubted the impact upon them: 'for the most part the institutional foundations of British Criminology remain intact and unaltered': S. Cohen, 'Footprints on the Sand: A Further Report on Criminology and the Sociology of Deviance in Britain' in M. Fitzgerald, G. McLennan, and J. Pawson (eds.), *Crime and Society: Readings in History and Theory* (London: Routledge & Kegan Paul, 1981) 236.

in the emergence of radically different competing conceptions of the criminological project.

The Emergence of Competing Paradigms

If the defining moments in the birth of 'modern' British criminology were the setting up of the Home Office Research Unit, the establishment of the Cambridge Institute of Criminology,[58] and, in 1966, the establishment of the Penal Research Unit at the University of Oxford under the direction of Max Grünhut's successor Nigel Walker; the key moment in the emergence of a rival conception of the discipline was undoubtedly the first National Deviancy Conference held at York in 1968.[59] It was here that sociologists of deviance and the forerunners of radical, critical, left realist, and later feminist and post-modern criminologies came together for the first time. So influenced was British criminology by the eclectic American sociologies of deviance (such as labelling theory, subcultural theory, and social disorganization theory), it has been described as 'an off-shore laboratory for the distillation of ideas fermented in the U.S.A.'.[60] The expansion of criminology within the universities had weakened the imperative of policy-relevance and brought with it a new imperative to adopt the intellectual aspirations of academic endeavour. The new sociologies of deviance were self-consciously theoretical, critical, and oppositional. They challenged the prevailing deterministic and individualistic understanding of crime and exposed the costs of correctionalist penal policies. Instead they sought variously to understand crime from the perspective of the controlled; to invest deviant action with meaning and rationality; and to replace the cosy consensus of welfarism with radical pluralism and differential definitions of normality.[61] The first National Deviancy Conference was convened as a deliberate break with the 'positivist methods and functionalist orthodoxy of much British sociology' and it ushered in a period of extraordinary creativity and productivity.[62] It has been described by one of its participants as 'the academic counterpart to

---

[58] Appointed Secretary to the Institute, Assistant Director of Research, and Director of Post-Graduate Studies in 1967, Roger Hood 'played a major role in the life of the Institute as a whole': Radzinowicz, n. 12 above, 240–1.

[59] D. Downes, 'The Sociology of Crime and Social Control in Britain 1960–1987' in Rock (ed.), n. 31 above, 45.

[60] Ibid., 46.   [61] Young, n. 3 above, 7–8.

[62] Downes, n. 59 above, 47–8.

the Big Bang'.[63] Even a former Head of the Home Office Research Unit acknowledged it as 'a turning point'.[64]

Radzinowicz dismissed the covert decision to found the National Deviancy Conference by a group of criminologists attending the mainstream 'National Conference' in Cambridge as the work 'of a group of naughty schoolboys playing a nasty game on their stern headmaster'.[65] Certainly this breakaway venture reflected growing frustration at the perceived dominance of the mainstream criminological agenda by the Home Office. But, whilst we may sympathize with Radzinowicz's sense of betrayal, it is hard to comprehend his denial of the importance of this event in the discipline's history. As Sparks has commented, 'Radzinowicz's rare but deep failure of perception on this point was amply repaid in the same coin and he came to be represented on a number of occasions as a more two-dimensional and conservative figure than was ever really just'.[66] Radzinowicz remained openly hostile to 'complex, long and expensive investigations with the self-assigned purpose of unravelling the origins of crime and constructing broad, flamboyant "theories"'.[67] Given the relatively small and intimate nature of the criminological academy at that time, it is not surprising that the York mutiny was read as a personal rebuff. And it may be partly for this reason that the magnitude of the intellectual schism opening up within criminology was not readily recognized.

The resistance of leading mainstream criminologists to the challenge posed by the sociology of deviance was mirrored also in the Home Office. A former head of the Research and Planning Unit, John Croft observed that 'the assault on orthodox criminological research by the new criminology...hardly deflected it from its course.... It is fair to say that research which concentrates on the solution of problems is likely to be parsimonious in the use of

[63] Rock, n. 9 above, 134.

[64] J. Croft, 'Criminological Research in Britain' in N. Morris and M. Tonry (eds.), *Crime and Justice: An Annual Review of Research* (Chicago, Ill.: University of Chicago Press, 1983) 269.

[65] Radzinowicz, n. 12 above, 229.

[66] R. Sparks' review of Sir Leon Radzinowicz *Adventures in Criminology* (1999) 39 *British Journal of Criminology* 452, at 455.

[67] Radzinowicz, n. 12 above, 223. And it is perhaps not surprising that, in turn, he 'had sometimes to bear stoically epitaphs of stodginess, anti-intellectualism, theoretical retardedness and even of narrow-mindedness which were, much too often, attached to me': ibid.

theoretical concepts.'[68] Far from feeling embattled by the challenge of the new theories, Croft appeared ever more confident: '[t]he wounds inflicted by the radical attack have not festered, and if they have not entirely healed, the patient has by inoculation gained a degree of immunity. Because of, and in spite of, this, criminological research is healthier, if perhaps a trifle complacent.'[69] Arguably Croft and his colleagues shared, and in sharing underestimated, this complacency. The 'radical attack' was no mere jab but a major *coup d'état*, after which 'mainstream' criminology could never again claim dominance within the academy.[70] Even if the criminological establishment appeared, and believed itself to be, unscathed, the new sociologies of deviance had set loose a series of ideas[71] that were eventually to percolate even into the innermost sanctums of policy formation.

The Strictures of Policy Relevance

Throughout the 1950s and 1960s the Home Office had regarded the independence of academic research from the Home Office as politically important and consistently preferred research to be undertaken by academics rather than within the Home Office.[72] This was to change rapidly in subsequent decades. In the 1970s the numbers of researchers within the Home Office grew significantly faster than in university criminology departments. It is difficult to discern whether this growth arose out of the institutional imperatives of empire building or was driven by antipathy to the very different intellectual preoccupations of the new sociologies of deviance. Certainly research was increasingly commissioned internally rather than solicited from universities. Within the Home Office, the twin imperatives of identifying policy areas to which research might contribute and designing research so as to maximize its policy

---

[68] Croft, n. 64 above, 270–1.   [69] Ibid., 275.

[70] As Young has pointed out, post 1968, radical criminology became at least an equal partner in Britain: the label 'mainstream' criminology had become a misnomer for what he prefers to term 'establishment' criminology: Young, n. 56 above, 164.

[71] Not least that conceptions of normality and deviance were constructed and contestable; that youth was a period of natural experimentation and the challenging of boundaries; and that labelling people as deviant was self-fulfilling and not without costs. Out of these ideas came such policies as diversion and, much later, reintegrative shaming.

[72] According to the testimony of T.S. Lodge (the first Director of the Home Office Research Unit): Lodge, n. 45 above, 22.

relevance became the dominant drivers of the research pro-gramme.[73] Perhaps subconsciously recognizing the revolutionary impact that the sociology of deviance had had within the academy, Home Office researchers tried to claim that the policy framework played a role analogous to that of theory in disciplining their own research. But if policy relevance provided the impetus and justifica-tion for Home Office research, how it was supposed to furnish conceptual, methodological and evaluative criteria for research was never spelt out. Moreover, the espousal of policy-relevance as the driver of Home Office endeavour thrust its researchers into the arms of the administrators to a degree that diminished their inde-pendence of thought and inhibited their ability to question the direction in which administrators were wont to go.

Where external research was commissioned, it was also subject to the strictures contained in the Rothschild Report (1971),[74] requiring that externally funded research satisfy tests of 'policy relevance'. As interpreted by the Home Office, this meant that any externally funded research must have a firmly identified 'customer' within the Home Office. Satisfaction of these customers became a primary test of successful research outcomes. Rothschild's customer-contractor principle thus created a climate in which policy-makers formulated or identified 'problems' which were then given to researchers to take away and 'solve'.[75] Research was thus institutionally reduced to a responsive, instrumental mechanism for resolving pre-identified problems. As Bottoms later observed, Rothschild's customer–contractor principle had been intended to pertain only to applied research and Rothschild had expected that there would be separate funding by the research councils for 'basic, fundamental or pure research'.[76] Yet the dominance of Home Office funding for crimino-logical research had had the effect of vastly inflating the importance of applied, at the expense of pure, research. For Bottoms, the princi-

---

[73] R.V.G. Clarke, 'Penal Policy-making and Research in the Home Office' in N. Walker (ed.), *Penal Policy-Making in England* (Cambridge: Institute of Crimin-ology, 1977) 116.

[74] Lord Rothschild, 'The Organisation and Management of Government R. & D.' in *A Framework for Government Research and Development*, Cmnd. 4814 (London: HMSO, 1971).

[75] Clarke, n. 73 above, 117.

[76] A.E. Bottoms, 'Reflections on the Criminological Enterprise' (1987) 46 *Cambridge Law Journal* 240, at 247.

pal cost of this development was the erosion of an autonomous university criminology capable of undertaking explanatory work unrelated to policy needs. It also made impossible both the pursuit of policy-relevant research in the public interest (but against the interests of ministers) and the creation of a forum for the necessary discussion of 'value-choices'.[77]

At the time, Stanley Cohen was driven to the derogatory description of establishment criminology as 'pragmatic, interdisciplinary, correctional, reformist and positivist'.[78] It is a deep irony that Home Office researchers Ron Clarke and Derek Cornish embraced his description as providing an 'effective framework for harnessing social science to policy' and advocated it as the basis for policy-relevant research both inside the Home Office and within the universities.[79] Their positivist, preferably quantitative and anti-theoretical conception of policy-relevant research was in every respect antithetical to prevailing conceptions within social science. This might hardly have mattered were it not for the fact that the Home Office was by then by far the largest source of funding, outstripping resources available to academics from the research-funding councils many times over.

In the face of this prevailing impetus to rein researchers ever more tightly to the customer–contractor principle, Roger Hood pulled off what now appears as a remarkable coup.[80] As Director of the Centre for Criminological Research at the University of Oxford, he secured from the Home Office a five-year 'rolling grant'.[81] This grant gave the Centre licence to suggest its own programme of research, subject only to Home Office approval. The academic freedom this form of funding provided enabled him to attract a number of very able criminologists with the prospect of a degree of continuity of employment not normally associated with Home Office funded research. This said, Oxford's reliance on Home Office funding required that

[77] Ibid., 247–8.

[78] Quoted in Clarke and Cornish, n. 8 above, 52.

[79] Bottoms, n. 76 above, 244–5.

[80] Having moved from the Institute of Criminology in Cambridge, he became Reader in Criminology and Director of the Penal Research Unit at the University of Oxford in 1973. In 1977 the PRU was renamed the Centre for Criminological Research in order to signal a broadening of its research agenda.

[81] Of £200,000, whereby every year the Centre was to be guaranteed security for a further five years.

its researchers engage in empirical research projects amenable to the Home Office's own agenda. Arguably, it could not afford them the academic freedom of enquiry now enjoyed by their counterparts in Cambridge who held permanent university posts and, therefore, were less reliant on outside funding.

Whilst the expansion of state-sponsored research during this period may be taken as a sign of the flourishing of criminology, seen another way it is but a happier reminder of the less than happy fact that criminology stood (and stands) at the mercy of government largesse. Aside from dependence on government funding, the need for government permission to gain access to the actors and institutions of criminal justice revealed the structural reliance of criminology on the exercise of state discretion. Examples litter the criminological literature of eminent academics whose re- search was curtailed by refusal of access, cutting off a commission, or other strictures so severe as to undermine basic academic free- doms. The decision by Stanley Cohen and Laurie Taylor to publish their research on the experience of maximum security conditions at Durham prison, in the face of threats by the Home Office to bring legal action under the Official Secrets Act, has rightly been ap- plauded by academics.[82] But it has been more rarely the cause for reflection on the strictures under which criminologists tacitly agree to work. Roger Hood and his colleagues were not exempt from the damaging exercise of this highly discretionary power.[83] And every academic conducting research on behalf of the Home Office was (and is) routinely subject to strictures surrounding access, publica- tion, and dissemination. Of course many of these strictures are necessary,[84] but there has been surprisingly little discussion, even

---

[82] S. Cohen and L. Taylor, *Psychological Survival* (Harmondsworth: Penguin, 1972). See Downes, n. 59 above, 47.

[83] An enquiry into sentencing practices in the Crown Courts set up by Roger Hood and carried out by A. Ashworth and colleagues was banned by the judiciary despite Home Office support: A. Ashworth, E. Genders, G. Mansfield, J. Peay, and E. Player, *Sentencing in the Crown Court* (Oxford: Centre for Criminological Research, 1984). Later Roger Hood's study *Race and Sentencing* (Oxford: Clarendon Press, 1992) was hindered by the fact that he was not allowed to speak to judges. See further Andrew Ashworth (this volume).

[84] Not least to protect civil servants and ministers who might otherwise find themselves embarrassed by the publication of critical comment that they were not ready to defend.

within the academy, about the extent of their necessity or about the limits on academic freedom that they impose.[85]

Despite the Home Office's conception of itself as impervious to the insights of the new criminology, as unashamedly wedded to a particular conception of 'scientific' rigour, and preferring quantitative over qualitative analysis, the intellectual ferment within academic criminology effected subtle changes in its administrative rival. Even within the Home Office, medico-psychological models of criminal behaviour were superseded by sociological models of background, socio-economic status, learning, and interaction.[86] And studies of crime and criminals were increasingly replaced by research on responses to crime and, in particular, the workings of the criminal justice process. The combined influences of the new sociology of deviance and emerging socio-legal studies had altered both the subjects of criminological enquiry and the methodologies employed to undertake it.

But we should not overstate the degree of change. The dominant requirement of policy relevance, both for Home Office research and that funded by it within the academy, served to shore up traditional criminological research. The schism between 'establishment' criminologists and the new sociologists of deviance grew only as the latter deplored the former's 'abstracted empiricism', excessive reliance on official criminal statistics, and insufficient concern for the process of their construction. Above all, they feared that the 'scientific' authority of 'findings could lend legitimacy to innovations in and extensions of the realm of social control'.[87] This last objection is particularly important. For this was no mere difference of intellectual taste but a grave political concern about the misuses to which criminological knowledge might unwittingly find itself put.

The 'Collapse of Faith'

For much of the 1970s, criminology's primary role in policy development lay in the evaluation of penal measures and, in particular, evaluating their efficacy in reforming offenders. Validation through

---

[85] Roger Hood has observed that the fact that Home Office commissioned research becomes ' "subject to Crown Copyright" must inevitably be an additional pressure to eschew too critical a stance': n. 19 above.

[86] Croft, n. 64 above, 271.

[87] D. Downes, 'Promise and Performance in British Criminology' (1978) 29 *British Journal of Sociology* 490.

research was central to the rehabilitative project and, ironically, therefore, responsible for generating the body of evidence that first cast doubt on its efficacy. The precise role played by academic research in the demise of rehabilitation has been the subject of extensive debate.[88] Criminologists were used to thinking of their contribution to policy development primarily in positive terms, in identifying social problems and suggesting means to their solution. In striking contrast, the dominant message of criminological research in the late 1970s was that 'nothing works'.[89]

These negative findings were neither new nor unequivocal and might, in different times, have simply been incorporated into the existing model as indicators of the need to modify, or find more effective, treatment programmes. What gave the 'Nothing Works' literature its force was less the strength of its empirical findings than a more generalized turning away from the rehabilitative ideal. Garland describes this phenomenon as 'a collapse of faith' and attributes it partly to the rejection of 'positivist' criminology by the new criminologies of the National Deviancy Conference and beyond.[90] For proponents of labelling theory, for example, the problem was not crime but the state's responses to it. For the most part, radical criminologists dismissed the correctionalists' claims of welfarism as a façade behind which lurked repression and control. In sum, the devastating force of the attack on rehabilitation lay less in empirical refutation of its claims to reform than in normative critique of its intrusive powers and rejection of the disciplinary foundations upon which it was based. Yet so bound up was criminology's self-conception with the reformative project of identifying the causes of crime and the means to its reduction, that the conclusion 'nothing works' severely damaged the discipline's own sense of self worth.[91]

---

[88] Most recently, Garland, n. 53 above, 63–73.

[89] R.L. Martinson, 'What Works—Questions and Answers about Prison Reform' (1974) 35 *The Public Interest* 22; S. Brody, *The Effectiveness of Sentencing: A Review of the Literature*, Home Office Research Study No. 35 (London: Home Office, 1976). This conclusion was not universal (Germany for example did not lose faith in the rehabilitative ideal) and was later revisited and largely reversed: see e.g. J. Maguire (ed.), *What Works: Reducing Re-offending Guidelines from Research and Practice* (Chichester: John Wiley & Sons, 1995).

[90] Garland, n. 53 above, 63–73.

[91] See S. Cohen, 'If Nothing Works, What is Our Work?' (1994) 27 *The Australian and New Zealand Journal of Criminology* 104.

Garland thus argues that 'the attack on welfarism was of necessity an attack also on mainstream criminology. The new criminologists... engaged in a critique of their own academic discipline and challenged the expert credentials that had been the basis of the criminologist's authority... they mounted an attack on the institutional epistemology of the criminological mainstream, showing the limits of its social vision and the patronising cast of its reformist politics.'[92] What Garland overlooks is the altogether more curious fact that rejection of the reformative impulses of positivism did not immunize the new criminologists against the sense that they too had failed.[93]

The demise of the rehabilitative project can be overplayed. Rehabilitative penalties like probation and community service continued to thrive, and even increased in use, in the 'post-rehabilitative era'. None the less as a framework for the production of useful knowledge, it is fair to say that by the 1980s, at least in Anglo-American debates, rehabilitation was so discredited as to form no significant part of the criminological endeavour. It was less clear what was to replace it.

The New Realism

The focus of the radical criminologies of the 1970s on victimless crimes and offences relating to sexual preference, drug use, and subcultural gang membership had down-played crime as a social problem and tended rather to reify it as an expression of alternative lifestyle choice. In the 1980s, the prevailing conservative political climate, combined with sharply increasing crime rates, made it more difficult to be dismissive of crime.[94] The response of 'new left realism' was to recognize that the burden of crime falls principally on those least able to bear it and that crime should therefore become an important political issue for the left.[95] New left realism spawned a series of studies on the costs of crime and, in particular, the extent and experience of victimization. Interestingly, much of this research was sponsored by radical local councils seeking data as a foundation

[92] Garland, n. 53 above, 67.   [93] Young, n. 3 above.
[94] Young, n. 56 above, 172.
[95] Key texts include: J. Lea and J. Young, *What is to be Done about Law and Order?* (London: Penguin, 1984); R. Kinsey, J. Lea, and J. Young, *Losing the Fight against Crime* (Oxford: Blackwell, 1986).

for and justification of urban regeneration programmes.[96] In place of radical criminology's oppositional stance to state crime policies, therefore, the new left realists found themselves working in collaboration with, and even within, the state itself.[97] At the same time, pioneering research was carried out at the Oxford Centre for Criminological Research providing for the first time extensive qualitative data on victims' experiences of crime and of the criminal justice system.[98]

The broadly leftist sympathies of realist criminologists in Britain, their commitment to feminism and anti-racism, stood in striking contrast to their North American realist counterparts. The latter's right wing politics fostered an entirely different, moralistic, punitively orientated agenda for what was to become known as the 'politics of law and order'.[99] None the less the peculiarly British brand of left realism served to usher in an altogether more pragmatic conception of criminology's contribution. As Ken Pease has observed, if the discipline in the 1970s could be characterized as a veritable 'Tower of Babel' of competing criminological voices, by the 1980s it had been 'replaced by an (arguably excessive) emphasis on piecemeal and pragmatic approaches to particular crime problems'.[100] No doubt the continued growth in recorded crime had brought with it 'a constant pressure for solutions',[101] but a more mundane explanation lies in the institutional expansion of governmental criminological research. By the start of the 1980s, the Home Office employed some fifty full-time research staff in its Research and Planning Unit alone, outstripping the number of academic re-

---

[96] e.g., inner London boroughs like Islington and Hammersmith and Fulham, and Merseyside in Liverpool.

[97] See discussion in R. Reiner, 'British Criminology and the State' in Rock, n. 31 above, 152–3.

[98] e.g. M. Maguire, *Burglary in a Dwelling* (London: Heinemann, 1982); J. Shapland, J. Willmore, and P. Duff, *Victims and the Criminal Justice System* (Aldershot: Gower, 1986); M. Maguire and C. Corbett, *The Effects of Crime and The Work of Victim Support Schemes* (Aldershot: Gower, 1987).

[99] J.Q. Wilson, *Thinking about Crime* (New York: Basic Books, 1975); for a highly critical appraisal of the contribution of the American realist school see T. Platt and P. Takagi, 'Intellectuals for Law and Order: A Critique of the New "Realists" ' in T. Platt and P. Takagi (eds.), *Crime and Social Justice* (London: Macmillan, 1981) 30–58.

[100] K. Pease, 'Methodological Developments' in Rock (ed.), n. 31 above, 70.

[101] A.E. Bottoms, 'Reflections on the Criminological Enterprise' (1987) 46 *The Cambridge Law Journal* 240.

searchers scattered throughout the universities.[102] Given that many of those working within the universities were employed on government funded projects, the dominance of the Home Office was significant. As Croft himself acknowledged, '[t]he proposition that the advancement of knowledge rests with the scientific community needs to be tempered by the realisation that the resources for that advancement are not under the direct control of scientists. In the United Kingdom they lie with government'.[103] Bottoms was certainly not alone in deploring the powerful influence of 'administrative criminology' over academic research.[104]

Managerialism and the New Economic Rationality

Under the Thatcher regime of the 1980s, the rise of managerialism in criminal justice, as elsewhere in government, generated pressures for research to be directed toward specific bureaucratic 'consumers', to give 'value for money', and to satisfy the demand for performance indicators (principally through evaluation research).[105] The Oxford Centre for Criminological Research was not protected from these pressures. In the early 1980s the rolling grant made by the Home Office to the Oxford Centre was ended.[106] Research funds were henceforth given for specific projects agreed on a 'customer-contractor' basis, usually for no more than two years for each project. Although by today's standards a two-year timeframe is relatively generous, this change represented a major contraction of academic freedom.[107] It was hardly surprising that many excellent criminologists who had been drawn to Oxford by the prospect of employment for the medium term were subsequently lured away to tenured positions in other universities.

[102] Croft, n. 64 above, 266–7.

[103] Ibid., 274.

[104] Bottoms, n. 101 above, 260. Roger Hood likewise argued that much policy research 'by definition, is narrow, often excessively narrow, technical evaluation of administrative procedures or decisions': Hood, n. 19 above.

[105] J.W. Raine and M.J. Wilson, *Managing Criminal Justice* (Hemel Hempstead: Harvester Wheatsheaf, 1993); C. Jones, 'Auditing Criminal Justice' (1993) 33 *British Journal of Criminology* 187.

[106] Though a moral commitment was made not to see the existing researchers unemployed.

[107] And it was, no doubt, changes such as this that led Roger Hood to reflect that the prevailing short-termism 'surely cannot be good for the intellectual development of any discipline': Hood, n. 19 above.

These fiscal pressures influenced not only the design and organization of research but even its very purpose. Prominent among the emerging roles of research identified by former head of the Home Office Research and Planning Unit, Croft was 'identifying options for the more economical and fruitful disposal of limited resources'.[108] This co-option of criminology as collaborator in the managerialist task of pursuing economy and efficiency was yet another sign of profound pessimism about any larger solution to the crime problem. As Croft observed, 'even if among some policy-makers there is still an expectation, originally generated by social scientists some thirty years ago but now abandoned, that criminological research will solve the problems that beset the penal system, realists have adjusted their utilitarian perspective to new horizons'.[109] The impact of economic reasoning served not only to constrain the ambitions of official criminology but to inform its very thinking.

The new post-welfare criminologies also drew directly on economic analysis. What Garland has termed the 'criminologies of everyday life'[110] regarded crime not as pathological but as normal and routine, and saw criminals as rational actors simply taking advantage of opportunities to serve their self-interest. Criminality was no longer a deviation from the norm but rather continuous with normal social interaction and motivated by the same urge to utility maximization. This re-conception of the criminal and of criminality owes much to the influence of rational choice theory, derived from economics and already influential in neighbouring social science disciplines. The impact of rational choice theory has been described as 'nothing short of the invasion of economic man . . . the ultimate imperialist assault of economics on sociology—the subordination of *homo sociologicus* to *homo economicus*'.[111] In criminology, rational choice theory gained currency partly because it provided an intellectually respectable explanation for the failure of the deviancy model and partly because it mirrored prevailing libertarian models of individual freedom, personal choice, and the pursuit of self-interest.

---

[108] Croft, n. 64 above, 274.   [109] Ibid., 273.
[110] Garland, n. 53 above, 16.
[111] P. Baert, *Social Theory in the Twentieth Century* (Cambridge: Polity, 1998) 154.

Perhaps because it was taken up first and most enthusiastically within the Home Office, rational choice theory in Britain generated few analyses of offending behaviour comparable to those carried out enthusiastically elsewhere.[112] But it has had a profound impact on thinking about responses to crime. If crime is rational and opportunistic, it is best combated by reduction of opportunity, finely calculated disincentives, imposition of controls, and modification of routines. The policy implications of this paradigm shift were quickly appreciated and applied. Routine activity theory, life-style analysis, and situational crime prevention are all important policy innovations arising out of the acceptance of crime as 'a normal social fact' and the criminal as rational man. Unlike the retrospective preoccupation of traditional criminology with crimes committed by individuals, the 'new penology'[113] operates prospectively to calculate risks, identify criminal opportunities, and target 'suspect' populations. This shift in temporal perspective necessarily entails a shift also in substantive focus, away from the workings of the criminal justice process, the trial, and punishment, and toward the physical environments and opportunity structures in which crime is committed. As Garland has commented, 'This is, in effect, "supply side criminology" shifting risks, redistributing costs, and creating disincentives'.[114] Arguably, therefore, some of the most important policy shifts of the closing decades of the twentieth century arose not from empirical, pragmatic policy-orientated criminological enquiry but from economic analysis.

Coda

By the closing decade of the twentieth century criminology had expanded enormously. By the mid-1990s the Home Office allocated a budget of £4.5 million for research, of which £1.5 million was devoted to external research. Between 80 and 90 per cent of external research depended upon the financial backing of the Home Office and the Economic and Social Research Council (ESRC).[115] The fact that most of this funding was for projects commissioned by

[112] e.g., R. Posner, *Economic Analysis of Crime* (5th edn., Boston Mass.: Little, Brown, & Co., 1998).

[113] M. Feeley and J. Simon, 'The New Penology: Notes on the Emerging Strategy of Corrections and its Implications' (1992) 30 *Criminology* 449.

[114] Garland, n. 53 above, 129.

[115] Radzinowicz, n. 12 above, 459.

government, directed by bureaucrats, or, at best, included in pre-determined programmes of enquiry was hardly consistent with any significant self-determination of academic research. A majority of criminologists were in receipt of government grants for pre-specified policy-orientated research projects and reliant upon securing further grants for their future employment. It is perhaps not surprising that truly critical positions, for example abolitionism, failed to flourish in Britain in the way they have done elsewhere.[116]

Overshadowed by the towering oak tree that is government-funded policy research, the undernourished sapling that is theoretical criminology is none the less flourishing.[117] Almost by definition, this is unsubsidized research, outside the policy arena and claiming no congress with it, and devoted instead to the deconstruction of social changes in crime and crime control.[118] Its myriad forms—'radical criminology', 'critical' criminology, deconstruction, discourse analysis, analyses of social control, risk, trust, security, of changing patterns of governance, and of post-modernity—attest to its vitality. Yet, for all its analytic subtlety and power of illumination, this criminology provides no clear implications for policy or politics.[119] In striking contrast to the oppositional stance of its immediate precursors, this criminology eschews political commitment and is unwilling to engage in normative theorizing. Lacking any larger political vision, any ideological allegiance, still less any blue-print for policy change, contemporary criminology can too easily be seen

---

[116] Most notably Scandinavia: see e.g. T. Mathiesen, *The Politics of Abolition* (London: Martin Robertson, 1974), also his *Prison on Trial* (London: Sage, 1990) and the Netherlands: see W. de Haan, *The Politics of Redress: Crime, Punishment and Penal Abolition* (London: Unwin Hyman, 1990).

[117] Whose scope and style is best illustrated by (but by no means limited to) the contributions to journals like *Punishment and Society* and *Theoretical Criminology*.

[118] Recent examples include J. Muncie, 'Deconstructing Criminology' (1998/9) 34 *Criminal Justice Matters* 4–5; P. O'Malley, 'Volatile and Contradictory Punishment' (1999) 3 *Theoretical Criminology* 175–6; I. Taylor, *Crime in Context* (London: Polity Press, 1999); J. Young, *The Exclusive Society: Social Exclusion, Crime and Difference in Late Modernity* (London: Sage, 1999); D. Garland and R. Sparks (eds.), *Criminology and Social Theory* (Oxford: Clarendon Press, 2000); T. Hope and R. Sparks (eds.), *Crime, Risk and Insecurity* (London: Routledge, 2000); K. Stenson and R.R. Sullivan (eds.), *Crime, Risk and Justice* (Cullompton: Willan Publishing, 2001); C. Shearing, 'Punishment and the Changing Face of Governance' (2001) 3 *Punishment and Society* 203; Garland, n. 53 above.

[119] This observation has also been made of previous generations of theoretical endeavour. See Reiner, n. 97 above, 282.

as a form of capitulation to the prevailing status quo. As such, it can lead to inadvertent collusion with penal policies that more politically engaged criminologists once felt minded to decry.[120]

Although the flourishing of theoretical criminology is a direct product of university expansion, academic criminology is of course a multifaceted entity. The proliferating masters (and even undergraduate) degree courses, full-time academic posts, research centres, conferences, colloquia, and seminar series, monographs, and journals cultivate criminology in all its many guises. Significantly also, the longest established centres of criminological research have attracted permanent university posts and diversified their sources of funding to permit a wider range of enquiry and greater academic freedom. The Oxford Centre for Criminological Research has grown from the single permanent university post to which Roger Hood was appointed as Reader in 1973 to the immediate prospect of employing one professor, four lecturers, and some twenty-five contract researchers. Oxford's one reader, Masters in Criminology and Criminal Justice, like those proliferating elsewhere, both meets the growing demand for criminologically-educated graduates[121] and, through this education, transmits criminological knowledge to the future practitioners of the criminal justice state.

Four Interim Conclusions

We began with two questions: in short, why is criminology torn between rival conceptions of its role and why does it consider itself impotent? Four interim conclusions can be drawn from the (avowedly incomplete) history told here. First, that the fractured nature of criminology derives as much from its institutional, as its intellectual, history. Secondly, that whilst the twin histories of the Home Office and the academy by no means furnish a perfect map of those fractures, they do frame the dominant intellectual allegiances and their concomitant rivalries. And the sense of rivalry should not be underplayed. At key historical moments, it seems that criminologists have

[120] L. Zedner, 'The Dangers of Dystopias in Penal Theory' [2002] *Oxford Journal of Legal Studies* 341. I am by no means the first to deplore this 'moral nihilism': see, e.g., W. de Haan, 'Fuzzy Morals and Flakey Politics: The Coming Out of Critical Criminology' (1987) 14 *Journal of Law and Society* 321–333.

[121] J. Braithwaite, 'The New Regulatory State and the Transformation of Criminology' (2000) 40 *British Journal of Criminology* 222.

more readily defined themselves by negative reference to rival conceptions of the discipline than by any strong positive model of what they do. The tendency to self-definition by negative allegiance has inhibited even the most intelligent minds from recognizing the value of an intellectual *rapprochement* between rival conceptions of the discipline. Thirdly, the schism between policy-orientated and theoretical criminology is based upon the shared delusion that only the former has the role of influencing policy-formation.[122] For reasons I will expand upon below, it is far from self-evidently the case that the most 'useful knowledge' is that which conceives of itself as such. Fourthly and finally, although criminology declaims its own impotence, this sense of failure derives less from any actual incapacity than from a collective tendency to underestimate the power of criminological knowledge.[123] The first two of these conclusions arise from, and I hope are adequately substantiated by, the brief history I have already traced. The third and fourth conclusions merit amplification.

The conclusion that only policy-orientated research can have influence rests upon a curiously constrained conception of relevance. It assumes that only empirical research can have anything to say to policy-makers, and it downplays the import for policy of critical and normative theory. Historically, policy-makers looking for 'off the shelf' solutions to pressing problems have been unwilling to accept the larger importance of the intellectual contribution to be made by criminology. The managerialist pressures that characterized Home Office policy in the 1980s and 1990s generated a further inhibition to recognizing the value in larger, but less readily auditable, criminological insights about crime, disorder, and social ordering practices. It has been assumed that only by providing hard data, by engaging directly with policy dilemmas, by proposing reforms, or evaluating existing initiatives can criminology influence policy.

This takes a too narrowly technocratic and mechanistic view of the relationship between academic research and policy-formation, namely 'that researchers' findings are supposed to fill a "knowledge gap" and provide policy-makers with authoritative *data* to make

---

[122] Though see Sanders and Young (this volume).

[123] Here I concur with Chan that 'the influence of criminological knowledge on public policy is more persuasive than we realise': J. Chan, 'Systematically Distorted Communication? Criminological Knowledge, Media Representation and Public Policy' (1995) 28 *The Australian and New Zealand Journal of Criminology* 23.

rational decisions'.[124] It assumes that criminological knowledge is useful only when it identifies a precise problem, studies it, formulates a solution, and persuades policy-makers to adopt that solution. It is as if 'criminology's utility depends on the validity with which it represents (reflects, describes, explains) some pre-existing social relations (the causes of crime, the motives of criminals and so on), which in turn is "implemented" by the institutions of government'.[125] Judged by these narrowly instrumental criteria of utility, it is hardly surprising that criminologists are rarely able to claim direct influence.[126] Clearly the more policy-orientated research is, the closer it shadows the concerns of government, or provides practical answers to prevailing social problems, the greater the likelihood of its warm reception in government. But the common assumption that criminological theory, with its tendency to radical critique and unverifiable abstraction, is incapable of influence is to misunderstand the subtle, indirect ways in which knowledge can generate social understanding and inform the policy agenda. Moreover research that blurs the boundaries of administrative and theoretical criminology, carried out independently of the imperatives of policy formation, none the less often furnishes the very data upon which subsequent policy initiatives rely. For example research into the dark figure of crime, into criminal careers, the impact of victimization, the uses of discretion within the criminal process, or, indeed, Roger Hood's own study of race and sentencing[127] contained few immediate policy proposals. But the knowledge these studies generated rapidly became a part of the policy-maker's repertoire, irrespective of whether its provenance was acknowledged or not.[128]

Understood this way, the problem is less the capacity of criminological knowledge to have influence than the failure of policy-makers to acknowledge their intellectual debts. Acknowledgement is not simply a matter of personal recognition: it has a direct impact also on funding. If this larger knowledge is, as I have argued, indispensable, then government needs to be willing to provide the financial support necessary for long-term projects whose immediate

---

[124] Ibid., 26.   [125] Hogg, n. 16 above, 146.   [126] Petersilia, n. 22 above.
[127] Hood, n. 83 above.
[128] This is not to say that policy-makers always acted upon these or other research findings. It is all too easy to cite occasions when policy decisions are made in the face of contrary evidence.

application or utility may not yet be clear.[129] To insist upon policy relevance (which the customer–contractor principle effectively does) is to deny funding to speculative, conceptual, exploratory, and experimental research despite the fact that this may, in the longer term, bear significant fruit. Equally, if criminologists allow their research agenda to be set by the immediate needs of policy-makers, the imaginative possibilities of their discipline will simply be lost. To this end, criminologists need to be more pro-active in seeking out other sources of funding that allow for longer time frames and larger enquiry.

It has been argued that the expansion of criminology within the academy and the rewards of academic recognition carry with them the danger of 'our growing isolation' from what goes on 'out there'.[130] Isolation would indeed be a dangerous failing in a criminologist. But it may be that such fears falsely conflate intimacy with policy-makers with intimate knowledge of policy. Whilst it is true that the power of criminology depends upon knowing what is happening 'on the ground',[131] it need not lie in subordination to the demands of policy-makers. Given the considerable body of criminologists working within government, together with the many academics who undertake governmental research, there is a strong case for fostering, not lamenting, the relative separation of academic criminology. Its value lies in the intellectual independence, the sense of perspective, and capacity for dispassionate analysis that are achieved only by securing a good measure of distance.

The Larger Influence of Criminological Knowledge

If we are to make the case for the larger influence of criminological knowledge, then we need to identify the means and manner by which this influence is had. In what follows, I argue that this larger contribution resides not only in empirical research but also in the provision of language and concepts with which to think about crime and its control; in the identification and definition of social problems; and

[129] To this end Roger Hood has called for the establishment of an independent Criminological Research Council: Hood, n. 19 above.

[130] Petersilia, n. 22 above, 10.

[131] And ethnographic studies, in particular, clearly require intimacy with those under scrutiny.

in critical and normative theory. As concerns the means by which influence is had, whilst our focus has been upon criminological research, it is clear that influence also occurs through interactions with policy-makers, through the media, and, not least, through education. Criminologists, as teachers, influence their pupils and their writings influence what others teach. This pedagogic influence is particularly important where those pupils are members of, or subsequently enter, the criminal justice professions as police, prison officers, or policy-makers. A more expansive account of criminological knowledge would recognize that influencing the way policy-makers think is likely to have more lasting, if less readily traceable, effects than narrowly instrumental endeavours.

If little recognition has been given to these more diffuse channels of influence, neither has there been sufficient consideration of the contexts in which criminological knowledge and ideas gain currency. In what circumstances, under what political or material conditions, does criminological knowledge acquire the power to influence and inform? Given the entrenched inertia built into the criminal justice system, the counter-influence of other pressures and constraints, and the necessary consideration given to public opinion, criminological knowledge has powerful competition for the minds (to say nothing of the hearts) of policy-makers. Historical analysis suggests that academic research can have enormous impact, but that that impact may have less to do with the power of what is being said than the time, place, and context in which it is said. The undeniable impact of Martinson's conclusion that 'nothing works', of J.Q. Wilson's 'broken windows' thesis, and of Stanley Cohen's concept of 'net-widening' (to cite just a few prominent examples) arose not only from the power of what was being said but from the fact that these potent ideas fell on fertile ground.[132]

Arguably criminology's most influential contribution resides in its ability to formulate conceptual frameworks within which to think about crime and its control. The development of criminological concepts may occur with little or no reference to the needs or interests of policy-makers. But, once developed, those concepts eventually percolate out of the academy and into the everyday

---

[132] Martinson, n. 89 above; J.Q. Wilson and G. Kelling, 'Broken Windows', *The Atlantic Monthly* (March 1982) 29; S. Cohen, *Visions of Social Control* (Cambridge: Polity Press, 1985).

working language of government researchers, from whom they may be taken up by civil servants, politicians, and the media.[133] As Chan has observed, 'social scientific theories, concepts and orientations are often taken over by lay actors in such a way that these concepts eventually shape how policy makers perceive social issues'.[134]

Criminology has also furnished key concepts in the language of crime and crime control. Criminological terms of art such as 'outsiders', 'the dark figure of crime', 'total institutions', 'decarceration', or 'moral panics' have entered the language of crime control precisely because they capture an important idea and irrespective of their immediate import for policy. In time, however, some become part of the policy-maker's toolkit and inform decision-making in more concrete ways.[135] The provocative power of criminological ideas to expose new ways of seeing crime and its solutions is important whether or not we share their ultimate conclusions. From the nineteenth-century identification of criminal physiognomy and phrenology through to the post-war 'discovery' of delinquency and its accompanying recognition of broken homes, poor upbringing, and inadequate opportunities as causes of crime, criminology has created novel objects of government intervention. And here, I would with agree with Hogg:

The utility of criminology is hard to deny. It authorises and validates judgement and decisions, it helps construct, allocate and sometimes efface criminal responsibility, it defines new horizons of social intervention and influences the deployment of government resources, and its provides 'vocabularies of motive' for the criminals who offend as well as the judges that send them down. It is, in an important sense, an indispensable component of the modern apparatuses of government.[136]

Criminological theory has also been important in defining the very social problems to which the policy-making process must respond. A good example here is the way in which feminist theory,[137] quite as much as empirical research, has led to the acknowledgement of domestic violence and sexual abuse as important social

---

[133] Though the speed with which they are taken up often depends upon the degree to which the concepts mesh with prevailing concerns or political agendas.

[134] Chan, n. 123 above, 26.

[135] Significantly, other concepts, notably 'white collar crime', are not taken up by policy-makers.

[136] Hogg, n. 16 above, 146.

[137] And, of course, feminist activism.

problems.[138] And just as theoretical insight can induce recognition of new social problems, so it can remove problems from the political and policy agenda. For example, the offender as the product of individual pathology (the focus of penal policy until the late 1960s) largely disappeared from the policy agenda in the 1970s in the wake of the radical new sociological theories of deviance which redefined offenders as the product of environment and socialization. Equally striking is the theoretical displacement of concern about social deprivation, inadequate socialization, and inequalities in wealth as causes of crime by rational-choice theory and free market economics in the 1980s. If criminology can 'create' and 'eradicate' social problems, it can also exercise more subtle influence by dispelling myths, by shifting the climate of informed opinion, and by revealing problems to be more complex than previously imagined.

Criminological theories that evolve with little regard, and even open hostility, to the policy process become no less part of the intellectual capital of policy-makers. And this is as true of normative as it is of explanatory theories (presuming the distinction itself is sustainable).[139] The post-war period is littered with examples of normative theories whose development could never have satisfied the customer–contractor principle but whose import has been no less significant for that. Desert theory, as developed most notably by Andrew von Hirsch,[140] was taken up and implemented in many countries including America, Sweden, and Britain. Similarly, restorative justice (advocated, amongst others, by John Braithwaite in Australia, by Mark Umbreit, Daniel van Ness, and Howard Zehr in the USA and by Martin Wright and Tony Marshall in Britain) has more recently achieved extraordinary influence around the world.[141] Both theories have in their turn had a powerful impact

---

[138] e.g., C. Smart, *Feminism and the Power of Law* (London: Routledge, 1989).

[139] R.A. Duff and D. Garland (eds.), 'Introduction: Thinking about Punishment' in R.A. Duff and D. Garland (eds.), *A Reader on Punishment* (Oxford: Oxford University Press, 1994).

[140] A. von Hirsch, *Doing Justice* (New York: Hill and Wang, 1976); A. von Hirsch, *Past or Future Crimes* (Manchester: Manchester University Press, 1986). In Britain Andrew Ashworth has also been a powerful advocate of desert theory. See his classic article 'Criminal Justice and Deserved Sentences' [1989] *Crim.L.R.* 340.

[141] Although there is scope for debate whether it was restorative justice theory or practice which first spawned the restorative justice movement, it is clear that the theoretical writings have been an important conduit for dissemination around the world.

on policy change and legislation.[142] Another powerful example of criminological theory effecting radical changes in responses to crime is the influence of what one might label criminological communitarianism on policy-making in the fields of community policing, community crime prevention, citizens' juries, community conferences, and some forms of restorative justice.[143] Indeed, it is arguable that the success of penal policies (in terms of take-up at least) is closely related to their theoretical sophistication.

Given the apparent power of normative theorizing, it is curious that more criminologists are not alive to its transformative potential. Yet, outside the narrow sphere of the philosophy of punishment, engagement in normative theorizing is sparse.[144] The major contributions of social and political philosophy have failed to capture the criminological imagination and the result is a dearth of theorizing about the ethics of criminal justice practices and penal measures, about the goals to be pursued outside punishment, or about the social values entailed in taking this decision over that. A striking example is that of situational crime prevention: an area dominated by technicist, instrumental research in which, with notable exceptions,[145] there has been worryingly little interest in the ethical parameters of what is being done. In part this may be a matter of intellectual taste (for descriptive or explanatory work over normative theorizing). In part it results from the positivist tradition wherein engagement with moral or political questions was regarded as unscientific. And in part it arises from the natural division of labour that tends to encourage specialism and inhibit attempts to

---

[142] In Britain the Criminal Justice Act 1991 can fairly be characterized as an attempt to structure sentencing according to desert theory, whilst the Crime and Disorder Act 1998 introduces several measures explicitly based upon restorative justice.

[143] N. Lacey and L. Zedner, 'Discourses of Community in Criminal Justice' (1995) 22 *Journal of Law and Society* 301; A. Crawford, *The Local Governance of Crime: Appeals to Community and Partnerships* (Oxford: Clarendon Press, 1997).

[144] As many of its proponents have observed: Bottoms, n. 101 above, 261–3; A. Ashworth, 'Criminal Justice and the Criminal Process' in Rock (ed.), n. 31 above; Jefferson and Shapland, n. 20 above, 266; J. Braithwaite, 'Republican Theory and Crime Control' in S. Karstedt and K.-D. Bussmann (eds.), *Social Dynamics of Crime and Control: New Theories for a World in Transition* (Oxford: Hart Publishing, 2000).

[145] Most notably A. von Hirsch, D. Garland, and A. Wakefield (eds.), *Ethical and Social Perspectives on Situational Crime Prevention* (Oxford: Hart Publishing, 2000).

develop expertise in theory as well as research (as if the two were separable). But to ignore normative theory constitutes a wilful refusal to recognize the moral and political implications of even the most hard-bitten policy-orientated research. Even criminological theorists are increasingly engaged in the kind of 'theoretical theory' that eschews political engagement in favour of the 'interrogation of...theoretical constructs and reflections on the conditions of possibility of criminological discourse'.[146] If criminological theory is to engage with and influence the *Realpolitik* of criminal justice, then it must concentrate on developing articulated values and principles, and attainable political objectives.[147] As Bottoms has remarked, 'criminology is itself inevitably linked to the political landscape, whether the criminologist likes it or not... doing criminology, in short, necessarily entails some engagement with normative issues'.[148] To do otherwise risks confining criminological theory to the academy and neutering its potential to bring about change.

Paradoxically, despite criminology's sense of collective failure, its practitioners share a surprisingly strong sense of their self-worth. Although they regret the impotence of their discipline to effect penal change, they are none the less confident that criminologically informed policy would be better policy. The presumption that the power of criminological knowledge is an invariable and incontrovertible good has invited little scrutiny. Yet it could be argued that one of the more serious problems of the recent past has been the potency of criminological ideas to influence the policy agenda in ways that their authors could not, or did not, foresee. Government researchers appear to recognize the need to be aware of the uses to which their results might be put.[149] Academics, particularly those who do not conceive of their work as policy-orientated, tend to be less farsighted about the possible uses and abuses to which their work may be subject. Striking examples spring to mind of moments

---

[146] Loader, n. 17 above, 202–3.

[147] See, e.g., the extended discussion of values, principles, and ethics in A. Ashworth, *The Criminal Process: An Evaluative Study* (2nd edn., Oxford: Oxford University Press, 1998).

[148] A. Bottoms, 'The Relationship between Theory and Research in Criminology' in R.D. King and E. Wincup (eds.), *Doing Research in Crime and Justice* (Oxford: Oxford University Press, 2000) 15.

[149] Clarke, n. 73 above, 122.

when criminology has been far from impotent and one might have wished for a little more resistance to its 'truths'. The devastating impact of Martinson's infamous conclusion that nothing works on rehabilitative policies is a case in point.[150] Those who criticized the treatment model of rehabilitation did so because they wished to see less intrusive, less punitive penalties in place. They did not imagine that their criticisms would help to usher in mandatory and incapacitatory sentencing, increased use of imprisonment, or, in some US states, revival of the death penalty.[151] The take-up of criminological concepts in ways their authors could not, or would not have wanted to, anticipate has not abated despite recent claims of criminology's impotence. Downes wryly observes 'that New Labour might have based their control policies on an inversion of every criminological warning of the past fifty years. "Net widening"—great idea. "Mesh-thinning"—no problem. "Penetration" (of the state into civil society)—why not?'.[152] Arguably then a major, but rarely contemplated, problem for criminology is less its impotence than the uncontrollable potency of ideas or research findings once in the public domain. Like the sorcerer's unfortunate apprentice, criminology all too easily finds itself as the helpless onlooker having unleashed a chain of events it has little power to control.

Conclusion

Seen one way, the failure of criminology to provide a solution to the problem of crime is just that, a failure. Seen another way, criminology fulfils the vital, if less immediately rewarding, functions of revealing complexities, of questioning certitudes, and of puncturing the false hope of simple solutions. It can be said to fail only on the false premises that crime is eradicable, that it should be eradicated, and that this can be achieved through the institutions of criminal justice. For policy-makers, academic devotion to the uncovering of complexity and concomitant reluctance to proffer easy ways out of

---

[150] A conclusion which he qualified even at the time of writing and from which he retreated a few years later: Martinson, n. 89 above; Martinson, 'New Findings, New Views: A Note of Caution Regarding Sentencing Reform' (1979) 7 *Hofstra Law Review* 242.

[151] Garland, n. 53 above, 72.

[152] D. Downes, 'Four Year Hard: New Labour and Crime Control' (2001) 46 *Criminal Justice Matters* 8.

policy dilemmas may be perceived as unhelpful,[153] but it is far from being a negative contribution. And historically it has certainly not inhibited criminology's continuing role in policy debates, still less limited its power to constitute the ways in which these debates are framed. In the widely differing interpretations and controversies that are the everyday stuff of academic life lies the possibility of seeing problems from every angle and, in so doing, securing robust, durable reforms that 'quick and dirty' policy-orientated research cannot supply. That there is a conflict between immediate and long-term goals is hardly a new insight. It reminds us, however, that whilst criminology can secure some measure of immediate impact through the provision of short-term, practical, reform proposals, its transformative power lies in revolutionary and utopian visions of what might be.[154] The value of academic criminology lies principally in its power to harness research evidence, to develop normative frameworks, to indulge in imaginative conjecture, and, in so doing, to look beyond the moment.

[153] As Ian Loader has observed, 'any modulated, research-based voice pointing out the effects of government policy, or unearthing information that unduly complicates simplistic political world views, is likely to prove troublesome and unpopular': Loader, n. 17 above, 197.

[154] Cohen, n. 91 above; P. Young, 'The Importance of Utopias in Criminological Thinking' (1992) 32 British Journal of Criminology 423.

5

Hearing, Not Listening: Penal Policy and the Political Prisoners of 1906–1921

Seán McConville

Policy and Knowledge

There is an etiquette for volumes of this kind. Contributors should have an association with the person to whom honour is being paid, and essays should pick up a theme in his or her work. This chapter falls well within these conventions. I was one of Roger Hood's earliest doctoral students and his supervision laid the basis for a continuing friendship. This chapter touches on his scholarly interests in several ways; I hope it also expands on some of his key values.

Penal history has been part of Hood's scholarly repertoire from the outset. His *Borstal Reassessed*[1] was part history and—another key element—part policy analysis and evaluation. Twenty-one years later there appeared the product of a fruitful collaboration with Sir Leon Radzinowicz, volume 5 of *A History of English Criminal Law and Its Administration from 1750*.[2] This project also spun off some valuable essays, including 'The Status of Political Prisoners in England'.[3] This was an elegant historical contribution to a policy dispute then gaining momentum and fierceness because of events in Northern Ireland and beyond. Neither Hood nor Radzinowicz gave support to the school which insists that lessons cannot or should not be taken from history.

---

[1] (London: Heinemann, 1965).
[2] (London: Stevens, 1986).
[3] Sir Leon Radzinowicz and R. Hood, 'The Status of Political Prisoners in England: The Struggle for Recognition' (1979) 65 *Virginia Law Review* 1421.

Roger Hood has consistently argued that public policy should be backed by research. He is not naïve about this, recognizing that facts (or the lack of them) may count for little in the face of political necessity, ideological preferences or party advantage. In his review essay 'Criminology and Penal Change' he considered penal policy in the period 1948–72, pointing to a repeated willingness to proceed without any kind of research. He concluded that 'the belief that expert advice based on criminological and penological research is the foundation for penal change, is only a screen behind which ideological and political factors, perhaps inevitably, shape those attitudes which imbue legislation'.[4]

This observation has not been a rationalization for abandoning research in the face of what sometimes appears to be the caprice of criminal and penal policy. Hood took the somewhat unpalatable truth as a spur for a career of research contributions and commentaries on policy which has been matched by few other British criminologists. Impressive as this body of work is in itself, it is all the more remarkable that Hood's impact has been made in years during which some senior politicians have not troubled to conceal their disdain, suspicion, or hostility to research or have overtly sought to bend it to party interest. And the academic climate has been scarcely more benign, with various strands of relativistic thought pushing criminological discussion towards epistemology and forms of always-on-the-starting-block historiography: plenty of room to patronize empirical research as a form of rustic confusion. But the caravan—politics, policy and administration—moves on.

These preliminaries are relevant to what follows—an examination of the contribution made to penal policy by political prisoners, particularly in the years around the First World War. Here is what today would be called the consumer's perspective, accounts of life in the institutions as it is lived, as distinct from ministerial briefs, renditions of annual reports, and the selections of committees of inquiry. I set out a sampling of these accounts and then consider the question of their effect on policy, before returning to some observations in the spirit of Hood's work.

---

[4] R. Hood, 'Criminology and Penal Change: A Case Study of the Nature and Impact of Some Recent Advice to Governments' in R. Hood (ed.), *Crime, Criminology and Public Policy: Essays in Honour of Sir Leon Radzinowicz* (London: Heinemann, 1974), 417.

The Quality of Evidence

More than eighty years ago Gilbert Murray, Professor of Greek at Oxford, asked whether prison reform would benefit from the testimony of those 'high-minded and utterly uncriminal people' who had recently been to prison. They were often perverse, he agreed, and some were no doubt also morally repulsive but 'when judged by any moderately intelligent and sensitive standard' some were considerably superior to the magistrates who sentenced them and also to the leaders of public sentiment. Their testimony could, in fact, be used with care. They were articulate, whereas the ordinary criminal was 'mostly inarticulate, uneducated, sullen; when he does speak he is often untruthful and almost never disinterested; also, to a greater extent than is always realised, he is hampered by shame'. It was a benefit to have the testimony of an intelligent man or woman who had been to prison.[5]

Murray gave a list of conscionable and political offenders which ranged from militant suffragists to Peculiar People to conscientious objectors to Sinn Féiners.[6] Then, as now, a political offence can include anything from a breach of the peace and criminal damage to arson, bank robbery, murder, and treason. If the motivation is political or conscionable rather than personal malice, vice, or gain, then no matter how much it goes against the grain to acknowledge it, the crime, despite its wickedness and harm, is not an 'ordinary' one, even though many lawyers and politicians insist it is.

Political offenders have always had the potential to influence policy. Most enter the criminal process with their character intact, even though they are called to justice and may be condemned for the methods they have chosen to further their objectives. They see the process and the institutions from a perspective not normally

[5] Preface to S. Hobhouse, *An English Prison From Within* (London: George Allen & Unwin, 1919), 6–7.

[6] These offenders clashed with the law in various ways. Militant suffragists, notably the Women's Social and Political Union (Suffragettes) were usually committed for public order offences connected with their votes for women campaigns. Peculiar People, a small protestant sect centred mainly on London, relied exclusively on prayer, and refused medical aid and vaccination, thus breaking the law. Sinn Féin after 1917 was a militant nationalist organization, whose armed wing was the Irish Republican Army. Its members came before the courts for a range of offences, including conspiracy, armed rebellion, and murder.

available to respectable middle-class or working-class society. They live the sequence of arrest and interrogation, remand, court appearance, sentence, and imprisonment. Sometimes these experiences embitter or anger, and while this may colour their accounts, anger can provide the motivation to publish and usually gives their stories fire and a testing quality of authenticity. It is remarkable that more often than not this version of events from the other side of the counter is even-handed, dealing fairly, for example with prison staff, even while criticizing attitudes and conditions.

Activists have several advantages as polemicists. There is usually a group of supporters and sympathizers in the wider community who concern themselves with their sentences and conditions, and who publish and join in their prisoners' complaints and observations on their experience of punishment. And there is a reciprocal benefit: a cause which has inspired the risk of lawbreaking and the sufferings of imprisonment is blooded: what is perceived as sacrifice validates in a curious way and adds energy and appeal. Letters to the newspapers, questions in Parliament, and prison demonstrations and vigils remind politicians and officials that their decisions, behaviour, and attitudes are being scrutinized; they are also a morale-boosting telegraph to the political prisoner. Self-justification, faithfulness to a cause and a sense of having been touched by history make it more likely that an account of trial and punishment will be written, disseminated, and preserved. Prison memoirs, whether long or short, in the form of a newspaper interview, pamphlet, or book, are likely to be more substantial than those of ordinary prisoners because of the intellectual capacity of the activist, the motivation, and the ability to make wider connections to politics and public policy. They will also have a guaranteed readership from supporters and the curious.

The careers of some political prisoners may later take a more conventional turn, one in which they may attain positions of influence or power. John Burns, for example, was imprisoned for his part in 'Bloody Sunday', the Trafalgar Square demonstration of 13 November 1887. For this he was sentenced to six weeks' imprisonment, without hard labour. Burns later became Liberal MP for Battersea and in Campbell-Bannerman's and then Asquith's administrations (1905–1914) was President of the Board of Trade. Six years after his imprisonment Burns was prominent in the group which, largely through the *Daily Chronicle,* secured the appointment of the Departmental Committee on Prisons (Gladstone Committee) in June 1894. He also took a leading part in the debates on the far-reaching Prison Bill of 1898.[7] Because of his experiences his views were given a respectful hearing by the House.[8] Burns' imprisonment was a cornerstone for his reputation and career.

The crusading journalist W.T. Stead, it could be said, made his mark upon national life not so much by his *Pall Mall Gazette* campaign against child prostitution and the disgusting trade in virgins as by his imprisonment. Although there were several remarkable features in the way in which he exposed the trade, there had been and would be other exposés of commercial vice. In November 1885 national indignation ran high when Stead was sent to prison for three months for a purely technical breach of the law in connection with his investigations. Churches, women's, and moral welfare organizations were enraged that he who should have been a hero, fully entitled to public gratitude for his work, was denigrated by the legal process and was being treated as a criminal. Determined lobbying by the churches and moral welfare agencies coerced a very reluctant Home Office into a probably illegal intervention in Stead's sentence, and his removal to the First Division.[9] So proud was Stead of what had thus been accomplished that thereafter he donned prison dress on the anniversary of his imprisonment.[10]

Irish Rebels

Burns and Stead were perhaps given to some embellishment of their prison experiences, and certainly reaped a lifelong harvest from the notoriety. Michael Davitt was in some ways a more substantial, and

---

[7] Enacted as 61 & 62 Vict., c. 41.

[8] See, e.g., HC Debs., vol. LVI, col. 98, 4 April 1898.

[9] There is an account of these events in my *English Local Prisons 1860–1900: Next Only to Death* (London: Routledge, 1995), 373–5. The First Division was, in effect, civil detention.

[10] Sylvia Pankhurst describes his appearance in prison uniform at an 'At Home' on 6 November 1906, 21 years after his incarceration: E.S. Pankhurst, *The Suffragette Movement: An Intimate Account of Persons and Ideals* (London: Longmans, Green & Co., 1913), 238. Eugene Debs, the American socialist, labour activist, and pacifist campaigned for the US Presidency in prison uniform. He had served almost three years of a 10-year sentence imposed for his opposition to US involvement in the First World War: see A. Neier, 'Confining Dissent: The Political Prison' in N. Morris and D. J. Rothman (eds.), *Oxford History of the Prison* (New York: Oxford University Press, 1995), 398–9.

certainly a more sombre figure—in the gravity of his offence, his sentence, and the time spent in prison. Sentenced in July 1870 to fifteen years' penal servitude for his part in Fenian arms procurement and smuggling, Davitt spent seven years and seven months' arduous confinement as a convict, before political circumstances procured his early release on licence. In 1881–2 he served a further fifteen months when his licence was withdrawn because of his activities and speeches in Ireland's Land War; he also spent four months in an Irish prison for seditious speech.[11] Davitt was elected as an MP in 1893 and again (for a four-year period) in 1895. Over the years his views on imprisonment were widely reported. In 1878 he gave evidence to a major committee of inquiry into the convict system.[12] During his second (and greatly ameliorated) spell of penal servitude he wrote a perceptive and surprisingly balanced account of prisons and prisoners, and on various aspects of the problem of crime.[13] Over the following decade and a half Davitt on a number of occasions wrote and spoke about prison conditions and penal policy. He also contributed to the debates on the 1898 Prisons Bill, making points about the treatment of political offenders and also (with several of his colleagues in the Irish Parliamentary Party) about the regime and prospects for the ordinary criminal prisoner.[14] Davitt's observations rang true and were respectfully received in the House. His shocking revelations about prison food led the then Home Secretary, Sir Matthew White Ridley, to set up the important Departmental Committee on Prison Dietaries—important in the sense that it recommended that food should cease to be an instrument for the punishment of prisoners.[15]

---

[11] For an account of Davitt's offence, trial, and imprisonment see T.W. Moody, *Davitt and Irish Revolution 1846–82* (Oxford: Clarendon Press, 1982), Chapters 3 and 5.

[12] This was the *Royal Commission to Inquire into the Working of the Penal Servitude Acts* (Kimberley Commission), Parliamentary Papers, 1878–9, C. 2368, XXXVII, 1.

[13] M. Davitt, *Leaves from a Prison Diary or Lectures to a 'Solitary' Audience* (London: Chapman and Hall, 1885) (2 vols.).

[14] See, e.g., HC Debs., vol. LV, cols. 1170–83, 24 March 1898. John Dillon, John Redmond, and T.P. O'Connor all condemned the state of English prisons, O'Connor denouncing them as 'a system of deliberate, calculated, scientific, cruel starvation': HC Debs., vol. LVI, col. 60, 4 April 1898.

[15] *Report of the Departmental Committee on Prison Dietaries*, Parliamentary Papers, 1899, C. 9166, XLII, 1, 3. Institutional inertia and the principle of less-eligibility largely thwarted this recommendation for many years.

But the penal views of Davitt and a few of his colleagues were not widely shared by the Irish MPs, and still less so by the revolutionists who came into the English prisons in the years following the 1916 Easter Rising. The majority view of the Irish politicals, MPs and non-Parliamentary activists alike, was far from sympathetic to the ordinary inmates of English prisons. These were seen in their corrupt criminal character as evidence of British moral degeneracy, a suppuration on the national body, and as part of the apparatus which, with the convict uniform and regime, was intended to contaminate and degrade Irish political offenders. (And it is noteworthy that such feelings were not expressed about ordinary *Irish* criminal prisoners, whose fallen state was conveniently seen as evidence of British misrule in Ireland.) This was a venerable and venerated doctrine of the Irish revolutionary canon. Seventy years before, John Mitchel, one of the Young Ireland leadership, was transported under the provisions of the tailor-made Treason Felony Act of 1848.[16] He possessed a vitriolic pen, and what acid he saved from his Anglophobia was flung at convicts. The dark genius of British penal discipline had, insisted Mitchel, brought them as near to being perfect friends 'as human wit can go. . . . What a blessing to these creatures, and to mankind, both in the northern hemisphere and the southern, if they had been hanged'.[17]

Later generations of Irish rebels generally adhered to the Mitchel rather than the Davitt view of their fellow convicts. Charles Kickham, a devout and pious man, and one of the mildest of the Fenian leaders imprisoned in 1865, told an official inquiry that being mixed with criminals was 'the greatest punishment in the power of man to inflict'. It was not their fault that he had been placed among them, 'but the loathing with which association with them had inspired me will cling to me while I live'. Kickham and his comrades bitterly complained that they were being treated in the same manner as persons convicted of appalling sexual offences.[18] Their relatives,

---

[16] 11 Vict. c. 12.

[17] J. Mitchel, *Jail Journal or Five Years in British Prisons* (London: R. & T. Washbourne, n.d.), 224. Elsewhere in the *Journal* he observed 'I gaze on them with horror, as unclean and inhuman monsters, due long ago to the gallows-tree and oblivion': ibid., 256. He was horrified by the thought that should he die in Van Diemen's Land his remains should mix with those of convicts 'in one of those devil's acres they name churchyards': *New York Daily Times*, 24 Nov. 1853, 3b.

[18] The Convict of Clonmel *Things Not Generally Known Concerning England's Treatment of Fenian Prisoners* (Dublin: The Irishman, 1869), 20, 21 and 26.

friends, and supporters took a similar line. The wife of one of the Fenian leaders (Mrs Ellen O'Leary) identified their enforced association with criminals as a particular form of wickedness and oppression: '[t]hat political prisoners some of whom are even of high intellect, refinement and education, should be placed on a level with the most degraded and basest of mankind—men stained with the worst crimes—is a thing which will reflect eternal disgrace on the British government'.[19]

By one set of criteria the Fenians were honourable men. They had conspired together and had taken steps to overthrow the government, but their revolutionary theory required an open contest between the forces of a resurgent Ireland and the British army. The Dynamitards, Irish-American conspirators of the 1880s, were hampered by no such rules of honour. The objective was the same— an independent Irish republic—but the method was terrorism. Dynamite, an explosive a hundred times more powerful than gunpowder, was the weapon, and its use against a variety of urban targets, including places where civilians congregated, was the tactic which would supposedly paralyse or even crush British power. By a series of mercies only one life was lost in the explosions, though a number of people were injured.

These groups were repudiated by mainstream Fenianism, and by others who opposed British authority in Ireland. The broader community, Irish and British alike, regarded the Dynamitards with revulsion. Yet the Dynamitards felt able to scorn their prison companions in much the same terms as John Mitchel. Thomas Clarke, one of the more intelligent of the imprisoned men, regarded the ordinary convicts as 'dregs raked in from the gutters'.[20] Some of the Dynamitards put the prison staff in much the same category as the criminals. James Egan complained of warders' language which was so 'filthy and disgusting' that he could not repeat the words when he made his complaint to the prison governor.[21]

---

[19]   *The Irishman*, 4 Aug. 1866, 93 a–b.

[20]   T.J. Clarke, *Glimpses of an Irish Felon's Prison Life* (Dublin and London: Maunsell & Roberts Ltd., 1922), 62. Clarke (1858–1916) served 15 years of a life sentence and was the central figure in the 1916 Easter Rising in Dublin.

[21]   *Report of the Visitors of Her Majesty's Convict Prison at Chatham as to the Treatment of Certain Prisoners Convicted of Treason Felony*, Parliamentary Papers, 1890, XXXVII, C. 6016, Minutes of Evidence, qq. 2100–2104, 63.

The hundreds of Irish political prisoners who entered British prisons in the five years following the 1916 Rising brought with them these traditional attitudes of contempt towards their fellow prisoners and prison staff. Countess Markievicz, whose socialism and work among the Dublin poor surely made her the foremost candidate for a sympathetic exploration of the prison world, easily adopted the usual patter. Her companion convicts included 'the lowest of the low'. The women's language was 'a torment to some of the ordinary prisoners, and a gradual training in vice to others'. Forcing the Irish rebels into association with such was a strategy on the part of the British government to destroy them morally, mentally and physically.[22]

Constance Markievicz was not immune to pity, however, and the plight of the 150 or so Borstal girls then at Aylesbury convict prison moved her beyond condemnation. The girls, a pathetic lot, had a high rate of suicide attempts and self-mutilation. During the months of Markievicz's incarceration several attempted hanging, another tried to cut her throat, yet another to set fire to her cell; several swallowed large needles. 'Poor girls', Constance observed, 'it seemed so wicked and futile to drive them to this.'[23] This sympathy did not prevent Constance's republican associates describing the Aylesbury women as 'the dregs of the population' and claiming that the Countess had been obliged to live in 'the atmosphere and conversation of a brothel'.[24] A noted female suffragist, internationalist, and labour activist friend of Constance, Miss Louie Bennett, also condemned the Aylesbury prisoners as 'the lowest type of criminals . . . prostitutes of infamous character'. She demanded a separation between 'moral women prisoners' and professional prostitutes.[25]

Among the Sinn Féin leaders detained, interned, and imprisoned in the years 1916–22 Markievicz was probably the only one to draw upon her prison experience to find even a smidgeon of sympathy for prisoners. She and her colleagues focused on their own plight and the struggle to force the British government to accord them prisoner of war or political status. The other prisoners (with whom most of the

[22] *San Francisco Examiner*, 7 Dec. 1919, 6 f–g. There was, stated the Countess (this was a retrospective interview), 'one horror always hanging over our heads, and that was the fear of catching loathsome diseases'.

[23] Ibid., 6 f.

[24] Public Record Office HO 144/1580/316818/10.

[25] Ibid. /20: Miss Louie Bennett to Home Secretary, 17 Feb. 1917.

men were generally not mixed) were England's criminals, doubly unfortunate, in the loss of their character and in being English. Forced association with these outcasts was a weapon in the British government's war against Ireland. Certainly when Ireland achieved independence the prison experience of many of its leaders had no discernible effect on Ireland's penal policy, and her prisons continued on their Victorian path, missing some of the very limited reforms introduced in Britain.[26]

Conscientious Objectors

It was an irony remarked upon at the time that there were concurrently in the English prisons persons whose crime was fighting the British Empire as well as those who refused to fight for it. So much a part did conscription become of twentieth-century life that we must remind ourselves of its novelty when introduced in 1916. To some it was inevitably associated with Continental despotism, a practice scarcely compatible with British ideas of liberty. Yet there was little room for dissenters—especially when refusal could so easily be portrayed as self-interest and self-preservation. It came in on a wave of popular sentiment against what were seen as shirkers and slackers, and in the face of at least some professional and political doubts about its immediate military necessity, or indeed of the ability of the army readily to absorb the conscripts.[27] Keeping trust with those who had enrolled and who had been killed, wounded, and maimed injected emotion and gave intensity and urgency to the conscription campaign.

The measure was introduced by a Liberal-led coalition government, and a concession had been made to minority opinion by providing an avenue of escape for those who had conscientious objections. Local tribunals heard appeals and could grant conditional or absolute exemption. These bodies of local worthies and tradesmen were generally unsympathetic to conscientious claims, imposed stringent and sometimes unattainable criteria for qualification, and rejected many appeals. Some men agreed to serve in a non-

---

[26] This was particularly marked in the regime for juveniles and young adult prisoners, normally the priority for penal reform. Contrast the situation before and after independence, as described by N. Osborough in *Borstal in Ireland: Custodial Provision for the Young Adult Offender 1906–1974* (Dublin: Institute of Public Administration, 1975), Chapters 2 and 4.

[27] A.J.P. Taylor, *English History 1914–1945* (Oxford: Clarendon Press, 1965), 53.

combative capacity, and were usually assigned to ambulance or other medical support work; 7,000 took this route. Labour camps of doubtful efficiency were set up (and, significantly, were administered by the Home Office), absorbing a further 3,000 men. A willingness to be removed from home, do meaningless work, and live in poverty in uncomfortable conditions was apparently taken as an earnest of sincerity in refusing conscription: another version of the 'workhouse test'.

The assessment of the conscionable and the indulgence of alternative work for those deemed genuine had the effect of intensifying feeling against the residue of men who had not won exemption and would not accept conditional service. About 1,350 men (the number remained firmly constant throughout the war) fell into this category and were subject to the coercive and punitive powers which the law provided. The motivations of this group (known as 'absolutists') included religious pacifism, political or moral unwillingness to accept state dictation over such an important matter of individual choice, and adherence to socialist, Marxist, or anarchist doctrines opposed to imperialist war. Alternative forms of service, whether in medical units or industry, were unacceptable to them. They argued (not unreasonably) that they would simply be substituting for and thereby releasing for combat men otherwise fit for military service. In the early weeks of conscription many of these absolutists were arrested, handed over to the military, ordered to put on uniforms, or forced into them, and were generally deemed to be under military command. Since they did not accept this authority and refused to obey orders they were brought before courts martial and sentenced to imprisonment.[28]

---

[28] With some military coercion went further. In one notorious incident 37 were taken to France where, considered to be on active service, refusal to obey an order could result in the death penalty. 17 men were subjected to further punishments, including Field Punishment (a form of non-lethal crucifixion). Death sentences were pronounced but, after a probably sadistic pause, commuted to 10 years' penal servitude. The political consequences of such treatment were recognized by government, and on the instructions of Asquith the men were returned to England. There were, especially in the first months, a number of other incidents of ill-treatment, severe beatings, and humiliations. While these were not officially sanctioned a blind eye seems to have been turned to them by various local commanders: Fenner Brockway, *Inside the Left: Thirty Years of Platform Press and Parliament* (London: George Allen & Unwin, 1942), 77–9.

The absolutists were the target of enforcement action throughout the war and indeed for a time thereafter. Most of the 1,350 were sentenced more than once to periods of imprisonment with hard labour. Some by the war's end had served nearly three years in instalments. Men continued to make their way into the prisons well into 1919. Fifty-four died following arrest—eight in prison, one in an asylum, eleven in the Home Office labour camps, and six by suicide. Thirty-seven became mentally afflicted and 189 were released on health grounds.[29] An examination of the files confirms the principal memoirs in most respects. Conscientious objectors who simply did not wish to fight were much more harshly treated and certainly granted far fewer privileges than the militant Sinn Féiners with whom they sometimes shared a prison, many of whom had used extreme violence or organized to do so.

Of the memoirs of the absolutists one of the most important is that of Stephen Hobhouse, son of the West Country landowner and Liberal MP, Henry Hobhouse, and of Margaret Hobhouse, née Potter, sister of Beatrice Webb. His cousin, Emily Hobhouse, had gained for herself a proud place in South African history by her investigation and condemnation of British concentration camps set up for Boer women and children during the South African war. A strong current of religious and political non-conformity ran in this well-connected and many-talented family. Stephen Hobhouse underwent a religious experience and conversion at Oxford in 1902 and committed himself to a life of asceticism, service, and searching along Tolstoyan and Quaker lines. On the outbreak of war he campaigned for the pacifist cause and involved himself in relief work. In August 1916 he refused conditional exemption (service in the Quaker Ambulance Unit). He failed to report for duty, and some weeks later was arrested, brought before Shoreditch magistrates (he had chosen to live in this very poor area), fined, and handed over to the army.

Hobhouse was to spend two periods of about five weeks each in regimental guardhouses, awaiting his courts martial. Those he did not find too onerous since by then (October 1916 on the first occasion) the harsher practices, such as stripping the conscientious objectors of their civilian clothes, beating them, and forcing them into uniforms or leaving them semi-naked, had stopped. With few

[29] Hobhouse, n. 5 above, 5.

exceptions the rank-and-file soldiers now treated the conscientious objectors decently.[30] A first sentence of imprisonment, six months' hard labour, was served at Wormwood Scrubs, and a second at Exeter. In December 1917, he and four other absolutists were on health grounds unconditionally released. From these experiences he published two pamphlets and became secretary and editor of an inquiry into the prison system put in hand by the Labour Research Department in January 1919.[31]

The perspective of Hobhouse and other religious and political conscientious objectors was very different from that of the Irish rebels. From a religious point of view other prisoners, far from being 'fiends', 'inhuman monsters', and 'dregs raked in from the gutters', were fellow beings to whom they owed the duty of love, respect, and concern as having been created in the image of God. A prison system that failed to respect the dignity of these fallen ones and to acknowledge their common humanity had to be exposed and condemned. The politically motivated conscientious objectors found in prison—in its inhabitants and its system of administration—ample support for their anti-capitalist doctrines. In these casualties was to be discerned a distillation of the wickedness of a system based on commodity, alienation, and oppression.

To the religious it was the moral deficiencies of the prisons which were most shocking. Hobhouse condemned the strict silence and debilitating separation. A prisoner who submitted to his isolation and did not attempt to communicate with his fellows endured an experience which 'inevitably tends to produce mental as well as moral decay'. Disobedience, on the other hand, promoted 'a special form of demoralisation, an undermining of the standard of truthfulness and sincerity'.[32] Hobhouse so objected to the moral effects of the silent regime that during his second imprisonment he informed the governor of Exeter prison that it was his intention to talk aloud

[30] See Brockway, n. 28 above, 83–8.

[31] Hobhouse, n. 5 above (originally in *Quarterly Review*, July, 1918, 21–37); S. Hobhouse, *The Silence System in British Prisons* (London: Society of Friends Bookshop, 1918) (originally in (1918) 52 *Friends Quarterly Examiner* 249–63). See also S. Hobhouse, *Forty Years and an Epilogue: The Autobiography of Stephen Hobhouse* (London: James Clarke, 1951), Chapters 15 and 16 and (with A. Fenner Brockway) *English Prisons To-Day: Being the Report of the Prison System Enquiry Committee* (London: Longmans Green & Co., 1922).

[32] Hobhouse, n. 5 above, 33.

to his companions. This was a demonstration against 'craftiness and deceit', in itself part of the more general protest against war. It was, moreover, his religious duty 'to pass on words of cheer and interest' to others.[33] Following this declaration of intent Hobhouse was placed in rigorously enforced solitary confinement, where he remained for almost three months until amnestied on health grounds.

Hobhouse considered the philosophy of imprisonment and its regime rotten to the heart. He saw this in the deprivation of all privacy and choice, the constant barrage of orders, the lack of any personal property ('and of that sense of self-expression and choice in things which is its chief spiritual value'), and the tedium and corroding and dehumanising dullness of prison life. Following a line of criticism eloquently addressed by Oscar Wilde twenty years before, he lamented the deliberate removal of all opportunities for the prisoner 'to serve his fellow, to do him a good turn, to interchange thoughts and greetings with him'.[34] He condemned the dietary ('[n]early all of us knew what hunger means'). There were also observations on the deplorable standards of hygiene—the promiscuous wearing of imperfectly laundered underclothing, and that changed only once a fortnight. But the thrust of the attack was moral: '[n]early every feature of prison life seems deliberately arranged to destroy a man's sense of his own personality, his power of choice and initiative, his possessive instincts, his conception of himself as a being designed to love and to serve his fellow-man'.[35]

Fenner Brockway also made numerous criticisms of imprisonment on the basis of the various sentences which he served (amounting to some thirty months). Some of these were on the moral plane, but more often they were pragmatic observations on the harshness of conditions and how to get around them. Unlike Hobhouse, Brockway had no qualms about evading the silence and non-communication rules. He quickly mastered the cell telegraph tapping code and was adept at concealing pencils and passing mes-

[33] Hobhouse, *Forty Years and an Epilogue*, n. 31 above, 165.

[34] Hobhouse, n. 5 above, 19–20. For Wilde's powerful letter (prompted by the dismissal from Reading prison of warder Thomas Martin for giving a biscuit to a hungry child) see the *Daily Chronicle*, 28 May 1897, 10 c–e; this text is given in full in M. Holland and R. Hart-Davis (eds.), *The Complete Letters of Oscar Wilde* (London: Fourth Estate, 2000), 847–55.

[35] Hobhouse, n. 5 above, 18.

sages; he even organized and circulated an illicit prison newspaper. Much more than Hobhouse, Brockway saw prison as an opportunity to hone his organizational skills, pit his intelligence and inventiveness against the authorities, and make socialist propaganda and converts wherever he could. He was trenchant in his condemnation of elements in the regime. Several mentally handicapped and insane prisoners at Walton (Liverpool) prison were accommodated in cage-like cells where '[t]hey gibbered like idiots or committed self-abuse with grinning faces'.[36] The long hours of cellular confinement (eighteen out of twenty-four), silence, one letter and one visit a month were hard to bear in themselves, disastrous for self-control, and drove prisoners to 'the verge of mental and nervous breakdown'. And he agreed with Hobhouse on the degradation and morally destructive effects of the experience: '[w]e were treated like caged animals, without minds or personality, and were starved of all beauty'.[37]

The Female Suffragists

More than any other political or campaigning group at this time the militants among the female suffragists saw that imprisonment could disadvantage authority as well as assert it, could advance a cause even while restricting individual members. On 13 October 1905, Christabel Pankhurst and Annie Kenny interrupted a Liberal Party election meeting at the Manchester Free Trade Hall; Sir Edward Grey was the principal speaker. The two young women were subsequently convicted of assault and fined. On refusing to pay they were sent to prison.[38] The publicity which this received encouraged others in disrupting such meetings and considerably strengthened support for the Women's Social and Political Union (WSPU) which had been founded two years before by Emmeline Pankhurst, Christabel's mother. The brief imprisonment of the two could be considered as

---

[36] Brockway, n. 28 above, 102.

[37] Ibid., 103. He recalled how a few blades of new grass growing between the flagstones in the exercise yard had given him great pleasure, and their removal by a work party had caused him to weep: '[p]erhaps the drabness of prison existence can be measured by that'.

[38] Emmeline Pankhurst went immediately to the court cells to pay the fines. Christabel protested and threatened, 'Mother, if you pay my fine I will never go home': E. Pankhurst, *My Own Story* (London: Eveleigh Nash, 1914), 49; S. Pankhurst, n. 10 above, 189–91.

the WSPU's proper launch. In the years that followed the organization went from strength to strength. Public disorder and disruption backed the campaign, with Liberal politicians being particularly targeted as the governing party and constantly procrastinating hypocrites. Protesters infiltrated election and other party meetings, dogged ministers, and there were incidents in Parliament and at Downing Street. At this stage of the campaign, however, there was little damage apart from the large-scale smashing of windows.

From the outset, the distinguishing feature of the WSPU was its singlemindedness wedded to claims of comprehensiveness. Here was a political philosophy wrapped around a single idea. Denial of the vote to women and women's counsel in government explained much that was wrong and rotten with the world: it followed that the female franchise would put right a deal more than the political, economic, and social disadvantages of women. What was on offer was a new beginning. To that end Emmeline Pankhurst demanded that '[n]o member of the WSPU divides her attention between suffrage and other social reforms'. Reason and justice demanded that women should take a hand in social reform, 'especially those evils bearing directly on women themselves', but before any of that— 'before any other legislation whatever'—there had to be 'the elementary justice of votes for women'.[39]

This sharp focus and world-explaining power undoubtedly contributed to the rapid and in some ways astonishing growth of the WSPU and the fanatical devotion of many of its members. There was no dissipation of energies on the many social, political, and international issues that then faced the conventional political parties and reform groups. And this powerful ideology was matched by simplicity in organization. There was no WSPU constitution or by-laws, no annual meetings, and no election of officers. Any woman became a member who paid a shilling, who agreed with the WSPU policy, and who pledged not to work for any other political party until the vote was won. The moment she suggested that some other policy be adopted, or that other policies be added to the franchise demand, she ceased to be a member. Emmeline Pankhurst adamantly defended this autocracy: '[t]he WSPU is simply a suffrage army in the field. It is purely a volunteer army, and no one is obliged to remain in it'.[40]

---

[39] E. Pankhurst, n. 38 above, 57.   [40] Ibid., 59.

With this intensity of purpose and remarkable efficiency in organization the WSPU waged one of the most effective direct-action campaigns in the country's history. The Pankhursts—especially Christabel—had the ability to approach issues in ways well beyond the conventional. This imagination and energy lent enormous flair to protest and demonstrations. Other members of the organization were almost equally inventive and certainly as determined: the act of public protest itself was personally liberating and transcended the ordinary cares. There is not space here for more than the briefest outline of the campaign, which in its various stages went from individual and small-scale protest to mass demonstrations, and from heckling to window-breaking to arson; in its final stages some procured and began to use explosives. As with other groups at other places and in other times the justness of the cause absolved in the activists' minds the destructiveness and violence of the action. (In fairness it must be said that great care was taken to avoid harm to people.) Over the course of the nine-year militant campaign of the WSPU several hundred members and supporters (including a few men) were sent to prison, sometimes in ones and twos, at other times in large batches. In January and February 1907, for example, 130 women were sent to prison for unlawful assembly and attempting to rush Parliament. In support of a Suffrage Bill the various suffrage organizations on 21 June 1910 organized a vast march, culminating in an overflowing meeting at the Royal Albert Hall, then the largest indoor venue in England. The march through the streets of London was headed by 617 women, dressed in white, each holding a silver pole topped by a broad arrow, to show that she had been imprisoned for the suffrage cause. Imprisonment had already been turned back on itself: from being a vital weapon of government it had become a suffragist tool.[41]

---

[41] As with other movements, the WSPU were not aware of the potential of prison propaganda at the outset. In 1906 Christabel Pankhurst's policy had been to ignore the conditions under which suffragists' sentences were served, lest this detract from the central issue of the vote. After her imprisonment Sylvia Pankhurst broke with this approach and gave 'dozens of interviews' on prison conditions, as well as distributing her prison sketches to the press: E.S. Pankhurst, n. 10 above, 238. Thereafter the WSPU was diligent in incorporating into its general campaign the prison conditions encountered by its members. The literature of the period (memoirs, interviews, etc.) suggests that for many of the women imprisonment was a stage in their personal emancipation and contributed significantly to a growth of self-confidence.

The Suffragette campaign will always be associated with the way in which the women continued to battle in prison. While some were allowed the privileges of the First or Second Divisions, others were sentenced to imprisonment with hard labour and subjected to the penal regime intended for ordinary criminals. This, as we have seen, comprised solitary confinement; coarse, poorly laundered, inadequate and ill-fitting clothes; a sparse diet; and the minimum of mental stimulation. Fortified by the justness of their cause as much inside as outside prison, the suffragettes soon embarked on acts and then routines of disobedience. At Holloway prison, Emmeline Pankhurst took exercise in the same ring as her daughter but was forbidden to speak to her. After two weeks she decided to endure this no longer: '[t]o forbid a mother to speak to her daughter was infamous'. Even closer and more punitive confinement followed. As suffrage prisoners were released so was the news of the punishment and its cause, and thousands of Suffragettes converged on the prison, marching around it, cheering and singing *March of the Women* and the *Women's Marseillaise*. Questions were asked in the Commons and the Home Office intervened to allow Mrs Pankhurst and her daughter to meet and talk each day for an hour.[42]

Political clout counted. In the landslide election of January 1906 the Liberal Party had secured a majority of eighty-four seats over all the other parties combined (Unionist, Irish Nationalist, and Labour). When Asquith succeeded Campbell-Bannerman in April 1908, by-elections had altered these figures but slightly. On paper, therefore, Asquith could afford to defy the Irish interest. In reality, the Irish had a considerable ability to create trouble in the Commons and outside it, and had many close ties with these margins of Liberalism which were fraying away as Asquith shifted his party more to the centre, and Labour grew in confidence. The great constitutional conflicts with the Lords were already discernible. The Irish, in short, were not to be ignored in Parliament. Then, as would later be the case with the Sinn Féin prisoners, Parliamentary leverage and nuis-

---

[42] E. Pankhurst, n. 38 above, 130–4. The fact that Mary Gordon, the first Lady Inspector of Prisons, was herself a committed suffragist and covert supporter of the WSPU may have had a bearing on the sometimes inconsistent treatment of the Suffragettes: see L. Zedner's excellent *Women, Crime and Custody in Victorian England* (Oxford: Clarendon Press, 1991), 128–9. Mary Gordon discussed the effect on penal policy of the imprisonment of the Suffragettes in her *Penal Discipline* (London: G. Routledge & Sons, 1922).

ance-value translated into better conditions for what at that time were a few Irish political prisoners. Sylvia Pankhurst noted that C.J. Farrell and other Irish members who were serving sentences for cattle driving were given the full privileges of the First Division.[43] Emmeline Pankhurst was campaigning for these privileges in Holloway, but was turned down by a Home Office seemingly unperturbed by accusations of differential treatment and double standards. And, after all, voteless women were of particularly little significance to the professional politician.

Hunger-striking began in July 1908, when Miss Wallace Dunlop arrived at Holloway to begin a sentence of one month's imprisonment for defacing the walls of St Stephen's Hall (on to which she had copied an extract from the Bill of Rights dealing with the right to petition Parliament). She informed the governor that Suffragettes had resolved not to submit to the regime for ordinary prisoners, and that she would not eat until this point was conceded by the authorities. No attempt was made to force-feed, but tempting and tasty food was left in her cell. Miss Dunlop remained steadfast, and a week later, on medical advice, was released.[44] On the day that she was freed fourteen new arrivals (window breakers) threatened hunger strikes. The prison governor charged them with mutiny. The Board of Visitors duly found them guilty, and the fourteen were severally sentenced to between a week and ten days in the punishment cells. This was farcical, since the chief part of the punishment regime was deprivation of food, and the women were being sentenced to a severe reduction in diet for the offence of refusing to eat. That there was little more that the authorities could do simply showed up the nonsense of their sentences and the weakness of their position. The hunger strike continued, and by the end of the following week all fourteen had been released not only from the punishment cells, but from prison.[45] Succeeding groups of suffrage

[43] E.S. Pankhurst, n.10 above, 291. The First Division privileges included unlimited correspondence, carrying on one's professional work, few restrictions on visitors, and an entitlement to own food, clothing, furniture, and medical advice and treatment; an ordinary prisoner could also be employed as a cleaner.

[44] At this time little was known of the body's capacity to withstand prolonged starvation. Medical officers, in particular, were unwilling to accept the responsibility for continued detention.

[45] Ibid., 151–2.

prisoners followed this pattern and displayed increasing self-confidence in active resistance in the prison.

Clearly this could not be allowed to continue. The women were circumventing the sentence of the court and undermining the state's authority. Forcible feeding of hunger-strikers commenced with Mrs Mary Leigh, sentenced to four months' imprisonment for hurling slates from a roof adjacent to a Birmingham hall in which Asquith was speaking.[46] The forced feeding technique was primitive. Food was poured through a funnel and a tube directly into the stomach of the hunger-striker. Refusal to open the mouth was countered by a species of jaw-jack. From the outset it was widely known that the procedure (made public under the euphemism 'hospital treatment') was both dangerous and exceedingly painful. Gums were torn and teeth broken by the jaw-jack, and food could relatively easily be poured into the lungs rather than the stomach. The rough handling of the women day after day as they resisted feeding, and the prostrate condition in which it left them, well publicized by the WSPU, electrified the faithful and generated indignation and deep concern well beyond suffrage ranks.[47] By 1913 the effect of the strikes and the growing inability of the prison administrators to cope with them led the government to the confession of failure signified by the 'Cat and Mouse Act'.[48]

Suffrage militancy showed no signs of slackening in the months following the introduction of the new legislation. Emmeline Pankhurst in April 1913 had been sentenced to three years' penal servitude for conspiracy to commit arson. Sent to Holloway, she added to

[46] Mrs Leigh's action against the governor of Birmingham prison, resulting in a ruling that the prison authorities were entitled and indeed obliged to keep a hunger-striking prisoner alive, became the leading case. The law stood thus for some 80 years: *Leigh v. Gladstone and Others* (1909) 26 *Times Law Reports* 139.

[47] Christabel Pankhurst wrote to all likely sympathizers about hunger strikers. In a letter to the MP C.P. Scott (a famous editor of the *Manchester Guardian*) she gave Miss Wallace Dunlop's opinion that it was 'a very terrible experience'. Other women were nevertheless considering it: 'I am sure you must now be feeling more strongly than ever how unworthy is the action of the Government as far as Women Suffrage and its advocates are concerned': C. Pankhurst to C.P. Scott, 13 July 1909 (Manchester: Manchester University, John Rylands Library, Manchester Guardian Collection 128/82).

[48] Prisoners (Temporary Discharge for Ill-health) Act 1913, 3 Geo. V. c.58. This allowed for the temporary release of prisoners whose health had deteriorated, and their rearrest when deemed by the authorities to be sufficiently restored.

the terrible effectiveness of the hunger strike a refusal to take liquid or to sleep.[49] Released after a few days, she was repeatedly re-arrested and over the following year served about one month in twelve monthly instalments. This, and many other suffrage activities, charged and drove the campaign ever more intensely. The resort to arson, attacks on museums and art galleries, the acquisition, planting, and detonation of explosives, showed that the stakes were being dangerously raised. The Derby Day death of Emily Davison shocked the nation and provided the movement with that most dangerous of weapons—a martyr. The WSPU continued efforts to broaden its appeal by linking the female franchise to an effective (if misleading) anti-vice campaign. With many tens and perhaps hundreds of thousands of women involved in one way or the other, it is unlikely that peace would have been re-established without female suffrage. In the event, domestic peace came through the most terrible war yet seen. Within days of the outbreak of hostilities an amnesty for all Suffragettes was announced. The WSPU leadership declared a halt in its campaign, threw its weight behind the war effort, and (speaking volumes) in 1915 the *Suffragette* was renamed *Britannia*.[50] In December 1917 a Franchise Bill passed the Commons and was endorsed by the Lords. The first steps had been taken to a full female suffrage. The part played by the WSPU, as distinct from less militant suffrage organizations, remains a topic of debate and judgement.

The Suffragette attitude towards ordinary criminals was sympathetic. Since theirs was a feminist organization there was a readiness to use the plight of women prisoners as examples of the wider injustices visited upon their sex. They did not see the criminal

[49] This technique had recently been pioneered by her daughter, Sylvia, who on release, and after five weeks' forcible feeding, had been 'emaciated in the extreme, with eyes heavily bloodshot, like cups of blood': E.S. Pankhurst, *The Life of Emmeline Pankhurst: The Suffragette Struggle for Women's Citizenship* (London: T. Werner Laurie, 1935), 125. For an account of the first hunger, fluid, sleeping, and sitting strike see S. Pankhurst's *The Suffragette Movement*, n. 10 above, 446–51.

[50] See David Mitchell's excellent *The Fighting Pankhursts* (London: Jonathan Cape, 1967), 50–62 for an account of the reaction of the WSPU and the Pankhursts to the Great War. Martin Pugh's *The Pankhursts* (London: Allen Lane, 2001), Chapters 14 and 15 gives an account of the different directions taken after the war; Sylvia Pankhurst, who disagreed sharply with her mother and sister on the issue of the war, the continuance of the suffrage campaign, and on Soviet Russia, gives her account of events in *The Life of Emmeline Pankhurst*, n. 49 above, Chapter 10.

prisoners as dregs, but as victims. Describing the awful effects of solitude upon Holloway prisoners, which made such an impression upon her during her first sentence, Emmeline pictured the ordinary petty offender 'sitting alone, day after day, in the heavy silence of a cell—thinking of her children at home—thinking, thinking. Some women go mad. Many suffer from shattered nerves for a long period after release. It is impossible to believe that any woman ever emerged from such a horror less criminal than when she entered it.'[51] After her first Holloway experience Emmeline was convinced that all prisons—men's as well as women's—should be razed. Giving examples of mothers who had been prosecuted and imprisoned under the 1906 'Children's Charter', despite the abject poverty and destitution under which they lived, she observed, '[t]hese sorry mothers, logical results of the subjection of women, are enough in themselves to justify almost any defiance of a Government who deny women the right to work out their destinies in freedom'.[52]

Lady Constance Lytton, who had to assume the identity of Jane Warton, a working woman, in order to avoid her family's string-pulling and actually serve her several sentences, was one of the Suffragette activists who was most concerned with imprisonment, but this strongly felt interest long antedated her WSPU membership. On the eve of what she expected to be her first imprisonment (for an attempted 'rush' on Parliament) she wrote a long explanatory and reassuring letter to her mother: '[w]hat maternity there lurks in me has for years past been gradually awakening over the fate of prisoners, the deliberate, cruel harm that is done to them, their souls and their bodies, the ignorant, exasperating waste of good opportunities in connection with them, till now the thought of them, the yearning after them turns in me and tugs at me as vitally and irrepressibly as ever a physical child can call upon its mother.'[53]

Constance was four times imprisoned—at Holloway twice, and at Newcastle and Liverpool. Her accounts of these sentences are full of interesting observations, permeated with a deep sense of compassion and laced with a determination to be truthful and fair. She encountered a deal of kindness not only from fellow prisoners, but also from wardresses and other staff: she also noted the deadening

---

[51] E. Pankhurst, n. 38 above, 101–2.   [52] Ibid., 193.
[53] C. Lytton and J. Warton, *Prisons and Prisoners: Some Personal Experiences* (London: William Heinemann, 1914), 33.

and dehumanizing effects of the regime on both. Her sympathy for the ordinary prisoners she encountered—an infanticide, an attempted suicide, a procession of remands she presumed to include debtors, thieves, prostitutes, and drunkards, led her to ask: '[w]hy are they there? What has driven these poor wrecks into this harbour? What is being done for them here to give them courage, self-reliance, hope, belief in better possibilities for themselves and their children ... ?'[54] She expressed disquiet about the plight of the young in court and in prison, and was greatly moved by the sight of a woman prisoner cooing and singing to her baby—'a sight as beautiful as the most beautiful picture in the world'.[55]

Sylvia Pankhurst, whose decision to organize for the WSPU in the East End was both an outcome and a reinforcement of left-leaning politics, was as focused as her sister and mother on female suffrage, but was apparently more moved by social conditions than either.[56] Her first imprisonment, moreover, was in the Third Division (her offence had been an altercation in the court of the apparently angry sentencing magistrate, Horace Smith). From the first, therefore she learned something of the prison experience of ordinary poor women. She recalled that in 1912, while campaigning in the East End, some ex-prisoners, ordinary offenders, told her that they had seen the Suffragettes at Holloway, where they had made things better.[57] Her memoir of this time includes cases of Dickensian piteousness, such as the man whose leg had been broken in an industrial dispute and whose wife had subsequently been sentenced to prison for selling laces in the street, attempting to support them both. An assiduous constable had arrested her when he noticed that several members of the public had paid but neglected to take the laces: an obvious (and presumably wicked) case of begging.[58] Such experiences, as well as the impact of living and organizing in the East End, left no room for illusions about the desperate plight of the very poor, and of the place of police, courts, and prisons in those straited lives. When suffrage had substantially been won, however, she took a broader view of these social issues, apparently agreeing with her sister about the inadvisability of getting lost in 'a quagmire of prison reform'.[59]

---

[54] Ibid., 133.   [55] Ibid., 279.

[56] In the early 1920s Sylvia's politics were such that she was criticized by Lenin himself in a pamphlet entitled 'Left Wing Communism: An Infantile Disorder'.

[57] S. Pankhurst, n. 10 above, 417. See n. 41 above.

[58] Ibid., 419.   [59] Ibid., 238.

So Much Turmoil, So Little Change

Elsewhere I have examined the remarkable persistence of the Victorian prison into and beyond the middle of the twentieth century.[60] Contemplating the prison experience of many countries and times it is clear that here is an institution highly resistant to change: the jails of pre- and post-revolutionary France and Russia, for example, were scarcely altered, if a large number of widely different memoirs are not to be disbelieved.[61] Part of the resistance may be explained by the relatively simple functions to which imprisonment may be reduced—containment, deterrence, and retribution. Other objectives may be added in happier, more prosperous, and liberal times, but the core functions remain and are pursued by equally simple and direct means—isolation and supervision, degrees of degradation, the enforcement of submission, a well-considered and finely-tuned list of deprivations, the confiscation of time, and the obliteration of choice.[62]

The First World War crystallized far-reaching changes in intellectual, artistic, social, and political spheres. Many of these were already under way, it is true, but some at least were surely presentiments of a break-up, or so loosened the intellectual guy-ropes that the turmoil of world war and the collapse of empires spread and penetrated beyond all expectation. Nor was this all destructive. Unprecedented levels of national and personal freedom began to grow at this time, while at least some of the elements of new economic theory and reorganization pointed the path to undreamt of levels of general prosperity and security in the metropolitan countries.

[60] S. McConville, 'The Victorian Prison: England, 1865–1965' in Morris and Rothman (eds.), n. 10 above, 131–67.

[61] Of the many memoirs which might be cited in support of this observation Arthur Koestler's *Darkness at Noon* (London: Jonathan Cape, 1940)—a fictionalized compound of experiences, most catches the irony of the unchanging gaol and its vital role in the engine of state. W.B. Carnochan provides a fine survey of prison literature, fictional and factual, in his 'The Literature of Confinement' in Morris and Rothman (eds.), n. 10 above, 427–55.

[62] It seems usual at this point to offer obeisance to Michel Foucault and the now extensive literature generated by his analysis of punishment as a critique of liberal politics and economics. Poor history (indeed sometimes paralysing epistemology and historiography) and a deal of ideological conformity and correctness give much of this literature a curious inward-looking sterility. This is not the place to address its claims, though they undoubtedly merit vigorous examination and debate.

All this is relevant to the events that have been described here. In the Irish rebels and their eventual success we have undoubtedly one of the tocsins of modernity, and an example which, widely studied, eventually helped to dismantle the British and other empires. The conscientious objectors cannot be said to have had any success at all in the short term, apart from demonstrating that there could exist even in times of national crisis an alternative moral evaluation of the state and the citizen's duty towards it, and that this could be upheld by an act of will and sacrifice. Whatever one's view of the merits of their case, this was a demonstration (ironically by not participating) in participatory democracy. The female suffragists prevailed in a case that no-one would now gainsay. Female suffrage may have made much less difference to general political and social outcomes than its supporters hoped, and certainly it failed to reshape the world but, like the Irish rebels and the conscientious objectors, the women challenged the very restricted doctrines of democracy then existing and raised perplexing questions about lawful authority and the process of change.

How then did it come that these strong political and moral currents made so little difference in the penal sphere? There were some changes, but against the impervious monolith of prison discipline they were small indeed. The greatest change was the creative development of the Borstal system under the inspired but frequently idiosyncratic leadership of Alexander Paterson. This, as Roger Hood points out,[63] achieved some notable successes in the inter-war period, and in the longer term the posting of Borstal-trained staff to adult prisons had an impact, particularly after 1945. But it is notable that whilst he was an unconventional public servant, Paterson was far removed from any kind of political protest. A social worker in Bermondsey before the war, he joined up with members of his community, accepting a commission only after an interval in the ranks.[64]

And, Paterson apart, there were few changes. In an attempt to get more work done by prisoners, the period of solitary confinement served by hard labour prisoners (who, contrary to what the terms of their sentence might suggest, were kept in their cells and away

[63] Hood, n. 1 above, 207.
[64] On his social ideas see his *Across the Bridges* (London: Edward Arnold, 1911); on his penal ideas see S.K. Ruck, *Paterson on Prisons* (London: Frederick Muller, 1951).

from hard labour for the first twenty-eight days of their sentences) was in 1919 reduced to fourteen days: hardly a rewriting of the rule-book. It was another twelve years before this preliminary period of solitary confinement was abolished. But so glacial was the rate of change that another vestige of the 1865 Prison Act was retained. Hard labour prisoners continued to be deprived of a mattress for the first fourteen days of their sentence, and had to endure the extreme discomfort of sleeping on bare boards. (This minor species of torture was not inflicted on women.) One could continue, but in general it can be said that the late Victorian prison was alive and well in the inter-war and even the post-war period, despite some minor tinkering.[65] Such a head of steam that there was for change was almost entirely stoked by officials, and culminated in the Criminal Justice Bill of 1938. This measure, thwarted by the war, did contain a number of innovations, but all ideas came from officials or departmental committees.

What then of the Irish, the women, and the conscientious objectors? The Irish are perhaps the easiest to explain. They had fought their war to opt out of the British state, and this is what they did. With one or two exceptions the Irish politicals never saw the criminal prisoners into whose company they were forced as companions; they despised them and had no concern for their fate in or out of prison. Nor was there any reform in Irish prisons after independence. During the years of civil war there was both severity and informality in the treatment of republican prisoners.[66] Ordinary crime was not a major problem in the largely rural and strongly Roman Catholic Irish Free State, and so without an intellectual or ideological impetus penal reform never found its way onto the policy agenda. Had it done so, there is in their general political philosophies and policies no indication that William Cosgrave (first Irish Premier) or Eamon de Valera (his successor and a dominant force in Irish politics), both of whom had served sentences of penal servitude in England, would have addressed the issues in any way that drew on

[65] There was a deal more interest and experimentation in penal policy for juveniles. This is examined in Victor Bailey's scholarly *Delinquency and Citizenship: Reclaiming the Young Offender, 1914–1948* (Oxford: Clarendon, 1987).

[66] There are several memoirs of this period, the most eloquent and perceptive of which is Ernie O'Malley's *The Singing Flame* (Dublin: Anvil Books, 1978), especially Chapters 12 to 17.

their own experiences or which took a broader and more informed view on criminal and penal issues.

The Suffragettes, as we have seen, were generally sympathetic to the plight of women prisoners and were well able to make the connections with wider social and economic conditions. But this had been a one-idea movement and its formidable energies evaporated in the post-war period. The remarkable Pankhurst women exploded apart. Emmeline and Christabel, who had taken a conservative, even jingoistic, position during the war, continued on that trajectory.[67] Sylvia continued on hers, for a time into ever more radical politics, and then brought her feminist convictions to bear on the health care given to mothers and babies. In the 1930s she formed an attachment to Ethiopia and its Emperor which dominated the rest of her days.

It was the conscientious objectors who made the most direct contribution to penal policy and reform in the post-war years, and that was a matter of fortuity. In the autumn of 1918 the Labour Research Department, in which Stephen Hobhouse's aunt, Beatrice Webb, was a leading light, decided on an inquiry into the prison system.[68] Since nationalization in 1877, and under the successive management of two autocratic Chairmen—Sir Edmund Du Cane and Sir Evelyn Ruggles Brise—prisons had been a fiercely-defended closed world. The Gladstone Committee of 1894–5 had shed some light on this dark recess of public administration, but the

[67] Emmeline stood for Parliament in the Unionist interest, and failed to be elected. Christabel became devoutly religious and awaited the Second Coming. Adela, the lesser-known sister, emigrated to Australia where she dabbled in socialism, trades unionism, imperialism, and a certain amount of appeasement of Hitler and Mussolini. She concluded her series of political misjudgements with an espousal of the cause of Japan—not a wise or happy choice for someone who had chosen to live in Australia in the 1930s and 1940s: see Mitchell, n. 50 above, 213–26 and 267–78.

[68] The Research Department had been founded by the Webbs, Bernard Shaw, and other leading Fabians. The Prison System Enquiry Committee which they appointed was intended to collect information and to make practical policy proposals. Besides the Webbs and Shaw members included Sir Sydney Olivier, a socialist and former governor of Jamaica, (Chairman); Margery Fry of the Howard League (and later Principal of Somerville College); Alexander Paterson, the social reformer; T. Edmund Harvey, Quaker and MP; some literary figures and (as adviser) the stipendiary magistrate, Sir William Clarke Hall. There were also two psychologists, a former prison chaplain, two lawyers, and other persons of substance. Despite its official-sounding title the Enquiry was denied government support and officials were forbidden to co-operate with it.

implementation of its recommendations had been long delayed, and such changes as were made were of the modest kind. The *facts* in which the Webbs rejoiced were hard to glean from the miserly and tightly worded annual reports and other official documents. The Webbs, Shaw, and their colleagues agreed that the passage through the prisons of the Suffragettes and the conscientious objectors should be seized as an opportunity to gather information. Strongly convinced of the moral superiority and mission of the British Empire, the Webbs and their colleagues evidently did not consider the Sinn Féin prisoners, of whom there had been several hundred, an acceptable source of information.

On the recommendation of Beatrice Webb, Hobhouse was appointed secretary to the Committee. Although his education and several years' experience as a civil servant doubtless commended him, his energy and confidence seem to have been sapped by imprisonment, and his was, in any event, a fragile psychology. Hobhouse and the Committee went about their work fairly mechanically, dividing the inquiry into a series of sequential topics. The absence of a philosophy and a guiding hand is all too evident in the accumulation. After two years or so of collecting in this mechanical and unreflective fashion Fenner Brockway was drafted onto the Committee as joint secretary. Brockway, an experienced and energetic journalist (and future MP) was able to sort the information that had been collected. By this time, however, the shaping and ordering could be little more than editorial. In 1922 the results appeared in the 728-page *English Prisons To-Day*.[69]

As Hobhouse ruefully observed, this was 'an expensive and unwieldy volume' bought and read by few outside the relatively small groups connected with penal reform. With thirty-eight chapters and three appendices *English Prisons To-Day* shows every sign of that familiar disorder of reports: a gigantic meal utterly beyond the digestive capacity of its compilers. The topic was dealt with methodically and minutely, but there was no attempt to set priorities or propose a programme; more importantly, there was no attempt to develop a penal philosophy. Politicians, the press, and even reform groups had little to grasp on to and carry forward as the nation appeared to return to normal in 1922. Within a few years penal

[69]   By S.H. Hobhouse and A.F. Brockway (London: Longmans, Green, 1922).

policy had retreated even further into the shadowy wings of public concern.

The Prison System Enquiry had some impact, but little of this was attributable to the effort of the committee itself, it was much more a matter of fortuity and serendipity. Alexander Paterson, who, as we have seen, had a long-established interest in social and penal issues, was propelled into the post of Prison Commissioner by his member-ship of the Enquiry and the authorship of the section of the report which dealt with Borstal. In this appointment, the retirement of Sir Evelyn Ruggles Brise and his replacement as Chairman of the Prison Commission by the more open-minded Sir Maurice Waller was probably the critical factor. Once established Paterson began his pioneering work to develop the Borstal system, and that in turn began to have an impact on the adult prisons in the inter-war years. But this was at best a tenuous connection with the experience of the conscientious objectors in wartime prisons.

The world of institutions had been shaken by the cataclysm of the Great War, but so also the world of perceptions and values. Loss, carnage, and destruction were dealt with in many different ways, one of which was to live in the here and now, and to distance oneself from past concerns. Political energies were more concentrated on the future—'never again'. Religious scruples and pacifism, always deli-cate and elusive, faded in such intense light and energy. As for the sufferings and moral degradation of imprisonment—how could these compare with the vast loss of life, the bestiality of trench warfare, the maimed, institutionalized and the physically and psych-ically wounded?

The problem of crime did not go away. Dropping to just over 200 per 100,000 of the population in 1915, reported indictable crimes almost doubled to 400 per 100,000 in 1930.[70] There was a less dramatic rise in the prison population. The average daily population dropped as low as 9,000 in 1915, and rose to just under 12,000 in 1930. But this merely restored the figure to its pre-war level, and the upward trend did not seem too worrying. The move away from short sentences meant that annual receptions on conviction (i.e. excluding remand prisoners) had fallen from about 165,000 in 1910 to just under 40,000 in 1930. This therefore was a mixed picture, not likely

[70] Adapted from L.W. Fox, *The Modern English Prison* (London: George Routle-dge, 1934), graph B, 223.

to strain public policy. Nor did the onset of the Great Depression change things, despite the rise in unemployment. By 1935 the prison population had stabilized at an average daily population of 10,600, a position more or less held until the outbreak of war.[71] There was no perceived crisis in criminal justice. The political parties were pre-occupied with the slump, coalition politics, and the threatening international scene. Criminal policy was left to officials and those reformers with whom they enjoyed a close and confidential working relationship. Professor Murray's 'high-minded and utterly uncriminal people' who had served their time in His Majesty's Prisons between 1906 and 1921 had no abiding interest in penal policy, and if they had the nation had little inclination to listen.

***

It is not true that the law of necessity determines all of politics, but its impact is great. Neither is it true that crisis is a determinant of all public policy, but it is indeed a great force. The political prisoners of 1906–22 opened a door into one of the darkest corners of public administration. Their number included persons who would by their energy, imagination, and commitment to principle have been outstanding in any generation. Here was the equivalent of a triple-engined Royal Commission, yet the impact was minimal. The public mood was unreceptive. Crime and punishment were of little interest to the professional politicians. Within public administration these remained minor fields of endeavour and offered little prospect for the advancement of able officials. Flawed though it was, the Prison System Enquiry was the only systematic independent compilation of penal information until the Cambridge, Oxford, and London studies in the years following the Second World War; academics found little of substance in the field in the inter-war period.

Inevitably subjective, sometimes partisan or self-serving, the books, essays, letters, and interviews of the political prisoners constitute a type of research. The prisoners could not possibly anticipate our wordy handbooks on participant observation, and they certainly

[71] *Report of the Commissioners of Prisons and the Directors of Convict Prisons for the Year 1935*, Parliamentary Papers, 1936–37 [Cmd. 5430], XV, 1, 16. In 1937 the average daily population was 10,562 and in 1938 11,086: *Report of the Commissioners of Prisons and the Directors of Convict Prisons for the Year 1938*, Parliamentary Papers, 1939–40 [Cmd. 6137], V, 261, 15.

were not practitioners of the rare arts of the survey. But in varying forms they did attempt to give a fair account of their experiences, of the prisoners and officials they encountered, of standards of hygiene, the dietary, and the effect of the penal regime as they saw and experienced its administration. Not a corrective to the bluebook version of imprisonment as much as a vivid alternative, they provided information unattainable or only partially available from other sources. And the fact that such a number of activists of so many different persuasions and opinions went to prison over this narrow span of years gave additional value to their observations. These accounts came close to comprehensiveness in detail, a *camera obscura* of the prison landscape then existing. As importantly, they capture and convey the human and moral element, a reality well beyond the mere statistics.

Alternative history, endlessly intriguing, can never venture beyond the suggestive. The centres and institutes of criminology now well established at the great universities emerged from a complicated interaction of disciplines, opportunities, personalities, academic politics, and even international affairs. The maturation of this field of study (to which Roger Hood has so importantly contributed) is very far from complete; public and political confidence in its values, methodologies, findings, and recommendations is fickle and uncertain. But had there been a more prominent and established criminological enterprise in Britain in the 1920s, a counterpart to departments then operating in certain Continental universities, it is arguable that the experiences of the political prisoners that we have discussed here would have been more effectively recorded, analysed, and investigated and perhaps would have been brought to bear on criminal and penal policy in the decades of political tranquility and bi-partisanship in these fields. Without a cohesive intellectual stimulus and absent institutional interest and resources, this criminological harvest was lost, dwindling into historical curiosity within a few years.

The connection between research and policy becomes fragile when an issue moves to centre stage. Relationships between public opinion, political parties, and government are fluid and reciprocal. The inter-war period, when criminal justice issues lay dormant, may well have offered opportunities for research to be fed into policy—but, as noted, there was little research being done. Crime trends, public concern, and political responses (responsible and opportunistic alike) have now given criminal and penal policy more prominence than at any time in the last two centuries. If not daily, then weekly announcements of 'initiatives' issue from the principal departments of state. Crime has joined health, education, and transport as a constantly debated and closely scrutinized measure of good government. It is indeed ironical that when informed and truly independent research is most needed, it stands less chance of being commissioned or supported and, if completed, used.

Despite the achievements of two or three generations of criminologists in Britain the relationship between research and policy therefore remains uncertain, at times even capricious. If political necessity and administrative crisis are the principal engines of policy, politicians and high officials *cannot* but ignore or selectively absorb the products of challenging or inconvenient research (or selectively commission and micromanage its conduct): that seems to be part of our political structure and culture. How much then have the constraints changed since Britain 'returned to normal' in the 1920s and simply ignored the penal experiences of an outstanding generation of political activists? Hood's 1974 contention that 'the belief that expert advice based on criminological and penological research is the foundation for penal change, is only a screen behind which ideological and political factors, perhaps inevitably, shape those attitudes which imbue legislation' is most likely a statement of business as usual, his own sterling contribution notwithstanding. And that being so, to adapt the words of the eighteenth-century blind and penniless Irish bard Raftery, are criminologists in their relations with policy-makers still simply 'playing music unto empty pockets'?

6

Ministers and Modernisation: Criminal Justice Policy, 1997–2001

Lord Windlesham

In his first speech as Home Secretary after the General Election in June 2001 David Blunkett declared that he had been asked by the Prime Minister to chair a committee that included the Lord Chancellor and the Attorney General.[1] Its remit was to oversee the modernisation of the criminal justice system and drive up its performance.[2] On returning to office with an overwhelming majority after a four-year tenure this statement was a clear signal that the Labour government's dedication to the imperatives of change and managerialism would continue, in criminal policy as elsewhere. Such a course could not be taken for granted, since it is commonplace for every political party when out of power to promise radical reform. Once in power, with all the hindrances which go with it, things can look very different. Thus the statement was a characteristic

---

[1] Peter Goldsmith, a leading QC and former chairman of the Bar, was created a life peer in 1999. He had spoken on criminal justice and legal issues from the Labour benches in the House of Lords before his appointment as Attorney General in the government formed in June 2001. Lord Irvine of Lairg continued as Lord Chancellor, while the previous Attorney General, Lord Williams of Mostyn QC, became Lord Privy Seal and Leader of the House of Lords.

[2] Transcript of a speech by the Home Secretary on sentencing reform, National Probation Service inaugural conference, 5 July 2001, para. 12. The membership of the Cabinet Committee on the criminal justice system was completed by: the Solicitor General, the Chief Secretary to the Treasury, the Minister without Portfolio and Party Chair, the Minister for the Cabinet Office and Chancellor of the Duchy of Lancaster, a Minister of State at the Home Office, and a Parliamentary Secretary at the Lord Chancellor's Department.

endorsement of Tony Blair's undiminished zeal for reform across the whole range of governmental activity, and beyond, for a further term. There was no hint of backsliding when, shortly before his party's second overwhelming election victory, he assured an interviewer that 'the real essence of modern government is the speed at which things change and therefore the constant need to revitalise and modernise and keep up to date'.[3]

Sufficient time has now elapsed to consider how such generalized objectives in the context of criminal policy were translated into practice between 1997 and 2001, and to draw some conclusions. In departmental terms the internal organization of the Home Office was restructured. Twelve responsibilities, several of them substantial and of long standing, were transferred to other departments or agencies.[4] Aims and objectives were set and published, with senior civil servants named and designated as aim owners. Since 1988 four Permanent Secretaries in succession had been brought in from outside the department,[5] each one a newcomer faced with adapting the distinctive customs and values of one of the most enduring components of the machinery of government.

Meanwhile other departments concerned with the justice system had been edging closer toward the front of the Whitehall stage. The Lord Chancellor's Department was greatly strengthened, led by an energetic and versatile senior civil servant as Permanent Secretary. Both the minister and his senior official continued in their posts after the 2001 General Election. With experience at the Home Office, the European Commission, the Treasury, and the Department for Culture, Media, and Sport, Sir Hayden Phillips was the first non-lawyer to be appointed as Permanent Secretary in an expansionist Lord

[3] A. Seldon (ed.), *The Blair Effect* (London: Little, Brown, 2001), Chapter 26; M. Cockerell, 'An Inside View on Blair's Number 10' 570.

[4] Responsibilities transferred from the Home Office to other Departments included Animal Welfare, Byelaws, Data Protection, Disaster Management, Electoral Law, Fire Safety and the Fire Service, HM Fire Services Inspectorate, Freedom of Information, Human Rights, Liquor and Gambling, Rolling Registration and Postal Votes, and Summer Time. A press notice from 10 Downing Street stated: '[t]he Home Office will be streamlined, losing a number of functions which are not central to its work, to allow it to focus on tackling crime, reform of the criminal justice system and asylum. As part of this, the UK Anti-Drugs Co-ordination Unit will transfer into the Home Office from the Cabinet Office' (8 June 2001).

[5] Sir Clive Whitmore (1988–94); Sir Richard Wilson (1994–7), Sir David Omand (1998–2000); and John Gieve (2001–).

Chancellor's Department. His skills complemented Lord Irvine's political weight and personal influence with the Prime Minister, with the result that a formidable challenger emerged to the criminal policy hegemony of the Home Office. The far smaller Law Officers' Department, with responsibility for the Crown Prosecution Service, the Serious Fraud Office, and the Treasury Solicitor's Department, also made the most of the opportunity to sit at the same table as the still dominant department of state, the Home Office, and its parvenu rival.

In the spirit of joined-up government, and despite the disparities in the extent of their responsibilities and spending power, the three ministers were presented as being jointly answerable for the overall performance of the criminal justice system. Whether or not this declaratory concept furthered the actual production of sought-after outcomes is open to debate. Yet the political risks were not great. In the early years at least, no more than containable political damage would be caused by shortfalls if the targets were set too high, provided the outcomes could be presented as an improvement on the performance of the Labour government's Conservative predecessors.

Counting Crimes

While institutional reform, in the shape of reorganizing ministerial responsibilities or departmental boundaries, is within the capacity of governments to produce intended results, policy reform is more elusive. Outcomes often turn on the disposition of large numbers of people to behave in a predicted way. Some reactions may be in the direction sought; others may be indifferent, or positively contrary. It is by the general public response to the implementation of their policies that governments eventually are judged; less on the basis of what they have said than on what they have done.

Ample evidence is available to show that crime is close to the top of issues of public concern. Consequently, high on the list of any incoming government's domestic priorities, irrespective of party, will be measures aimed at reducing the frequency of criminal offending. Evaluating success or failure in securing this objective is complicated by the fact that there is no single method of measurement. After steep increases in the total of all crimes recorded by the police between 1991 and 1993, both the police statistics and the

British Crime Survey (BCS)[6] began to indicate downward trends. Following a small rise between 1995 and 1997 in the BCS figures, both methods of measurement showed a decline, the BCS falls being the larger.[7] Post-1997, the year Labour came to power, the trends were on a generally downward path, although with a setback occurring in 1999–2000 when an increase of 3.8 per cent in the number of notifiable offences was recorded by the police in England and Wales. In the following twelve months to March 2001, a total of 5.2 million offences were recorded by the police in England and Wales, representing an estimated fall of 2.5 per cent over the previous twelve months.[8] There were falls in the areas covered by thirty-four of the forty-three forces.

When published in October 2001 the first results of the British Crime Survey presented a still more encouraging picture. Between 1999 and 2000 there had been a fall in nearly all of the offence categories measured. Statistically significant falls were recorded of burglary (17 per cent), vehicle-related theft (11 per cent), other household theft (16 per cent), and violent crime (19 per cent). The overall decline was a fall of 12 per cent in crimes against people living in private households.[9] Consequently, while there was still a significant difference in the scale of reduction between the BCS and police-recorded incidents, with both under-reporting the actual incidence of offending, nevertheless there was reliable evidence of a downward trend. If it continued, in the cautious comment of the Home Office Director of Research, Development, and Statistics, a century-long historical trend of ever-increasing recorded crime rates would have been broken.[10]

---

[6] The British Crime Survey (BCS) is a large-scale survey which measures crimes against persons aged 16 and over living in private households in England and Wales, whether or not reported to the police. It has been conducted by the Home Office nine times between 1982 and 2001.

[7] Home Office, *Recorded Crime: England and Wales, 12 months to March 2001*, Statistical Bulletin 12/01, July 2001.

[8] Ibid., 3, 10–12. Recorded crime refers to notifiable offences recorded by the police according to Home Office rules on counting and classification.

[9] Home Office, *The 2001 British Crime Survey: First Results, England and Wales*, Statistical Bulletin 18/01, Oct. 2001, p. iv.

[10] *The Times*, 26 Oct. 2001. Paul Wiles, Professor of Criminology (1988–99) and Dean of the Faculty of Law (1990–6) at Sheffield University, was appointed as Director of Research, Development and Statistics at the Home Office in 1999.

The political significance accorded to the publication of the crime statistics was shown by the fact that, despite the pressing demands of the international crisis following the attacks on the World Trade Center and the Pentagon in the United States on 11 September 2001, the Prime Minister found time to join the Home Secretary soon afterwards at a well-publicized meeting with police officers from two areas whose forces had recorded larger than average falls in criminal offending. Although the presentational advantage for ministers in being able to report falling crime rates is clear enough, by no means all of the causative factors are within the control of government. For example, improved household security has made burglary at private dwellings more difficult, while thefts of and from motor vehicles are countered effectively by more sophisticated alarms and locking devices. Nor was the trend of declining property crime since the high levels reached in the early 1990s peculiar to the UK. Elsewhere the picture was similar. Between 1995 and 1999 there was an average fall of 14 per cent in police-recorded domestic burglary across all European Union Member States. The greatest decreases were in England and Wales (31 per cent) and Germany (29 per cent). Austria (26 per cent), the Netherlands (22 per cent), and France (20 per cent) also recorded significant falls over the same period.[11] In the United States too, reliable sources reported falls of 19 per cent in domestic burglary between 1995 and 1999, and of all crime by 16 per cent.[12]

Whilst recognizing the extensive harm caused by property offences and the fear they generate, media attention and public comment are typically more focussed on crimes of violence. Here too the 2001 BCS survey held out some hope, reporting significant falls in the high proportion of people who had been victims of some type of violent crime once or more during the year. The number of violent crimes fell between 1999 and 2000, from 3,246,000 to 2,618,000, a decrease of 19 per cent. Among individual categories of violent crime there was a statistically significant fall of 34 per cent in offences of wounding.[13] Overall trends in violent crime fell for the

[11] Home Office, n. 9 above, p. i.

[12] Ibid. After a sharp rise in violent crime in the mid-1980s, continuing until 1991, there was a decline over the next seven years to levels not experienced in the USA since the 1960s. See A. Blumstein and J. Wallman (eds.), *The Crime Drop in America* (Cambridge and New York: Cambridge University Press, 2000), 1–12.

[13] Home Office, n. 9 above, p. viii.

third successive year, although the total number of crimes of violence was still in excess of two and a half million. This meant that an average 3.7 per cent of the population of England and Wales experienced at least one incident of violence in 2000, down from 4.2 per cent in 1999.[14] While there was some reduction in overall trends measuring fear of crime, levels of worry about personal safety were greater amongst certain defined categories. These included people living in high crime areas; recent victims; those who considered it likely that they would be victimized; and those who were socially or economically vulnerable.[15] Such factors combined to ensure that many elected representatives in local and central government would keep the necessity for effective crime control at the forefront of their political priorities.

Flawed Initiatives

Policy initiatives between 1997 and 2001 fell under three heads. There were manifesto and later commitments leading to a fundamental recasting of criminal legal aid, the reorganization both of the Probation Service and the Crown Prosecution Service, a new structure for youth justice, and the development of local crime and disorder partnerships. In marked contrast to these planned reforms, broadly termed evidence-based, were responses to unwelcome events, ranging from large-scale evasion of immigration controls and the anti-social behaviour of unruly football supporters to protection from international terrorism. The full horror of the latter threat had not yet become apparent, although some ominous incidents outside mainland Britain were beginning to point the way.

On an altogether more mundane scale was the pursuit of political advantage in domestic politics. This trait was manifest in an eclectic series of populist inspired initiatives. Several found a place in the legislative programme despite falling well short of the ideals implicit in the concept of criminal justice. Examples were the peremptory withdrawal or reduction of social security benefits for alleged breach of a community order; automatic forfeiture of a driving licence for failure to pay maintenance ordered by the court after marital breakdown; compulsory tests for drugs before bail; mandatory custodial sentences for breach of community orders; and on-the-spot fines for

---

[14] Home Office, n. 9 above, 30.   [15] Ibid., p. ix.

disorderly behaviour in public places. Each of these had origins that were essentially presentational. Their enactment was made easier by being inserted into omnibus bills implementing a range of larger, and more carefully considered, policy issues.

In a personal memorandum addressed to his advisers, headed *Touchstone Issues*, the Prime Minister had emphasized the 'need to highlight tough measures to offset a rise in street crime, especially in London. The police are putting in place measures to deal with it; but, as ever, we are lacking a tough message along with the strategy. We should think now of an initiative e.g. locking up street muggers. Something tough, with immediate bite, which sends a message through the system'.[16] Direct instructions of this kind were then followed up by an expanding cadre of paid political appointees working within ministerial offices. In February 1997, the final year of the previous Conservative administration, there were thirty-eight special advisers to Ministers in post.[17] By October 2001, the total had more than doubled, amounting to eighty-one special advisers attached to government departments. Of these a significant number were concentrated in the policy directorate at 10 Downing Street.[18]

Although mostly enacted by the time of the General Election in June 2001 some of these initiatives were amended during their passage through Parliament. The size, and general docility, of Labour's majority in the Commons meant that ministers had little to fear in getting their proposals accepted. But in the House of Lords the government was defeated over its initial attempt to withdraw or reduce the payment of social security benefits for reported failure to conform to the conditions of a community order.[19] The principal objection was that such a potentially drastic sanction would bite before the court hearing to establish whether or not there had been a breach of the order. If it was found that the offender had failed to comply, the court would then decide on the appropriate penalty without taking account of the administrative sanction already incurred.

With hindsight, it is hard to see how ministers and their advisers failed to recognize that the imposition of punitive sanctions before a finding of fact by due process of law not only defied a fundamental

---

[16] A stolen copy of the memorandum was published verbatim in *The Times* on 17 July 2000. Its authenticity was subsequently confirmed.

[17] HC Debs., vol. 295, col. 97, 2 June 1997.

[18] HL Debs., vol. 627, col. 473, 16 Oct. 2001.

[19] HL Debs., vol. 614, cols. 848–51, 27 June 2000.

precept of justice, but also amounted to a double penalty. The face-saving compromise was that the misconceived loss of entitlement to benefit would be retained, but deferred until after a court had made a determination that an offender had failed to comply with the conditions of a community sentence. By this means the Government could claim that its policy aim had been preserved, while its critics could claim that the rule of law had been upheld.[20]

The Child Support, Pensions and Social Security Bill, incorporating this inappropriate administrative sanction for the breach of a criminal order, was followed by a related provision in the Criminal Justice and Court Services Bill which was subject to Parliamentary scrutiny in the same session. It too claimed to strengthen the enforcement of community orders by providing a mandatory sentence of imprisonment for a second unacceptable failure to comply with the conditions of a community sentence. The singular result was that, whether by accident or design, two separate measures, each intended to achieve the same outcome, were introduced by different departments in the same session of Parliament.

The presumption of imprisonment, as it became known, caused widespread concern throughout the Probation Service, and was brought to the notice of the newly appointed Lord Chief Justice. In June 2000 Lord Woolf had succeeded Lord Bingham, and later that year he devoted the first Parliamentary speech in his new office to pointing out the shortcomings of the presumption of imprisonment for breach of a community penalty, irrespective of the individual circumstances. What was the evidence, he asked, that magistrates or judges were being unduly lenient when offenders were brought back before the courts for breach of a condition imposed as a non-custodial sentence? It was not the impression of probation officers with whom he had discussed the matter. If offenders were being treated unduly leniently, training plus guideline decisions from senior judges could produce the required result. Why place a judge in the entirely artificial situation of having to impose an artificial sentence of imprisonment?[21]

---

[20] For a more detailed account of this dispute, see Windlesham, 'Loss of Benefit: A Misplaced Sanction' [2000] *Crim.L.R.* 661. Ss. 62–66 (excluding the sub-sections relevant to Scotland) of the Child Support, Pensions and Social Security Act 2000 were brought into effect in October 2001, thus enabling pilot projects to be launched in four probation areas.

[21] HL Debs., vol. 616, col. 1609, 4 Oct. 2000.

Faced with judicial opposition at the highest level, as well as the prospect of a further Parliamentary reverse in the Lords, ministers decided that tactical withdrawal was necessary. The resulting formula must have taxed Parliamentary draftsmen to the full. On behalf of the government the Attorney General, Lord Williams of Mostyn, moved amendments which he claimed were a 'proportionate, reasoned, and reasonable response to the criticisms which were made'.[22] Be that as it may, they were far from straightforward. Where a court found that an offender over the age of 18, who was subject to a community order to which statutory warning provisions applied, had breached the conditions of the order, it would proceed to a further step. This was to decide whether, notwithstanding the current breach, the offender's response to the sentence as a whole was such that it was likely the order would be successfully completed. If the court took the view that successful completion was likely, it would allow the order to continue, but would be under a duty to punish the breach by imposing a community punishment order, a curfew order, or, where the appropriate age applied, an attendance centre order. If, however, the court did not believe there was a likelihood the order would be successfully completed, there would be a requirement to impose a custodial sentence, other than in exceptional circumstances. If the original offence was punishable by imprisonment, a prison sentence would be imposed for the original offence. If the original offence was not so punishable, the prison sentence should be limited to not more than three months. The existing exclusions, i.e. those under the age of 18, and those who failed to comply with a requirement to refrain from using Class A drugs, would remain.[23]

It was not surprising that Woolf should have broadened the scope of his critique by citing the improvements so recently accomplished by consolidating many enactments dealing with the sentencing and treatment of offenders in the Powers of Criminal Courts (Sentencing) Act 2000. That measure, the work of the Law Commission and Scottish Law Commission, brought together legislation spread across numerous Acts of Parliament and, he vouched, was very much a step to be commended. Yet once again the mistakes of the past were being repeated by trying to deal piecemeal with particular problems. While complexity had been reduced in the civil justice

---

[22] Ibid., col. 1606.   [23] Ibid., cols. 1605–6.

system in recent years, what was being done now, and in previous years, was to move in the opposite direction with regard to the criminal justice system.[24]

Awkward Issues

The volume of legislation needed to implement the government's changes to the criminal justice system during the Parliament of 1997–2001 was unusually heavy. Other than the Powers of Criminal Courts (Sentencing) Act 2000, five omnibus crime bills were enacted. They were the Crime and Disorder Act 1998, Access to Justice Act 1999, Youth Justice and Criminal Evidence Act 1999, Criminal Justice and Court Services Act 2000, and Criminal Justice and Police Act 2001. The greater part of these measures resulted from the commitments of Labour's pre-election agenda, as adjusted by the realities of office. Two awkward issues, neither matters of party policy, came in at a tangent. The first was the age of consent for homosexual acts, and the second a continuing controversy over restricting entitlement to jury trial. On each issue popular feelings were strong, but divided, and political loyalties weak.

The Sexual Offences (Amendment) Bill, which reduced the age at which a person may consent to homosexual acts from 18 to 16, resulted from an undertaking given by the government in the resolution of a contested application which had been declared admissible by the European Commission of Human Rights and referred to the Court of Human Rights in October 1997. Proceedings at Strasbourg had been stayed before the final stage on the basis that at the earliest opportunity the government would arrange a free vote in the House of Commons on whether the age of consent for homosexual acts should be reduced from 18 to 16. If a majority of MPs voted in favour of a reduction, the government undertook to bring forward legislation to implement the will of Parliament in time for it to be completed by the end of the next session at the latest. What this formula overlooked was that law reform by statute requires the consent of both Houses of Parliament.

Eight months later, in a free vote at the Report Stage of the Crime and Disorder Bill on the floor of the Commons, an amendment to equalize the age of consent at 16 was carried by a majority of over

[24] HL Debs., vol. 616, col. 1610.

200. 336 MPs voted for the new clause and 129 against. Thirteen Labour members voted against, and seventeen Conservative members voted in favour. The Prime Minister, Home Secretary, and eight Cabinet Ministers voted for reduction, but ten other Cabinet Ministers did not vote.[25] Soon after, the Bill containing the amendment was returned to the House of Lords in which it had been introduced.

The composition of the Lords meant that a substantial and influential group of cross-bench peers included several Church leaders. On the morning of the vote *The Times* published an article by the Archbishop of Canterbury explaining why he could not support a reduction in the age of consent to 16.[26] The Bishop of Winchester, intervening early in the debate on a motion to disagree with the Commons amendment, said that in the unavoidable absence of the Archbishop his speech would represent the statements of the House of Bishops of the Church of England as published shortly before. He was unable to accept the widespread assumption that homosexual activity in general was as appropriate and desirable as heterosexual activity, with the choice between them being presented as equal options. Such an assumption was not consistent with the Christian teaching that sex was a gift of God for the enriching of lives within the context of marriage. Parliament should be very wary indeed, he warned, about deserting the wisdom in these matters not only of the Christian faith, but of other faiths too.[27] While the former Archbishop of York, Lord Habgood, also argued against reduction in the age of consent at this stage, another Bishop, with experience as chairman of the Children's Society, spoke and voted to the contrary.[28] The most vehement denunciation by a religious leader of the Sexual Offences Act 1967, which legalized homosexual acts in private, provided the parties consented and attained the age of 21, went well beyond the dispute over the age of consent. To the retired Chief Rabbi, Lord Jakobovits, such unnatural acts were violations of the laws of God and nature that could not endure in the long run.[29]

[25] They included David Blunkett, who had voted against reduction to the age of 16 four years earlier. For the full Division list, see HLC Debs., vol. 314, cols. 805–8, 22 June 1998.

[26] 22 July 1998. [27] HL Debs., vol. 592, col. 943, 22 July 1998.

[28] The Bishop of Bath and Wells, ibid., cols. 952–4. Two other Bishops (Lincoln and Oxford) also voted for the amendment.

[29] Ibid., col. 950.

After a long debate, during which deeply felt feelings were articulated for and against the change, 290 peers voted against the new clause which had been passed by the Commons, while 122 supported it.

This outcome left ministers in a quandary. In the interests of Parliamentary management it had been their decision that the clause should be enacted by way of a private Members' amendment to a major government bill. The tactic had allowed dissenters on their own benches, as well as in the opposition parties, to argue their case and vote accordingly. But the Lords had proved to be a stumbling block. Meanwhile, implementation of the Crime and Disorder Bill was pressing. Some of its clauses were due to come into force on Royal Assent, which had been expected by the end of July, with a further twenty-five planned to come into effect by the end of September. Thus it was the restrictions imposed by the Parliamentary timetable, interacting with the views of a majority in the Lords, which exacerbated the setback.

In the Commons the Home Secretary, Jack Straw, gave another undertaking, this time that the government still intended to honour the formal undertakings which it had given in the document lodged at the European Court of Human Rights the previous year. In each of the next two sessions a separate Sexual Offences (Amendment) Bill was passed by the Commons, giving effect to the reduction of the age at which a person might consent to male homosexual acts from 18 to 16. Having been defeated again in the Lords in the first session, 1998–9, it was re-introduced in the following session. Although given a second reading by the Lords in April 2000 the bill was radically amended in Committee six months later. Subsequently it received the Royal Assent in the form originally agreed by the Commons under the terms of the Parliament Act 1949 at the end of the session without being further discussed.[30]

Trial by Jury

Confrontation between the two Houses arose also over access to jury trial. The extent to which an accused person was entitled to opt for trial by jury was not a new issue, but one that had been rumbling on

---

[30] House of Lords, *Annual Report and Accounts, 2000–2001* (London: The Stationery Office, 2001), 9.

for some years. In 1993 the Royal Commission on Criminal Justice, noting that there had been a large increase in the proportion of cases 'triable either way' (i.e. summarily in the Magistrates' Courts or on indictment in the Crown Court) had recommended that in contested cases involving either-way offences the defendant should no longer have the right to insist on trial by jury.[31] Neither the more serious contested cases triable only on indictment before a jury in the Crown Court nor the less serious cases triable summarily by the Magistrates' Courts would be affected. Although not widely understood by the general public, the coming conflict was confined only to persons charged with offences of intermediate gravity which were triable 'either way'.

Ministers past and present, Conservative and Labour alike, and their advisers had convinced themselves that there were benefits to be gained in terms of saving court time and hence cost by curtailing the right of a defendant to opt for trial by jury if charged with an either-way offence. In the year ending in September 1996 as many as one quarter of the total Crown Court case-load for the year was made up of defendants in the either-way category who had elected trial in the Crown Court. A large majority of these defendants, estimated at about two-thirds, then went on to plead guilty.[32] It was the forthright conclusion of a one-man review by a Home Office official,[33] who had been appointed to investigate the causes of delay in the criminal justice system, that a substantial proportion of such elections were 'little more than an expensive manipulation of the criminal justice system', and were not concerned with 'any wish to establish innocence in front of a jury'.[34] In an equally brusque recommendation he proposed that what amounted to an 'automatic veto' on the magistrates' decision on mode of trial should be removed.

---

[31] Royal Commission on Criminal Justice, *Report*, Cm. 2263 (London: HMSO, 1993), Recommendation 114, 198.

[32] A research study by C. Hedderman and D. Moxon, *Magistrates Court or Crown Court? Mode of Trial Decisions and Sentencing*, Home Office Research Study No. 125 (London: HMSO, 1992), was influential in informing the debate on mode of trial, up to and including the Auld report in 2001.

[33] Martin Narey held a variety of posts both in the Prison Service and at the Home Office before being appointed as Director General of the Prison Service in December 1998 at the unusually early age of 43.

[34] Home Office, *Review of Delay in the Criminal Justice System*, A Report, Feb. 1997, 2.

At times the vocabulary of officialdom can indicate a changing outlook, later reflected in legislation. No better example can be found than the transformation of what previously had been regarded as the established right of a defendant, when charged with an offence of intermediate seriousness, to opt for trial by a jury into an automatic veto on the discretion of the magistrates. Michael Howard, while still Home Secretary, instinctively realized the sensitivity of the issue and had avoided committing the Conservative government to legislation by the time of the general election in May 1997. The shadow Home Secretary had been less inhibited. Earlier in that year Jack Straw had rejected cutting down the right to jury trial as making the system less fair. Amongst other factors, he gave weight to the loss of reputation which would result if, for example, 'a police officer, or an MP or even the Secretary of State was charged with an offence of dishonesty, would they not insist on being tried by a jury?'[35] If that was the case, why should others be denied the same right of election?

Reducing access to jury trial in the interests of saving time and eliminating misuse was not among the objectives of the incoming Labour government. It had not featured in the manifesto, could be criticized as illiberal, and might be expected to encounter stiff Parliamentary opposition. Moreover, there were indications that trial by jury had a public resonance which did not correspond with the conclusions of the Home Office review. Had it not been for a non-political turn of events, an incoming Home Secretary with other things on his mind might well have left it alone. But while the majority of elected politicians had shown no more than tepid interest in reform, the judiciary had been considering the merits. In a speech at the Mansion House, the Lord Chief Justice, Lord Bingham, announced publicly that with one important proviso the higher judiciary was not opposed to changes being made in the mode of trial. The proviso was that there should be a right of appeal for a defendant denied trial by jury in any either-way case.

If the higher judiciary was potentially supportive, endorsing the conclusions both of the Royal Commission and the Narey review, the perceived balance of advantage shifted towards change. After further ministerial consultations, the government decided to introduce a Criminal Justice (Mode of Trial) Bill in the House of Lords in

---

[35] *The Independent*, 27 Mar. 1997.

November 1999. Although it received a Second Reading on 2 December 1999, there were unmistakable warning signs that a powerful challenge would be mounted at the Committee stage early in the New Year. These were duly borne out when an all-party amendment was carried by a large majority against the government on 20 January 2000. The effect was to retain the right of an accused person to opt for a trial on indictment. The composition of the partly reformed House, still including the Law Lords, enabled Bingham to make an eloquent speech in support of the change. But it was to no avail. Labour backbench peers either abstained or voted against the government in such numbers that an opposition amendment was carried by nearly 100 votes. That the outcome had been foreseen was demonstrated by the Leader of the House announcing that, as amended, the Bill no longer represented government policy and would not be proceeded with. A replacement measure would be introduced in the Commons in the current session.[36]

Ministers were as good as their word, and no time was lost in introducing a Criminal Justice (Mode of Trial) (No. 2) Bill in the House of Commons. But here too the government experienced antagonism from its own benches. A reasoned amendment moved by a Labour backbencher to decline to give the Bill a Second Reading on the ground that it failed properly to safeguard or maintain the right to jury trial in either-way offences attracted 214 votes, mainly Conservative or Liberal Democrat, but also twenty-nine cast by Labour MPs.[37] Many others abstained. Whereas a revolt on this scale might have forced a change of course at times of smaller overall majorities, the government could afford to ride it out. What had begun as a cost- and time-saving policy had turned into a test of strength, to be persevered with even when serious doubts had emerged over the extent of the claimed savings of time and money.

The drafting of the original Bill resulted in at least one unintended consequence. In the course of the debates it was argued that in attempting to preserve the reputation and livelihood of persons accused of criminal offences in the Magistrates' Courts, a bias would be created against defendants with no reputation or livelihood to preserve. Since many of those falling into the latter category would belong to racial minorities, an unwelcome ethnic perspective

---

[36] HL Debs., vol. 608, col. 1297, 20 Jan. 2000.
[37] HC Debs., vol. 345, col. 969, 7 Mar. 2000.

was added to the fear that a two-tier system of justice would risk the poor or unemployed being less favourably treated than defendants with higher economic or social status.

The government's stubborn defence of the deteriorating justifications for persisting with the policy, despite its flaws, was further weakened by doubts over the validity of the projected savings in court time and cost. The initial assumptions, as published in the Explanatory Notes to the original Bill, estimated the likely financial effects as an annual reduction of about 12,000 Crown Court trials per year, resulting in a net annual saving of £105 million. This calculation had been used by the Royal Commission, but in the intervening period, partly as a consequence of the introduction of the plea before venue system in 1997 and the courts' greater use of the practice of reflecting early pleas in sentencing, the annual number of those electing trial in the Crown Court had fallen from about 35,000 at the time of the Royal Commission report to about 18,500.[38]

To cap it all, when the No. 2 Bill came on to the Lords near to the end of the Parliamentary session in the Autumn of 2000, the government business managers made another rod for their own backs. In a maladroit attempt to meet the objections to the reputation clause, it was simply deleted. The result was that whatever the circumstances of the accused, no reference could be made to a defendant's standing in the community. For example a young black resident of a crime-ridden inner-city estate, who had been charged with an either-way offence while trying to prevent a fight, would be unable to ask the magistrates to take account of his good reputation and character, perhaps as a youth club leader. But the Bill was doomed in any event, and the result was a foregone conclusion. It is not often that the House of Lords defeats a government Bill on Second Reading, but that outcome had become inevitable. As few as three peers on the government benches spoke in support of the Attorney General, out of a total of twenty-one speakers in a five-hour-long debate. The upshot was that 184 peers voted to amend the motion that the Bill be read a second time, substituting a delay of six months. With only eighty-eight on the government side of the House dissenting (less

---

[38] Review of the Criminal Courts of England and Wales, *Report*, by Lord Justice Auld (London: The Stationery Office, 2001), para. 141, 190.

than half of the nominal total) the result was that the Criminal Justice (Mode of Trial) (No. 2) Bill was abandoned.[39]

Expert Review

In sharp contrast to the intense, single issue, Parliamentary controversies over the age of consent and mode of trial were two far-reaching reviews, each commissioned by the government and carried out by an individual well versed in the operation of the system of criminal justice. The approach represented a deliberate departure from the ponderous, and by no means always unanimous, Royal Commissions and departmental Committees of Inquiry of the past. The first was primarily a review of the organization, practices, and procedures of the criminal courts, but went further in examining the relationships between the courts and the wider criminal justice system of which they were part. To carry out this task ministers, in the shape of the Lord Chancellor, the Home Secretary, and the Attorney General, had chosen a Court of Appeal judge, Sir Robin Auld.[40]

The second review was of the sentencing framework, a complex mixture of law and administrative practice, falling within the ministerial responsibility of the Home Secretary. Here too an ideal person for the job was on hand. John Halliday, the most experienced civil servant on the criminal side of the Home Office and a veteran of past legislation and its consequences, intended or otherwise, was nearing retirement.[41] As a final assignment he was appointed, with the help

[39] HL Debs., vol. 616, cols. 1033–4, 28 Sept. 2000. The controversy over mode of trial is fully described in *Dispensing Justice* (Vol. 4, of Windlesham, *Responses to Crime*) (Oxford: Oxford University Press, 2001), 198–232.

[40] Judge of the High Court of Justice, Queen's Bench Division, 1987–95; Presiding Judge, Western Circuit, 1991–4; Senior Presiding Judge of England and Wales, 1995–8; Chairman, Criminal Committee, Judicial Studies Board 1989–91; Lord Justice of Appeal, 1995–.

[41] Although Halliday had been the senior official in charge of criminal policy at the Home Office since 1990, his successive designations reflected the changes in management style over a decade. From 1990 to 1995 he was a Deputy Under-Secretary of State, one rank below the Permanent Under-Secretary, with responsibility for the Criminal and Research and Statistics Departments. In 1995 he was redesignated as Director, Criminal Policy Group. After the change in government in 1997, as part of the process of modernisation, he became aim-owner, Home Office Aim 2. One of seven stated aims, No. 2 was 'delivery of justice through effective and efficient investigation, prosecution, trial and sentencing, and through support for victims'.

of a support team, to consider what principles should guide sentencing decisions and the types of disposal which should be made
available to the courts. The costs of different proposals, and their
relative effectiveness in reducing offending, should also be considered.[42] This remit recognized that changes would need to be
made in the sentencing framework established by the Criminal
Justice Act 1991. Specific reference was also made to the likely
impact of any recommendations in terms of cost and the effect on
the prison population. Finally the review was enjoined to keep in
mind 'the desirability of promoting flexibility in the use of custodial
and community based approaches'.[43]

When the weighty report (686 pages) of the Auld review was
published in October 2001 the most significant of its 328 recommendations was the proposed replacement of the existing court
structure by a unified criminal court.[44] Instead of the present
Crown Court and Magistrates' Courts, there should be a unified
Criminal Court consisting of three divisions. The Crown Division,
constituted as the Crown Court now is, would continue to exercise
jurisdiction over all indictable-only matters, as well as the more
serious 'either-way' offences allocated to it. The District Division
would be an innovation, such courts comprising a professional judge
(normally a District Judge or Recorder) and at least two magistrates.
This division would exercise jurisdiction over a mid-range of 'either-
way' matters of sufficient seriousness to merit up to two years'
custody on conviction. The Magistrates' Division would exercise
the present jurisdiction of Magistrates' Courts over all summary
matters, as well as the less serious 'either-way' cases allocated to
them. The courts in that division would allocate all of the either-way
cases according to the seriousness of the alleged offence and the
circumstances of the defendant, looking at the possible outcome of
the case at its worst from the point of view of the defendant, and
bearing in mind the jurisdiction of each division. In the event of
a dispute about venue, the District Judge would determine the

[42] HC Debs., vol. 350, col. 72W, 16 May 2000.   [43] Ibid.

[44] The Auld Report (n. 38 above) included some references to empirical research in
its discussion of jury trial and the unified criminal court. See the references to Sanders,
Morgan, and Russell, and Seago, Walker, and Wall at 104–7, and again at 110,
118–19. In addition, Appendix V lists a useful bibliography of published research
findings up to the year 2000 compiled by P. Darbyshire, A. Maughan, and A. Stewart,
680–6.

matter after hearing representations both from the prosecution and defendant.[45]

Under the Auld proposal, the defendant would have no right of election to be tried in any division, thus relinquishing the much-contested elective right to trial by jury in either-way cases. It was this feature of the proposed changes that re-ignited the embers of the Parliamentary dispute over mode of trial which were still smouldering. Almost without exception, national media coverage concentrated on this aspect of the reform proposals, much of the commentary being critical.[46]

The Halliday report on the sentencing framework, which followed in July 2001, was a classic example of the genre of expert review. In its analysis it was thorough, sensitive to prevailing currents of opinion, and carefully balanced. Having identified a range of purposes and principles of sentencing persons convicted of criminal offences, and consulted widely, the review examined the various types of sentence that are, or may be made, available to the courts. The overall aim was stated as being the need to design more flexible sentences so as to work effectively, whether the offender was in prison or in the community. The costs and benefits of a new-style sentencing framework were estimated, and the factors critical for the successful implementation of such a policy identified. The most compelling of the flaws in the present system of criminal sentencing was seen as 'the unclear and unpredictable approach to persistent offenders, who commit a disproportionate amount of crime'.[47] Short prison sentences of less than twelve months evidently had failed to make any meaningful intervention in the criminal careers of many of those who received them.

The review acknowledged candidly that while the case for change was strong, shorter prison sentences in particular being peculiarly ill-suited for their purposes, many practitioners feared that after a period of incessant change further reforms might not be for the better. Nevertheless, some of the present deficiencies cried out for reform. For offenders sentenced to less than twelve months' imprisonment, many of them recidivists who commit a disproportionate

---

[45] Review of the Criminal Courts of England and Wales, *Report*, n. 38 above, 24.

[46] For a wide-ranging critical commentary see M. Zander QC, *Lord Justice Auld's Review of the Criminal Courts, A Response* (London: LSE Law Department, 2001).

[47] *Making Punishments Work: Report of a Review of the Sentencing Framework for England and Wales* (London: Home Office, 2001), Executive Summary, p. i.

amount of crime, the solution proposed was that they should remain subject to penal sanctions for the whole period of the sentence, although only part of it would be spent in prison. The custodial element would normally consist of a maximum period of three months, followed by a period of supervision in the community. Undergoing participation in programmes designed by the Probation Service to tackle offending behaviour would be compulsory until the end of the duration of the sentence. Failure to co-operate could result in return to custody.

Described as 'custody plus', the proposal was aimed at the large numbers of short-term inmates annually serving prison sentences of less than twelve months. Even if combined with the probable ending of the home detention curfew scheme, it was anticipated that sufficient space would be created in prison establishments for inmates sentenced to twelve months' imprisonment or more. For this category, it was recommended that convicted offenders should serve the sentence imposed by the courts in full, whether in custody or under supervision in the community. Halliday proposed that after serving half of the sentence in custody the remainder should be served in the community, subject to conditions the breach of which could result in recall to prison. Supervision and conditions would extend until the end of the sentence. The most dangerous offenders, defined as those convicted of specified violent or sexual offences, with a high risk of reoffending and the potential to cause serious harm, would no longer be released on licence automatically after serving two thirds of their sentences in custody. Instead, discretionary release would depend on an assessment of risk by the Parole Board. In addition, the court would have power to order an extended period of supervision up to a maximum of ten years for sexual offences and five years for violent offences.[48]

By these means Halliday produced a report that was in tune with the prevailing political culture. The language was tough sounding, often reflecting public and practitioner views. In making a cautious attempt to retain the principle of proportionality in sentencing, but to reconcile it with the protection of the public from future offending, and with a keen awareness of the practical limitations

[48] The Halliday report made considerable use of research, although including no direct citation of research studies. Appendices 3, 5, and 6 contain summaries of research, assembled by Home Office researchers. Chapters 1 and 2 contain references to that research.

imposed by cost and the capacity of the prison estate, the report is a directional signpost for the future. If it marks a final departure from the principled structure of the Criminal Justice Act of 1991, it is not so much because of the perceived weaknesses of that legislation, the most conspicuous of which were quickly remedied,[49] but rather because of changed political expectations.[50]

The professional knowledge and experience of each reviewer, reinforced by the pressure of timetable, meant that there was less reliance on criminological research than might have been the case with a broader-based inquiry including laymen. The Royal Commission on Criminal Justice, for example, chaired by Lord Runciman earlier in the 1990s, albeit with a much wider remit, commissioned and published a series of no fewer than twenty-two research studies. While there is little indication that either Auld or Halliday sought to extend the bounds of criminological research, both took account of the existing state of knowledge and consulted widely. In addition, the Lord Chancellor, with the agreement of the Home Secretary and the Attorney General, appointed twelve well-qualified consultants to assist Auld.[51] Although Halliday gave no direct citations, he too sought and received much expert advice based on research as well as practical experience. Nevertheless the overall conclusion must be that criminological research as such played little more than a supporting role in this pre-legislative episode, and that it was political imperatives which were the driving force of policy changes.

The Politics of Reform

There can be no questioning the thoroughness and political independence of the Auld and Halliday reviews. Each resulted from lengthy and painstaking inquiries, and a well-informed assessment of the results. The structure of the courts and the sentencing framework are both central features of the criminal process, and it is

[49] See Windlesham, n. 39 above, iii, 'Legislating with the Tide', 3–36.

[50] This is the conclusion of David Faulkner, prime architect of the 1991 Criminal Justice Act at a time when he was the senior civil servant in charge of the Criminal and Research and Statistics Departments at the Home Office. See his paper for 26th Cropwood Round Table Conference, University of Cambridge Institute of Criminology, 29 Nov.–1 Dec. 2001.

[51] Review of the Criminal Courts of England and Wales, *Report*, n. 38 above, 3.

important that they should be subjected to periodic scrutiny. By July ministers were ready to announce their plans for the future. Three documents were published simultaneously under the title *Justice for All*. The most substantial was a White Paper representing 'the Government's view as to what should be done to modernise and improve the criminal justice system so its aims can be achieved more effectively'.[52] The 181-page document was accompanied by two others. The first summarized the Government's response to each of the numerous recommendations made in the Auld and Halliday reports, with reasons for their acceptance or rejection. The second was a short summary of the proposals contained in the White Paper.

In November two separate Bills were introduced at the start of the new session; the Courts Bill by the Lord Chancellor in the House of Lords, and a Criminal Justice Bill by the Home Secretary in the House of Commons. The main feature of the Courts Bill was the decision to set up a new executive agency as part of the Lord Chancellor's Department, replacing both the existing Court Service and the forty-two local Magistrates' Courts' Committees. The contentious recommendations by Auld for a unified criminal court were not pursued.

Although the Courts Bill did not set out a blueprint for the new agency, and ministers stressed the importance of maintaining a strong local dimension of decentralized management and local accountability, it was precisely this feature that attracted the strongest criticism. One of the most forthright libertarian challenges came from the former Conservative Attorney General, Lord Mayhew of Twysden. Neither in the pursuit of the objective of modernisation and greater efficiency or at all, he declared, were the Bill's proposals for the magistrates' courts justified. They constituted 'a quite unjustified exercise in centralization, one which has the potential to impinge dangerously upon the independence of the lay judiciary'.[53]

The Criminal Justice Bill, the latest in a long line, was more diverse, ranging from crime prevention to the punishment and rehabilitation of offenders. Procedural reforms included involving the

---

[52] Both reports were subject to a period of public consultation. The Government response was published on 17 July 2002 (Cm 5563).

[53] See HL Debs., vol. 642, col. 45, 9 Dec. 2002.

Crown Prosecution Service in charging decisions; reforming the system for allocating cases to court; and increasing magistrates' sentencing powers so that fewer cases would go to the Crown Court. A new presumption against bail would be introduced for those tested positive for class A drugs who refuse to go into treatment. Controversial provisions included the disclosure to the court of a defendant's previous similar convictions; the ending of the double-jeopardy rule to enable retrial for serious offences, if sanctioned by the Court of Appeal; and trial by a judge alone in serious or complex cases of fraud or where there is a risk of jury intimidation.

Thus in the next phase in the development of national criminal justice policy in England and Wales it will be politics, rather than expert review, which will be paramount. Legislation incorporating, in whole or in part, many of the Auld and Halliday recommendations is already before Parliament with the prospect of being enacted before the end of the 2002–3 session. Such practical considerations as the adequacy of financial resources; crisis management; the capacity of the prison estate; and the availability of Parliamentary time will co-exist with opportunism and overtly political objectives and values. Aims and expectations differ, not just between the parties, but at a deeper level between ministerial colleagues in the government. There is an irony that David Blunkett, a communitarian politician with a strong, and repeatedly proclaimed, antagonism to lawyers, finds himself joined at the Cabinet Committee on the Criminal Justice System by the government's two most prominent lawyers, the Lord Chancellor and Attorney General.[54]

Since some Home Secretaries have left a mark on what is still one of the great offices of state, whereas others have made no more than soon-forgotten impressions, it is instructive to be aware of personal attitudes and goals. In October 2001, a few months after his appointment as Home Secretary following the General Election in June of the same year, David Blunkett explained the basis of his political beliefs in the following terms:

our goal should be this: a truly participative democracy, one in which everyone feels their voice is heard and they have a stake in their communities and their future. How can we support this? Through greater redistribution of power and responsibility across society and towards local communities, and through open and honest two-way communication

[54] Lord Irvine of Lairg QC and Lord Goldsmith QC.

between government and communities. Only then can we forge a sense of common membership that allows us to shape our common future.[55]

Fine words and warm sounding. But what if local communities, or those claiming to speak or act on their behalf, want to impose additional post-sentence community-based sanctions on identified sex offenders or threaten alleged paedophiles? How about those who resent what they caricature as foreign judges in the European Court of Human Rights imposing their will on a reluctant national government which is obliged to accept and implement their findings? Is the return of capital punishment for the most heinous of all homicides, including the possibility of terrorist offences of unimaginable horror, still off the agenda? Would the promotion of populist dogma renew democracy and civil society or debase it?

[55] D. Blunkett, *Renewing Democracy and Civil Society*, a Lecture presented to Civitas: the Institute for the Study of Civil Society, Oct. 2001.

Part 3

Criminological Research and Policy Change: Three Case Studies

7

Sentencing and Sensitivity: A Challenge for Criminological Research

Andrew Ashworth*

The career that has taken Roger Hood to the top of his profession began with empirical research into sentencing, and he has revisited this field many times, both as a researcher and in the course of his influential writings on the relationship of criminology to policy-making. Sentencing presents one of the most public faces of the criminal justice process. It also has an importance internal to the system, in that it determines the workload of the prisons, the probation service, and other agencies. This chapter will focus on two aspects of the relationship between criminology and sentencing—the effect of research findings on decisions to propose a new form of sentence, or on the rise and fall of certain rationales for sentencing; and the effect of research findings on sentencing practice in the magistrates' courts and the Crown Court. First, however, recent events in criminal justice policy will be sketched in order to provide a context for the discussion.

Introduction

Histories of criminal justice in the last decade of the twentieth century are likely to include the crisis in judicial legitimacy as one of the major themes. A major theme it was, but, even with respect to the judiciary, only one of several interweaving strands. The decade began with the notorious cases of miscarriage of justice, when the

*I am grateful to Jill Peay, Elaine Player, Stephen Shute, and Lucia Zedner for their comments on a previous draft of this chapter.

Court of Appeal overturned the convictions of the Birmingham Six, the Guildford Four, the Maguire Seven, and others. Some of these convictions had already been upheld by the Court on a previous occasion, a fact which called into question the integrity of judicial processes as well as that of the police and prosecutors whose earlier acts and omissions rendered the convictions unsafe. In 1993, however, the judiciary and magistracy scored a success, and one that they shared with the government of the day. Two years earlier the Criminal Justice Act 1991 had been passed in an attempt to impose a consistent framework on English sentencing, but parts of it met with resistance from sentencers. Their call to repeal certain sections of the Criminal Justice Act 1991, notably those dealing with unit fines and with previous convictions, was heeded by the Home Secretary and Parliament passed the Criminal Justice Act 1993.[1] Indeed, the higher judiciary had already sabotaged one key element of the Criminal Justice Act 1991, by reinstating general deterrence as a sentencing aim through a defiant and subversive reinterpretation of the statutory phrase 'commensurate with the seriousness of the offence',[2] and the government accepted this without demur.

After that there was a progressive distancing between the judiciary and the government. Opposing positions were defiantly taken up towards the end of 1995, as the then Home Secretary (Michael Howard) announced the government's intention to introduce mandatory minimum sentences for certain crimes, and the then Lord Chief Justice (Lord Taylor of Gosforth) responded swiftly with a public denunciation of that policy.[3] Both sides kept up this public debate for over a year until the enactment of the Crime (Sentences) Act 1997, which introduced mandatory sentences for three types of offender but with certain concessions that acknowledged the strength of the counter-arguments.[4] The incoming Labour govern-

---

[1] Lord Windlesham, *Responses to Crime, volume 3: Legislating with the Tide* (Oxford: Oxford University Press, 1996), Chapter 1.

[2] These are strong words (for fuller discussion see A. Ashworth, *Sentencing and Criminal Justice* (3rd edn., London: Butterworths, 2000), 85–7), but it is now accepted that this is what the Court of Appeal did: see the Halliday Report, *Making Punishment Work* (London: Home Office, 2001), para. 1.34.

[3] A. Ashworth, 'The Decline of English Sentencing' in M.H. Tonry and R. Frase (eds.), *Sentencing and Sanctions in Western Countries* (Oxford: Oxford University Press, 2001); Lord Windlesham, *Responses to Crime, volume 4: Dispensing Justice* (Oxford: Oxford University Press, 2001), Chapter 1.

[4] In brief, a mandatory sentence of life imprisonment for the second serious or violent offence; a mandatory minimum of seven years for the third offence of drug

ment, which had not voted against the Bill when in opposition, chose to implement the sentencing provisions of the 1997 Act. But at the same time it initiated another debate, by announcing its intention to introduce the measure that became the Human Rights Act 1998. Here was a policy on which most members of the higher judiciary and the government were at one, whilst some of the strongest critics of the measure opposed it because of the great power it bestowed on the judiciary.[5] Interestingly, one way in which that power has been exercised by the judiciary is to reinterpret the statutory provisions on the automatic sentence of life imprisonment for the second serious offence, introduced by the Crime (Sentences) Act 1997, so as to broaden the saving clause for 'exceptional circumstances' in a way that the judiciary would have preferred from the outset.[6]

This brief account of the 1990s identifies an ambivalence in the political standing of the judiciary: although there is evidence of a crisis in judicial legitimacy, best exemplified in the miscarriage of justice cases, there is also evidence of the continuing political power of the judiciary, in terms of an ability to influence and even, occasionally, to subvert policy. Thus, in relation to sentencing in particular, the judiciary joined with the then Home Secretary in criticizing aspects of the Criminal Justice Act 1991, and the result was the amending Act of 1993. But only a couple of years later the judiciary and the then Home Secretary stood on opposite sides over the introduction of mandatory sentences. The constant element in the judicial position is an insistence on maximum discretion in sentencing: any measure that constrains judges or magistrates is criticized as tending to produce injustice by preventing courts from responding to the facts of individual cases. Sometimes the way in which the position is elaborated suggests that it has a constitutional foundation—that determining what sentence should be given to an offender is a proper function only of the judiciary—but this is without substance. There is nothing constitutionally improper in Parliament constraining judicial discretion or even introducing mandatory

dealing or trafficking; and a mandatory minimum of three years for the third offence of domestic burglary. The last two were made subject to the court's power to pass a lower sentence if the statutory minimum would be unjust in all the circumstances.

[5] e.g. K.D. Ewing, 'The Human Rights Act and Parliamentary Democracy' (1999) 62 *Modern Law Review* 79.

[6] *Offen (No. 2)* [2001] 1 Cr. App. R. 372; there are those who argue that this decision would have been the same even if the Human Rights Act had not been in force.

sentences.[7] The true meaning of the principle of judicial independence is to ensure impartiality in decision-making, within whatever parameters the legislature has provided.

The crisis of judicial legitimacy, evident in public reactions to the miscarriage of justice cases, is also reflected in the lack of public confidence in the courts and their sentencing practices. This may be illustrated by the results of the 1996 and 1998 British Crime Surveys, which included detailed questions on the subject.

Eighty-two per cent of the sample thought that judges were out of touch with the public; the figure for magistrates was 63 per cent. Four-fifths of people think that sentences are too lenient, half saying that they are much too lenient. Judges were thought to be doing the worst job amongst criminal justice professionals.[8]

This appears to be a damning indictment of judicial sentencing, lending strong support to the notion of a crisis of judicial legitimacy. Yet the same surveys also show that those public opinions are largely based on mistaken assumptions and gross misunderstandings. To summarize again:

Findings of particular interest are:

—the mistaken belief among the majority that recorded crime had rapidly increased
—substantial overestimates of the proportion of recorded crime involving violence
—a tendency to underestimate the proportion of the population with criminal records
—large minorities being unaware of the upward trend in the use of imprisonment
—widespread ignorance of sentences available to the court
—very substantial underestimates of the courts' use of imprisonment for three types of crime: rape, mugging and burglary.[9]

---

[7] The arguments are set out in Ashworth, n. 2 above, Chapter 2.

[8] M. Hough and J. Roberts, *Attitudes to Punishment: Findings from the British Crime Survey*, Home Office Research Study 179 (London: Home Office, 1998), p. viii; see also, to the same effect, J. Mattinson and C. Mirrlees-Black, *Attitudes to Crime and Criminal Justice: Findings from the 1998 British Crime Survey* (London: Home Office, 2000).

[9] Hough and Roberts, n. 8 above, pp. vii–viii; also Mattinson and Mirrlees-Black, n. 8 above, p. vii.

Even presented in this crude form, such research findings raise important questions about any crisis in judicial legitimacy. It does seem that there is an unhealthy deficit of public confidence in judges and their sentencing. It also seems that this deficit is the result of such far-reaching misconceptions that it would be unsound to take it at face value. The public thinks that judges are out of touch with it, but the public is out of touch with the realities of crime and sentencing. In this particular context it would therefore be preferable to abandon the apparent objectivity of the term 'legitimacy' and instead to refer to 'public confidence', a term which has a clearer link to public perceptions.[10]

Problems with public confidence in the sentencing practices of the courts are not new. If one looks back over a period of fifty years, one finds that two focal points of public dissatisfaction with sentencing have been recurrent—disparity of sentencing and undue leniency. The criticism of leniency has doubtful foundations, given the public misunderstandings outlined above. Successive research projects have shown that, when individuals are asked about the sentence they would think appropriate on a given set of facts, their preferred sentence is quite close to, and rarely above, the average given by the courts in such cases.[11] What about disparity? Here the evidence provides some basis for the criticism, in respect of both judges and magistrates. When introducing their exploration of the criminological evidence of disparity, Roger Hood and Richard F. Sparks quoted from a paper prepared by the United Nations secretariat in 1965:

In most countries there is, admittedly, a varying degree of disparity and inconsistency in the sentencing process, and this tends to engender disrespect and even contempt for the law.[12]

The issue of disparity was thus linked not merely to what is here termed 'public confidence' but also, more deeply, to what some would call the 'legitimacy' of judges and magistrates—a failure to

[10] There is evidence that supplying information designed to dispel misconceptions about criminal justice and sentencing has some effect on public views: B. Chapman, C. Mirrlees-Black, and C. Brown, *Improving Public Attitudes to the Criminal Justice System: The Impact of Information*, Home Office Research Study 245 (London: Home Office, 2002).

[11] Hough and Roberts, n. 8 above, 27–30.

[12] R. Hood and R. Sparks, *Key Issues in Criminology* (London: Weidenfeld and Nicolson, 1970), 142.

observe the principle of equality of treatment or, as Roger Hood would prefer, equality of consideration.

Research and New Forms of Sentence

There are plenty of examples of decisions to propose a new form of sentence being taken more on political grounds than on a careful consideration of the evidence. This is not simply a recent phenomenon. In his masterly essay on 'Criminology and Penal Change', Roger Hood laid bare the shallowness of the criminological foundations of several new forms of sentence. Analysing the reasons for introducing the suspended sentence (1967) and the community service order (1972), he wrote:

My argument is that the adoption of both these methods of punishment was due to the appeal of their ideologies and that, particularly in the case of community service, there was no attempt to justify the new penalty in terms of a coherent analysis of crime, criminal behaviour or the effects of penalties. In other words, the part played by criminological analysis, theory and research was minimal.[13]

Hood's critique of the assumptions that apparently underpinned the decision to introduce the community service order was devastating, and was followed by further strictures on the Wootton Committee[14] for its failure to examine the reasons for the inadequacy of existing forms of sentence before proposing new ones:

there was no analysis of the prison population, of sentencing practice, of those who were regarded as unsuitable for available alternative penalties even though the A.C.T.O. in 1957 had specifically stated that it would need 'the most extensive research to form even a tentative estimate of the numbers' of prisoners who could be dealt with by means other than imprisonment.[15]

[13] R. Hood, 'Criminology and Penal Change: A Case Study of the Nature and Impact of Some Recent Advice to Governments' in R. Hood (ed.), *Crime, Criminology and Public Policy* (London: Heinemann, 1974), 380.

[14] This was a committee of the Advisory Council on the Penal System, chaired by Baroness Wootton, which produced the Advisory Council's report on *Non-Custodial and Semi-Custodial Penalties* (London: HMSO, 1970), on which subsequent reforms, including the introduction of the community service order, were based.

[15] Hood, n. 13 above, 413; the reference to ACTO was to the Advisory Council on the Treatment of Offenders, the predecessor of the Advisory Council on the Penal System. ACTO had reported in 1957 on *Alternatives to Short Terms of Imprisonment*

These were clearly examples of poor policy-making, although some would argue that, even if an adequate amount of criminological information had been assembled, it would not have been conclusive and a leap of faith would still have been required in order to decide for or against the introduction of each new measure.[16] It is possible that there was another influence at work, too. There is some evidence of an attitude of deference to the courts, yielding a belief that it would be improper for committees to make proposals about the way in which sentencers should use the powers they were to be given. Thus the Wootton Committee made this startling comment when proposing the introduction of the community service order:

We have not attempted to categorise precisely the types of offender for whom community service might be appropriate, nor do we think it possible to predict what use might be made by the courts of this new form of sentence.[17]

The use of the term 'predict' in this context is extraordinary. A conscientious committee ought to offer guidance on how the measure should be used, for what types of offender, and in place of which forms of existing sentence. The Wootton Committee's comments suggest either great deference to the independence of the courts in sentencing matters or an unquestioned separation between the Committee's business and sentencing principles and practice.

A modest step away from this separation was taken a decade later when the combination order was proposed. This order (now termed a 'community punishment and rehabilitation order') combines a requirement of community service with an element of probation supervision, and was intended to be the most demanding of all community penalties. In its 1990 White Paper, the government stated:

(London: HMSO, 1957). In the present day it seems strange to write about committees of independent people making recommendations on matters of criminal justice policy after enquiry and assessment.

[16] Baroness Wootton, seeking to defend herself, asked where 'is that "body of criminological and penological knowledge" to which Hood so lightly refers, which would enable anybody to predict with confidence the reaction of different classes of offenders to different forms of treatment?': B. Wootton, 'Official Advisory Bodies' in N.D. Walker (ed.), *Penal Policy-Making in Britain* (Cambridge: Institute of Criminology, 1977), at 19. Hood's point was more about the method adopted by the committee, and about their failure to make certain enquiries or to commission research.

[17] Advisory Council on the Penal System, *Non-Custodial and Semi-Custodial Penalties* (London: HMSO, 1970), para. 37.

This new order should be particularly suitable for some persistent property offenders. About 10,000 of those in custody sentenced for burglary, theft, handling, fraud and forgery, have three or more previous convictions.[18]

This stands as a rare indication of the group for whom a new measure was intended, but it adopts no more than a small part of Roger Hood's prescription. Not only was there no attempt to examine how such offenders might respond to the new measure (particularly since most of them would already have re-offended after being given other community penalties on previous occasions), but there was also no real attempt to steer the courts towards using the measure for this group of offenders. Perhaps the attitude of deference was still exerting an influence. Indeed, one of the features of the final two decades of the last century is that, although proposals for new measures were still heavily influenced by the ideological and political factors to which Roger Hood drew attention many years earlier, there was also a distinct push in the direction of what sentencers themselves wanted. In its 1988 Green Paper the Home Office invited sentencers to state what kinds of non-custodial measure they would be prepared to use:[19] this approach is either a manifestation of deference to the courts (that it would be wrong to tell the courts what to do, either by ministerial speeches or by introducing restrictions into the new powers) or a pragmatic recognition that the policy goal could not be achieved unless the courts were prepared to co-operate in the enterprise of using community penalties more and custodial sentences less.

In relation to the introduction of new forms of sentence, have we therefore arrived at a position in which criminological evidence of the kind outlined by Roger Hood has a minimal influence, and in which either political attractiveness or deference to the judiciary is the most powerful factor? In a sense this would not be unexpected. The interest of criminologists in carrying out 'effectiveness studies' declined in the 1980s, even within the Home Office,[20] and non-consequentialist rationales for sentencing were making headway. If

[18] Home Office, *Crime, Justice and Protecting the Public* Cm 965 (London: HMSO, 1990), para. 4.16.

[19] Home Office, *Punishment, Custody and the Community* (London: Home Office, 1988).

[20] After the publication of two important studies—S.R. Brody, *The Effectiveness of Sentencing*, Home Office Research Study 35 (London: HMSO, 1975), and S.R. Brody and R. Tarling, *Taking Offenders out of Circulation*, Home Office Research Study 64

the aim is to have sentences that are proportionate to the degree of wrongdoing, measuring their effectiveness in terms of reconviction rates is at best an evaluation of a secondary function (although still worthwhile, since theories of proportionate punishment are more concerned with the quantum than with the content of sentences). However, in view of the recurrent finding of effectiveness studies 'that different community and custodial penalties did not seem to be differentially effective in preventing reconviction, once demographic and criminal record variables were taken into account',[21] the focus was understandably on other forms of criminological enquiry.

The last quarter of the twentieth century saw a burgeoning interest among criminal justice scholars in reassessing, both empirically and philosophically, the rationales for sentencing. Rehabilitation had been a prominent rationale in the 1960s, especially in the United States, but its influence began to wane in the early 1970s as the promise of significant changes in behaviour following 'treatment' seemed not to be borne out by research findings, as autonomy-based worries about compulsory programmes of behaviour modification came to be more widely shared, and as the elements of discretion allowed by the rehabilitative approach raised concerns about the absence of proper controls on what was undoubtedly the exercise of coercive power by officials.[22] Thus the gathering criticisms ran much deeper than the failure of many programmes to show positive results, which is how the 'decline of the rehabilitative ideal' is often represented. As Roger Hood wrote as early as 1974:

Beyond all these criticisms there is of course a political point, namely that the State should not use its powers to punish in order to stifle diversity in life-styles; that it should not use the power to punish in order to deny the offender's view of his social situation as unjust or as uncaring if indeed it is;

(London: HMSO, 1981)—very few studies of the comparative effectiveness of penal measures were undertaken. The next Home Office publication of this general kind struck a much more sceptical note: C. Lloyd, G. Mair, and M. Hough, *Explaining Reconviction Rates: A Critical Analysis*, Home Office Research Study 136 (London: HMSO, 1994).

[21] Ibid., introduction by R. Tarling, p. iii.

[22] This is to simplify a process which was quite sudden and significant in criminal justice discourse (see D. Garland, *The Culture of Control* (Oxford: Oxford University Press, 2001), Chapter 3) but which had much less of an effect on penal practice both in prisons and in the community, as Lucia Zedner points out: 'Dangers of Dystopias in Penal Theory' (2002) 22 *Oxford Journal of Legal Studies* 341.

that the penal system cannot act as a major instrument of social change, and that if it attempts to do so it is in danger of adopting a stance whereby social deprivation is attributed to individual pathology which can be 'corrected' by a 'treatment' service ... [23]

But where did these powerful reservations about the rehabilitative approach leave the rationale of sentencing? Roger Hood, in the same vein as the most influential American reports of the 1970s,[24] argued in favour of combining proportionality in sentencing with greater restraint in the use of custody. To this end he urged criminologists to turn their attention to normative questions:

What weight should be given to harm done? To previous record? To poor environment? To cultural differences in the interpretation of challenges to personal status or integrity? To marital stress or to inadequate income? Which offences should be regarded as the most socially injurious? Have we placed traffic offences in their right order compared with most petty thefts or common-or-garden assaults?[25]

Moreover he directed a particular challenge to sentencers themselves: he chided the judiciary for its vague references to 'the gravity of the offence' when sentencing, and he wrote of 'forcing judges' to be explicit 'about the way in which they "evaluate social behaviours" and "to articulate the moral judgements on which their sentence is based" '.[26] These comments ignited a vigorous debate, not least because they more or less charged the 'reductivist' approach (which favoured what might now be termed risk-based sentencing) with producing 'greater punishments for the lower social classes, leaving many sociologists wondering whether the criminal justice system is not simply a means of scapegoating those with little social

---

[23] R. Hood, *Tolerance and the Tariff: Some Reflections on Fixing the Time Prisoners Serve in Custody* (London: NACRO, 1974); the quotation may be found in the slightly abridged version reprinted in J. Baldwin and A.K. Bottomley (eds.), *Criminal Justice: Selected Readings* (Oxford: Martin Robertson, 1978), at 301–2.

[24] His 'Tolerance and the Tariff' was written a couple of years after the publication of the report of the American Friends' Service Committee, *The Struggle for Justice* (New York: American Friends' Service Committee, 1971), but two years before the Report of the Committee for the Study of Incarceration, now much more widely known: A. von Hirsch, *Doing Justice: The Choice of Punishments* (New York: Hill and Wang, 1976).

[25] 'Tolerance and the Tariff', n. 23 above, 302.

[26] Ibid., 302–3.

power'.[27] However, Roger Hood's critique was somewhat ahead of its time in this country,[28] and it was not until 1990 that the principle of proportionality, combined with at least a partial commitment to restraint in the use of custody, found its way into official policy statements.[29]

At the same time other rationales, particularly incapacitation, were attracting both official and criminological attention. And both the judiciary and politicians refused to let go of deterrent rationales for sentencing, despite the rather unpromising research evidence. The last few years of the millennium were to witness a remarkable *pas-de-deux* of denial and affirmation, with the Lord Chief Justice castigating the then Home Secretary (Michael Howard) for his unfounded assumptions about the deterrent effects of sentences when proposing mandatory minimum sentences, and yet continuing to preside over a Court of Appeal that routinely upheld sentences based on deterrence, and with a subsequent Home Secretary (Jack Straw) commissioning research into the state of knowledge about the effects of deterrent sentencing and then neglecting its results in his policies.[30] Such duplicitous approaches are to be expected of politicians, perhaps. As the judiciary engages more frequently in debates about policy, it is not surprising (although sad) to see senior judges falling into the same habit. Desperate to preserve as much discretion in sentencing as possible, they made claims about deterrence that contradicted their own sentencing practice. Deterrence remains one of the most difficult subjects in

---

[27] Ibid., 302, with a footnote reference to D. Chapman, *Sociology and the Stereotype of the Criminal* (London: Tavistock, 1968). His predecessor at Oxford, Nigel Walker, took up the cudgels in defence of the 'reductivist' approach, of which he was probably the leading exponent. The ensuing pair of articles placed more emphasis on parole than on sentencing: N. Walker, 'Release by Executive Decision: a Defence' [1975] *Crim.L.R.* 540, and R. Hood, 'The Case against Executive Control over Time in Custody: a Rejoinder to Professor Walker's Criticisms' [1975] *Crim.L.R.* 545.

[28] Many criminologists in influential positions (such as those on the Advisory Council on the Penal System) still pursued rehabilitative or other reductivist aims: see the previous note.

[29] Home Office, *Crime, Justice and Protecting Society* (London: HMSO, 1990).

[30] See Lord Taylor, 'Continuity and Change in the Criminal Law' (1996) 5 *King's College L.J.* 1, and A. von Hirsch, A.E. Bottoms, E. Burney and P.-O. Wikström, *Criminal Deterrence and Sentence Severity* (Oxford: Hart Publishing, 1999), and the general discussion by A. Ashworth, 'The Decline of English Sentencing' in M. Tonry and R. Frase (eds.), *Sentencing and Sanctions in Western Countries* (Oxford: Oxford University Press, 2001), at 76–84.

criminology, but that is no excuse for the holders of so much public power to say one thing and do another.

We arrive at a position in which a large number of rationales for sentencing can still be said to be 'in play'. Incapacitation and deterrence continue to have attractions for policy-makers; proportionality (or desert) retains considerable support, albeit in more or less constraining forms;[31] and the 'what works' movement has led to a revival of interest in rehabilitative schemes, including 'accredited programmes' based on 'cognitive-behavioural' methods, which is drawing some criminologists back to effectiveness research.[32] Behind these rationales, the principle of restraint in the use of custody flits in and out of official dialogue—apparent in some form in the 1990 White Paper;[33] abandoned, in favour of 'prison works', in 1994 and for the remaining years of the 1990s; and then beginning to re-appear in the early years of the new century, as the Lord Chief Justice urges the courts to use prison more sparingly for less serious offenders,[34] and the government proposes a refocusing of custodial sentences.[35] We should also note the rise of a fifth rationale: the last few years of the millennium saw a marked increase of interest in

---

[31] See, e.g., the Halliday report (Report of a Review of the Sentencing Framework for England and Wales, *Making Punishments Work* (London: Home Office, 2001)).

[32] Some of this work is being carried out by the Probation Research Unit at the Centre for Criminological Research in Oxford: see, e.g., P. Raynor, J. Kynch, C. Roberts, and S. Merrington, *Risk and Need Assessment in Probation Services: An Evaluation*, Home Office Research Study 211 (London: Home Office, 2000). From among the broader evaluative literature see J. Vennard, D. Sugg, and C. Hedderman, *Changing Offenders' Attitudes and Behaviour: What Works?*, Home Office Research Study 171 (London: Home Office, 1997), and S. Rex, 'Beyond Cognitive-behaviouralism? Reflections on the Effectiveness Literature' in A.E. Bottoms, L. Gelsthorpe, and S. Rex (eds.), *Community Penalties: Change and Challenges* (London: Willan, 2001).

[33] See n. 29 above: it was in para. 2.7 of this White Paper that the government declared that, unless prison can be 'justified in terms of public protection, denunciation and retribution . . . it can be an expensive way of making bad people worse'. It is also to be noted that deterrence found no place in this list of justifications.

[34] See the judgment of Lord Woolf C.J. in *Kefford* [2002] *Crim.L.R.* 432. The overcrowding argument is fickle because it can always be answered by building more prisons, a policy that has been pursued in recent years but which runs directly counter to the principle of restraint in the use of custody. In *Kefford* Lord Woolf expressed the hope that the prison building programme 'in the future would alleviate the situation', thus amply demonstrating the fickle nature of his approach and departing from some of his own previous pronouncements on the relative futility of imprisonment.

[35] Home Office, *Justice for All* (London: The Stationery Office, 2002), paras. 5.6, 5.7, and 5.9.

restorative justice, which insists on the value of processes which are fair to all stakeholders (including the victim), and which makes various claims about its effectiveness for victim and for offenders. Research and writings on restorative justice are already considerable,[36] and, although there are different views about what the criterion or criteria of effectiveness should be (e.g. forms of victim satisfaction, reconviction rate of offenders, community acceptance), it is likely that it will attract the attention of many criminologists in the coming years. Yet the criticisms made and the questions asked by Roger Hood in 1974 about rehabilitation may be applied no less to aspects of restorative justice.[37]

Criminological research in the broadest sense has therefore played some part in the rise and fall of various rationales for punishment. So far as empirical research on effectiveness is concerned, there has been a resurgence of interest in this kind of criminological enquiry after many years in which enthusiasm was low. It is not the norm, however, for empirical research to inform decisions to introduce new forms of sentence in the methodical way rightly urged by Roger Hood in his 1974 papers. Typically, effectiveness research is now carried out after a measure has been introduced, sometimes on a pilot basis, and it is often focused on whether the sentence is workable (in logistical terms) rather than whether it 'works' (in terms of reconvictions, let alone any comparative reconviction study that includes similar offenders given other sentences).[38] Research of this kind is usually commissioned by the Home Office, and whether it has some influence on decisions to press ahead with a particular

---

[36] See the reviews by D. Miers, *An International Review of Restorative Justice* (London: Home Office, 2001), and by D. Miers and 10 others, *An Exploratory Evaluation of Restorative Justice Schemes* (London: Home Office, 2001); see also C. Hoyle, R. Young, and R. Hill, *Proceed with Caution: An Evaluation of the Thames Valley Police Initiative in Restorative Cautioning* (Oxford: Centre for Criminological Research, 2002).

[37] A. Ashworth, 'Responsibilities, Rights and Restorative Justice' (2002) 42 *British Journal of Criminology* 578.

[38] Examples of this genre might be the various reports on electronic monitoring: G. Mair and C. Nee, *Electronic Monitoring: The Trials and their Results*, Home Office Research Study 120 (London: HMSO, 1990); G. Mair and E. Mortimer, *Curfew Order with Electronic Monitoring: An Evaluation of the First 12 Months of the Trials in Greater Manchester, Norfolk and Berkshire*, Home Office Research Study 163 (London: Home Office, 1996); E. Mortimer and G. Mair, *Electronic Monitoring in Practice: The Second Year of the Trials of Curfew Orders*, Home Office Research Study

form of sentence can only be speculation.[39] The story of electronic monitoring is instructive, in that the first research report was largely negative,[40] but such was the political appeal of 'tagging' that the government returned to it a few years later and conducted action research in order to devise a workable system.[41] On the other hand, much of the research activity surrounding restorative justice is not state funded:[42] it tends to be broader in its coverage of the issues and far less focused on policy decisions.

Research into Sentencing Practice

We noted earlier the argument that it makes little sense to propose new forms of sentence unless it is clear either how any such sentence *would* be used by the courts or how the sentence *should* be used by the courts. Either way, an understanding of how the courts approach the task of sentencing must be the foundation. How can such an understanding be acquired? So far as the Crown Court is concerned, the pioneering work of David Thomas in the 1960s led him to construct, out of the decisions of the Court of Appeal,[43] a framework of sentencing principles which has subsequently been de-

177 (London: Home Office, 1997); I. Walter, D. Sugg, and L. Moore, *A Year of the Tag: Interviews with Criminal Justice Practitioners and Electronic Monitoring Staff About Curfew Orders*, Findings 140 (London: Home Office, 2001); D. Sugg, L. Moore, and P. Howard, *Electronic Monitoring and Offending Behaviour—Reconviction Results for the Second Year of Trials of Curfew Orders*, Findings 141 (London: Home Office, 2001).

[39] It would not be scandalous to suggest that governments have been ideologically committed to electronic monitoring, and would have pressed ahead unless real disasters were brought to light by the research. Similarly in 1975 the Home Office's own research on the reconvictions of offenders sentenced to community service was held back until after the government had announced that community service orders would be extended from the pilot areas to all courts. The research showed a rather unflattering reconviction rate: K. Pease, S. Billingham, and I. Earnshaw, *Community Service Assessed in 1976*, Home Office Research Study 39 (London: HMSO, 1976), Chapter 3.

[40] G. Mair and C. Nee, *Electronic Monitoring: The Trials and their Results*, Home Office Research Study 120 (London: HMSO, 1990).

[41] See Ashworth, n. 2 above, 283–5.

[42] For a recent review see D. Miers, *An International Review of Restorative Justice* (London: Home Office, 2001).

[43] The ground-breaking articles by D.A. Thomas culminated in the publication of his book *Principles of Sentencing* (London: Heinemann, 1970; 2nd edn., 1979).

veloped by the Court itself. Later the Court introduced the guideline judgment as a technique for structuring sentences, and, as the reporting and citation of sentencing decisions have increased, so there has been a gradual spread of 'rule of law' values into the substantially discretionary sphere of sentencing. It was developments of this kind that led Lord Lane, when Lord Chief Justice, to conclude that:

In his view the available textbooks give a fairly clear account of the factors which judges take into account in sentencing, and he could not think of any aspects of judicial sentencing upon which research might prove helpful.[44]

No criminologist would find this acceptable. In the first place, there was and is plenty of evidence of disparities among courts in their sentencing practices, which indicates that (in Lord Lane's terms) the 'factors' may be given different weight by different judges and magistrates. That, in turn, suggests a need to explore the reasons for these different approaches. And, secondly, Lord Lane's view implies that sentencing decisions are taken in isolation from the wider system, whereas they are likely to be shaped by the practices of probation officers, prosecutors, defence lawyers, and others, at least in the selection and presentation of information to the court.

What, then, has criminological research been able to offer on these and other issues? And what influence, if any, have the findings of such research had on policy development? A selective account of sentencing research in England over the last half century should indicate some answers to these questions. For reasons that will become apparent, the magistrates' courts are discussed separately from the Crown Court.

Sentencing in Magistrates' Courts

Interest in studying the sentencing practices of the courts was kindled in the 1950s, particularly in respect of young offenders. Max Grünhut, holder of the first criminology post at Oxford University, wrote in 1956 that:

Criminological interest today has shifted from the causes of crime to the effects of treatment. However, even such treatment research must not lose

[44] This reportage of Lord Lane's words constitutes the final sentence of A. Ashworth, E. Genders, G. Mansfield, J. Peay, and E. Player, *Sentencing in the Crown Court: Report of an Exploratory Study* (Oxford: Centre for Criminological Research, University of Oxford, 1984), 64.

sight of the characteristics of the juvenile delinquents who appear before the courts and are put on probation or committed to institutions, and of any changes in the types of young offender with whom magistrates and social workers have to deal.[45]

Grünhut's study demonstrated not only changes in the characteristics of the young girls coming before local courts in Oxfordshire, but also wide disparities in the use of fines and probation orders in juvenile courts across the country (and sometimes between courts in neighbouring areas).[46] Around the same time Hermann Mannheim and others reported the first stage of their research into sentencing in eight London juvenile courts in the mid-1950s.[47] They attempted a 'scientific study' to test the hypothesis that sentencing in these courts was consistent. They concluded that the hypothesis could not be supported, and that 'it is the intuitive assessment of individual cases which in the main prevails'.[48] Some effort was made to assess whether courts were dealing with significantly different mixes of cases, by examining the numbers of larcenies of different kinds sentenced at each court, and by assessing the family characteristics of the boys, but in both respects 'a fairly even distribution' was found. The authors recognized that their information was not complete, and suggested that research from court records could not capture certain factors of probable relevance, such as 'the general demeanour and manner of the boy and his parents in the court during the hearing of the case' and 'the general delinquency situation in the court areas at the time'.[49]

The findings from this study led Mannheim to believe that the next stage 'might very usefully consist of a study of magistrates' attitudes to the different methods of treatment at their disposal'.[50] This was the study that Roger Hood completed and published as *Sentencing in Magistrates' Courts*.[51] It was a study of twelve urban

[45] M. Grünhut, *Juvenile Offenders before the Courts* (Oxford: Oxford University Press, 1956), 119.

[46] For similar results a decade later, testing some of Grünhut's observations, see K.W. Patchett and J.D. McClean, 'Decision-Making in Juvenile Cases' [1965] *Crim. L.R.* 699.

[47] H. Mannheim, J. Spencer, and G. Lynch, 'Magisterial Policy in the London Juvenile Courts' (1957) 8 *British Journal of Delinquency* 13 and 119.

[48] Ibid., 138.

[49] Ibid., 135. It is interesting that the authors raise no doubts about the relevance of these two factors, particularly the first one.

[50] Ibid., 138.   [51] (London: Tavistock, 1962).

courts, including some with high, medium, or low rates of imprisonment. Among other results it found that the differential use of imprisonment could not be explained by differences in the cases coming before the courts: indeed, courts were dealing differently with offenders who had similar characteristics, and therefore appeared not to be giving equal consideration to those factors. It also emerged that the use of probation varied independently of the use of custody—the court using probation most frequently also made ample use of imprisonment. This led Roger Hood to speculate that 'differences in sentencing policy are not so much a reflection of opposing views on the aims of punishment, but a reflection of different beliefs on how to achieve these aims'.[52] However, the study also led him to conclude that:

The imprisonment policies of the magistrates appear to be related to the social characteristics of the area they serve, the social constitution of the bench, and its particular view of the crime problem: factors which are themselves highly associated.... There is some evidence in favour of the hypothesis that middle-class magistrates dealing with working-class offenders, in relatively small and stable middle-class communities, are likely to be relatively severe. The material at least gives an indication that the type of community served by the court, and the social composition of the bench, may influence sentencing policy.[53]

These were challenging findings so far as the Magistrates' Association was concerned; and Roger Hood concluded his study by observing that the rota system of sitting in many courts meant that the justices never met as a whole to decide on basic issues. He quickly added that he was not arguing 'that a rigid scale should be made out, but just that a decision should be made on the circumstances which should be present before imprisonment is imposed'.[54]

Shortly after the publication of *Sentencing in Magistrates' Courts* the Magistrates' Association contacted Roger Hood and invited him to carry out a study of disparities in the sentencing of motoring offenders.[55] Concern about consistency in sentencing also led the Magistrates' Association to consider drawing up a list of basic penalties for certain motoring offences. Some courts had already drawn up suggested scales of penalties,[56] and so the Association's Road Traffic

---

[52] Ibid., 123.   [53] Ibid., 119–20.   [54] Ibid., 124.

[55] The Magistrates' Association, *43rd Annual Report, 1962–63* (London: The Magistrates' Association, 1963), 11–12.

[56] There is reference in ibid., 17, to the scale used by the Amersham justices.

Committee considered the matter and prepared a draft scale of penalties, submitted to the Association's Council in July 1963 and then passed to the Lord Chancellor.[57] Further discussions about the momentous step of issuing such a document then ensued, but the amount of public concern about magistrates' sentencing did not abate. Indeed, at its July 1964 meeting the Association's Council took the unusual step of drawing up a statement on 'Consistency of Penalties',[58] which was subsequently released to the press. Work on the proposed guidelines continued: references to a tariff or to basic penalties were removed, and the Association's draft document was circulated to benches for comment in 1965 and ultimately, after further discussions[59] and adjustments, issued to members of the Magistrates' Association in May 1967 as 'Suggestions for Traffic Offence Penalties'.

It is evident that throughout this period the Association was both showing a genuine interest in the results of research and fighting a 'public relations' battle with some newspapers and some critics from within. As soon as a word such as 'guidance' or 'guideline' was uttered, it was misinterpreted by some as a call for rules, even for rigid rules. The critics of disparity now turned their fire towards the vices of rigidity, tariffs, and slot-machine justice. Lord Gardiner, the Lord Chancellor at the time of the first Magistrates' Association starting-points for road traffic offences, responded thus:

The public and the press cannot have it both ways. In one breath they object to variations in sentence and in the other they attack a genuine and quite proper attempt to lessen the variation. There can be nothing wrong in justices themselves getting together and discussing the problems of sentencing and indicating a level of penalty which they think right for certain of the more straightforward minor offences, where the facts reveal neither extenuating nor aggravating circumstances.[60]

---

[57] The Magistrates' Association, *44th Annual Report, 1963–64* (London: The Magistrates' Association, 1964), 5.

[58] The Magistrates' Association, *45th Annual Report, 1964–65* (London: The Magistrates' Association, 1965), Appendix VIII; in effect, the document attempted to repudiate the suggestion that the Association supported 'tariff' sentencing, and to advance the view that 'each case ought to be judged on its merits' but that this does 'not exclude the establishment of a greater measure of consistency'.

[59] There was opposition from the Lord Chancellor to the inclusion of serious traffic offences, such as dangerous driving and drunk driving, and these were omitted from the 'Suggestions'.

[60] Lord Gardiner, 'Presidential Address' (1967) 23 *The Magistrate* 183, quoted by R. Hood, *Sentencing the Motoring Offender* (London: Heinemann, 1972), 66–7.

Despite criticisms from within and outside the magistracy, the 'Suggestions' gradually established themselves and have become a permanent feature of sentencing in the magistrates' courts—never accepted by some benches or clerks, adapted to a greater or lesser degree by several benches, but widely referred to and up-dated every few years by the Magistrates' Association.[61]

When Roger Hood began his research into sentencing for the very types of offence included in the 'Suggestions', and a few more serious road traffic offences, he contacted thirty-two courts to find out their approach to road traffic cases, and found that only sixteen had responded to the Magistrates' Association's call to adopt the starting points as a basis for discussing and articulating their own local lists of starting points. Those local lists varied considerably, not only in the offences included (many included dangerous driving and the more serious motoring offences, whereas the Magistrates' Association excluded them) but also in the starting points indicated. Thus, for example, 'the 14 courts which included driving whilst disqualified varied in their suggestions from a fine of £25 with no stated period of disqualification to "imprisonment or a heavy fine plus at least 12 months' disqualification" '.[62] This shows that the idea of starting points took some time to be accepted, and that, even where the idea was adopted, some local benches preferred to develop their own guidance rather than accepting a national approach.

One of the most significant findings of Roger Hood's research on *Sentencing the Motoring Offender* is the influence of membership of a particular bench. The research design required magistrates to assign sentences to hypothetical cases in their homes, in an endeavour to minimize the risk of group pressure. Yet the findings revealed a strong and pervasive association between magistrates' sentences and membership of a particular bench. Sometimes this reflected local lists of suggested penalties, but in some courts there was no such list. Interestingly, the presence or absence of a local list did not affect the probability of magistrates from the same bench adopting similar approaches to sentence.[63] This, therefore, indicated the influence of magistrates' training,[64] of the justices' clerk and/or the

---

[61] They are now incorporated into the Sentencing Guidelines for Magistrates' Courts, discussed at 316–318 below.

[62] Hood, n. 60 above, 67.

[63] Ibid., 146.

[64] The training of lay magistrates became compulsory in 1965.

chairman of the bench, and of the groups sitting on different days according to the rota system.[65] However, Roger Hood concluded that 'uniformity of *approach* cannot be achieved simply by adopting lists of "starting points"', and this was largely because different magistrates made differing assessments of the relative seriousness of certain types of offence.[66] Divergences were particularly frequent when cases presented unusual features. One effect of starting points or suggested penalties, it seemed, might be to draw magistrates away from a discussion of principles towards a particular figure:

The danger is that attempts to achieve uniformity in sentencing through booklets, scales or more informal methods (such as the steady influence of the clerk) may well inhibit change—whether it be adapting present methods, or experiments with new approaches.... The fears of 'computer justice' are a natural outcome of too great a reliance on tariff principles.[67]

These were salutary warnings, but they did not tell against the notion of sentencing guidelines as a means of reducing disparity. The argument was that guidelines might have other, unwanted effects, to which attention should be paid.

However, in the opposite direction there lay a flawed argument about the value of experience in sentencing. The early studies highlighted the views of many magistrates that sentencing was largely the application of experience, not of rules, to the differing facts of cases.[68] Roger Hood tackled this oft-repeated sentiment head on:

Magistrates and judges... place particular value upon their experience in sentencing. Now, if this experience is to be of value, then all cases cannot be unique, they must be comparable in at least some respects; and even if it is agreed that all cases are unique in some sense, this cannot be decisive in the practice of sentencing, for frequently decisions are reached with the aid of 'experience.' There are, then, certain observable factors which magis-

---

[65] Hood commented that 'the organizational aspects, including the roles occupied by senior members, and clerks in particular, need to be studied in depth': n. 60 above, 153. Cf. P. Darbyshire, *The Justices' Clerk* (Chichester: Barry Rose, 1984).

[66] Hood, n. 60 above, 148.

[67] Ibid., 150.

[68] Mannheim *et al.*, n. 47 above, took this seriously and called for further research into it. 'It would be as difficult for any magistrate to describe what he or she meant by 'court experience' as it would be for the research worker to measure it... Experience may teach the court that factors which appear important are, quite often, relatively insignificant in assessing particular cases': at 136.

trates will take into account in their consideration of the appropriate sentence.[69]

Thus, unless magistrates and judges maintain that the 'experience' they use derives from some inarticulable 'hunch' or 'feeling', it must be possible to concretize it and to express it in some way. If this is so, it opens up the possibility of writing down guidance of some kind—not necessarily in the form of a tariff, but certainly in the form of starting points or normal ranges.

Concern about sentencing disparity remained a major issue. Roger Tarling began his 1979 report thus:

Apparent inconsistencies and anomalies in the sentences awarded at magistrates' courts are frequently commented on in the press, and lead to criticisms by members of the public, offenders (and organisations representing them) and on occasion by magistrates themselves, on the quality of justice meted out.[70]

Tarling's study confirmed the persistence of considerable disparities. Among the thirty courts whose records he studied there were variations in the use of probation between 1 and 12 per cent, in imprisonment between 3 and 19 per cent, in fines between 46 and 76 per cent, and so on—variations not explained by differences in the mix of cases at the courts.[71] He carried out interviews at twenty-eight of the benches, and twenty-four of them used a recommended penalty list for the sentencing of road traffic offences (four adopting the Magistrates' Association's suggested penalties as they stood, and the others adapting them to a greater or lesser degree).[72] Tarling's study was unusual for Home Office research of the time because it concluded by setting out possible reforms to the system: whereas Roger Hood had been rather guarded about the probable effects of sentencing guidelines, the Tarling study proposed a number of reforms including the extension of sentencing guidelines to forms of crime other than road traffic offences.[73] One particular target was local traditions and divergences, of which Tarling found ample evidence. A similar finding emerged a decade later from the study by Parker, Sumner, and Jarvis of four magistrates' courts following the Criminal Justice Act 1982. They commented that:

[69] Hood, n. 51 above, 16.

[70] R. Tarling, *Sentencing Practice in Magistrates' Courts*, Home Office Research Study 56 (London: HMSO, 1979), 1.

[71] Ibid., 9.   [72] Ibid., 31.   [73] Ibid., Chapter 6.

One of the most remarkable features of each court we investigated was the all-embracing nature of the local version of the magistrates' ideology. Wherever we went, Benches emphasised the importance of their *rite de passage* to becoming a real magistrate through watching and sitting with the more experienced colleagues[74]

By the late 1980s, however, the seeds sown by Tarling and others were beginning to take root. In particular, two initiatives were to emerge during this period—structured sentencing for magistrates and national sentencing guidelines. The structured sentencing initiative began with two publications in 1986,[75] and was carried forward energetically by a prominent member of the Magistrates' Association, Rosemary Thomson, who was subsequently appointed to the Judicial Studies Board and persuaded the Board to issue 'structured decision-making cards' for decisions on remand, mode of trial and sentencing.[76]

The sentencing guidelines movement had already begun in certain quarters. Some local courts had drawn up lists of recommended penalties that went beyond motoring offences. The Portsmouth bench had a list of suggested penalties for over 600 offences, i.e. almost all those that would normally come before the summary courts. In Cheshire the local liaison judge, Judge David, had joined with the county's magistrates to develop an agreed set of guidelines for a limited number of frequent offences. Lord Hailsham, the Lord Chancellor at the time, commended the Cheshire guidelines as 'designed to secure consistency in the area and to give individual benches confidence that, although each case is a separate problem, they are working on lines likely to meet with the approval of colleagues'. He went on:

These are encouraging signs. At the national level the Magistrates' Association has not yet felt able to suggest guidelines outside the field of traffic offences, but so many benches are producing their own local guidelines that

---

[74] H. Parker, M. Sumner, and G. Jarvis, *Unmasking the Magistrates* (Milton Keynes: Open University Press, 1989), 171.

[75] A. Ashworth, 'Structuring the Sentencing Decision' [1986] *The Magistrate* 5, and K. Barker and J. Sturges, *Decision Making in Magistrates' Courts* (London: Fourmat, 1986).

[76] Judicial Studies Board, *Report for 1983–87* (London: HMSO, 1988), paras. 7.20 and 12.13.

I wonder whether the time has not come to reconsider the national option, based on the experience of benches.[77]

In fact a sub-committee of the Magistrates' Association had already been convened to work on the project. It decided to develop guidelines for twenty common offences, and in late 1988 sent out drafts to local benches for discussion.[78] The draft guidelines were then revised and sent early in 1989 to the Lord Chancellor and the Lord Chief Justice. The former gave them his approval, whereas Lord Lane reacted rather strongly against them—a reaction that seemed to be a mixture of feelings of affront that mere magistrates were taking such an initiative, together with surprise and concern that so many drugs offences (including production and supply) were thought suitable for sentencing in magistrates' courts. By the time his strong objections had come to the attention of the chairman of the Magistrates' Association, the Lord Chancellor had already signified approval and the Association was moving towards publication. Boldly the Association's chair declined to be deflected by Lord Lane, although some of the drugs offences were removed and the pocket guide was marked 'Provisional' out of deference to the Lord Chief's reservations.[79] The guidelines were sent out to magistrates in September 1989, accompanied by a four-page leaflet on 'The Case for National Sentencing Guidelines'.

Reception of the guidelines across the country was variable. Some justices' clerks made the obvious point that the guidelines had no legal standing, but of course this may just have been a respectable way of repelling a threat to their own power as training officers for local justices. One of the consequences of Lord Lane's disquiet about the 1989 guidelines was that, when the Association began to revise the guidelines in 1992 to take account of the implementation of the Criminal Justice Act 1991, a circuit judge was co-opted to the committee. He read all the committee's proposals, and commented on them from the judicial point of view. His comments were positive and helpful, but it was typical of the prevailing culture that his final

---

[77] In his Presidential Speech to the Association, printed in [1987] *The Magistrate* 119, at 120.

[78] The fact that guidelines were being prepared was well publicized: see, e.g., the letters to *The Times* on 9 Dec. 1988.

[79] The term 'provisional' was explained on the ground that guidelines for mode of trial decisions needed to be drawn up, and would inevitably have implications for the sentencing guidelines: see, e.g. *The Guardian*, 16 Aug. 1989.

communication on the 1992 guidelines was that he was pleased with them, but that he would not be recommending them in his own area because the East Midlands had developed its own guidelines![80] This was yet another example of the dominance of local traditions, originally associated with powerful bench chairmen, then often linked with the influence of justices' clerks, and more recently a manifestation of the growing power of liaison judges.

In their survey of sentencing in the mid-1990s, Flood-Page and Mackie reported continuing inconsistency in sentencing by magistrates' courts. They pointed out that efforts were being made to draw the attention of local benches to variations in sentencing practice for twelve types of offence, variations which persisted despite the advent of the Magistrates' Association's guidelines.[81] Research into fining in 1995 found that some 55 per cent of magistrates' courts substantially adopted the Magistrates' Association's guidelines, that a further 28 per cent had devised a significant modification of those guidelines for local use, and that 17 per cent were still using a form of unit fine approach to guide their sentencing (despite abolition of the statutory unit fine scheme in 1993).[82] Attempts were made during the 1990s to increase acceptance of the guidelines among those to whom they were intended to apply, by bringing some stipendiary magistrates (now District Judges) into decision-making on the content of the guidelines and by increasing the number of justices' clerks on the working group,[83] and the 2000 version of the guidelines is now titled 'Magistrates' Courts Sentencing Guidelines' to signal their approval by the Justices' Clerks' Society and the District Judges. This did not prevent resistance to the guidelines in two localities—hardly surprising, given the lengthy and ingrained tradition of local approaches to summary justice, and given the

---

[80] For further evidence of separatism in the East Midlands see D. Riley and J. Vennard, *Triable-Either-Way Cases: Crown Court or Magistrates' Court?*, Home Office Research Study 98 (London: HMSO, 1988), 12.

[81] Home Office, *Local Sentencing Patterns in Magistrates' Courts* (London: Home Office, the Justices' Clerks Society and the Magistrates' Association, n.d.).

[82] E. Charman, B. Gibson, T. Honess, and R. Morgan, *Fine Impositions and Enforcement following the Criminal Justice Act 1993*, Research Findings 36 (London: Home Office, 1996).

[83] The working group that drew up the first national guidelines in 1989 also contained two academics. Both were dropped from the group when it was working towards the tougher 1993 guidelines, but one of them was invited to join the working group again for the many meetings that led to the 2000 guidelines.

absence of legal force behind the guidelines (even though they are commended by the Lord Chancellor and the Lord Chief Justice).

This overview of sentencing developments in magistrates' courts during the last fifty years testifies to a strong tradition of welcoming researchers and, to a considerable extent, of paying attention to their findings. However, it is apparent that there is now an urgent need for fresh detailed research into the impact of the guidelines on sentencing in magistrates' courts. All guidelines issued by the Magistrates' Association have contained strong warnings against treating them as a tariff,[84] but there are some who think that it is too easy and natural for magistrates to treat the guidelines thus and not to go through with the proper thought processes. This was a reservation expressed by Roger Hood many years ago,[85] and it is now time for a substantial study of the effects of the guidelines on sentencing in a sample of courts.

Sentencing in the Crown Court

The above survey of research into sentencing in the magistrates' courts[86] is sufficient to demonstrate that both the Magistrates' Association and local benches have shown themselves willing to welcome criminological researchers and to give serious consideration to some of the results. The position in the Crown Court has been quite different. There have been some studies of court records on sentencing, discussed below. But the most penetrating studies of magistrates' sentencing have included interviews with justices, participation in sentencing exercises, and response to questionnaires about their background and personality. Only recently have some small studies of this kind been permitted in the Crown Court, and those do not involve close observation of judicial sentencing practices. The sentencers who deal with the most serious cases, and who impose the most severe sentences, have not allowed researchers to get close to their working practices and assumptions in this way. The one attempt to conduct such a study lasted for only a few months before the Lord Chief Justice of the day called it to a halt.

---

[84] The 'Suggested Penalties' document always had, printed in bold at the beginning, the words 'This is *not* a tariff'. The Guidelines document always emphasized that it indicated starting points, not finishing points.

[85] N. 67 above and accompanying text.

[86] It does not purport to be a complete survey.

In 1980 the Centre for Criminological Research at Oxford University obtained funding from the Home Office for a team of researchers to carry out a three-year research project which would examine sentencing practices in the Crown Court in the context of the attitude, knowledge, and beliefs of the judges and of the practices of others who might be thought likely to exert some influence on sentencing (prosecuting and defence lawyers, probation officers, court administrators, and so on). Not only was this an 'obvious' topic for research, in view of what had been learnt from research into magistrates' sentencing, but it might also have been thought to be a propitious time for such a study—public concern about consistency in sentencing had just been acknowledged by the Lord Chief Justice, Lord Lane, in a judgment in which he called for judges to adopt 'uniformity of approach' to the sentencing of crimes of moderate seriousness.[87] When Lord Lane was approached for his permission to conduct the study, he replied that he would permit a pilot study and would then consider its results before deciding whether to allow the main project to proceed.

The pilot study set out to conduct interviews with twenty-five judges, each of whom would also be left with a questionnaire to complete; to carry out observational research in one court, during which the researcher would sit in court, see all the documentation, and discuss the cases with the judge; and to conduct a detailed study of the practices of two judges at a particular court, constructing a sentencing profile from court records and then discussing their practices with them in the light of the record research.[88] There were three early signs that the going would be difficult. A consultant who was invited to advise the team on techniques of interviewing and questionnaire research warned the team that they should treat the exercise as if they were approaching a remote tribe in Africa. And a randomly selected list of judges whom the team wished to interview was rejected by the Presiding Judges of the South Eastern Circuit as unacceptable: some were mere 'fledgling' judges whom it would be inadvisable to interview, he stated, and it was also thought proper for the team to interview the senior judge at any court they visited. The five High Court judges were nominated by the Lord Chief

[87] *Bibi* (1980) 2 Cr. App. R. (S) 177.
[88] The details are set out in Chapter 2 and Appendices A and B of the Oxford pilot study, n. 44 above.

Justice. So the twenty-five judges who participated in the pilot study were selected for the team, and not randomly. And, thirdly, a request to study the operation of the processes whereby leave to appeal from the Crown Court to the Court of Appeal is granted was peremptorily refused.[89]

It would be wrong to regard the outcome of such a small exploratory study as yielding 'findings', but at least it served to indicate several fruitful avenues for further research—the way in which judges construct 'the facts of the case' and the influence of the defendant's attitude in court; judicial views about certain types of offence and offender; judicial views about public opinion and its relevance to sentencing; the degree of awareness of the sentencing practices of others; attitudes towards pre-sentence reports and pleas in mitigation; trial judges' views about the Court of Appeal; the limited extent to which judges were aware of their own sentencing practices; and the influence of court administrators. Although these and other points were put to the Lord Chief Justice in a report on the pilot study, it was known that the nature of the researchers' enquiries had offended some judges, notably the questions about the judges' backgrounds, families, and social contacts. The report to Lord Lane had been prepared with care, and on advice from the Home Office Research Unit, but when Roger Hood and I were summoned to meet Lord Lane and Lord Justice Watkins on 8 December 1981, we were told that access to judges for any further study would be refused.[90] Lord Lane put forward the view that the principles on which judges pass sentence are well known from the textbooks, and that it would not be worth the judicial time and public money to continue with the research. Moreover, he argued that:

research into the attitudes, beliefs and reasoning of judges was not the way to obtain an accurate picture: sentencing was an art and not a science, and the further judges were pressed to articulate their reasons the less realistic the exercise would become.[91]

---

[89] See further n. 105 below and text.

[90] The original proposal for the research came from Roger Hood, but he soon invited me to take over the project because of the pressure of his other commitments. He continued to advise on the project, and all significant correspondence with the Lord Chief Justice was in his name.

[91] Oxford pilot study, n. 44 above, 64.

This amounted to a total rejection of the idea of criminological study of sentencing, dismissing the possibility that differing views on the aims or the effectiveness of sentences might influences judges in their sentencing. Whether for convenience or out of conviction, Lord Lane and some of his senior colleagues propounded a view of sentencing largely as the application of settled principles to the facts of individual cases or, to the extent that there was discretion, as 'balancing' such competing factors as emerged from the particular case.

The story does not end there. The Home Office was rightly concerned that the banning of this research should not prevent further approaches to the higher judiciary in the future. It was accepted that the Oxford pilot study was, to adopt the terminology of the time, 'a shipwreck in the channel', around which future applicants would need to navigate. The tactic was to ensure, so far as possible, that the channel was not entirely obstructed. One consequence was that, when the time approached to publish a report of the pilot study, substantial pressures were exerted. The Home Office was concerned that the report did not alienate the judiciary further, and considerable time passed while the draft report was subjected to various criticisms in the hope of avoiding this result.[92] For example, it was suggested that the discussion of judicial attitudes which regarded tax fraud as less serious than social security fraud should be removed, on the ground that it might make some judges appear to be biased in their views—which, of course, was a reflection of what the researchers had found.[93] After various amendments the report of the pilot study was eventually published in 1984. In typical fashion the press devoted almost all its attention to a short section of the report—the three pages that recounted how administrators at one court tried to keep serious cases away from reputedly lenient sentencers, and how at another court a prosecutor was heard to ask for and obtain the listing of a case in front of a particular judge.[94] The higher judiciary was ready for the attack, and both Lord Hailsham and Lord Lane denounced the research publicly. Lord Lane

[92] Another element in the delay was the need to find other projects for the four researchers when the sentencing study collapsed, and to ensure that those other projects were properly set up.

[93] See Oxford pilot study, n. 44 above, 25, for the final formulation, which was only slightly modified.

[94] Ibid., 58.

memorably declared that the listing practices we recorded had not taken place, or, if they had, then they should not have done—a manifest failure to confront what had been found. After Lord Hailsham had given a speech that also questioned the integrity of the researchers,[95] he was tackled about his grounds for doubting their word and was told that this was simply what the researchers saw and heard. He replied indignantly that the matter should have been reported to him immediately and he would have taken action—a rather naïve approach to the conduct of empirical research.

For many years afterwards, research into sentencing in the Crown Court was based only on court records, or at least observation from the back of the court, without any interviews or interaction with judges. The opening pages of David Moxon's study refer, immediately after mentioning the Oxford study, to the 'lack of detailed information about the sentencing process' and to the need for 'a better understanding of Crown Court practice'.[96] His study yielded some valuable findings about the factors that seem strongly associated with decisions to impose certain kinds of sentence, and also showed how (for example) judges were flouting the Court of Appeal's guidance on suspended sentences. When Flood-Page and Mackie conducted their sentencing research in the mid-1990s, it was plain to all how their methodology differed between the two levels of courts: in magistrates' courts they were able to interview magistrates and justices' clerks on general issues, whereas in the Crown Court there was no such possibility.[97]

After the Oxford research had been blocked, the judiciary had set up a procedure of its own to deal with applications from researchers for access to the Crown Court. Very few researchers obtained permission to talk to judges, and it is strange that probably the first application to be approved came from Jill Peay, a member of the

---

[95] Newspapers for 13 Sept. 1984. The Oxford pilot study was reviewed in *The Guardian* on 14 Sept. 1984 by Hugo Young, who wrote that Lord Lane had 'enshrined ignorance as a judicial virtue, and intellectual privacy as the hallmark of the priesthood over which he presides. Rarely have such eminent heads been so piously buried in the sand, and never, I would hazard, at such social cost.'

[96] D. Moxon, *Sentencing Practice in the Crown Court*, Home Office Research Study 103 (London: Home Office, 1988), 2.

[97] C. Flood-Page and A. Mackie, *Sentencing Practice: An Examination of Decisions in Magistrates' Courts and the Crown Court in the mid-1990s*, Home Office Research Study 180 (London: Home Office, 1998).

Oxford research team.[98] However, when in the late 1980s Roger Hood applied for access to Crown Courts in the West Midlands in order to carry out his research into race and sentencing, it was made clear to him that, whilst access to court records would be permitted, discussions with judges would not. This was a decision that was to back-fire, at least in the opinion of some senior judges. For when Roger Hood presented his outline findings to members of the senior judiciary in 1992, in advance of publication of his book, they were astonished to hear that one of the courts studied had a much higher proportionate use of custody for black offenders than the others.[99] Their immediate reaction was to ask what comments the judges of the Dudley Crown Court made when it had been discussed with them, but Roger Hood's reply was that permission to speak to the judges had not been granted. At this stage one of the senior judges commented that matters might be different now—a suggestion that the judicial defensiveness associated with the policies of Lord Lane was beginning to recede following his retirement as Lord Chief Justice.

In the ten years since the publication of Roger Hood's race study the senior judiciary has become far more open. The 'Kilmuir rules' against judges speaking to the press have been relaxed. Whatever one might think of Kilmuir's view that 'so long as a judge keeps silent, his reputation for impartiality remains unassailable', the three most recent Lord Chief Justices have changed the climate. Lord Taylor, Lord Bingham, and Lord Woolf have all spoken out for and against certain penal policies—indeed, Lords Taylor and Bingham were vociferous in 1995–7 in their opposition to the introduction of mandatory and minimum sentences, as we saw earlier. The senior judiciary has acquiesced in the creation of the Sentencing Advisory Panel, which might be thought to have encroached on what judges conceived to be their own task of deciding on what subjects sentencing guidelines are required and drawing them up.[100] And Lord

---

[98] For the process of obtaining permission for the conduct of semi-structured interviews with judges sitting on Mental Health Review Tribunals, see J. Peay, *Tribunals on Trial* (Oxford: Oxford University Press, 1989), 79.

[99] R. Hood, with G. Cordovil, *Race and Sentencing* (Oxford: Oxford University Press, 1992), Chapter 6, comparing Dudley and the other Crown Courts in the study.

[100] For discussion see A. Ashworth, *Sentencing and Criminal Justice* (3rd edn., London: Butterworths, 2000), 48 and 357–62; see also www.sentencing-advisory-panel.gov.uk.

Justice Auld has called for the regular appraisal of judges, an unprecedented step towards greater accountability.[101] In respect of access to judges for researchers, the climate is also beginning to change. Roger Hood and Stephen Shute have been granted permission to talk to judges as part of their research into race and the criminal courts, and other researchers have been given access for the conduct of sentencing exercises, etc.[102] Perhaps, in time, access will be granted for sentencing research in the Crown Court which includes close observation of judges and the opportunity to discuss with them the details of their reasoning when deciding upon sentence in particular cases—that, rather than general discussions or sentencing exercises, will be the crucial step.[103] It remains unlikely that guidelines and guidance will achieve their goals so long as there is insufficient understanding of the factors that actually influence sentencers, as Roger Hood argued in his 1972 study of magistrates' sentencing of motoring offenders.[104]

In discussions about disparity in sentencing, one counter-argument over the years has been that the Court of Appeal is there to correct aberrant sentences. But we know little about the operation of that Court, or about the reception of its judgments by sentencers in the Crown Court. One of the requests made by the Oxford team when approaching Lord Lane for the first time in 1981 was to study the operation of the Court of Appeal, and particularly the processes for deciding on the grant or refusal of leave to appeal against sentence. The reason given for declining even to allow a pilot study in that field was that it might add to the pressures under which the Court was already working. Understandable as this reason may be, it

---

[101] Sir Robin Auld, *Review of the Criminal Courts* (London: The Stationery Office, 2001), 266–8.

[102] See, e.g., M. Davies and J. Tyrer, 'Filling in the Gaps—a Study of Judicial Culture' [2003] *Crim. L. R.* 243; cf. R. Henham, *Sentence Discounts and the Criminal Process* (Aldershot: Ashgate, 2001).

[103] The Crime and Disorder Act 1998 states that sentencing guidelines should take into account, among other things, 'the need to promote public confidence in the criminal justice system': s.80(3)(d). The Sentencing Advisory Panel has commissioned research on perceptions of burglary and of rape: see Sentencing Advisory Panel, *Annual Report 2000–2001* (London: Home Office, 2001), 13–16; but its funds are insufficient for large-scale research into sentencing processes of the kind that is surely necessary.

[104] Above at 314.

is hardly a sound justification for refusing research into this vital aspect of due process. Moreover, as recently as the mid-1990s Lord Taylor, Lord Lane's successor, refused a request from Professor Michael Zander for permission for Kate Malleson to interview judges about their role in the criminal appeal system. No reasons for the refusal were given; Lord Taylor suggested that retired Lords Justice of Appeal could be contacted.[105]

Research into sentencing in the Crown Court has therefore not been productive, largely because it has not been possible to observe the judges at close quarters and to discuss with them their approach to sentencing. This is not exclusively a British phenomenon: reports from the Council of Europe in 1974[106] and again in 1992[107] called for more and detailed research into sentencing, recognizing that in most countries little more than quantitative research based on court records had been accomplished. More has been achieved in Scotland, where the judiciary has worked with researchers from Strathclyde University to develop a Sentencing Information System, which records sentences according to the type of case and the presence of certain key factors, and thus enables judges to use their computers to see what sentences were given by their colleagues in similar cases.[108] However, the participation of judges in the Scottish system has been a matter of controversy and delicate negotiation over the years, and even that falls short of the kind of fundamental qualitative research advocated here.

Conclusions

Through his empirical research and his writings on policy, Roger Hood has made a telling contribution to the development of sentencing. But the programme he set out in the 1960s and 1970s has stalled: governments (and, where they still exist, advisory committees) rarely plan their consideration of new penal measures in the

---

[105] Personal communication from Dr. Malleson.

[106] European Committee on Crime Problems, *Sentencing* (Strasbourg: Council of Europe, 1974), 13.

[107] Council of Europe, *Consistency in Sentencing* (Strasbourg: Council of Europe, 1992), para. J4.

[108] C. Tata and N. Hutton, *A Sentencing Information System for the High Court of Justiciary in Scotland* (Glasgow: Centre for Sentencing Research, University of Strathclyde, 1998).

methodical way he advocated, and knowledge about the influences that shape sentencing practice has advanced little since his 1972 book. We know a fair amount about magistrates' sentencing, at least in the era before guidelines began to play such an apparently significant part, but further research is now needed. We know virtually nothing about the processes by which Crown Court judges decide on sentence.

Why should governments be so reluctant to plan the introduction of new penal measures methodically, and by considering all the available knowledge and relating it to the sentencing system into which it is proposed to introduce the new measure? In part the answer is to be found in the decline in studies of the comparative efficacy of penal measures, but far more prominent are the political attractions of 'law and order' rhetoric and 'populist punitiveness'. Advisory committees have gone, civil servants have been relegated in influence, and now it is government advisers who wield considerable power. The concern is far more with achieving the desired political effect than with measured and research-based initiatives. True, there are often pilot schemes before a new form of sentence is adopted nationally, and this may tempt the government to claim that an initiative is 'evidence-based'. But these pilot schemes tend to be focused on logistical viability rather than on concerns about the effect on sentencers' behaviour, the pursuit of equality of consideration and treatment, and other possible goals of sentencing (including preventive effectiveness).

Why should the judiciary be so reluctant to welcome researchers? Three substantive reasons might be a fear of unfairly adverse criticism, apprehension about the use of research findings by the government, and beliefs about judicial independence. The fear of unfairly adverse criticism is related to the conviction that it is difficult for people outside the judiciary to grasp the nature of the judicial task and the range of issues that courts have to take into account. Thus in 1981 Lord Lane dismissed the suggestion that research could be justified on the ground that it would ensure that the public was better informed about Crown Court sentencing:

In his view, neither the press, nor the public nor politicians would take any notice of such findings. The judiciary would continue to be subjected to ill-informed criticism, and they were experienced at dealing with that.[109]

[109] Reported in the Oxford Pilot Study, n. 88 above, 64.

There is undoubtedly some substance in this position: as we saw earlier,[110] public attitudes towards sentencing are both adverse to the judiciary and largely ill-founded. Most people simply do not have even an elementary understanding of the sentencing system. Criticisms are therefore often wide of the mark, but are still strongly expressed. It is easy to declare that this is a problem of education and information;[111] it is also easy to understand the judges' doubts about the possibility of alleviating public ignorance, whether directly or indirectly, through academic research.

Judicial apprehension about the use of research findings by the government has some historical foundations. In the late 1970s there was Home Office research suggesting that custodial sentences were no more effective in preventing reconviction than non-custodial sentences:[112] the Advisory Council on the Penal System seized on this to propose a lowering of the severity of sentencing,[113] and the government took the unusual step of ensuring that every sentencing judge and magistrates' court received a copy of the report. Around the same time the House of Commons Expenditure Committee propounded a view of the judiciary as a branch of the public services which makes decisions about public expenditure (particularly when offenders are sentenced to imprisonment), and there were suggestions of requiring a kind of financial accountability for the expenditure committed through sentencing.[114] During the 1980s the government tried various approaches to control the prison population, again using economic arguments. This drew a critical response from many judges: on the one hand they argued that their task was to impose the appropriate sentence on the facts of each case, and that the government's duty was to provide the facilities for carrying out those sentences, and on the other hand they deprecated what they saw as the government's attempts to undermine their sentences, since the government's preferred approach was to increase remission and

---

[110] Nn. 7–9 above, and accompanying text.

[111] The Home Office website carried a quiz on criminal justice in autumn 2001, in an attempt to educate people, or at least to show them how little they understood about sentencing levels etc.

[112] See particularly the study by Brody, n. 20 above.

[113] Advisory Council on the Penal System, *The Length of Prison Sentences* (London: HMSO, 1977).

[114] House of Commons Expenditure Committee, *Reduction of Pressure on the Prison System* (London: HMSO, 1978).

parole and thus to diminish the significance of the sentence passed.[115] In this climate it is hardly surprising that judges should be apprehensive about research, even academic research,[116] for fear that research findings could be used to thrust upon the judiciary unwanted changes, whether managerial or substantive. This fear was and is probably enlarged by the judicial insistence on maximum discretion in sentencing, since much research carries implications about the need to control or structure discretion.

A third factor lay in feelings about respect for the position of the judiciary. The late 1970s and early 1980s were the heyday of judicial sensitivity, often expressed through a brazenly over-expansive notion of judicial independence. For example, consider the response of some judges to a call for a programme of judicial training, as described by the Bridge Committee:

It is said that 'training' implies that there are 'trainers' who can train people to be judges, and so long as this concept is capable of influencing the thought of those concerned with the provision of 'judicial training' this must, despite all protestations to the contrary, represent a threat to judicial independence.[117]

These sentiments did not prevail, but that they were expressed so strongly demonstrates the climate of opinion at the time. Thus some would think it improper for researchers to come close to judges in their work, and might even suggest that this closeness would jeopardize their independence—surely a far-fetched suggestion, unless it is claimed that there is some mystery in sentencing, the exposure of which would have calamitous consequences. More likely is the suggestion that the findings of any such research might be used to undermine what some regard (wrongly) as the notion of judicial independence, by providing ammunition for those who wish to curtail judicial discretion.[118]

---

[115] The judges' complaints on the latter score eventually received a response, in the form of the appoi. ment of the Carlisle committee to review the parole system. Roger Hood was an influential member of this committee. See Report of the Review Committee, *The Parole System in England and Wales* (London: HMSO, 1988).

[116] The Oxford research in 1981 was funded by the Home Office, and this may have been a factor that made some judges wary.

[117] Lord Bridge, *Report of the Working Party on Judicial Studies and Information* (London: HMSO, 1978), para. 1.6.

[118] As stated earlier, the principle of judicial independence requires impartiality and sentencing without fear or favour; it does not require maximum discretion: see n. 7 above.

This is where the alleged conflict between independence and accountability comes to the fore. One of the effects of good criminological research ought to be to enable people to understand how a key public service operates, and how decisions about the exercise of state power over citizens and companies are taken. This is not necessarily to claim too much for research: after all, research into sentencing in the magistrates' courts may be thought to have led to some improvements, but it cannot be claimed to have achieved transparency. But research can be justified, in part at least, as a means to accountability. There is undoubted value in research that uncovers the motivations and practices of judges, assesses their knowledge of sentencing law, examines their reliance on others such as counsel and probation officers, and so forth. By making known the way in which judges typically approach the task of sentencing, research can bring greater transparency to this essential public function. It might also be argued that greater public understanding could be fostered, but perhaps a more realistic objective would be better to inform those who discuss and make policies about sentencing—the government as the promoter of legislation, the Sentencing Advisory Panel as the proposer of guidelines, and even the senior judiciary themselves as the promulgators of sentencing guidelines.

Research findings can be embarrassing, of course. The police have always been relatively open to researchers, but some of the findings have caused considerable difficulties within the service.[119] Nevertheless, there has generally been the response that the organization ought to change in order to match reasonable public expectations. The Crown Prosecution Service has been less welcoming, and was reluctant to agree to the publication of research it had commissioned when it discovered significant criticisms.[120] If the judiciary were to agree to academic research, it would have to be prepared for this kind of scrutiny and, if the evidence justified it, criticism. It might also be asked whether goals such as accountability and transparency are inappropriate in relation to the judiciary. Such 'managerialist'

---

[119] e.g. D. Smith and J. Gray, *Police and People in London* (London: Policy Studies Institute, 1983).

[120] See J. Baldwin, 'Understanding Judge Ordered and Directed Acquittals in the Crown Court' [1997] *Crim.L.R.* 536, among whose findings were the controversial assertion that some CPS lawyers 'share a common value system with the police' (551)—from whom, of course, they ought to be independent.

concerns are proper in relation to the police and the Crown Prosecution Service, it might be said, but the judiciary should stand above that. Those issues run beyond the topic of this chapter, since they lead into questions of judicial appointments, tenure, appraisal, and so forth.[121] But there remains another point about the effects of research: if it were to uncover divergent practices and inconsistent approaches, might not politicians use it as ammunition for the introduction of more mandatory sentences?

That, surely, is a challenge that must be confronted directly. Sentencing is a vital realm of public policy, and it should not be shrouded in secrecy simply because of fears about the possible reactions to research findings of the press and of politicians. In this important sphere, researchers should no longer be repelled with the claim that sentencing is a kind of ineffable art, which can never be understood or conveyed without distortion. Even supposing that there were some truth in that characterization of the process, there is a strong public interest in ensuring that the considerable power over citizens' lives that is wielded by sentencers is exercised along appropriate lines, ensuring equality of consideration and equality of treatment. The details of sentencing practice are a matter of deep social concern, and they cannot even be discussed properly until they are made known. It is highly unlikely that judges simply apply Court of Appeal decisions faithfully when they are passing sentence, as Lord Lane claimed in 1981,[122] and it would certainly be untrue to claim that those decisions cover all relevant issues in sentencing.

And, lastly, a word about research and teaching in universities. Could judges fairly retort that university teachers and researchers would not welcome research into their own working practices? My response to this would be to welcome such research. There is already a considerable degree of accountability in higher education and, although the details can be debated, it is right that university staff should be generally accountable for their use of public money.

---

[121] K. Malleson, *The New Judiciary: The Effects of Expansion and Activism* (London: Dartmouth, 1999).

[122] N. 91 above.

8

The Forester's Dilemma: The Influence of Police Research on Police Practice

Richard Young and Andrew Sanders

This chapter looks at the potential impact of different styles of police research on police policy and practice. We say 'potential' in acknowledgement of the fact that policy changes are always brought about through a myriad of influences; it would take a brilliantly designed, lavishly funded, perfectly executed research project to assess accurately the actual impact of research on policy. Since there has never been such a research project (and is never likely to be one) the best we are able to do is explore theoretically and empirically the potential impact of research on policy. We focus on policing because both of us have conducted large research projects in this area and because these projects were, as far as their intended influence on policy was concerned, of radically different design.

The first-named author co-directed (with Carolyn Hoyle) an 'action-research' research project from 1998 to 2001 which examined the Thames Valley Police initiative in restorative cautioning. The funding was provided by the Joseph Rowntree Foundation and the ostensible aim of the project was to contribute to the development and evaluation of an innovatory set of police practices. In other words, the project was *designed* to influence policy and practice. The 'Hawthorn effect', where the researcher influences what is being observed, was actively sought during the lifetime of the project itself. The research project generated a series of publications from 1999 onwards, culminating in the national launch by the Joseph Rowntree Foundation of the 'final report', *Proceed with Caution*, in

May 2002.[1] A book, *Policing Restorative Justice*, is also in preparation.

The second-named author co-directed two projects to be examined in this chapter. The first (with Roger Leng and Mike McConville) was a study of decision-making by police officers and prosecutors in three police force areas in respect of criminal cases. This research was funded by the Economic and Social Research Council (ESRC) and the fieldwork was carried out between 1986 and 1988. The research formed the basis of a book, *The Case for the Prosecution* (CFP),[2] and several other publications. There was no intention to influence policy or practice during the lifetime of this project, the Hawthorn effect was seen as something to be minimized, and the authors conclude *CFP* by arguing that police practice was so bound up in protecting the interests of the state that it could not be radically changed.

The second project (with Lee Bridges), *Advice and Assistance in Police Stations* (*AAPS*) was a study of decision-making by police officers, defence lawyers, and suspects in relation to custodial legal advice. This research was funded by the Lord Chancellor's Department and the fieldwork was carried out largely in 1988. A full report of the research was published in 1989,[3] and several other publications summarized and/or drew upon it. There was no intention to influence policy or practice during the lifetime of this project, although (unlike in *CFP*) one of the explicit aims was to exert influence in the short and medium term.

As we shall see, all three projects have contributed to the development of police policy, albeit often in obscure ways. The argument of this chapter is that these different styles of research are, or at least should be, complementary. The rest of the chapter falls into three parts. In the first, we examine the interrelationships between theory, research, and policy and argue in favour of a synthesized model of criminological endeavour. In the second, we seek to illustrate some central features of this model through recounting some of our own police research 'war stories'. Finally, we offer a brief conclusion.

---

[1] C. Hoyle, R. Young, and R. Hill, *Proceed with Caution: An Evaluation of the Thames Valley Police Initiative in Restorative Cautioning* (York: York Publishing Services, 2002).

[2] (London: Routledge, 1991).

[3] A. Sanders, L. Bridges, A. Mulvaney, and G. Crozier, *Advice and Assistance at Police Stations and the 24 Hour Duty Solicitor Scheme* (London: Lord Chancellor's Department, 1989).

The Criminological Enterprise

Theory, Research, and Policy

The title of this chapter raises an issue that faces all social scientists, that of being able to see the wood for the trees. This is one of the more confusing proverbs encountered in childhood. It could mean that when one is deep within a forest of detail the larger picture, the wood, is obscured. Alternatively, it could mean that the potential for trees to be refashioned, as the raw material wood, is overlooked. Whatever its linguistic origins, it can be understood as meaning both. Either one misses the larger picture by focussing on the detail, or one misses the subtleties of what is being observed, and its potential for transformation, by concentrating on outline external appearances.

This sense of ambiguous dualism is also to be found in criminology. Should we focus on the bigger picture, the macro changes taking place at a societal or global level and their multiple implications for the differential distribution of legitimate and illegitimate opportunities, and material and cultural resources, as well as for the prevalence, frequency, and nature of offending, victimization, and criminal justice responses? To do so risks glossing over much local variation, and, by placing too much emphasis on structural changes in society, under-stating the potential for things to be other than they are. Should we instead carry out careful case studies of situations and institutions, perhaps with a special focus on innovatory practices which appear to offer the hope of bringing about progressive reforms and reconfigured social relations? To do so risks exaggerating the significance of local detail as well as overlooking and, therefore, under-stating the structural impediments to change.

The problem is not just one of deciding on which vantage point to adopt when making empirical observations, but also of how to theorize the process and outcome of data collection itself. We agree with Bottoms that:

some engagement with theory is inevitable if one is to practise social science (including criminology) at all. Neither the natural nor the social world can be neutrally observed and reported upon by the research analyst, for we always approach our empirical observations through some kind of theoretical understandings.[4]

---

[4] A. Bottoms, 'The Relationship between Theory and Research in Criminology' in R. King and E. Wincup (eds.), *Doing Research on Crime and Justice* (Oxford: Oxford University Press, 2000), 16.

Thus the choice is not between theoretical and atheoretical approaches to criminology but rather between the various theories that have been developed for making sense of social life. 'Atheoretical' criminology, on this analysis, comprises studies that fail to make explicit and coherent the theory or theories which underpin them. Theory guides decisions on what to observe (what constitutes 'the big picture' or 'the local detail'?), how to observe it (ethnography or the collection of statistical data?), how to analyse the data obtained (grounded theory or hypothesis testing?), and how to interpret the results (in an isolated apparently 'value-free objective' manner, or in the context of wider sociological, philosophical, and theoretical debates?). Criminologists who eschew explicit theorizing may miss the all-important wood. By the same token, however, those committed to a particular theoretical model may be blind 'to whole tracts of significant social practice'.[5] This was the accusation made by Gwynn Davis of the authors of *CFP* at an 'authors meet critics' session of the British Criminology Conference in 1993.[6] But his remark that we should let 'the facts speak for themselves' shows his lack of awareness of Bottoms' point.

The relationship between research and policy introduces a third layer of complexity. For much of the last century many criminologists regarded engagement with moral, normative, and policy debates as beyond their scientific remit. Even David Garland, in *The Culture of Control*, tells us that he has 'chosen to subdue' his 'normative voice' until completing his sociological analysis of current methods of controlling crime and doing justice.[7] In consequence the normative positions he adopts, although not difficult to unearth, are under-developed and, as such, unlikely to make much of an impact on policy-makers.[8] In the last third of the twentieth century the policy-neutral tradition was challenged by politically activist criminologists, such as feminists, Marxists, and new-left realists.

---

[5] N. Lacey, 'Introduction' in N. Lacey (ed.), *A Reader on Criminal Justice* (Oxford: Oxford University Press, 1994), 34.

[6] Rod Morgan made a similar point at the same conference, written up as 'Authors meet Critics: *The Case for the Prosecution*' in L. Noaks, M. Levi, and M. Maguire (eds.), *Contemporary Issues in Criminology* (Cardiff: University of Wales Press, 1995). The authors' response is in the same volume.

[7] D. Garland, *The Culture of Control: Crime and Social Order in Contemporary Society* (Oxford: Oxford University Press, 2001), 3.

[8] R. Young, 'Review of "The Culture of Control" ' (2002) 65 *Modern Law Review* 143.

Committed to changing aspects of social life, they were naturally drawn to more evaluative modes of analysis and writing. Thus Kathy Daly recorded her frustration with naturalistic researchers who chose not to engage in normative debates: 'I am impatient with the descriptive exercise alone when consequential decisions are made daily about life and liberty. How shall we evaluate those decisions? Are they just?'[9] These criminologists also rightly argued that choice of subject matter, methods, and presentation of results inevitably has political implications.

However, political-activist criminologists may also fail to persuade policy-makers of the need for change. Policy-makers may suspect that politically activist criminologists are blind to data that would be unhelpful to a favoured political outcome. This may lead to their research findings being ignored or, alternatively, subjected to testing of a far more searching nature than the norm.[10] That the social changes favoured by politically activist criminologists may not mesh with dominant political values provides another reason why this style of research may fail to influence policy.

To illustrate this, compare the reception of the findings of two different projects. First, there are Sherman's (contentious) findings that mandatory arrests reduce domestic violence. These have led to mandatory arrest legislation and other policy changes.[11]

Secondly, there are the results of the second-named author's research with Hoyle, Morgan, and Cape which suggested that victim impact statements did little to help victims.[12] The most important of these results were not so much ignored as misleadingly used to justify an extension of the 'Personal Statement Scheme' (PSS). In a television news programme the sponsoring Minister insisted that 'this [the PSS]

---

[9] K. Daly, *Gender, Crime and Punishment* (London: Yale University Press, 1994), 12–13.

[10] This is the argument in M. Travers, 'Preaching to the Converted? Improving the Persuasiveness of Criminal Justice Research' (1997) 37 *British Journal of Criminology* 359, discussed in the second part of this chapter.

[11] See L. Sherman, 'The Influence of Criminology on Criminal Law: Evaluating Arrests for Misdemeanour Domestic Violence' (1992) 83 *Journal of Criminal Law and Criminology* 1 and A. Sanders, 'Victim Participation in an Exclusionary Criminal Justice System' in C. Hoyle and R. Young (eds.), *New Visions of Crime Victims* (Oxford: Hart Publishing, 2002).

[12] C. Hoyle, E. Cape, R. Morgan, and A. Sanders, *Evaluation of the 'One Stop Shop' and Victim Statement Pilot Projects* (London: Home Office, 1998); and R. Morgan and A. Sanders, *The Uses of Victim Statements* (London: Home Office, 1999).

is what victims want' and simply repeated this mantra when it was put to him that these results cast doubt on whether this remained the view of many victims by the end of 'their' cases.[13] Sebba rightly concludes about policy formation generally that: 'policy is more influenced by other factors such as ideology, pressure groups and personalities. Research findings, if invoked at all, are generally used merely to buttress policies advocated for other reasons.'[14] Thus research that resonates with the prevailing political ethos is far more likely to be welcomed and acted upon than that which strikes a discordant note.

The relevance of the discussion for this collection hardly needs spelling out. The influence of research on policy has been one of Roger Hood's abiding concerns.[15] Most academic social science disciplines connect with theory at one end and policy at another, with analysis of social, economic, or political arrangements linking the two. As we have seen, many academics attempt to work at one or more of these levels in an entirely dispassionate way, while others, including Roger Hood, incorporate an explicitly normative dimension into their work. In a recent paper, at a conference convened to honour Sir Leon Radzinowicz' memory, Hood endorsed his friend and mentor's view that empirical work shorn of its moral element is valueless and approvingly quoted his view that criminological work needed 'a little more humanity and reality'.[16]

The desire to promote both 'humanity' and 'reality' is evident from much of Hood's work. Take, for example, parole and executive release from custody. In his debate with Nigel Walker in the 1970s and his work as a member of the Carlisle Committee on parole these twin concerns are married with clear argument and detailed knowledge. Extensive discretion could not, he concluded in 1975, 'be justified empirically, logically or morally'.[17] He viewed it as incon-

---

[13] 'Newsnight', June 2000. The PSS was announced in a Home Office Press Notice, 26 May 2000, 147/2000.

[14] L. Sebba, 'On the Relationship between Criminological Research and Policy: The Case of Crime Victims' (2001) 1 *Criminal Justice* 27 at 44–5.

[15] See, for an early example, R. Hood, 'Criminology and Penal Change: A Case Study of the Nature and Impact of some recent Advice to Government' in R. Hood (ed.), *Crime, Criminology and Public Policy* (London: Heinemann, 1974).

[16] For an account of the importance of Roger Hood's professional relationship with Sir Leon see the chapter by Zedner in this collection.

[17] R. Hood, 'The Case against Executive Control over Time in Custody: A Rejoinder to Professor Walker's Criticisms' [1975] *Crim.L.R.* 545 at 552. Walker's article, to which this is a reply, is in the same volume at 540.

sistent with his objective of 'greater legality in the treatment of prisoners'.[18] However, pragmatist that he was and is, he sought to retain executive discretion for the most dangerous offenders, with a view to both effectiveness and the ways in which sentences are received by the public. This approach was adopted, in part, by the Carlisle Committee over a decade later and partially implemented in the Criminal Justice Act 1991. In his study of the death penalty, Roger Hood's moral stance is less explicit but not difficult to discern.[19] He advocates the collection and analysis of empirical evidence so that decisions with moral dimensions—in this case, concerning the death penalty—are taken on the basis of as accurate an understanding of their implications as possible in order to, again, minimize unfairness and maximize effectiveness. For Hood, criminologists 'are duty bound to contribute our knowledge to achieve, as best we can, a just and effective penal policy'.[20]

So, on the one hand we have a concern for morality, fairness, and legality. On the other, reality, effectiveness, and efficiency. Traditionally, these are seen as two incompatible sets of values—both vital to some extent, but impossible to reconcile. Packer famously encapsulated them as, respectively, 'due process' and 'crime control'. He said that anyone espousing one to the exclusion of the other would be a fanatic.[21] Hood is no fanatic, and nor are we. However, this chapter will not concern itself with how one might set about reconciling these sets of values, nor with defending our view that the pursuit of efficiency and effectiveness within criminal justice is not necessarily an amoral stance.[22] Rather we here pursue the question of how *best* to minimize unfairness and maximize effectiveness through research. Persuasive evidence may be a necessary condition of rational reform, but it is not a sufficient one. Indeed, as we have already illustrated, policy-makers sometimes act in ways that run directly counter to research that they themselves have commissioned. What needs to be considered is whether we can conceptualize the

---

[18] Ibid.

[19] R. Hood, *The Death Penalty*: a World-Wide Perspective (Oxford: Clarendon Press, 3rd edn., 2002).

[20] R. Hood, 'Penal Policy and Criminological Challenges in the New Millennium' (2001) 34 *The Australian and New Zealand Journal of Criminology* 1 at 6.

[21] H.L. Packer, *The Limits of the Criminal Sanction* (Stanford, Cal.: Stanford University Press, 1968), 154.

[22] Our views on these matters are set out in A. Sanders and R. Young, *Criminal Justice* (2nd edn., London: Butterworths, 2000), Chapter 1.

relationship between research and policy in a way that makes the former more likely to influence the latter.[23]

In Favour of Oscillation and Synthesis

We have argued that the different approaches evident within criminology to the inter-relations between theory, research, and policy have both strengths and weaknesses. Ideally, we should combine the best elements of each, thus minimizing their disadvantages. For example, Daly proposes that empirical researchers should oscillate between 'logico-scientific and narrative modes of reasoning'. Large-scale quantitative analysis is necessary to establish a representative picture of patterns of decision-making, whereas narrative analysis (based on observation, case-studies, and small-scale qualitative interviewing) adds depth and meaning. For Daly, the objective is not to combine these approaches since the two modes of reasons are regarded as irreducible to each other.[24] Rather they should be seen as poles 'from which we can glimpse distinctive representational possibilities [allowing us] to think more systematically about narrative and more meaningfully about numbers'. Crucially, Daly advocates such oscillation as a means of developing a normative stance on the justice of criminal justice practices.[25] A commitment to oscillation is also evident in Lacey's recommendation that those studying criminal justice should adopt a 'self-consciously eclectic approach which entails moving back and forth between general conceptions and hypotheses, on the one hand, and the specificity of social practices, on the other'.[26]

As Bottoms notes, eclecticism is not the same as synthesis, if by the latter term we mean the practice of taking one's views from a variety of sources in ways that make 'no strenuous effort to create intellectual harmony between discrete elements'.[27] To achieve such har-

[23] This is not a call for empirical evidence to *lead* policy, since policy should ultimately be led by values, not evidence. Where evidence is important is in the testing of the factual assumptions on which value choices are (usually) based, and in thinking through the implications of those choices.

[24] A similar approach is adopted by D. Garland, *Punishment and Modern Society* (Oxford: Oxford University Press, 1990). See his discussion at 279–80 in particular.

[25] K. Daly, *Gender, Crime and Punishment* (London: Yale University Press, 1994), 264–7.

[26] Lacey, n. 5 above, 34. To like effect see Garland, n. 7 above, at p. vii.

[27] A. Flew (ed.), *A Dictionary of Philosophy* (New York: St Martin's Press, 1997), 24 quoted in Bottoms, n. 4 above, at 23. On this basis we see Lacey's essay cited above as one of synthesis rather than eclecticism.

mony he advocates the use of 'adaptive theory' as developed by Layder.[28] This approach requires:

(i)   An acceptance that there are no theory-neutral facts;

(ii)   A willingness to test hypotheses rigorously but not in such a way that one becomes blind to fresh data that do not easily mesh with the pre-existing line of inquiry;

(iii) A willingness to use to the full the method of grounded theory;

(iv)   An unwillingness to foreclose inquiry too quickly, recognizing that theories may require reformulation in response to new data or interpretations of data;

(v)   An openness to the relevance of concepts from general social theories at all stages of the developing theoretical analysis;

(vi)   A willingness to utilize appropriately both quantitative and qualitative sources of data.[29]

Bottoms recognizes that 'no-one has all the necessary skills to be a fully rounded criminologist ... some who are adept at unravelling the intricacies of Michel Foucault's theoretical arguments will have no idea how to interpret the results of a multivariate statistical analysis; and the same is also true in reverse ... Hence, there has to be some division of labour among criminologists.'[30] Nonetheless, he insists that because there are no such things as theory-neutral facts, and because an important test of any theoretical account is whether it interprets social reality more convincingly and accurately than other theoretical accounts, all criminologists must grapple with the theory–research relationship at an individual level to at least some degree. So we are left with another kind of oscillation: between the pole of individual theoretical and empirical endeavour, and the pole of seeking to deploy, test, and build on the insights gained previously by the scholarly community as a whole.[31] As we shall argue below, this kind of oscillation is crucial when considering the influence of different styles of police research on police practice.

---

[28] D. Layder, *Sociological Practice: Linking Theory and Social Research* (London: Sage, 1998).

[29] This list is a simplified version of the points set out by Bottoms, n. 4 above, at 44.

[30] Ibid., 16.

[31] To like effect see Garland, n. 7 above, p. vii.

Synthesis of the kind described above may bolster the persuasiveness of research findings and thus increase the likelihood that they influence policy, but there still remains the problem of those findings not meshing with the dominant political discourse. To some extent, academics are stuck with that. However, the state is not monolithic: practitioners, public officials, and politicians vary within and among themselves. Practitioners, in particular, play a crucial role in mediating high-level policy such that it becomes reformulated 'at the coal-face'.[32] So one obvious strategy is to use the research process in a way that maximizes the chances of influencing and shaping these 'intermediate factors'. This can be done by showing how particular groups of practitioners can be helped to do their job better in their, as well as in the researchers', own normative terms and by placing short articles, stripped of sociological jargon and technical statistical detail, into practitioner journals and pressure group publications. Even at a time when there is no obvious window of opportunity to influence policy the strategy of disseminating summaries of research in a variety of settings can pay dividends. As Rock's analysis of the construction of British victim policy makes clear, such activity does not necessarily 'trigger direct political activity' but it can shape more general understandings by officials of particular social issues or problems, understandings which then play a part in shaping policy responses.[33]

This is not to argue that production of lengthy books and scholarly articles in prestigious academic journals are policy-irrelevant gestures. Rather, it is yet another argument for oscillation, the need to move between different levels of dissemination, oral and written, statistical and narrative, scholarly and summary, nakedly policy-oriented and subtly policy-relevant, remaining reflexively aware of the advantages and disadvantages of each approach and staying alert to how findings are being received by different individuals and groups.

The synthesized approach to the inter-relations between theory, research, and policy outlined in this section seems to hold out the

---

[32] See, e.g., K. Haines and M. Drakeford, *Young People and Youth Justice* (Houndmills: Macmillan, 1998), 55–61 on youth justice practitioners; and C. Hoyle, *Negotiating Domestic Violence* (Oxford: Oxford University Press, 1998) on street level police officers.

[33] P. Rock, *Helping Victims of Crime* (Oxford: Clarendon Press, 1990), 301–2. See also Zedner, this volume.

best hope of criminology impacting on policy in a beneficial way. To make our case more persuasive we now provide a more extended analysis of some of these relationships in the context of a specific area of criminological endeavour, research into police and policing.

The Policy Relevance of Police Research

Police Research

In a recent essay Reiner highlights shifts in the style of police research over the last forty years. He identifies a critical/theoretical phase of police research that flourished in the 1970s and early 1980s. At the start of this phase the 'key theoretical influences were symbolic interactionism and the labelling perspective, which saw policing as an important process in shaping (rather than merely reacting to) the pattern of deviance through the exercise of discretion'.[34] Later, the phase was characterized by more structural critiques of policing (for example Marxism) which focussed on the 'inadequacy of existing mechanisms for holding the police to account, whether as individuals through the complaints process or the courts, or force policy and operations as a whole through the institutions of police governance'.[35] Although these studies were not focussed on short-term policy issues, the findings they produced were unmistakably policy-relevant.

In the late 1980s and 1990s the predominant style of police research became managerialist, and policy-oriented, concerned above all with issues of effectiveness, often embracing formal evaluations of crime control initiatives. These speedy and focussed projects 'may not shed light on the low visibility practices of everyday policing ... the way day-to-day decisions about the use of powers are made, and other key aspects of cop culture'.[36] Reiner recognizes that critical and theoretical work has continued to be undertaken, citing *The Case for the Prosecution* as an 'influential and much debated' example of the genre, but argues that replication 'of the classic observational studies of routine police work is badly needed'.[37] The dominant crime control-oriented political agenda makes it more difficult both to obtain funding to carry out critical/theoretical studies of the police and to gain access to police services

---

[34] R. Reiner, 'Police Research' in King and Wincup (eds.), n. 4 above, 214.
[35] Ibid., 215.   [36] Ibid., 226.   [37] Ibid.

for the purpose of collecting data for such studies, whether by making observations, scrutinizing police files, or through interviewing officers.[38] The upshot seems to be that the kind of policy that research is likely to inform is short-term, narrowly conceived, and largely pre-determined by prevailing ideological considerations. That appears to limit greatly the extent to which research can contribute to policy formulation.

Criminologists committed to synthesis need not despair at this state of affairs, lamentable as it is. Rather, the aim should be to build broader theoretical concerns into the design, implementation, and reporting of policy-relevant evaluations. There is ample scope to do this, even under current conditions. First, not all funding bodies are committed to funding short-term evaluations to the exclusion of other styles of policing research. For example, the research which led to *The Case for the Prosecution* was funded by the Economic and Social Research Council during the period Reiner identifies as dominated by effectiveness studies, and *Proceed with Caution* is based on *three years'* worth of funding from a charity.

Secondly, even when funding has been provided by a policy-obsessed body such as a government department, there remains the potential to use the research process to engage with critical concerns. As Morgan puts it:

it is always open to an imaginative and critically minded researcher to view the data collected within a broader theoretical frame of reference. ... If Home Office-funded research projects are limited in their outputs ... this typically has more to do with self-censorship or the interpretative failure of academic researchers to realize and seize opportunities than any constraints imposed by the Home Office.[39]

Naturally, it is easier to recognize and seize such opportunities if the theoretical frame of reference informed the design of the research in the first place and was then kept in mind as data collection and analysis took place.[40] But even where this is not done, there are still possibilities for re-interpreting data in the light of theoretical frameworks only discovered once a project is formally

---

[38] R. Morgan, 'The Politics of Criminological Research' in King and Wincup (eds.), n. 4 above.

[39] Ibid., 77.

[40] For a case-study based discussion of how general social theory can inform criminological research see Bottoms, n. 4 above, 38–9.

concluded.[41] But the optimum research design is that based on adaptive theory, where the research process is *informed* by coherent theorizing rather than being *driven* by it towards a pre-destined conclusion. The essential point is that it is for the theoretically informed researcher to define the policy problem, not for the policy-maker to do it.[42] We shall offer *AAPS* as an example of such a project.

Thirdly, it is a mistake to assume that the police are uninterested in broader theoretical concerns. Bottoms records his surprise at the 'widespread interest' shown by senior police managers, during professional training, in aspects of his own work on late modernity theory.[43] He argues that a senior police manager:

inevitably realizes that there are many interconnections between different parts of the complex world that they are supposed to 'manage'. They would like to have some fuller understanding of these interconnections, and that is precisely what theoretical frameworks, when adequately understood and internalized, can begin to provide.[44]

Similarly, the first-named author well remembers being taken aback by one of his earliest conversations with a Thames Valley Police officer assigned to its restorative justice consultancy. On being asked what literature the police had looked at in designing its

---

[41] Examples stemming from our own research on the police include R. Young, 'Integrating a Multi-Victim Perspective into Criminal Justice Through Restorative Justice Conferences' in A. Crawford and J. Goodey (eds.), *Integrating a Victim Perspective within Criminal Justice* (Aldershot: Ashgate, 2000), in which the concept of 'the victim' was deconstructed, and R. Young, 'Just Cops Doing "Shameful" Business?: Police-led Restorative Justice and the Lessons of Research' in A. Morris and G. Maxwell (eds.), *Restorative Justice for Juveniles* (Oxford: Hart Publishing, 2001) in which Foucault's account of 'discipline' was used to explore the extent to which restorative cautioning can be conceptualized as a punitive practice. For a non-police research example see A. Sanders, 'Victim Participation in an Exclusionary Criminal Justice System' in Hoyle and Young (eds.), n. 11 above, which draws on the research of Hoyle *et al.*, n. 12 above, and Morgan and Sanders, n. 12 above, but also applies the ideas Garland develops in *The Culture of Control*, n. 7 above.

[42] This point is elaborated, through discussion of an earlier prosecution research project in which case construction was 'discovered' at a late stage, by A. Sanders, 'Some Dangers of Policy-oriented Research—the Case of Prosecutions' in I. Dennis (ed.), *Criminal Law and Justice* (London: Sweet and Maxwell, 1987).

[43] The first-named author of this chapter contributed to this training programme in 2001 and was similarly surprised by the degree of interest and skill shown by senior police officers in integrating late modernity theory into their assessed essays.

[44] Bottoms, n. 4 above, 21.

cautioning initiative, the officer called out to his colleagues: 'What's that book we all read last year, it was "Pride, Sex, Shame and the Birth of Self" wasn't it?' Various responses were shouted back, all offering variations on this theme, not one of them containing a hint of jocularity. This was as far from stereotypical notions of 'canteen culture' ribaldry as could be imagined and provided an indication of the extensive theoretical work that preceded and underpinned the early stages of the implementation of this initiative.[45] It follows that the incorporation of theoretical concerns into police-funded or police-facilitated research may be welcomed, even sought.

Case Studies 1 and 2: The Case for the Prosecution and Advice and Assistance in Police Stations

In 1981 The Royal Commission on Criminal Procedure proposed wide-ranging reforms of police and prosecution processes.[46] They were aimed, in an optimistic attempt to square a circle, at strengthening police powers in order to secure more convictions of the guilty, and also at strengthening protections for suspects in order that there be fewer prosecutions of innocent people. Most of its recommendations were enacted—in the Police and Criminal Evidence Act 1984 (PACE) and the Prosecution of Offences Act 1985. The latter created the Crown Prosecution Service (CPS), introduced in 1986, with the Director of Public Prosecutions (DPP) (whose office had been established over one century earlier) as its Head. An equally significant event in 1981, for academics if not for government, was the publication of Doreen McBarnet's book, *Conviction*.[47] This was perhaps the most influential British criminology book concerning pre-trial procedure of the 1980s, but its roots lay in the structural critiques of policing that, we saw earlier, were characteristic of work in the 1970s and early 1980s.

In the midst of the debate fuelled by the Royal Commission report, in 1984 ESRC announced a 'Crime and Criminal Justice System' initiative, inviting bids for research. With all of the (theoret-

---

[45] In particular those at Headquarters responsible for developing the initiative were familiar with J. Braithwaite, *Crime, Shame and Reintegration* (Cambridge: Cambridge University Press, 1989); D. Nathanson, *Shame and Pride: Affect, Sex and the Birth of the Self* (New York: Norton & Company, 1992); and T. Tyler, *Why People Obey the Law* (New Haven, Conn.: Yale University Press, 1990).

[46] Cmnd 8092 (London: HMSO, 1981).

[47] (London: MacMillan, 1981).

ical and policy) events of the previous few years in mind the second-named author joined Mike McConville and Roger Leng in a success-ful bid to research 'Discretion to Charge and to Prosecute'.[48] The object was to examine the factors shaping police decisions whether or not to prosecute, how these decisions were affected by (and affected) the relationship with the then-new CPS, and the role played by the then-new PACE framework. The result was, eventually, *CFP*.

One of the most important due process elements of PACE was the introduction, in sections 58 and 59, of a right for all suspects to free legal advice and assistance; and the mechanism—a duty solicitor scheme—by which that right could be made real. With a touching concern for the autonomy of suspects, the government was unwilling to force suspects to accept legal advice, or even to provide advice to all who did not explicitly refuse it. Instead, PACE established an opt-in system, which only 25 per cent of suspects sought to use. One fifth of these suspects did not get the advice they sought, and many of those who did were advised over the telephone (rather than in person) and still had to undergo interrogation alone. The Lord Chancellor's Department, which was responsible for the scheme, asked for bids for research to evaluate the scheme. The second-named author, with Lee Bridges, was successful, and work began on *AAPS* in 1987.

In securing the *Case for the Prosecution* grant, the main 'pitch' to ESRC was theoretical. However, the research needed the co-operation of the police and the new CPS, so it was sold to them as an evaluative project. None of these bodies was misled as the project contained both theoretical and evaluative strands.

McBarnet argued that criminal justice agencies adopt due process rhetoric if they have to. However, they (and the police in particular) will continue to use crime control policies and practices whilst this fits both the adversarial relationship between police and suspect and the material conditions of the broader society. She argued that due process measures are sometimes even used to subvert due process policy. Further, a 'case' is not a value-neutral collection of facts, but

[48] McConville had extensive experience of empirical criminal justice research; see, e.g., (with J. Baldwin), *Courts, Prosecution and Conviction* (Oxford: Oxford University Press, 1981). Sanders had also carried out empirical research on police and prosecutorial discretion, the results of which led him to express misgivings about the new prosecution arrangements. See his 'An Independent Crown Prosecution Service?' [1986] *Crim.L.R.* 27.

something 'built' or 'constructed' by the police with the (usually successful) aim of conviction.

We wanted to see if McBarnet's thesis applied to the new ostensibly due process-inspired policies embodied in PACE and the CPS, particularly when tested by more systematic research than she had been able to carry out. Although our theoretical questions were at the forefront, several policy questions followed logically and were not distracting. These questions included whether PACE and the CPS work as ostensibly intended; whether suspects and defendants are now better protected than before, reducing the danger of miscarriages of justice; and what changes are needed to make the reforms work better. For the policy debate on the CPS had been conducted in terms of 'strong' and 'weak' cases. In other words, the CPS was introduced to 'weed out' weak cases and only prosecute strong cases. If it worked, this would be good for some suspects and also be more efficient for the system. Only by employing McBarnet's *theoretical* idea of case construction could this idea be adequately *researched*. For if the police could (and, prompted by the advent of the CPS, would be more likely to) construct 'weak' cases in such a way that they became 'strong', then the existence of the CPS would be inadvertently jeopardizing people who might otherwise be acquitted.

As far as *AAPS* was concerned, the initiative was that of government, so the immediate research agenda was explicitly policy-relevant. However, for us the policy and theoretical questions were the same as in *CFP*, except that the former, not the latter, were at the forefront. Like the ESRC research, this project allowed us to examine policing, and broader criminal justice processes, through both a theoretical prism and the prism of new reforms and the need to work with other agencies (defence lawyers in this project, and the CPS in the ESRC project). The published report, *Advice and Assistance in Police Stations*, was not explicitly theoretical in the way *CFP* was to be, but later articles and book chapters were.[49] For example, a crucial element in case construction in many cases is the confession. Part of the controversy over criminal justice in the 1980s concerned

---

[49] See, in particular, A. Sanders, 'Access to Justice in the Police Station—an Elusive Dream?' in R. Young and D. Wall (eds.), *Access to Criminal Justice* (London: Blackstone, 1996); and the use of this material in A. Sanders and R. Young, 'The Rule of Law, Due Process, and Pre-trial Criminal Justice' (1994) 47 *Current Legal Problems* 125.

coerced and false confessions. One purpose of legal advice and assistance for suspects is to prevent the police from pressuring suspects into false or coerced confessions. We were therefore interested at the theoretical level in how far case construction was obstructed by the legal advice provisions we were researching.

Since our theoretical perspective was based on McBarnet's argument that the police used due process rhetoric to pursue crime control practices, the methodology in both projects was designed to ascertain what the police did, not what they said they did. Where there was a gap between the two, this was not unexpected, and was therefore something to be explained and understood, not to be explained away. In *CFP* this was operationalized by examining police records, including prosecution files and then interviewing the officers whose reports constituted those files. By gaining the trust of those officers we hoped that they would reveal their real thinking and actions, rather than simply repeating written scripts.

To some, inevitably uncertain, extent we were successful in this. Officers talked about stops and arrests on the basis of little or no 'reasonable' suspicion, the virtual rubber-stamping of detention following arrest, getting round the PACE restrictions on access to lawyers and on interrogations, and how they would persuade the CPS to 'give a prosecution a run' when there was little evidence. The files in the corresponding cases revealed little or nothing of these practices, and usually conformed to the due process requirements of the law. When, occasionally, the mask did slip and a prosecution file did reveal a breach of PACE or a glaring evidential gap, the CPS generally berated the police for this. This did not make it less likely that the malpractice would recur, but simply made it less likely that it would be revealed. The CPS, in other words, inadvertently encouraged police case construction instead of acting as a brake on it.

In *AAPS* we were able to compare what the police said with what they actually did a little more directly. This was done by observing the treatment of suspects in the custody suite, by observing interrogations, and by interviewing suspects. There may have been a 'Hawthorn effect' as a result of all this, but if there was, it would have minimized the gap between law and practice. Much of PACE is elaborated in Codes of Practice to which the police should adhere. One particularly striking finding was that, on our observations (not including what suspects told us), the police breached Code C (on the treatment of suspects in custody) in around 10 per cent of cases—three times as often as was revealed by their own custody records.

In both projects a synthesized approach to theory, research, and policy was adopted, and, without knowing it, a loose version of Layder's adaptive theory, as discussed in the first section of this chapter, was employed. In both projects the nature of the 'facts' we 'uncovered' was understood as being dependent in part on the theoretical ideas we employed. Our suspicion of the police, for example, led us to methods such as those that explored the gap between what they say they do and what they actually do. But we were, at the same time, open to 'facts' and explanations for them that did not fit our existing ideas.

Most of the findings[50] in both projects fitted the McBarnet thesis and our adaptation of it to the new conditions of the CPS and PACE. In *CFP* we argued that the police were not bound by most of the stop-search, arrest, custody, legal advice, and interrogation restrictions imposed by PACE. This was fleshed out in detail in relation to legal advice and interrogation by *AAPS*. Indeed, we argued that most of these rules were either presentational or enabling rules—forms of rules that enabled the police to continue to practise crime control policing.[51] This is not to say that all rules were either breakable or flexible enough to allow the police *carte blanche* (although that is true of many). But we found, as have many other police researchers, that more or less all rules that were not breakable or flexible were avoidable. The police breached and found ways round many of the rules on stops, arrest, detention, interrogation, access to legal advice, prosecution, and so forth.

Thus it was (and is) true that it is now rare and unacceptable to use violence. But the police have recourse to psychological methods of securing confessions that make violence redundant,[52] use 'informal interviews' to avoid tape recordings and time limits, and use covert policing methods when interrogation fails. The police deal with suspects and other agencies (including the CPS)[53] on their own

---

[50] Only a very brief account is given here. For a summary of the up-to-date research on the topic, see Sanders and Young, n. 22 above, Chapters 2–5.

[51] See further Sanders and Young, n. 22 above, 73–5.

[52] R. Leo, 'Police Interrogation and Social Control' (1994) 3 *Social and Legal Studies* 93.

[53] Much of *CFP* was concerned with the CPS and police control over it and with plea-bargaining. None of this is dealt with here, nor in the next section on policy

terms, and so exercise more *real* power than those other agencies, regardless of the formal powers conferred by legislation. One of the results of this was that the police were often able to construct cases to be strong. Whereas the policy debate was couched in terms of whether or not cases were weak or strong (and how weak cases should be dealt with) the important question, arrived at only from a theoretical starting-point, was how cases come to be weak or strong.

At the time we did the *AAPS* research we found that the police used a variety of 'ploys' to persuade suspects not to seek advice, or not to wait for their lawyers when they did seek it. Combined with the structural problems (such as having to wait in the cells for a lawyer), the confused and nervous suspects who never made their wishes clear (and who were therefore denied a lawyer), and the often unhelpful or non-adversarial attitudes and practices of the lawyers themselves, this meant that many suspects did not secure the protection that the Royal Commission envisaged.

We found in both projects that the police were able to hide their rule breaches and rule avoidance effectively much of the time by constructing custody records, stop-search records, and so forth to comply with the law, this often being a vital part of the overall case constructions. Having to appear to comply with due process, in other words, helped the police to pursue their (usually crime control) agendas. But we were able to verify this part of our theoretical perspective only because that perspective alerted us in the first place to investigate the gap between what the police said and what they did. Without this approach the research projects, and their policy implications (discussed in the next section), would have been very different.

Our argument is not that the police (or other agencies) *always* subverted due process provisions to their own ends or that police–suspect encounters are generally an unmitigated dystopian hell.[54] In

---

implications, as space does not permit the 'research on policing' brief to be interpreted this widely. Similarly, much of *AAPS* was concerned with defence lawyer practices and the organization of duty solicitor schemes. This is not discussed for the same reasons.

[54] Thus the argument of many critics of our work, that it portrays the police as irredeemably 'bent' and is therefore misleading and inaccurate, is based on a false premise. For two examples of such writers, discussed in more detail in the next section, see M. Travers, 'Preaching to the Converted? Improving the Persuasiveness of Criminal Justice Research' (1997) 37 *British Journal of Criminology* 359; D. Smith, 'Case Construction and the Goals of the Criminal Process' (1997) 37 *British Journal of Criminology* 319.

the cases that mattered to the police, they usually managed to subvert due process protections. But many cases do not matter that much to the police, and then the police simply accepted that they had the wrong person or that that person would, for example, see a lawyer. We found that the police constructed cases 'down' (away from conviction) as well as up, whilst some of the latter cases ended in acquittal, showing that there are limits to the effectiveness of case construction.

So our theory had to be adaptive, in order to allow for cases that the police did not win. We had to go beyond McBarnet's focus on the individual case to the broader and longer term process. Even when the police really wanted to win they did not always succeed—that day. There was always another day. As we argued in *CFP*, stop-search enables the police to harass and arrest anyone who is in the broadest sense 'suspicious', which means, *inter alia*, people whom the police have put, or wish to put, behind bars. The police have a long-term relationship with the suspect community.[55] Again, to understand the empirical facts of the police–suspect encounter, that encounter has to be understood theoretically. To 'count' releases from police custody, for example, without seeing whether the police ultimately 'get their man' Mountie-fashion, is to miss the point, just like researchers who 'count' silences in a suspect's interrogation miss the point if that suspect eventually confesses (as happened in the Cardiff Three case, for example). These are classic examples of not seeing the wood for the trees.

The policy implications of both projects were fairly obvious. It is true that our theoretical orientation led us to conclude that the police were largely unreformable in relation to important cases and the suspect groups in whom they were most interested for as long as the material conditions and adversary system alluded to earlier remained. However, this does not necessarily lead to the conclusion that all criminal justice processes are necessarily unreformable. Following McBarnet's thesis, we argued that the police behaved as they did because it was their adversarial job to do so. By the same reasoning, defence lawyers could do their job equally vigorously. However, this will be true only if lawyers are given the appropriate powers and structures within which to work—which we will return to later. So we argued, in short articles aimed at practitioners, policy-makers, and the general public, for specific changes in policy.

---

[55] S. Choongh, *Policing as Social Discipline* (Oxford: Clarendon, 1997).

For example, we argued that many police powers (especially those that had been enhanced in PACE) should be reduced, because the crime control manner in which they are used enables the police to exercise greater power over suspects than would be so if the police adopted due process approaches to the exercise of power. For the same reasons, the police should not be expected to act as 'gatekeepers' for the rights of suspects—for how could they be expected to protect the very group of people with whom they have an adversarial crime control relationship? Further, legal advice should be provided automatically, or at least on an opt-out basis, for our analysis of ploys led us to conclude that many suspects do not choose to forgo advice 'freely' in any meaningful sense of that term. This all led us to argue that defence lawyers should be given the means to challenge police constructions rather than requiring the police themselves and the CPS to quality-control those constructions. For we saw police (and CPS) 'error', as discussed earlier, as a predictable result of their structural position in the criminal justice system, not as a result of bureaucratic pressures or failures of training which could be remedied without structural change.

Another policy implication was that it was not just weak cases that should create concern—indeed, strong cases were an even greater cause for concern. For legal strength was no more indicative of 'true guilt' than legal weakness, as the victim of many a miscarriage in cases originally pronounced by the courts as undoubtedly guilty (such as Judith Ward and the Birmingham Six) will testify. A similar point relates to police-generated records. These are supposed to protect suspects but, as we have seen, they often have the opposite effect and, we therefore argued, are worthless as due process mechanisms.

None of these reforms came to pass. In some instances, such as giving the defence more power, this was doubtless because our suggested reforms would have been too radical for the government of the day. But providing advice on an opt-out, instead of opt-in, basis would not, in principle be a radical step, although in practice it might be as it could lead to the right becoming meaningful in most cases. In fact the direction of reform has gone mainly in the opposite direction in the last ten years or so. There is now, for example, more self-assessment than ever before of police performance through police-generated records.

On the other hand, some of the reforms of the last few years have been due process oriented, and were probably introduced at least in part because of these research findings, particularly those of *AAPS*. For example, Code A covers stop-search (discussed in *CFP*) and Code C covers suspects in custody (discussed in both projects). Both Codes were tightened up in 1995. Many police ploys in relation to legal advice, for example, were banned in Code C. Custody officers became obliged to inform suspects of all their important rights, including the crucial fact that advice was free. Also, the rules provided for solicitors advising at police stations were changed, requiring them to give a better service to suspects.[56] Many of these changes, particularly in Code A, probably had little or no effect.[57] But some, in Code C, probably did, and the proportion of suspects seeing a lawyer, and having that lawyer in the interrogation, has now risen considerably. In 1995 around 40 per cent of suspects requested advice, and around 34 per cent received it.[58]

This victory for the influence of research on policy, and (wearing our normative hats explicitly) for due process over crime control, should not be underestimated. It is important in practical policy terms, in terms of the modifications needed to our theoretical approach, and for the general argument of this chapter. But nor should this apparent victory be overestimated, as we shall see in the third section of this chapter. Further, the police arguably had the last laugh. *AAPS* includes a table of 'ploys' that we reproduced in a *Criminal Law Review* article.[59] Such ploys included saying to a suspect:

—'You're too young to have a solicitor';
—'You'll have to wait in the cells if you want a solicitor';
—'What's the name of your solicitor? You don't know? Well, you can't have one then, can you?'.

---

[56] For discussion of these changes see A. Sanders and L. Bridges, 'The Right to Legal Advice' in C. Walker and K. Starmer (eds.), *Miscarriages of Justice* (London: Blackstone, 1999).

[57] Home Office research on stop-search conducted in the late 1990s is discussed by A. Sanders and R. Young, 'From Suspect to Trial' in M. Maguire, R. Morgan, and R. Reiner (eds.), *The Oxford Handbook of Criminology* (3rd edn., Oxford: Oxford University Press, 2002).

[58] T. Bucke and D. Brown, *In Police Custody: Police Powers and Suspects' Rights under the Revised PACE Codes of Practice*, Home Office Research Study 174 (London: Home Office, 1997).

[59] A. Sanders and L. Bridges, 'Access to Legal Advice and Police Malpractice' [1990] *Crim.L.R.* 494.

On several occasions we have been told of police stations where this table has been pasted up on a wall, presumably to help officers with insufficient imagination of their own to deal with awkward suspects who want to exercise their rights.

Why did we fail to influence policy in major ways? Is it because of the oppositional stance we adopted, particularly in *CFP*, which, Travers argues, makes research less persuasive?[60] Certainly our findings and arguments are often treated dismissively by government researchers.[61] But it seems to us at least as likely that the research is dismissed because its policy implications are unpalatable as that the policy implications are unpalatable because of the nature of the research. After all, the victim participation research discussed earlier was Home Office sponsored, Home Office designed, and saturated with Home Office values (in that it was, put simply, victim-oriented). But that did not stop the Home Office rejecting the type of reform that we believed followed logically from our findings (although the new PSS scheme does 'raid' our findings in order to improve on the original scheme in small ways).[62]

Travers' argument to the contrary comes down to two main points. First, he simply disagrees with our theoretical position and asserts that our interpretation of our data is primarily a product of that position. But he provides no reason or evidence to support his case. Secondly, he suggests that a 'thick' ethnomethodological account would be more convincing to practitioners than the research methodologies that we adopted. This takes no account of the possibility that his chosen methodology might not be the methodology of choice of others (his claim for its supremacy rests solely on its supposedly greater persuasiveness to practitioners); nor of the need for the chosen methodology to fit the aims of the project.

Moreover Travers talks of 'thick' accounts being more persuasive to the practitioners in question because they will recognize what is

---

[60] M. Travers, 'Preaching to the Converted? Improving the Persuasiveness of Criminal Justice Research' (1997) 37 *British Journal of Criminology* 359; Also see D. Smith, 'Reform or Moral Outrage—the Choice is Yours' (1998) 38 *British Journal of Criminology* 616 (a response to the reply to Smith's critique of *CFP* by M. McConville, A. Sanders, and R. Leng, 'Descriptive or Critical Sociology—the Choice is Yours' (1997) 37 *British Journal of Criminology* 347.

[61] See, e.g., D. Brown, *PACE Ten Years On*, Home Office Research Study 155 (London: Home Office, 1997).

[62] A. Sanders, C. Hoyle, R. Morgan, and E. Cape, 'Victim Impact Statements: Don't Work, Can't Work' [2001] *Crim.L.R.* 447.

being described. But he does not discuss whether policy-makers are likely to find such accounts persuasive. Maybe they would find other types of account (more heavily statistical accounts in particular) more persuasive. He states that progressive change is likely to occur 'only' if practitioners and academics work together to raise professional standards. This clearly reflects his own theoretical position on the types of reform needed as well as a narrow conception of the types of reform that are possible. The influence of research on reform is far more likely to be related to underlying social and political interests than to the intrinsic qualities of the research or its methodology, as we shall argue in the third section.

A major advantage of explicitly policy-relevant research over theoretically-led research, particularly if, as with *AAPS*, it is initiated by a government agency, is that access to places, documents, and personnel is almost guaranteed. The *AAPS* research was far more intrusive (into interrogations for example) than *CFP* where the research was carried out under police and CPS sufferance. We have argued that *AAPS* lost nothing, in terms of its intellectual independence, as a result of this orientation; but *CFP* encountered major problems that would have been less likely to arise had it been sponsored.

First, of the three co-operating police forces, one withdrew co-operation when it discovered that Mike McConville was one of the principal investigators. Much of his previous research, with John Baldwin, had been carried out in that force, and that too had been critical of the police. The second-named author remembers, in an earlier research project, a Detective Inspector asking him if he worked 'for' McConville. I hastily replied that, though I knew him, our work was not connected. The Inspector reflected on the way they had all thought McConville was a 'nice bloke' until 'he shafted us'. That force was clearly not prepared to be 'shafted' by him again, but luckily we were able to find another force we could study, so no harm was done in the end.

Secondly, the DPP agreed to co-operate only on condition that direct quotations from prosecutors and files be made only with his permission. When the DPP returned the final draft of *CFP* to us, a number of quotations had been eliminated. He did not like our observing that prosecutors often knowingly allowed prosecutions to continue when cases did not meet the official criteria. We pointed out that rejecting the quotations that put the CPS in a bad light, and allowing the more flattering ones to remain, did not reflect well on the CPS, but this did not alter the stance of the DPP. We had no choice but to accept this, although we did paraphrase the quotations so that their meaning was preserved (and we noted the censorship on each occasion in the book). As with changing police forces, this was an irritant created by the need to secure the co-operation of official agencies, which is often the penalty attached to policy-oriented research, but it did no great harm to the integrity of the research or our analysis of our material.

The second-named author's experience in another project makes an interesting contrast. Research in the late 1990s into vulnerable witnesses found, among other things, that prosecutors often went to great efforts to prosecute cases in which there were vulnerable victims, even if this meant allowing prosecutions to continue when they did not meet the official criteria.[63] The finding that the formal norms were being ignored echoed what we said in *CFP*. But this time a CPS that was battling to establish victim credibility was proud of this fact. Rather than trying to suppress our findings, the CPS asked us if they could highlight this point prior to publication! Now, the data obtained in this research were no 'thicker' than in *CFP*. The methodology was no more rigorous. The results were simply more palatable to the CPS and government because the climate had changed over the first part of the 1990s from victim invisibility to victim consciousness.

This section has illustrated some of the compromises that have to be made if one's research is to be carried out and published at all, let alone have a chance of influencing policy. Unlike the ones revealed here, some compromises are clearly not worth making, and yet others involve very hard choices indeed. These last points are taken up in the next case study.

Case Study 3: Proceed with Caution

Police cautioning is a practice of major significance within the criminal justice system. In recent years, about one in three of all formal disposals resulting in a criminal record have been cautions rather than convictions. The police determine whom to caution without any oversight from prosecutors or the courts. This gives

---

[63] A. Sanders, J. Creaton, S. Bird, and L. Weber, *Victims with Learning Disabilities* (Oxford: Centre for Criminological Research, 1997).

rise to due process concerns about people receiving cautions for crimes they did not commit or which could not have been proved. There are also equal treatment concerns, as cautioning rates have been found to vary from area to area and across time.[64] A caution is supposed to take the form of a warning from a police officer that the record of this formal disposal may influence future prosecution and court decisions if the cautioned person should offend again. Whilst this may sound like quite a low-key encounter, an observational study by Lee[65] in four police force divisions revealed that the police sometimes used a cautioning session to humiliate and stigmatize young people. Interviews with Thames Valley Police officers in the initial stage of the *Proceed with Caution* (PWC) research were replete with references to 'old-style police cautioning' as amounting to a 'bollocking' by a senior police officer (usually an inspector) in which the aim was to make the cautioned person cry. They explained how there had been no training on how to administer a caution, no supervision of practice, and no expectation of consistency.

Following *ad hoc* experimentation from the mid-1990s onwards, the Thames Valley Police initiative in 'restorative cautioning' began formally on 1 April 1998. A 'restorative caution' involves two distinct innovations. The first is that the cautioning police officer is supposed to invite all those affected by the offence, including any victim, to the cautioning session. The second is the structuring of the session according to a 'script' which requires the cautioning officer to put certain questions to those present according to a definite order. This script derived from the police-led model of restorative cautioning developed in Wagga Wagga, Australia. The Wagga Wagga model's main influences were the New Zealand system of family group conferences and the quite separate criminological theory developed by John Braithwaite of reintegrative shaming.[66] The latter posits that the best way to control crime is to induce a sense of shame in offenders for their actions whilst maintaining respect for them as people (as to condemn them as 'bad people' might push them towards deviant identities, commitments, or sub-

[64] The research on cautioning is discussed by Sanders and Young, n. 22 above, 347–64.

[65] M. Lee, *Youth, Crime and Police Work* (Basingstoke: Macmillan, 1998).

[66] D. Moore with L. Forsyth, *A New Approach to Juvenile Justice: An Evaluation of Family Conferencing in Wagga Wagga* (Wagga Wagga: Centre for Rural Social Research, Charles Stuart University, 1995).

cultures). It further posits that this kind of reintegrative shaming is best achieved not by the police or the courts but rather by exposing offenders to the emotionally-charged opinions of those whom they most care about, such as parents, partners, and friends.

Officers in Thames Valley can facilitate restorative cautions and conferences only if they have first received specialist training. During this training they are provided with a practice manual which includes modules on the underlying theories, practice standards, and the script. Once trained they are allocated cases by local co-ordinators who also endeavour to monitor whether the practice standards are adhered to. In addition a team of officers at police headquarters, known as the Restorative Justice Consultancy, oversees all aspects of the initiative and maintains a database of all restorative cautions and conferences.

The fact that the restorative cautioning initiative represented an attempt to transform a large-scale and controversial policing practice had a number of implications for the research methods adopted. The existing body of critical/theoretical studies of the police helped us to appreciate that initial interactions between police and arrestees might prove crucial in understanding the practice and effect of restorative cautioning. So it was decided to focus on direct observation of the cautioning sessions and, to a lesser extent, to question participants about their treatment by the police, and to examine police case files closely.

In this way, what appeared to be a narrow evaluation of a 'crime control' initiative was able to achieve something rather more radical: the collection of systematic observational and other forms of data on a routine everyday police activity, cautioning, in the manner of a critical, explicitly theoretical, research project. Moreover, the organizing theoretical idea of 'case construction', as deployed in the *Case for the Prosecution*, was built into the design of the *PWC* research and informed much of the subsequent data collection and analysis. For example, it sensitized the research team to cases in which harm was exaggerated within the cautioning session in an attempt to make the maximum impact on cautioned persons[67] and it aided

---

[67] This facet of restorative cautioning was first identified in the exploratory study which led to the *Proceed with Caution* research. See R. Young and B. Goold, 'Restorative Police Cautioning in Aylesbury—From Degrading to Reintegrative Shaming Ceremonies?' [1999] *Crim.L.R.* 126 at 134–5.

understanding of the few cases where restorative cautions took place despite the 'offender' denying responsibility for the offence.[68]

The *Proceed with Caution* study was designed on the assumption that a formal evaluation of the programme's impact should be attempted only following a period of action-research in which the researchers helped the police implement its model as planned. For several reasons a large initial gap between the blueprint for restorative cautioning and the actual practice of police officers when facilitating cautioning sessions was to be expected. First, all programmes tend to suffer from teething difficulties. Secondly, many promising initiatives fail due to weak implementation rather than because the underlying ideas are faulty.[69] Thirdly, an exploratory study in the Thames Valley had highlighted the likelihood of such a gap.[70]

Fourthly, and more fundamentally, a 'wide implementation gap' was expected on the basis of the body of critical, explicitly theoretical research into policing including *The Case for the Prosecution*. The *PWC* research team assumed at the outset that restorative cautioning was best theorized not as a stand-alone new practice capable of being evaluated in isolation but rather as an attempt to transform a long-existing policing practice. The initiative would necessarily involve some accommodation and conflict between two sets of philosophies and practices, the first, restorative justice, the second, established policing. It made sense, therefore, to evaluate restorative cautioning as something embedded within wider policing structures and understandings. The difficulties of changing entrenched policing practices had been forcefully reiterated by *The Case for the Prosecution* and *AAPS* as well as by other recently published research.[71] The *PWC* team accordingly expected to find that established policing culture, structures, and patterns of

[68] See Hoyle, Young, and Hill, n. 1 above, 31–2.

[69] See C. Hollin, 'The Meaning and Implications of "Programme Integrity"' in J. McGuire (ed.), *What Works: Reducing Reoffending* (Chichester: John Wiley, 1995), and T. Bennett, 'Problem-Solving Policing and Crime Prevention: An Assessment of the Role of the Police in Preventing Crime' in T. Bennett (ed.), *Preventing Crime and Disorder: Targeting Strategies and Responsibilities* (Cambridge: The Institute of Criminology, University of Cambridge, 1996).

[70] See R. Young and B. Goold, 'Restorative Police Cautioning in Aylesbury—From Degrading to Reintegrative Shaming Ceremonies?' [1999] *Crim.L.R.* 126.

[71] See, e.g., J. Chan, 'Changing Police Culture' (1996) 36 *British Journal of Criminology* 109.

behaviour would shape and often distort the supposedly 'restorative' nature of cautioning sessions.

The *PWC* team aimed to measure the gap between theory and practice, understand its causes and effects, and test whether it was possible for the police to close this gap once these matters had been documented. This might enable the position taken in *The Case for the Prosecution*, that there was no real possibility of major substantive changes to existing modes of policing, to be tested in the way suggested by adaptive theory. It would also allow measurements to be taken of the impact of police-led restorative justice, as opposed to police-led cautioning sessions masquerading as such. The action-research design thus allowed the research team to pursue both parts of its dualistic agenda, the theoretical and the practical.

The fact that the *PWC* research had this dualistic agenda (crime-control evaluation and theoretically informed critical research) also had implications for research access. Access was achieved with few of the usual problems that those researching the police have typically encountered.[72] No objections were raised to the proposal that tape-recordings be made of restorative cautions, and no *a priori* restrictions were placed on access to information or on the form or content of any publications arising out of the research. This was because the *PWC* team was seen by the police, to a degree that varied from place to place and over time, more as partners than as critical outsiders. It was important to Thames Valley Police, as an organization, that independent research was undertaken into its restorative cautioning initiative. This was in part because of its genuine commitment to providing a better service to victims and a more educational experience for offenders. However, as documented in more detail below, this police service also wanted to influence national and international policy debates on the place of restorative justice within the criminal justice system. It thus sought the involvement of academic researchers in order to give credibility to the claims it was already making about the benefits of restorative cautioning. Therefore, unlike the case with many avowedly critical/theoretical projects, the police organization had a clear incentive to facilitate the process of the research. The incentive for individual officers responsible for administering restorative cautions to co-operate in the research process was less

---

[72] For an analysis of the problems of researching the police see R. Reiner, 'Police Research' in King and Wincup (eds.), n. 4 above, 218–24.

clear-cut, and their perspective will be considered in more detail below.

In order to test whether the police could change their practices, a 'before and after' component was built into the research design. Systematic 'base-line' measurements, based on observations of twenty-three cautioning sessions, and 135 interviews relating to these cases, were made in the interim study carried out between January and April 1999. A confidential report was produced in October 1999. The 'full evaluation' was conducted between January and April 2000. 'After' data were collected through observing a further fifty-six cases and by conducting 483 interviews with the 242 participants in these cases.

Base-line data. In the interim study the main conclusion was that only two of the twenty-three cases we observed merited the label of 'restorative justice' in that they adhered closely to the Thames Valley model and were therefore 'restorative' in nature. Each of the other cases involved major deviations from the Thames Valley Police model. In particular, facilitators tended to dominate the exchanges that took place and behaved in ethically questionable ways, as by re-investigating the offence or seeking admissions to prior offending.[73] However, the practices observed were in most cases significantly different from 'old-style' cautioning, in that they included at least some commitment to broader 'community' involvement, procedural fairness, and the use of a coherent criminological theory. The interim report was designed to leave the police as an organization in no doubt about the scale and nature of the deviations by its facilitators from the scripted model. The report included eighty-one recommendations designed to close (or at least narrow) the gap detected between the programme's protocols and the behaviour of the facilitators observed. All of these recommendations were accepted by the police officers based at headquarters with responsibility for overseeing the initiative. As a direct result, the restorative justice script was revised and facilitators received top-up training designed to eradicate poor practice.[74] The interesting question is

[73] For an in-depth discussion of the policing practices witnessed during the interim study see Young, n. 41 above.

[74] The interim report also influenced the content of the restorative justice training that Thames Valley Police provided (with Youth Justice Board funding) for staff from other police forces and youth justice agencies. The training was designed to support the implementation of the Crime and Disorder Act 1998.

whether the resulting policy changes made any difference to the practices of individual police officers.

The full evaluation. In some respects the full evaluation data suggested that facilitators remained the dominant figures that the interim study had showed them to be. As in the interim study, there were many instances of offenders, victims, and their respective supporters saying proportionately very little, with facilitators contributing, on average, half of all the words spoken during a restorative session. However, closer analysis demonstrated there was a much greater degree of fidelity to the script in the full evaluation.[75] For example, facilitators asked irrelevant or improper questions in 57 per cent of interim study cases as compared with 26 per cent of full evaluation cases. On the other hand, progress was clearly patchy, and there remained substantial room for improvement in facilitation practice. For example, the fact that a third of offenders' supporters observed in the full evaluation were not asked what they would like to see come out of the restorative caution is a significant failing, even if it does represent a considerable improvement over the corresponding interim study figure of 59 per cent. Overall, however, the *PWC* researchers conclude that Thames Valley Police has effected a transformation of cautioning practices which is remarkable in its scope and intensity.[76] Whilst this police service has yet to secure full implementation of its own model, it clearly has moved a long way from old-style cautioning practices.

Just a research effect? Like any other agency, the police may modify their behaviour in the presence of observers. The *Proceed with Caution* team spent eight months in the field prior to undertaking formal tape-recorded observations in an attempt to win the trust of individual facilitators, but the presence of researchers undoubtedly made facilitators more self-conscious and more concerned to do and say 'the right thing'. This was particularly evident during the full evaluation stage, as by then facilitators had been given the opportunity to digest the critical remarks made in the interim study report. As one facilitator remarked to us at the end of a restorative session we had

---

[75] For fuller discussion of the improvements in practice witnessed in the full evaluation see R. Young and C. Hoyle, 'New Improved Police-Led Restorative Justice?' in A. von Hirsch, A. Bottoms, J. Roberts, K. Roach, and M. Schiff (eds.), *Criminal Justice and Restorative Justice: Competing or Complementary Paradigms?* (Oxford: Hart Publishing, 2003).

[76] Ibid.

observed: '[w]hen you've finished collecting your cases, you should come back and see how I really do them'. However, not all the changed practice observed could be attributed to cynical or instrumental behaviour. Some facilitators had clearly accepted the arguments presented in the interim report and altered their behaviour accordingly.[77]

Demonstrating the value of changed practices. Regardless of the reasons why practice changed, to the extent that the presence of researchers put facilitators on their 'best behaviour', the *Proceed with Caution* full evaluation represents police-led restorative justice under 'optimal conditions', in other words, a 'best case' scenario. To reiterate, one objective of the research was to find out whether police behaviour could be changed. The research process helped Thames Valley Police, in the aggregate, change facilitators' behaviour in the desired direction. It might be argued that there is little value in changing police practice through research if, as soon as the researchers leave the field, behaviour in large part reverts to normal. But this is to overlook another objective of the research, which was to measure the impact on participants of something that could justifiably be called police-led restorative justice.

The research team tested whether cases run 'according to script' were associated with more positive outcomes than those where facilitators run the session more in line with their own instinctive feel for what is appropriate. It was found that the better outcomes tended to result from the cases where the facilitator adhered reasonably closely to the script.[78] For example, 80 per cent of those who experienced the 'most restorative' cautions considered that the meeting had helped offenders to understand the effects of their behaviour compared with just 56 per cent of those who attended the 'least restorative' cautions. The results of the study thus provided a new incentive for Thames Valley Police, and other organizations using the scripted model of restorative justice, to put in place policies designed to secure the full implementation of this model. No such incentive could have been provided if the action-research had failed to secure at least a short-term improvement in policing practices.

In leaving the field the research team's final assessment was that its work had influenced many facilitators to change their practices in

---

[77] See further ibid.
[78] See Hoyle, Young, and Hill, n. 1 above, 58–60 for full analysis and discussion of this aspect of the research.

the short-term, a few of whom did so for principled reasons. More speculatively, the team believed that many more facilitators will be persuaded to alter their behaviour by the dissemination of the results of the research, and by the related renewed policy commitment by Thames Valley Police to its model of restorative cautioning. Whether front-line officers' working assumptions and norms about what constitutes best practice will in fact change in the light of the renewal of policy and the dissemination of the research findings is ultimately an empirical question.

The mere fact of carrying out research. One of the rarely acknowledged effects of research on policy is to keep vulnerable new initiatives in place, if only so that the research process can be brought to a conclusion. For example, the police-led experiment in reintegrative shaming in Canberra appears to have had its life substantially prolonged because of the huge research investment made in evaluating its effects. By contrast, across the rest of Australia police-led restorative justice was seen as problematic and other agencies have tended to adopt or take over the leading role.[79] In the case of the Thames Valley Police, there was never any suggestion that the research study was helping to maintain support for restorative cautioning within the police service, but it did become apparent that the involvement of researchers was helping to bolster the credibility of the initiative on the national and international stage.[80] This became problematic at one point in the research process, as we shall see later.

The dissemination strategy. Academics have become used to thinking in complex terms about the processes by which social institutions such as the police undergo change.[81] As noted in the first section of this chapter, the very complexity of policy formulation and its uncertain relationship with changes in practice mean that the lessons of the research process may be most likely to have an impact on policy (whether direct or indirect) if disseminated in a variety of

[79] K. Daly, 'Conferencing in Australia and New Zealand: Variations, Research Findings, and Prospects' in A. Morris and G. Maxwell (eds.), *Restorative Justice for Juveniles* (Oxford: Hart Publishing, 2001), 63–6.

[80] For an example see the way in which a reference to the Oxford University research was used by the then Chief Constable to introduce a paragraph setting out 'early findings' (none of which flowed from our research) in relation to the Thames Valley initiative: C. Pollard, 'If Your Only Tool is a Hammer, All Your Problems Will Look like Nails' in H. Strang and J. Braithwaite (eds.), *Restorative Justice and Civil Society* (Cambridge: Cambridge University Press, 2000) at 171.

[81] For examples see Garland, n. 24 above, 281–3 and Chan, n. 71 above.

settings. In the *Proceed with Caution* project the research team conceptualized the dissemination task as an ongoing one that involved producing 'position papers' for a variety of audiences as the fieldwork progressed. Examples include: a short piece in a police journal on the advantages of police services and academics working together in action-research projects;[82] three chapters in academic collections designed, respectively, to encourage the police and others to think critically about the notion of 'the victim', the relationship between restorative justice and punishment, and the process of translating police policy into police practice;[83] a shorter piece reflecting on how 'restorative justice' initiatives funded by the Youth Justice Board might best be evaluated, in a publication which specializes in providing briefings on topical matters;[84] a short piece in a journal aimed at practitioners working within the prison;[85] an overview of restorative justice for a reference work on criminal justice;[86] and reports prepared for dissemination within Thames Valley Police itself.

The research team also orally disseminated the emerging findings of the research in a variety of contexts and settings, all of which had the potential to influence policy. Sometimes there was scope to influence high-level policy-making, as with presentations made to the Youth Justice Board of England and Wales,[87] the Home Office,[88] and the Police Authority of Thames Valley Police.[89] Sometimes the

---

[82] N. Preston, C. Hoyle, and R. Young, 'Restoring the Faith' (a title substituted by the sub-editor of the journal for that originally submitted: 'Bloody Researchers and Hairy Big Officers') [1999] *Police Review*, 17 July, 28–30.

[83] R. Young, 'Integrating a Multi-Victim Perspective into Criminal Justice Through Restorative Justice Conferences' in A. Crawford and J. Goodey (eds.), *Integrating a Victim Perspective within Criminal Justice* (Aldershot: Ashgate, 2000), Young, n. 41 above, and Young and Hoyle, n. 76 above.

[84] R. Young and C. Hoyle, 'Examining the Guts of Restorative Justice' (2000) 40 *Criminal Justice Matters* 33–4.

[85] C. Hoyle, 'Restorative Justice in the Thames Valley: Changes in the Complaints and Discipline Process' (2000) 133 *Prison Service Journal* 37–40.

[86] C. Hoyle and R. Young, 'Restorative Justice' in M. McConville and G. Wilson (eds.), *The Handbook of The Criminal Justice Process* (Oxford: Oxford University Press, 2002).

[87] *Summary of the Restorative Cautioning Action-Research Project (revised)*, 17 Jan. 2002.

[88] *What are the Prospects for Police-Led Initiatives in Restorative Justice?*, paper delivered at a Home Office Research and Statistics Directorate Seminar, London, 8 Oct. 1999, and to the Thames Valley Restorative Justice Steering Group, Bicester, 13 Oct. 1999.

[89] *Summary of the Restorative Cautioning Action-Research Project*, 19 Oct. 2001.

objective was to influence police facilitators and their line managers, as in the case of several presentations of the interim study findings made to Thames Valley Police officers. Sometimes the influence of policy, if any, was bound to be more indirect, as in the case of presentations to academics, postgraduates, and practitioners at various universities and international conferences.[90] The final report of the research written for the Joseph Rowntree Foundation was itself 'launched' at national, local, and international events in May, June, and August 2002 respectively, resulting in a great deal of media attention.[91]

One oft-noted danger of spending too long in the field is that researchers 'go native', that is to say that they begin to identify with, rather than merely to 'appreciate', the perspective of those studied.[92] In this study the problem was more that the research team considered it necessary to criticize the natives mid-way through the research process itself.

It was noted above that there was no clear incentive for individual police facilitators to co-operate with the research project. In the early stages of the research the 'sales pitch' the research team adopted was that of helping individual cautioning officers improve the effectiveness of their practice. However, following the dissemination within the police service of a confidential report of the interim research findings, some facilitators became more wary about being observed, and facilitators at one research site withdrew all co-operation for a time. With the help of the Restorative Justice Consultancy, based at police HQ, permission to collect further cases from this area was eventually secured. This episode represented in

---

[90] e.g., papers were delivered by the research team at the conference 'Integrating a Victim Perspective within Criminal Justice: An International Conference', held by the University of Leeds at York in July 1998, at the British Society of Criminology Conference, John Moores University, Liverpool, 14 July 1999, at the international seminar held at Fitzwilliam College, University of Cambridge Seminar, 8 Oct. 2000, at the public session of the international seminar on restorative justice held at the University of Toronto in May 2001, at the University of Cambridge (diploma course for senior police officers) on 11 Sept. 2001, and at the University of Leuven (fifth international conference on restorative justice for juveniles) on 17 Sept. 2001.

[91] e.g., in May 2002 Carolyn Hoyle and Richard Young between them gave some 20 interviews to journalists from local and national newspapers, radio stations, and television programmes.

[92] See the discussion by C. Hoyle, *Negotiating Domestic Violence* (Oxford: Oxford University Press, 1998), 45–6.

microcosm a much larger problem faced in the research process. It is worth exploring this further as it bears directly on the issue of the relationship between research, policy, and practice.

The decision to combine in the interim report lengthy quotations from transcripts of cautions with sharply worded criticisms of facilitator behaviour was one of the most difficult taken during the course of this research project. The almost inevitable consequence was that individual facilitators would be able to discern when their own personal behaviour was being criticized and that this would cause resentment. Not only did the researchers regret the damage this was likely to do to the genuinely warm personal relations they had with some of these facilitators, but they feared that the research access needed for the full evaluation would be jeopardized. However, there was no point in collecting 'after' data through a full evaluation unless the research team had first made it crystal clear that current practice was often unethical, counter-productive, and non-restorative in orientation. If this was not done, it was extremely unlikely that policing practice would change. The critical/theoretical literature on policing indicates that to bring about changes in policing practice requires something more than an abstract summary of aggregate findings delivered in moderate language.[93]

This is not to suggest that action-research must always be carried out in this somewhat confrontational manner. Much of the action-research literature emphasizes the need for the researcher to facilitate a process of change that is owned by practitioners.[94] In various contexts and settings this may well be the most fruitful way for research to influence policy and practice, since it seems to hold out the hope of practitioners making an internal commitment to change, indeed of changing operational culture itself.[95] However, this facilitative style of action-research is likely to work best when there is room for practitioners to determine and implement the changes of practice thought desirable. In the case of the Thames Valley Police

[93] The stance of the research team was also influenced by the relative failure of a previous large-scale attempt by an academic team at carrying out action-research with the police. See C. Horton and D. Smith, *Evaluating Police Work: An Action Research Project* (London: Policy Studies Institute, 1988), 191–2.

[94] See, e.g., P. Reason and H. Bradbury (eds.), *Handbook of Action Research: Participative Inquiry and Practice* (London: Sage, 2001).

[95] See, e.g., A. Liebling, C. Elliot, and H. Arnold, 'Transforming the Prison: Romantic Optimism or Appreciative Realism?' (2001) 1 *Criminal Justice* 161.

initiative the task was different. It was the research team's job to examine a particular model in operation, and to do that it had to ensure that that model was implemented properly. In some cases this meant getting facilitators do things which ran directly contrary to their beliefs about effective practice.

Problems caused by 'attacking the natives' were also encountered at a police service level. Thames Valley Police, as an organization, responded constructively to the interim report. The confidential nature of the report meant that it was unlikely to arouse media, academic, or political concern about the restorative cautioning initiative. This probably helped to shape the reception it received within the police service, as subsequent events seem to suggest. For when the researchers indicated that they wished to publish some of the interim findings in a chapter in an edited collection devoted to international perspectives in restorative justice, some within the police service became (understandably) concerned about the political reception that might given to such a publication.[96] One reader of a draft, not a police officer, provided just one darkly worded oral comment on the piece: 'you should think carefully about whether you ever want to have research access to the police again'. Some officers in the police service made clear their view that the piece should not be published as it could prove 'damaging'.

However, the research team again took the view that the risk of endangering relations with the police, and of 'damaging' the restorative cautioning initiative, was one worth taking. Throughout the research process, senior Thames Valley Police officers were promoting the restorative cautioning initiative by talking and writing about it in various national and international settings.[97] But the implementation difficulties the research team had identified were not being discussed publicly, creating the danger that other police services might rush towards implementing the scripted model without any appreciation of the difficulties involved, or of the safeguards that needed to be in place. The team had also become aware of the view amongst some Thames Valley officers that implementation

---

[96] This piece was eventually published as Young, n. 41 above.

[97] See, e.g., the following publications by the then Chief Constable of Thames Valley Police: Pollard, 'Victims and the Criminal Justice System: A New Vision' [2000] Crim.L.R. 5, and n. 80 above. The extent to which the scripted model is shaping national and international policy on restorative justice is discussed in Young, n. 41 above, 195–7.

problems needed to be openly acknowledged and discussed, and some had encouraged us to make the interim findings more widely available.[98] As noted earlier, it is mistaken to assume that any criminal justice agency has a monolithic outlook.

In order to influence policy formation, both within Thames Valley Police and more broadly, the team thought it important to press ahead with publication. We explained our reasoning to the police and provided them with ample opportunity to suggest additions, corrections, and different interpretations of the evidence. Most suggestions made by the police for change were accepted and the draft chapter was improved in consequence, but this episode inevitably placed a strain on our relations with at least some parts of the Thames Valley Police service. Some potentially important chances to contribute to policy debates within, or hosted by, that service may have been lost as a result. On the other hand, the publication in question could now be drawn upon by others in those very same debates. Indeed, in the year of its publication it was included as part of the materials photocopied for use in the accredited training run by Cambridge University and Bramshill Police Training College for senior officers from forces throughout the United Kingdom.

Despite all these tensions and the determination of the team to maintain its independence, Thames Valley Police has facilitated a new two-year study by the same researchers of its use of restorative justice in the police complaints and discipline system.[99] This turn of events provides perhaps the best evidence of the determination of this police service to learn from research and improve its practice. The ominous warning that access to the police would be lost forever if the research team published its interim findings has proved to be baseless. Indeed, the decision to press ahead with publication may ultimately have helped our standing with the police. Individual officers have indicated repeatedly that they understand that our findings (whether positive or negative) would not be credible if the research team was seen as having lost its independence or critical

---

[98]   e.g., key police officers accepted our suggestion that all of the 40 or so restorative justice projects set up with funding from the Youth Justice Board in 1999–2000 should receive a copy of the interim report so that they could learn from the implementation difficulties encountered in the Thames Valley.

[99]   The full research team for this project is Karen Cooper, Roderick Hill, Carolyn Hoyle, and Richard Young, all based at the Centre for Criminological Research, the University of Oxford.

edge. Once again we can see that the inter-relationships between the research enterprise and policy are complex and the considerations militating for or against any given course of action are always more finely balanced than might first appear.

Conclusion

In this chapter we have attempted to show the complexity of the inter-relationships between theory, research, and policy. An argument has been advanced for oscillating between different levels of theory, different styles of research, and different settings within which to influence policy. Through a discussion of 'adaptive theory' we have explored how critical/theoretical research and policy-led evaluations may complement one another. The former can inform the latter, and the results of the latter may serve to confirm, refute, or call for modification of the positions taken in the former. When these research traditions are brought together in a synthesized manner the persuasiveness of criminological knowledge, and thus its impact on policy and practice, can be enhanced.

However, in studying the police we need to see not only the forest, the trees, the wood from which the trees are made, and the potential for that wood to be refashioned. We also need to understand the environment which shapes the forest and everything in it. In other words the political, social, cultural, and economic context within which the police operate must be taken into account when seeking to understand police culture, police practice, and the potential for it to be changed. This needs to be made more concrete, as follows.

This chapter has identified an apparent contradiction and an apparent truth. *CFP* had little influence on police policy, and *AAPS* more so but less than *PWC*. The apparent contradiction is that both of the latter projects drew heavily on the theoretical foundations of *CFP*, where, we saw earlier, it was declared that the police were unreformable in major respects without fundamental socio-economic and political change.[100] Is the difference in the impact of these projects due to *PWC* being action-research, while the others were less explicitly reform-oriented? There is an element of truth to

---

[100] The success of *CFP* in influencing policy should be noted by commentators like Travers, n. 60 above, who insist that the preconceptions of 'political' researchers undermine the effectiveness of their policy recommendations.

this, though it begs the question why the police service in *PWC* sought reform and wanted to act on the results of research, while in *AAPS* and *CFP* they (and the Home Office) did not. Perhaps the important question is not 'do they want reform?', but 'what kind of reform do they want?'. The victim research discussed earlier shows that no matter how closely researchers identify with the ostensible policy goals of government and criminal justice agencies, when governments decide to adopt a particular policy, the persuasiveness or otherwise of applicable research becomes irrelevant. Government wanted reform of victim participation procedures, but not the type of reform that the researchers believed followed logically from their results.

We do, however, still hold to the position that there is no contradiction. *CFP* made the point that policing in general was crime control oriented, but did not claim that all policing was unfair, repressive, or counter-progressive. A restorative approach to cautioning goes no more against the fundamentals of policing in capitalist society than does old-style cautioning. From this perspective, the shift to restorative cautioning requires cultural change of a fairly modest kind (and securing that change was difficult enough), but it does not require any change to the majority of policing activity. This is less true of Thames Valley Police's broader restorative justice programme. Thames Valley Police itself quite explicitly intended that its restorative cautioning initiative would have a beneficial impact on its organizational culture and has also recognized the need to reform other aspects of its practices. It has introduced restorative justice values and processes into other aspects of its work, including dispute resolution, the handling of internal personnel matters, and the handling of complaints by members of the public against police officers. It remains important, however, to recognize the enormity of the task the police have undertaken and to argue the case for keeping in focus the need for still wider structural reforms of policing, reforms that may be possible only if social relations more generally are reconfigured.[101]

The apparent truth is that the more policy oriented a research project is the more influential it will be on policy. This would be a

---

[101] The importance of such structural changes is discussed in Chan, n. 71 above. The importance of the reforms of policing which accompanied the introduction of family group conferencing in New Zealand is discussed by H. Blagg, 'A Just Measure of Shame?' (1997) 37 *British Journal of Criminology* 481 at 485.

naïve and superficial reading. Instead, we argue that the more peripheral to core policing a theoretically/critically-based project is, the more influential it is likely to be, in the same way that a non-theoretical/critical project that is central to policing is also likely to be highly influential. To put this another way, theoretical projects that are highly critical of peripheral police practices may bring about policy change and perhaps even changes in practice, but projects in this tradition which criticize core policing activities are likely to be brushed aside. Similarly, action-research aimed at helping the police service achieve its own goals more effectively is more likely to bring about change than research that seeks to bring a crime control-oriented police force into line with due process norms.

How, then, do we account for the moderate success of *AAPS* in the light of this discussion? Changes to PACE Code of Practice C almost certainly led to a reduced use of ploys by the police. Coupled with changes to the solicitors' own 'rule books' to make them more responsive to the needs of their clients, the take-up of legal advice in police stations and its effectiveness in protecting suspects and challenging coercive interrogation and custody practices undoubtedly rose. Is this not fundamental to policing? This is answered by observing two developments. First, the police, spurred on by bodies such as the Audit Commission, have become more 'problem-oriented' and proactive in policing. The use of informers and surveillance techniques to gather evidence went up dramatically in the mid to late 1990s. These techniques supplement interrogation-based ways of securing evidence, reducing the police dependence on interrogation.[102] Policing, in other words, adapts to changes in its legal and policy environment (as we documented in many ways in *CFP* in the light of the immediate changes brought about by PACE). Policing does not stay the same in detail, but it tends to remain similar in essence, and identical in objectives and the capacity to achieve those objectives.

Sometimes, though, the police need the help of government legislation. No sooner had legal advice levels and effectiveness risen than the government drastically eroded the right of silence in the Criminal Justice and Public Order Act 1994. Following this Act the provision of legal advice to suspects has impeded interrogation only infrequently. In many situations the ethical advice to suspects is now to the effect that answering police questions could be damaging and

---

[102] For a longer discussion see Sanders and Young, n. 22 above, Chapter 12.

that not answering them could be damaging. The obstacles to defence lawyers could be removed because they had been, in reality, 'sidelined'.[103]

As we argued earlier, research on, and aimed at improving, policing has to take a broader and longer look at policing than the particular practice or power in question—something that ethnomethodologically-based 'thick' accounts such as advocated by Travers cannot do. It may even be that on a longer view of restorative cautioning the apparently beneficent effects of *PWC* will be less apparent. That is why we have written elsewhere that it remains unclear whether the recent enthusiasm for restorative justice will result in more inclusionary freedom-enhancing ways of responding to street-level crime or simply create new sites for unaccountable extensions of state power wielded to exclusionary ends.[104] The first-named author adheres to a more fluid and open-ended model of social change than that inherent in the Marxist-inspired position taken by the second-named author, and is thus somewhat more optimistic on this point. Only time, and critical/theoretical research, will tell.

As if the world 'out there' were not difficult enough to deal with, there is also the academic world in which we work to consider. First, the deadlines for bidding for Home Office contracts have become increasingly tight, to the point of absurdity. Sometimes as little as two weeks is provided for potential research teams to be identified, designs to be drawn up, literature reviews completed, and tender documents submitted. Secondly, the typical specification of how quickly the Home Office wishes the research to begin and be completed, how many interim reports it will need, how many data it demands be collected and analysed, and how little money it is prepared to pay, is designed to depress the most indefatigable researcher. Good quality research is very difficult to conduct under such a regime.[105]

---

[103] E. Cape, 'Sidelining Defence Lawyers: Police Station Advice after *Condron*' (1997) 1 *International Journal of Evidence and Proof* 386.

[104] A. Sanders and R. Young, 'From Suspect to Trial' in M. Maguire, R. Morgan, and R. Reiner (eds.), *Oxford Handbook of Criminology* (3rd edn., Oxford: Oxford University Press, 2002).

[105] One of us recently decided not to bid for some Home Office work of this nature. No other academic did either. The Home Office therefore had to carry out the work itself with the aid of a market research company. It quickly realized that its initial research specification set out in the tender documents was unrealistic and drastically cut back on the planned data collection.

Thirdly, academics are currently under enormous pressure to do more with less. As staff–student ratios worsen, as library budgets and research grants are cut, as responsibility (but rarely power) is devolved to academic departments (now 'budget centres'), so increases the pressure to run several research projects simultaneously (to generate income for one's department in the form of 'overheads', income which is maximized by seeking funding from *non*-charitable sources), publish scholarly books and articles (so as to generate more income through the Research Assessment Exercise), to teach better (to satisfy external funding bodies), to teach more students (to bring in more income), and to carry ever greater administrative burdens. In this new research context it becomes difficult to justify writing short articles for practitioner journals (since these count for nothing in the Research Assessment Exercise) and to engage in other forms of activity designed to influence policy (but with no measurable outputs or gain to the university). During term-time, in particular, the priority of most academics has to be to deal with the next pressing duty or engagement, and this militates against the kind of reflective oscillation between theory, research, and policy that we have advocated. In a state of near exhaustion it is difficult to see beyond the next tree. The very analyses we deploy when analysing the police can be turned on us to interesting effect. The habitus of the typical academic is becoming ever more miserable in the light of structural changes in the field of academia.

But let us end on a happier note. As past collaborators with Roger Hood in teaching and research, we can testify to his immense breadth and depth of criminological knowledge, his ability to integrate historical, sociological, and philosophical insights in his praxis, his capacity to juggle the competing demands of university, college, journal and book editors, and grant-givers, and to his challenging habit of pointing out all the ways in which our ingrained habits of thinking about crime and criminal justice are blinkered. Long may he continue to call us out of our narrow glens.

9

The Development of Parole and the Role of Research in its Reform

Stephen Shute*

Since its inception in 1967 the parole system in England and Wales has been the subject of much comment and criticism.[1] It has also undergone many fundamental changes. From tentative beginnings it has, in thirty-five years, become a significant form of release for long-term prisoners. The purpose of this chapter is to examine the extent to which both the creation of the scheme and the numerous reforms that have been made to it subsequently can be attributed to the influence of criminological research. The term 'research' has been construed widely to include not just the findings of empirical studies but also the arguments of academics and others who have examined parole's shortcomings from a theoretical or principled standpoint.

It is fitting that a chapter on this topic should appear in a book published in honour of Roger Hood. During his long and distinguished career he has taken a keen interest in parole. Between 1972

*I am grateful to the Max-Planck Institute for the Fellowship awarded me which made it possible to devote time to this chapter.

[1] Professor Donald West's 1973 definition has stood the test of time: '[p]arole, as it is understood in the United Kingdom, is a procedure whereby a sentence imposed by a court of justice may be varied by administrative action': see D.J. West, 'Parole in England: An Introductory Explanation' in D.J. West (ed.), *The Future of Parole* (London: Duckworth, 1972), at 1. For the purposes of this chapter use of the term 'parole' will be confined to the discretionary release of those serving determinate sentences of imprisonment. The chapter will not, therefore, discuss the release of those serving sentences of 'life imprisonment'. It is also confined to parole as it operates in England and Wales.

and 1973 he served as a member of the newly-constituted Parole
Board. In the mid-1970s he wrote a series of influential papers which
explored the system's defects and put forward radical proposals for
change. In the late 1980s he became a member of the Carlisle
Committee which had been asked to review the creaking structures
and suggest possible reforms. Astute readers of that Committee's
Report will readily detect his influence on its thinking. Finally, in the
1990s, he and I joined forces to work on a longitudinal study which
had been designed to examine the impact on the system of the
changes made by the Criminal Justice Act 1991. These factors
alone would be reason enough to write a chapter of this kind. But
for me, a former student who was moved to take up criminology
professionally by Roger Hood's inspirational teaching in Oxford
in the 1980s, it has been a special privilege to be asked to be its
author.

The Roots of the Modern Parole System

The first significant step towards the development of a modern
system of parole in England and Wales was the creation of a 'ticket
of leave' system for transportees. This empowered the executive to
reduce the restrictions placed on convicts once they had been in the
colonies for a certain period of time.[2] As transportation drew to an
end—it finally concluded in 1867—the perceived advantages of a
system of early release were sufficient to convince the Government
that the penalty of 'penal servitude' (first introduced in 1853[3])
should include a mechanism whereby an offender could be released
early on 'licence' after having served a stipulated portion of his
sentence.[4] Although a critical report from a Royal Commission in

---

[2] Paradoxically, however, the existence of the ticket of leave system may have
'helped to postpone the introduction of a more formal parole system in England'.
See A.K. Bottomley, 'Parole in Transition: A Comparative Study of Origins, Develop-
ments, and Prospects for the 1990s' (1990) 12 *Crime and Justice*, M. Tonry and
N. Morris (eds.), 319–74, at 326. Bottomley served as a member of the Parole
Board from 1980 to 1982.

[3] Penal Servitude Act 1853.

[4] The sentence of penal servitude was eventually abolished by s. 1(1) of the
Criminal Justice Act 1948.

1863[5] led to that scheme being supplemented by a system of 'marks', this did not signify a general loss of confidence in early release, and around the turn of the century two further developments occurred. First, in the wake of the Gladstone Committee Report of 1895, the Prison Act 1898 introduced a system of unconditional remission for all prisoners serving ordinary sentences of imprisonment. Then, the Prevention of Crime Act 1908 included in the new sentences of Borstal Detention and Preventive Detention a procedure whereby preventive detainees could be released by the Home Secretary on the advice of an advisory board, subject to a maximum period of detention of ten years, and Borstal trainees could be released at the direction of the Prison Commissioners, subject to a maximum period of detention of three years.[6]

While these developments provided the foundation for later changes, some sixty years were to pass before any serious attempt was made to turn them into a national system of parole. The stimulus for reform was the publication in 1964 of an influential report entitled *Crime—A Challenge To Us All* by a Labour Party Study Group chaired by Lord Longford. The Study Group was concerned about the 'gross overcrowding' plaguing British prisons.[7] As a way of easing this overcrowding it recommended that the Home Secretary should establish a 'Parole Board' with a power similar to that of the Prison Department in respect of Borstal trainees to release prisoners under supervision once they had served at least a quarter of their sentences.[8] Soon that idea was adopted by other leading figures in the House of Lords, notably Viscount Dilhorne, a former Lord Chancellor, and Lord Parker of Waddington, the then Lord Chief Justice. Concerned that the Murder (Abolition of Death Penalty) Bill would put long-term determinate prisoners in a less favourable

[5] *Report of the Commission Appointed to Inquire into the Operation of the Acts Relating to Transportation and Penal Servitude* (Reports from Commissioners, XXI Sess., 1863). The Commission looked into the operation of the legislation relating to transportation and penal servitude and concluded that penal servitude was not 'sufficiently dreaded' (see *Report and Appendix*, vol. 1, para. 31). The Commission recommended (para. 40) that 'a system of marks', such as that found in Western Australia, 'might with advantage be introduced into this country, with some modifications'.

[6] For an excellent account of these events see Sir Leon Radzinowicz and R. Hood, *A History of English Criminal Law and Its Administration from 1750, Volume 5, The Emergence of Penal Policy* (London: Stevens and Sons, 1986).

[7] (London: Labour Party, 1964), 43.   [8] Ibid., 44.

position than lifers, who at that time could on average expect to be released from prison after about nine years, they argued that the Home Secretary should be given 'much wider powers of releasing on licence in all cases—and not just murder cases—where long sentences have been imposed'.[9] They also moved an amendment to the Bill which would have given the Home Secretary the power to release murderers on licence once they had spent five years in custody.[10] That amendment was ultimately withdrawn, but as a *quid pro quo* the Government agreed to put forward proposals of its own, a pledge that was honoured with the publication in 1965 of a White Paper, *The Adult Offender*.[11] A 'central feature' of the White Paper was the suggestion that prisoners whose 'character and record' rendered them 'suitable' should be released on parole earlier than would otherwise have been the case. The White Paper offered the following argument in support of this proposal:

Prisoners who do not of necessity have to be detained for the protection of the public are in some cases more likely to be made into decent citizens if, before completing the whole of their sentence, they are released under supervision with a liability to recall if they do not behave. Other countries have used systems of this kind with success and the Government have concluded that the time has come to ask for powers to adopt a system of early release on licence in this country.[12]

As the above passage reveals, developments overseas, particularly in other common law jurisdictions, had a strong influence on the Government's thinking. It had not gone unnoticed that every Ameri-

---

[9] See H.L. Debs., vol. 269, col. 406, 5 Aug. 1965, *per* Viscount Dilhorne. He further argued (col. 408) that 'there should be a Parole Board to advise the Home Secretary in all these cases'. Lord Parker of Waddington supported Viscount Dilhorne's suggestions and recommended to the Government that it should 'invite the Royal Commission on Penal Reform' to consider the matter. See also H.L. Debs., vol. 268, col. 473, 19 July 1965, where Viscount Dilhorne said: 'I have long been in favour of there being much wider powers to release on licence, for I think that a moment may come when it would be to the advantage of society and of the prisoner if a man could be released on licence, and if that chance is not taken reformation may become impossible'.

[10] Ibid., col. 405. See also Carlisle Committee Report, *The Parole System in England and Wales* Cm 532 (London: HMSO, 1988), para. 19, but note that the *Report* mistakenly states that the amendment applied to 'those serving long determinate sentences'. In fact, Viscount Dilhorne made it quite clear (see col. 406) that the amendment applied only where there had been 'a conviction for murder'.

[11] Cmnd 2852 (London: HMSO, 1965).

[12] Ibid., at para. 4.

can state had by the mid-1930s established some system of discretionary early release,[13] that a national parole board had been in existence in Canada since the late 1950s,[14] and that parole boards were by then operating in both Australia and New Zealand.[15] But it was also important that parole had the support of a number of leading British academics. Three figures—Professors Rupert Cross, Nigel Walker, and J.E. Hall Williams—made particularly important contributions.

Writing in *The Listener* in 1962, Cross suggested that 'the Prison Commissioners (or some body of persons acting on their behalf)' should be empowered to release a prisoner early on licence if they thought him 'suitable'.[16] Such an arrangement, Cross argued, would maintain protection for society, as a prisoner would be released only after he had mended his ways. It would also, he said, ensure that there was no adverse effect on deterrence, since a longer sentence would have originally been passed.[17] Walker, a career-long champion of greater indeterminacy in sentencing, was the second senior

---

[13] See Bottomley, n. 2 above, 322, drawn from D.J. Rothman, *Conscience and Convenience: The Asylum and Its Alternatives in Progressive America* (Boston, Mass.: Little, Brown, and Co., 1980). Parole was also a feature of the US Model Penal Code. For a comparison between the English parole system and that provided for in the Model Penal Code see E. Shea, 'Parole Philosophy in England and America' in West, n. 1 above, 66.

[14] The board was set up under the provisions of the Parole Act 1958. For an excellent discussion of the development of parole in Canada and the United States, see Bottomley, n. 2 above.

[15] Many of those who spoke in favour of parole in Parliament also referred to developments overseas. Sir John Hobson, e.g., observed that, in 1964, 60% of all releases from prisons in America were on parole. See the debate on the Second Reading of the Criminal Justice Bill, H.C. Debs., vol. 738, col. 194, 12 Dec. 1966. This figure may have been drawn from an article by Manuel López-Rey which stated that 'by 1964 63.7% of all those released from State and Federal institutions were released conditionally': see 'Release and Provisional Release of Sentenced Prisoners' (1966) 6 *British Journal of Criminology* 236 at 258.

[16] 'Indeterminate Prison Sentences' (1962) 67 *The Listener* 289 at 289. Cross was willing to consider a minimum qualifying period of six months' imprisonment (for further discussion of the minimum qualifying period see 402–406 below) but did not want the judiciary to have a discretionary power to set the minimum at the point of sentence.

[17] Cross regarded it as an advantage of his scheme (see ibid., 289) that cases could be 'reconsidered from time to time in the light of the effect of prison life on the prisoner'. He admitted that the retributive principle of just deserts might be threatened, but he said that the threat was small because deserts were not 'the kind of things that can be measured in terms of the length of a prison sentence'. Four years

academic to favour the introduction of parole. Under the terms of his proposal the executive would be allowed 'to grant earlier release under supervision to those who seem ready for it'.[18] This, he said, would 'make it possible to ensure that the penal measures applied to a serious offender were based on experience of dealing with similar offenders, and could be modified when his progress justified this, instead of being rigidly prescribed for years ahead'.[19] The final member of the distinguished triumvirate, Hall Williams,[20] though more sceptical about the benefits of indeterminate sentencing, nonetheless supported the idea that the prisoner or the Home Secretary should be given a right, once a certain portion of the sentence had been served,[21] to apply to a 'Sentence Review Board' for early release.[22] On receipt of such an application, Hall Williams argued, a 'private hearing' should be convened at which the prisoner would have 'the right to be represented and to be heard'. At its conclusion the decision and reasons would be 'publicly announced'.[23]

later he again defended his position, saying that it was 'high time that some kind of parole system was tried out': see R. Cross, 'Penal Reform in 1965—A Mass of Unexplained and Unfounded Assumptions' [1966] *Crim.L.R.* 184 at 190. He added, however, (at 194) that the proposals with regard to parole in *The Adult Offender*, n. 11 above, were 'based on the unexplained though, it is hoped, correct, assumptions that release on licence at different times of prisoners serving sentences of the same length will not produce prison discontent of unmanageable proportions, and that means exist for determining the optimum moment of release'. See also R. Cross, *The English Sentencing System* (London: Butterworths, 1971), at 2: '[t]here is no magical accuracy in the pronouncement of a prison sentence of a particular length by a judge and that is why the introduction of parole by the Criminal Justice Act 1967 is so devoutly to be welcomed'.

[18] N. Walker, 'The Sentence of the Court' (1962) 67 *The Listener* 1099 and 1121, at 1100. Unlike Cross, however, Walker saw this as only the first phase of reform and argued that later the executive should be allowed 'to operate within the limits fixed by the law, as the courts operate at the moment'. Walker served as a member of the Parole Board from 1986 to 1989.

[19] Ibid., 1121.

[20] See J.E. Hall Williams, 'Alternatives to Definite Sentences' (1964) 80 *Law Quarterly Review* 41 at 57. Hall Williams served as a member of the Board from 1970 to 1972.

[21] Hall Williams suggested six months.

[22] Hall Williams envisaged that a judge, who would be 'assisted by a number of persons with experience of prisoners and with social science or psychological training', would chair the Board.

[23] Hall Williams, n. 20 above, 61. Hall Williams estimated that 'something like 700 cases would fall to be reviewed annually'.

These suggestions may have had their merits, but they all relied on a questionable assumption, *viz.* that the relevant decision-making body would be able to detect reliably when a prisoner was 'suitable' (Cross) or 'ready' (Walker) for release.[24] That view had a long pedigree in Anglo-American criminology. Prominent exponents were Ernest W. Burgess and Thorsten Sellin, who said in their introduction to Lloyd E. Ohlin's 1951 monograph, *Selection for Parole: A Manual of Parole Prediction*:

> If parole is to be most effective, a prisoner should be placed on parole at the moment when—taking into account the limitations of the law and the sentence, the effect of institutional life, and the prospect of social rehabilitation—both he and the community could profit most by such a step.[25]

Yet no strong empirical evidence had emerged to back up this claim. Nor was there evidence to support the related claim that many prisoners reach a point in their sentence (a 'peak') at which their propensity to reoffend is at its lowest, and after which a deterioration sets in and the threat posed by them starts to rise. Some politicians picked up on this issue in the ensuing Parliamentary debates. Mr T.L. Iremonger, for example, speaking for the Conservative opposition, quoted at length from a well-known book, *Criminology and Penology*,[26] in which the American writers Richard Korn and Lloyd McCorkle argued that, although much attention had been given to the importance of selecting the 'right moment' to release a prisoner on parole, little guidance had been forthcoming on how this might be achieved.[27]

But the warnings of a few Parliamentarians and academics— Rupert Cross, for example, who was, as we have seen, otherwise favourably disposed to parole, asked whether the idea of a peak in

---

[24] See also Mr Sam Silkin's suggestion, made during the debates on the Second Reading of the Criminal Justice Bill in 1966, that it would be desirable to develop 'a far more thorough system of classification procedure, such as exists in California, after a man has been committed to a custodial institution, so that it is possible, within the limits of human judgment, to foretell the kind of response a man is likely to make both while within the institution and ultimately when he is placed on parole': H.C. Debs., vol. 738, col. 176, 12 Dec. 1966.

[25] (New York: Irvington Publishing, 1951), at 10.

[26] (New York: Holt, Rinehart and Winston, 1959), at 613.

[27] Standing Committee A, H.C. Debs., session 1966–67, vol. 2, col. 723, 7 March 1967. He also said (col. 726): '[i]n my own view, the word "treatment" as a term of art in penal jargon fills me with the utmost scepticism'.

training was 'an empirically established proposition or a statement of Prison Department lore'[28]—made little impact on the Government's thinking. Thus, in an influential passage of the White Paper, the Government supported the introduction of parole by linking it both to the discredited notion of a 'peak' and to the then emerging ideas of treatment, training, and rehabilitation:

What is proposed is that a prisoner's date of release should be largely dependent upon his response to training and his likely behaviour on release. A considerable number of long-term prisoners reach a recognisable peak in their training at which they may respond to generous treatment, but after which, if kept in prison, they may go downhill. To give such prisoners the opportunity of supervised freedom at the right moment may be decisive in securing their return to decent citizenship.[29]

And later the Home Secretary, Mr Roy Jenkins, relied upon the same argument as part of his Parliamentary defence of the new scheme.[30]

[28] See R. Cross, 'Penal Reform in 1965—A Mass of Unexplained and Unfounded Assumptions' [1966] Crim.L.R. 184 at 191. Other subsequent critics included: (i) Roger Hood who described the 'peak in training' as 'mythical' (see 'The Case against Executive Control over time in Custody: A Rejoinder to Professor Walker's Criticisms' [1975] Crim.L.R. 545 at 547); (ii) E.E. Barnard, a member of the Board from 1974 to 1977, who wrote (see 'Parole Decision-Making in Britain' (1976) 4 International Journal of Criminology and Penology 145 at 147): '[i]t is safe to say that the theory underlying the proposal to introduce parole to Britain rested on weak empirical foundations'; and (iii) Neil Morgan (see 'The Shaping of Parole in England and Wales' [1983] Crim.L.R. 137) who said (at 142): '[i]t is unclear where the idea of a peak in training originated; certainly it has never found empirical support'. See also 144 where he described the notion of a specific peak as 'outrageous'.

[29] N. 11 above, para. 5. See also Crime—A Challenge To Us All, n. 7 above, 44, where rehabilitative language was also used: '[w]e doubt the value of keeping men in prison after they have learned their lesson'.

[30] See the debate on the Second Reading of the Criminal Justice Bill, H.C. Debs., vol. 738, col. 70, 12 Dec. 1966. Similarly, Lord Stonham, the Minister of State, said in the debates in the House of Lords on the committee stage of the Criminal Justice Bill that one of the considerations to be taken into account when granting parole was whether a prisoner 'has reached a point in his sentence in which further training is unlikely to improve his prospects of leading a good and useful life on release': H.L. Debs., vol. 283, cols. 746–747, 12 June 1967. The Parole Board made it clear in its first Annual Report (see Report of the Parole Board for 1968 (London: HMSO, 1969), 290, at para. 49) that the White Paper's statement had been of considerable assistance to it in formulating criteria for the selection of suitable candidates for parole, although in the Board's hands the idea was stripped of much of its rehabilitative baggage and recast in terms of a notion of a gradual decline rather than a 'peak' (para. 52): '[c]ustodial conditions too long continued', the Board said, 'can undermine a man's good resolutions or destroy such beneficial changes of attitude as may have taken place'.

Why might policy-makers have been drawn to claims with so little empirical foundation? The most likely answer is that they offered a convenient way of providing a veneer of theoretical respectability to policies which were driven by other, more pragmatic, concerns.[31] One of these was the belief that parole might contribute to the maintenance of discipline in prisons.[32] Even more significant, though, was the thought that parole would provide a quick and relatively inexpensive solution to the pressing problem of prison overcrowding. That idea had been at the heart of Lord Longford's 1964 report and was also relied upon, albeit in more muted terms, by the Government's White Paper, which saw it as an advantage of parole that it 'would incidentally... go some way to relieve the existing overcrowding in prisons'.[33] In the years that have followed, this justification has (as we shall see) continued to play an important part in determining the shape of the scheme.[34]

---

[31] Indeed, the *Carlisle Committee Report* (n. 10 above, para. 22) took the view that the scheme had been 'conceived for primarily political and pragmatic reasons'. Neil Morgan, however, argues that the 'vacuum cleaner thesis'—the idea that parole was introduced to reduce the prison population—and the 'control thesis'—the idea that parole would assist in maintaining prison discipline—are 'too simplistic' an explanation. Observing that the 'first formulations of parole predate the particularly serious overcrowding crisis of 1966/67', Morgan claims that it was 'ideological factors' that 'both promoted and shaped the system': see N. Morgan, 'The Shaping of Parole in England and Wales' [1983] *Crim.L.R.* 137 at 137–9.

[32] See *The Adult Offender*, n. 11 above, at para. 8, where it was argued that parole would 'greatly assist the task of prison administration'. The belief that parole can have a beneficial effect on prison discipline has endured. In 1981 the *Home Office Review of Parole in England and Wales* (London: Home Office, 1981), May 1981 argued (at para. 28): '[t]here can be little doubt that, however cynically the parole system may be regarded by some prisoners, its discretionary nature plays a part in control within prisons.... The balance of advantage is difficult to assess but the net effect of the parole system is probably a benefit to prison discipline'.

[33] See n. 11 above, para. 8. P. Morris and F. Beverly, *On Licence: A Study of Parole* (London: Wiley, 1975), 159, argue that when parole was introduced it 'was regarded as a piece of penal machinery designed to do little more than reduce the prison population and to negate the necessity for a large and expensive programme of prison building'. See also F.H. McClintock, 'The Future of Parole' in J. Freeman (ed.), *Prisons Past and Future* (London: Heinemann, 1978), at 125; and T.P. Morris, 'The Parole System—Executive Justice' in C. Brewer *et al.* (eds.), *Criminal Welfare on Trial* (London: The Social Affairs Unit, 1981), at 28–9.

[34] The 1981 *Home Office Review of Parole*, n. 32 above, stated that one of parole's main justifications was its effect on the prison population (see paras. 50–52).

The Structure of the New Scheme

The publication of the 1965 White Paper marked a watershed in the history of parole. Over the next few years the discussion centred not so much on the general merits of the scheme but on its detailed structure. Particularly contentious was the Government's proposal that parole decisions should be taken by the Home Secretary.[35] This encountered fierce opposition in Parliament on the ground that it would place too much power in the hands of the minister. One fear was that ministerial control would result in an over-generous use of parole, especially if a Home Secretary felt it necessary to use the scheme to ease prison overcrowding.[36] Others took the opposite view. They worried that ministers might use parole too parsimoniously. Sir John Hobson (a former Attorney General), for example, argued that the Minister would be 'apt to be timid and rigid' and would not be willing to take the risks that 'a strong body with independence' might be able to take.[37]

In the end, the combined influence of these two groups was sufficient to cause the Government to rethink its strategy, and revised proposals were drawn up based on a three-tier system: a Local Review Committee (LRC) would first consider the case; next, the Home Office would forward some of these cases to a Parole Board ('a non-judicial, independent, advisory body'[38]) for it to make its recommendation; and, finally, the Home Secretary would consider the Board's recommendations and make the ultimate decision on release. This 'compromise'[39] was enshrined in legislation with the enactment of the Criminal Justice Act 1967, sections 59 to 62.[40] A

---

[35] The idea was that he would first receive advice from informal local committees in each prison.

[36] See the remarks of Mr T.L. Iremonger, Standing Committee A, H.C. Debs., session 1966–67, vol. 2, col. 724, 7 Mar. 1967. For the Home Secretary's attempts to allay those fears, see col. 734.

[37] Standing Committee A, H.C. Debs., session 1966–67, vol. 2, col. 706, 1 Mar. 1967. Sir John had been a former member of the Home Office's Advisory Committee on the Treatment of Offenders. On an earlier occasion he supported his argument by referring to information about the USA that had been provided to him by the Cambridge Institute of Criminology. This, he said, revealed that there was 'no example there where the power of release on parole is done by executive administration, and none where it is done by a political Minister': see H.C. Debs., vol. 738, col. 193, 12 Dec. 1966.

[38] *Home Office Review of Parole*, n. 32 above, at para. 6.   [39] Ibid.

[40] Although a statutory scheme, the power to release prisoners on parole is said to derive ultimately from the Royal Prerogative of Mercy: see S. McCabe, 'The Powers

Parole Board was first constituted in November 1967, and in the same year a Parole Unit was established within the Home Office to handle the administrative arrangements. Prisoners became eligible for parole under this system once they had served one-third of their sentence or twelve months, whichever expired later. But they retained their existing entitlement to one-third remission.[41] The first releases on parole began on 1 April 1968.

Which Cases Reached the Board, 1968–93?

A key feature of the agreed compromise was that the decision whether or not to refer a case considered by an LRC to the Parole Board would lie not with the Board but with the Home Office. Initially this power was used very sparingly: in the first few months of the scheme almost all LRC 'unsuitables' and the majority of 'suitables' were filtered out.[42] But the Board objected to this restriction, and in June 1968 its representations bore some fruit when the Home Secretary announced his intention to refer all 'suitables' and some 'unsuitables' to the Board.[43] The new policy was clearly of great benefit to the former group. However, the referral rate for 'unsuitables' remained extremely low: just 2.5 per cent of such cases were referred to the Board between 1 April and 31 December 1968 (see Table 9:1).[44] This low referral rate underscored the importance of the LRC's decision—if it was against parole a prisoner's

and Purposes of the Parole Board' [1985] *Crim.L.R.* 489 at 490. McCabe was a member of the Parole Board from 1981 to 1984. For a good general discussion see A.T.H. Smith, 'The Prerogative of Mercy' [1983] *Public Law* 398.

[41] In 1940 remission had been standardized for prisoners and convicts and increased to one-third of the sentence: see S.I. 1940 No. 1217, reg. 5(1), 10 July 1940.

[42] There were 4,764 prisoners who became eligible for parole on 1 April 1968. After 417 prisoners had opted out, this left 4,347 prisoners whose cases were considered by LRCs (see Table 9:2 below). Of these, 1,032 (23.7%) were considered 'suitable'. However, only 480 (46.5%) of these 'suitables' were then referred to the Board. A further 3,315 (76.3%) were considered 'unsuitable' (see Table 9:1 below) and just 61 (1.8%) of these cases were referred to the Board.

[43] See H.C. Debs., Written Answers, vol. 767, col. 63, 25 June 1968. But the Home Secretary (Mr Callaghan) also made it clear that he intended to retain his right to veto any favourable recommendation made by the Board where he felt it appropriate to do so. For a discussion of this right, see 407–412 below.

[44] Between 1 April 1968 and 31 December 1968, 5,008 prisoners became eligible for parole. After 493 prisoners had opted out, this left 4,515 whose cases were considered by LRCs (see Table 9:2). Of these, 1,053 (23.3%) were considered 'suitable'. All these

TABLE 9:1   Local Review Committee 'Unsuitables', 1968–1993 (source: *Parole Board Annual Reports*)

Year	Number of Prisoners Considered 'Unsuitable' by LRCs	Number and Percentage of 'Unsuitables' Referred to the Parole Board		Number and Percentage of 'Unsuitables' Recommended for Parole by the Parole Board		Percentage of Referred Cases Recommended for Parole by the Parole Board
	N	N	Per Cent	N	Per Cent	Per Cent
1968*	3315	61	1.8	18	0.5	29.5
1968**	3462	85	2.5	33	1.0	38.8
1969***	4585	373	8.1	164	3.6	44.0
1970	5243	996	19.0	295	5.6	29.6
1971	6193	1124	18.1	299	4.8	26.6
1972	5524	1040	18.8	275	5.0	26.4
1973	5914	1302	22.0	284	4.8	21.8
1974	5830	1774	30.4	385	6.6	21.7
1975	5561	1691	30.4	581	10.4	34.4
1976	5212	1539	29.5	538	10.3	35.0
1977	5123	1593	31.1	513	10.0	32.2
1978	5023	1765	35.1	406	8.1	23.0
1979	5028	1794	35.7	358	7.1	20.0
1980	5038	1972	39.1	569	11.3	28.9
1981	4557	1908	41.9	638	14.0	33.4
1982	4165	1636	39.3	570	13.7	34.8
1983	4338	1925	44.4	679	15.7	35.3
1984	6991	2250	32.2	609	8.7	27.1
1985	8026	2653	33.1	560	7.0	21.1
1986	8551	3071	35.9	463	5.4	15.1
1987	8579	2791	32.5	405	4.7	14.5
1988	9222	2816	30.5	492	5.3	17.5
1989	8958	2776	31.0	592	6.6	21.3
1990	9344	3244	34.7	602	6.4	18.6
1991	9122	3728	40.9	606	6.6	16.3
1992	9837	3768	38.3	799	8.1	21.2
1993****	5154	2525	49.0	514	10.0	20.4

*Cases eligible on 1 April 1968.
**Cases eligible between 1 April 1968 and 31 December 1968, excluding cases shown in the 1968 *Annual Report* which were considered by LRCs but not decided by the Parole Board at 31 December 1968.
***Excluding 14 cases shown in the 1969 *Annual Report* as 'deferred' which were in fact decided in 1970.
****LRCs were phased out in the last quarter of 1994.

[*n. 44 contd.*] cases were, as the Home Secretary had promised, referred to the Board. But the same was true of just 85 (2.5%) of the 3,462 (76.7%) considered 'unsuitable' by LRCs (see Table 9:1). Most of the 'unsuitables' referred were accomplices of prisoners deemed 'suitable' by their LRC: see C.P. Nuttall, with E.E. Barnard, A.J. Fowles, A. Frost, W.H. Hammond, P. Mayhew, K. Pease, R. Tarling, and M.J. Weatheritt, *Parole in England and Wales*, Home Office Research Study No. 38 (London: HMSO, 1977) at 24.

chances of early release were virtually nil. It also prompted the Home Office Research Unit to embark on a programme of research that was to have a profound effect on the parole system for many years to come.

The Research Unit combined reconviction data with information from the newly created *Parole Index*[45] to develop a statistical model capable of predicting the probability of a particular parole applicant being reconvicted within two years of his release from prison. The resultant scores were then used as a control device to examine consistency in parole decision-making.[46] The researchers were able to demonstrate 'that different LRCs seemed to be applying different selection standards'.[47] It also appeared that referral decisions made in the Parole Unit were not, as had been hoped, 'ironing out' unjustified variations between LRCs.

The study had an immediate impact on the system. Soon after its completion an agreement was reached between the Parole Unit and the Research Unit to allow the Parole Board to review more of the cases which had been judged 'unsuitable' by LRCs, especially where the prisoner was in an open prison.[48] To assist in this process a new selection method was devised based on a prisoner's risk of reconviction prediction score.[49] From October 1969 all 'unsuitables' with low actuarial risks (under 35 per cent) were forwarded to the Board.[50] This more than doubled the referral rate for 'unsuitables': from 8.1 per cent in 1969 to 19.0 per cent in 1970.

[45] Developed by the Parole Unit in the Home Office in collaboration with the Research Unit, the *Index* recorded information about prisoners going through the parole system, including information about their criminal records and social backgrounds.

[46] The scores, based on 16 predictive factors, were derived from a sample of 2,276 male prisoners who were discharged from prison in 1965, before the parole system was introduced.

[47] Nuttall *et al.*, n. 44 above, at 39.

[48] Ibid., 5–6. See also *Home Office Review of Parole*, n. 32 above, at para. 23: '[t]he intention behind this measure had been to ensure that unfavourable recommendations by committees at open prisons or other establishments where the proportion of good parole risks is high, do not cause the rejection of cases which, had they been seen at other prisons against the background of a collection of much worse cases, might have been favourably reviewed'.

[49] Lord Stonham announced the introduction of the new procedure to the Board at a meeting in July 1969: see *Report of the Parole Board for 1969* (London: HMSO, 1970), 48, at para. 37.

[50] The prediction model allowed scores to be calculated for male prisoners only. As a result, all female 'unsuitables' were routinely referred to the Board.

Two years later the Board sought permission to review an even broader range of cases.[51] It proposed that it should consider all prisoners rejected by LRCs who had a risk score of up to 50 per cent, as well as some prisoners with higher risk scores if they were either 'petty persistent offenders' or more serious offenders serving their first terms of imprisonment.[52] The first of these changes, implemented in May 1973, further raised the referral rate for 'unsuitables': from 18.8 per cent in 1972 to 30.4 per cent in 1974. The second suggestion, that certain 'unsuitables' with risk scores of 50 per cent or higher might be referred to the Board, was not adopted immediately, but late in 1977 the Home Office asked the Board whether it would consider a batch of these cases for a short period to see if some of them might be suitable for release. The experiment proved a success. Within a year the proportion of 'unsuitables' considered by the Board had risen to 35.1 per cent and the arrangement was made permanent in 1979.[53]

At the same time the Board indicated that a further relaxation in the referral rules would be desirable.[54] The upshot was that by the mid-1980s 'unsuitables' with prediction scores of 50 per cent or higher were routinely referred to the Board if: (i) the LRC had not been unanimous in refusing parole; (ii) the prisoner was a co-defendant of another prisoner whose case was being considered by the Board; (iii) the prisoner was serving a sentence of nine years or more and was at his third or subsequent review;[55] (iv) the prisoner had previously been considered by the Board;[56] or (v) some other factor warranted 'a second look'.[57] By 1983 no less than 44 per cent

---

[51] The Board felt encouraged to take on this extra work by its reduced workload following the enactment of s. 35 of the Criminal Justice Act 1972 (for a discussion of this provision, see 394–396 below).

[52] See Morris and Beverly, n. 33 above, 5. But, according to Nuttall, men serving long sentences for violent offences who were at their first review were excluded: see Nuttall *et al.*, n. 44 above, at 6.

[53] See *Report of the Parole Board for 1979* (London: HMSO, 1980), 651, at para. 5. However, the proportion of 'unsuitables' who were *recommended for release* by the Board declined sharply: from 32.2% in 1977 to 23.0% in 1978. There was a further fall in 1979 (to 20%) but in 1980 the figure recovered to 28.9%. See Table 9:1.

[54] See *Report of the Parole Board for 1979*, n. 53 above, at para. 6.

[55] See *Report of the Parole Board for 1980* (London: HMSO, 1981), 340, at para. 6.

[56] See S. Mackey, *Prospects for Parole* (London: NACRO, 1980), at 3.

[57] See McCabe, n. 40 above, at 493, fn. 16. Compare the Carlisle Committee's somewhat different account of the rules: 'if the LRC has recommended against parole

of all 'unsuitables' were reaching the Board and, despite the introduction of the so-called 'restricted policy',[58] this figure never fell
below 30 per cent[59] until the LRCs were phased out in 1994.

Parole and the Paroling Rate, 1968–93

In the debates on the second reading of the Criminal Justice Bill
1966, the Home Secretary told Parliament that he expected 'about
4,500' prisoners to be eligible for parole as soon as the Bill was
enacted, but that no more than 'say, 20 per cent' would be granted
parole, either when they became eligible or at a later stage.[60] This
estimate proved to be accurate for the first year of the scheme's
operation. Of the 4,347 prisoners who became eligible for parole
on 1 April 1968, 541 (12.4 per cent) were considered by the Board
and 406 (75 per cent) were recommended for parole: an overall
paroling rate of 9.3 per cent (see Table 9:2). Between 1 April and
31 December 1968 the Board considered a further 1,138 of the
4,515 prisoners who had become eligible for parole during that
period, recommending 751 (66 per cent) of them for release: an
overall paroling rate of 16.6 per cent.[61] These low paroling rates
were said by NACRO to have caused 'great disappointment on the

by three votes to two the case goes to the Board'. But if the recommendation 'is
unanimous or there has been only one dissenting vote' the case will go to the Board
only if the RPS is 45% or below, or if the offender is female, or if the prisoner is serving
nine years or more and it is his third or subsequent review (*Carlisle Committee Report*,
n. 10 above, at para. 130). See also *Home Office Review of Parole*, n. 32 above, at
para. 43: '[i]f the LRC unanimously recommend refusal of parole and the prediction
score is over 50% then parole is normally refused'. 'All other cases are sent to the
Parole Board for further consideration'.

[58] See 400–402 below.

[59] By the early 1990s it had also become standard practice to refer to the Board all
prisoners who were at their last review, irrespective of what their prediction score may
have been.

[60] See H.C. Debs., vol. 738, col. 70, 12 Dec. 1966. This, Mr Roy Jenkins said,
would lead to a reduction in the average daily prison population of 'about 600'. Some
four months later he said that he expected that 'another 4,000 would become eligible
each year': see Standing Committee A, H.C. Debs., session 1966–67, vol. 2, col. 735, 7
Mar. 1967.

[61] A word of caution is needed here. Christopher Nuttall pointed out as early as
1973 (see his 'Parole Selection' (1973) 13 *British Journal of Criminology* 41) that the
'true paroling rate' is not the proportion of cases considered each year for whom
parole is recommended (the calculation, drawn from *Parole Board Annual Reports*,

TABLE 9:2   Parole Reviews and Decisions, 1968–1993 (source: *Parole Board Annual Reports*)

Year	Number of Prisoners Considered by LRCs	Number and Percentage of Prisoners Released Directly by LRCs		Number and Percentage of Prisoners Considered by the Parole Board		Number and Percentage of Prisoners Recommended for Parole by the Parole Board		Overall Parole Rate (excluding Home Secretary's vetoes)
	N	N	Per Cent	N	Per Cent	N	Per Cent	Per Cent
1968*	4347	-	-	541	12.4	406	75.0	9.3
1968**	4515	-	-	1138	25.2	751	66.0	16.6
1969***	6774	-	-	2576	38.0	1835	71.2	27.1
1970	7813	-	-	3566	45.6	2210	62.0	28.3
1971	9653	-	-	4584	47.5	2971	64.8	30.8
1972	8934	-	-	4450	49.8	2926	65.8	32.8
1973	9846	813	8.3	4421	44.9	2531	57.2	34.0
1974	9877	676	6.8	5145	52.1	2831	55.0	35.5
1975	9455	923	9.8	4662	49.3	3106	66.6	42.6
1976	10077	2115	21.0	4289	42.6	2880	67.1	49.6
1977	10344	2018	19.5	4796	46.4	3200	66.7	50.4
1978	10183	1622	15.9	5303	52.1	3193	60.2	47.3
1979	10156	1925	19.0	4997	49.2	2846	57.0	47.0
1980	10070	1998	19.8	5006	49.7	3090	61.7	50.5
1981	9620	1916	19.9	5058	52.6	3363	66.5	54.9
1982	9193	2042	22.2	4626	50.3	3158	68.3	56.6
1983	9534	1903	20.3	5218	54.7	3460	66.3	56.3
1984	19071	8446	44.3	5884	30.9	3463	58.9	62.4
1985	22912	11138	48.6	6401	27.9	3293	51.4	63.0
1986	24380	11245	46.1	7655	31.4	3560	46.5	60.7
1987	23778	10482	44.1	7508	31.6	3524	46.9	58.9
1988	23136	9027	39.0	7703	33.3	3749	48.7	55.2
1989	23772	9167	38.6	8423	35.4	4614	54.8	58.0
1990	23170	9697	41.9	7373	31.8	3221	43.7	55.8
1991	22300	8099	36.3	8582	38.5	3819	44.5	53.4
1992	25048	10623	42.4	8201	32.7	3713	45.3	57.2
1993****	11426	2514	22.0	6234	54.6	3026	48.5	48.5

*Cases eligible on 1 April 1968.
**Cases eligible between 1 April 1968 and 31 December 1968, excluding cases shown in the 1968 *Annual Report* which were considered by LRCs but not decided by the Parole Board at 31 December 1968.
***Excluding 14 cases shown in the 1969 *Annual Report* as 'deferred' which were in fact decided in 1970.
****Excluding 30 new-style DCR cases decided in that year.

[*n. 61 contd.*] used in Table 9:2) but the proportion of parole eligible prisoners released on parole at some point in their sentence. Because of the effect of multiple reviews for parole eligible prisoners serving longer sentences, the latter will be larger than the former.

part of prisoners'. They also produced 'an outcry in the press'.[62] Yet it would be wrong to blame the Board for this outcome, since it recommended for release more than two-thirds of the prisoners it considered in 1968. Rather, the problem lay in the fact that only one in six cases reached the Board.[63]

When the rules on referral were relaxed, this situation eased.[64] By 1970 the proportion of cases reaching the Board had gone up to 45.6 per cent and, as the Board continued to recommend at least 60 per cent of these prisoners for release, there was a corresponding rise in the overall paroling rate: from 16.6 per cent in 1968 to 28.3 per cent in 1970.[65] Encouraged by this, and by the fact that it had occurred without any loss of public confidence in sentencing,[66] the Board resolved to be a 'little more flexible' in its approach, particularly with regard to so-called 'persistent petty offenders' who might have high risks of reconviction but who were unlikely to commit very serious crimes when released. It admitted that in the past it had

---

[62] See P. Cavadino, N. Hinton, and S. Mackey, *Parole: The Case for Change* (Chichester and London: Barry Rose, 1977), 14. See also H.C. Debs., vol. 761, col. 1695, 28 Mar. 1968, where Mr Brooks spoke of 'reports of widespread despair among prisoners about the number of them granted release on licence'. It has been claimed that the press furore was sparked by an article in the *Sunday Times* which dubbed parole 'a cruel hoax': see C.H. Rolph, 'Two Cheers for Parole' (1970) 9 *Prison Service Journal* 13, at 14. Rolph described the line taken by the national press as 'a real hatchet job'. 'Here was a new idea—kill it somebody'.

[63] As this was prior to the enactment of s. 35 of the Criminal Justice Act 1972 (see 394–396 below), any prisoner whose case was not considered by the Board could not be granted parole.

[64] At the same time the Board urged LRCs 'to make a greater number of positive recommendations': see *Report of the Parole Board for 1971* (London: HMSO, 1972), 274, at para. 49. In 1972 J.P. Martin, 'The Local Review Committee', in West, n. 1 above, 32, at 50, observed that many members of LRCs found it 'difficult to contemplate a man being granted the full period of parole possible under the legislation'. Professor Martin was a member of an LRC.

[65] See Table ? ?.

[66] Some suggested that the introduction of parole would cause a general upward pressure on sentence lengths as judges sought to compensate for the fact that many prisoners would now serve a smaller proportion of their sentences in prison. Indeed, in the Parliamentary debates in 1967 on the Criminal Justice Bill, it was said that this was exactly what had happened in Canada (see the remarks of Sir John Hobson, Standing Committee A, H.C. Debs., session 1966–67, vol. 2, col. 708, 1 Mar. 1967). However, analysis of data from the *Prison Department Annual Reports* for the years 1966–72 conducted by Nigel Walker showed 'no sign of an upward shift in [the length of parole-eligible sentences] in the two years after 1968': see 'A Note on Parole and Sentence-Lengths' [1981] *Crim.L.R.* 829 at 829.

treated such cases 'cautiously'. Now, it said, they would stand a greater chance of parole.[67]

In the event, this new approach produced an increase of just 2.8 percentage points in the proportion of prisoners recommended by the Board[68] and, although the Board indicated that 'further experiments in the operation of a more liberal policy' were warranted,[69] enthusiasm for a liberalization of parole turned out to be short-lived. Thus, in 1973, the Board observed that while opinions among its members differed, 'caution continued to prevail in the councils of the Board over those who would have preferred a more adventurous policy'. And the Board harked back to the first years of the scheme, reminding readers of its *Annual Report* that there had been 'two serious failures' at that time which, it said, 'served as a warning that risks of this order could readily bring parole into disrepute'.[70]

Given such a conservative release policy it was perhaps inevitable that governments worried about the size of the prison population would wish to use their muscle to influence the paroling rate. Indeed, of the five important changes that were made to the system in the 1970s and 1980s, four were overtly designed to increase the number of prisoners granted parole.

Direct Release by LRCs

There had long been debate in the academic community about whether it was necessary for every release decision to be filtered through the Board. Alec Samuels, for example, suggested in 1969 that LRCs might be allowed to release some short-term prisoners without reference to the Board,[71] and Professor Donald West argued three years later that it was 'wasteful of public money and experts' time' for low-risk, short-term cases which had been recommended

---

[67] See *Report of the Parole Board for 1970* (London: HMSO, 1971), 437, at para. 41.

[68] From 62% in 1970 to 64.8% in 1971: see Table 9:2.

[69] See *Report of the Parole Board for 1971*, n. 64 above, at para. 62. It promised that 'the timid path of over caution which might falsely project an image of its wisdom' would be 'eschew[ed]': see ibid., at para. 65.

[70] See *Report of the Parole Board for 1973* (London: HMSO, 1974), 143, at para. 98. The two cases are discussed in detail in *Report of the Parole Board for 1968*, n. 30 above, at paras. 125–129.

[71] A. Samuels, 'Parole: A Critique' [1969] *Crim.L.R.* 456 at 462. Samuels suggested that the procedure could be used where 'not more than six months' parole was involved'.

by an LRC to be considered again by the Board.[72] These arguments, which were bolstered by a study conducted by the Home Office Research Unit that concluded that the proposed change in procedure would not lead to an increase in reconviction rates, appear to have made an impression because, in 1972, the Government enacted section 35 of the Criminal Justice Act which allowed the Home Secretary, after consultation with the Board, to designate certain categories of prisoner who could be paroled without reference to the Board.[73]

At first such 'fast-track' cases were limited to prisoners who had been unanimously recommended by their LRC and who were serving sentences of imprisonment of less than three years for an offence other than violence, sex, arson, or drug trafficking.[74] But in subsequent years the categories were extended.[75] On 1 July 1974 prisoners serving exactly three years who had been unanimously recommended by their LRC and who had not been imprisoned for an offence of violence, sex, arson, or drug trafficking were included. Then, from 1 July 1976, as part of the so-called 'Jenkins initiative',[76] the class of

[72] See D.J. West, 'Parole in England: Some Comments on the System at Work' in West, n. 1 above, 21 at 27. (West was one of the first members of the Board. He resigned in December 1969 before the end of his three-year term.) It would be sufficient, West said, if these cases were scrutinized by 'one or two Board members or by officials of the Parole Unit, with referral to a full panel of the Board only if some cause for doubt emerged'. He had in mind, particularly, 'ordinary offenders against property', who might be released 'only a month or two in advance of normal discharge'. See also J.P. Martin, who argued that in 'lesser cases . . . perfectly adequate decisions might well be taken by LRCs' ('The Local Review Committee' in West, n. 1 above, 32 at 55).

[73] The section came into force on 1 Jan. 1973. For the study see Nuttall *et al.*, n. 43 above, at 6.

[74] See *Report of the Parole Board for 1973*, n. 70 above, para. 34. West welcomed the change: see his 'Report of the Parole Board for 1971' (1973) 13 *British Journal of Criminology* 56 at 59. The Home Office reserved the right to order a referral to the Board if it considered the individual circumstances of the case warranted it, and discussions between the Parole Board and the Home Office eventually resulted in an agreed list of criteria, although the Home Office also made it clear that the list 'could not cover every eventuality'.

[75] The then Chairman of the Board, Lord Hunt, writing in January 1973, favoured extension: see 'Foreword' (1973) 13 *British Journal of Criminology* 1 at 4.

[76] The announcement of the change was made to Parliament by the then Home Secretary, Mr Roy Jenkins, in the form of a written answer: see H.C. Debs., Written Answers, vol. 897, cols. 25–26, 4 Aug. 1975. The 'initiative' is discussed further in the section on 'New Criteria', see 396–400 below.

case was widened again to include prisoners who had been unanimously recommended by their LRC and who were serving sentences of up to and including four years, so long as they had not been sentenced for one of the proscribed offences.[77] The net effect of these measures was to increase the proportion of 'suitables' released without reference to the Board from 16.7 per cent in 1974 to 43.6 per cent in 1976 (see Table 9:3).[78] And in the 1980s two more changes were made. First, it became possible for a prisoner to be released by the direct route if there had been one dissenting vote at the LRC.[79] Secondly, on 24 November 1989, prisoners serving less than four years became eligible *irrespective* of their offence type, although prisoners serving exactly four years were apparently now excluded.[80] The effect of these changes was to push the proportion of 'suitables' released directly by LRCs up to 55.7 per cent in 1990 (see Table 9:3).

New Criteria

A surprising feature of the 1967 scheme was that neither the Government nor the Board produced any comprehensive criteria for parole. The then Attorney General, Sir Elwyn Jones, did make a statement to the Commons, in which he outlined some 'principles' on which the scheme would be based.[81] But his guidance was much less detailed than that found in other jurisdictions,[82] and, despite the

---

[77] Prisoners sentenced for the latter crimes were eligible for 'fast track' release only if their sentences were for a period of two years or less: see *Report of the Parole Board for 1975* (London: HMSO, 1976), 432, at paras. 10–11.

[78] As Table 9:2 reveals, there was a fall in the proportion of LRC 'suitables' released directly in 1977 and in 1978. Commenting on this fall the 1981 *Home Office Review of Parole*, n. 32 above, said (see para. 32): '[t]he main factor seems to have been that case-workers within the Home Office were exercising more caution about accepting local review committee recommendations under section 35 arrangements'. It added that 'an investigation showed this to be the case'.

[79] See the *Carlisle Committee Report*, n. 10 above, at para. 128.

[80] See *Report of the Parole Board for 1989* (London: HMSO, 1990), 385, at para. 18.

[81] See H.C. Debs., vol. 738, col. 205, 12 Dec. 1966. The statement was repeated by the Minister of State, Lord Stonham, during the Committee stage of the Bill in the Lords: see H.L. Debs., vol. 283, cols. 746–747, 12 June 1967.

[82] Compare, for instance, the 'Criteria for Determining Date of First Release on Parole' and the 'Data to Be Considered in Determining Parole Release' found in the American Law Institute's *Model Penal Code*, ss. 305.9 and 305.10. S. 305.9(1) creates a presumption in favour of release on parole which can be displaced only for one of four identified reasons; s. 305.9(2) lists 13 factors which must be taken into account.

TABLE 9:3 Number and Percentage of Prisoners Granted Parole By Local Review Committees Under Section 35 Without Reference to the Board, 1973–1994 (source: *Parole Board Annual Reports*)

Year	Number of Prisoners Considered by LRCs (N)	Section 60 Cases (sentence two years or more) 'Suitable' for Parole (N)	Section 33 Cases (sentence less than two years) 'Suitable' for Parole (N)	Total 'Suitable' for Parole*** (N)	Total 'Suitable' for Parole*** (Per Cent)	Section 60 Cases (sentence two years or more) Released Directly**** (N)	Section 60 Cases (sentence two years or more) Released Directly**** (Per Cent)	Section 33 Cases (sentence less than two years) Released Directly***** (N)	Section 33 Cases (sentence less than two years) Released Directly***** (Per Cent)	Total Released Directly (N)	Percentage of LRC 'Suitables' Released Directly (Per Cent)
1973	9846	3932	-	3932	39.9	813	20.7	-	-	813	20.7
1974	9877	4047	-	4047	41.0	676	16.7	-	-	676	16.7
1975	9455	3894	-	3894	41.2	923	23.7	-	-	923	23.7
1976	10077	4865	-	4865	48.3	2115	43.5	-	-	2115	43.5
1977	10344	5221	-	5221	50.5	2018	38.7	-	-	2018	38.7
1978	10183	5160	-	5160	50.7	1622	31.4	-	-	1622	31.4
1979	10156	5128	-	5128	50.5	1925	37.5	-	-	1925	37.5
1980	10070	5032	-	5032	50.0	1998	39.7	-	-	1998	39.7
1981	9620	5063	-	5063	52.6	1916	37.8	-	-	1916	37.8
1982	9193	5028	-	5028	54.7	2042	40.6	-	-	2042	40.6
1983	9534	5196	-	5196	54.5	1903	36.6	-	-	1903	36.6
1984	19071	6346	5734	12080	63.3	2767	43.6	5679	99.0	8446	69.9
1985	22912	6359	8527	14886	65.0	2732	43.0	8406	98.6	11138	74.8
1986	24380	7494	8335	15829	64.9	3045	40.6	8200	98.4	11245	71.0
1987	23778	7858	7341	15199	63.9	3291	41.9	7191	98.0	10482	69.0
1988*	23136	8185	5729	13914	60.1	3408	41.6	5619	98.1	9027	64.9
1989	23772	9463	5351	14814	62.3	3935	41.6	5232	97.8	9167	61.9
1990	23170	8729	5097	13826	59.7	4859	55.7	4838	94.9	9697	70.1

(continued overleaf)

TABLE 9:3 (continued)

Year	Number of Prisoners Considered by LRCs	Section 60 Cases (sentence two years or more) 'Suitable' for Parole	Section 33 Cases (sentence less than two years) 'Suitable' for Parole	Total 'Suitable' for Parole***		Section 60 Cases (sentence two years or more) Released Directly****		Section 33 Cases (sentence less than two years) Released Directly*****		Total Released Directly	Percentage of LRC 'Suitables' Released Directly
	N	N	N	N	Per Cent	N	Per Cent	N	Per Cent	N	Per Cent
1991	22300	8585	4593	13178	59.1	4103	47.8	3996	87.0	8099	61.5
1992	25048	9759	5452	15211	60.7	5517	56.5	5106	93.7	10623	69.8
1993	11426	5463	809	6272	54.9	1827	33.4	687	84.9	2514	40.1
1994**	4627	N.K.	N.K.	1991	43.0	N.K.	N.K.	N.K.	N.K.	736	37.0

*On 13 April 1987 half remission was introduced for those serving sentences of 12 months or less. This effectively excluded these prisoners from eligibility for parole.
**LRCs were phased out in the last quarter of 1994.
***The percentages in this column refer to the proportion of all cases considered by LRCs that were regarded as 'suitable' for parole.
****The percentages in this column refer to the proportion of section 60 'suitables' that were released directly without reference to the Board.
*****The percentages in this column refer to the proportion of section 33 'suitables' that were released directly without reference to the Board.

Board's attempt to give these 'principles' respectability by claiming that they were based on considerations which had been 'identified by criminological research as the factors significant for success or failure after release from custodial sentence',[83] their lack of specificity was rightly criticized by academic writers.[84] In 1975 this issue was partially resolved by the 'Jenkins' initiative'.[85] As the Board was later to observe, the intention behind the initiative was 'that more prisoners should be released on parole, provided that this was not at the cost of a substantially increased risk to the safety of the community'.[86] The mechanism used to bring about this change was the introduction of new Criteria for Selection for Parole which distinguished between *serious* offenders, those guilty of 'grave crimes' who were likely to present a considerable threat to the public, and *less serious* offenders, those who had not committed grave crimes and who were 'unlikely to present a grave threat to the public'.[87] For less serious offenders there became, in effect, a 'presumption in favour of parole'. And a similar presumption operated in respect of two other groups:

[83] See *Report of the Parole Board for 1971*, n. 64 above, at para. 55. No research was named by the Parole Board to support its assertion. However, it was claimed in 1974 by P.A. Banister, K.J. Heskin, N. Bolton, and F.V. Smith that the Board was 'using those variables as criteria for release which American studies have shown to be most indicative of non-recidivism': see 'A Study of Variables Related to the Selection of Long-Term Prisoners for Parole' (1974) 14 *British Journal of Criminology* 359 at 367.

[84] See, for instance, West, n. 1 above, at 20, who pointed out that: '[s]ince it is nowhere laid down what level of reconviction risk is tolerable, what kinds of offences make a prisoner unlikely to deserve parole, or what is the relative importance attached to the contradictory demands of deterrence and rehabilitation, it is impossible to know whether the system is operating a consistent policy'. See also Shea, n. 13 above, at 74; but compare J.E. Hall Williams, 'Natural Justice and Parole' [1975] *Crim.L.R.* 82 and 215, at 219, who argued that 'no list of criteria can tell us what is likely to be decisive in an individual cases'.

[85] The Home Secretary's 'broad statement of policy' was made in a Parliamentary written answer on 4 August 1975: see H.C. Debs., Written Answers, vol. 897, col. 25. In its wake, the Home Office (after consultation with the Board) issued 'revised guidance on paroling criteria' to LRCs and the Board. The full text is to be found in Appendix 4 of the *Report of the Parole Board for 1975*, n. 77 above.

[86] See *Report of the Parole Board for 1981* (London: HMSO, 1982), 388, at para. 4. See also the comments of the then Chairman of the Board, Sir Louis Petch, made to the House of Commons Expenditure Committee: Fifteenth Report from the Expenditure Committee (Session 1977–78), *Minutes of Evidence, Vol. 2* (London: HMSO, 1978), at para. 824.

[87] See Appendix 4 of the *Report of the Parole Board for 1975*, n. 77 above, at paras. 19–21.

so-called 'one-offence-in-a-lifetime' offenders and prisoners who had committed offences of a violent or sexual nature but of a less serious kind and for whom the potential benefits of compulsory parole supervision were considered 'particularly important'.[88]

The initiative had an immediate effect. The proportion of prisoners recommended by the Board rose by 11 percentage points,[89] and there was a concomitant rise in the overall paroling rate from 35.5 per cent to 42.9 per cent. In the following year the overall paroling rate rose again and, in 1977, for the first time more than half of all parole applicants were recommended for release (see Table 9:2). This prompted a confident Parole Board to say that whereas at the beginning of the scheme the onus was on the prisoner 'to demonstrate that he was worthy of parole and had earned it', now the emphasis was on 'the desirability of giving the prisoner the encouragement of release on parole and the blend of control and support provided by compulsory supervision'.[90]

The Restricted Policy

That bolder approach was maintained throughout the late 1970s and into the 1980s. During this period a new mood of optimism dominated the Board's thinking, as the following remarks from the Parole Board's 1981 *Annual Report* indicate:

the Board is conscious of the importance of protecting the community by not exposing it to undue risk. At the same time, members are also aware of the prison situation and the severe problems caused by overcrowding. Against this background the Board was prepared in 1981 to recommend release in certain cases, where the arguments were finely balanced in the expectation that should the licensee fail to respond to the conditions of his licence he would be recalled to prison. The parole system is well established, and enjoys the confidence of the public at large; those operating it can afford, therefore, to be sensibly venturesome in their approach.[91]

---

[88] See *Report of the Parole Board for 1981*, n. 86 above, at para. 4.

[89] From 55% in 1974 to 66.6% in 1975 (see Table 9:2).

[90] See *Report of the Parole Board for 1976* (London: HMSO, 1977), 388, at para. 3.

[91] See *Report of the Parole Board for 1981*, n. 86 above, at para. 16. It is interesting to note that, in its written evidence to the Carlisle Committee in November 1987, the Board claimed that '[d]espite considerable expansion and modification over the years' the criteria for release still adhered 'closely to the Attorney General's statement in 1966': see *Report of the Parole Board for 1987* (London: HMSO, 1988), 509, at para. 17.

But within two years that mood had changed. The transformation was caused by Mr Leon Brittan's announcement on 11 October 1983 at the Conservative Party Conference in Blackpool that he intended to use his discretion to ensure that certain categories of prisoner—those serving sentences of more than five years for a single offence of sex, violence, or drug trafficking, set out in Schedule 1 to the Criminal Justice Act 1982, including attempting, conspiring, inciting, and aiding and abetting these offences—would not be released on parole, except where a few months' supervision was likely to reduce the long-term risk to the public or where the circumstances were genuinely exceptional. The Board indicated that it wished to continue to review all cases that fell within what came to be known as the 'restricted category' in order to ascertain whether, in its view, there were 'genuinely exceptional circumstances' or whether the public interest would best be served by releasing the prisoner on supervision for a few months before his normal release date.[92] The Home Secretary acceded to this request but insisted that these reviews must take account of the new policy.[93] It was thus recognized by all concerned that the policy, which applied both to existing prisoners and future prisoners with immediate effect, placed very real constraints on the Board's powers.[94]

The policy was driven by political expediency, not principle or empirical research, and as such was disliked by both academics[95] and the Board.[96] Indeed, one member (Dr Candy, a Consultant Psychiatrist at St John's Hospital, Aylesbury) was so outraged by

[92] Ministers eventually informed the Board that 'a few months before his normal release date' should be taken to mean, at most, a period of up to eight months on licence.

[93] The Home Secretary's statement was amplified in Parliament on 30 November 1983 to take account of this: see H.C. Debs., vol. 49, col. 506.

[94] Professor Mike Maguire, a member of the Board between 1988 and 1991, says that following the introduction of the restricted policy the Board generally adopted a 'realistic approach, rarely recommending release for a longer period than it knows to be acceptable to Ministers': see M. Maguire, 'Parole' in E. Stockdale and S. Casale (eds.), *Criminal Justice Under Stress* (London: Blackstone Press, 1992), 179–209 at 186.

[95] See, e.g., McCabe, n. 40 above, 489: '[i]t can be argued that such a class definition negates the intention of the 1967 statute, which was concerned to make provision for individual offenders. Whether that be the case or not, some offenders will now be refused parole not on grounds of desert or risk but of offence category'.

[96] In its 1992 *Annual Report* the Board said that it 'had long argued for abolition of the restricted policy': see *Report of the Parole Board for 1992* (London: HMSO, 1993), 712, at para. 5.

the change that he resigned from the Board in protest in November 1983.[97] Although a challenge to the policy in the courts was unsuccessful,[98] criticism continued, and in 1988 it was condemned by the Carlisle Committee as 'flawed in principle and harmful in practice'. The policy, the Committee noted, 'cut right across the normal criteria for parole' and 'forced inmates, subject to the option of declining to be considered (which very few, if only for family reasons, feel able to do), to be party to a process which they know is almost bound to be futile'.[99]

It was therefore only a matter of time before the policy was abandoned, and the end finally came when the decision was taken in the Criminal Justice Act 1991 to postpone the review of prisoners serving four years or longer until they had reached the halfway point of their sentence. In this setting the policy was plainly untenable and, on 29 June 1992, the Home Secretary (Mr Kenneth Clarke) announced its abolition.[100] This led to a period of readjustment for the Board which admitted that it had become used to relying on the policy to short-circuit discussion in difficult cases:

We have had some difficulty after nearly nine years of the restricted policy, in coming to terms with the concept of releasing violent offenders on licences of more than a few months, and we have noted similar difficulties on the part of Ministers, who have demonstrated reluctance to accept such recommendations. In these cases the decisions are rarely easy.[101]

Minimum Qualifying Period Reduced to Six Months

Alongside the introduction of the restricted policy came a simultaneous liberalization in the parole system. The groundwork for this change, which had long been favoured by the Board[102] and by some

[97] See *Report of the Parole Board for 1983* (London: HMSO, 1984), 463, at para. 10. Nonetheless, at its Annual Meeting in February 1984, the Board felt compelled to confirm amendments to its criteria for selection to take account of the Brittan changes.

[98] It was held to be lawful by the House of Lords in *R. v. Secretary of State for the Home Department, ex parte Findlay and Others* [1984] 3 All ER 801. For a note on this case see G. Richardson, 'Judicial Review of Parole Policy' [1985] *Public Law* 34.

[99] See *Carlisle Committee Report*, n. 10 above, at paras. 190 and 191.

[100] See H.C. Debs., Written Answers, vol. 210, col. 388, 29 June 1992. See also the 1990 White Paper, *Crime, Justice and Protecting the Public*, Cm 965 (London: HMSO, 1990), at para. 6.23.

[101] See *Report of the Parole Board for 1992*, n. 96 above, at para. 55.

[102] The idea was discussed first by the Board in 1972.

senior academics,[103] was laid in 1982 when, in response to renewed concerns about unacceptable overcrowding in prisons, the Government agreed to an amendment to the Criminal Justice Bill which had been proposed by the All-Party Penal Affairs Group.[104] The new clause, which eventually became section 33 of the Criminal Justice Act 1982, altered the Criminal Justice Act 1967 to allow the Home Secretary to change the minimum qualifying period for parole, subject to an affirmative resolution by both Houses of Parliament. That approval was obtained on 29 December 1983 and, as of 1 July 1984, the minimum qualifying period was lowered to six months.[105] Prisoners sentenced to terms of imprisonment of as little as ten-and-a-half months thus became eligible for consideration.[106]

'Section 33 prisoners', as they came to be known,[107] were dealt with under somewhat different procedures: police and probation reports were not required and, as with section 35 cases, if the LRC thought the prisoner 'suitable' he would almost always be released without the need for his case to be referred to the Board.[108] However, unlike in section 35 cases, a negative LRC recommendation would normally be decisive, since the shortness of the sentence meant that there would usually be insufficient time to refer the

[103] In 1972 D.J. West suggested that the minimum qualifying period should be reduced to six months (see n. 72 above, at 26). In 1962 Cross (see n. 16 above) was thinking of a minimum qualifying period of six months, as was Hall Williams in 1964 (see n. 21 above). In 1984 A. Keith Bottomley argued for a change in the eligibility rules to allow all prisoners to become eligible for parole after having served one-third of their sentence (see A.K. Bottomley, 'Dilemmas of Parole in a Penal Crisis' (1984) 23 *Howard Journal of Criminal Justice* 24 at 37).

[104] As the *Carlisle Committee Report*, n. 10 above, was later to observe (see para. 31): '[i]n the light of subsequent events it is interesting to note that this amendment aroused not the slightest controversy in Parliament'. There was a suggestion, however, which was not adopted, that the Act itself should reduce the minimum qualifying period from one year to six months.

[105] See The Eligibility for Release on Licence Order 1983, S.I. 1983 No. 1958.

[106] This was because the Home Secretary had directed that inmates should not be reviewed for parole unless they would be in a position to be released for at least one month on licence if parole were to be granted, and because no change was made to the one-third remission rule.

[107] i.e., prisoners serving sentences of less than two years who would not formerly have qualified for parole but who were now eligible.

[108] Thus, in 1984, 99% of those regarded as 'suitable' by an LRC who were serving sentences of less than two years were released without reference to the Board (and in the six years that followed the figure never fell below 94%): see Table 9:3.

case to the Board.[109] LRCs were also told that section 33 cases should, like certain other groups of inmates previously identified by the Board,[110] benefit from a 'presumption in favour of parole',[111] and that special licence conditions would rarely need to be imposed. This therefore became automatic release in all but name.[112] Indeed, in 1984, as Table 9:4 shows, 77 per cent of eligible section 33 inmates were paroled, compared with 53 per cent of all other inmates in the year as a whole;[113] and seven years later, in 1991, as many as 83 per cent were being released.[114]

The change in the minimum qualifying period might, at first blush, seem relatively minor when compared with the introduction of the 'restrictive policy'. In fact it sounded the death knell for the old system of parole.[115] The problem was that most prisoners sentenced to terms of imprisonment of between ten and eighteen months were

[109] If the LRC were split, the decision would be on the basis of the majority view. Some s. 33 cases found 'unsuitable' by the LRCs were referred to the Board where the recommendation of the LRC 'seemed significantly out of line with those of LRCs at similar establishments' (see Table 9:4 for the proportion of s. 33 'unsuitables' referred annually to the Board). The *Carlisle Committee Report*, n. 10 above, noted in 1988 (see para. 129) that 'one routine check built into the system is that if any LRC panel which considers six or more of these section 33 cases turns down more than 50% of the inmates the Home Office sends the cases to the board for a second opinion'. 'In addition,' the *Report* said, 'the Parole Unit will sometimes send the cases of co-defendants who are held in different establishments to the board in the interests of equality of treatment'. As Table 9:4 shows, the proportion of s. 33 'unsuitables' considered by the Board increased dramatically in 1991 to 42.6%.

[110] i.e., offenders, such as property offenders, who were unlikely to pose a grave threat; so-called 'one-offence-in-a-lifetime' offenders; and those who had committed offences of a violent or sexual nature, not of the most serious kind, for whom the potential advantages of compulsory parole supervision were particularly important. See *Report of the Parole Board for 1981*, n. 86 above, at para. 4. See also text at n. 88 above.

[111] See *Report of the Parole Board for 1986* (London: HMSO, 1987), 5, at para. 11.

[112] But see 'Editorial' [1985] *Crim.L.R.* 413 and the letter from the Chairman of the Board, Lord Windlesham, [1985] *Crim.L.R.* 687.

[113] In 1984, 19,071 inmates were considered by LRCs (see Table 9:2). Of these, 7,575 were 's. 33' cases (see Table 9:4). Of the 11,496 'other' cases, 6,065 (52.8%) were released.

[114] See Table 9:4.

[115] Indeed, the *Carlisle Committee Report* (n. 10 above, at para. 33) stated that the effect of the restrictive policy and the reduction in the minimum qualifying period were so profound that 'they were the main reason why the judicial and political consensus, which had hitherto existed, broke down'.

TABLE 9:4   Number and Percentage of Section 33 LRC 'Unsuitables' Referred to the Board, 1984–1993 (source: *Parole Board Annual Reports*)

Year	Section 33 Cases Considered by LRCs N	Section 33 Cases Considered 'Unsuitable' for Parole by LRCs N		Section 33 LRC 'Unsuitables' Referred to Board N		Section 33 'Unsuitables' Granted Parole by Parole Board N		Total Section 33 Cases Granted Parole N	
			Per Cent		Per Cent		Per Cent		Per Cent
1984	7575	1841	24.3	199	10.8	110	55.3	5844	77.1
1985	10966	2439	22.2	432	17.7	131	30.3	8658	79.0
1986	10603	2268	21.4	474	20.9	133	28.1	8468	79.9
1987	9397	2056	21.9	236	11.5	68	28.8	7409	78.8
1988	7585	1856	24.5	150	8.1	40	26.7	5769	76.1
1989	6917	1566	22.6	151	9.6	54	35.8	5405	78.1
1990	6536	1439	22.0	287	19.9	157	54.7	5254	80.4
1991	5926	1333	22.5	568	42.6	323	56.9	4916	83.0
1992	7055	1623	23.0	351	21.6	124	35.3	5556	78.8
1993*	1028	219	21.3	127	58.0	57	44.9	866	84.2

*LRCs were phased out in the last quarter of 1994.

now released at the same time (i.e., after six months), irrespective of the length of their sentences. This infuriated the judiciary, whose hackles were raised still further by two speeches made in 1985. The first, given by the sentencing expert Dr David Thomas to an academic conference in Manchester, claimed that section 33 had reduced sentencing to 'a complete farce';[116] the second, given by Lord Lane CJ (a member of the Board from 1970 to 1972) to judges at the Lord Mayor's Dinner, asked whether, given the gap between what 'the court orders and what happens to the criminal in fact', the time had not arrived 'when the very existence or place of parole in our system of detention and release of prisoners should be subjected to a strenuous review'.[117]

The Home Office responded to these criticisms by embarking on a review of section 33 procedures which was completed in 1986.[118]

---

[116] An extract of this speech was later published as 'Parole and the Crown Court' (1985) 149 *Justice of the Peace* 344 at 344. Thomas also played a major role in Judicial Studies Board seminars and acted as a consultant to the Board.

[117] Quoted in Lord Windlesham, *Responses to Crime* (Oxford: Oxford University Press, 1986), i, at 285. As a result of these concerns, informal discussions took place between the Home Office and representatives of the judiciary about the matter.

[118] In 1984 the Home Office had announced its intention to conduct such a review after the first year of the section's operation.

The review concluded that police reports should be added to the dossier, so as to ensure that there was more information about the nature of the offence, and that the guidance given to LRCs 'should be clarified'.[119] Since this guidance had been based on the Board's own criteria for selection in respect of cases of lesser gravity, it was suggested that the Board should look again at these in order to ensure that the two documents—the Home Office's Guidance to LRCs and the Board's *Criteria for Release*—were consistent. This the Board did, and in 1986 its General Purpose Committee decided to excise any reference to a 'presumption' in favour of parole, emphasizing instead 'that each case should be considered on its merits'.[120] The revised version took effect on 1 January 1987.

However, tinkering with the procedures and making changes to the criteria did nothing to allay judicial concerns about the erosion of sentencing differentials. Nor did it have any great effect on the proportion of section 33 prisoners adjudged 'unsuitable' by LRCs, which remained stable during the late 1980s and early 1990s.[121] Furthermore, as is so often the case with parole reform, a wider agenda was at work, *viz.* the need to control the prison population.[122] Thus, as the Carlisle Committee was later to observe,[123] when the Home Office communicated the change in the criteria to LRC chairmen on 10 June 1987, its letter did not state 'explicitly that the presumption had been withdrawn'.[124] The reason for this obfuscation (at least according to the Carlisle Committee) was the Home Office's wish not to stimulate a dramatic downturn in the paroling rate, with all the inevitable knock-on effects that that would have had on the prison population.

---

[119] See *Report of the Parole Board for 1986*, n. 111 above, at para. 11.

[120] Ibid., para. 12.

[121] See Table 9:4.

[122] In a statement to Parliament on prison overcrowding on 30 March 1988 the Home Secretary (Mr Douglas Hurd) noted that the restricted policy had increased the prison population by about 2,000 (see H.C. Debs., vol. 130, col. 1083). This must have almost eliminated any savings obtained by the liberalization effected by s. 33.

[123] See para. 188.

[124] The outcome was that, at the time of the *Carlisle Committee Report* (n. 10 above) in 1988, a large number of LRC members met by the Committee still thought that the presumption in favour of parole for s. 33 cases applied (see para. 188).

50 per cent Remission for Prisoners Serving Twelve Months or Less

The last major change to the system before it was completely over-hauled by the Criminal Justice Act 1991 came on 13 August 1987, when the Home Secretary introduced 50 per cent remission for prisoners serving sentences of twelve months or less.[125] Given the requirement of a six-month 'minimum qualifying period' for parole, this effectively removed from the scheme prisoners serving sentences of between ten-and-a-half and twelve months.[126] The need to reduce prison numbers was, once again, the motivation for the change, but, as with the lowering of the minimum qualifying period, the conse-quence was to erode further sentencing differentials. As such, it became the final nail in the coffin of the old parole system.[127]

The Rise and Fall of the Home Secretary's Veto

Before turning to the general reforms that occurred as a result of the Carlisle Committee's 1988 report we should examine one other aspect of the scheme, the Home Secretary's veto.[128] As part of the compromise arrived at in 1967 it was the Home Secretary, not the Parole Board, who retained the ultimate power to decide whether a prisoner should or should not be released on parole. In the debates on the Second Reading of the Criminal Justice Bill, Mr Quintin Hogg (later Lord Hailsham) made it clear that the Conservative opposition was against this idea. Parole, he argued, should not 'be a matter within the day-to-day responsibilities of a political Minister... [I]t should be not only detached from politics... but should be seen to be

---

[125] See The Prison (Amendment) Rules 1987, S.I. 1987 No. 1256.

[126] Across a year the Board estimated that this reform reduced its caseload by about 4,000 cases. See *Report of the Parole Board for 1988* (London: HMSO, 1989), 412, at para. 20.

[127] As with many reforms of parole, the change had been discussed over many years. For example, in its *1981 Annual Report*, the Parole Board noted that some of its members favoured the introduction of 50% remission as a more desirable way of reducing the prison population than the introduction of automatic release for short-term prisoners. Other members, however, 'thought that 50% remission would be counter-productive, as it might lead to longer sentences being imposed': see *Report of the Parole Board for 1981*, n. 86 above, at para. 6.

[128] For a view that use of the term veto is 'inappropriate' as it inverts a positive power of release which is conferred on the Minister by statute into a negative right to 'deny' a prisoner release see Windlesham, n. 117 above, at 256.

detached from politics'.[129] And Mr Mark Carlisle (later to chair the most important inquiry into parole), also speaking for the Conservative Party, said that 'on balance' he would prefer the Board to have mandatory rather than advisory powers of release.[130] Nonetheless, once the principle of an independent parole board had been accepted, the opposition parties for the most part came round to the idea that the Home Secretary should retain the power to veto a recommendation for release made by the Board.[131]

At first the practice was for the Minister of State,[132] in 'certain categories of case involving critical decisions',[133] to review the dossier and inform the Parole Board in advance if the Home Secretary would wish to exercise his right to refuse release regardless of the Board's recommendation. However, in July 1969, it was decided to postpone ministerial scrutiny until after the Board had reviewed the case.[134] Although the Parole Board welcomed this reform,[135] it did not meet the more fundamental opposition from academic researchers and campaigning organizations. Evelyn Shea, for example, argued that it was neither 'logical' nor 'desirable' for the Home

---

[129] Debate on the Second Reading of the Criminal Justice Bill, H.C. Debs., vol. 738, col. 78, 12 Dec. 1966. He repeated these views even more forcefully in the Standing Committee discussions on the Bill, when he said that it was 'constitutionally unacceptable' for a political officer to have 'power over individuals in custody' (Standing Committee A, H.C. Debs., session 1966–67, vol. 2, col. 745, 7 Mar. 1967), although he appeared to moderate his views later when he said (at col. 749) that he accepted that the Board should be advisory in nature.

[130] Standing Committee A, H.C. Debs., session 1966–67, vol. 2, col. 763, 7 Mar. 1967.

[131] Sir John Hobson, e.g., speaking for the Conservative opposition, said that his party had considered whether it should be made obligatory for the Home Secretary to accept the Board's recommendation, but in the end concluded that it was right that the Home Secretary should be able, if he wished, to 'veto the recommendation of the Board'. After all, he continued, the Home Secretary might 'have additional knowledge of security or other factors' which the ordinary members of the Board would not know: see Standing Committee A, H.C. Debs., session 1966–67, vol. 2, col. 708, 1 Mar. 1967.

[132] Then Lord Stonham.

[133] See *Report of the Parole Board for 1969*, n. 49 above, at para. 35.

[134] A longstanding convention developed whereby a positive Parole Board recommendation would be rejected only on the personal authority of the Home Secretary: see the *Carlisle Committee Report*, n. 10 above, at para. 138.

[135] In the *Report of the Parole Board for 1969*, n. 49 above, at para. 35, the Board said that it was 'well able to recognise cases in which Ministers would feel particular concern'.

Secretary to be able to veto positive recommendations but to have no power to overrule negative recommendations,[136] and Keith Hawkins[137] and Donald West[138] voiced equally powerful objections to its retention. In the short term this hostility left the executive unmoved. Successive Home Secretaries showed no wish to relinquish the veto, and the Parole Board showed no inclination to try to persuade them otherwise. Furthermore, in 1981, the veto received strong support from the Home Office in its *Review of Parole*:

Few though the cases are in which the Home Secretary rejects a Parole Board recommendation for release on licence, they include cases in which the difference of opinion relates to the estimation of dangerousness, and this long-stop safeguard would be lost if the Home Secretary no longer had power to intervene.[139]

But the campaign against the veto continued, and in the longer term the weight of these criticisms started to tell, particularly when, in the mid-1980s, they were supplemented by an empirical study conducted by Professor Martin Wasik and Professor Ken Pease.[140] The researchers asked two general questions: first, whether the proportion of vetoes increased just before and at the time of general elections; and, secondly, whether the proportion varied with the party of government. In an attempt to control for the fact that the parole system is always subject to change, the authors compared the mean number of vetoes in election and pre-election years with the mean number in post-election and pre-pre-election years. For all three elections in their period of study (the period before 1971 was ignored) they found that vetoes on release decisions 'were more

---

[136] See Shea, n. 13 above, at 71–2.

[137] See K. Hawkins, 'Parole Procedure: An Alternative Approach' (1973) 13 *British Journal of Criminology* 6 at 23. Hawkins argued that, apart from a few cases where national security was in issue, the Home Secretary should be removed entirely from the parole process. He pointed out that members of the Board were 'responsible people, sensitive to public opinion and aware of their obligations to the public' and their membership included High Court judges. Hawkins became a member of the Board in 1977, ceased to be a member in 1979, but served again from 1983 to 1986.

[138] See West, n. 74 above, at 59.

[139] See *Home Office Review of Parole*, n. 32 above, at para. 86. Table 9:5 below shows the extent to which the Home Secretary's veto was used during the years 1969 to 1999.

[140] M. Wasik and K. Pease, 'The Parole Veto and Party Politics' [1986] *Crim.L.R.* 379. Professor Pease was a member of the Board from 1987 to 1991.

TABLE 9:5   Use of the Home Secretary's
Veto in Determinate Sentence Cases, 1969–1999
(source: *Parole Board Annual Reports*)

Year	Vetoes Used
1969	2
1970	9
1971	15
1972	11
1973	16
1974	5
1975	0
1976	4
1977	5
1978	7
1979	13
1980	11
1981	8
1982	20
1983	17
1984	23
1985	25
1986	15
1987	12
1988	16
1989	30
1990	36
1991	13
1992	7
1993	16
1994	13
1995	46
1995/6	49
1996/7	22
1997/8	2
1998/99	0

common in the period of electoral sensitivity than in the surrounding period'. From this they concluded that 'the evidence of the relevance of political interest on parole veto decisions in determinate sentence cases is as strong as it could be given the small number of elections since parole was introduced'.[141]

On the basis of their findings Wasik and Pease argued, like so many academics before them, that the Home Secretary's veto should be removed. And in 1988 the Carlisle Committee, convinced by the force of these arguments, also recommended its abolition. But the

[141] See n. 140 above, at 380.

Board was strangely hesitant. It worried that if the veto were to be abolished the role of the Chairman would need 'to be greatly expanded' and would probably have to become a full-time position; that 'some similar safeguard' would need to be built into a reformed system to ensure consistency between panels; and that anomalies would be created between those serving determinate sentences of imprisonment and those serving life imprisonment.[142] Nonetheless, the Government's 1990 White Paper, *Crime, Justice and Protecting the Public*, made it clear that the Home Secretary intended to grant the Board sole jurisdiction over the release of prisoners serving sentences of less than seven years,[143] and in the subsequent Parliamentary debates on the provisions of the 1991 Criminal Justice Bill very few spoke against the Home Secretary's plan.[144] An attempt was made by Lord Richard to force the Government to go further and remove the veto completely, as Carlisle had intended, but Earl Ferrers (who was supported in his approach by the former Chairman of the Board, Lord Hunt) resisted that move and the proposed amendment was withdrawn.[145] The consequence was that the 1991 Act gave the Home Secretary the power to make an order delegating his responsibilities to the Board,[146] and in 1992 he exercised this power in relation to prisoners serving sentences of less than seven years.[147] The Board, having undergone something of a change of heart, applauded the decision and expressed the wish that some time in the future the Home Secretary's trust in it would be sufficient to allow the threshold 'to be raised or abolished'.[148] In 1998 that wish was granted and the

[142] See *Report of the Parole Board for 1988*, n. 126 above, at para. 5.

[143] See n. 100 above, at para. 6.16.

[144] But see the comments made by Lord Boyd-Carpenter, H.L. Debs., vol. 527, col. 123, 12 Mar. 1991, who also said that he regarded the abolition of capital punishment to have been a great mistake. The Chairman of the Parole Board, Viscount Colville of Culross, told the House of Lords (col. 115) that he was confident that the Parole Board would be able to take on the responsibility of releasing prisoners serving less than seven years without the need to refer the case to the Home Secretary for the final decision to be taken.

[145] H.L. Debs., vol. 528, cols. 11–15, 22 Apr. 1991.

[146] See s. 50(1) and (2). The section obliges the Home Secretary to consult with the Board before making an Order and any Order requires the approval of each House of Parliament.

[147] See The Parole Board (Transfer of Functions) Order 1992, S.I. 1992 No. 1829. The Order affected prisoners serving sentences imposed on or after 1 Oct. 1992.

[148] See *Report of the Parole Board for 1993* (London: HMSO, 1994), 450, at para. 10.

Board was empowered, from 26 December onwards, to release prisoners serving sentences of up to (but not including) fifteen years.[149]

The Carlisle Committee's Report

There was, as we have seen, mounting pressure in the late 1980s for a
radical overhaul of the parole system. On the one hand, the judiciary
was concerned that sentencing differentials had become dangerously
eroded and that parole was 'virtually an entitlement' for section 33
cases.[150] On the other hand, academics saw irreconcilable tensions in
the system and were critical of a lack of due process. In 1987 the
Conservative Party bent to this pressure, and included in its election
manifesto a promise to review the system.[151] After winning the election the Home Secretary kept that promise by establishing, in July
1987, a Review Committee under the chairmanship of the Rt Hon
Mark Carlisle QC (later Lord Carlisle of Bucklow). Nine other
members were also appointed to the Committee, one of whom was
Roger Hood.

The Committee's terms of reference were to examine both the
operation of the parole system in England and Wales and the relationship between parole and the arrangements for remission, time
spent in custody, and suspended sentences. The Committee therefore
felt compelled to rule out not only the complete abolition of parole
(which had been favoured by some writers[152]) but also the highly

---

[149] See The Parole Board (Transfer of Functions) Order 1998, S.I. 1998 No. 3218.

[150] *Carlisle Committee Report*, n. 10 above, at para. 36.

[151] There had been earlier calls for an independent inquiry into the parole system.
The Association of Chief Probation Officers, NACRO (see Mackey, n. 56 above, 22)
and the Howard League (twice) (see L. Blom-Cooper's 'Preface' to the League's
Freedom on Licence: The Development of Parole and Proposals for Reform (Sunbury:
Quartermaine House, 1981), at p. vii) had suggested such a move, as had the House of
Commons Expenditure Committee in 1978 (see Fifteenth Report from the Expend-
iture Committee (Session 1977–78), *The Reduction of Pressure on the Prison System,
Vol. 1: Report; Vols. 2 and 3: Minutes of Evidence* and *Appendices* (London: HMSO,
1978), at para. 56: J.E. Hall Williams and S.D.M. McConville were appointed to act
as Specialist Advisors to the Committee). Following a question tabled by Lord Longford, the matter was also discussed in a debate in the House of Lords in July 1980: see
H.L. Debs., vol. 412, cols. 626–653.

[152] See S. Cohen and L. Taylor, *Prison Secrets* (London: National Council for Civil
Liberties/Radical Alternatives to Prison, 1978), at 88: '[w]e . . . would argue for the
total abolition of parole'.

pared down version suggested by Roger Hood in the 1970s.[153] Implementation of either of these options without a complete restructuring of sentencing tariffs (something that was not within its terms of reference), the Committee said, would be bound 'to provoke a further unwarranted and unacceptable increase in the prison population'.[154]

The Committee's report, published in November 1988, was based primarily on the different arguments for and against various reform options and on its assessment of previous empirical studies, rather than on an extensive body of specifically commissioned research.[155] The Committee was, however, able to collect information from the *Parole Board Annual Reports* and present this in a way that made it easier to identify long-term trends.[156] The Committee also asked for three small-scale research studies to be conducted on its behalf. The first established that, in 1986, 'all but 3.5 per cent of LRC decisions were unanimous', which confirmed the Committee's impression 'that there was a strong momentum towards consensus within the panels'.[157] The second, carried out by the Board's Secretariat in October 1987, showed that 'all but seven per cent of 325 cases

---

[153] Hood had argued that parole should be used only for 'a very limited category of offenders': those serving sentences longer than three (or possibly four) years whom the trial judge considered 'dangerous'. His view was that in these cases the court should 'fix the minimum period for parole eligibility, which would not be less than the period for statutory release on licence [one-third] nor greater than, say, three-fifths of the sentence': see 'Some Fundamental Dilemmas of the English Parole System and a Suggestion for an Alternative Structure' in D.A. Thomas (ed.), *Parole: Its Implications for the Penal and Criminal Justice Systems* (Cambridge: Institute of Criminology, 1974), esp. at 15. See also his *Tolerance and the Tariff: Some Reflections on Fixing the Time Prisoners Spend in Custody* (London: NACRO, 1974), 13; his 'Comments on the Report of the Advisory Council on the Penal System' (1974) 14 *British Journal of Criminology* 388; and his 'The Case against Executive Control over Time in Custody: A Rejoinder to Professor Walker's Criticisms' [1975] *Crim.L.R.* 545.

[154] See *Carlisle Committee Report*, n. 10 above, at para. 233.

[155] The Committee was also influenced by developments in parole and sentencing in the USA and particularly in Canada. Members of the Committee visited both countries.

[156] This prompted the Parole Board to do the same, beginning with its *Report of the Parole Board for 1988*, n. 126 above, Table 7.

[157] See *Carlisle Committee Report*, n. 10 above, at para. 126. The *Report* does not say who carried out the research, but it likely to have been the Home Office's Parole Unit.

considered over a fortnight's period were decided unanimously'.[158]
The final study, conducted by Dr Carol Hedderman at the Home
Office, looked into decision-making in section 33 cases. Hedderman
examined the parole dossiers of 300 section 33 cases (all involving
male prisoners) that had been obtained from the Parole Unit during
the first two months of 1998, half of which were LRC 'suitables' and
half 'unsuitables'. She found that these prisoners differed in a
number of ways. The 'unsuitables' had longer criminal records,
poorer job histories and prospects, and worse prison disciplinary
records than the 'suitables'. They were also less frequently recommended for parole by prison staff and by their home probation
officers, and were more likely to have breached previous licences.[159]
The Committee concluded from this that the selection of section 33
cases was 'not entirely a lottery', but said that it was clear from its
own observations of LRC meetings that 'there was no common
understanding of the test to be applied in assessing the suitability
of a short sentence prisoner for parole'.[160]

After considering these studies, and a mountain of other evidence
which had been submitted by various interested parties, the Committee eventually opted for a scheme in which short-term prisoners
would be released automatically without the need for their cases to

[158] Ibid., at para. 134. This can be compared with the position in 1968 when one of
the first two 'criminologist' members of the Board, Dr Donald West (the other was Mr
R.D. King), suggested that members should record their opinions, whether for or
against release on parole licence, both before and after panel discussions. Analysis of
these records at the end of the year revealed that in '64 cases, out of an unselected series
of 100 offenders considered for parole, there was a unanimous consensus of recorded
opinion before arrival at the panel meetings'. The Board concluded from this that
'members had achieved considerable consistency in their preliminary assessments of
the majority of case dossiers': see *Report of the Parole Board for 1968*, n. 30 above, at
para. 37. Little had changed when Roger Hood and I examined the system in the late
1990s. In *The Parole System at Work: A Study of Risk Based Decision-Making*, Home
Office Research Study No. 202 (London: Home Office, 2000) at 23–4, we found that
in eight out of 10 of the observed decisions the lead member's initial preference was
followed by the two other members of the panel, with neither of them voicing any
dissent.

[159] See C. Hedderman, 'Short Sentence Prisoners: The Characteristics of Those
Judged Suitable and Unsuitable for Parole By Local Review Committees' (1988) 25
Research Bulletin 14, esp. at 17. Dr Hedderman was appointed a member of the
Parole Board in September 2001.

[160] See *Carlisle Committee Report*, n. 10 above, at para. 187.

be considered by the Board.[161] It was 'wrong in principle' and 'unworkable in practice', the Committee said, 'to try to operate a selective parole system for short sentence prisoners'.[162] That idea was not new. It had first been suggested by Hood in a seminal paper in 1974,[163] had been supported by Lord Donaldson of Kingsbridge in the House of Lords,[164] and had found favour with the Home Office in its 1981 *Review of Parole*.[165] The fact that it was omitted from the 1981 Criminal Justice Bill was, it seems, largely because of opposition from the judiciary[166] and concern amongst the grass-roots of the Conservative party. Now its time had come.

[161] Ibid., para. 299(a).   [162] Ibid., para. 186.

[163] Hood, n. 153 above, 14. Hood proposed that 'for all prisoners serving sentences of up to and including three years (or possibly four), release on licence should be automatic after serving one third, say, of the sentence (subject to any loss of remission) with supervision on licence up to the end of the sentence' (fn. omitted).

[164] Hood's scheme, he said, was 'the best solution before us': see H.L. Debs., vol. 412, col. 645, 24 July 1980. Lord Donaldson was chairman of NACRO from 1966 to 1974.

[165] See n. 32 above, at paras. 53–60. The *Review* suggested that the introduction of automatic conditional release for prisoners serving less than three years might reduce the prison population by up to 7,000: see para. 60. The 1981 proposal was considered by the Parole Board's General Purposes Committee, which was broadly in favour of the reform. The Committee recommended, however, that the scheme be confined to prisoners serving up to two years: see *Report of the Parole Board for 1981*, n. 86 above, at para. 7. Similar proposals for prisoners sentenced to less than three years were endorsed by the Howard League's Working Party on Parole chaired by Lord McGregor: see n. 151 above. The other members were Paul Cavadino, Rachel Dickson, David Jenkins (Secretary), Terence Morris, Ken Pease, Andrew Rutherford, Richard Whitfield, and Martin Wright.

[166] See Bottomley, n. 2 above, at 354–5. Mike Maguire observes that in 1981 a BBC *Panorama* programme claimed that 'a cabal of senior judges' made it clear to the Home Secretary that automatic release at the one-third point was simply unacceptable: see n. 94 above, at 191. However, in a speech to the House of Lords made in 1982, the then Lord Chief Justice, Lord Lane, said that the real sticking point for the judiciary was the Conservative Government's refusal to contemplate its suggestion that judges be given a power not to apply the 'third-third-third' rule—whereby a third of the sentence should be served in prison, a third served on supervised release, and a third remitted—in specific cases, 'particularly where the public required protection'. This suggestion was, as Lord Lane put it, 'turned down flat'. But if it had been accepted, he said, there could be 'no possible objection to the scheme': see H.L. Debs., vol. 429, col. 880, 28 Apr. 1982.

Once the decision had been taken to exclude short-term prisoners, a number of other recommendations fell easily into place, especially in the light of the Committee's commitment to due process and to 'restoring some meaning to the full sentence imposed by the court'.[167] The Committee concluded that LRCs were unnecessary;[168] that unconditional remission should be abolished;[169] that licence conditions set by the Parole Board should be available irrespective of whether the prisoner was granted parole;[170] that parole criteria should be based on 'an evaluation of the risk to the public of the person committing further serious offences at a time when he would otherwise be in prison';[171] that these criteria should be prescribed by statute;[172] that parole decision-making should be open and that reports should be disclosed except where, in exceptional circumstances, the Board considered that disclosure would cause specific harm;[173] that prisoners should be given reasons for refusal;[174] that the Home Secretary should no longer have a veto; and that the parole eligibility date for longer-term prisoners should be moved from one-third of the sentence to one-half[175] (a proposal that one writer claims was adopted in order to appease the judiciary[176]).

The Criminal Justice Act 1991

It is a testimony to the quality of the Carlisle Committee's report that, despite its controversial nature, most of its recommendations were eventually accepted by Government: they were endorsed first by the 1990 White Paper, *Crime, Justice and Protecting the Public*,[177] and finally received legislative approval in the Criminal Justice Act 1991. As a result, long-term prisoners sentenced to determinate

[167] See *Carlisle Committee Report*, n. 10 above, para. 240.
[168] Ibid., paras. 314–317.
[169] Ibid., para. 240.
[170] Ibid., para. 383.
[171] Ibid., paras. 321–324.
[172] Ibid., para. 324.
[173] Ibid., paras. 331–336.
[174] Ibid., paras. 354–357.
[175] Ibid., paras. 269–274.
[176] See Maguire, n. 94 above, 190, who claims that this move was 'prompted above all by the desire to produce a system palatable to the judiciary'.
[177] See n. 100 above

terms of imprisonment on or after 1 October 1992, the date on which the sections of the Act relating to parole were brought into force, were now eligible for parole only at the halfway point of their sentences, were released at the two-thirds point if not granted parole, were required to submit to statutory supervision until the three-quarters point, and for the rest of their sentences remained 'at risk' of being returned to prison for the unexpired portion if they were convicted of another offence committed before the sentence terminated—all of which was exactly what Carlisle had intended.

Other aspects of the new scheme, however, differed from Carlisle. One departure was that prisoners serving sentences of exactly four years were not released automatically at the halfway point of their sentence as Carlisle had intended—an alteration that was made in part, it seems, because the Board had lobbied hard to persuade the Government that four-year sentences should—*pace* Carlisle—be brought within the scope of the discretionary scheme.[178] Another departure was that parole criteria were not prescribed by statute as Carlisle had wished. Instead, section 32(6) of the 1991 Act empowered the Secretary of State to give directions to the Board on the matters it must take into account when considering an application for parole.[179] The Home Secretary (Mr Kenneth Clarke) exercised this power in 1992[180] and new and more detailed criteria, which applied to both 'new' and 'old style' cases,[181] were promulgated.

The revised criteria are noteworthy in a number of respects. Not only did they clarify for the first time the level of further re-offending to be regarded as a risk,[182] but they expressly stated that 'a risk of violent offending [was] to be treated as more serious than a larger risk of non-violent offending'. That greater specificity meant they provided 'a much clearer basis for decision-making' than the criteria

[178] See *Report of the Parole Board for 1988*, n. 126 above, at para. 3.

[179] When issuing such directions s. 32(6) requires the Secretary of State to have particular regard to: '(a) the need to protect the public from serious harm from offenders; and (b) the desirability of preventing the commission by them of further offences and of securing their rehabilitation'.

[180] See H.C. Debs., Written Answers, vol. 211, col. 981, 16 July 1992.

[181] Nevertheless, the Board indicated that applying the criteria to 'old style' cases required a degree of 'flexibility' in their interpretation: see *Report of the Parole Board for 1992*, n. 96 above, at para. 7.

[182] See para. 1.3, which stated that the relevant risk was 'of further *imprisonable* offences being committed' (emphasis added).

they had replaced.[183] However, they also represented 'a somewhat tougher line' than had been taken in the past,[184] and in May 1996 the noose around parole was tightened further when the Board was told in another revision to the directions that it must 'take into account that safeguarding the public may often outweigh the benefits to the offender of early release'.[185] The Carlisle Committee had hoped that its proposals would lead to an increase in the number of prisoners being granted parole.[186] In fact, by restricting the criteria for release in this way, the Government confounded Carlisle's expectations and a prisoner's chances of being granted parole at some time in his sentence became lower than they had been under the old system.[187]

Two Procedural Issues

The 1967 scheme had been based on the idea that parole was a 'privilege' not a 'right'. It was therefore thought unnecessary to offer prisoners the full range of procedural protections. Not surprisingly, academics and organizations with an interest in parole were highly critical of this approach and campaigned for more than twenty years to have it rectified. Their efforts were finally repaid when the reforms that followed the publication of the *Carlisle Report* put due process at the heart of the new system and swept away the old idea that parole decision-making was none of a prison-

---

[183] See *Report of the Parole Board for 1992*, n. 96 above, at para. 7. Nevertheless, one commentator has expressed the fear that risk assessment will be 'used, consciously or unconsciously, to camouflage other grounds for decisions, in particular those of deterrence and retribution': see Maguire, n. 94 above, 195–6.

[184] See *Report of the Parole Board for 1992*, n. 96 above, at para. 9. The Board repeated this view in its 1993 *Annual Report*: 'the new directions are tougher than the old criteria and will eventually contribute to a lower paroling rate': see *Report of the Parole Board for 1993*, n. 148 above, at para. 21.

[185] Miss Ann Widdecombe announced the revision to the House of Commons in a written answer on 10 May 1996. The new directions, she said, contained 'a more explicit statement about the need to protect the safety of the public being a paramount factor': see Written Answers, H.C. Debs., vol. 277, col. 308.

[186] See *Carlisle Committee Report*, n. 10 above, at para. 280.

[187] In other words, the criteria brought about a fall in the 'any time' parole rate. For an analysis see Hood and Shute, n. 158 above, 25–7. In the last two years the parole rate has recovered somewhat: see *Annual Report and Accounts of the Parole Board for England and Wales 2001/2002*, HC 1203 (London: Stationery Office, 2002), at 4, 46, and 52.

er's business.[188] In the context of this chapter it is instructive to examine in detail two of these issues—the membership and composition of the decision-making bodies and the giving of reasons—so as to get a better idea of the effects of 'research' on the various reforms that were made.

Membership and Composition of Decision-making Bodies

LRCs. The composition of LRC panels was a matter of debate even at the outset of the scheme. A particular anxiety was that prison employees would be able to wield a disproportionate influence on parole outcomes. Indeed, Lord Brooke of Cumnor tabled but ultimately did not press an amendment to the 1967 Criminal Justice Bill which would have prevented 'any person employed in the prison service' from being a member of an LRC,[189] and Lord Parker of Waddington (the Lord Chief Justice) also expressed concern that 'any local review committee would pay the greatest attention to the governor'.[190] The Minister of State, Lord Stonham, sought to reassure the House of Lords on this matter. He forthrightly asserted that LRCs would 'certainly not be under the control of the governor'.[191] In the end it was this view that prevailed and the Local Committee Rules 1967[192] provided that LRCs must consist of 'the governor of the prison'; a probation officer; a member of the Board of Visitors; and a fourth, so-called 'independent member', who was not a probation officer or a member of the Board of Visitors.[193]

As with so many issues surrounding parole, however, the problem did not go away, and in the late 1960s and early 1970s two pieces of empirical research revived fears that governors might be exercising

---

[188] However, the Committee was split on whether hearings involving prisoners were necessary (see para. 353). Although these might be thought to be an essential feature of a regime which takes 'due process' seriously, they were not introduced in the wake of the Criminal Justice Act 1991.

[189] See H.L. Debs., vol. 283, col. 737, 12 June 1967. He suggested that LRCs should include 'at least one person who is not connected by any official relationship whatever with the prison service' and (at col. 738) expressed concerns about possible inconsistencies in LRC decision-making.

[190] Ibid., col. 749.

[191] Ibid., col. 745.

[192] S.I. 1967 No. 1462, r. 1(2).

[193] This fourth 'independent' member was added at the suggestion of Mr T.L. Iremonger. See Standing Committee A, H.C. Debs., Session 1966–67, vol. 2, cols. 728–730, 7 Mar. 1967.

inappropriate control over LRC decision-making. In the first of these studies Professor A.K. Bottomley analysed the parole outcomes of 207 prisoners serving sentences of five years or longer whose applications for parole had been reviewed at a closed training prison in Hull between March 1969 and March 1970. Bottomley found that the assistant governor's general assessment of the prisoner, which was included in the parole dossier, was 'a good guide' both to his chances of being favourably recommended by the Parole Board and to his chances of being favourably recommended by his LRC.[194] The second study, carried out by Christopher Nuttall and his colleagues at the Home Office, examined 159 decisions made by LRCs in 1973. It confirmed Bottomley's conclusion. In Nuttall's sample of cases recommendations made by assistant governors were followed 86 per cent of the time.[195]

It was natural to infer from these studies that assistant governors were exerting a disproportionate influence at panel meetings, and the Government responded to this suggestion by introducing two measures which were designed to increase LRCs' autonomy: first, the Local Review Committee (Amendment) Rules 1973 added a fifth, independent, person to the membership;[196] secondly, a change was made to the administrative practice that had grown up in the early days of the scheme whereby governors chaired LRC meetings—now they were precluded from doing so.[197]

The Parole Board. When it was first constituted in 1967 the Parole Board consisted of a part-time Chairman (Lord Hunt)[198]

---

[194] A.K. Bottomley, 'Parole Decisions in a Long-Term Closed Prison' (1973) 13 *British Journal of Criminology* 26 at 37. When the assessments of assistant governors were divided into five classes (good, fair, uncertain, doubtful, poor) 'the prospects of three-quarters of those recommended were assessed as good or fair (compared to only 13 % of those not recommended), and none of them was assessed as having poor prospects (compared to half of those not recommended)': see 32–3. The assessments of assistant governors were equally influential at the Board. 'Thus, well over half of those paroled (57 %) were assessed as having good prospects on parole (compared to only a fifth of the recommendations turned down), and a further 26 % as having "fair" prospects; conversely, only 17 % had uncertain or doubtful prospects on parole, compared to 35 % of those turned down. No one in either group was assessed as having *poor* prospects': see 36.

[195] See Nuttall *et al.*, n. 44 above, 38.

[196] S.I. 1973 No. 4, r. 2(c), 29 Jan. 1973.

[197] See *Home Office Review of Parole*, n. 32 above, at para. 17.

[198] In all the Board has had eight Chairs: Lord Hunt (1967–74), Sir Louis Petch (1974–9), Lord Harris (1979–82), Lord Windlesham (1982–8), Viscount Colville

and sixteen other part-time members who were drawn from (but not limited to) four statutory categories: judges; psychiatrists; probation officers (described in the legislation as persons who have 'knowledge and experience of the supervision or after-care of discharged prisoners'), and criminologists (described as persons who have 'made a study of the causes of delinquency or the treatment of offenders').[199] Appointments to the Board were made in such a way that at least two persons from each category were members.[200] The Board's initial practice when considering cases was to divide itself into two panels,[201] but within a year or so the workload had become such that three panels were needed. There was also a requirement for more members.[202] Thus, in the late 1960s three new members were added, and a further eleven were appointed at the beginning of the 1970s. This upward trend continued, and by 1990 the Board consisted of seventy-six members plus the Chair (see Table 9:6). Three years later the requirements of Discretionary Lifer Panels pushed the ordinary membership up to eighty-four.

As the membership increased, so panel size reduced. In the early 1970s panels consisted of 'about five members',[203] but by the mid-1980s panel size had been cut to four,[204] and a further reduction in 1993 meant that just three members sat.[205] With fewer members on each panel representatives from the four statutory categories began

(1988–92), Lord Belstead (1992–7), Baroness Prashar (1997–2000), and David Hatch (2000–present). See Table 9:6 below.

[199] See Sched. 2, para. 1, to the Criminal Justice Act 1967.

[200] See *Report of the Parole Board for 1968*, n. 30 above, at para. 24.

[201] The Parole Board Rules 1967 stated that a case could be dealt with 'by any three or more members of the Board': see S.I. 1967 No. 1685, r. 1.

[202] In the 1960s the Board had concerns about expanding its membership: '[a]dding more members', it said, 'is a policy that has diminishing returns in efficiency, since the problems of co-ordination and consistency must increase with the size of the Board in almost geometric progression': see *Report of the Parole Board for 1969*, n. 49 above, at para. 120.

[203] Normally including 'a judge, a psychiatrist and a principal probation officer and whenever possible a criminologist': see *Report of the Parole Board for 1973*, n. 70 above, para. 32. See also *Report of the Parole Board for 1974* (London: HMSO, 1976), 432, at para. 20, where the Parole Board said, 'Whilst the statutory quorum for a panel is three, for practical purpose it is preferable that four or five members are nominated for each one'.

[204] See *Report of the Parole Board for 1987*, n. 91 above, at para. 21.

[205] The *Report of the Parole Board for 1992* (n. 96 above, para. 57) states that in 1992 it met in panels of 'either three or four members'. The suggestion that panels

TABLE 9:6   Parole Board Membership, 1968–2002* (source: *Parole Board Annual Reports*)

Year	Chair	Number of Part-time Members	Number of Full-time Members
1968	Lord Hunt	16	-
1969	"	16**	-
1970	"	19	-
1971	"	19	-
1972	"	30	-
1973	"	31	-
1974	Sir Louis Petch	33	-
1975	"	33	-
1976	"	37	-
1977	"	38	-
1978	"	35	-
1979	Lord Harris	45	-
1980	"	45	-
1981	"	48	-
1982	Lord Windlesham	44	-
1983	"	46	-
1984	"	49	-
1985	"	53	-
1986	"	54	-
1987	"	66	-
1988	Viscount Colville	68	-
1989	"	66	-
1990	"	76	-
1991	"	62	-
1992	Lord Belstead	61	-
1993	"	84	-
1994	"	77	6
1995	"	59	4
1996	"	66	4
1997	Baroness Prashar	68	4
1998	"	76	4
1999	"	92	4
2000	Mr David Hatch	101	2***
2001	"	107	2
2002	"	109	2

*For the years 1968 to 1996 inclusive the figures are as at 1 January; for the years 1997 to 2002 inclusive the figures are as at 31 March.

**It is unclear from the 1969 *Annual Report* when one member (Mrs Jacobson) resigned, but it has been assumed for the purposes of this Table that her resignation was after 1 January 1969.

***One of the former full-timers (Dr Richard Osborn) transferred to a part-time capacity in July 1999.

to play less of a role in parole decision-making. Indeed, Roger Hood and I found in our second study of parole decision-making that 'independent' members outnumbered experts on more than two-thirds of the panels we observed.[206]

The early 1990s also brought another important change: the appointment of full-time members. Although this idea had long been promoted by some academics who considered it to be in 'the interests of fair procedure and proper consideration of cases',[207] it was vigorously opposed by the Parole Board on the ground that it would create 'undesirable distinctions of role and commitment within the Board'.[208] The Government brushed aside this objection, and the first full-time Chair, Lord Belstead, was appointed in October 1992.

might be reduced to three had been made in the 1990 White Paper (n.100 above, para. 6.19). The Board was opposed to this. In particular, it objected to the suggestion that there could be a quorum of two. (Lord Hunt, the former Chairman of the Board, also spoke against these ideas in the debates on the 1991 Criminal Justice Bill in the House of Lords: see H.L. Debs., vol. 527, col. 107, 12 Mar. 1991: 'the minimum number should be four with a quorum of three'.) The Board favoured the existing system in which each panel would usually include 'a member of the judiciary or a criminologist, a psychiatrist, a probation officer, and an independent member'. This, said the Board, provided the 'best mix' and enabled 'all the issues in each case to be thoroughly and properly considered': see *Report of the Parole Board for 1989*, n. 80 above, at para. 10. These concerns were repeated in *Report of the Parole Board for 1991* (London: HMSO, 1992), 43, at para. 27. The Board noted that many of its members actually favoured increasing panel size to five and cautioned against the suggestion that the membership of the Board might be reduced. Yet, in November 1999, the Board established two-member panels to consider cases involving the revocation of licences and recall to prison. This change was prompted by the extra work created by the implementation on 1 January 1999 of s. 103 of the Crime and Disorder Act 1998 which transferred to the Board responsibility for considering the recall of short-term prisoners as well as long-term prisoners (see 430–431 below). Initially, one two-member panel was convened each week but, by 31 March 2001, the case-load was such that it was necessary to convene four of these panels weekly. See the Parole Board's *Annual Report and Accounts of the Parole Board 2000–2001*, HC 235 (London: Stationery Office, 2001), 20.

[206] R. Hood and S. Shute, *Paroling With New Criteria, Evaluating the Impact and Effects of Changes in the Parole System: Phase Two*, Occasional Paper No. 16 (Oxford: University of Oxford Centre for Criminological Research, 1995) at para. 14. And, by the time of our third parole study, the position had been exacerbated by the fact that judges had been asked to chair discretionary lifer panels and so were no longer available to sit on determinate sentence panels: see Hood Shute, n. 158 above, at 21.

[207] See Hawkins, n. 137 above, 21.

[208] See *Report of the Parole Board for 1969*, n. 49 above, at para. 120.

Five months later the Minister of State, Mr Peter Lloyd, told the Board's Annual General Meeting that the Home Secretary had decided to make other full-time appointments.[209] Predictably, the Board again resisted this proposal,[210] but its efforts came to naught and six full-time members were appointed in September 1993. At the same time the number of part-time members was scaled down.[211]

It was not long, however, before the Government's enthusiasm for full-time members started to wane. When one full-time member died and another resigned they were not replaced,[212] nor were two of the other full-time members once their contracts had come to an end. Accordingly, by March 2000, only two full-time ordinary members were sitting on the Board, and the new Chairman, Mr David Hatch, was also part-time. This drop in the number of full-time members meant that there was a need for yet more part-timers, and two years later no fewer than 109 were members of the Board.

Reasons

Under the terms of the 1967 scheme, reasons had to be given whenever a parole licence was revoked, but not when the original decision to deny a prisoner parole was taken.[213] For some academic writers this was as it should be. Hall Williams, for example, drew an analogy between parole decisions and decisions made by juries: in each case, he said, it was better for the reasoning to remain 'inscrutable'.[214]

---

[209]   The meeting was held in March 1993.

[210]   *Report of the Parole Board for 1993*, n. 148 above, at para. 25. The Board argued that 'sufficient management expertise existed within the Board' already and pointed out that other methods could be adopted if it was felt that there was a need to improve consistency in decision-making. The Board did, however, recognize that the Home Secretary had the right to make such appointments if he wished to do so. See also 'Clarke accused of "packing" the Parole Board', *Independent on Sunday*, 4 Apr. 1993.

[211]   From 77 in 1994 to 59 in 1995.

[212]   Mr J.C.L. Wright resigned in December 1993 and Mr B.C. Sullivan died after a short illness in April 1994.

[213]   Criminal Justice Act 1967, s. 62(3): '[a] person recalled to prison . . . may make representations in writing with respect to his recall and shall on his return to prison be informed of the reasons for his recall and of his right to make such representations'.

[214]   See his Sixth Denis Carroll Memorial Lecture, *Ten Years of Parole—Retrospect and Prospect* (Croydon: Institute for the Study and Treatment of Delinquency, 1978), 18. Other writers were opposed to the giving of reasons on purely practical grounds. See, for example, D.J. West who thought that it was 'probably impractical to do more than inform prisoners of the range of considerations taken into account in all cases': n. 72 above, 28. See also Rolph, n. 62 above, at 15.

The weight of academic opinion, however, regarded reason-giving not just as desirable but as obligatory,[215] with notable contributions to this debate being made by Keith Hawkins,[216] Roger Hood,[217] J.P. Martin,[218] Alec Samuels,[219] and Evelyn Shea.[220]

Yet the Board vacillated. Its first Chairman, Lord Hunt, who saw some merit in reason-giving,[221] introduced a practice whereby, for administrative purposes, the chair of the panel would summarize the main points that had been taken into account when making the decision. These would then be recorded by the panel secretary,[222] but that record was never made available to prisoners and, although discussions took place with the Home Office, Lord Hunt was unable or unwilling to force through more radical change.[223] When the next Chairman, Sir Louis Petch, arrived in 1974 the Board's position hardened. While it admitted that reason-giving was a matter that

---

[215] It also had some support in Parliament when the legislation was debated. See Mr T.L. Iremonger's comments in the Committee stage of the Criminal Justice Bill: Standing Committee A, H.C. Debs., session 1966–67, vol. 2, col. 729, 7 Mar. 1967.

[216] Hawkins, n. 137 above, 21. Hawkins noted (at 17) that in the USA a number of states had 'adopted the practice for some time' and that the Chairman of the Federal Board of Parole had announced its intention to give reasons as of April 1972.

[217] Hood, n. 153 above, 13: 'I believe it is essential, whether parole is granted to a minority or the majority, for those who are refused to have the opportunity of a personal hearing and be given reasons for the refusal.... But to make this the only change would, I believe, be a mistake. To give reasons in a system operating with such diverse and sometimes conflicting criteria for selection might have a worse impact on the morale of prisoners than giving no reasons at all'.

[218] Martin, n. 64 above, 56.

[219] Samuels argued that '[r]easons should always be given, shortly and simply, except where the Board expressly for good reasons decides otherwise': see n. 71 above, at 459.

[220] N. 13 above, 77–8.

[221] Initially, he qualified his support by saying that it must be done 'in the context of a personal interview and discussion'. See 'Foreword' (1973) 13 British Journal of Criminology 1, at 4. Later, he became more strongly persuaded. See H.L. Debs., vol. 399, col. 1382, 22 Mar. 1979, where he said that in this area there had been 'a failure to fulfil a matter of natural justice for too long'.

[222] See Report of the Parole Board for 1969, n. 49 above, at para. 64. Hawkins, n. 137 above, 15 and 16, reasonably asks why, if the Board could formulate reasons for administrative purposes, it could not do so for disclosure to prisoners.

[223] See Report of the Parole Board for 1969, n. 49 above, at para. 115, which states that the prevailing view of the Board was, at the present stage of development of the parole scheme, that reason giving 'would not be helpful'.

'frequently exercised the minds' of its members,[224] the Board clearly felt that there were insuperable obstacles to it doing so.

Eventually, though, the Home Secretary responded to continued pressure from critics[225] by announcing in a speech at the Mansion House on 12 July 1976 that an experiment would be conducted within the Parole Board using standardized 'causes for concern'.[226] The Board did not relish having to construct such a list, but after some delay it eventually came up with sixteen factors for determinate sentence prisoners. The experiment was then extended to five prisons of different security categories in order 'to test the practicality of LRCs selecting appropriate standardised reasons in all cases' and 'to obtain subjective assessments from governors as to the likely effect on prisoners were such reasons to be given'.[227] As the 1981 *Home Office Review of Parole* later observed, the results of the experiment were 'disappointing':

> Even with careful advice and feedback LRCs were still having as much difficulty in selecting appropriate reasons from the standardised list after 12 months as at the outset of the experiment ... [And] of those cases considered by both a LRC and the Parole Board and recommended for refusal by both, different causes for concern were given by the two bodies in about a quarter of the cases.[228]

So when, on 28 February 1979, the Board sent a letter to the Home Secretary outlining its opposition to reason-giving,[229] and also called

[224] See *Report of the Parole Board for 1975*, n. 77 above, at para. 19. See also paras. 21–25 where the Board lists a number of its objections to reason giving.

[225] Lord Longford argued in the House of Lords in 1980 that 'the reformative benefits of the system would be vastly increased if reasons for refusing parole were given' (see H.L. Debs., vol. 412, col. 628, 24 July 1980) and that 'a good many more people would in fact get parole, if only because the Parole Board would not be able to defend the sort of reasons which are tending to weigh with them all too often now' (col. 630). The Howard League's Working Party on Parole in 1981 pointed out that Mental Health Review Tribunals, which dealt with equally sensitive cases, gave reasons for their decisions and allowed hearings and representation. See n. 151 above, at para. 121.

[226] The experiment is described in the *Home Office Review of Parole*, n. 32 above, paras. 75–79.

[227] Ibid., para. 77.

[228] Ibid., para. 78. The *Review* came out against the giving of reasons (see para. 74).

[229] This was later reproduced in its 1979 *Annual Report*, n. 53 above, as Appendix 5. '[T]wo detailed and one fundamental objection to the giving of reasons' were offered. All look weak now. The first detailed objection was that it would concede

for the 'Reasons Experiment' to be abandoned,[230] it found that it was pushing at an open door. By July 1979 the Government's *volte-face* was complete. Lord Belstead, Parliamentary Under-Secretary of State at the Home Office and later a Chairman of the Parole Board, replied to a Parliamentary Question in the following terms:

The Government feel it right...to say that, on the available evidence, the giving of reasons would be incompatible with the present parole scheme and would make unacceptable demands on resources.[231]

Over the next few years little changed. The Board was now routinely recording refusals under categories *A* to *F* of the *Criteria for Selection*[232] but this information was not transmitted to prisoners. The Board took comfort in the fact that the Court of Appeal in *Payne* v. *Lord Harris of Greenwich and another*[233] had held that there was no duty on the part of either the Parole Board or the LRCs to give reasons for refusing parole, and in its written submission to the Carlisle Committee it stood by its longstanding position: providing reasons to prisoners, it said, would be 'incompatible with the operation of the parole system' in its current form.[234]

---

the principle that its decisions were open to legal challenge. The second was that it would be 'merely to invite disclosure of the reports which the Board considered supported that reason'. The third, more fundamental, objection was that reason-giving was incompatible with a system in which parole was 'a privilege to be earned' and not 'a right to be claimed'. Since this was the system Parliament had created, the Board argued, it should not be altered without Parliamentary intervention.

[230] Once the results of the 'causes for concern' experiment had been analysed, the Board said, 'it was clearly the opinion of the great majority of Board members that it would be impracticable to communicate reasons for refusal, even in the form of "causes for concern" ': see *Report of the Parole Board for 1979*, n. 53 above, at para. 3. The Board also reported that its Chairman had visited New South Wales where the Parole Board provided written reasons in every case where parole had been refused. These consisted of 'a brief statement identifying the main factors which influenced the Board's decision'. They were taken from a standardized list and were not unlike the 'causes for concern' which had been developed experimentally by the Board. The Board observed, however, that even in this condensed form the reasons 'had failed to satisfy prisoners': see para. 56.

[231] See H.L. Debs., vol. 401, col. 4, 2 July 1979.

[232] The alphabetical designations first appeared in the Criteria in the Board's 1980 *Annual Report*, n. 55 above.

[233] [1981] 2 All ER 842. Lord Denning MR made much play of the 'practical difficulty' of giving reasons and the danger that 'reasons would become short and stereotyped, rather than full and informative': see 846.

[234] See *Report of the Parole Board for 1987*, n. 91 above, at para. 28.

The Carlisle Committee, however, took a different view. It strongly recommended that reasons should be provided to all prisoners.[235] The Government finally accepted the wisdom of that approach, and the 1990 White Paper said that the aim was to move towards a position in which the Board gave reasons for its decisions.[236] Although a requirement to do so was not included in the 1991 Act, the Home Secretary announced less than two years later that (as from April 1993) all parole applicants who had received determinate sentences of imprisonment on or after 1 October 1992 would be given reasons for the decisions taken in their case.[237] In 1994 this practice was extended to include so-called 'existing prisoners'.[238]

Since that time the Board has made considerable efforts to ensure the quality of the reasons it provides.[239] Its *Policy and Procedures Manual* has been changed to include specific guidance to members on the drafting of reasons and it has tried to encourage the dissemination of good practice by launching a quarterly newsletter for its members and staff.[240] It has also changed its policy on appointing panel chairs. At one time the Board thought it sensible to allow all members to have the opportunity to chair panels,[241] and a rotation system was used. Now, only 'the most experienced' members are allowed to chair panels, and chairs are provided with 'specific training' to prepare them for the task.[242]

---

[235] See *Carlisle Committee Report*, n. 10 above, at paras. 354–357.

[236] *Crime, Justice and Protecting the Public*, n. 100 above, at para. 6.26.

[237] The Home Secretary also said that prisoners would have their dossiers disclosed to them.

[238] See Hood and Shute, n. 206 above, Chapter 5, for an empirical study of reasons giving by the Board in 'old system cases'. In *The Parole System at Work: A Study of Risk Based Decision-Making*, n. 158 above, 27–31, we looked at reasons giving in the new system.

[239] One important stimulus for this has been the increased tendency on the part of prisoners to take their cases to the courts for judicial review.

[240] The newsletter was first launched in March 1998.

[241] See *Report of the Parole Board for 1969*, n. 49 above, at para. 64.

[242] See *Report of the Parole Board for 1997–98* (London: Stationery Office, 1998), 1089, at 19. The responsibilities of chairs increased further in 1998–9 when panel secretaries were removed from determinate panels. See *Report of the Parole Board for 1998–99* (London: Stationery Office, 1999) HC 809, at 5.

Recent Developments, 1996–2002

The parole system continues to evolve and, as always, the relation-ship of policy to criminal research is ambivalent. In this last section I will examine a few of the most significant recent developments.

The Crime (Sentences) Act 1997 and the Crime and Disorder Act 1998

In 1996 the Government published a controversial White Paper, *Protecting the Public: The Government's Strategy on Crime in Eng-land and Wales*,[243] which, *inter alia*, proposed that both automatic conditional release for prisoners serving short sentences and discre-tionary conditional release for those serving longer determinate sentences should be abolished. The Parole Board's response was, not surprisingly, hostile. It defended parole on the basis that it provided 'an incentive to reduce the risk of re-offending in the future' and so played a part 'in breaking the cycle of offending behaviour and hence reducing the overall level of serious crime'.[244] The Gov-ernment's proposals were also criticized, albeit on different grounds, in an article (based on an empirical study) that Roger Hood and I published in the *Criminal Law Review* in 1996.[245]

Unmoved, the Government incorporated its proposals into the Crime (Sentences) Bill. But by now serious opposition was building up in the House of Lords. With a general election looming the

---

[243] Cm 3190 (London: HMSO, 1996).

[244] See *Report of the Parole Board for 1995 and 1995/96* (London: Stationery Office, 1996), 506, Appendix E, para. 8. The Board also considered it wrong that 'carefully prepared risk assessments' would be discarded 'in favour of mechanically adding up days earned for good behaviour' (para. 5); and that the decision on early release would be the responsibility of the Prison Service (para. 10). The Board said that the reforms would 'lead to an abandonment' of rehabilitation, which was a crucial plank in the 'prison works' strategy of then Conservative Gover-nment, and replace 'a system which is effective in dealing with the release of dangerous and persistent prisoners with one which is worse in almost every respect' (para. 14). In order to salvage something, the Board suggested a compromise: 'a reduction in remission whereby a prisoner would be eligible for discretionary conditional release with a full risk assessment after serving 85% of the sentence': see para. 6.

[245] See 'Protecting the Public: Automatic Life Sentences, Parole and High Risk Offenders' [1996] *Crim.L.R.* 788. This article was later referred to by the then Chair of the Board, Lord Belstead, in the debates in the House of Lords on the Crime (Sentences) Bill: see H.L. Debs., vol. 577, col. 1019, 27 Jan. 1997.

Government sought to save its legislation by introducing amendments which retained parole for prisoners serving sentences of three years or more, but postponed their eligibility date until five-sixths of their sentences had been served—a change which would have had the effect of cutting the parole window in half for a second time. The power to assess these prisoners and direct their release was to remain with the Board. The compromise worked, and the Crime (Sentences) Act received its Royal Assent in March 1997, just before the general election. However, the incoming Labour Government soon made it clear that it had no intention of implementing the provisions relating to parole,[246] and they were finally repealed a year later by section 107(2) of, and Schedule 10 to, the Crime and Disorder Act 1998.[247]

The Crime and Disorder Act 1998 also made another important change to parole[248] by bringing the recall arrangements for released prisoners who were serving sentences of less than four years into line with those for prisoners who were serving sentences of four years or longer: henceforth both groups would be subject to recall by the Home Secretary on the recommendation of the Board.[249] There had been a longstanding convention whereby recall cases were considered by ordinary panels of the Board before they turned their attention to other work. However, because of the increased number of recall cases now reaching the Board, this became impractical, and the Board was forced to establish separate panels to deal with these cases. This modification is very much to be welcomed. For far too long recall cases had been the waifs and strays of the system, con-

---

[246] See the speech to Parliament made by the Home Secretary (Mr Jack Straw), H.C. Debs., vol. 299, col. 342, 30 July 1997.

[247] See also s. 120(2). For a full account of the history of this matter, see Lord Windlesham, *Dispensing Justice: Responses to Crime* (Oxford: Oxford University Press, 2001), iv, Chapters 1 and 2.

[248] The Crime and Disorder Act 1998 also made provision for prisoners recalled to prison after release from an 'extended sentence' (a sentence which consists of a custodial term and an extended period of community supervision) to have their representations against recall reviewed by the Parole Board, and then for their continued detention to be reviewed again on an annual basis. To comply with the terms of the European Convention on Human Rights it was decided by the Board that an oral hearing should be provided in these cases similar to that offered to discretionary life sentence prisoners.

[249] See s. 103, which was brought into force on 1 January 1999. S. 150 of, and Sched. 10, para. 70 to, the Criminal Justice and Public Order Act 1994 had earlier amended the provisions relating to emergency recalls.

sidered on the basis of tabled papers at the beginning of a meeting with an already full agenda.

The Comprehensive Review of Parole

A second important development to the parole system occurred on 11 February 2000 when the then Home Office Minister for Prisons and Probation, Mr Paul Boateng, told Parliament that the Prison Service would be carrying out a first Quinquennial Review of the Parole Board.[250] While such reviews are a requirement for all Non-Departmental Public Bodies (which the Board now is[251]) the scope of the review was extended to enable issues raised in 'three significant research reports'—the research into parole decision-making conducted by Roger Hood and me;[252] the National Audit Office's value-for-money study of the parole system;[253] and the study of discretionary lifer panels carried out by Nicola Padfield and Alison Liebling[254]—to be considered together.

When it was published in 2001 the *Review* made more than 100 recommendations for change.[255] For the most part these were accepted by the Parole Board, although it did express 'strong concerns' about two of the more radical suggestions, both of which were based on ideas that Roger Hood and I had floated in 2000: i.e., that interviews might be conducted not by Board members but by volunteers or paid interviewers; and that some or all determinate sentence cases might be decided by a single panel member, subject to a right of appeal to a three-member panel if requested by the prisoner. Whether or not these controversial proposals are eventually implemented will turn on the decisions that are taken concerning the

[250] See H.C. Debs., Written Answers, vol. 344, cols. 317–318. The terms of reference for the Quinquennial Review are set out in the Parole Board's *Annual Report and Accounts of the Parole Board 1999–2000* (London: Stationery Office, 2000) HC 894, at 24.

[251] The change was effected by s. 149 of the Criminal Justice and Public Order Act 1994 (see also Sched. 10, para. 70) and took effect as of 1 July 1996.

[252] *The Parole System at Work: A Study of Risk Based Decision-Making*, n. 158 above.

[253] *Parole*, HC 456, Parliamentary Session 1999–2000, May 2000.

[254] *An Exploration of Decision-making at Discretionary Lifer Panels*, Home Office Research Study No. 213 (London: Home Office, 2000).

[255] *The Comprehensive Review of Parole and Lifer Processes* (London: Sentence Management Group, HM Prison Service, October 2001).

Halliday Review of the Sentencing Framework for England and Wales.[256]

The Halliday Report

Completed in 2001, the Halliday Report, *Making Punishments Work*,[257] proposed that parole should be abolished except for persons considered by the courts to be 'dangerous' violent or sexual offenders. Those deemed to fall into the latter category would receive a 'special sentence', rendering them eligible for release at the halfway point of their sentence if (but only if) the Parole Board thought them suitable for release.[258] Those not thought to be 'dangerous' by the courts would be released from custody automatically at the halfway point of their sentence and would then serve the rest of their sentence in the community.[259]

These proposals, which bear a striking resemblance to ideas developed by Roger Hood, have the advantage of ensuring that sentencing and parole decisions are based on the same criteria.[260] They thus resolve many of the tensions within the parole system that Hood so eloquently discussed almost thirty years ago[261] and they were, for the most part, adopted by the 2002 White Paper, *Justice For All*.[262] However, the White Paper departed from Halliday in one important respect. Whereas the *Halliday Report* envisaged the use of a special *determinate* sentence for 'dangerous' violent and

---

[256] See the *Annual Report and Accounts of the Parole Board 2000–2001* (London: Stationery Office, 2001) HC 235, at 15.

[257] See *Making Punishment Work: A Review of the Sentencing Framework in England and Wales* (London: Home Office, 2001).

[258] The courts would also have the power to order a period of extended supervision for up to 10 years after the normal expiry date of the sentence (or the maximum for the offence, whichever was the lesser).

[259] Ibid., Chapter 4.

[260] See R. Hood and S. Shute, 'The Changing Face of Parole in England and Wales: A Story of Some Well-Intentioned Reforms and Unintended Consequences' in C. Prittwitz, M. Baurmann, K. Günther, L. Kuhlen, R. Merkel, C. Nestler, and L. Schulz (eds.), *Festschrift für Klaus Lüderssen* (Baden-Baden: Nomos Verlag, 2002), 835, at 849.

[261] See nn. 153 and 163 above. Roger Hood served as a member of the External Reference Group to the Halliday Review Team (see Appendix 1, Annex B for a full list) and undoubtedly had an influence on its deliberations.

[262] e.g., para. 5.45 of the White Paper states that discretionary release will 'only apply to dangerous, sexual and violent offenders'.

sexual offenders, the White Paper advocated the use of an *indeterminate* sentence: 'dangerous' violent and sexual offenders, the White Paper stated, should 'be required to serve a minimum term', and after the expiry of that term should remain in prison until the Parole Board is 'completely satisfied' that the risk to the community has diminished 'sufficiently' to warrant their being released and supervised in the community. The arguments against indeterminate sentencing are, of course, well known,[263] and the Government's proposals may yet encounter opposition when they are debated in Parliament. Furthermore, on the face of it, there seems to be no need for a new sentence of this kind, since the courts already have the power in many cases to impose a discretionary life sentence if a serious sexual and violent offender appears to them to be dangerous. Only time will tell whether they become law.[264]

Conclusion

Over the years the shape of the parole system in England and Wales has been affected by many different factors. Research has certainly played a part.[265] Empirical studies were behind the changes made to the LRC referral system in the late 1960s and early 1970s; provided new impetus to the efforts made to reform the membership of LRCs in the mid-1970s; gave heart to campaigners seeking to devolve authority from the Home Secretary to the Board in the mid-1980s; assisted the Carlisle Committee in its deliberations in the late 1980s; had a hand in saving the parole system from abolition in the mid-1990s; and served as a spur to

---

[263] See, e.g., Sir Leon Radzinowicz and R. Hood, 'A Dangerous Direction for Sentencing Reform' [1978] *Crim.L.R.* 713 and 'Dangerousness and Criminal Justice: A Few Reflections' [1981] *Crim.L.R.* 756.

[264] Compare A. Bottomley's prescient remarks made in 1990: '[i]t is possible that this groundswell of popular feeling might lead to the disappearance of parole as we have known it and its replacement by a system of preventive detention for dangerous offenders': see n. 2 above, 368.

[265] Research into parole has had a long history in other jurisdictions. Manuel López-Rey, e.g., said in 1966 that 'parole policies have provoked wide and interesting research in parole practices and that contrary to some expectations that research has demonstrated that in more than one respect parole needs a serious overhaul': see 'Release and Provisional Release of Sentenced Prisoners' (1966) 6 *British Journal of Criminology* 236 at 257–8.

the establishment of the Comprehensive Review of Parole in 2001. Furthermore, with the notable exception of the restrictive policy, academics or others with an interest in the system had, at one time or another, recommended most of the other reforms that occurred.

The difficult task, however, is to explain exactly why some proposals for reform were taken up with alacrity by policy-makers while others either lay dormant for years or were never implemented at all. There is, of course, no straightforward answer to this question—decisions about penal policy are almost always the product of a multitude of different influences.[266] Nonetheless, a few general comments can be made.

In the first place, it is significant that the parole scheme in England and Wales was created not only at a time when there was a widespread belief in the rehabilitative potential of prison but also when criminology in general and empirical research in particular were, at least in some quarters, held in high regard. That this is so can be seen from the debates on the Second Reading of the Criminal Justice Bill 1966 where a number of Members of Parliament spoke forcefully about the need to monitor the development of the new system. Mr Bill (later Lord) Deedes, for example, asked, 'Where is the research to evaluate the results which will flow from this? This I regard as absolutely crucial. What plans are there for increasing the amount of research being done? . . . Research is the handmaiden of these ideas. Without it we shall not even learn from our mistakes.'[267] The Government's response to this call was positive. Sir Elwyn Jones, the Attorney General, agreed that 'any marked change in the penal system should be carefully observed where possible so that the precise effect of the change can be objectively ascertained

---

[266] As Sir Leon Radzinowicz pointed out in 1961, 'the specific solution of many legal and penal problems cannot be determined exclusively, or even predominantly, by the factual criminological evidence which [criminologists] can provide. There are deep-rooted and far-reaching issues of public morality, of social expediency, of the subtle but vital balance between the rights of the individual and the protection of the community, which underlie decisions of penal policy, and must often override the conclusions of the experts': see his *In Search of Criminology* (London: Heinemann, 1961), 179, quoted by R. Hood in R. Hood (ed.), *Introduction to Crime, Criminology and Public Policy* (London: Heinemann, 1974), at p. xiv.

[267] H.C. Debs., vol. 738, col. 97, 12 Dec. 1966. In the same debate Sir John Hobson also called for research into 'the operation and effects of the Bill': see H.C. Debs., vol. 738, col. 190, 12 Dec. 1966.

and checked against the intended objective' and he promised that the effects of the Bill would be 'fully studied', either by the Home Office Research Unit or by universities.[268] A further indication of the esteem in which criminology and criminologists were held at that time was the inclusion in the 1967 legislation of a provision, surely unique in English law, whereby criminologists—persons who had 'made a study of the causes of delinquency or the treatment of offenders'— became one of the four statutory categories of member qualified to sit on the Board. Indeed, of the sixteen 'founder members', two—Mr R.D. King and Dr Donald West—were established criminologists,[269] and their presence on the Parole Board in those early years may have helped to ensure that it, too, recognized the value of criminological research. Thus, in its first *Annual Report*, the Board asserted, 'The effectiveness or otherwise of the methods of operating a parole system needs to be demonstrated by empirical research; and the possibilities of improvement need to be systematically explored'.[270] As a way of furthering this goal the Board established a research sub-committee 'to act as a liaison with the Home Office Research Unit'. It also announced its intention 'to co-operate with appropriate experts' and do all in its power 'to further constructive projects'.

This commitment to empirical research on the part of policy-makers and the Board provides part of the explanation why the reconviction prediction scores developed by Christopher Nuttall and his colleagues at the Home Office Research Unit in the late 1960s were so swiftly incorporated into the new procedures for LRC referrals. Established a decade earlier, the Home Office Research Unit, which had by that time built up a strong reputation for its work on prediction studies, was going through a period of expan-

---

[268] See H.C. Debs., vol. 738, col. 201, 12 Dec. 1966. See also Mr Sam Silkin's remarks, Standing Committee A, H.C. Debs., session 1966–67, vol. 2, col. 721, 7 Mar. 1967.

[269] As of 31 March 2002, however, just five of the 109 members were criminologists: Dr Carol Hedderman, Professor Roy King (returning to the Board after 30 years), Professor Andrew Rutherford, Mr Nigel Stone, and Dr Anne Worrall. And with panel size reduced to three, fewer and fewer panels now contain a criminologist member: see Hood and Shute, *Parole in Transition, Phase One, Establishing the Base-Line*, 1994, University of Oxford Centre for Criminological Research, Occasional Paper No. 13, at para. 45; Hood and Shute, n. 206 above, at para. 15; and Hood and Shute, n. 158 above, at 21–2.

[270] *Report of the Parole Board for 1968*, n. 30 above, at para. 145.

sion and plainly enjoyed the confidence of Government.[271] It would be wrong to assume, though, that even in the halcyon days of the late 1960s there was always a close connection between policy formation and research. The founders of the parole system, it will be remembered, made much play of the importance of a supposed 'peak in training' despite the fact that there was no convincing evidence to back this up. Not only had empirical research in the 1950s and 1960s cast doubt on Donald Clemmer's notion of 'prisonization' on which the idea of a 'peak in training' seems to have been based[272]—'prisonization' measures the extent to which prisoners become socialized into the culture, customs and mores of a prison community and the degree to which their behaviour conforms to staff norms[273]—but it had also undermined a related claim made by Hulin and Maher[274] that a prisoner's attitude to law and to those who enforce the law generally deteriorates the longer he remains in prison.[275] Moreover, within a few years, there was a marked decline in the Government's enthusiasm for research, and its promise that

[271] See T.S. Lodge, 'The Founding of the Home Office Research Unit' in Hood (ed.), n. 266 above, 20 and 21. Lodge identifies 21 March 1957 as the 'date on which the Research Unit was formally founded'.

[272] See S. Wheeler, 'Socialization in Correctional Communities' (1961) 26 *American Sociological Review* 697. Wheeler's results 'strongly supported' the prisonization theory when inmates were classified according to the length of time they had served, but when they were classified according to whether they were in the early, middle, or late phase of their sentence the theory was found to be 'inadequate as a description of changes over time', because it failed 'to account for the U shaped distribution of high conformity response' (see 708). In the late 1960s R.C. Atchley and M.P. McCabe tried to replicate Wheeler's work (see 'Socialization in Correctional Communities: A Replication' (1968) 33 *American Sociological Review* 774) but their research was not able to sustain either Clemmer's or Wheeler's theory concerning the development of prisonization.

[273] Clemmer, who was Director of the Department of Corrections for the District of Columbia Government, published his famous study, *The Prison Community* (New York: Holt, Rinehart and Winston) in 1940. He considered the deleterious effects of imprisonment to be such that they would probably so disrupt a prisoner's personality that 'a happy adjustment in any community' would be 'next to impossible': see 300.

[274] See C.L. Hulin and B.A. Maher, 'Changes in Attitudes Towards Law Concomitant With Imprisonment' (1959) 50 *Journal of Criminal Law and Criminology* 245. Hulin and Maher were careful to qualify their findings, however, by noting that they could have been affected by reluctance on the part of some newly-sentenced prisoners to express their true feelings.

[275] See K.J. Heskin, N. Bolton, F.V. Smith, and P.A. Banister, 'Psychological Correlates of Long-Term Imprisonment' (1973) 13 *British Journal of Criminology* 150.

the effects of the Bill would be 'fully studied' started to look hollow: a frequent academic complaint at the time was that while a considerable quantity of research had been initiated, especially by the Home Office Research Unit, 'little systematic information had been published'.[276] And the Board, too, appeared to be changing its attitude towards research. Its research sub-committee had fallen into abeyance,[277] and in 1980 it 'reluctantly' came to the conclusion that it did not have the necessary facilities itself to embark on any major empirical study of the system.[278] Overall, the paucity of research was such that it led the Carlisle Committee to say in 1988, '[t]he public and political mood continues to be conditioned more by hunch and gut-feeling than by the considered fruits of research'.[279]

The researchers studied 175 men serving either determinate sentences of 10 years or more or sentences of life imprisonment in a number of English prisons. See also G. Hawkins, *The Prison: Policy and Practice* (Chicago: University of Chicago Press, 1976). Nonetheless, the idea of a 'peak' continued to have an influence on parole decision-making. For example, in 1973, A. Keith Bottomley found in his study of 207 prisoners serving sentences of five years or longer in a closed training prison in Hull that, 'in relation to a man's response to prison, in a fifth of the [recommended] cases the local review committee considered that the "optimum" time had come for release, beyond which the chances of rehabilitation were likely to decrease': see n. 194 above, at 33. In the late 1980s the Board referred to the idea without scepticism in its written evidence to the Carlisle Committee. The Board's evidence, which was submitted in November 1987, is reproduced in its entirety in its *Report of the Parole Board for 1987*, n. 91 above, at paras. 1–30. Hood has suggested that the appeal of the theory of peak response to training followed by deterioration may best be explained by the concept of 'cognitive dissonance': '[h]ow better to resolve the conflict between the belief that prison has a deleterious effect and the belief that training is provided in prisons than to say that training occurs for a while and is later, if not tested in conditions of freedom, followed by deterioration?': see 'Some Fundamental Dilemmas of the English Parole System and a Suggestion for an Alternative Structure' in Thomas (ed.), n. 153 above, 4, n. 14.

[276] See Bottomley, n. 194 above, 26. See also E.E. Barnard, 'Parole Decision-Making in Britain' (1976) 4 *International Journal of Criminology and Penology* 145 at 149.

[277] It was, however, revived briefly in 1978 and started to look for 'areas that might be suitable for further research': see *Report of the Parole Board for 1978* (London: HMSO, 1979), 105, at para. 5.

[278] See *Report of the Parole Board for 1980*, n. 55 above, at para. 4. Nonetheless, the Study Group recommended that the Board should establish 'its own research advisory group' which would have 'the dual purpose of informing members of research findings and suggesting research topics to the Home Office'. Compare the 1997–8 *Annual Report* where the Board stated that a 'key element' of its strategy to explain its role and functions better will be for it to 'undertake small-scale research projects': see *Report of the Parole Board for 1997–98*, n. 242 above, 21.

[279] See *Carlisle Committee Report*, n. 10 above, at para. 198.

A second important consideration is that, as we have seen, many other factors apart from research were also at work. Decisions taken both by the Government and the Board were influenced, on the one hand, by the administrative benefits of parole (in particular the need to keep the prison population under control) and, on the other hand, by the political imperative to be seen to be 'doing something about crime' and the fear that public support for the system might drain away if too liberal a release policy were to be adopted. Hence, in its 1970 report, the Board noted that the success of the scheme depended 'to a considerable extent upon the confidence that members of the general public have in it';[280] and in 1973 the then Chairman of the Parole Board, Lord Hunt, wrote that it was 'a basic condition that public opinion about the development of the scheme should always be taken carefully into account'.[281]

During the next few years the parole system will once again be going through a further period of fundamental change, and public opinion will undoubtedly continue to play a part in determining its future. Some of the tensions that have plagued the system since it was conceived in the late 1960s will, it seems, be resolved by the planned reforms. But others will remain. The difficult problem of identifying accurately 'true positives'—prisoners who will definitely re-offend during their licence period if they are released—from 'true negatives'—prisoners who will not re-offend—will not go away.[282] Nor will the ever-present fear that a few widely reported 'mishaps' will bring the parole system into disrepute and threaten its continued existence. If the proposals in the 2002 White Paper are enacted, then the restructured system will deal only with those prisoners who have been identified as 'dangerous' at the time of their trial. In these

---

[280] See *Report of the Parole Board for 1970*, n. 67 above, at para. 95. See also *Report of the Parole Board for 1977* (London: HMSO, 1978), 497, at para. 32: 'we are very much aware that our work can only succeed if we have the confidence of the public'.

[281] N. 75 above, 2. See also his article 'Parole. Where Next?' (1974) 10 *Prison Service Journal* 2, at 3. Informed academic commentators made the same point. Donald West, e.g., observed in 1972 that the Board needed 'the backing of a well-informed public capable of tolerating the disasters which must occasionally ensue when serious offenders are paroled': see n. 72 above, 24.

[282] See R. Hood, S. Shute, M. Feilzer, and A. Wilcox, 'Sex Offenders Emerging from Long-Term Imprisonment: A Study of Their Long-Term Reconviction Rates and of Parole Board Members' Judgements of Their Risk' (2002) 42 *British Journal of Criminology* 371.

circumstances, it is quite possible that the Board's release policy will become even more risk-averse than it is at present. It is therefore imperative that the new scheme is monitored and evaluated by a sustained programme of empirical research, conducted either by the Home Office or universities. But whether the lessons of that research will be taken up by policy-makers is, at this stage, a matter of speculation.

Part 4

International Comparisons

10

The Renaissance of the Victim in Criminal Policy: A Reconstruction of the German Campaign

Heike Jung

Introduction

A rationally based criminal policy cannot be conceived of and implemented as a 'single issue campaign', since it will have to take into account a complex network of ideas, institutions, and actors, as well as the normative and empirical setting which constitutes the system of crime control. Changes in criminal policy do not take place rapidly and radically from one year to the next. They come about by a gradual process.[1] This holds true for today's emphasis on victims' rights, too, even though the rediscovery of the victim might fairly be described as a turning point in the history of criminal justice. This makes it an attractive topic for a policy evaluation. Of course, this is not the first attempt to reconstruct the victim movement and its impact on criminal policy. In particular, we can draw on Rock's brilliant analytical narrative of the Canadian Justice for Victims of Crime Initiative,[2] difficult to surpass in its density and its masterly knit of empirical details, and many other comparative overviews and victimological

---

[1] On the slow and meandering course of changes in criminal policy see H. Jung, 'New Perspectives or More of the Same? Criminal Law and Criminal Science in the 21st Century' [1993] *Keio Law Review* 41.

[2] P. Rock, *A View from the Shadows. The Ministry of the Solicitor General of Canada and the Justice for Victims of Crime Initiative* (Oxford: Clarendon Press, 1986).

stock-takings.[3] My account will not have the depth of an empirical study. Rather, I shall rely on personal observations underpinned, however, by some documentary evidence.

Why another evaluation of the victim movement and why Germany? There has been a vigorous exchange of policy-oriented information and research on victims of crime, in particular in the 1980s.[4] However, victim-oriented policy targets have not been consistent throughout. The 'victim protection movement' has, for example, increasingly turned into a 'witness protection movement'—which denotes a slight shift of accent. Also, it is a matter of debate whether this 'new collective victimhood', as Garland calls it,[5] is not about to destabilize the balance of the criminal justice system.[6] We can also note a rise in 'popular punitiveness' liable to smother the more socio-constructive intentions which united many protagonists of the victim movement. Studies relating to a particular jurisdiction may reveal that the thrust and concrete output of such campaigns will, despite the international scope of the movement and a similar dedication to the victim's cause, depend on the particularities of that legal system.

[3] Cf. the several profound evaluations by M. Joutsen, *inter alia: The Role of the Victim of Crime in European Criminal Justice Systems* (Helsinki: HEUNI, 1987); 'Research of Victims and Criminal Policy in Europe' in R. Hood (ed.), *Crime and Criminal Policy in Europe* (Oxford: 1989), 50–3; 'Criminal Policy and Victims of Crime: A European Perspective' in R. Hood and N. Courakis (eds.), *The Changing Face of Crime and Criminal Policy in Europe* (Oxford: 1999), 36; also M. Delmas-Marty, 'Des victimes: répères pour une approche comparative' [1984] *Revue de science criminelle et de droit pénal comparé* 209; K. Sessar, 'Über das Opfer', in T. Vogler (ed.), *Festschrift für Jescheck* (Berlin: Duncker & Humblot, 1985), 1137; A. Eser, 'Zur Renaissance des Opfers im Strafverfahren' in G. Dornseifer *et al.* (eds.), *Gedächtnisschrift für Armin Kaufmann* (Cologne: Heymanns, 1989), 723; H.J. Schneider, 'Der gegenwärtige Stand der kriminologischen Opferforschung' (1998) 81 *Monatsschrift für Kriminologie und Strafrechtsreform* 316.

[4] *Inter alia*, in the context of the Proceedings of the first Colloquia uniting European Criminologists: R. Hood (ed.), *Crime and Criminal Policy in Europe* (Oxford: 1989), 50 ff.; H.J. Albrecht and G. Kaiser (eds.), *Crime and Criminal Policy in Europe*, Proceedings of the II. European Colloquium (Freiburg: Eigenverlag Max-Planck-Institut für ausländisches und internationales Strafrecht, 1990), 249 ff.

[5] Cf. D. Garland, *The Culture of Control* (Oxford: Oxford University Press, 2001), 144.

[6] e.g. J. Gardner, 'Crime: in Proportion and in Perspective' in A. Ashworth and M. Wasik (eds.), *Fundamentals of Sentencing Theory* (Oxford: Clarendon Press, 1998), 31, 52, who expresses concern about the preoccupation with the position of the victim in the criminal process.

Criminal Policy: Actors, Ways and Means

Traditionally, the focus of criminal policy research lay on legislative reforms in the field of criminal justice to the extent that *Strafrechts-reform* had almost become a synonym for criminal policy. Of course, criminal policy has never been a *domaine réservé* of the legislator,[7] though in parliamentary democracies legislation is the preferred vehicle for major criminal policy moves. However, we cannot disregard the fact that the activities of the legislator build upon the 'normative consensus' in society (*normative gesellschaftliche Verständigung*) which emerges in a differentiated process of interactions. This formula recognizes that the legislator is dependent on social values and social change which develop in an unsystematic way. In most instances this process is not initiated, but only endorsed by the legislator.[8]

Thus, the formulation and implementation of criminal policy are not a prerogative of parliaments, governments, and administrative bodies at the federal or state level. State agencies, important as they may be, cannot pass as the only policy-makers though they have the monopoly when it comes to formal processes. 'My family has a voice in what our government does?' This question which formed part of a questionnaire addressed to US American High School seniors and their German counterparts[9] may illustrate what I mean: we are to a certain extent all potential policy-makers. Some may even aspire to the leading role of moral entrepreneurs.[10] This holds true in particular, but not exclusively, for members of the German academic profession who, due to their position as experts, can be sure of a wider resonance if they engage in public debates, in particular if they manage to bring about some joint action and/or to engage the support of the mass media. Interestingly enough many academics in Germany may conceive of their position as a kind of 'public office'

---

[7] See my own attempt to answer M. Zander's question 'Who are the Real Legislators?' (*A Matter of Justice* (Oxford: Oxford University Press, 1989), 239), in *Sanktionensysteme und Menschenrechte* (Bern: Haupt, 1992), 183.

[8] For further details cf. W. Hassemer, *Theorie und Soziologie des Verbrechens* (Frankfurt am Main: Athenäum, 1973), 153.

[9] Cf. W. Hastings and K. Payne, 'Democratic Orientations Among High School Seniors in the United States and Germany' [1990] *Social Education*, Nov./Dec., 458, 459.

[10] Cf. Rock, n. 2 above, 100 ff. with a particularly impressive portrait of Irvin Waller as the Canadian moral entrepreneur of the victim campaign.

authorizing them to speak up if needed. This 'private' reform potential increases if existing non-governmental organizations get involved or if a particular issue gives rise to the *ad hoc* foundation of action groups and initiatives. In many instances such groups, which we tend to localize under the slightly overworked heading of 'community involvement',[11] will, by way of their individual members, be linked to public authorities.

This all goes to show that a valid reconstruction of the German or any policy campaign is in itself a painful, if not impossible, exercise, the more so since any such evaluation will have to take into account the interaction with international institutions and networks. Above all, policy developments will not be documented in daily bulletins and records of achievement. Rather, they take a meandering course; even retrospectively it is difficult to assess the significance of simple events and the relevance of a particular initiative.[12] Still we are forced to identify such events and initiatives unless we want to resign ourselves to remain in the abstract, embodied in formulae such as the 'general political climate'. This said, criminologists may have to concede that the 'general political climate'—somewhat like the *Zeitgeist*—diffuse and ephemeral as it may be, is a socio-psychological fact. Of course, this general climate will be influenced by the mass media. However, the media rarely carry on a consistent and persistent criminal policy campaign. Rather, they focus on particular spectacular incidents.[13] Still, it may be fair to say that the media have a tendency to side with the law enforcement agencies and to reinforce fear of crime.

The Decline and the Rise of the Victim: Some Theoretical Considerations

The development of criminal justice is closely linked to the state or, we should rather say, to the emergence of central powers acting

[11] See D. Nelken, 'Community Involvement in Crime Control' (1985) 38 *Current Legal Problems* 239; and, with special reference to Germany, N. Lacey and L. Zedner, 'Discourses of Community in Criminal Justice' (1995) 22 *Journal of Law and Society* 301.

[12] Very illuminating in this respect is Rock, n. 2 above, 46.

[13] For a general assessment of the role of the media in criminal policy debates cf. H. Jung, 'Was können die Medien in der kriminalpolitischen Meinungsbildung leisten?' in G. Kielwein (ed.), *Entwicklungslinien der Kriminologie* (Cologne: Heymanns, 1985), 47.

in the public interest.[14] Consequently, criminal law has traditionally been defined by the formula 'the State vs. the Accused', or the 'State vs. the Offender'. This preoccupation led to a certain 'neutralization'[15] of the victim whose distinct interests were integrated into and deformed by the paternalism of an administrative system which increasingly acquired traits of a 'self-perpetuating bureaucracy'.[16] 'Public interest' took over, disregarding to a large extent the personal impact of such conflicts. The personal aspects, losses, emotions, and suffering of victims, as well as of suspects and offenders, were downplayed in a process of rationalization. Of course, such rationalization is an indicator of an advanced 'civilized' system of criminal justice which requires some form of conflict resolution. However, the acceptance of criminal justice as a state-bound activity may mean that victims are not being taken seriously 'in their own right' and that they are being discarded as 'flat characters'[17] in the plot.

Moreover, in some instances, state interference is to the detriment of all parties, since it has a tendency to give rise to counterproductive effects. Here, the personal character of the conflict prevails to the extent that the parties to the conflict should try to come to a resolution without the repressive potential of the criminal justice system. This is the domain of 'regulated self-regulation'.[18] The term reminds us that this way of handling conflicts links our topic to the privatization debate, and thereby to the very function of law. The more we accept that law has to do with 'consensus',[19] the more we can accept dispute settlements at a situational or sub-community level. Lawyers will,

[14] From a historical point of view: E. Wadle, 'Die Entstehung der öffentlichen Strafe' in H. Jung, H. Müller-Dietz, and U. Neumann (eds.), *Perspektiven der Strafrechtsentwicklung* (Baden-Baden: Nomos, 1996), 9.

[15] The formula used by W. Hassemer, *Einführung in die Grundlagen des Strafrechts* (2nd edn., Munich: Beck, 1990), 70.

[16] An expression taken from Sir Leon Radzinowicz, 'Penal Regressions' (1991) 50 *Cambridge Law Journal* 422, 428.

[17] Borrowed from literary critique: cf. E.M. Forster, *Aspects of the Novel and Related Writings*. Abinger Edition (London: Edward Arnold, 1974), xii, 46.

[18] On the relevance of this concept for criminal law see e.g. H. Jung, 'The Concept of Regulated Self-Regulation' (2001) 86 *Svensk Jurist Tidning* 121.

[19] e.g. W. Naucke, 'Versuch über den aktuellen Stil des Rechts' [1986] *Kritische Vierteljahresschrift für Gesetzgebung und Rechtswissenschaft* 189, 190 ff.; for a general rehearsal of the concept of Law ('Recht') see K. Seelmann, *Rechtsphilosophie* (2nd edn., Munich: Beck, 2001), 5.

whatever the nature of the conflict, tend to protect institutions, and perhaps this is what justice, in the 'abstract sense', is about.[20] Stable institutions guarantee living conditions for individuals. Yet forms of participatory justice which are detached from the state may be more suitable for the settlement of very personalized conflicts. Of course, it is difficult to draw the line. Since we cannot resolve this question here, we should now turn to more solid observations of a more empirical and evaluative nature.

The Course of the Campaign

The use of the term 'campaign' suggests that we are dealing with co-ordinated action over a specific period of time. Though neither of these conditions is met in full, it is apparent that, in Germany, moves in favour of victims' rights become more frequent, direct, and powerful at the beginning of the 1970s. It is revealing that the *Weiße Ring* organization, a strong lobby for victims' interests, was founded in 1976.[21] In the beginning, the emphasis lay on victim compensation. Yet the scope of the debate was, from the outset, broader and covered the whole range of victim interests ranging from participation to protection, well illustrated by the first comprehensive German textbook on victimology, which appeared in 1975.[22] In 1976, the German Victim Compensation Act introduced a state-based compensation scheme for victims of serious crimes of violence, which forms part of the social security system. Of course,

---

[20] As opposed to L. Nader's concept of 'situational justice': cf. L. Nader, 'The Direction of Law and the Development of Extra-Judicial Processes in Nation State Societies' in P.H. Gulliver (ed.), *Essays in Memory of Max Gluckman* (Leyden: F.J. Brill, 1978), 78, 86.

[21] Among the 17 founding members there were two prominent criminologists and penologists, H.J. Schneider and Alexander Böhm.

[22] H.J. Schneider, *Viktimologie, Wissenschaft vom Verbrechensopfer* (Tübingen: Mohr (Siebeck), 1975), dwelling on a rich international bibliography including such names as Amir, Drapkin, Ellenberger, von Hentig, Miyazawa, Schäfer, and Wolfgang. This book was preceded in Germany by several articles on victimology by criminal lawyers, criminologists, and psychologists, *inter alia* H. Zipf, 'Die Bedeutung der Viktimologie für die Strafrechtspflege' (1970) 53 *Monatsschrift für Kriminologie und Strafrechtsreform* 1; H. Schüler-Springorum, 'Über Victimologie' in *Festschrift für Richard Honig* (Göttingen: Schwartz, 1970), 201; H. Maisch, 'Victimologie' in W. Arnold, H. J. Eysenck, and K. Meili (eds.), *Lexikon der Psychologie* (Freiburg *et al.*: Herder, 1972), iii, 720–1; G. Kaiser, 'Viktimologie' in G. Kaiser, F. Sack and H. Schellhoss (eds.), *Kleines kriminologisches Wörterbuch* (Freiburg *et al.*: Herder, 1974), 380.

such legislation did not come out of the blue; rather it was preceded by a lengthy public debate. It is noteworthy that this statute was enacted in the same year as the Criminal Corrections Act. Speculation that the Victim Compensation Act may well have served as a back-up strategy to bring the prison reform debate to a constructive end may not be totally unfounded.[23] Indeed, the prison reform debate had positive effects on the victim movement and vice versa, a fact which the popular 'either/or' arguments tend to overlook.

The concern for victim compensation led to several still tacit modifications in the repertoire of sanctions. When, in 1975, the German legislator introduced the possibility of conditional non-prosecution for certain crimes (§ 153 a StPO), one of the conditions to choose from was 'victim compensation'. Though this debate focussed originally on financial aspects, it was permeated by symbolic tunes which led to wider debates on reparation and restorative justice. This principled turn is reflected *inter alia* in the orientation of two of the several *habilitation* theses which have been devoted to the larger area of compensation and reparation. Whereas Frehsee, in 1987, still concentrated on compensation,[24] Walther, in 2000, reached out much further in her attempt to reconstruct the whole system of sanctions and, consequently, of criminal justice.[25]

In a way, the compensation issue has, at least in Germany, triggered off a more general debate. It has raised awareness of the shortcomings of stated-based punitive systems which have disowned the victim, not to speak of their inherent deficiencies in dealing with offenders. Of course, the shortcomings of victim compensation have not been the real breeding ground for the emergence of 'participatory justice'. However, this new paradigm, developed *inter alia* by Christie[26] and McClintock,[27] profited from the fact that victim

---

[23] Cf. H. Jung, 'Gesetz über die Entschädigung für Opfer von Gewalttaten' (1976) 16 *Juristische Schulung* 478.

[24] D. Frehsee, *Schadenswiedergutmachung als Instrument strafrechtlicher Sozialkontrolle* (Berlin: Duncker & Humblot, 1987).

[25] S. Walther, *Vom Rechtsbruch zum Realkonflikt* (Berlin: Duncker & Humblot, 2000).

[26] N. Christie, 'Conflicts as Property' (1977) 17 *The British Journal of Criminology* 1.

[27] F. McClintock, 'Some Aspects of Discretion in Criminal Justice' in M. Adler and S. Asquith (eds.), *Discretion and Welfare* (London: Heinemann, 1981), 185.

compensation was, to put it mildly, badly organized. The next stage of the debate is marked by a widening of perspectives. The victim was acknowledged as a participant on the criminal justice scene with particular interests which did not necessarily coincide with those of the legal apparatus. Research on the decision to report,[28] and victimization surveys in general,[29] produced a close-up of victims' real interests and concerns.

In 1981, the criminal law professors' congress (*Strafrechtslehrertagung*) had, in a role-oriented agenda of topics related to the criminal process, included the victim.[30] Only three years later, the 55th Deutsche Juristentag, a bi-annual reform-oriented lawyers' congress,[31] took up the position of the victim in its criminal law section.[32] In 1986, the German legislature passed the *Opferschutzgesetz*,[33] which tried to promote victim compensation by the offender as well as victim protection in the course of the trial.

The legislator had conceived this reform as a first step only.[34] Indeed, instead of putting an end to an already intensive debate it added more steam to it. A group of the *Alternativprofessoren*

[28] Cf. W. Heinz, *Bestimmungsgründe der Anzeigebereitschaft des Opfers*, thesis Freiburg, 1972.

[29] *Pars pro toto*: E. Stephan, *Die Stuttgarter Opferbefragung* (Wiesbaden: BKA-Forschungsreihe/Deutschland, Bd. 3, Bundeskriminalamt, 1976).

[30] H. Jung, 'Die Stellung des Verletzten im Strafprozeß' (1981) 93 *Zeitschrift für die gesamte Strafrechtswissenschaft* 1147.

[31] The Deutsche Juristentag had been founded as a private organization in 1860 with the purpose of discussing and promoting law reform. It comprises members from all legal professions; professors have, due to their expertise, always figured among the opinion leaders; for the history of the Deutsche Juristentag and its impact on the development of German law see e.g. H. Conrad, G. Dilcher, and H.-J. Kurland, *Der Deutsche Juristentag 1860–1994* (Munich: Beck, 1997).

[32] P. Rieß, *Die Rechtsstellung des Verletzten im Strafverfahren, Gutachten zum 55. Deutschen Juristentag* (Munich: Beck, 1984). Rieß' assessment of the matter and the subsequent discussion have been particularly influential, which may be partly due to the fact that Rieß himself held an influential position in the Federal Ministry of Justice. The Deutsche Juristentag has since then twice taken up victim-oriented topics: cf. H. Schöch, 'Empfehlen sich Änderungen und Ergänzungen bei den strafrechtlichen Sanktionen ohne Freiheitsentzug?' *Gutachten für den 59. Deutschen Juristentag* (Munich: Beck, 1992); T. Weigend, 'Empfehlen sich gesetzlichen Änderungen, um Zeugen und andere nicht beschuldigte Personen im Strafprozeß besser vor Nachteilen zu schützen?', *Gutachten für den 62. Deutschen Juristentag* (Munich: Beck, 1998).

[33] Cf. the overview by T. Weigend, 'Das Opferschutzgesetz—Kleine Schritte zu welchem Ziel?' (1987) 40 *Neue Juristische Wochenschrift* 1170.

[34] Cf. Bundestags-Drucksache 10/5305, 20 ff.

published a model draft for reparation in 1992.[35] Only two years later the legislator adopted this approach, providing for the possibility of preferring reparation to punishment (§ 46a StGB). Recently, this option has been underpinned by a new procedural framework. This last move acknowledges that in the meantime mediation has brought new tunes into the traditional melody of the criminal justice system, not only in Germany, but world-wide.[36] The issue of victim protection, already addressed by H.J. Schneider in his *Viktimologie* and having permeated public debate ever since, has led to yet another widening of the debate from victims to witnesses. In 1998, the legislator made a first attempt to reconcile witness/ victim protection with the procedural rights of the accused. This *Zeugenschutzgesetz*[37] will certainly not be the last word on the matter.[38]

This necessarily brief account may be wanting in many respects. One particular aspect needs to be explained: I did not allude to developments in the former German Democratic Republic. Some of its legal instruments, for example the *gesellschaftliche Gerichte* (roughly, 'mediation boards'), might have deserved further attention: they were, at least as a theoretical model, received

---

[35] J. Baumann *et al.*, *Alternativ-Entwurf Wiedergutmachung (AE-WGM)* (Munich: Beck, 1992). The group of the *Alternativprofessoren*, which also includes members from Austria and Switzerland, has, ever since it came up with the model draft of a general part of the Criminal Code in 1966, been actively engaged in setting the reform agenda and in structuring reforms. Among the founding members of the group were Jürgen Baumann, Arthur Kaufmann, Werner Maihofer, Ulrich Klug, and Peter Noll. The affiliation of Baumann, Maihofer, and Klug to the Freie Demokratische Partei helped introduce the proposal into the parliamentary process in 1966. Generally speaking, the group pursues a line which is characterized by dedication to good legal reasoning and a progressive criminal policy. Each campaign has traditionally been terminated by the publication of collective proposals in the form of an annotated bill. Membership is acquired by co-optation. At present, the group consists of 22 members. It has periodically been intertwined with the Deutsche Juristentag, since some of its members, at present Heinz Schöch, have played a prominent role in the criminal law section of the Deutsche Juristentag.

[36] Cf. H. Jung, 'Mediation—Paradigmawechsel in der Konfliktregelung' in H.-D. Schwind, E. Kube, and H.-H. Kühne (eds.), *Festschrift für H. J. Schneider* (Berlin/New York: de Gruyter, 1998), 913.

[37] Bundesgesetzblatt I, p. 820.

[38] On the activities of the Council of Europe in the matter cf. H. Jung, 'Europe vs. Organized Crime—the Case of Victim Protection' in Rüßmann (ed.), *Keio Tage 1998* (Baden-Baden: Nomos, 2000), 29.

favourably[39] and are still noted on the 'positive list'. However, their integration into the procedural system would have required considerable structural changes. Some of the reluctance with regard to their practical implementation probably stemmed from the fact that it is difficult to disentangle these legal instruments from the underlying socialist ideology and the accompanying social pressure on individuals.[40] In a way, the experiences of socialist systems remind us that any procedural reforms will have to take into account the various human rights guarantees which are the embodiment of our normative aspirations regarding criminal justice. Therefore, the Recommendation of the Council of Europe on 'Mediation in Penal Matters' devotes a special chapter to the relevance of human rights guarantees in mediation proceedings.

From Financial to Personal: the Change of Perspective

In the beginning it was the aspect of victim compensation that overshadowed other victim interests in public debate. Presumably, this had to do with the fact that monetary categories allow for a 'rough and ready' assessment of interests. Also, the real dimension of the victim as a person had yet to be discovered. The criminal justice system had to learn from victims that financial remedies were appreciated, but still considered insufficient help to alleviate the suffering. Still, the 'compensation issue' was the forerunner. This may have been due to the fact that procedural mechanisms for victim compensation were not altogether new. They existed in many systems, though in most instances they operated inefficiently. But systems

---

[39] e.g. A. Eser, *Die gesellschaftlichen Gerichte* (Tübingen: Mohr (Siebeck), 1971); T. Feltes, 'Gesellschaftliche Gerichte, Schlichtungs- und Schiedskommissionen' (1991) 24 *Zeitschrift für Rechtspolitik* 94. U. Ebert, 'Aus Recht wird Unrecht? Deutsche Wiedervereinigung und Strafrecht' in E. Koch (ed.), *10 Jahre Deutsche Rechtseinheit* (Tübingen: Mohr-Siebeck, 2001), 21, 42, 44.

[40] This pressure is well captured by contemporary DDR novelists, e.g. Jurek Becker's novel *Schlaflose Tage* (Frankfurt am Main: Suhrkamp, 1979) and Erich Loest's novel *Es geht seinen Gang oder Mühen in unserer Ebene* (Munich: Deutscher Taschenbuch Verlag, 1980). It has also been confirmed by recent research summarized by F. Herzog, 'Rechtspflege—Sache des ganzen Volkes? Bericht über eine Studie zu den Gesellschaftlichen Gerichten in der DDR' in T. Vormbaum (ed.), *Jahrbuch der Juristischen Zeitgeschichte* (Baden-Baden: Nomos, 2001), ii, 180.

which did not provide such mechanisms—like those in the UK—also addressed the compensation issue first.[41]

Thus, the initial preoccupation with compensation helped to attract a wider audience for the more complex concerns of victims on victimology's differentiated agenda. In particular, the criminal justice authorities began to adopt a more sensitive approach to crimes of violence and sexual offences. Here, the victim movement and the emancipation movement joined forces. Research[42] showed the inefficiency of responses to these phenomena, in particular in the case of domestic violence.[43] Such research led to a re-personalization of the abstract *Rechtsgutslehre*.[44] Procedural steps aimed at victim and witness protection followed. The need for victim assistance and therapy was recognized, though practical implementation is still wanting.[45]

Increased victimological knowledge about the genesis of conflicts also stimulated a reappraisal of criminal attribution: relational,

---

[41] For a comparative discussion of the English and Scottish compensation order cf. H. Jung, 'Die compensation order in Großbritannien' in A. Eser, G. Kaiser, and K. Madlener (eds.), *Neue Wege der Wiedergutmachung im Strafrecht* (Freiburg: Eigenverlag Max-Planck-Institut für ausländisches und internationales Strafrecht, 1990), 93; also, concentrating on England, the thorough account by L. Zedner, 'England' in A. Eser and S. Walther (eds.), *Wiedergutmachung im Kriminalrecht. Reparation in Criminal Law* (Freiburg: Edition Iuscrim, 1996), 109, as well as, for a general overview on the development of the victim's stand in the English criminal procedure, J. Spencer, 'Improving the Position of the Victim in English Criminal Procedure' (1997) 31 *Israel Law Review* No 1–3, 286.

[42] Cf. K. Weis, *Die Vergewaltigung und ihre Opfer* (Stuttgart: Enke, 1982).

[43] Cf. B. Bannenberg, E. Weitekamp, D. Rössner, and H.J. Kerner, *Mediation bei Gewaltstraftaten in Paarbeziehungen* (Baden-Baden: Nomos, 1999).

[44] U. Neumann, 'Die Stellung des Opfers im Strafrecht' in W. Hassemer (ed.), *Strafrechtspolitik. Bedingungen der Strafrechtsreform* (Frankfurt: Lang, 1987), 225; W. Hassemer, 'Grundlagen einer personalen Rechtsgutslehre' in H. Scholler and L. Philipps (eds.), *Jenseits des Funktionalismus* (Heidelberg: Decker & Müller, 1989), 85. Likewise see X. Pin, 'La vulnérabilité en matière pénale' in F. Cohet-Cordey (ed.), *Vulnérabilité et droit* (Grenoble: Presses universitaire de Grenoble, 2000), 119, has revisited French criminal law under the angle of 'vulnerability'. The *Rechtsgutslehre* (roughly: 'theory of legally protected goods') is meant to offer a basis for a (critical) appraisal of the protection of a particular interest by way of criminalization. It is somewhat related to, but not identical with, the harm concept. For further discussion cf. A. von Hirsch, 'Der Rechtsgutsbegriff und das "Harm Principle"' in (2002) 149 *Goltdammer's Archiv* 2.

[45] Cf. G. Kaiser, 'Brauchen wir in Europa neue Konzepte der Kriminalpolitik?' (2000) 33 *Zeitschrift für Rechtspolitik* 150.

interactional, and contextual concepts gained ground, although criticized by some for blurring the borderline of a concept which traditionally focussed on the individual wrongdoer. This had consequences not only for the theory of punishment[46] but also for the construction of defences (e.g. the 'battered wife syndrome') and for the interpretation of statutory provisions (e.g. the concept of 'threatening').

Above all, this trend towards personalization also imposed itself on the system of response. At least for a sizeable segment of conflicts, arrangements of conflict resolution were propounded and adopted which were more personal, more socio-constructive, and more democratic than traditional punitive responses. The path from compensation to mediation and restorative justice can be traced back nicely in the rhetoric of German publications in the matter which moved gradually from *Schadenswiedergutmachung*[47] to *Täter-Opfer-Ausgleich*, a term which was introduced into statutory language in 1986.

The Impact of the International Debate

One need not be an expert in the matter to realize that the course of events in Germany is in line with the general trend. This impression becomes even stronger if we take into account the standing advice by comparativists to disregard the positivistic niceties of a particular system in favour of a problem-oriented functional approach. However, since it has, in the era of globalization, become customary to level off differences and to assume that 'elsewhere' the problems and their solutions are more or less the same as in one's own jurisdiction, it is appropriate to look into the matter more closely.

The international stimuli are not difficult to identify. Above all, victimology and the growing awareness of victimological research

[46] Cf. A. Duff, *Punishment, Communication, and Community* (Oxford: Oxford University Press, 2001), with A. Norrie, *Punishment, Responsibility, and Justice* (Oxford: Oxford University Press, 2000). On the emergence of 'relational concepts' see also A. Garapon, 'La justice reconstructive' in A. Garapon, F. Gros, and T. Pech, *Et ce sera justice. Punir en démocratie* (Paris: Odile Jacob, 2001), 247.

[47] Cf. Bundesministerium der Justiz (ed.), *Schadenswiedergutmachung im Kriminalrecht*, Untersuchung des Fachausschusses I, 'Strafrecht und Strafvollzug' des Bundesverbandes der Straffälligenhilfe e.V. (Bonn: Forum Verlag Godesberg, 1988).

have fuelled the debate.[48] Pioneering empirical research into e.g. the status of the victim in criminal procedure[49] and the question of assistance to victims[50] set the tone. Victimology itself is a truly international branch of criminology. This international scope is embodied and expresses itself in cross-border international victimological research, collected works, and, above all, the existence of scientific networks and organizations, like the World Society of Victimology founded in 1979. Of course, as M. Joutsen[51] has pointed out, we still have to strive for a true internationalization of victimological research, since the developing countries are lagging behind. At the European level, the Council of Europe has rapidly caught on, producing victim-oriented colloquia and recommendations which imposed themselves in the subtle way of soft law on policy discussions in some Member States.[52] Empirical knowledge of how and to what extent such guidance is received by Member States is still lacking, though Member States are aware of the fact that their compliance is liable to be evaluated in a follow-up procedure.[53] In countries like Germany it does not function as a checklist-like reminder for policy-makers; rather, it infiltrates the general discourse. Reference to what international organizations have to say in the matter has increasingly become part of the 'state of the art'.

The 'negative' stimulus, i.e. a certain loss of faith in offender-oriented policy, also has an international dimension. It relates in particular to the world-wide reception of the misleading 'nothing

[48] Cf. Rock, n. 2 above, 71.

[49] Cf. J. Shapland, J. Willmore, and P. Duff, *Victims in the Criminal Justice System* (Aldershot: Gower, 1985).

[50] Cf. M. Maguire and C. Corbett, *The Effects of Crime and the Work of Victims Support Schemes* (Aldershot: Gower, 1987).

[51] M. Joutsen, 'The Internationalization of Victimology' in n. 36 above, 353; illuminating in this respect is also M. Cain, 'Orientalism, Occidentalism and the Sociology of Crime' (2000) 41 *British Journal of Criminology* 239.

[52] For an account of the relevant activities of the Council of Europe in the 1980s see A. Tsitsoura, 'Victims of Crime—Council of Europe and United Nations Instruments', in *Changing Victim Policy. The United Nations Victim Declarations and Recent Developments in Europe*, HEUNI Publications No. 16 (Helsinki: HEUNI, 1989), 197.

[53] For a general outlook on the role of the Council of Europe in criminal matters see H. Jung, 'European Criminal Policy: Actors, Issues, Challenges' in A. Eser and C. Rabenstein (eds.), *Neighbours in Law, Papers in Honour of Barbara Huber on her 65th Birthday* (Freiburg: Edition Iuscrim, 2001), 143.

works' slogan which has, in recent years, been replaced by the more optimistic formula of 'something works'.[54] There are also definite structural similarities. One has to do with the fact that a re-orientation towards the victim struck a popular note in all jurisdictions. The rationale of a rehabilitation-oriented policy has never been easy to sell. Admittedly, it can only flourish with the solid back-up of social élites and in a situation of relative financial affluence.

The neo-classical wave which had swept across the Atlantic led to a reorientation among criminal justice personnel. Social workers who had, to some extent, 'undermined' the traditional pre-eminence of lawyers in the criminal justice system[55] had, in tendency, been dedicated to the offender's cause. Many of them reoriented themselves towards victim/offender work, partly in order to avoid being caught in the neo-classical 'trap'.[56]

The German specificities of the debate are less obvious. Of course, one is always tempted to identify particular trends in penal history in support of present-day developments.[57] This often ahistorical perspective has been popular with the protagonists of the victim movement throughout. We should not, however, overvalue the fact that the idea of *Wiedergutmachung* had already found some resonance in the nineteenth century philosophical debate.[58] What counts more is the fact that the victim has always had standing in German criminal procedure. German procedural law has endowed the victim with several rights and remedies. To begin with, there is a series of

[54] For a balanced account cf. R. Hood, 'General Report' in Council of Europe (ed.), *Psychosocial Interventions in the Criminal Justice System* (Strasbourg: Council of Europe Press, 1995), 191; see also H. Kury, 'Zum Stand der Behandlungsforschung oder: Vom nothing works zum something works' in W. Feuerhelm, H.-D. Schwind, and H. Bock, *Festschrift für Böhm* (Berlin/New York: de Gruyter, 1999), 251.

[55] On this rivalry see R. Zauberman, 'Victim-Related Alternatives and the Criminal Justice System: Mediation, Compensation and Restitution, Commentary' in Kaiser and Albrecht (eds.), n. 4 above, 301, 306 ff.

[56] For an account of the different streams in restorative justice see T. Marshall, 'The Evolution of Restorative Justice in Britain' (1995) 4 *European Journal on Criminal Policy and Research* 21.

[57] Cf. Rock's similar observation: '[t]here has even arisen the apparent convention that discussions of services to victims should allude first to the code of Hammurabi and then move into a disquisition about early Anglo-Saxon law': n. 2 above, 68.

[58] For a rehearsal of Karl Theodor Welcker's 'Wiederherstellungstheorie' cf. H. Müller-Dietz, 'Vom intellektuellen Verbrechensschaden—eine nicht nur historische Reminiszenz' (1983) 130 *Golddammer's Archiv für Strafrecht* 481.

offences which normally are (or have to be) prosecuted privately by
the victim—the so-called *Privatklagedelikte*. In certain cases the
victim may initiate a supplementary prosecution (*Nebenklage*). Furthermore, the so-called *Klageerzwingungsverfahren* entitles the
victim to challenge a prosecutor's decision not to prosecute in cases
where the principle of compulsory prosecution applies. The victim
may even pursue the civil claims in a special follow-up procedure,
the *Adhäsionsverfahren*. Though this system of victim participation
lacked the necessary clarity and cohesion to be effective, and though
the 'professionals' may not always have taken the victim's rights
seriously enough, there was no need to conceive of the position of
the victim from scratch, as has been the case with the Anglo-American concept of an adversarial trial. The debate about victim impact
statements and the implementation of constitutional rights for
victims[59] is somewhat tainted by this 'structural gap' in Anglo-
American procedure, though it cannot be denied that the emphasis
on (effective) victims' rights has become a more or less universal
characteristic of the campaign.[60] Still, the German debate focussed
rather on a reappraisal of existing remedies, with the result that some
were more or less sorted out, whereas others were developed
more fully. In particular, we had to learn that having a right and
being able to exercise it effectively within the framework of a criminal trial are two different things. This is a question of competence
and burden, but it also has to do with the fact that not even the best
procedural remedy can make offenders solvent.

It may be due to this pre-existing structure that moral entrepreneurs, though present in the German debate as well, lacked the
missionary zeal of some of their US-American and Canadian counterparts.[61] Speaking of pre-existing structures, it is, on the other
hand, not surprising that the very developed German doctrinal
concept of individual blame (*Schuldprinzip*), as well as the strict
divide betwe n private law and criminal law responses, made it

---

[59] Cf. L. Lamborn, 'Victims' Rights' in the United States: From Statutory to Constitutional' in H. Kühne, *Festschrift für K. Miyazawa* (Baden-Baden: Nomos, 1995),
215.

[60] Cf., e.g., R. Cario, *Victimologie* (Paris/Montreal: L'Harmattan, 2000), 135 ff.

[61] Cf. Rock's remark, n. 2 above, 96: 'at a seminar meeting given by Marlene Young
at Carleton University, for instance, a senior Ministry official murmured sotto voce:
"there's no point in saying anything. It's a religious meeting"'.

difficult to opt for a strategy of compensation instead of punish-ment.[62]

Also it seems to me that the German debate has paid particular attention to potential antagonism between victims' rights and the rights of the accused,[63] an issue which has been somewhat neglected in the Anglo-American discourse. This may have to do with the fact that, in Germany, lawyers have had a strong voice in the campaign.

Finally, it seems to me that the tradition of a codified system of law imposes itself onto the structure of the debate. It focusses on the legislative process, one advantage of which is to channel discussion towards a clear policy output. Its distinct disadvantage consists in the fact that implementation is not taken seriously enough, even though this very same system will attach particular importance to the equality principle, i.e. to the idea that criminal justice facilities should be provided as a general service. However, it seems that there is a universal problem about how to make space for innovative individual initiatives without jeopardizing the idea of civic cohesive-ness that calls for generalization. Speaking of initiatives, I think it is fair to say that, in Germany, the backing of projects and schemes by 'official criminal policy' was of greater importance than for example in the much less 'state-oriented' set-up of the UK, which seems to be more favourable to 'grassroots' developments.

The Role of the Academic Profession

The role of academic lawyers and criminologists or, more generally, of experts in the process of shaping and defining criminal policy has always attracted attention. It used to be discussed from a per-

[62] Cf. the opposing views of H.J. Hirsch, 'Wiedergutmachung des Schadens im Rahmen des materiellen Strafrechts' (1990) 102 *Zeitschrift für die gesamte Straf-rechtswissenschaft* 534 on the one hand and A. Brauneck, 'Trennendes und verbin-dendes Denken' in F. Haft, W. Hassemer, U. Neumann, W. Schild, and U. Schroth (eds.), *Festschrift für Arthur Kaufmann* (Heidelberg: C.F. Müller, 1993), 417, on the other hand.

[63] For a recent assessment of this delicate issue cf. H. Jung, 'Einheit und Vielfalt der Reformen des Strafprozeßrechts in Europa' (2002) 149 *Goltdammer's Archiv für Strafrecht* 65, 71; see also, with reference to the European Court of Human Rights, A. Ashworth, 'Further Notes on Coherence in Criminal Justice' in P. Asp, C.E. Herlitz, and L. Holmqvist (eds.), *Festskrift till Nils Jareborg* (Uppsala: Iustus Förlag, 2002), 11, 15.

spective of criminological self-understanding. Scholars would ask themselves whether and to what extent they should get involved in public policy debates, in particular to what extent their research should respond to public demand[64] and be defined by external funding. Today, the interest has somewhat shifted to the role of experts in policy debates, namely whether, in a democratic society, the scholar's voice should have special weight in public policy debates at all.

Roger Hood has recently diagnosed a 'widening gulf' in the relationship between criminology and penal policy;[65] he attributes this *inter alia* to a steady loss of credibility and acceptance of criminologists. At first sight the victim campaign seems to prove the opposite. Scholars have contributed substantially to the thrust and the course of the victim campaign on the national and on the international level. The identification and formulation of the different problems and targets were to a large extent owed to scholarly research and advice. In Germany, scholars definitely had an agenda-setting function. Scholars have been engaged at all levels of the debate. The influential Max-Planck-Institut at Freiburg launched several victim-related research projects.[66] Victim-related issues were addressed in the more academically oriented discourse of *Festschriften* as well as in legal periodicals aiming at a wider (legal) audience. Scholars participated in seminars often at an interdisciplinary level within the framework of academies or other institutions of learning.[67] Scholars also introduced the topic into academic teaching.[68] Moreover, their advice was requested at parliamentary

[64] On this controversy between '*Grundlagenforschung*' and '*anwendungsorientierter Kriminologie*' cf. K.L. Kunz, *Kriminologie. Eine Grundlegung* (3rd edn., Bern: Haupt, 2001), 15 ff.

[65] R. Hood, 'Penal Policy in the Public Debate and Criminological Challenges' in (2001) 34 *Australian and New Zealand Journal of Criminology* 1.

[66] Cf. *inter alia* G. Kaiser, H. Kury, and H.J. Albrecht (eds.), 'Victims and Criminal Justice' (Freiburg: Eigenverlag Max-Planck-Institut für ausländisches und internationales Strafrecht, 1991); A. Eser and S. Walther (eds.), *Wiedergutmachung im Kriminalrecht, Reparation in Criminal Law* (Freiburg: Edition Iuscrim, 1996–2001) i–iii; M. Kilchling, *Opferinteressen und Strafverfolgung* (Freiburg: Edition Iuscrim, 1995).

[67] An early example is D. Krauß, 'Subjekt im Strafverfahren?' in Evangelische Akademie Hofgeismar (ed.), *Das Tatopfer als Subjekt*, Protokoll No 177/1981, Hofgeismar, 44.

[68] Noteworthy in this respect is M. Will (ed.), *Schadensersatz im Strafverfahren. Rechtsvergleichendes Symposium zum Adhäsionsprozeß* (Kehl: Engel, 1990), assembling *inter alia* several contributions by students.

hearings. The proposals of the *Alternativprofessoren* found considerable resonance in the public debate, at least in their general direction.

Victimologists did not encounter any serious opposition. Rather, victimological research tended to underscore public anxieties and concerns about the running of the criminal justice system. Perhaps, unintentionally, scholars reassured the general public, and, in turn, the media as well as the politicians in their punitive sentiments. Once again Roger Hood's realistic if not sceptical position is confirmed: '[i]ndeed, the belief that expert advice based on criminological and penological research is the foundation for penal change, is only the screen behind which ideological and political factors, perhaps inevitably, shape those attitudes which imbue legislation'.[69]

Victimologists could be sure of a wider audience. Their proposals connected with a general predisposition to reinstate victims into criminal justice. It is fair to say that the campaign had such sweeping success because it was possible to bring together an uneasy yet powerful coalition of differentiated new empirical knowledge, socio-constructive demands, and strands of 'law and order' philosophy. As could have been expected, once the agenda was reset, the more socio-constructive positions lost ground to the punitive element, which was reaffirmed by being projected onto the victim's role. What looks like a real 'success story' needs to be reassessed in the light of this aspect. From the point of view of a rational humanistic criminal policy dedicated to minimizing punitiveness, those scholars who have fought for a criminal justice system which takes victims' interests more seriously have, in some respects, to content themselves with what may, despite mediation and definite advances in victim protection, be called a Pyrrhic victory after all.[70]

---

[69] R. Hood, 'Criminology and Penal Change: A Case Study of the Nature and Impact of some Recent Advice to Governments' in R. Hood (ed.), *Crime, Criminology and Public Policy. Essays in Honour of Sir Leon Radzinowicz* (London: Heinemann, 1974), 375, 417.

[70] Cf. Joutsen's warning that victim movements might easily turn into 'offender-bashing campaigns' (n. 59 above, 72) or D. Garland's assessment: '[m]any supporters of victims' rights are embarassed to find themselves associated with retributive policies, though it seems undeniable that the social roots of the two phenomena are closely intertwined': N. MacCormick and D. Garland, 'Sovereign States and Vengeful Victims: The Problem of the Right to Punish' in Ashworth and Wasik (eds.), n. 6 above, 11, 15 ff.

Thus, the victim campaign is a good indicator of the potential influence of professional expertise. The input of academics into a campaign will be particularly welcome and fruitful if it endorses public predispositions or else allows for interpretations which suit different audiences and purposes. But it also shows that scholars are not in a position to steer or to predict the outcome of a campaign.

Generally speaking, scholars in social sciences operate in a controversial field. Neither their research nor their argument will convince *per se*. Crime and criminality are popular issues; everybody has—or claims to have—an opinion and a say in the matter.[71] The wholesale reception of the victimological agenda may have to do with the fact that the public at large felt reassured by its approach to offenders and victims.

Scholars will rightly emphasize that the 'victimological turn' is neither directed against offenders nor intended to justify greater punitiveness. Indeed, 'populist punitiveness' is by no means the inevitable flip-side of the 'victimological turn'. Criminologists should not refrain from emphasizing the complexity of the various issues, in particular the risks of punitiveness, since they should try to enhance the rationality in criminal policy debates.

In this respect, David Garland's sceptical account of the contemporary Anglo-American culture of control[72] calls *inter alia* for a reassessment of the role of US-American criminologists who may have, as regards the so-called populist punitiveness, resigned themselves too much to the 'inevitable'.[73] Going public and getting involved does not, as our example shows, guarantee that such moves will produce the desired result and only this result. However, progress in criminal policy requires a constant input of—to use Bourdieu's expression[74]—a *savoir engagé*.

---

[71] For the very same observation with regard to the social sciences at large cf. Bourdieu, *Science de la science et réflexivité* (Paris: Raisons d'Agir Éditions, 2001), 170.

[72] Cf. Garland, n. 5 above.

[73] Apparently the ASC is reluctant to take sides in policy issues. Cf. L. Stern, 'Welchen Einfluß hat die Kriminologie auf die Kriminalpolitik in den USA?' [2001] 2 *Neue Kriminalpolitik* 32. This holds true for Garland as well whose position in *The Culture of Control* is characterized and criticized by L. Zedner, 'Dangers of Dystopias in Penal Theory' (2002) 22 *Oxford Journal of Legal Studies* 341, 365, as an 'abandonment of political commitment and of normative theorizing'.

[74] P. Bourdieu, 'Pour un savoir engagé' Le *monde diplomatique*, February 2002, 3.

Conclusion

Reconstructing a policy campaign is no easy task. It does not become easier if one has, in some way or another, been involved in it. Still, more research into the development and orchestration of criminal policy campaigns is needed. It requires an interdisciplinary approach which draws on both empirical and analytical methods. Theorizing about criminal policy forms part of the more general domain of social theory and lends itself to lofty abstractions. A project-oriented design has the advantage of a more realistic appraisal. In this sense, my own account—giving no more than some 'consolidated impressions'—is meant to illustrate the need for further comparative and international criminal policy research.

The German victim campaign may well pass as an example of how the input of scholarly expertise can trigger policy changes. In this respect, Germany with her tradition of pressure groups, rooted in or at least inclined towards academia, such as the Deutsche Juristentag and the group of *Alternativprofessoren*, is perhaps a special case. Still, my account confirms Roger Hood's warning that criminologists should not overestimate their influence. The 'victimological turn' was well received because it struck a popular chord: scholars had at last rediscovered the victim as a person.[75] At the same time, they found themselves in an uneasy coalition with 'law and order' protagonists. Perhaps the time has come to help forge a new alliance against the resurgence of punitiveness.

[75] In the sense of H. Schüler-Springorum, *Kriminalpolitik für Menschen* (Frankfurt am Main: Suhrkamp, 1991).

11

Influencing Policy: Successes and Failures of Criminological Research in Australia

Richard Harding*

Hood's Own Observations

In a series of lectures presented in 1986–7, Roger Hood explored the question of the relationship of criminology to policy.[1] At that time he had been Director of the Centre for Criminological Research at Oxford University since 1973, so this was a question that had by then become part of his daily working life. Research centres do not run themselves, nor do the funds that enable a team of accomplished researchers to be kept together grow on trees. The Director has the never-ending task of reconciling a wish list of challenging research questions with the priorities of funding agencies. In Hood's case at that time, this principally meant those of the Home Office Research and Planning Unit.

Despite his own excellent personal relations with both John Croft (Head of the Home Office Research and Planning Unit until 1983) and his successor (Professor Ron Clarke), Hood was becoming concerned that the Home Office had started to be too dominant in

---

* In preparing this chapter I wrote to about 25 leading Australian criminologists to seek their views of their own impact upon policy, rather than merely imposing my own evaluations. Helpful responses were obtained from the following, to whom I extend my thanks: David Biles, John Braithwaite, David Brown, Dennis Challinger, Duncan Chappell, Richard Fox, Arie Freiberg, Peter Grabosky, Ross Homel, Peter Loof, Rick Sarre, Adam Sutton, Rob White, and Paul Wilson. Where any of the above persons are quoted without another source being identified, it can be assumed that this is a quotation from their letters to me.

[1] These lectures were consolidated into a single paper, 'Some Reflections on the Role of Criminology in Public Policy' [1987] *Crim.L.R.* 527.

setting agendas and too controlling about publication. Nils Christie's plea that 'independent research should be institutionally as well
as intellectually protected against embracement by authorities' already seemed, in Hood's view,[2] 'merely a dream'. This was because
Ministries of Justice or their equivalents had become the primary
source of funding; because governments already had in their direct
employ the largest groups of full-time researchers working in the
area of criminology; and because the agenda for research—including
the scope of projects, timetables, methodologies, access to subjects
and data, and even control over the final publication—was heavily
influenced by bureaucratic or political perceptions of problems.
These factors 'surely cannot be good for the intellectual development
of any discipline', Hood commented.[3]

Even so, he had no sympathy for the view that criminology
should be quarantined from policy and practice. This attitude was
epitomized by Stanley Cohen's comment that 'it simply is not the
professional job [of criminologists] to advise, consult, recommend or
make decisions'. Such an approach, stated Hood, was 'startling. . . .
By its very nature, the study of crime cannot be logically separated
from the study of criminal policy. The one is shaped by the other, and
vice versa.'[4] Hood endorsed the view of his mentor and long-time
collaborator and friend, Sir Leon Radzinowicz, that 'to rob criminology of this practical function is to render it sterile'.[5]

In making this point, Hood could not resist tweaking the tails of
those who in earlier times would have subscribed to Cohen's views.
Prominent amongst them was Jock Young, who had by the mid-
1980s moved on from the rather nihilistic postures of *The New
Criminology* to 'left realist' concerns about safety on the streets
and in their homes for those citizens, particularly the poor, who
suffer most from crime—a change of stance made with the avowed
intention of bringing about policy changes.[6]

---

[2] Hood, n. 1 above, 536. The quotation from Christie is found in *Limits to Pain*
(Oslo: Universitetsforlaget, 1981), 110.

[3] Ibid., 537.

[4] Ibid., 529. The Cohen quotation is taken from *Visions of Social Control* (Cambridge: Polity Press, 1985), 110.

[5] Ibid., 531. The Radzinowicz quotation is taken from *In Search of Criminology*
(London: Heinemann, 1961), 168.

[6] I. Taylor, P. Walton, and J. Young, *The New Criminology: For a Social Theory of
Deviance* (London: Routledge and Kegan Paul, 1973). 'We are now in Britain witnessing the mushrooming of empirical surveys of crime carried out by criminologists who at

Comparable Australian Experience

My own career in Australia, running a few years behind Hood's, has thrown up identical dilemmas. These first became manifest to me as Director of the Australian Institute of Criminology (1984–7) and later as the Foundation Director of the Crime Research Centre at the University of Western Australia (1988–2000). The first of these bodies was funded entirely by the federal government, and the establishment of the second had been dependent upon my supplicating successfully to the state government.

To be fair, it should be put on the record that pressures upon me were fairly infrequent and mostly indirect. Nevertheless, I have, like Hood, witnessed inappropriate attempts at agenda-setting by people who lack any theoretical understanding of the issues; but like him—although he does not explicitly say so in the article I have cited—I have learned that the agenda-setters can subtly be guided down more suitable paths. Like Hood, I also have been convinced by a lifetime's experience that the notion of criminology as a policy-free zone is absurd, doomed to sterility; and I have also had the amusing opportunity of observing 'radical criminologists' who would once have preferred never to be in the same room as a bureaucrat leading the charge to try to seize the policy agenda (and, even more urgently, the funding).

Given, then, that informing and thereby influencing policy is a legitimate purpose of criminological research, is there some optimum way of achieving this? A series of questions is encapsulated within this broad question. They can best be teased out by considering work situations, funding sources, publication means, and so on.

Categories of Research Situation

There are four main types of situation:

- Research, often unfunded, by an unaligned researcher, usually university-based;
- Research supported by a competitive research grant;
- Commissioned research, with the granting body (usually public but occasionally private) specifying with more or less precision the problem it believes requires analysis; and
- Research carried out by people working for a government criminological research body.

one time took the radical position but now call themselves left realists': Hood, n. 1 above, 530.

Obviously, reading down the page one goes from the area of greatest researcher choice to that of greatest external direction; and, likewise, from the area of least likely receptivity by policy-makers to that of greatest receptivity. In other words, one would expect unfunded research by outsiders to have the least and research by paid employees to have the greatest impact, in the sense of policy adoption. This point is diagrammatically represented by Figure 11:1.

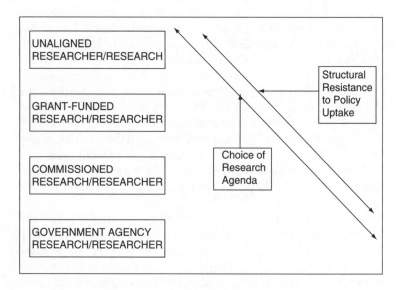

FIGURE 11:1.   Postulated Impact of Research upon Policy

What I shall briefly explore in this chapter is whether these patterns are linear and consistent; in other words, whether the dominance of agenda-setting funding bodies and government agencies, in terms of subsequent policy uptake, is quite as great as one's hypothesis might suggest. My broad conclusion will be that, in an Australian context, the patterns are mixed; that, although there is a broad correlation between proximity of the researcher and the research topic to official agencies and the uptake of research findings, this is by no means uniform. It is necessary to spell out these categories a little more to bring these points alive.

Unfunded, Independent Research

The first category is self-explanatory. In criminology, as in Classics or Literature or Pure Mathematics, the talented person who thinks about issues, re-analyses known data, expands the knowledge base, and re-orders theoretical understanding of issues can still be found, despite the advent into the university world of performance indicators and time management and all the paraphernalia of managerialism. This is as true in Australia as it is in the UK.

Competitive Research Grants

Competitive research grants for Australian criminologists emanate from two sources: the Criminology Research Council (CRC) and the Australian Research Council (ARC). The first of these funds is pathetically small,[7] but to the extent that it can underwrite major empirical research it recently has come to have a Home Office feel about it. Assessment of applications and funding decisions of the Council are made by a group of senior criminal justice system administrators from each state. At present, only the Chairman and one other member have any research qualifications. Previously, for quite a long time, this group had mostly acted with the guidance of its scientific adviser. Its working premise was that professional researchers could be relied upon to identify significant topics, so that their own role was to keep an eye on costs, ensure a spread across crime areas, and achieve accountability.

However, they have now moved towards a pattern of identifying a 'problem' and seeking bids from researchers to find a 'solution'. To applicants this often seems like pure hubris; to funding bodies it is their version of accountability. About half of the available funds are now allocated on this basis. The remainder is mostly allocated to projects that are congruent with the administrators' perceptions of current 'problems', even though brought to their attention by the applicant. Over its thirty-year life, the CRC has thus moved inexorably to the point where bureaucrats are setting and tightly controlling the agenda.

---

[7] Peter Loof, who was intimately involved in the establishment of the Australian Institute of Criminology and the Criminology Research Council and who served for many years as Chairman of each, described the level of CRC funding as 'disturbingly low'. He added, 'In 1971 we contemplated a similar level of funding to that proposed for the Institute.' In fact, at ca. A$500,000 p.a., its funding is now about one-eighth.

Without rancour, let me highlight this trend from my own experience. In 1973 I was one of the first recipients of a grant from the newly created CRC; funds were needed to conduct a national survey of firearms ownership. At that time, gun control was on the action agenda of absolutely no Australian policy-maker. However, I had brought it onto the research agenda by earlier Western Australian work, and the scientific adviser to the Council recommended funding. The Council agreed. The proposal promised to shed light on matters which were currently hidden from view and which could provide a context for other debates—the extent and nature of armed crime; the epidemiology of suicide and the extent to which completed suicides were a function of the chosen means, particularly a firearm; what impact that in turn had on rates by socio-demographic patterns; the efficacy if any of a 'house-gun' as a defence against crime; and so on. The subsequent work led to the publication of the first ever book about firearms ownership, use, and misuse in Australia.[8] This was the beginning of gun control as a serious social and criminological issue in Australia, and the landmark 1996 national gun control legislation[9] can be traced back intellectually through the work of other researchers[10] to my own book and that first research grant. With hindsight, the Council's funds had been well spent; and a research-oriented Council had had the foresight to recognize that this might turn out to be so.

A quarter of a century later, in 1999, I sought a grant to add a national and deeper dimension to some earlier work carried out on

---

[8] *Firearms and Violence in Australian Life* (Perth: University of Western Australia Press, 1981).

[9] On 28 April 1996 a deranged gunman, armed with several automatic and semi-automatic firearms, killed 35 people in a rampage at Port Arthur, a popular historical tourist site in Tasmania. The federal government has no direct legislative power in relation to gun control, but the Prime Minister used a combination of the moral mandate brought about by this event and the financing powers of his government to bring about matching laws in all states, the Territories and the Commonwealth. The laws involved: prohibition of certain categories of firearm; stricter licensing requirements for users; a national gun registration system; safe storage and training requirements; and an extensive buyback scheme. The key elements of this were later replicated in the UK gun control laws passed after the killing of 17 people, mostly children, at Dunblane Primary School on 13 March 1996.

[10] Such as Chappell: see below at 474.

road rage.[11] The scientific adviser to the Council stated that this application was the only one of the twenty or so for consideration that was 'outstanding', and recommended funding. However, it did not fit the current agenda of the administrators, and it was knocked back. Projects of a more immediately 'practical' kind were funded in that round. That was a perfectly legitimate decision. However, if the earlier Council had taken a similar approach in 1973, the essential foundation of what is now a respectable *œuvre* of Australian gun control literature would not have come into existence.

The ARC is broadly similar to the Economic and Social Research Council (ESRC) in the UK. It is funded by the federal government, and operates according to the principle of peer review. Criminology comes within the general field of Social Sciences. Each year broad areas of priority are indicated, but they are neither exclusive nor unduly prescriptive. In seeking a 'Discovery' grant, criminologists must pit themselves competitively against anthropologists, political scientists, economists, psychologists, and so on—something that is probably very good for the intellectual development of the discipline, to pick up Hood's earlier observation.

The make-up of the evaluation panels—eminent researchers from the social sciences—ensures that criminal justice administrators cannot control research agendas. A small personal illustration of this was found in the road rage proposal, mentioned above. This was funded on its merits—indeed much better funded—when an application was subsequently made to the ARC. Australian criminologists were perhaps a little tardy in perceiving the potential of the ARC (just as, anecdotally, British criminologists were in relation to the ESRC). However, my clear impression is that the number of successful applications is now increasing.[12]

---

[11] The original work is published as R.W. Harding, F. Morgan, D. Indermaur, A. Ferrante, and H. Blagg, 'Road Rage and the Epidemiology of Violence: Something Old, Something New' (1998) 7 *Studies on Crime and Crime Prevention* 221.

[12] Data are not published by sub-discipline, but only under the generic head of 'Social Sciences'. However, perusal of the website upon which successful national applications are published underpins my impression that the numbers are increasing. The Australia and New Zealand Society of Criminology, as the professional association, could perhaps act as a clearing-house for this important information.

Commissioned Research

Commissioned research is undoubtedly the growth area. Ministries of Justice, Police Departments, child welfare agencies, Aboriginal peak bodies, and the like, as well as some private or commercial bodies such as shopping centre managements or banks, have increasingly started to let research contracts for pre-identified problems. Local councils also are increasingly becoming aware of research needs. Criminologists—whether bidding individually or, more likely, in conjunction with colleagues and on behalf of their university departments—often find themselves in competition with 'Big Five' management companies (Ernst Young, Touche Ross, etc.) or with local mini versions of these. In other words, subject-matter knowledge and understanding are diminishing qualifications for this kind of research; the generic 'scans' of secondary sources that pass for research in these companies are increasingly regarded as adequate. Not surprisingly, the success rate of university researchers is correspondingly reduced.

Less drastically in terms of intellectual integrity, the federal government has through the agency of 'National Crime Prevention' commissioned research, in a way comparable to that in which the much less well-funded CRC had started to discharge its function. However, the people setting the agenda at National Crime Prevention on the government's behalf initially were scholar-bureaucrats rather than administrators, as with the CRC, and the protocols reflected this fact.[13]

Accountability mechanisms in relation to these projects have been strong but not stifling. Examples of funded projects include: 'Developmental and Early Intervention Approaches to Crime in Australia';[14] 'Preventing Crime and Victimisation among Homeless Young People';[15] 'Working with Adolescents to Prevent Domestic Violence';[16] and 'Young People and Domestic Violence'.[17]

Another form of research, which one might describe as semi-commissioned, is funded by the ARC under its 'Linkage' scheme.

[13] A committee that included members of the Criminology Research Council was responsible for the allocation of the very first grant, but this pattern did not continue.

[14] Published as *Pathways to Prevention* (Canberra: Attorney General's Department, 1999).

[15] Published as *Living Rough* (Canberra: Attorney General's Department, 1999).

[16] Published under that name (Canberra: Attorney General's Department, 1999).

[17] Published under that name (Canberra: Attorney General's Department, 2001).

The linkage is between universities and 'industry'—a concept that includes government agencies. The 'industry' body is required to match the ARC grant on a dollar-for-dollar cash and kind basis. Here university researchers have the opportunity for agenda setting; but of course it is only if the industry—most typically in the realm of criminology a criminal justice or related government department—believes that it will derive problem-solving value from the project that it will normally support the application. In that sense, the researchers must be receptive to the perceptions of administrators—though there is also an opportunity to influence administrators to be receptive to the perceptions of researchers.

Two such projects with which I myself have been associated have been: with the Queensland Department of Corrective Services a project to evaluate the impact of private prisons upon public prisons; and with the Western Australian Department of Justice a project to identify factors that bear upon crime patterns in rural areas. The relevance of the first, from a linkage point of view, was that the Queensland Department had been the first in Australia to commission a privately-managed prison, and in 1997—the date of the application—was considering the future direction of this policy. The relevance of the second was that regional crime patterns were very uneven as regards volume and type and, even allowing for the Aboriginal overlay, the explanations were far from obvious. Yet service needs were either unresponsive or, in some cases, over-responsive to these patterns.

Each issue, then, possessed challenging intellectual aspects, but with outcomes that should inform policy and practice. One could say that the agenda was mutually set; it suited both parties. My impression is that the majority of Linkage projects, from whatever discipline, broadly reflect this sort of balance.

Research by Government Agencies

As in the UK, numerically and financially this is the largest source of criminological research. Most Ministries of Justice and the like have some in-house capacity to conduct research.[18] In addition, there are

---

[18] Continuity of employment and growth of a research culture do not always rate highly in some agencies. In difficult financial times, these groups can receive rather cavalier treatment, and their personnel become first cab off the redundancy rank.

at least four general criminological research bodies in Australia that are funded by governments and available to carry out directed or endorsed research. These are: the Australian Institute of Criminology; the New South Wales Bureau of Crime Statistics and Research; the South Australia Office of Crime Statistics; and the Queensland Criminal Justice Commission Research Unit. The total number of persons working in these bodies is about 130. Of course, not all of these are directly involved in research; however, the numbers certainly far exceed the total of those working in the most mature and established university departments in Australia—*viz.* the Melbourne University Department of Criminology, the Griffith University Centre for Crime Policy and Public Safety, and the University of Western Australia Crime Research Centre.

Whilst these government agencies each have some degree of nominal independence (some being more assertive in this regard than others), they inevitably are very much aware of governmental agendas. If they do not reflect them voluntarily to a significant degree, they can be directed to do so. This is reflected in their outputs. If they do not always seek to solve pre-identified problems, they certainly work around the edges or against the background of these problems.

Research Efficacy: The Socio-political Context and Timeliness of Proposals

The argument of this chapter, to reiterate, is that policy uptake of research is likely to be related to the proximity of the research group or project to governmental agendas, but that this pattern is by no means linear or consistent. Policy uptake is also very much a matter of whether the prevailing social and political ethos is receptive to the directions pointed by the research findings.

In this regard, one would expect independent researchers to encounter higher hurdles than, progressively, research grant recipients, those carrying out commissioned research, and government-employed researchers. This is because researchers often see problems before politicians and bureaucrats do so. Their timing can be, at best, embarrassing and, at worst, open to ridicule. The politico-bureaucratic culture, understandably, is very much committed to the approach that '[i]f it works, don't fix it. To address something that is only a *potential* problem is to risk doing something that may never need to be done if you do not do it in the first place'. That is why, for example, long-term crime prevention planning has such a hard time, particularly in the ultra-pragmatic Anglo-Saxon tradition.

So, when one thinks of policy uptake, individual researchers have considerable barriers to overcome. Neither their agendas nor their standing are necessarily taken on their merits. Research grant recipients are on somewhat firmer ground, for they have already managed to convince others of the academic relevance of their work. Commissioned researchers are working to an agenda that already seems to have passed some of the tests of timeliness and relevance. Finally, the government research group is normally tied in closely with policy concerns and purported problem-solving needs of government. Nevertheless, the examples that follow suggest that policy uptake patterns are by no means uniform.

Violence within Aboriginal Communities

This example fits into the expected mould—work carried out by an independent researcher working to his own agenda and identifying a problem that policy-makers were not ready to address. It relates to Paul Wilson's 1982 work on Aboriginal violence against other Aboriginals.[19] At that time, surprising as it must now seem, criminological study of issues relating to Aboriginal people was still in its infancy. When I commenced duty as Director of the Australian Institute of Criminology in 1984, I discovered that the research staff did not even include a qualified researcher in this area. To the extent that Aboriginal issues were at last getting on to the agenda, they mostly revolved around identifying discriminatory contacts and outcomes within the legal system (police contacts, attitudes of judicial officers, numbers in juvenile detention and prison, and so on). This was a crucially necessary and long overdue phase of debate and analysis.

Wilson leapt past all of this to the point of highlighting victimization trends *within* communities. But no one was yet sufficiently interested; policy-makers were only just starting to grasp the first-level discrimination aspect of the debate. In policy terms, Wilson's cogent book made no impact at all at this time. Now, of course, twenty years on, the question of violence—sexual and other—within Aboriginal communities is mainstream—indeed, the single biggest item on the Aboriginal criminal justice agenda.

[19] P. Wilson, *Black Death, White Hands* (Sydney: George Allen and Unwin, 1982).

Gun Control

Not merely individual researchers but also, at the other end of the scale, government researchers can be before their time. I have already referred to my own work, published between 1976 and 1981, on gun control and its lack of any discernible impact on contemporary policy. That work was done as an independent researcher.

In the late 1980s, the issue was taken up again under the auspices of the government-funded Australian Institute of Criminology. Duncan Chappell, then the Director, vigorously and with intellectual rigour took up the question as an aspect of the National Campaign against Violence.[20] In other respects this turned out to be a markedly successfully campaign. But the gun control agenda was still ahead of its time. Chappell has stated:

Despite this report being tabled and debated in virtually all of the Australian Parliaments, no significant changes occurred to Australian gun control laws, and the work of the National Campaign against Violence...was fiercely attacked by the proponents of guns like the Sporting Shooters and similar groups.[21]

Five years later, after the Port Arthur massacre in which a single gunman killed thirty-five people,[22] the timing was at last right. Now, Chappell pointed out, 'those who were urging immediate gun law reform had a...reference point upon which to base their arguments for change'. This brings out an important point, that things that are before their time sometimes find that time catches them up.

Random Breath Testing

Timing is, of course, simply a matter of the level of social and political awareness of the essential nature of a problem and the understanding of what can be done about it. The anti-smoking campaign is a prime example of an issue that started as an obsession of cranks and has become a mainstream medical, lifestyle and etiquette matter. Activists—lobbying, debating, litigating, advertising, ridiculing—brought about its changed status, so that the time was ripe for the radical change that has subsequently occurred.

---

[20] The main thrust of this campaign is best encapsulated in *Violence: Directions for Australia* (Canberra: Australian Institute of Criminology, 1990).

[21] Letter to the author, 6 Aug. 2001.   [22] See n. 9 above.

The criminological researcher sometimes faces the same challenge and must become a lobbyist or activist. Perhaps the best example in Australia concerns random breath testing (RBT). Whilst Ross Homel is careful 'not to exaggerate [his] own role and claim an undue share of any credit for the injuries prevented [and lives saved] as a result of RBT',[23] it is true to say that he has been the greatest single contributor to this national crime prevention and harm reduction strategy. Homel's campaign began when he was an unfunded, independent researcher. His work was very much a case of re-ordering existing research carried out by Laurence Ross[24] in the light of the appropriate theoretical framework and effectively synthesizing it for Australian—particularly New South Wales—purposes. Homel describes his work as follows:

The analysis [Laurence Ross] presented in his review demonstrated clearly...that police enforcement had considerable unrealized potential in public health terms, even if in the end the deterrent impact could not be sustained. The main conclusions I drew from his work were that to influence perceived probabilities of apprehension (and hence behaviour), police enforcement must be highly visible in a threatening kind of way, must be sustained at a high level, and...supported by extensive publicity.[25]

He goes on to describe the sustained campaign that he and others mounted and its ultimate success. The issue, which started out well ahead of the received political agenda, was transformed into one for its time. The academic work alone would not have achieved this. Homel states:

One lesson from many attempts to influence policy...is that an enormous amount of time is required. One must take the time not only to read the literature and do all the other normal academic things; one must also take the time to talk to police, government, researchers and other key players. ...

A further lesson, reinforced by innumerable appearances in the media and before audiences of non-academics, is that one must keep one's message simple.[26]

---

[23]   R. Homel, 'Random Breath Testing in Australia: Getting It to Work According to Specifications' (1993) 88 (Supplement) *Addiction* 28S.

[24]   Homel (ibid.) cites a corpus of work spanning the period 1973 to 1990.

[25]   Ibid., 28S.   [26]   Ibid., 32S.

The Cannabis Expiation Notice Scheme

This story illustrates that what is timely in one place may not be so in another. Research carried out by the South Australia Office of Crime Statistics in the mid-1980s, under the directorship of Adam Sutton and with considerable input from Rick Sarre amongst others, led to the passage in 1987 of laws that made the cannabis laws of that state significantly different from those of the other Australian states. Sutton describes the scheme as follows:

Rather than continuing to treat possession, private use and cultivation [of amounts suitable for personal use] as 'normal' summary offences, to be dealt with by arrest or summons and a formal appearance in a court of summary jurisdiction, it implemented a system of expiation notices.... Police were required to issue a written notice to any adult detected committing a 'simple cannabis offence'. By paying the fine...within a specified period, recipients could avoid both the requirement of attending the court and the possibility of incurring a criminal conviction.[27]

The aim of this law was to avoid the collateral effects (stigma, prejudice to employment, contact with established dealers) of bringing within the criminal justice system many young adults for whom cannabis use was a socially acceptable and normal activity and who were otherwise not involved in criminal activities. The law was controversial, even within South Australia. Opponents argued that this would open the floodgates to increased cannabis use, thus increasing in turn the number of users who might 'graduate' to use of harder drugs.

More than a decade on, there is no evidence that these fears have been borne out; indeed, the evidence is to the contrary.[28] The scheme has been intensively and frequently evaluated, and is working reasonably well and achieving much of its primary purpose. But its national impact has been slight, with only the two numerically insignificant jurisdictions of the Northern Territory and the Australian Capital Territory replicating versions of it. For the other states, the timing may never be right—at any rate, it is still premature.

[27] A. Sutton, 'Cannabis Law and the Young Adult User: Reflections on South Australia's Cannabis Expiation Notice System' (2000) 28 *International Journal of the Sociology of Law* 147.

[28] A. Sutton and E. Macmillan, 'Criminal Justice Perspectives on South Australia's Cannabis Expiation Notice Procedures' (2000) 19 *Drug and Alcohol Review* 281 at 285.

Corporate Regulation

John Braithwaite's book, *Responsive Regulation*,[29] co-authored by Ian Ayres, represents the culmination of many years' thought and research about the nature of corporate criminal activity. It was written whilst he was a Research Professor at the Institute of Advanced Studies at the Australian National University—probably the least 'directed' position available in Australian academic life.

This book could well be said to be one of the most influential in Australian and, indeed, international criminology. Braithwaite's concern was to get away from regulatory legalism, on the one hand, whilst avoiding unbridled self-regulation, on the other hand. His well-known 'enforcement pyramid' lies at its crux—the notion that regulators should carefully graduate their enforcement responses, an aspect of this being that they should primarily regulate and monitor corporate standards and compliance systems rather than directly police substantive corporate activities.

I have some concerns about this model, which some businesses and regulators have purportedly adopted whilst in reality stripping it of its subtleties and balance in its daily application. But that is not the point for present purposes. What matters is that Braithwaite, as an independent researcher, has by the sheer intellectual quality of his work, drawing its strength from his long-term research observations, achieved a degree of policy uptake that is enormous. A linear model that regards outsiders as inevitably and invariably lacking in influence could not absorb this experience.

Of course, Braithwaite's work had been exquisitely timed; the ever-increasing complexity of corporate activities and the palpably diminishing capacity of governments to deal on equal terms with global businesses meant that a new regulatory model had urgently to be developed. Timing is not just a question of luck, but one of the marks of a good researcher.

Corporate Crime in the Pharmaceutical Industry

However, Braithwaite had had to learn his sense of timing the hard way. One of the first tasks that I had to carry out on arriving at the Australian Institute of Criminology in 1984 was to sort out some residual legal correspondence arising out of Braithwaite's book of

---

[29] I. Ayres and J. Braithwaite, *Responsive Regulation: Transcending the Deregulation Debate* (Oxford: Oxford University Press, 1992).

the above title.[30] The pharmaceutical industry is powerful, rich, averse to criticism, and litigious. Efforts had been made, unsuccessfully, to interfere with publication of this excellent book.

However, neither its excellence nor the fact that Braithwaite had been sheltering under the wing of a government research institute could make it efficacious. In policy terms, it had no discernible impact.[31]

Other Examples

It would be tedious to continue indefinitely. A few more outline examples will suffice. Ron Clarke's approach to situational crime prevention has a strong following in Australia, not only from a theoretical perspective but also distributed through agencies and university researchers carrying out empirical funded research. The policy uptake has been tangible.

National Crime Prevention-funded research projects have also been widely picked up—for example, Ross Homel's *Pathways to Prevention*[32] and Harry Blagg's *Crisis Intervention in Aboriginal Family Violence.*[33]

On the other hand, Homel's work commissioned by the Western Australian Police on High Speed Police Pursuits was completely ignored, if not rejected out of hand.[34] The researcher got the 'wrong answer'; in other words, the commissioning body, whilst sufficiently self-aware to recognize the need for independent research, was still not mature enough to accept unpalatable findings.

The Research Unit of the Royal Commission into Aboriginal Deaths in Custody—a government-funded group set up to help 'solve' an identified 'problem'—has had virtually all of its technical recommendations implemented—on cell design, visitors' schemes, double-bunking, alarm buttons, and so on.[35] However, whilst the temper of the times was ready for those initiatives, the main thrust of

---

[30]   (London: Routledge and Kegan Paul, 1984).

[31]   Actually, the choice of subject matter was more akin to that of an independent researcher than a government employee. Protocols subsequently developed at the AIC would ensure that nothing as personal as this would get on to the agenda again.

[32]   See n. 13 above.

[33]   (Canberra: Attorney General's Department, 2000).

[34]   'High Speed Police Pursuits In Perth: A Report to the Police Department of Western Australia' (Perth: Police Department, 1990).

[35]   D. Biles and D. McDonald, *Deaths In Custody Australia, 1980–89* (Canberra: Australian Institute of Criminology, 1992).

the recommendations, which was to reduce contact between Aboriginal people and the criminal justice system and personnel, came too soon.

Robert White's work on the utilization of public space by juveniles is an interesting example. As he has explained, it is often taken up avidly by local councils and shopping centre managements but then undermined by general 'law and order' policies that regard visible juveniles as potential law-breakers.

In summary of this part, the pattern of policy uptake in Australia is mixed. Government agency research can be rejected; commissioned research can be ignored; research grant work can disappear from view; independent research can be taken up. And the obverse of each of these situations can occur. The matrix in Figure 11:2 attempts to reflect these themes in relation to the examples covered in this chapter.

This is actually a very heartening conclusion for criminologists. It means that, whatever their work situations, they are not cut off from 'making a difference'. Certainly, the closer one is to government, the more one might expect to influence policy through research. But the independent researcher can also do so if s/he picks an issue that is timely, does the work well, and is prepared to 'sell' it. Inputs into

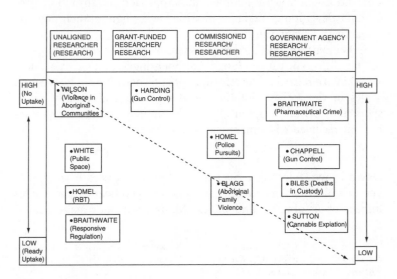

FIGURE 11:2. Representation of Actual Resistance to Policy Uptake

government policy genuinely do seem to come from a multiplicity of sources.

Other Policy Inputs by Criminologists

The criminologist may be an activist, a teacher, an author, a consultant, or a bureaucrat. Much that is relevant to these roles is self-evident but goes to make up the total picture of how policy can be influenced. Let me refer briefly to each of these categories.

Activist

Homel's role as an activist in the RBT campaign has already been mentioned. In a sense, he and his colleagues created the optimum timing for the reception of their own research. Less dramatically, researchers may plug into a social movement or value system that is already evolving. In the UK and Australia, many aspects of the victims' movement and victims' research can be characterized this way. As the movement grows, the research may take root; and as the results of the research become known, the movement may consolidate.[36]

The restorative justice movement, led in Australia by Braithwaite, likewise fits this pattern. Braithwaite and his team, like their New Zealand counterparts, adopted this approach as an action programme developing and being modified in the light of their ongoing research and evaluation.

Other activism preceded the social movement—for example, that of David Brown, Russell Hogg, Gil Boehringer, and George Zdenkowski with regard to the reform of prison conditions in New South Wales in the 1970s. But the social movement eventually came, sparked by prison riots and a Royal Commission, and activist values became received wisdom, at least for a time.

Teacher

David Brown referred to his teaching and the related monographs and/or collections of materials as being very significant aspects of his impact upon practice and policy. Many academics make similar

---

[36] The seminal work conducted at Hood's Centre in the early 1980s fits this description: see J. Shapland, J. Willmore, and P. Duff, *Victims in the Criminal Justice System* (Aldershot: Gower, 1985).

claims. It is, after all, part of our very *raison d'être*—something we have to believe in to keep the spirits up.

However, these aspirations are essentially non-quantifiable. The processes of cognitive learning and the assembling of value systems are too complicated for measurement. That in itself does not diminish the validity of the claim, but merely alerts one to rein in such claims.

Author

Richard Fox's response emphasized that it is not just the research itself but the manner, place, and timing of its publication that bears upon the ability of the scholar to influence policy. A textbook that 'targets' possible High Court citations—a 'top down' approach—will have a different impact from one that tries to change community understanding of a problem—a 'bottom up' approach. Fox himself has been notably successful in working this way.

Consultant

Ministries of Justice and the like mostly call in consultants only when they have a broad notion of what their problem is or what direction they believe they should head in but they cannot really fathom out the detail. It was very much in that situation that Arie Freiberg was called in by the Victoria Department of Justice in 1989 to redraft legislation that subsequently was passed as the Sentencing Act 1991. That legislation introduced important new concepts, in particular by spelling out the purposes of sentencing, introducing a clear hierarchy of punishments, and relating pecuniary penalties (by way of penalty units) to each other punishment in the hierarchy.

Freiberg rightly emphasizes that these innovations were not made *ad hoc* but drew upon theoretical principles explored and refined, in conjunction with Richard Fox, over a considerable period.[37] Subsequently, Victoria has managed to maintain its position as the Australian state with the lowest rate of imprisonment—a fact that seems to have had no adverse impact upon its crime rate.

---

[37] Homel makes the same point about the crucial importance of a strong theoretical position when developing his RBT campaign: see n. 20 above, 315.

An achievement such as this makes nonsense of Cohen's view that it is not the job of the criminologist to consult or advise.[38] The impact of Freiberg's work has been to make hundreds, probably thousands, of citizens' lives in Victoria less oppressive than they otherwise would have been, in that they have not been imprisoned when otherwise they probably would have been. It would be perverse to downgrade that for a point of abstract principle.

Bureaucrat/Administrator

Australian criminologists move in and out of the bureaucracy more than might be expected. For example, Tony Vinson became Commissioner of Corrective Services in New South Wales[39] before returning to academic life; Sandra Egger was Deputy Director of the New South Wales Bureau of Crime Statistics; Adam Sutton spent some time as Director of the Office of Crime Statistics in South Australia; both Duncan Chappell and George Zdenowski were federal law reform commissioners; Satyanshu Mukherjee and David Brereton have each been Directors of the Research Unit of the Queensland Criminal Justice Commission. Comparable patterns may be found in the UK.

Recently I myself have taken up the position of Inspector of Custodial Services in Western Australia. For English readers, the nearest equivalent is that of HM Chief Inspector of Prisons, though the statutory base of my own position is stronger. In the UK, Rod Morgan has even more recently become HM Chief Inspector of Probation. It would be premature to write my own valedictory, but it can be said that the capacity to bring about change by direct involvement in the process of government is considerable. The great advantage the criminologist has over other possible incumbents is a theoretically based strategic sense—something usually

[38] Cohen's position should be seen as one of personal preference, suiting doubtless his own temperament and value structure, and thus maximizing for him the quality and perspicacity of his work. Many would say that it is the very objectivity and clarity that come from standing off from the fray that have made his contribution to criminology so outstanding. However, to deny the validity or legitimacy of alternative approaches is not helpful, nor is it necessary to sustain the legitimacy of his own position.

[39] See T. Vinson, *Wilful Obstruction: The Frustration of Prison Reform* (Sydney: Methuen, 1982).

lacking in career public servants. I am sure Rod Morgan will be finding this also in his position.

Influencing Policy: A Summation

It has been interesting to discover how pessimistic some of my high-achieving colleagues have been about the ability of criminologists to influence policy. John Braithwaite wrote that he 'did not think anything I have written has had a lot of influence for good or ill on Australian criminal justice policy'. David Biles said that 'the more I think about it, the more I am coming to the view that the notion that criminological research should primarily be to influence criminal justice policy is just too simplistic'. Peter Grabosky modestly emphasized the team side of his own achievements.

This brief review has brought home to me, and I hope to others, the range and extent of policy influence that criminologists can have. Perhaps as an academic or professional group we are too keenly aware of our failures—three strikes laws, immigration detention centre conditions, drug laws, and many others—to recognize all our own achievements. There has actually been a dazzling array of effective inputs.

In the UK the pattern is no less diverse. Roger Hood, both directly and as a strategist, has epitomized the way in which the scholar can with dignity, integrity, and perspicacity enrich the national criminological scene. The range of his work is enormous—from sentencing in magistrates' courts through the history of English criminal law to global humanitarian issues related to capital punishment. The work of others that he has nurtured includes literally dozens of projects that have worked their way into English crime policy—anti-racism policies in prisons; awareness of race bias in sentencing; the proper concern for victims in the criminal justice system; the due process operation of the Mental Health Review Tribunal; the watchdog role of Boards of Visitors; multiple issues concerned with the effectiveness of probation; the problems of prisoner victimization; and so on.

Roger Hood's career has demonstrated for the UK what I set out to explore in this chapter about Australia—that if the integrity and quality of the research are good enough and the sense of timeliness and social relevance is acute enough, the criminologist can influence policy whatever his formal position in the overall scheme of things and however he chooses to bring his work to public notice.

12

Criminology and Public Policy in the USA and UK

Michael Tonry and David A. Green

For at least fifty years, academics have been urging the relevance to criminal justice policy-making of systematic knowledge based on research, and decrying the failure of policy-makers to take account of research findings. That sentence could be construed as evidence that criminology, not economics, is the dismal science: science in its aspirations, dismal in its influence. The story of the interactions between knowledge and policy is not, however, so bleak, though the pattern of interactions is complex.

Roger Hood has on a number of occasions written about the ways that research can, should, and does influence policy-making.[1] In this chapter we explore a number of themes and issues he has discussed and, with the benefit of hindsight, comment on how things have changed since he began writing on these matters. To do this, we need at the outset to distinguish among a number of separate issues and claims.

First, a distinction needs to be drawn between researchers' specialized knowledge and their personal beliefs and policy preferences. Few people, at least outside the heat of political battle, disagree with

---

[1] R. Hood, 'Criminology and Penal Change: A Case Study of the Nature and Impact of Some Recent Advice to Governments' in R. Hood (ed.), *Crime, Criminology and Public Policy: Essays in Honour of Sir Leon Radzinowicz* (London: Heinemann, 1974), 153–172; R. Hood, 'Some Reflections on the Role of Criminology in Public Policy' [1987] *Crim.L.R.* 527; R. Hood, 'Penal Policy and Criminological Challenges in the New Millennium' (2001) 34 *The Australian and New Zealand Journal of Criminology* 1; R. Hood, 'Criminology and Penal Policy: The Vital Role of Empirical Research' in A.E. Bottoms and M. Tonry (eds.), *Ideology, Crime and Criminal Justice* (Cullompton: Willan, 2002).

the proposition that sensible policy-making should take account of systematic evidence. Few people outside academic circles, however, believe that researchers' beliefs and preferences about policy are entitled to any special weight. Many policy issues implicate moral values, political philosophies, and practical considerations about which reasonable people disagree. The proposition that researchers lack credible claims to special wisdom in these matters is so obvious, and straightforward, as almost not to warrant mention. We mention it, however, because some academics seem to believe otherwise. More in England than in the United States, some researchers see themselves as engaged simultaneously in research and policy advocacy. This is a serious problem in its own right, because, as the recent ESRC Initiative on Violent Crime illustrates, mixing advocacy with research distorts research priorities and produces bad research.[2] It is an even more serious problem in relation to policy-making because advocacy research undermines the credibility of social science research generally, and feeds 'lies, damn lies, and statistics' stereotypes. In the longer term advocacy research makes policy-makers less likely to take research findings seriously. Social science researchers start with credibility problems, since most people who self-select to become academic social scientists are political liberals. Many policy-makers are conservative (though most might themselves use such adjectives as 'practical' or 'hardheaded' or 'moderate') about criminal justice issues or feel required by public opinion to act as if they, and seem often to be predisposed to believe that social scientists have axes to grind. Advocacy research that masquerades as non-partisan, even-handed scientific research confirms that predisposition. Our interest in this chapter is in how systematic knowledge influences policy, and not in whether policy decisions accord with researchers' preferences.

Secondly, consideration needs to be given to the ways in which research might influence policy. Few people outside elementary school imagine that research findings translate directly into policy. Research in the USA in the late 1980s, for example, showed that sending offenders to correctional boot camps did not achieve lower recidivism rates than those of comparable offenders given other

---

[2] e.g., generally N. Gilbert, 'Advocacy Research and Social Policy' in M. Tonry (ed.), *Crime and Justice—A Review of Research* (Chicago, Ill.: University of Chicago, 1997), xxii, 101–148 and, particularly, Hood, 'Criminology and Penal Policy', n. 1 above.

sentences.[3] Few researchers or policy-makers were surprised when American states continued to operate boot camps and establish new ones. Conversely, research in England and the United States found that Neighbourhood Watch schemes have no discernible effects on crime rates,[4] and in the United States researchers found that Operation DARE (Drug Abuse Resistance Education), a widespread police-in-the-classroom drug-abuse prevention programme, has no long-term effects on drug use.[5] Few people are surprised that governments continue to fund such programmes.

Several filters separate knowledge from policy. One is the filter of prevailing punishment paradigms.[6] The individualized sentencing ethos of indeterminate sentencing was not sympathetic to research findings that 'nothing works' (whether things worked or not), but the retributive ethos of determinate sentencing was. Scholars had raised empirical and normative questions about individualized sentencing for a quarter of a century[7] before Martinson's famous article was published in 1974,[8] but until paradigms shifted many people were not ready to pay attention. When a new determinate sentencing ethos predicated on retributive conceptions of justice took hold, people were ready to attend to the arguments in Martinson's article and acted on what they thought they learned.

Prevailing ideology is another filter. Clear majorities of the population and of elected officials in the United States today justify the

[3] D.G. Parent, 'Boot Camps Failing to Achieve Goals' in M. Tonry and K. Hamilton (eds.), *Intermediate Sanctions in Overcrowded Times* (Boston, Mass.: Northeastern University Press, 1995), 139–149; D.L. MacKenzie, 'Boot Camps—A National Assessment' in ibid., 149–160.

[4] T. Hope, 'Community Crime Prevention' in M. Tonry and D. Farrington (eds.), *Building a Safer Society: Strategic Approaches to Crime Prevention* (Chicago, Ill.: University of Chicago Press, 1995), 21–89.

[5] L.W. Sherman, D. Gottfredson, D. MacKensie, J. Eck, P. Reuter, and S. Bushway, *Preventing Crime: What Works, What Doesn't, What's Promising* (Washington, DC: US Department of Justice, Office of Justice Programs, 1997), Chapter 5.

[6] T.S. Kuhn, *The Structure of Scientific Revolutions* (3rd edn., London: University of Chicago Press, 1996).

[7] e.g., F.A. Allen, *The Borderland of Criminal Justice* (Chicago, Ill.: University of Chicago Press, 1964); C.S. Lewis, 'The Humanitarian Theory of Punishment' in R.J. Gerber and P.D. McAnany (eds.), *Contemporary Punishment: Views, Explanations and Justifications* (Notre Dame, Ind.: University of Notre Dame Press, 1972), 194–199.

[8] R. Martinson, 'What Works?—Questions and Answers about Prison Reform' (1974) 35 *Public Interest* 22–54.

use of capital punishment on the moral ground that people who commit heinous violent killings deserve to die. It should come as no surprise that research findings questioning capital punishment's deterrent effects have little influence.[9] Partly this is because death penalty supporters do not think the research findings relevant, and partly because they are predisposed to disbelieve them. In both England and the United States, public officials and much of the public believe that crime is controllable through changes in the severity or certainty of punishment, and thus are not very open to evidence that suggests the contrary.[10] Ideological filters are especially frustrating to academics because many believe (we do) that research on public opinion, the deterrent and incapacitative effects of penalties, and crime prevention raises serious doubts about the wisdom and effectiveness of many contemporary crime control policies.

Short-term political considerations are still another filter. In the USA and the UK, the Democratic Party and the Labour Party were from the 1950s to the 1980s associated with relatively more humane criminal justice and social welfare policies than their rivals.[11] In recent years they have sought, through their rhetoric and their policies, to assure voters that they are no less tough on crime than the Republicans and Tories. As a result, criminal justice policy debates are stalemated in both countries. In such an environment, few elected officials are prepared in public to risk being called 'soft on crime' for proposing or making policy changes that research findings might suggest are desirable. It is not uncommon, in private settings, by contrast, for senior policy-makers to say that they do not

---

[9] e.g., A. Blumstein, J. Cohen, and D. Nagin, *Deterrence and Incapacitation: Estimating the Effects of Criminal Sanctions on Crime Rates* (Washington, DC: National Academic Press, 1978); R. Hood, *The Death Penalty: A World-Wide Perspective* (3rd edn., Oxford: Oxford University Press, 2002).

[10] e.g., A. von Hirsch, A.E. Bottoms, E. Burney, and P.-O. Wikström, *Criminal Deterrence and Sentence Severity: An Analysis of Recent Research* (Oxford: Hart Publishing, 1999), 62; D. Nagin, 'Deterrence and Incapacitation' in M. Tonry (ed.), *The Handbook of Crime and Punishment* (New York: Oxford University Press, 1998), 345–368.

[11] T. Gest, *Crime and Politics: Big Government's Erratic Campaign for Law and Order* (New York: Oxford University Press, 2001); D. Downes and R. Morgan, 'The Skeletons in the Cupboard: The Politics of Law and Order at the Turn of the New Millennium' in R. Maguire, R. Reiner, and R. Morgan, *The Oxford Handbook of Criminology* (3rd edn., Oxford: Oxford University Press, 2002), 286–321.

favour particular policies or proposals but that they feel unable to take the political risks of opposing them publicly.

Short-term bureaucratic considerations and inertia are a final filter. Norval Morris often illustratively quotes a possibly apocryphal Victorian administrator's exclamation, '[r]eform, reform, don't speak to me of reform. Things are bad enough as it is.' A bit exaggerated maybe, but it does capture the resistance to change that characterizes most organizations. It is comfortable to continue doing what we know how to do and is familiar, and it is always easy to imagine all the things that can go wrong with proposed changes. Research findings are seldom so clear and the foreseeable benefits from change so compelling as to make the need for policy change self-evident. And when the need for change is not obvious, the tendency toward inertia kicks in.

The filters are real, but do not mean that policy-making is impervious to influence from research findings and other systematic evidence. They do mean that influence is often indirect and partial and that researchers and others need to give careful thought to how findings are disseminated and how they could more usefully inform policy-making.

Thirdly, assuming that research findings should and do influence policy, consideration should be given to ways in which the quality of research can be improved and its scope expanded. Proposals to establish national research-and-statistics institutes that are governmentally funded but operationally independent have been made in the USA and the UK for three-quarters of a century.[12] Arguments in favour include the desirability of separating research and statistics from day-to-day political influence and of organizing research agendas around both basic and operational issues. Health research agencies, which are typically operationally independent and support long-term basic research, are often invoked as appropriate models for criminal justice research.

Roger Hood has several times written about interactions among researchers, research, and policy. In *Key Issues in*

---

[12] M. Tonry, 'Building Better Policies on Better Knowledge' in *The Challenge of Crime in a Free Society: Looking Back, Looking Forward, Symposium on the 30th anniversary of the President's Commission on Law Enforcement and Administration of Justice* (Washington, DC: US Department of Justice, Office of Justice Programs, 1998), 93–122.

Criminology,[13] he and Richard F. Sparks asserted that criminologists cannot 'decide what the *aims* of penal policy should be, but by discovering how much crime is committed, and by showing how and why it is committed, criminologists can help to show what policy goals are reasonable; and if given certain aims, they can try to discover by research the best means of accomplishing them'.[14] In later writings, Hood elaborated on that theme. In a 1974 *festschrift* honouring Sir Leon Radzinowicz,[15] he explored ways in which policy and knowledge interact and, adverting to Radzinowicz's similar 1965 proposals,[16] argued for government funding of independent research institutes. A 1987 article is less optimistic:[17] Hood's principal assertion is that researchers should be interested in policy and the main, if wistful, proposal is a reiteration of the 1974 suggestions for development of a governmentally funded but independent national institute for criminological research. Finally, in 2002, Hood revisited themes explored earlier,[18] and concluded, '[t]he relationship between criminology as an academic discipline and penal policy makers is . . . facing a crisis'.[19] He once again reiterated the proposal for creation of a free-standing criminological research institute.

In this chapter we examine three strands pulled from Hood's writings. First, we examine ways in which research findings have influenced policy, and conclude that prevailing pessimism is exaggerated. The filters we described a few paragraphs back do make policymakers more or less susceptible to influence, but that is not the end of the story. While it is true that sanctioning policies in the USA and the UK in recent years have largely not reflected relevant research findings, research has importantly informed the development of crime prevention policies and had major influence on policy-making in police, probation, and prison agencies, and in other spheres. Secondly, we explore some of the literature on how social science findings influence policy. Optimistic expectations of the founders of the earliest criminology departments in Cambridge, Melbourne,

---

[13] R. Hood and R.F. Sparks, *Key Issues in Criminology* (London: Weidenfeld and Nicolson, 1970).
[14] Ibid., 9 (emphasis in the original).
[15] Hood, 'Criminology and Penal Change', n. 1 above.
[16] L. Radzinowicz, *The Need for Criminology* (London: Heinemann, 1965).
[17] Hood, 'Some Reflections', n. 1 above, 527–538.
[18] Hood, 'Criminology and Penal Policy', n. 1 above.
[19] Hood, 'Penal Policy and Criminological Challenges', n. 1 above, 1.

and Berkeley that investment in sound research would generate findings that would guide policy-making soon proved over-ambitious. Frustrations about this, however, are somewhat misconceived because the optimistic expectations were overblown and over simple. New knowledge seldom leads directly to policy changes, though occasionally it does. Even when research does not directly or in the short term change policies, however, in the longer term research provides a backdrop to policy whose influence is insufficiently recognized. Thirdly, we examine the evolution of related proposals, by Radzinowicz in 1965 and by the US President's Crime Commission in 1967, and echoed by Hood in 1974, 1987, 2001, and 2002, for creation and funding by governments of independent research institutes to undertake basic and long-term research on crime and the justice system. Those proposals have never been fully realized, but they remain as valid today as when repeatedly they have been made.

The Influence of Criminological Knowledge on Policy

Anyone who has devoted a life to trying to understand crime and the workings of the justice system, as one of us has and the other may, must believe that knowledge matters. We believe, with Winston Churchill's much-quoted 1910 rhetoric, that 'the treatment of crime and criminals is one of the most unfailing tests of the civilisation of any country', and that research findings can improve and enrich the ways in which crime and criminals are handled.

Many researchers, including Roger Hood, are doubtful that research has much influence on policy in our time: '[m]ost developments in penal policy over the last decade have emerged', he has written, 'not through the influence of criminological ideas or from the application of findings from research on the nature, incidence or trajectories of criminality, or on the effectiveness of ways to respond to and control it, but from ideological and political considerations fueled by populist concerns and impulses.'[20] To like effect, in the United States, Joan Petersilia and Alfred Blumstein, both past presidents of the American Society of Criminology, wrote: '[i]t may be that policies intended to address crime and criminal justice are so strongly driven by fundamental ideological convictions that neither

---

[20] Ibid., 1–2.

side wants to confront empirical reality because that might undermine their deeply held beliefs ... [W]e believe this is a major reason
why policy has so largely ignored research findings'.[21]

Both observations are true but overly ambitious, and too pessimistic. What Hood and Petersilia and Blumstein appear to have in
mind is legislation concerning criminal penalties and decisions about
relative investments in criminal justice and other preventive strategies and measures. If that is right, they are overly ambitious because
it is unrealistic to expect research findings easily to pass through
paradigmatic, ideological, political, and bureaucratic self-interest
filters, especially when the most symbolically salient policy questions are at issue. They are too pessimistic because they overlook an
enormous range of policy judgements that are influenced by research
findings.[22]

Policy-makers are, for a variety of reasons, not likely to look to
research to inform major penal policy decisions. Many politicians
and citizens believe that crime policy is a matter of simple common
sense, so there is no particular reason to look for specialist knowledge or to defer to specialist expertise. The first American national
crime commission, the Wickersham Commission,[23] observed in
1931: '[m]ost of those ... who speak on American criminal justice
assume certain things to be well known or incontrovertible'. Norval
Morris put it thus:[24] '[p]eople are born experts on the causes and
control of crime; they sense the solutions in their bones. The solutions differ dramatically from person to person, but each one knows,
and knows deeply and emotionally, that his perspective is the way of
truth.'

Crime and punishment issues raise disputed normative questions.
Criminologists, like everyone else, have opinions on normative questions, but neither normatively nor politically is there any good

---

[21] A. Blumstein and J. Petersilia, 'Investing in Criminal Justice Research' in J.Q.
Wilson and J. Petersilia (eds.), *Crime: Twenty-Eight Leading Experts Look at the
Most Pressing Problem of Our Time* (San Francisco, Cal.: ICS Press, 1995), 465–488,
at 468.

[22] Hood, n. 19 above; Blumstein and Petersilia, n. 21 above.

[23] Wickersham Commission (US National Commission on Law Observance and
Enforcement), *Report on Criminal Statistics* (Washington, DC: US Government
Printing Office, 1931), i–vi, 3.

[24] M. Tonry and N. Morris, 'Introduction' in M. Tonry and N. Morris (eds.), *Crime
and Justice—An Annual of Research* (Chicago, Ill.: University of Chicago Press,
1983), iv, pp. vii–ix, at p. vii.

reason why criminologists' opinions should count more than anyone else's. If the answers to policy questions—capital punishment, longer or shorter prison sentences, life imprisonment—derive primarily from normative analyses, empirical evidence is by definition irrelevant, or relevant only at the margins. In political terms, it is much more important that policy proposals be facially plausible and consistent with widely held beliefs and intuitions than that they be soundly based on reliable evidence.

Moreover, confident assertions based on research tend not to be galvanizing. Typically they are either negative—two-officer squad cars are no more effective than single-officer cars[25] or Neighbourhood Watch or boot camp programmes do not reduce crime rates— or highly qualified—a well-managed treatment programme for carefully targeted offenders will reduce re-offending by a few percentage points.[26] Neither kind of claim gives policy-makers clear guidance on what to do. Negative findings, such as those on boot camps' effects on re-offending, address only a small part of what motivates policy-makers when they support or create such programmes. The claimed instrumental reasons for creating boot camps typically were reduction in re-offending, diversion of offenders from prison, and cost savings resulting from the diversions. If, then, research findings show, as they did, no effects on recidivism, net-widening rather than net diversion, and cost increases, the formal logic would suggest abandonment of boot camps.[27] If, however, boot camps are adopted because the case for them seems intuitively strong, it is easy to reject research evidence as counter-intuitive and therefore probably wrong. Moreover, it is likely that focusing on stated instrumental goals of boot camps is a mistake because a variety of latent goals were at least as important in their creation. These included symbolic political goals of assuring citizens that policy-makers are serious about holding offenders accountable and punishing them severely, and expressive goals of denouncing bad acts and bad actors. If the latent goals were as important as or more important than the stated

[25] L. Blake and R.T. Coupe, 'The Impact of Single and Two-officer Patrols on Catching Burglars in the Act' (2001) 41 British Journal of Criminology 381–396.
[26] G.G. Gaes, T.J. Flanagan, L.L. Motiuk, and L. Stewart, 'Adult Correctional Treatment' in M. Tonry and J. Petersilia (eds.), Prisons, Crime and Justice: A Review of Research Vol. 26 (Chicago, Ill.: University of Chicago Press, 1999), 361–426.
[27] M. Tonry, Sentencing Matters (Chicago, Ill.: University of Chicago Press, 1996), Chapter 4.

instrumental goals, we should not be surprised if research on instrumental effects alone did not lead to redirections in policy. And highly qualified claims about modest but discernible sought-after effects, important though they are, seldom support a sense of excitement likely to lead to major new initiatives or changes in policy direction.

Evaluation findings may have limited influence because they measure the wrong things. The durability of Neighbourhood Watch programmes in England and of Operation DARE in the USA, despite chastening research findings concerning effects on crime and drug use, may occur because the programmes' real purposes are other things. Neighbourhood Watch, for example, may be successful (as measured by durability) because it serves as a symbol of community action and efficacy and because it provides occasions for structured community interactions. It may also provide increased interactions and communications between citizens and the police that both find satisfying. Operation DARE, similarly, may survive because citizens and police value the interactions they provide between police and children in positive settings. Police may value them as forms of community outreach and public relations, and individual police officers may enjoy participating in programmes that are concerned with socialization of children and may value the belief that they are helping change children's lives (whether they are or not). If Neighbourhood Watch, Operation DARE, and boot camps existed primarily or largely to achieve things other than their stated purposes, evaluation research might have more influence if it targeted major latent functions and tried plausibly to measure the extent of their realization, in addition to evaluating achievement of nominal goals.

The programmes discussed in the preceding few paragraphs do not raise the most controversial or politically salient of penal policy issues—the severity of sanctions, the nature of street-level law enforcement, the death penalty—but they illustrate some of the reasons the influence of knowledge on policy is complex. Latent, symbolic, and expressive goals are even more central concerning issues like the death penalty or the severity of punishments than in relation to narrower programmes, and it would accordingly be surprising if research were more influential concerning the former than the latter.

Looking only at the largest issues of penal policy, however, gives a misleading impression. On different kinds of questions, and in relation to policy-makers at agency rather than legislative or senior executive branch levels, research and researchers have plenty of influence. And governments have demonstrated with cash their realization that researchers have important roles to play. Governments in England and the United States, for example, have invested heavily in the development of cadres of social scientist researchers, in the creation of statistical systems and databases that enhance understanding of crime, and in the maintenance of government departments that fund, synthesize, and conduct research.

In both countries governments have supported bodies of research that, though looking haphazard and short term as they unfolded, in retrospect look like the kinds of strategic research programmes academics favour—long-term, incremental, and cumulative. In England, examples include work on crime prevention in general,[28] situational crime prevention in particular,[29] and multiple victimization even more particularly.[30] In the United States, examples include work on prediction and classification,[31] criminal careers,[32] community penalties,[33] developmental crime prevention,[34] and community policing.[35] In both countries, representative national victimization surveys have become entrenched and respected, and other national statistical systems have steadily improved.

In both countries, particular topics received focused attention that is consistent with rational bureaucratic notions of how policy should be developed. In the United States, the Minneapolis Domestic Violence Experiment[36] concluded in a random allocation experiment that a mandatory arrest policy for alleged domestic violence

---

[28] Tonry and Farrington (eds.), n. 4 above.

[29] R.V. Clarke, 'Situational Crime Prevention' in ibid., 91–150.

[30] G. Farrell and K. Pease (eds.), *Repeat Victimization* (Monsey, NY: Criminal Justice Press, 2001).

[31] D.M. Gottfredson and M. Tonry (eds.), *Prediction and Classification, Criminal Justice Decision Making* (Chicago, Ill.: University of Chicago Press, 1987).

[32] A. Blumstein, J. Cohen, J. Roth, and C. Visher (eds.), *Criminal Careers and 'Career' Criminals* (Washington, DC: National Academy Press, 1986).

[33] J. Petersilia, 'Probation and Parole' in M. Tonry (ed.), *The Handbook of Crime and Punishment* (New York: Oxford University Press, 1998), 563–588; M. Tonry, 'Intermediate Sanctions' in ibid., 683–711.

[34] R.E. Tremblay and W.M. Craig, 'Developmental Crime Prevention' in Tonry and Farrington (eds.), n. 4 above, xix, 151–326.

[35] W.G. Skogan and S.M. Hartnett, *Community Policing, Chicago Style* (Oxford: Oxford University Press, 1997).

[36] L.W. Sherman and R.A. Berk, 'The Specific Deterrent Effects of Arrest for Domestic Assault' (1984) 49 *American Sociological Review* 261–272.

misdemeanours reduced later victimization when compared with other police responses. The US National Institute of Justice then funded replications using experimental designs in Omaha, Milwaukee, Charlotte, Colorado Springs, and Metro-Dade in Miami to learn whether the results were replicable.[37] In some places they were not, and in other places they were, but only for some demographic subgroups (employed and married) under certain conditions (when suspects were present when police arrived). In Omaha, Milwaukee, and Charlotte, for some minority and unemployed subgroups mandatory arrest had the iatrogenic effect of exacerbating subsequent victimization.[38] The initial findings thus had some validity, but the replications showed they did not have broad generalizability, suggesting that more textured and situation-specific policies are preferable and more effective than any single approach, including mandatory arrest.

In England, the former Home Office Research Unit, transmogrified after several reorganizations and name changes into the Research and Statistics Directorate ('RDS'), supported a series of research programmes on community penalties that looked strikingly rational and knowledge-based. Concerning unit fines (the English term chosen for what are called day fines in other countries), for example, pilots were undertaken in four magistrates' courts, evaluated,[39] and the resulting evidence of achievement of sought-after goals was cited as the basis for legislation in 1991 to establish a unit-fine system.[40] More recently, as part of the Blair Government's evidence-based policy strategy, RDS was given hundreds of millions of pounds for evaluation of new initiatives and the related 'What Works' movement gave rise to accreditation processes for correctional treatment programmes.

The recent establishment in England of the Joint Prison/Probation Accreditation Panel is another nod to evidence-based

---

[37] L.W. Sherman, *Policing and Domestic Violence: Experiments and Dilemmas* (Oxford: Maxwell Macmillan International, 1992), 3–4.

[38] Ibid., 3.

[39] D. Moxon, M. Sutton, and C. Hedderman, *Unit Fines: Experiments in Four Courts*, Home Office, Research and Planning Unit, Paper 59 (London: Home Office, 1990).

[40] Although the one major change from the pilot studies—the raising of the maximum fine per unit from £25 to £100—seems to have been strongly related to the unit fine's demise.

policy.[41] In 1999–2000, it assessed twenty-one programmes and found only one to be worthy of accreditation, four to be provisionally eligible on condition that specified changes were made promptly, nine to be 'encouraging, and two to be unworthy of continuance' (more information was needed to assess the remaining five).[42] By the end of the Panel's second year, fifteen prison or community programmes had acquired accredited or provisionally accredited status.[43]

Along similar lines, on the rationale that research findings should inform policy processes, national governments in both countries have invested in exhaustive reviews of crime-prevention research. The US National Institute of Justice has since 1977 funded *Crime and Justice—A Review of Research*, which has as its primary purpose the publication of state-of-the-art essays on topical research subjects.[44] The National Institute of Justice funded the University of Maryland to prepare a systematic review of over 500 research evaluations measuring the effects of crime prevention efforts in seven settings—communities, families, schools, labour markets, and places, by police, and by criminal justice agencies after arrest. Each evaluation was analysed and rated on the strength of its design and methodology, and credible substantive conclusions were identified.[45] In England, the RDS commissioned and published two such surveys.[46] Similarly, two reports published in 1998, as part of the

---

[41] Joint Prison/Probation Accreditation Panel, *What Works: First Report from the Joint Prison/Probation Accreditation Panel* (London: Home Office, 2001), (www. homeoffice.gov.uk/cpd/probu/jppapar.pdf), para. 4.

[42] Ibid., paras. 10, 18.

[43] Joint Prison/Probation Accreditation Panel, *What Works: Second Report from the Joint Prison/Probation Accreditation Panel 2000–2001, Towards Effective Practice* (London: Home Office, 2001), (www.homeoffice.gov.uk/cpd/probu/whatwork. pdf), 3.

[44] *Crime and Justice—A Review of Research* (Chicago, Ill.: University of Chicago Press), 30 vols. (to 2002).

[45] Sherman, Gottfredson, MacKensie, Eck, Reuter, and Bushway, n. 5 above; summary also available in *Research in Brief* (Washington, DC: National Institute of Justice, July 1998).

[46] Home Office, *Changing Offenders' Attitudes and Behaviour: What Works?*, Home Office Research Study No. 171 (London: Home Office Research and Development & Statistics Directorate, 1997); Home Office, *Reducing Offending: An Assessment of Research Evidence on Ways of Dealing with Offending Behaviour*, Home Office Research Study No. 187 (London: Home Office Research and Development & Statistics Directorate, 1998).

What Works Project of Her Majesty's Chief Inspector of Probation, sought to establish evidence-based principles for the supervision of offenders.[47] Agencies of both national governments are supporting the crime and justice component of the Campbell Collaboration, an international programme to develop cumulative and dynamic data bases on research findings on selected subjects.[48]

At administrative levels, criminal justice system agencies in both countries fund management research. One subject receiving particular attention in England is the development, and more recently the validation, of prediction instruments to be used in risks and needs assessments of probationers and parolees.[49] Another is risk assessments for sex offenders.[50] Both Petersilia[51] and Blumstein and Petersilia[52] provide long lists of illustrations of instances in which research findings have influenced policy.

Both governments have funded and acted upon materials research on such things as electronic monitoring, speed cameras, CCTV, police body armour, automated data systems, and credit card technology. These are not kinds of research, nor subjects, that many university-based social scientists celebrate, but they demonstrate a government research culture in which systematic knowledge is sought and used for policy purposes.

Finally, in both countries, but especially in England, academics and researchers are regularly called upon to work with government departments, serve as members of commissions and policy bodies, and advise ministers. The chair and two members of the Sentencing Advisory Panel are academics. In addition to the seven individuals

[47] HM Inspectorate of Probation, *Strategies for Effective Offender Supervision* (London: HMIP, 1998); HM Inspectorate of Probation, *Evidence Based Practice: A Guide to Effective Practice* (London: HMIP, 1998).

[48] D.P. Farrington and A. Petrosino, 'The Campbell Collaboration Crime and Justice Group' (2001) 578 *Annals of the American Academy of Political and Social Science* 35–49.

[49] P. Rayonor, J. Kynch, C. Roberts, and S. Merrington, *Risk and Need Assessment in Probation Services: An Evaluation* (London: Home Office, 2000).

[50] R. Taylor, *Predicting Reconviction for Sexual and Violent Offences Using the Revised Offender Ground Reconviction Scale* (London: Home Office, 1999).

[51] J. Petersilia, *The Influence of Criminal Justice Research* (Santa Monica, Cal.: Rand, 1987); J. Petersilia, 'Policy Relevance and the Future of Criminology—The American Society of Criminology 1990 Presidential Address' (1991) 29 *Criminology* 1–15, at 5.

[52] Blumstein and Petersilia, n. 21 above, 465–488, at 465–466.

who represent government agencies, the Joint Prison/Probation Accreditation Panel includes thirteen independent members, of whom a majority are researchers.[53] The head of the RDS, Paul Wiles, is on secondment from the University of Sheffield. Many senior English criminologists have served as members of the Parole Board. A very large number of academics, including our Cambridge colleagues, Sir Anthony Bottoms and Adrian Grounds, have served on government bodies charged to remake the justice system of Northern Ireland. American academics would give their eye teeth to be invited so often into the corridors of power, and once there to be taken seriously.[54]

All of that suggests that researchers' specialized knowledge is valued and sought, and that many individual academics influence both policy formulation and day-to-day administration. Where many academics want influence, and rightly believe they have little, is on the fundamental questions of policy—severity of penalties, choices between repressive and preventive crime and drug control policies, relative law enforcement emphases on street crime and white collar crime, and investment in social programmes aimed at the root causes of crime. On these big questions most elected officials, and probably most citizens, believe they know what needs to be known, and see little reason to defer to any asserted expert knowledge of criminologists.

Policy-making Based on Systematic Knowledge

Criminology has existed as a discipline in the English-speaking countries for little more than a half-century. Before that, though the word existed and individuals in law schools, sociology departments, and a few other university departments thought of themselves as doing criminological research, there were no free-standing criminology departments and no doctorates in criminology *per se.* Within a decade, however, the first departments were established

[53] Joint Prison/Probation Accreditation Panel, n. 41 above, para. 4.

[54] Petersilia, 'Policy Relevance', n. 51 above; Blumstein and Petersilia, n. 21 above; A. Blumstein, 'Editorial: Probing the Connection Between Crime and Punishment in the United States' (1995) 5 *Criminal Behaviour and Mental Health* 67; A. Blumstein, 'Interaction of Criminological Research and Public Policy' (1997) 12 *Journal of Quantitative Criminology* 349–361.

in the USA (University of California at Berkeley, 1950),[55] Australia (Melbourne University, 1951),[56] and England (Cambridge University, 1959).[57]

This was during the hey-day of what David Garland calls 'penal welfarism',[58] and many of the founding fathers believed that they would produce new knowledge on which improved policies would be based. The Cambridge Institute, the Melbourne Department, and Berkeley's School of Criminology were founded on a set of pragmatic and optimistic beliefs that criminal justice policy could be made better informed and more effective as a result of independent scientific inquiry. The perspective of Sir John Barry and Norval Morris in the 1950s in Melbourne 'was one which sought the development of a research base on key issues of crime and punishment which might then inform more effective and just policy'.[59] Establishment of the School of Criminology at the University of California was preceded in 1941 by a meeting that led to formation in 1946 of the Society for the Advancement of Criminology, later in 1958 renamed the American Society of Criminology. Both the School and the Society were co-founded by August Vollmer, the first Police Chief of Berkeley, with practical visions and commitments to the 'extension and improvement of police training'.[60]

The context in Cambridge was similar. In the White Paper which first proposed an Institute of Criminology, R.A. Butler, the Conservative Party Home Secretary, wrote, '[t]he institute should be able, as no existing agency is in a position to do, to survey with academic impartiality—in the light of the results of the research effort as a whole—the general problem of the criminal in society, its causes, and

[55] A. Morris, 'The American Society of Criminology: A History, 1941–1974' (1975) 13 *Criminology* 123–167.

[56] N. Morris, *University of Melbourne Department of Criminology 50th Anniversary 1951–2001 Commemorative Booklet* (www.criminology.unimelb.edu.au/about/history/htm).

[57] L. Radzinowicz, *The Cambridge Institute of Criminology: Its Background and Scope* (London: HMSO, 1988).

[58] D. Garland, 'The Culture of High Crime Societies: Some Preconditions of Recent "Law and Order" Politics' (2000) 40 *British Journal of Criminology* 347–375.

[59] M. Finnane, 'Sir John Barry and the Melbourne Institute of Criminology: Some Other Foundations of Australian Criminology' (1998) 31 *The Australian and New Zealand Journal of Criminology* 69–82, at 73.

[60] Morris, n. 55 above, 127.

its *solution*.[61] Butler's aspirations were optimistic, and Sir Leon Radzinowicz distanced himself from that part of Butler's statement,[62] but Radzinowicz's own optimism was not much different. As he put it in 1940, '[a]lthough the first task of criminal science is to ascertain the origins of crime this is not its main purpose. The main purpose is ... to ascertain how best to fight against crime.'[63]

Lord Butler later observed:

I was determined that there should be a long-term plan: a course of action that would lay a path for an enlightened penal policy. In particular I believed that changes should not be based on swings in emotion and opinion, prone as they are to the influence of dramatic events and bizarre cases, but upon reliable information about the phenomenon of crime, its social and personal roots and the effectiveness of the preventive and penal measures available.[64]

In 2002, reducing and preventing crime and formulating sensible public policies appear more intractable problems than they did forty and fifty years ago. Partly this is because, 'in the circumstances of late modernity', as some might say,[65] belief in government's capacity to do good has diminished. Partly it is because research findings have often punctured unrealistic expectations of programmes' effects. Partly it is because of advances in understanding of how knowledge shapes policy.

Criminologists' frustration at what many perceive as their lack of influence on policy may result partly from too mechanical a set of assumptions about how knowledge influences policy. The four filters described in the introduction, however, constrain policy-makers' openness to proposals for change based on new knowledge. An hypothesis that credible evidence will result in adoption of new policies or alteration of existing ones is much too simple. However,

---

[61] Home Office, *Penal Practice in a Changing Society*, Cmnd. 645 (London: HMSO, 1959), 6, para. 21 (emphasis added).

[62] L. Radzinowicz, *Adventures in Criminology* (London: Routledge, 1999), 194.

[63] L. Radzinowicz and J.W.C. Turner, 'The Language of Criminal Science' (1940) 7 *Cambridge Law Journal* 224–237, at 233.

[64] R.A. Butler, 'The Foundation of The Institute of Criminology' in Hood (ed.), *Crime, Criminology and Public Policy*, n. 1 above, 1–10, at 1.

[65] D. Garland, *The Culture of Control: Crime and Social Order in Contemporary Society* (Oxford: Oxford University Press, 2001); A.E. Bottoms, 'The Philosophy and Politics of Punishment and Sentencing' in C. Clarkson and R. Morgan (eds.), *The Politics of Sentencing Reform* (Oxford: Clarendon, 1999), 17–49.

as scholarship on the influence of social science knowledge on policy shows, more nuanced understandings suggest that social scientists have more influence that they realize.

Carol H. Weiss summarized the conventional conception prevalent until the 1970s of how research findings would influence policymaking:

policy research would add a measure of rationality to the hurly-burly of policymaking. By providing objective evidence, such research would counteract the special pleading and selfish interest that seemed to dominate the political process. Somehow it was expected that however self-seeking politicians might be and however cautious and inert public bureaucracies might be, research would be above the fray. By producing objective, valid, nonpolitical data and conclusions, research would win attention on its merits and help overcome the excesses of 'politics' in its most pejorative sense. Research was a quintessentially rational way to help solve policy problems. Although political actors were often irrational, as these observers saw it, they would somehow *have* to use the evidence that research provided. Why they would use it—in violation of all their accustomed modes of operation—was not clear, but the tacit assumption seemed to be because it was there.[66]

Mark Moore described this as a 'social research-and-development model'[67] in which decision-making relies heavily upon the systematic testing and evaluation of a range of possible policy options. He also believed it to be a narrow and naïve conception of the research/policy nexus, as it presumes direct relations between research results and policy-makers' activities that seldom exist.

Knowledge utilization research (a horrible phrase, but it is a term of art, so we use it) suggests that criminological research has had more influence on policy than is generally recognized because insufficient attention has been paid to the diffuse ways that knowledge influences policy. Weiss recalled how, by the early 1970s, an array of evaluation and policy studies indicated that criminological and other

[66] C.H. Weiss, 'Ideology, Interests, and Information: The Basis of Policy Decisions' in D. Callahan and B. Jennings (eds.), *Ethics, the Social Sciences, and Policy Analysis* (London: Plenum Press, 1983), 213–245, at 213–214.

[67] M.H. Moore, 'Learning by Doing: Linking Knowledge to Policy in the Development of Community Policing and Violence Prevention in the United States' in P.-O. Wikström, R.V. Clarke, and J. McCord (eds.), *Integrating Crime Prevention Strategies: Propensity and Opportunity* (Stockholm: National Council for Crime Prevention, 1995), 301–331, at 303.

social science research had had a low, barely perceptible impact on policy decisions. She referred to the ways in which social science research results gradually and often untraceably weave their way into practice as 'diffuse enlightenment', 'decision accretion', and 'knowledge creep'.[68]

As Weiss explained:

Rarely does research supply an 'answer' that policy actors employ to solve a policy problem. Rather, research provides a background of data, empirical generalisations and ideas that affect the ways that policymakers think about problems. It influences their conceptualisation of the issues with which they deal; affects those facets of the issue they consider inevitable and unchangeable and those they perceive as amenable to policy action; widens the range of options that they consider; and challenges some taken-for-granted assumptions about appropriate goals and appropriate actions.[69]

Political scientists in the 1970s developed theoretical frameworks for understanding how public policies take shape. Charles Lindblom and David Cohen[70] explored the ways in which the learning generated by systematic research, what they called 'professional social inquiry (PSI)', influences policy. They use the concept of 'social learning' to explain how PSI, as contrasted with more fallible and commonsensical 'ordinary knowledge', is often powerless to alter the assumptions of ordinary knowledge. As they explain, 'until the required learning occurs, PSI may be futile. . . . The common opinion "things will have to get worse before they get better" testifies to the possibility that a problem cannot be solved until people have had— or suffered—such experiences as will bring them to new attitudes and political dispositions'.[71]

Tied closely to the construct of social learning are two other useful notions. The first is 'boundedness', a concept developed by Weiss.[72] She used the term to designate limits on decision-makers' organizational room for manœuvre in a particular time and place. It should

---

[68] C.H. Weiss, 'Research and Policy-Making: A Limited Partnership' in F. Heller (ed.), *The Use and Abuse of Social Science* (London: Sage, 1986), 214–235, at 230; Weiss, n. 86 below, 278.

[69] Ibid., 217.

[70] C.E. Lindblom and D.K. Cohen, *Usable Knowledge* (London: Yale University Press, 1979).

[71] Ibid., 19.

[72] Weiss, n. 68 above, 214–235, at 220.

be broadened to encompass wider limits set by contemporaneous political and cultural arrangements. Practical and ideological constraints that limit scope for policy-making in a given period in history are acknowledged in all of Hood's work on the relationship between research and policy. As he put it in 1974, '[i]ndeed, the belief that expert advice based on criminological and penological research is the foundation for penal change, is only a screen behind which ideological and political factors, perhaps inevitably, shape those attitudes which imbue legislation'.[73]

The second notion is what Moore refers to as 'windows of opportunity'[74] for decision-making. Windows are created by the coalescence of political wills in a place and time to act on a problem. Often this occurs cyclically, and policy issues raised and dealt with at one time come round again later. Windows are also created by the weight of growing social problems, or by the perceptions of growing problems, that have become so urgent that a policy response seems required.

Moore's windows of opportunity, turned around, are other people's moral panics.[75] The assassinations of John F. Kennedy, Martin Luther King, and Robert Kennedy in the United States in the 1960s are generally seen as creating the windows of opportunity in which mould-breaking federal civil rights, welfare, and gun control legislation was enacted. Depending on whose values and preferences count, these were at the time seen as good or bad things. From the perspective of liberal reformers, those tragic deaths opened a window of opportunity for progressive change. To social and political conservatives, those deaths precipitated the enactment of unwise laws. In retrospect, much of the 1960s welfare and gun control legislation was seen by later federal administrations and Congresses as unsound and was fundamentally revised. Most commonly, and particularly as developed by Stanley Cohen and his sociological successors, moral panics are generally seen as bad things that lead to poorly considered populist legislation.

However conceptualized, whether as opportunities for constructive policy change or dangerous times when risks of repressive policy-

---

[73] Hood, 'Criminology and Penal Change', n. 1 above, 375–417, at 417.

[74] Moore, n. 67 above, 301–331, at 309.

[75] See S. Cohen, *Folk Devils and Moral Panics* (New York: St Martin's, 1972); P. Jenkins, *Moral Panic: Changing Conceptions of the Sex Offender in America* (New Haven, Conn.: Yale University Press, 1998).

making are high, windows of opportunity make changes more likely than at other times. Windows that enable policy responses to drug abuse, for example, open and close cyclically as prevailing cultural sensibilities change.[76] Exceptional, high-profile cases often open windows to ambitious or radical policy responses. Drug abuse and drug-related crime, for example, were politically salient issues in the USA in the 1980s, but it was the death by cocaine overdose of University of Maryland basketball player, Len Bias, in 1986 that precipitated the enactment of the Anti-Drug Abuse Act of 1986, which prescribed the severest drug-law penalties in US history.[77] The murders of Polly Klaas in California and of Megan Kanka in New Jersey respectively catalyzed enactment of three-strikes laws in California[78] and Megan's Laws in all fifty American states.[79] A comparable English example is the murder of toddler James Bulger in 1993, which changed the policy climate for several years afterwards.[80] Another English example is Michael Stone, who murdered Lin and Megan Russell in 1996 after asking for, but failing to receive, treatment for his psychiatric problems. The case highlighted gaps in treatment options for individuals with severe personality disorders, and moved the Department of Health and the Home Office to propose indefinite detention of individuals described as 'dangerous severe personality disordered (DSPD)'.[81]

Boundedness interacts with windows of opportunity. When windows of opportunity are circumscribed by boundedness in a particular place at a given time, policy prescriptions that fail to take account of that—those that attempt to push social learning

[76] See M. Tonry, 'Unthought Thoughts: The Influence of Changing Sensibilities on Penal Policies' [2001] *Punishment and Society* 167–181.

[77] *Annual Report for the Year 1986 of the Select Committee on Narcotics Abuse and Control 99th Congress Second Session*, Report 99–1039 (Washington, DC: US Government Printing Office, 1987); cited in B.A. Stolz (ed.), *Criminal Justice Policy Making: Federal Roles and Processes* (London: Praeger, 2002), 78.

[78] F.E. Zimring, G. Hawkins, and S. Kamin, *Punishment and Democracy: Three Strikes and You're Out in California* (New York: Oxford University Press, 2001).

[79] R. Lieb, V. Quinsey, and L. Berline, 'Sexual Predators and Social Policy' in M. Tonry (ed.), *Crime and Justice: A Review of Research* (Chicago, Ill.: Chicago University Press, 1998), 43–114.

[80] A. Young, *Imagining Crime: Textual Outlaws and Criminal Conversations* (London: Sage, 1996).

[81] Department of Health, Home Office, *Managing Dangerous People With Severe Personality Disorder* (London: Home Office, 1999), 9.

beyond its boundaries—will not be taken seriously.[82] Even if, for example, a major breakthrough showed how community psychiatric treatment could humanely, irreversibly, and undisputedly prevent reoccurrence of sexual offences, the sentencing of Sarah Payne's killer would for a considerable time have closed the window to its adoption as a policy option for treatment of sex offenders.

Earlier work by Weiss offers another framework in which to understand the relationship between research knowledge and policy action.[83] Weiss calls this the 'I–I–I framework'. It takes account of the conflict that arises in policy-making among 'Ideology', the values and political orientation of a group or political administration; 'Interests', primarily the self-interest of particular bureaucrats and public officials; and 'Information', both PSI and ordinary knowledge. This model embodies the congeries of conflicting interests that constrain policy-making. Information of all kinds, much of it intuitive and experiential and in competition with the findings of research, must compete with self-interest and ideology.

There is nothing new about the proposition that scientific knowledge must overcome impediments if it is to inform policy-making. Resistance to incorporation of the implications of research knowledge into policy was as likely in earlier decades, when prevailing ideologies were different, as now. Garland and Sparks offer this comment on the status accorded social researchers in the 1960s:

Governments do not always listen to reason, and certainly not to criminological reason. They operate in a context that is defined by instrumental rationality but also by emotions and values, insistent demands and political imperatives. Governments were doing just this in the heyday of modern criminology, but criminologists did not always notice because they shared its politics and took its gestures for real commitments.[84]

The most convincing pictures of policy influence are likely to be drawn in retrospect. Findings from individual projects seldom have

---

[82] B.A. Stolz, 'Congress and Criminal Justice Policy Making: The Impact of Interest Groups and Symbolic Politics' in B.A. Stolz (ed.), *Criminal Justice Policy Making: Federal Roles and Processes* (London: Praeger, 2002), 81–94, at 86–87.

[83] Weiss, n. 66 above, 213–245.

[84] D. Garland and R. Sparks, 'Criminology, Social Theory, and the Challenge of our Times' in D. Garland and R. Sparks (eds.), *Criminology and Social Theory* (Oxford: Clarendon Press, 2000), 1–22, at 19.

direct effect on policy decisions.[85] It is usually the cumulative effects of numerous studies that gradually influence emerging conventional wisdom and widely shared understandings, and as a result shape policy. Effects on decision-making tend to be diffuse as implications of findings slowly 'seep' into and 'percolate'[86] through the policy community. Often, as Lindblom and Cohen point out, the time lag is such that the findings of one generation of researchers are acted upon by subsequent generations of policy-makers.[87]

The notion of diffuse enlightenment is useful when trying to understand shifts in policy and public opinion. Widespread political and popular support for current punitive trends in penal policy cannot be understood without reference to its boundedness. As we noted in the introduction, until faith in rehabilitative methods of penal treatment declined, people were not ready to assimilate accumulating research findings on the ineffectiveness of treatment programmes at reducing recidivism. Similarly, the rehabilitative ideal that characterized the United States from the Progressive Era to the 1970s[88] cannot be understood without appreciation of widely-shared optimism about reliance on scientific knowledge. Both trends required shifts in the ways individuals understood the problems facing them, and each had antecedents that fostered or impeded change.

Other policy realms offer analogies. Research on mental health agencies has shown that three criteria must be met if research findings are to inform policy.[89] Research must be relevant to the policy-makers' agendas. It must be of high methodological quality, especially if it is to challenge existing practice.[90] It must point in clear directions for action.

---

[85] Though there are conspicuous exceptions, such as the Minneapolis domestic violence experiment which influenced adoption of mandatory arrest policies for misdemeanour domestic violence throughout the United States in the 1980s: see Sherman, n. 37 above.

[86] C.H. Weiss, 'The Circuitry of Enlightenment: Diffusion of Social Science Research to Policymakers' (1987) 8 *Knowledge: Creation, Diffusion, Utilization* 274–281, at 275; Weiss, n. 68 above, 218.

[87] Lindblom and Cohen, n. 79 above, 2.

[88] D. Rothman, *Conscience and Convenience* (New York: Addison-Wesley, 1980).

[89] C.H. Weiss and M.J. Bucuvalas, 'Truth Tests and Utility Tests: Decision-Makers' Frames of Reference for Social Science Research' (1980) 45 *American Sociological Review* 302–313.

[90] Ibid., 307.

Weiss and Bucuvalas found that research challenging traditional practices or ways of thinking, or indicating clear prescriptions for action, was deemed valuable by policy-makers, provided the conditions were right and windows of opportunity were open. To the three criteria of relevance, rigour, and clarity, Lempert[91] added that research must be 'congenial' if it is successfully to merge with other knowledge. Research can be both congenial and a challenge to the status quo as it can embolden like-minded, sympathetic policy actors to exploit open windows by contesting vulnerable conventional thinking. Criminological research findings presumably also need to satisfy these four criteria in order for policy-makers to influence policy-making.

Influence of knowledge on policy-making often results from face-to-face encounters between individuals.[92] Andrew Rutherford's account[93] of James Q. Wilson's influence in the United States offers an example. Wilson's conversation with then President Gerald Ford about the deterrent effects of imprisonment, as well as a copy of *Thinking About Crime* Wilson sent to Ford, presaged his appointment to policy advisory posts by President Ronald Reagan several years later. Ford later wrote of the exchange with Wilson in his autobiography, stating that Wilson's 'points made a lot of sense to me . . . I decided to use his arguments for the detailed proposals that I would submit to Congress' in 1975.[94]

The evidence supporting Wilson's deterrence arguments was no less contested or ambiguous then than it is now,[95] but the arguments were consistent with prevailing sensibilities—the 'window' was open to them, they passed boundedness tests, and American officials were ready to be persuaded. Their influence was due in great measure to their intuitive resonance. In Wilson's words, '[t]he most influential intellectuals were those who managed to link a concept or a

---

[91] R. Lempert, ' "Between Cup and Lip": Social Science Influences on Law and Policy' (1998) 10 *Law and Policy* 167–200, at 184–185.

[92] Weiss, n. 66 above, 214–245.

[93] A. Rutherford, *Transforming Criminal Policy* (Winchester: Waterside Press, 1996).

[94] Ibid., autobiography, 31–46, quoted at 31–32.

[95] See e.g. A. Blumstein, J. Cohen, and D. Nagin, *Deterrence and Incapacitation: Report to the National Academy of Sciences Panel on Deterrent and Incapacitative Effects* (Washington, DC: National Research Council, National Academy Press, 1978) and von Hirsch *et al.*, n. 10 above.

theory to the practical needs and ideological predispositions of political activists and government officials.'[96]

Research findings influence policy less often and powerfully than researchers believe is appropriate, partly as a result of the differences between policy-makers' and researchers' interests, needs, and institutional contexts. This disjunction has been characterized by the 'two-communities metaphor',[97] in which policy-makers and researchers occupy divergent cultures that are inadequately bridged. Petersilia,[98] studying the information needs of practitioners in US criminal justice agencies, found that practitioners repeatedly complained of researchers' failure to focus on practical problems: 'criminal justice practitioners have repeatedly said that if researchers want to have an effect, they must focus on "real problems." Practitioners want more efficient, less expensive, and less complicated ways of solving operational and management problems.'[99] The status and career incentives of the academic world, however, typically reward the creation of knowledge, not its practical application. Petersilia's practitioner-informants, concerned with practical policy questions, saw the academic world as concerned primarily with esoteric as distinguished from real world knowledge.[100]

A second impediment to communication is a fundamental debate on whether researchers are obliged even to consider the policy relevance of their work. Stanley Cohen, describing a detachment he suggested should pervade academic criminology, wrote, 'I am convinced that the role of the sociologist of crime and punishment is no different from that, say, of the sociologist of religion. We should not be priests, theologians or believers, and social scientists who have taken up equivalent positions in regard to crime are misguided.'[101] Roger Hood disagreed, finding Cohen's analogy inapt. More appropriate, he suggested, are the relationships between

---

[96] J.Q. Wilson, '"Policy Intellectuals" and Public Policy' (1981) 64 *The Public Interest* 31, at 33.

[97] W.N. Dunn, 'The Two-Communities Metaphor and Models of Knowledge Use: An Exploratory Case Study' (1980) 1 *Knowledge: Creation, Diffusion, Utilization* 515.

[98] Petersilia, n. 51 above.

[99] Ibid., 106.

[100] J. Petersilia, 'Defending the Practical Value of Criminological Research' (1993) 30 *Journal of Research in Crime and Delinquency* 497–505.

[101] S. Cohen, *Visions of Social Control* (Cambridge: Polity, 1985), 238.

economics and fiscal planning or urban geography and town planning.[102]

A thousand flowers should be allowed to bloom in criminology as everywhere else. No doubt there will always be room for research that is not directly germane to policy debates. Nonetheless, there are good reasons why people working in so applied a field should do work which can facilitate policy-making that is evidence-based. Most researchers in such parallel fields as developmental psychology or urban planning would have difficulty imagining high-priority work that is not policy-relevant in the short or longer term.

Some researchers worry that emphasis on policy relevance may complicate efforts to obtain funding for research that cannot promise to inform policy-making and that they may have difficulty justifying research projects that yield little knowledge that is directly policy relevant.[103] No doubt there is some validity to this concern. Research funding is a market like any other, and funders are likely to want to invest in work that they regard as useful or important. The image, however, of the 'basic' researcher who receives little support because pushed aside in favour of applied researchers is at war with a different stereotype of researchers who are frustrated by their sense of impotence in having their findings taken seriously. In any case, researchers who have the luxury of university appointments have substantial discretionary time in which they can carry out research without a need to rely on external funding. Large-scale quantitative projects do generally require external funding if they are to be done at all, but much of the work of British criminologists—including armchair theorizing, small-sample qualitative projects, and the preparation of edited volumes—does not.

The Case for an Independent Institute of Justice Research

Research influences policy but often indirectly and with considerable time lags. There is value in facilitating the achievement of systematic knowledge that is sound, generalizable, and replicable. There is also value in capacity building. Unless high-quality special-

[102] Hood, 'Some Reflections', n. 1 above, 527–538, at 529.
[103] Petersilia, n. 51 above, 1–15.

ized institutions exist and cadres of experienced and talented researchers are available, little high-quality research will be done.
These may be thought of as among the most important express
(build knowledge) and latent (build infrastructure and intellectual
capital) functions of research funding.

The organization and funding of criminal justice research in
England is not well designed to perform express or latent functions,
and conditions are only a little better in the United States. In both
countries the movement of government into crime research funding
in the 1960s and 1970s led private foundations to move out. If
government was prepared to invest major resources in criminal
justice research, it appeared sensible to foundations to shift funding
programmes in other directions. This is not quite an instance of bad
money driving out good, but it did result in substitution of government's shorter-term, applied, and political interests for longer-term,
more basic, and less partisan interests that foundations often
promote.

By the early 1980s, according to John Croft,[104] at the time head of
the Home Office Research and Planning Unit, the Home Office was
the principal source of research funding in England. The private
foundations had largely ceased funding crime research when government became active in the field, and the Social Science Research
Council at the time made few awards to criminologists. Also by the
mid-1980s changes in Home Office policies tied research closer to
government's short-term policy interests. Projects could not be
funded unless a Home Office 'customer', usually a minister or a
civil servant in a policy office, was prepared to support it. Researchers found themselves with little choice but to accept a redefined,
more restrictive role. Administrators presented researchers with pre-
formulated problems to solve.[105]

Gaping holes exist in English mechanisms for funding social
and behavioural science research on crime and criminal justice.
Funding is seldom available for projects requiring more than a few
years to complete (though all serious longitudinal studies and intervention follow-ups require more than a few years); for projects that

---

[104] J. Croft, 'Great Britain and the Council of Europe' in M. Tonry and N. Morris
(eds.), *Crime and Justice, A Review of Research, Vol. 5* (Chicago, Ill.: University of
Chicago Press, 1983), 265–280.
[105] R.V.G. Clarke and D.B. Cornish, *Crime Control in Britain: A Review of Policy
Research* (Albany, NY: SUNY Press, 1983).

investigate subjects that are not seen as policy-relevant by contemporary standards (though these standards change); for evaluation projects using experimental designs and multi-year follow-ups (though these are likeliest to provide valid generalizable findings); for evaluations not of current interest to government (though interests change), nor for 'basic' research that may shed light on important human or social problems but whose policy relevance is unclear. Except for minor and serendipitous funding by a handful of British foundations, most crime and criminal justice research is funded by the Home Office or the Economic and Social Research Council (ESRC), and neither typically funds the types of work just described.

Two- and three-year Home Office funding for research on more basic topics was available in the 1970s and early 1980s. More recently, however, the Home Office Research and Statistics Directorate mostly has funded small-scale, short-term evaluation research on subjects that officials deem to be policy relevant. Much of this is funded following solicitations that describe research projects designed by Home Office staff, not by independent researchers; that are to be overseen by Home Office-appointed advisory committees; and that must keep to short timetables. Strong research designs are seldom used, and post-intervention follow-ups are typically short. The conventional explanation is that Home Office research is driven by the policy and political agendas of ministers and governments that are interested in doing something this year or next, and that fast-and-dirty research is all that is possible under the circumstances. That may be, but it means that little high-quality rigorous evaluation research is carried out and that other kinds of research go unsupported. It also means that young researchers are being acculturated into bad habits and accordingly that the latent function of building a cadre of high-quality researchers is not being well served. In recent years there have been small programmes for unsolicited proposals for small-budget projects, but so far at least they tended to be meagrely funded and to fall victim to what ministers see as higher-priority work.

The ESRC mostly funds small-scale, short-term research projects, with the exception of periodic solicitations for up-to-five-year proposals for research networks and centres. Only one of these latter solicitations in recent years has been on crime or a related topic. And, as Bottoms pointed out, Home Office funding for policy-relevant research 'so far outstrips that available from the relevant research council for basic research that even when the latter produces a special initiative, its funds are small by comparison'.[106]

The situation in the United States is somewhat better. Although foundations largely abandoned criminal justice research as a programme area in the 1970s, by the late 1990s increasing numbers of large foundations began to revive interest in the subject and to support research on delinquency, crime, and criminal justice. In the 1980s and 1990s the directors of the National Institute of Justice were persuaded of the merits of evaluation research using strong research designs, and many projects with random allocation and strong quasi-experimental designs were funded. Both the National Institute of Justice and the federal Office of Juvenile Justice and Delinquency Prevention agreed to support decade-long longitudinal studies addressing basic etiological issues.

But the situation in the USA is only somewhat better. As in England, little money was invested in building research institutions or providing career incentives and structures for young researchers. Most government-funded research followed the English command pattern in which government chose the topics to be investigated. In many areas, as for example sentencing and corrections about which we know a little, command research has followed a stop-and-start pattern. There have been three bursts of NIJ-funded research on sentencing and sanctions—in 1978–82 on determinate sentencing, in 1985–9 on intermediate sanctions, and in 1995–7 on truth-in-sentencing and sentencing guidelines. As a result of that lack of continuity there is little if any overlap in the institutions and individuals who have carried out those three generations of research. This means that each new set of research teams brings little specialized expertise to the subject, and that the latent goal of building a cadre of sentencing researchers has, again, not been realized. In the physical and biological sciences, those would be seen as serious failures in institution-building and research strategy.

Outside the US Department of Justice (as outside the Home Office), few other government agencies invest in crime and criminal justice research. The National Science Foundation budgets about US$2,000,000 annually for 'law and society' (including crime)

---

[106] A.E. Bottoms, 'Reflections on the Criminological Enterprise' (1987) 46 *Cambridge Law Journal* 240–263, at 247.

research, and the National Institute of Mental Health provides support for some crime-related psychological research.

If government-funded research in England and America were to be indicted, a number of points would be made. First, political appointees and elected officials often want answers faster than good research can deliver them, with the result that much research is funded with timetables that are too tight, research designs that are too weak, follow-up periods that are too short, and budgets that are too small. This is a bigger problem, we suspect, in England, than in America, because the Research and Statistics Directorate is organizationally much more closely integrated with policy operations than is the US National Institute of Justice with operating components of the US Department of Justice.[107]

Secondly, in England and the USA, the agencies that fund criminal justice research have been placed in government departments whose principal mission is law enforcement. Under the best of circumstances, it is not surprising that the principal interests are in research subjects that have immediate or short-term policy significance, and in evaluations of pilot and new initiatives. There is comparatively little structural reason for agencies infused with law-enforcement values to invest in long-term strategic research programmes or in basic research.

Thirdly, government research programmes on crime and criminal justice are seldom cumulative or strategic. They respond to the policy fashions and preoccupations of the moment. Medical research, in which long-term research programmes including long-term support for individual projects and individual researchers are not uncommon, might suggest a better model.

---

[107] English co-mingling of research, policy, and political agendas, however, may simultaneously produce comparatively more fast-and-dirty research and yet give research findings a comparatively larger role in influencing policy implementation. In the USA, constitutional separation-of-powers traditions radically separate legislative policy-making from executive branch responsibilities for implementation and day-to-day management. In England and Wales, the Home Office has responsibility both for developing proposed legislation and, if it is enacted, for planning its implementation and management. Policy offices that 'commission' research are also often involved in planning implementation of related policy initiatives. It may be ironic that American institutional arrangements conduce to production of stronger research of lesser policy influence and English arrangements to comparatively weaker research of greater influence.

Fourthly, operating criminal justice system agencies are unlikely, in contrast to medical-sector agencies, to give high importance to such latent funding goals as development of the institutional infra-structure for research, and development of career opportunity ladders and structures that will build qualified research cadres. This is why, when as in the USA in the mid-1990s and in England in 1999–2001 the political salience of crime produced unusually large research budgets, much of the work went to for-profit contract research funds, which can quickly gear up and gear down, rather than to universities, and why much of the resulting work was typically of low quality.

Recommendations for the creation of independent research institutes have for these reasons been offered for three-quarters of a century. Earlier we adverted to Radzinowicz's 1965 call for the creation of an independent institute for criminological research and to Hood's successive reiterations of that proposal. Here we offer it once again, briefly, and then discuss both the tortured story of America's failure to create such an institute and the more promising Dutch experience which shows that, at least in a humane and rationalistic country, such a body can be created and survive. It is important to note that thoughtful research administrators recognize both the limits of governmental research strategies and the need for independence. That is why Paul Wiles, the current RDS head, beginning in 2000 created a small unsolicited research programme. John Croft, one of Wiles's predecessors, was strongly of the view that independent centres for research should be supported. It is desirable, Croft wrote, in explaining why the Home Office for many years provided core funding to the Cambridge Institute of Criminology and the Oxford Centre for Criminological Research, 'for governments to assist independent research... the results of which may sometimes be unpalatable to it'.[108]

The first full-blown proposal for the creation of an independent national institute for crime research was offered in 1931 by the US National Commission on Law Enforcement and Observance,[109]

---

[108] J. Croft, *Research in Criminal Justice*, Home Office Research Study No. 44 (London: HMSO, 1978), 10; cited in Hood, 'Some Reflections', n. 1 above, 527–538, at 537 n. 36.

[109] Wickersham Commission (US National Commission on Law Observance and Enforcement), *Reports. Volume 1—Prohibition, Criminal Statistics, Prosecution* (Washington, DC: US Government Printing Office, 1931).

better known as the Wickersham Commission. Empirical data are needed, the Wickersham Commission urged, 'to tell us, or at least help tell us, what we have to do, how we are doing it, and how far what we are doing corresponds to what we have to do. They are important in so far as they may be made to give us an accurate picture both as to the basis of criticism and as the basis of making laws and administrative regulations.'[110] The Commission was adamant that research and statistics (it mostly discussed statistics) should be handled by an independent agency—it recommended the US Bureau of the Census[111]—not directly engaged in law enforcement: 'it is important that the compiling and publication of statistics should not be confided to any bureau or agency which is engaged in administering the criminal law'.[112] The commission then discussed at length various kinds of organizational and political interests that might motivate operating agencies to distort the data they publish. No independent criminal justice statistics or research agency was established. Such national crime and criminal justice statistics and research programmes as existed were housed and managed in the Federal Bureau of Investigation and the US Department of Justice.

Nearly forty years later, shortly after Radzinowicz's 1965 proposals, the US President's Commission on Law Enforcement and Administration of Justice in 1967, proposed the creation of an independent federal 'National Foundation for Criminal Research', patterned on the existing National Science Foundation, and augmented by 'a number of [independent] research institutes in various parts of the country'.[113] Three major rationales were put forward for why the proposed institute should be independent of the US Department of Justice. The department's legal culture was incompatible with a research institution's scientific orientation. The department's short-term operational and political emphases would distort and politicize research activities. A research organization in an operating agency would have difficulty attracting first-rate behavioural and social scientists into its employ.

---

[110] N. 23 above, i, 3.   [111] Ibid., i, 17.   [112] Ibid., i, 4–5.

[113] President's Commission on Law Enforcement and Administration of Justice, *The Challenge of Crime in a Free Society* (Washington, DC: US Government Printing Office, 1967), 276.

In the event, new statistics (the Bureau of Justice Statistics) and research (the National Institute of Justice) offices were established, but within, not outside, the US Department of Justice. The early experience was disastrous, as a 1977 review by a panel of the National Academy of Sciences demonstrated.[114] One of the Panel's comments hits close to home in contemporary England where policy-makers regularly set blue-sky goals of reducing particular crime levels by particular amounts in particular places. The Panel described repeated efforts to tie research to short-term policy initiatives, including 'an intensification of the Institute commitment to directly reducing crime;... this effort has generally been considered not only a failure but wrong-headed as well'.[115]

When the US Congress held hearings on the Panel report, it received much testimony recommending yet again the establishment of an independent research agency. Griffin Bell, a former US Attorney General, noted in a memorandum to President Jimmy Carter that 'a major cause of weakness in LEAA's [NIJ's] research programs has been the failure to insulate research activities from the demands of policy makers and program managers for immediate results'.[116] Bert Early, Executive Director of the American Bar Association, testified:

A research institute which is part of an 'action agency' such as the Department of Justice will inevitably be influenced by the Department's policy decisions and operational needs. Numerous studies of the current National Institute of Law Enforcement and Administration of Justice have cited such pressures as primary causes of the Institute's disappointing record in performing justice research.[117]

In response, the Congress reorganized the research and statistics agencies, leaving them inside the Department of Justice but making their directors presidential appointees, confirmed by the US Senate,

[114] See n. 12 above; S. White and S. Krislov (eds.), *Understanding Crime: An Evaluation of the National Institute of Law Enforcement and Administration of Justice* (Washington, DC: National Academy of Science, 1977).

[115] Ibid., 21.

[116] B. Early, 'Testimony before the Senate Committee on the Judiciary, Tuesday, March 13, 1979' in *Federal Drug Enforcement and Supply Control Efforts: Hearings Before the Committee of the Judiciary, United States Senate, 96th Congress, 1st Session on S.241. 9, 15, 28 February and 7, 13, March 1979. Serial No 96-5* (Washington, DC: US Government Printing Office, 1979).

[117] Ibid., 357.

who have final authority over their own budgets (but are dependent on other offices of the Department of Justice for support, including budget review and legal services).

This recital of successive unsuccessful US calls for the creation of an independent criminal justice research institute, and the successive failures of national research institutes to deliver adequate results, should be chastening and add weight to Roger Hood's repeated calls for the creation of an independent research-funding agency in England. The arguments in favour are compelling.

That such proposals are not impossible of realization is illustrated by the establishment in the Netherlands in 1992 of the Netherlands Institute for the Study of Crime and Law Enforcement (often called NISCALE). Explaining its importance requires a bit of background. The largest criminology agency in the Netherlands is the Research and Documentation Centre (RDC) of the Dutch Ministry of Justice. It has long rivalled the Home Office RDS in size and (in its country) domestic influence. It funds extra-mural research by social scientists in universities and research institutes, and it funds many programme evaluations and descriptive base-line research projects carried out by RDC staff. Much of this work, given the RDC's Ministry of Justice situs, is policy-focused and relatively short term. Recognizing this as a problem, the Ministry of Justice and the Dutch National Science Foundation established and agreed jointly to fund NISCALE for five years with an assumption of continuous funding for at least another five years if things went well (ten years have passed and further funding has been provided). NISCALE was established as an independent research institute affiliated to the University of Leiden, and was given sufficient funding to employ a director and four to six senior research staff and a larger junior and support staff, and was given control over its own research budget. The goal was that NISCALE avoid duplicating the RDC's specialization in evaluation and other short-term, immediately policy-relevant, research but instead specialize in mid- and long-term work nested within long-term research strategies. Some would argue that it should have achieved more, but its performance has been sufficiently good to support the extension of its funding. If the necessary political will should come into being in England and Wales or the United States to create an independent criminological research institute, NISCALE's experience should be examined closely.

Conclusion

Research influences criminal justice policy-making, though generally incrementally and partially. At managerial and administrative levels, research findings are welcomed and used. The work of England's correctional accreditation panel is an example. Probation and Prison Service decisions about investment in programmes and personnel turn directly on accreditation decisions. Some penal policy issues, however, such as the severity of punishments, or in the United States the death penalty, involve normative beliefs that resist inconsistent evidence. Cynical disregard for research findings or other empirical evidence that contradicts political ideologies or politicians' self-interest are a reality in the United States and England (elsewhere also, of course, though differences in national history and culture no doubt create distinctive 'windows').

Lindblom placed the importance of research, relative to other factors considered by policy-makers, in perspective:

If social scientists and other experts cannot approach conclusiveness on empirical questions about the appropriateness of means to given ends for complex social problems, then inquiring citizens and functionaries must choose, with the help of experts willing to probe rather than to hold tightly to conventional scientific inquiry.[118]

This statement makes three important points. First, policy will be made with or without expert knowledge. Ordinary knowledge is a powerful competitor for the attention of policy-makers. Secondly, the research knowledge base must grow if it is to contend with other forces that influence policy-makers. Thirdly, new roles must be created if bridges are to be built between the two communities of research and policy-making.

Criminological knowledge must compete with other forms of information and other pressures for change. The proliferation and durability of policies that are ineffective in terms of their stated goals—for instance, boot camps and mandatory minimum sentences in the USA, Neighbourhood Watch and mandatory minimum sentences in England—is partly testament to the failure of research findings to influence policy. It is also testament to the significance of other latent or functional goals such as policy-makers' aims to

---

[118] C.E. Lindblom, *Inquiry and Change: The Troubled Attempt to Understand and Shape Society* (New Haven, Conn.: Yale University Press, 1990), 10.

respond to public anxieties and to demonstrate that they are doing *something*.

Roger Hood,[119] to illustrate how public opinion has dominated penal policy-making, pointed to public health for comparison. Public health officials do not defer to public opinion in responding to a health crisis as much as justice system officials do. In relation to crime, few informed observers are surprised that policies such as mandatory minimum sentence laws are adopted for expressive or symbolic reasons, even when it is known that they are unlikely to achieve their putative purposes.[120] In relation to public health, nearly everyone would be surprised if policies were adopted that were known or strongly believed to be instrumentally ineffective. Perhaps one reason for this is that public health and medical research are widely seen as being more scientific and value-free than is criminal justice research. Of course, that is often not true, as recent policy debates over women's health, AIDS prevention, and needle exchange programmes demonstrate. Nonetheless, it is true that the findings of criminological research receive much less public and political deference than do findings of medical and public health research.

The history of criminology, however, has been defined by ideological struggles that have undermined its substantive policy impact. Furthermore, a persistent notion survives that existing basic research knowledge is insufficient realistically to expect it to have a real impact on penal policy. Criminological research has been less successful in mapping a way forward in matters of penal policy than many would have liked. As Croft put it:

if criminological research has achieved anything in recent years, it has helped to destroy popular myths about the causes and consequences of crimes, to expose the complexity of the problems facing those whose concern is the enforcement of the law, and to suggest options less for the positive commitment of resources than for the avoidance of the dissipation of such resources.[121]

In 1998, for example, HM Inspectorate of Probation evaluated all programmes delivered since 1992 and found only four out of 210 to have demonstrable preventive effects on reconviction

---

[119] Hood, 'Penal Policy', n. 1 above.

[120] Garland, n. 65 above.

[121] J. Croft, *Managing Criminological Research*, Home Office Research Study No. 69 (London: Home Office, 1981), 3.

rates.[122] Evidence of what does not appear to work inevitably has less galvanizing effect on policy-makers than would be convincing evidence of what does work.

Despite the confidence expressed in the 1960s by R.A. Butler and others about the potential of criminology to uncover the roots of crime and to base subsequent interventions on that knowledge, it is clear that we still do not know nearly enough to do that. The persistence of the problems facing criminological research outlined by Roger Hood over the course of nearly three decades is striking. The continued call for more basic research is a consistent point:

I do not deny the merits of research aimed to increase our understanding of recidivism, but it needs to be broadened. The studies undertaken so far tell us very little, if anything, about the effects of various kinds of penal and other sanctions as a criminal career develops and wanes. We need to know more about the realities of how and why punishments of different severities increase or decrease prospects of reconviction.[123]

This need to know more is evident in the persistence of the issues that have dominated policy-makers' concerns over the years. When he lobbied for the establishment of an Institute of Criminology as Home Secretary in 1959, Lord Butler was principally concerned with the question of how to deal with persistent offenders and with the role of 'statutory after-care' for released prisoners.[124] Though 'prolific'[125] has become the latest successor to 'persistent' or 'chronic' to describe offenders, and the concept of 'after-care' is often referred to as 'post-custody supervision',[126] the proposals in Halliday's recent sentencing review[127] show that these issues are as salient today as they were forty years ago.

One side effect of a lack of a definitive understanding of the processes that underlie criminal behaviour and the effective inter-

---

[122] Home Office, *Towards a Seamless Sentence*, Criminal Justice Conference, 27–28 Feb. 2001 (Liverpool: Home Office Special Conferences Unit, 2001).

[123] Hood, 'Some Reflections', n. 1 above, 527–538, at 535.

[124] R.A. Butler, *Penal Practice in a Changing Society: Aspects of Future Development*, Home Office White Paper, Cmnd. 645 (London: HMSO, 1959), p. iv.

[125] HM Inspectorates of Prisons and Probation, *Through the Prison Gate: A Joint Thematic Review by HM Inspectorates of Prisons and Probation* (London: HMIP, 2001), para. 3.16.

[126] Home Office, *Making Punishments Work: Report of a Review of the Sentencing Framework for England and Wales* (London: Home Office, 2001), para. 0.11.

[127] Ibid.

ventions to alter it is what Weiss has called 'endarkenment'.[128]
When policy-makers are faced with a deluge of contradictory research on a subject, research findings can produce confusion instead
of enlightenment. In the absence of a solid consensus of opinion on
which line of research is more valid, inadequate and shoddy research
that confirms preconceptions finds ready acceptance.

Under pressure to 'do something' policy-makers must often settle
for options which are not ideal or even advisable. They are forced to
'satisfice', as Herbert Simon[129] put it, that is to make the best choice
possible under the circumstances. Lawrence Sherman's Minneapolis
Domestic Violence Experiment and its replications provide an
example. As Sherman explained:

The question of how much research is enough to serve as a basis for policy-
making is troublesome.... Researchers, who are trained to be cautious,
may prefer to keep research out of policy-making until results are well
replicated and conclusions are quite firm. Policymakers and the taxpayers,
who are worried about today's problems today, prefer to know what
early results show, on the premise that some research is better than
none.[130]

The choice between acting without a strong evidence basis and
postponing action until all the facts are in is easily made.

Policy-makers may not be unaware of foreseeable consequences
and downsides of punitive measures. Blumstein observed:

It is not unreasonable to believe that the people who establish the high-
sanction policies fully understand the limitations of the policies but need
some means to respond to public pressure to 'do something.' Lacking any
better alternative to propose, they merely increase the sanctions, not so
much because they think it will work, but because they have come to
realize that it is an effective way to relieve the political pressure.[131]

This process of successive adoptions of ineffective practices may
further undercut public confidence in justice system institutions,
and feed into the notion that 'something *else*' must be done. Julian

[128] C.H. Weiss, 'Research and Policy-Making: A Limited Partnership' in F. Heller
(ed.), *The Use and Abuse of Social Science* (London: Sage, 1986), 214–235, at 219.

[129] H.A. Simon, *Administrative Behavior* (New York: Free Press, 1947); cited in
Weiss, n. 128 above, 214–235, at 220.

[130] Sherman, n. 37 above, 20.

[131] A. Blumstein, 'Making Rationality Relevant—The American Society of Criminology 1992 Address' (1993) 31 *Criminology* 1–16, at 9.

Roberts[132] makes this point when he identifies dangers in attempting to devise, as the Home Office[133] has done, a sentencing framework intended to increase public confidence. A framework of this sort is built on the supposition that sufficient is known on which to base a sentencing system that will effectively reduce rates of re-offending. If these promises are not kept, 'public confidence is likely to sink still further'.[134]

So long as empirical information is weak, 'endarkened' policy-making is likely to remain highly susceptible to political interests, unreliable information, and ideological fashion. Without providing strong empirical support that prison regimes based on restorative justice ideas would, for instance, reduce recidivism rates, such programmes are unlikely to elicit a great deal of public or political backing. Without evidence to break the deadlock of ideologies, these arguments are no more compelling to those on the right than are arguments for more repressive regimes to those on the left. Without strong foundations provided by basic research, policy is likely to be fragmented, ineffective, iatrogenic, and often self-defeating. Without a pragmatic application of its findings, criminological research will be lifeless and 'sterile', to use Radzinowicz's term.[135]

Some suggest that the two intellectually, culturally, and socially distinct communities of research and policy can be bridged. Researchers need first to acquire greater sensitivity to the possible policy implications of particular research studies while remaining aware of the forces with which policy-makers must contend. One suggestion is for researchers to learn to write reports in a style that is more accessible to the non-social scientist layperson. Studies filled with jargon and specialized terminology are unlikely to compete successfully with other forms of information. Others recommend social science and policy-making adopt more collaborative models of problem solving that allow policy-makers and practitioners to

---

[132] J.V. Roberts, 'Public Opinion and Sentencing Policy' in S. Rex and M. Tonry (eds.), *Reform and Punishment: The Future of Sentencing* (Cullompton: Willan, 2002), 18–39.

[133] Home Office, n. 126 above.

[134] Cf. Roberts, n. 132 above, 31.

[135] L. Radzinowicz, *Adventures in Criminology* (London: Routledge, 1999), 457.

provide feedback to researchers on the applicability of their studies in a real world context.[136]

Some have suggested more controversial, larger scale adaptive strategies that could bring research knowledge more to bear on policy decisions.[137] Blumstein and Petersilia[138] have suggested what essentially amounts to a research brokerage, in which research results are reviewed and mined for their policy implications, and relevant findings are disseminated to appropriate parties. This proposition would provide a buffer between the traditional 'two communities' and would allow each community to get on doing what it is they do.

When criminal justice policy-making is viewed as a swirling whirlwind of emotional conflict and political compromise, it is not surprising that inferences based on research findings seldom undermine beliefs based on ideology and conventional wisdom. Ideologies, interests, and various forms of non-scientific information dominate policy-making to differing extents at different places at different times. The reasons for this need to be better understood, but Weiss doubts that any refashioning of the research enterprise will enhance its influence on policy-making.[139]

Criminologists need to think much harder about the ways systematic evidence does and does not, can and cannot, influence policy processes. The picture at the outset of the twenty-first century is not all bleak. While policy-making concerning the biggest, most controversial, and most politically topical issues of crime and punishment is *largely* impervious to influence by research findings, that is not always the case. A notch lower in terms of political symbolism and saliency, though, as we demonstrated in the introduction, policy-makers and managers sometimes hunger for reliable evidence that can make their decision-making less risky.

If researchers recognized that research findings are influential in relation to policy-making on most subjects at least some of the time, and on many subjects most of the time, attention could shift from

---

[136] See e.g. ibid.; M.H. Moore, 'Learning by Doing: Linking Knowledge to Policy in the Development of Community Policing and Violence Prevention in the United States' in Wikström, Clarke, and McCord (eds.), n. 67 above, 301–331.

[137] See e.g., Blumstein and Petersilia, n. 21 above, 465; Weiss, n. 128 above, 214–235, at 228.

[138] Cf. Blumstein and Petersilia, n. 21 above.

[139] Weiss, n. 128 above, 214–235, at 232.

complaints about impotence to practical ways to make the research base stronger and researchers more credible. The case for an independent National Institute of Justice Research is as cogent as it has ever been. Governments should in any case invest more on research, research infrastructure, and intellectual capital, and should do it more strategically. Funding programmes and institutions like NIS-CALE should be created that can focus on mid- and long-term research strategies and programmes. Shorter-term evaluation research needs to be made more rigorous—using stronger research designs and more reasonable time schedules—and more strategic—pursuing subjects iteratively so that findings cumulate. Governments need to invest in programmes like the Campbell Collaboration, *Crime and Justice*, and National Academy of Sciences expert panels, all of which in various ways distill strong findings from mountains of research and provide authoritative statements of what we know. Information sources such as these show that, compared with thirty or even ten years ago, a great deal is known about the operations and effects of justice system programmes and policies and about the courses and causes of criminal careers. Policy-relevant research knowledge exists and influences policy-making. The promised land is not in sight, but things are not as bad for research and researchers as often they appear, and can be made substantially better.

Index of Names

Subject Index